Hands-On Software Engineering with Python

Move beyond basic programming and construct reliable and efficient software with complex code

Brian Allbee

BIRMINGHAM - MUMBAI

Hands-On Software Engineering with Python

Commissioning Editor: Merint Mathew
Acquisition Editor: Sandeep Mishra
Content Development Editor: Anugraha Arunagiri
Technical Editor: Ashi Singh
Copy Editor: Safis Editing
Project Coordinator: Ulhas Kambali
Proofreader: Safis Editing
Indexer: Tejal Daruwale Soni
Graphics: Tania Dutta
Production Coordinator: Shantanu Zagade

First published: October 2018

Production reference: 2061118

Published by Packt Publishing Ltd.
Livery Place
35 Livery Street
Birmingham
B3 2PB, UK.

ISBN 978-1-78862-201-1

www.packt.com

`mapt.io`

Mapt is an online digital library that gives you full access to over 5,000 books and videos, as well as industry leading tools to help you plan your personal development and advance your career. For more information, please visit our website.

Why subscribe?

- Spend less time learning and more time coding with practical eBooks and Videos from over 4,000 industry professionals

- Improve your learning with Skill Plans built especially for you

- Get a free eBook or video every month

- Mapt is fully searchable

- Copy and paste, print, and bookmark content

Packt.com

Did you know that Packt offers eBook versions of every book published, with PDF and ePub files available? You can upgrade to the eBook version at `www.packt.com` and as a print book customer, you are entitled to a discount on the eBook copy. Get in touch with us at `customercare@packtpub.com` for more details.

At `www.packt.com`, you can also read a collection of free technical articles, sign up for a range of free newsletters, and receive exclusive discounts and offers on Packt books and eBooks.

Contributors

About the author

Brian Allbee has been writing programs since the mid-1970s, and started a career in software just as the World Wide Web was starting to take off. He has worked in areas as varied as organization membership management, content/asset management, and process and workflow automation in industries as varied as advertising, consumer health advisement, technical publication, and cloud-computing automation. He has focused exclusively on Python solutions for the best part of a decade.

> *There are more people deserving of my thanks than I have room to thank. It's 99% certain, if you've ever worked with me, I learned something about this craft from you.*

> *Thank you!*

> *Special thanks to Erik, Saul, Tim, and Josh for lobbing ideas, and Dawn, for being there, always.*

> *#GNU Charlie Allbee and Sir Terry Pratchett — Mind how you go...*

About the reviewers

Chad Greer's focus lies in helping others find excellence. He works to replace typical "systems thinking" with talent-based approaches, breaking the mold of traditional business processes. Embracing the principles of agility, he works to respond to changing market and societal needs in order to ensure that the best solutions are created and delivered. He has worked in many different industries, including real estate, accounting, construction, local government, law enforcement, martial arts, music, healthcare, and several others. He draws on his breadth of experience to help others around him develop and prosper.

Nimesh Kiran Verma has a dual degree in maths and computing from IIT Delhi and has worked with companies such as LinkedIn, Paytm, and ICICI for about 5 years in software development and data science. He co-founded a micro-lending company, Upwards Fintech, and presently serves as its CTO. He loves coding and has mastered Python and its popular frameworks, Django and Flask. He extensively leverages Amazon Web Services, design patterns, and SQL and NoSQL databases to build reliable, scalable, and low latency architectures.

To my mom, Nutan Kiran Verma, who made me what I am today and gave the confidence to pursue all my dreams.

Thanks, Papa, Naveen, and Prabhat, who motivated me to steal time for this book when in fact I was supposed to spend it with them.

Ulhas and the entire Packt team's support was tremendous. Thanks, Varsha Shetty, for introducing me to Packt.

Packt is searching for authors like you

If you're interested in becoming an author for Packt, please visit authors.packtpub.com and apply today. We have worked with thousands of developers and tech professionals, just like you, to help them share their insight with the global tech community. You can make a general application, apply for a specific hot topic that we are recruiting an author for, or submit your own idea.

Table of Contents

Preface

Ultimately, the purpose of this book is to illustrate pragmatic software engineering principles and how they can be applied to Python development. To that end, most of this book is dedicated to exploring and implementing what I'd consider to be a realistically scoped, but probably unrealistic project: a distributed product-management and order-fulfillment system. In many cases, the functionality is developed from scratch, and from first principles—the fundamental concepts and assumptions that lie at the foundation of the system. In a real-world scenario, the odds are good that ready-made solutions would be available to deal with many of the implementation details, but exposing the underlying theories and requirements is, I think, essential for understanding why things work the way they do. That, I believe, is an essential part of the difference between programming and software engineering, no matter what languages are in play.

Python is a rare beast in many respects—it's a dynamic language that is nevertheless strongly typed. It's an object-oriented language too. These, taken together, make for an amazingly flexible and sometimes surprisingly powerful language. Though it can be taken as my opinion, I strongly believe that you'd be hard-pressed to find another language that is as generally capable as Python that is also as easy to write and maintain code in. It doesn't surprise me in the least that Python has racked up the kinds of success stories that are listed on the language's official site (`https://www.python.org/about/success/`). It also doesn't surprise me that Python is one of the core supported languages for at least two of the big name public cloud providers—Amazon and Google. Even so, it's often still thought of as only a scripting language, and I sincerely hope that this book can also show that view to be wrong.

Who this book is for

This book is aimed at developers with some Python experience looking to expand their repertoire from "just writing code" to a more "software engineering" focus. Knowledge of Python basics—functions, modules, and packages, and their relationship to files in a project's structure, as well as how to import functionality from other packages—is assumed.

What this book covers

Chapter 1, *Programming versus Software Engineering*, discusses the differences between programming (merely writing code), and software engineering—the discipline, mindset, and ramifications of them.

Chapter 2, *The Software Development Life Cycle*, examines a detailed software development life cycle, with particular attention to the inputs, needs, and outcomes that relate to software engineering.

Chapter 3, *System Modeling*, explores different ways of modeling and diagramming functional, data-flow, and interprocess-communication aspects of systems and their components, and what information those provide with respect to software engineering.

Chapter 4, *Methodologies, Paradigms, and Practices*, delves into current process methodologies, including a few Agile process variants, looking at the advantages and drawbacks to each, before reviewing **object-oriented programming** (**OOP**) and functional programming paradigms.

Chapter 5, *The hms_sys System Project*, introduces the concepts behind the example project used through the book to exercise software engineering design and development mindsets.

Chapter 6, *Development Tools and Best Practices*, investigates some of the more common (or at least readily available) development tools—both for writing code and for managing it in ways that reduce ongoing development efforts and risks.

Chapter 7, *Setting up Projects and Processes*, walks through an example structure that could be used for any Python project or system, and the thought processes behind establishing a common starting-point that is compatible with source control management, automated testing, and repeatable build and deployment processes.

Chapter 8, *Creating the Business Objects*, starts the first iteration of the hms_sys project, defining core library business-object data structures and capabilities.

Chapter 9, *Testing the Business Objects*, closes the first iteration of the hms_sys project after designing, defining, and executing repeatable automated testing of the business object code defined during the iteration.

Chapter 10, *Thinking about Business Object Data Persistence,* examines the common need for data persistence in applications, some of the more common mechanisms, and criteria for selecting a "best match" data-storage solution for a variety of implementation requirements.

Chapter 11, *Data Persistence and BaseDataObject,* starts the second iteration of the hms_sys project with the design and implementation of a common, abstract data-access strategy that can be re-used across any of the project's components.

Chapter 12, *Persisting Object Data to Files,* continues the second iteration's efforts with a concrete implementation of the abstract **Data Access Layer** (**DAL**), which persists business-object data into local files.

Chapter 13, *Persisting Data to a Database,* implements a concrete DAL that stores and retrieves data from a commonly used NoSQL database—MongoDB—and compares that approach with the requirements of an equivalent SQL-based DAL.

Chapter 14, *Testing Data Persistence,* concludes the second iteration of the hms_sys project by implementing automated tests against the varied implementations of both DAL strategies built during the iteration.

Chapter 15, *Anatomy of a Service,* analyzes the common functional requirements for free-standing services, and works through the construction of abstract service/daemon classes, which are reusable for creating a variety of concrete service implementations.

Chapter 16, *The Artisan Gateway Service,* starts the third iteration of the hms_sys project with an analysis of the communication needs of the system components, several options for implementing those communications, securing them, and finally working them into the concrete implementation of the core service for the project.

Chapter 17, *Handling Service Transactions,* considers all of the necessary business-object communications between hms_sys components, extracts some common functionality for all of them, and walks through the processes required to implement them.

Chapter 18, *Testing and Deploying Services,* wraps up the hms_sys development in the book, and investigates and resolves some common automated-testing concerns for service/daemon applications.

Chapter 19, *Multi-Processing and HPC in Python*, walks through the theory and basic practices involved in writing Python code that can scale to multiple processors on a single machine, or to multiple machines in a clustered-computing environment, and provides starting-point code-structure variations for executing Python code on common high-performance computing systems.

To get the most out of this book

You should know, specifically, about the following:

- How to download and install Python (3.6.x was used while writing this book, but the code here is expected to work in 3.7.x with little or no modification)
- How to write Python functions
- How to write basic Python classes
- How to install Python modules with pip, and how to import modules into your code

Download the example code files

You can download the example code files for this book from your account at www.packt.com. If you purchased this book elsewhere, you can visit www.packt.com/support and register to have the files emailed directly to you.

You can download the code files by following these steps:

1. Log in or register at www.packt.com
2. Select the **SUPPORT** tab
3. Click on **Code Downloads & Errata**
4. Enter the name of the book in the **Search** box and follow the onscreen instructions

Once the file is downloaded, please make sure that you unzip or extract the folder using the latest version of:

- WinRAR/7-Zip for Windows
- Zipeg/iZip/UnRarX for Mac
- 7-Zip/PeaZip for Linux

The code bundle for the book is also hosted on GitHub at `https://github.com/PacktPublishing/Hands-On-Software-Engineering-with-Python`. We also have other code bundles from our rich catalog of books and videos available at `https://github.com/PacktPublishing/`. Check them out!

Download the color images

We also provide a PDF file that has color images of the screenshots/diagrams used in this book. You can download it here: `https://www.packtpub.com/sites/default/files/downloads/9781788622011_ColorImages.pdf`.

Conventions used

There are a number of text conventions used throughout this book.

`CodeInText`: Indicates code words in text, database table names, folder names, filenames, file extensions, pathnames, dummy URLs, user input, and Twitter handles. Here is an example: "Within the `src` directory is the package tree for the project."

A block of code is set as follows:

```
def SetNodeResource(x, y, z, r, v): n = get_node(x,y) n.z = z
n.resources.add(r, v)
```

When we wish to draw your attention to a particular part of a code block, the relevant lines or items are set in bold:

```
def __private_method(self, arg, *args, **kwargs):
print('%s.__private_method called:' % self.__class__.__name__)
print('+- arg ...... %s' % arg) print('+- args ..... %s' % str(args))
print('+- kwargs ... %s' % kwargs)
```

Any command-line input or output is written as follows:

```
$python setup.py test
```

Bold: Indicates a new term, an important word, or words that you see on the screen, for example, in menus or dialog boxes, also appear in the text like this. For example: "Select **System info** from the **Administration panel**."

 Warnings or important notes appear like this.

 Tips and tricks appear like this.

Get in touch

Feedback from our readers is always welcome.

General feedback: Email customercare@packtpub.com and mention the book title in the subject of your message. If you have questions about any aspect of this book, please email us at customercare@packtpub.com.

Errata: Although we have taken every care to ensure the accuracy of our content, mistakes do happen. If you have found a mistake in this book, we would be grateful if you would report this to us. Please visit www.packt.com/submit-errata, selecting your book, clicking on the Errata Submission Form link, and entering the details.

Piracy: If you come across any illegal copies of our works in any form on the Internet, we would be grateful if you would provide us with the location address or website name. Please contact us at copyright@packt.com with a link to the material.

If you are interested in becoming an author: If there is a topic that you have expertise in and you are interested in either writing or contributing to a book, please visit authors.packtpub.com.

Reviews

Please leave a review. Once you have read and used this book, why not leave a review on the site that you purchased it from? Potential readers can then see and use your unbiased opinion to make purchase decisions, we at Packt can understand what you think about our products, and our authors can see your feedback on their book. Thank you!

For more information about Packt, please visit `packtpub.com`.

The Software Development Life Cycle

1

All software development, Python or otherwise, above a certain level of complexity follows repeatable patterns, or has a life cycle. A **Software** (or **System**) **Development Life-Cycle** (**SDLC**) might be used as its own distinct development methodology, providing a set of tasks and activities that apply to the development process. That is, even if there is no formal process wrapped around an SDLC, any or all of the activities that go on through one may still take place, and any or all of the artifacts that come out of them may be available during the development of a project.

From the perspective of the actual development, not all of the artifacts resulting from an SDLC, formal or otherwise, may be significantly useful, either, particularly those coming out of the first few phases of the life cycle's process. Even so, the more knowledge that is available during the development process, the less likely it is that development efforts will go in directions that run contrary to the intentions of the system on a longer-term basis.

In order to fully explore what an SDLC might provide, we'll use one of the more detailed ones that can be found on the internet. It breaks the life cycle down into ten phases, which would be executed in the following order, barring process alterations from a development methodology:

- Initial concept/vision
- Concept development
- Project management planning
- Requirements analysis and definition
- System architecture and design
- Development (writing code) and quality assurance
- System integration, testing, and acceptance

- Implementation/installation/distribution
- Operations/use and maintenance
- Decommissioning

 Many of these individual phases can be merged together, or might be broken out into smaller sub-phases, but this breakdown—these ten phases—is a useful grouping of similar activities with similar scopes.

The first three phases may all occur before any code is written, defining the high-level concepts and goals, and planning for how to accomplish those goals. The last three generally happen after code is complete, though as new features are thought of, or as bugs surface, code development may restart to address those items. The balance, phases 4 through 7, are loosely classifiable as **during development**, though, except for the actual writing of code in phase 6, that classification may depend on what development processes or methodologies are in play, something that is likely decided during phase 3 if it isn't already determined by external policies or forces.

 Different software development methodologies (Agile ones in particular) may well address these in more of an on-demand manner, grouping phase activities iteration by iteration, story by story, or out of the sequence they are listed in here. A deeper exploration of these variations can be found in Chapter 4, *Methodologies, Paradigms, and Practices*.

Pre-development phases of the SDLC

Before the first line of code is written, there is the potential for a fair amount of thought and work going into a project. Not all of the work is going to be visible by the time development starts, and, realistically, not all of what could be produced pre-development will be, in many cases. Even those artifacts that are created may not have any formal structure or documentation around them, or may not be as complete or detailed as might be desired. Despite all of that, knowing what might be available that is of use or interest during development can at least help answer questions that can arise during the actual writing-of-code portion of a system/project.

Initial concept/vision

The very first thing that happens in a project's or system's life is its conception. Behind the scenes, that usually involves the recognition of some unfulfilled need, or something that isn't working the way it should, though other variations might occur as well. As part of that realization, there will frequently be a collection of capabilities that the conceived system will provide, benefits or functionality that will drive the system's development, and determine when that development is complete. At this initial, very high-level overview, there may not be much in the way of detail—we need a better way to manage inventory, maybe for the entire vision, for example—but it's possible that more detail will enter the picture, too.

The concept and the benefits might come from anyone with a stake in the system: business staff who are looking for a better way of doing things, developers who perhaps recognize that an existing system isn't as effective as it could be, or maybe that it's difficult to maintain. System administrators might have concerns about how easily managed an in-place system is and want a newer, better approach taken, or the initial vision might be for something completely new, at least in the context of the business setting—we need a way to keep track of fuel efficiency across our delivery truck fleet, maybe. What about if our customers could order our products online?

Hopefully, if off-the-shelf solutions or products are available that meet parts of these needs, those options will have been investigated in some detail—maybe even to the point where the vision owner would be able to point to some feature set(s) of those products and say, "We want something like this." Having examples of functionality that's close to what's actually wanted can be a significant time-saver during pre-development design and development alike, and it's almost always worth asking if there are examples of what's wanted as the design and development processes move along. If that sort of investigation was undertaken and no options were found that were even close, that, too, has useful information embedded in it—what was missing? What did product X do that wasn't meeting the needs in the concept? If no investigation was undertaken, or if nothing came out of an investigation, it's quite possible that the initial concept would be no more than a sentence or two. That's alright, though, since more detail will be extracted later on as the concept development gets underway.

 The "no investigation was undertaken" scenario, in the author's experience, happens more frequently than might be expected, particularly in businesses that are heavily invested in the development of their own products, or where there is a desire to own all the code.

In more formal processes, other analyses may also take place, looking for things such as the following:

- **Specific user needs**: What users must be able to do within the system, and probably what they should be able to do. There may also be a collection of nice-to-have features—things that users would like to be able to do, but that are not a functional necessity.
- **Specific functional needs**: What problems the system needs to solve, or at least mitigate in a significant fashion.
- **Risks**: Usually business-process-related risks, but those may also serve to guide design and development in later phases.
- **Costs**: Both in money and resources. Odds are that this information won't yield much use from a development process perspective, but it's not impossible for an occasional significant nugget of information to come out of this either.
- **Operational feasibility**: Examining how well the conceptual system addresses the needs it's been thought up to address. Like with cost analysis, the odds are good that there won't be much that comes out of this that's directly useful for development purposes, but it might identify operational or design areas where there is doubt about feasibility, and those doubts, in turn, may well shape design and/or implementation by the time the system is in development.

At best, then, given either a formal process, or sufficient attention to detail in an informal one, the initial concept might produce information or documentation about the following:

- Benefits or functionality expected from the system (usually at a high level, at least to start with):
    - A collection of specific, high-level functional needs
    - A collection of specific user needs
- Specific features or functionality that were not provided by an off-the-shelf system (thus justifying custom development effort)
- Specific risks to mitigate against
- Specific functional or feasibility concerns to address

All of these have at least some value once development is underway and will hopefully make their way into design or requirements, and from there into development.

Concept development

Concept development is concerned mostly with fleshing out some of the high-level details that come out of the initial concept, providing details and direction for efforts later in the life cycle. One of the more significant aspects of this step is the generation of various System Modeling artifacts—and there's enough involved in those efforts that they'll be covered in a separate chapter. The balance of the development-related information that comes out of this phase is probably focused more on marrying business processes and system functionality, and providing some detail around system goals. There is also room here for a definition of at least a basic user experience and/or user interface, especially as they connect to the process/functionality.

Defining the business processes embedded in a system includes identifying the business objects that the system keeps track of, the actions that can be taken with respect to those objects, and the outcomes of those actions, at a minimum. Applying of the sort of questioning described earlier in `Chapter 1`, *Programming versus Software Engineering*, can yield a fair bit of that information, if more detail is needed.

 This same system concept will be revisited in `Chapter 3`, *System Modeling*, to illustrate how fleshing out the high-level technical design aspects of a system might progress.

By way of example, consider a system whose concept begins with the knowledge that they need a way to keep track of fuel efficiency across their delivery truck fleet. Working out the business objects and activities from there could answer some very basic questions, such as the following:

- **What is the system keeping track of?**: The individual trucks in the fleet, the mileage on the odometers of those trucks at irregular intervals, and the refueling of those trucks, at a minimum.
- **What does a refueling look like?**: A fuel quantity and the odometer reading at the time of refueling, to start with. Those two data points would allow for the calculation of fuel efficiency, which is calculated in whatever units each uses (gallons or liters for fuel, miles or kilometers for the odometer). Fuel efficiency becomes a calculation of any given refueling for any given truck, and the current odometer reading for any given truck can be retrieved from the odometer reading at its last refueling.

- **How many refuelings should be kept for any given truck?**: If one of the goals of the system is to detect when a truck's fuel efficiency has dropped, in order to flag it for maintenance, perhaps, or to trigger a review of the delivery scheduling associated with it, then there is an obvious need to keep track of more than one such refueling—maybe all of them.
- **Who will be using the system, how, and where?**: There would need to be at least two types of physical access point: one from mobile devices (when fueling a truck), and one from in-office computers (for reporting purposes, if nothing else). That set of use cases tells us that we're looking at either a web application, or some sort of dedicated phone and computer application set, with access to some common data stores, possibly through a service layer.

There may be other questions that could be asked, but these four alone probably give enough information to make the most of major concept design decisions, though the latter may require a bit more exploration before they can be finalized. Similar questioning, asking things such as What can (a specific type of user) do with the system until there aren't any more users and activities, can also yield more specific system goals:

- Various users can log refuelings, providing the current odometer reading, and the quantity of fuel involved:
    - Delivery drivers (at local fuel stations)
    - Fleet maintenance staff (at the main office, where there is a company fuel station)
- Fleet maintenance staff will be alerted when a truck's calculated fuel efficiency drops to lower than 90% of its average, so that the truck can be scheduled for an examination
- Office staff will also be alerted when a truck's calculated fuel efficiency drops to lower than 90% of its average, so that the truck's delivery rounds can be examined

The question of how and where users will interact with the system may well spark some discussion and design decisions around user experience and interface design as well. In this case, perhaps after discussion about whether the system is a web application or dedicated phone and desktop application, the decision is made to make it a web application and to use the **Clarity Design System** for the UI, because the primary stakeholder in the system's vision likes the way it handles on-screen **cards:**

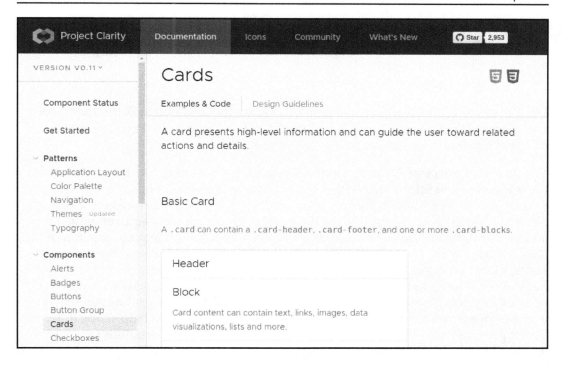

Project management planning

This phase of the life cycle is where all of the conceptual items come together, hopefully in a form or fashion that's ready for the actual creation of code to start. If there is a formal PMP document as a result, its outline might look something like this:

- Business purpose
- Objectives
- Goals
- What's included
- What's excluded
- Key assumptions
- Project organization:
    - Roles and responsibilities
    - Stakeholders
    - Communication

- Risks, issues, and dependencies
- Preliminary schedule of deliverables
- Change management
- Risk and issue management

Developers won't need all of these items, but knowing where to look for various bits and pieces of the information they will need (or, in some cases, who to contact for information) is advantageous, so:

The **Business purpose**, **Objectives**, and **Goals** sections should, ideally, collect all of the original vision information (from the initial concept/vision phase) with whatever details have been added or changes made after the concept design was complete. These will, in all probability, include the starting points for the **Requirements analysis and definition** efforts that go on during the development-specific phases of the life cycle. In addition, the **What's included**, **What's excluded**, and **Key assumptions** sections, between them, should expose what the actual scope of development looks like, as well as providing high-level design decisions and any relevant high-level system modeling information. **Risks, issues,** and **dependencies** may provide specific items of concern or other interests that will help shape the development efforts. Finally, **Change management** will set expectations (at a high level, at least) for what processes are expected or planned for as changes to the system are made.

People in a position to answer questions or make decisions about the system's implementation that fall outside the scope of pure development will probably be listed in the **Roles and responsibilities** and/or **Stakeholders** sections, though there may be specific established processes for raising those questions in the **Communication** section.

Even without formal documentation around project management expectations, much of the information noted previously should still be made known to development staff—the less time spent having to track down who can answer a question, the more time can be devoted to actually writing code, after all.

Development – specific phases of the SDLC

Since the advent of Agile methodologies, and the widespread adoption of many of them, the specific shapes of the development-specific phases of an SDLC can vary substantially. Different methodologies make different decisions about what to prioritize or emphasize, and those differences can, in turn, yield significantly different processes and artifacts to accomplish the goals of formal SDLC phases that focus directly on developer needs and activities. Whole books have been written about several of the Agile processes, so a complete discussion of them is well beyond the scope of this book, but all of them address the following activities.

Requirements analysis and definition

Requirements analysis and definition are concerned with discovering and detailing the specific requirements of a system—what the system needs to allow users to do with it. Users obviously includes end users, ranging from office workers using the system to conduct day-to-day business, to external end users such as customers. Less obviously, users should also include system administrators, staff who receive data from the system through some reporting processes, and perhaps any number of other people who interact with the system in any fashion, or who are acted upon by it—including the developers themselves.

Requirements are, first and foremost, about those interactions, and developers have to know what is expected of the system in order to write code to provide those capabilities.

System architecture and design

If requirements analysis and definition are about what a system provides, system architecture and design are primarily about how those capabilities work. The differences in how various development methodologies deal with architecture and design is less about that how and more about when they are defined. Essentially, given a set of requirements (the intentions behind the system, or the why), the implementation details (the how) will almost certainly be determined more by those requirements and the specifics of how best to implement them in the programming language than by when they are identified, consolidated, or formalized.

Developers need to know how best to implement the required functionality, and that is what this phase is concerned with.

Development and quality assurance

The development part of this phase probably requires the least explanation: it's when the actual code gets written, using the defined requirements to determine what the goals of the code are, and the architecture/design to determine how to write the code. An argument could probably be made that the quality assurance part of this phase should be broken out into its own grouping, if only because many of the activities involved are substantially different—there's less code authoring going on, if there is any at all, in executing a manual test plan, after all. That said, the concept of automated testing, which may be able to replace a lot of the old-style manual test plan execution activities, does require a substantial amount of code, at least at first. Once those test suites are established, regression testing becomes much simpler and less time-consuming. Development methodologies' concerns with the QA aspects of this phase are usually centered around when QA activities take place, while the actual expectations of those activities are usually a combination of development standards and best practices.

Developers need to know what quality assurance efforts are expected of them, and plan (and perhaps write code) accordingly during development.

Automated testing is also a critical foundation for increasingly popular Continuous Integration (CI) and Continuous Delivery/Deployment (CD) practices.

System integration, testing, and acceptance

If a system is above a certain size or degree of complexity, it's just a matter of time before new code coming out of development efforts will have to be incorporated into the larger system environment. Attention may also need to be paid to interactions with other systems, and any of the implications that are raised in those scenarios. In smaller, less complex systems, this integration may be achievable during development.

In either case, the integration of new (or modified) functionality needs to be tested to assure that it hasn't broken anything, both in the local system and in any other systems that interact with it.

 Developers need to know how and where their code fits into the larger system, and thus how to integrate it. As with the Quality Assurance portion of the previous phase, developers also need to know what testing efforts are expected of them, for much the same reasons.

Post-development phases of the SDLC

The portions of the SDLC that happen after the core code of a system is written can still have significant impacts on the development cycle. Historically, they might not involve a lot of real development effort—some code may be written as a one-off for various specific purposes such as packaging the system's code, or facilitating its installation on a target environment, for example. If the structure of the system's code base or, rarely, the language that the system is written in doesn't somehow prevent it, most of any code that was written in support of post-development activities would probably be created very early on in the development process in order to meet some other need.

As a case in point, packaging the code-base, and/or the creation of some installation mechanism is pretty likely to be undertaken the first time the code-base needs to be installed on an environment for user acceptance testing. If that expectation is known ahead of time—and it should be, at some level—then efforts to write the packaging process in order to write the installer may well start before any real code is created. After that point, further efforts will usually happen infrequently, as new components need to be added to a package structure, or changes to an installation process need to be undertaken. Changes at that level will often be minor, and typically needed with less and less frequency as the process matures and the code base installation. This sort of process evolution is at least a starting point for DevOps and some Continuous Delivery practices.

 Developers will need to know how the system is supposed to be distributed and installed so that they can plan around those needs, writing code to facilitate them as required.

The last two phases of the SDLC, concerned with the day-to-day use of the system and with its eventual retirement, will have less relevance to the core development process in general. The most likely exception to that would be re-entry into the development cycle phases in order to handle bugs or add new features or functionality (the *Use and Maintenance* part of the *Operations/Use and Maintenance* phase).

From the perspective of system administrators, the staff responsible for the execution of activities in those phases, developers are contributors to the knowledge and processes they need in much the same way that all of the pre-development contributors to the system's development were with respect to developer knowledge and processes. System administration and maintenance staff will be looking for and using various artifacts that come out of the development process in order to be able to execute their day-to-day efforts with respect to the system. The odds are good that those artifacts will mostly be knowledge, in the form of documentation, and perhaps the occasional system administration tool.

 Developers will need to know what kind of information is needed for post-development activities in order to be able to provide the relevant documentation or to write code to facilitate common or expected tasks.

Finally, with respect to the process of decommissioning a system, taking it offline, presumably never to be used again: someone, probably at a business decision level, will have to provide direction, or even formal business policies and procedures around what needs to happen. At a minimum, those will likely include the following

- Requirements for preserving and archiving system data (or how it should be disposed of, if it's sensitive data)
- Requirements for notifying users of the system's decommissioning

There may well be more, even a lot more—it's very dependent on the system itself, both structurally and functionally, as well as any business policies that might apply.

 Developers will need to know what should happen when the system is finally shut down for good so that they can plan and document accordingly.

 Knowing how things will be handled during a complete and permanent shutdown may give significant insight into how system processes and data can or should be handled when normal data deletion is executed during normal system operation.

Summary

Even if there is no formal SDLC in place, a lot of the information that would come out of one is still advantageous for developers to have access to. If enough of it is available, and if it's sufficiently detailed, readily accessible, and, above all, accurate, it can certainly help make the difference between a project just being programmed and being well-engineered software.

Another significant contributor to making that difference is the availability of similar information about the system itself, in any or all of several *System Model* artifacts. Those provide more implementation-oriented details that should be at least as useful as the policy and procedure-level information from the various SDLC artifacts. We'll take a look at those next.

Summary

2
System Modeling

The goal of any **system modeling** process is to define and document a conceptual model of some aspect of a system, usually focusing individually on one (or many) specific faces of that system. System models may be defined in a formal architecture description language, such as **Unified Modeling Language (UML)**, and can, in those cases, get very detailed – down to the minimum required property and method members of classes. Details at that level are generally fluid – or at least not finalized – until the requirements analysis processes in Agile methodologies, and will be discussed in more detail in `Chapter 4`, *Methodologies, Paradigms, and Practices*.

At a higher, less granular level, there are still several system-model views that are of particular interest going into the development process, particularly with respect to the bigger picture:

- Architecture, both logical and physical
- Business processes and rules
- Data structure and flow
- Interprocess communication
- System scope/scale

Architecture, both logical and physical

The goal of both logical and physical architecture specifications is to define and document the logical and physical components of a system, respectively, in order to provide clarity around how those component elements relate to one another. The artifacts resulting from either effort could be text documentation, or diagrams, and both have their own advantages and drawbacks.

Text documentation is usually quicker to produce, but unless there is some sort of architectural documentation standard that can be applied, the formats can (and probably will) vary from one system team to another, at a minimum. That sort of variance can make it difficult for the resulting artifacts to be understandable outside the team that it originated with. If there is not a lot of movement of developers between teams, or a significant influx of new developers to teams, that may not be a significant concern. It can also be difficult to ensure that all of the moving parts or the connections between them are fully accounted for.

The primary advantage to diagrams is the relative ease with which they can be understood. If the diagram has obvious indicators, or symbols that unambiguously indicate, for example, that one component is a database service and another is an application, then the difference between them becomes obvious at a glance. Diagrams also have the advantage of being more easily understandable to non-technical audiences.

In both cases, text-based or diagram-based documents are, obviously, most useful if they are well-constructed, and provide an accurate view or model of the system.

Logical architecture

Development is often going to be more concerned with the logical architecture of a system than with the physical. Provided that whatever mechanisms needed are in place for the actual code in a system to be deployed to, live on, connect to, and use the various physical components that relate to the logical components, and that any physical architecture constraints are accounted for, little more information is generally needed, so where any given component lives just isn't as important from that perspective. That often means that a physical architecture breakdown is at best a nice-to-have item, or maybe a should-have at most. That also assumes that the structure in question isn't something that's so commonplace that a need for it to be documented surfaced. There are, for example, any number of systems in the wild that follow the same common three-tier structure, with a request-response cycle that progresses as follows:

1. A user makes a request through the **Presentation Tier**
2. That request is handed off to the **Application Tier**
3. The application retrieves any data needed from the **Data Tier**, perhaps doing some manipulation or aggregation of it in the process

4. The **Application Tier** generates a response and hands it back to the **Presentation Tier**
5. The **Presentation Tier** returns that response to the user

Diagrammed, that structure might look as follows:

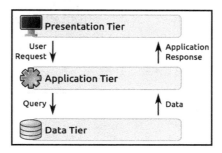

This three-tier architecture is particularly common in web applications, where:

- The **Presentation Tier** is the web-server (with the web browser being no more than a remote output-rendering component)
- The **Application Tier** is code called by, and generating responses to, the web server, written in whatever language and/or framework
- The **Data Tier** is any of several back-end data-store variants that persist application data between requests

Consider, as an example, the following logical architecture for the refueling-tracking system concept mentioned earlier. It serves as a good example of this three-tier architecture as it applies to a web application, with some specifically identified components:

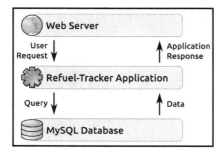

Physical architecture

The primary difference between logical and physical architecture documentation is that, while logical architecture's concerns end with identifying functional elements of the system, physical architecture takes an additional step, specifying actual devices that those functional elements execute on. Individual items identified in logical architecture may reside on common devices, physically. Really, the only limitations are the performance and capabilities of the physical device. This means that these different physical architectures are all logically identical; they are all valid ways of implementing the same three-tier web application's logical architecture:

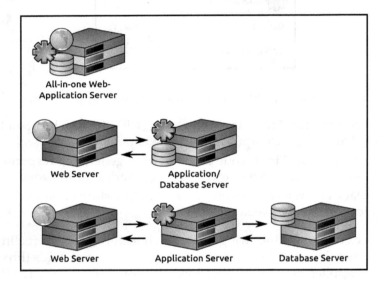

With the current enthusiasm for virtualization, serverless, and cloud-based technologies in the industry, provided by public and private cloud technologies such as Amazon Web Services and VMware, whether a physical architecture specification really is a physical architecture often becomes something of a semantics quibble. While, in some cases, there may not be a single, identifiable physical computer the way there would be if there was a dedicated piece of server hardware, in many cases that distinction is irrelevant. If it acts like a distinct physical server, it can be treated as one for the purposes of defining a physical architecture. In that case, from a documentation standpoint, there is no knowledge value lost in treating a virtual server like a real one.

When considering many serverless elements in a system, several can still be represented as a physical architecture element as well – so long as it acts like a real device from the perspective of how it interacts with the other elements, the representation is adequate. That is, given a hypothetical web application that lives completely in some public cloud, where:

- That cloud allows serverless functions to be defined
- Functions will be defined for processing the following, with back-end databases for each of those entities also living in the cloud:
    - Customers
    - Products
    - Orders

A corresponding physical architecture might look something as follows:

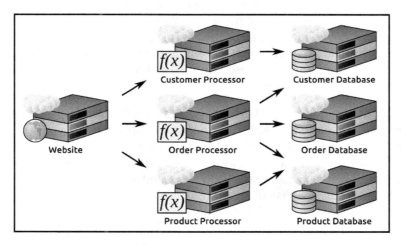

An example real-world implementation of this serverless architecture can be implemented in all three of the big-name public clouds: **Amazon Web Services** (**AWS**), Azure, and **Google Cloud Platform** (**GCP**). Each of these public cloud platforms provides virtual server-instances that could serve the website and maybe databases. The processor servers in this structure could use serverless functions (AWS Lambda, or Cloud Functions in Azure and GCP) to drive the interactions between the website and the databases as the website sends events to the functions in the processor elements.

Collectively, logical and physical architecture specifications provide development with at least some of the information needed to be able to interact with non-application tiers. Even if specific credentials will be required but are not supplied in the documentation, knowing, for example, what kind of database drives the data tier of a system defines how that data tier will be accessed.

Use cases (business processes and rules)

In any system, the most important thing is whether it's doing what it's supposed to do for all of the use cases that it's supposed to support. Code has to be written for each of those use cases, and each use case corresponds to one or more business processes or rules, so it's only logical that each of those use cases needs to be defined and documented to whatever extent is appropriate for the development process. As with the logical and physical architecture, it's possible to execute those definitions as either text or some sort of diagram, and those approaches have the same advantages and drawbacks that were noted before.

The Unified Modeling Language (UML) provides a high-level diagramming standard for use cases, useful mostly for capturing the relationship between specific types of users (actors, in UML's terminology) and the processes that they are expected to interact with. That's a good start, and may even be sufficient all by itself if the process itself is very simple, already extensively documented, or known across the development team. The use case diagram for the Refuel-Tracker application concept that was discussed earlier in *Use Cases* section is, so far, very simple, and harks back to the system goals that were established for it in the Chapter 2, *The Software Development Life Cycle*. This time, though, we'll attach some names to them for reference in the diagram:

- **Refuel**: Various users can log refueling's, providing the current odometer reading and the quantity of fuel involved:
    - Delivery drivers (at local fuel-stations)
    - Fleet maintenance staff (at the main office, where there is a company fuel station)
- **Maintenance Alert**: Fleet maintenance staff will be alerted when a truck's calculated fuel efficiency drops to lower than 90% of its average, so that the truck can be scheduled for an examination.

- **Route Review Alert**: Office staff will also be alerted when a truck's calculated fuel efficiency drops to lower than 90% of its average, so that the truck's delivery rounds can be examined.

Those three use cases are simple to diagram, if that's the preferred documentation. The following list of processes is also a viable option. In some ways it's actually better than a standard diagram, since it provides some business rules of the system that a standard use case diagram doesn't capture:

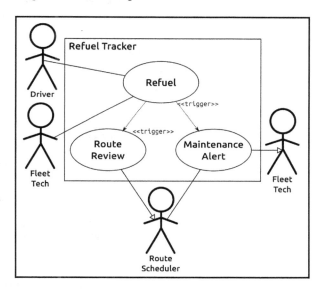

Even if the diagram were modified to include some of the missing information (what a refueling is, and what the rules around the two «trigger» items are), it still only tells part of the story: who is expected (or allowed) to use specific process functionality. The balances, the actual processes underneath the use cases, are still unknown, but need to be exposed so that code can be written around them to actually make them work. This also can be handled either as plain text of some sort, or through a diagram. Looking at the Refuel process that's been identified, it breaks down to something as follows:

- A **Driver** or **Fleet Tech** logs a refuel of a truck, providing:
  - The current odometer reading
  - The amount of fuel used to fill the truck
- Those values are stored (probably in an application database, though that may not be part of the actual requirements) with an association to the truck (how that gets specified has yet to be determined).

- The application calculates the fuel efficiency for the refueling: (current odometer reading minus previous odometer reading) ÷ quantity of fuel.
- If the efficiency is less than or equal to 90% of the most recent efficiency value for that truck, the **Route Review** alert is triggered .
- If the efficiency is less than or equal to 90% of at least half of the previous four efficiency values for that truck, the **Maintenance** alert is triggered.

Whether a diagram (such as the following flowchart) would add any value to the documentation will likely depend on the process being described, and on team or even personal preferences. These five steps, as a simple flowchart, are simple enough that going any further than a text description of them is probably not going to add any value, but more complex processes might benefit from a diagram:

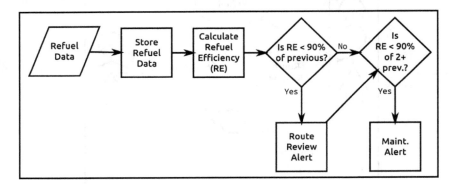

From a developer's perspective, use cases map out to one-to-many functions or methods that will have to be implemented, and if there are process flows documented, those explain how they will execute at runtime.

Data structure and flow

Between the two of them, basic use-case and business-process documentation may provide enough information to make the structure and flow of the data through the system obvious, or at least transparent enough that development won't need any additional information. The Refuel process we've been looking at probably falls into that category, but let's see what a data-flow diagram for it might look like anyway.

The data that's coming in (the **Refuel Data** in the flowchart) was defined earlier in *Use Cases* section, and at least some of the related data flow was also noted, but having some names to associate with those values, and knowing what types of value they are, will be helpful:

- `odometer`: The current odometer reading (probably an `<int>` value)

- `fuel_quantity`: The amount of fuel used to fill the truck (probably a `<float>` value)

- `truck_id`: The truck being refueled (a unique identifier for the record of the truck in the application's database – to keep things simple, we'll assume it's also `<int>`)

During the process, a refuel-efficiency value is also being created that might need to be passed along to the **Route Review** alert and/or **Maintenance** alert processes:

- `re`: The calculated refuel-efficiency value, a `<float>` value

In this very simple case, data elements are simply being noted, by name and type. The diagram indicates where they start being available, or when they are explicitly passed to a process – otherwise they are assumed to be available all the way through. Then the data elements are just added to the previous flowchart diagram:

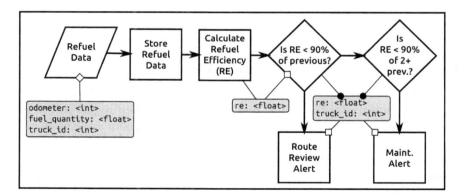

In a more complicated system, something that has more complex data structures, more data structures in general, more processes that use those, or any of several combinations of those factors, a source and destination oriented flow-diagram may be a better option – something that doesn't really pay attention to the inner workings of the processes, just to what data is needed, and where it comes from.

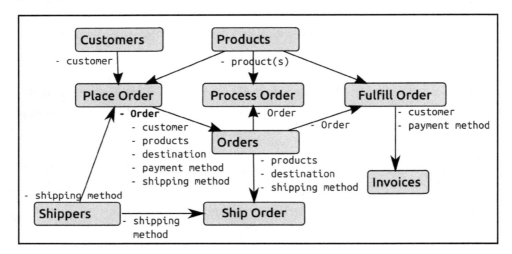

 Data-flow documentation/diagrams tell developers what data is expected, where it's originating from, and where/whether it's going to live after the processes are done with it.

Interprocess communication

It's very common for different processes to communicate with each other. At the most basic level, that communication might take the form of something as simple as one function or method calling another from somewhere in the code they share. As processes scale outward, though, especially if they are distributed across separate physical or virtual devices, those communication chains will often get more complex themselves, sometimes even requiring dedicated communications protocols. Similar communication-process complexities can also surface, even in relatively uncomplicated systems, if there are interprocess dependencies that need to be accounted for.

In pretty much any scenario where the communication mechanism between two processes is more complicated than something at the level of methods calling other methods, or perhaps a method or process writing data that another process will pick up and run with the next time it's executed, it's worth documenting how those communications will work. If the basic unit of communication between processes is thought of as a message, then, at a minimum, documenting the following will generally provide a solid starting point for writing the code that implements those interprocess communication mechanisms:

- **What the message contains**: The specific data expected:
    - What is required in the message
    - What additional/optional data might be present

- **How the message is formatted**: If the message is serialized in some fashion, converted to JSON, YAML, or XML, for example, that needs to be noted

- **How the message is transmitted and received**: It could be queued up on a database, transmitted directly over some network protocol, or use a dedicated message-queue system such as RabbitMQ, AWS SQS, or Google Cloud Platform's Publish/Subscribe

    - **What kinds of constraint apply to the message protocol**: For example, most message-queuing systems will guarantee the delivery of any given queued message once, but not more than once.

    - **How messages are managed on the receiving end**: In some distributed message-queue systems – certain variants of AWS SQS, for example – the message has to be actively deleted from the queue, lest it be received more than once, and potentially acted upon more than once. Others, such as RabbitMQ, automatically delete messages as they are retrieved. In most other cases, the message only lives as long as it takes to reach its destination and be received.

Interprocess-communication diagramming can usually build on the logical architecture and use-case diagrams. One provides the logical components that are the endpoints of the communication process, the other identifies what processes need to communicate with each other. Documented data flow may also contribute to the bigger picture, and would be worth looking at from the perspective of identifying any communication paths that might've been missed elsewhere.

The refuel tracker, for example:

- Can access the database for the existing route-scheduling application, which provides a dashboard for the route schedulers.

- The maintenance alert functionality can leverage a web service call belonging to an off-the-shelf fleet-maintenance system that was purchased, which has its own dashboard used by the fleet technicians.

The relevant messaging involved for the route-review and maintenance-alert processes is very simple under these circumstances:

- An update in the route-scheduling database, perhaps flagging the last route that the truck was scheduled for as an inefficient route, or maybe some sort of notification that'll pop up on the dashboard to alert a route scheduler to review the route

- A JSON-over-REST API call made to the maintenance-tracking system

That messaging would fit on a simple variant of the use case diagram already shown:

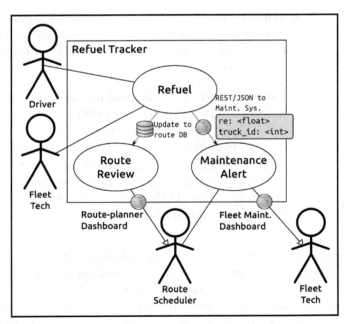

The order-processing, fulfillment, and shipping system might use RabbitMQ messaging to deal with order-fulfillment, passing entire orders and simple inventory checks from the products datasource to determine whether an order can be fulfilled. It might also use any of several web service API calls to manage order shipment, pushing the shipping information back into the order over a similar web service call. That message flow (omitting the data structure for brevity) might then look as follows:

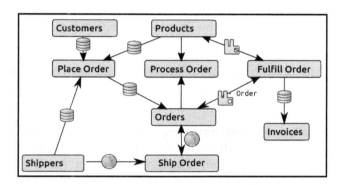

 The main takeaway from a development focus on Interprocess Communication is how the data identified earlier gets from one point in the system to another.

System scope and scale

If all of these items are documented and/or diagrammed, if it's done thoroughly and accurately, they will, collectively, provide a holistic view of the total scope of a system:

- Every system component role should be identified in the Logical Architecture
- Where each of those components actually resides should be identified in the Physical Architecture
- Every use case (and hopefully every business process) that the system is supposed to implement should be identified in the use-case documentation, and any of the underlying processes that aren't painfully obvious should have at least a rough happy-path breakdown

- Every chunk of data that moves from one place or process to another should be identified in the Data Flow, with enough detail to collate a fairly complete picture of the structure of that data as well
- The formats and protocols that govern how that data move about, at least for any part of the system that involves more than just passing system objects from one function or method in the code-base to another, should be identified
- A fair idea of where and how those data are persisted should be discernible from the Logical, and maybe Physical, architectures

The only significant missing piece that hasn't been noted is the scale of the system. If the scope is how many types of object are being worked with or are moving around in the system, the scale would be how many of those objects exist, either at rest (stored in a database, for example) or actively at any given time.

Scale can be hard to anticipate with any accuracy, depending on the context of the system. Systems such as the hypothetical refueling tracker and order-processing/fulfillment/shipping system that have been used for illustration are generally going to be more predictable:

- **The number of users is going to be reasonably predictable**: All employees and all customers pretty much covers the maximum user base for both of those

- **The number of objects being used is also going to be reasonably predictable**: The delivery company only has so many trucks, after all, and the company running the order system, though probably less predictable, will still have a fair idea of how many orders are in flight at most, and at typical levels

When a system or application enters a user space such as the web, though, there is potential for radical variation, even over very short periods of time. In either case, some sort of planning around expected and maximum/worst-case scale should be undertaken. That planning may have significant design and implementation effects – fetching and working with a dozen records at a time out of a few hundred or thousand total records doesn't require nearly the attention to efficiency that those same twelve records out of several million or billion would, just as a basic example – on how code might be written. If planning for even potential massive surges in use involves being able to scale out to multiple servers, or load-balance requests, that might also have an effect on the code, though probably at a higher, interprocess-communication level.

Summary

All of the components, data, and documentation from this chapter, as well as the previous two chapters, are potentially available in any software engineering effort. How much is actually is available probably depends in part on how much discipline is involved in the predevelopment processes, even if there isn't anything formal associated with it. That discipline might be present because of a singularly talented project manager.

Another contributor to when, how much, and what quality of data is available is often the development methodology in play through the life of a project, system, or team. Several of the more common methodologies manage these predevelopment efforts in significantly different manners, and their treatment can make a substantial difference.

3
Methodologies, Paradigms, and Practices

It could be argued that software engineering, at least as it's usually thought of now, really came into being with the first formally identified software development methodology. That methodology (which was eventually dubbed Waterfall in 1976) made people start thinking about not just how the software worked, or how to write the code, but what the processes around writing the code needed to look like in order to make it more effective. Since then, roughly a dozen other methodologies have come into being, and in at least one case, the collection of various Agile methodologies, there are nearly a dozen distinct sub-variants, though Scrum is almost certainly the most widely known, and Kanban may be a close second.

While those methodologies were growing and maturing, the increase in computing power also led, eventually, to newer, more useful, or more efficient development paradigms. **Object-Oriented Programming (OOP)** and **Functional Programming (FP)** are probably the most well-known advances on the original procedural programming paradigm that dominated the scene for decades. Automation of code integration and promotion practices (Continuous Integration and Delivery, respectively) have also become popular in recent years.

In this chapter, we will cover the following topics:

- Process methodologies
- Waterfall
- Agile:
  - Scrum
  - Kanban
- Development paradigms:
  - Object-Oriented Programming (OOP)
  - Functional Programming (FP)

- Development practices:
  - Continuous Integration
  - Continuous Delivery

Process methodologies

At some level, all development process methodologies are variations on the theme of managing development within the boundaries of some common realities:

- There are only so many useful working hours per person per day that can be devoted to a project
- There is a limit to the available resources, whether in terms of people, equipment, or money, available to a project
- There is a minimum acceptable quality standard for the project when it's complete

This is sometimes expressed as the **Iron Triangle** of project management:

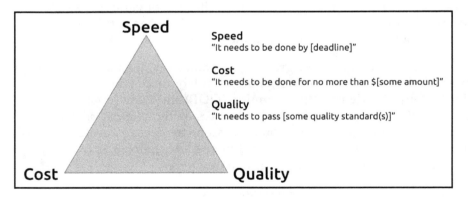

The primary concern with respect to the **Speed** point is time—the most common focus is probably on a project needing to be complete by a specific deadline, or there is some other time constraint that may only be surmountable by adding developers to the team (an increase in **Cost**), or by cutting corners (a decrease in **Quality**).
 Budget variations are a common theme for the **Cost** point—anything that costs money, whether in the form of additional developers, newer/faster/better tools, and so on.
Reducing the available resources/staff decreases the **Speed** of project completion and/or the final **Quality**.

The **Quality** point is, obviously, concerned with quality measures—which might include specific internal or external standards—but could easily include less obvious items such as longer-term maintainability and support for new features and functionality. Prioritizing **Quality**, at a minimum, requires more developer hours, decreasing **Speed**, and increasing **Cost**.

Often, significant priority (whatever value for significant might apply) can only be given to two out of the three points of the triangle at most, yielding three priority possibilities:

- Fast, inexpensive development, at the cost of quality
- Fast, high-quality development, but at greater cost
- High-quality, inexpensive development that takes a longer time to complete

The **Lean Startup Method** (or just Lean) is sometimes cited as an alternative process methodology that can overcome the constraints of the Iron Triangle, but is beyond the scope of this book. A reasonable introduction to its concepts can be found at https://www.castsoftware.com/glossary/lean-development.

There are three specific development process methodologies that are worth an in-depth examination in the context of this book. The first, Waterfall, will be examined in order to provide a frame of reference for two Agile methodologies, Scrum and Kanban, and a few others will be looked at as well, at least briefly. A full discussion of any of them is well beyond the scope of this book, but the intention is to provide enough detail on each of them to illustrate what their focuses and priorities are, as well as their advantages and drawbacks. At a minimum, this should provide a baseline of what to expect while working in any of them, tying the phases of each methodology back to the phases of the model SDLC from Chapter 3, *System Modeling*, to show what happens, when, and how.

Waterfall

Waterfall's ancestry can probably be traced back to manufacturing and/or construction planning. In many respects, it's a very simple approach to planning and implementing a development effort, and is essentially broken down into defining and designing what to build, building it, testing it, and deploying it.

More formally, it's six separate phases, intended to be executed in this order:

- Requirements
- Analysis
- Design
- Implementation
- Testing
- Installation and Operation:

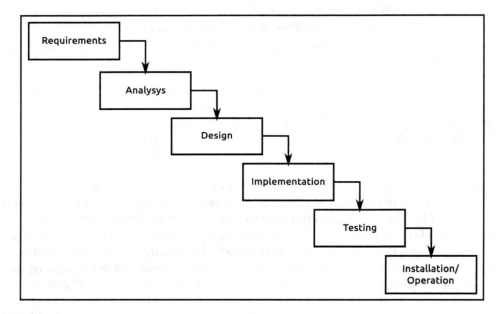

These phases correspond fairly neatly with the sequence of phases in the SDLC. They are very similar, whether by accident or design, and are intended to accomplish many of the same goals. Their focus is probably best summarized as an effort to design, document, and define everything that's needed for development to succeed, before handing that design off to development for implementation. In an ideal execution, the design and requirement information will give developers everything they need, and the project manager may be completely hands-off once implementation starts.

Conceptually, there is some merit to the approach—if everything is thoroughly and accurately documented, then developers will have everything that they need, and they can focus entirely on writing code to accomplish the requirements. Documentation, as part of the initial project specifications, is already created, so once the software is deployed, anyone managing the resulting system will have access to that, and some of that documentation may even be user-oriented and available to them.

If done well, it almost certainly captures and allows for dependencies during implementation, and it provides an easily followed sequence of events. Overall, the methodology is very easily understood. It's almost a reflexive approach to building something: decide what to do, plan how to do it, do it, check that what was done is what was wanted, and then it's done.

In practice, though, a good Waterfall plan and execution is not an easy thing to accomplish unless the people executing the **Requirements**, **Analysis**, and **Design** phases are really good, or sufficient time is taken (maybe a lot of time) to arrive at and review those details. This assumes that the requirements are all identifiable to begin with, which is frequently not the case, and that they don't change mid-stream, which happens more often than might be obvious. Since its focus is on documentation first, it also tends to slow down over long-term application to large or complex systems—the ongoing updating of a growing collection of documentation takes time, after all—and additional (and growing) expenditure of time is almost always required to keep unmanageable bloat from creeping in to other support structures around the system.

The first three phases of a Waterfall process (**Requirements**, **Analysis**, and **Design**) encompass the first five phases of the SDLC model:

- Initial concept/vision
- Concept development
- Project management planning
- Requirements analysis and definition
- System architecture and design

These would ideally include any of the documentation/artifacts from those phases, as well as any *System Modeling* items (Chapter 3, *System Modeling*), all packaged up for developers to use and refer to. Typically, these processes will involve a dedicated Project planner, who is responsible for talking to and coordinating with the various stakeholders, architects, and so on, in order to assemble the whole thing.

In a well-defined and managed Waterfall process, the artifact that comes out of these three phases and gets handed off to development and quality assurance is a document or collection of documents that make up a Project plan. Such a plan can be very long, since it should ideally capture all of the output from all of the pre-development efforts that's of use in and after development:

- Objectives and goals (probably at a high level)
- What's included, and expected of the finished efforts:
    - Complete requirement breakdowns
    - Any risks, issues, or dependencies that need to be mitigated, or at least watched for

- Architecture, design, and system model considerations (new structures or changes to existing structures):
    - Logical and/or physical architecture items
    - Use cases
    - Data structure and flow
    - Interprocess communication
- Development plan(s)
- Quality assurance/testing plan(s)
- Change management plans
- Installation/Distribution plans
- Decommissioning plans

The **Implementation** and **Testing** phases of a Waterfall process, apart from having the Project plan as a starting point reference, are probably going to follow a simple and very typical process:

- Developer writes code
- Developer tests code (writing and executing unit tests), fixing any functional issues and retesting until it's complete
- Developer hands finished code off to quality assurance for further testing
- Quality assurance tests code, handing it back to the developer if issues are found
- Tested/approved code is promoted to the live system

This process is common enough across all development efforts and methodologies that it will not be mentioned again later unless there is a significant deviation from it.

Waterfall's **Installation and Operation** phase incorporates the **Installation/Distribution** and **Operations/Use and Maintenance** phases from the SDLC model. It may also incorporate the **Decommissioning** phase as well, since that may be considered as a special **Operation** situation. Like the **Implementation** and **Testing** phases, chances are that these will progress in an easily anticipated manner—again, apart from the presence of whatever relevant information might exist in the Project plan documentation, there's not really anything to dictate any deviation from a simple, common-sense approach to those, for whatever value of common-sense applies in the context of the system.

While Waterfall is generally dismissed as an outdated methodology, one that tends to be implemented in a too-rigid fashion, and that more or less requires rock-star personnel to work well on a long-term basis, it can still work, provided that one or more conditions exist:

- Requirements and scope are accurately analyzed, and completely accounted for
- Requirements and scope will not change significantly during execution
- The system is not too large or too complex for the methodology to manage
- Changes to a system are not too large or too complex for the methodology to manage

Of these, the first is usually not something that can be relied upon without policy and procedure support that is usually well outside the control of a development team. The latter two will, almost inevitably, be insurmountable given a long enough period of time, if only because it's rare for systems to become smaller or less complex over time, and changes to larger and more complex systems tend to become larger and more complex themselves.

Agile (in general)

By the early 1990s, a sea change was under way in how development processes were viewed. The Waterfall process, despite widespread adoption, even in government contractor policies in the US, started to show more and more of the flaws inherent to its application to large and complex systems. Other, non-Waterfall methodologies that were in use were also starting to show signs of wear from being too heavy, too prone to counter-productive micro-management, and a variety of other complaints and concerns.

As a result, a lot of thought around development processes started focusing on lightweight, iterative, and less management-intensive approaches, that eventually coalesced around the Agile Manifesto and the twelve principles that underlie it:

- We are uncovering better ways of developing software by doing it and helping others do it. Through this work, we have come to value:
    - Individuals and interactions over processes and tools
    - Working software over comprehensive documentation
    - Customer collaboration over contract negotiation
    - Responding to change over following a plan

That is, while there is value in the items on the right, we value the items on the left more. We follow these principles:

- Our highest priority is to satisfy the customer through early and continuous delivery of valuable software.
- Welcome changing requirements, even late in development. Agile processes harness change for the customer's competitive advantage.
- Deliver working software frequently, from a couple of weeks to a couple of months, with a preference for the shorter timescale.
- Business people and developers must work together daily throughout the project.
- Build projects around motivated individuals. Give them the environment and support they need, and trust them to get the job done.
- The most efficient and effective method of conveying information to and within a development team is face-to-face conversation.
- Working software is the primary measure of progress.
- Agile processes promote sustainable development. Sponsors, developers, and users should be able to maintain a constant pace indefinitely.
- Continuous attention to technical excellence and good design enhances agility.
- Simplicity—the art of maximizing the amount of work not done—is essential.
- The best architectures, requirements, and designs emerge from self-organizing teams.
- At regular intervals, the team reflects on how to become more effective, then tunes and adjusts its behavior accordingly.

You may refer to The Agile Manifesto at `http://Agilemanifesto.org/` for more details.

In an application, these principles lead to a few common characteristics across different methodologies. There may be exceptions in other methodologies that are still considered Agile, but for our purposes, and with respect to the specific methodologies discussed here, those common traits are as follows:

- Development happens in a sequence of iterations, each of which has one to many goals
- Each goal is a subset of the final system
- At the conclusion of each iteration, the system is deployable and operational (perhaps only for a given value of operational)
- Requirements are defined in detail in small chunks, and may not be defined at all until just before the iteration that they're going to be worked on

Scrum is claimed to be the most popular, or at least most widely used, Agile development methodology (the 12th *Annual State* of *Agile Report* puts it at 56% of Agile methods in use), and as such is probably worth some more detailed attention. Kanban is another Agile methodology that bears some examination, if only because it's closer to how the main system project in this book is going to be presented.

There are a few other Agile methodologies that also bear at least a quick look-over for some of the specific focus they can bring to a development effort, either on their own, or as a hybrid or mix-in with other methodologies.

 Businesses are also exploring additions and modifications to textbook Agile processes to improve them and address needs that weren't encompassed by the original concept. One such process is the **Scaled Agile Framework**, which is used to improve the use of Agile processes at larger scales.

Scrum

Scrum has the following moving parts, broadly:

- The Scrum methodology centers around time-limited iterations called Sprints:
    - A Sprint is defined as taking some fixed length of time that the development team (and sometimes stakeholders) can agree upon
    - Sprint durations are usually the same duration each time, but that duration can be changed, either temporarily or permanently (until the next time it's changed) if there is reason to do so
- Each Sprint has a set of features/functionality associated with it that the development team has committed to completing by the end of the Sprint.
- Each feature/functionality item is described by a **user story.**
- The team determines what user stories they can commit to completing, given the duration of the Sprint.
- The priority of user stories is determined by a stakeholder (usually a Product Owner), but can be negotiated.
- The team gathers periodically to groom the backlog, which can include:
    - Estimating the size of stories that don't have one
    - Adding task-level detail to user stories
    - Subdividing stories into smaller, more manageable chunks if there are functional dependencies or size-related execution concerns, and getting those approved by the relevant stakeholder(s)
- The team reviews the Sprint at the end, looking for things that went well, or for ways to improve on things that went less-than-well.
- The team meets periodically to plan the next Sprint.
- The team has a short, daily meeting (a stand-up), the purpose of which is to reveal what status has changed since the last update. The best-known format, though not the only one for these meetings, is a quick statement from each participant on:
    - What they have worked on since the last stand-up, complete or otherwise.

- What they are planning on working on until the next stand-up.
- What roadblocks they are dealing with, that someone else in the team might be able to assist with.

Story sizing should not be based around any sort of time estimate. Doing so tends to discount any assessments of complexity and risk that might be critically important, and implies an expectation that all developers will be able to complete the same story in the same length of time, which is probably not going to be the case. Use story points or t-shirt sizes (extra small, small, medium, large, extra large and extra-extra large) instead!

1. From beginning to end, a typical Sprint will unfold something like this, assuming all goes well:
2. **Day 1 Sprint start-up activities**:
    1. Stories and tasks are set up on the task board, whether it's real or virtual, all in a **Not Started** status, in priority order.
    2. Team members claim a story to work on, starting with the highest priority item. If more than one person is working on a single story, they each claim one of the tasks associated with it. Claimed stories are moved to an **In Progress** status on the task board.
3. **Day 1 –day before end of Sprint**: Development and QA.
4. **Daily stand – up meeting** (probably skipped on the first day).
5. **Development**:
    1. As tasks are completed, their status is updated on the task board to indicate as much.
    2. As stories are completed, they are moved to the next status on the task board after development. This column might be **Dev-Complete**, **QA-Ready**, or whatever other status description makes sense given the team's structure.
    3. If roadblocks are encountered, they are notified to the **Scrum Master**, who is responsible for facilitating resolving the blocking issue. If it cannot be resolved immediately, the status of the blocked story or task should be updated on the task board, and the developer moves on to the next task or story that they can tackle.

4. As roadblocks get resolved, the items they were blocking reenter development status, and progress as normal from that point on. There is nothing to say that the developer who encountered the block initially has to be the one to continue work on the item after the block is resolved.

- **Quality Assurance activities**:
    - If QA staff are embedded into the development team, their processes are often similar to development activities, except that they'll start by claiming a story to test from whichever column indicates **Dev-Complete** items
    - Testing a story should include, at a minimum, the **acceptance criteria** of that story
    - Testing may well (and probably should) include functional tests that are not part of the acceptance criteria
- **Story Acceptance**: If there are any stories completed that haven't been accepted, they can be demonstrated and accepted or declined by the relevant stakeholder(s). Declined items will probably go back to the **In Development** or **Not Started** status, depending on why they were declined, and what can be done to resolve the reason for being declined.
- **Sprint-Close Day**:
    - Demonstration and acceptance of any remaining stories.
    - If time has not been available to do so before, preparation for the next Sprint should take place:
        - **Sprint Planning**, to prepare the user stories for the next Sprint
        - **Backlog Grooming**, to prepare and define details and tasks for any user stories that need those details
    - Acceptance of remaining stories.
    - **Retrospective meeting**—the team gathers to identify the following:
        - What worked well in the Sprint, in order to try and leverage what made it work well
        - What worked poorly, or not at all, in order to avoid similar scenarios in the future

All of the daily activities orbit around a task board, which provides a quick mechanism for easily seeing what's in progress, and what the status of each item is:

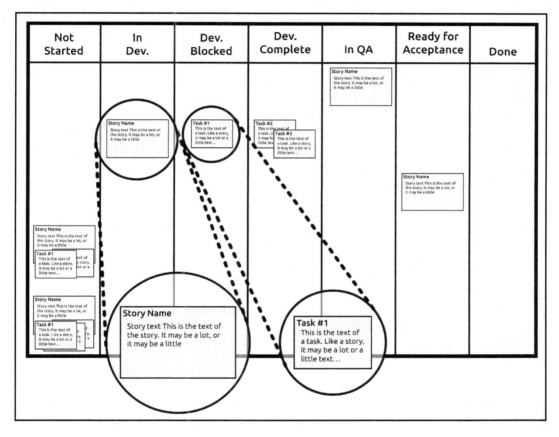

An example task board, showing stories and tasks in different stages of development

The task board shown has more detailed status columns than are technically required—the bare-minimum column set would be **Stories**, where the top-level stories' details live until they are done, **Not Started**, and **In Progress** for tasks that are part of the Sprint, and **Done**, where tasks (and possibly stories) land when they are complete, tested, and ready for acceptance.

Scrum's priorities are its focus on transparency, inspection, and self-correction, and its adaptability to changing needs and requirements. The task board is a significant part of the transparency aspect of the methodology, allowing anyone with any interest to see at a glance what the current status of development efforts is. But it doesn't end there—there is a role known as the **Product Owner**, who acts as the central communications point between the development team and all of the stakeholders of the system. They attend the daily stand-ups, in order to have near-real-time visibility into progress, roadblocks, and so on, and are expected to speak for and make decisions on behalf of the entire collection of stakeholders. They are also responsible for connecting team members with external stakeholders in the event that questions or concerns arise that the Product Owner cannot address themselves. Their role is critical in assuring a good balance between providing transparency into ongoing development efforts to the stakeholders and and not burdening the development team with ongoing status reporting from them.

Scrum expects a fair amount of self-inspection in the process itself, and encourages a similar inspection of the results of the process—the software being created, and the practices and disciplines used in creating it—by prioritizing team openness and member intercommunication, providing a mechanism for raising visibility into risks and blocking conditions, and even, to some degree, by encouraging user stories that entail the smallest amount of effort to achieve a given functional goal. When concerns or issues arise, the emphasis on immediate communication and the ready availability of someone who can provide direction and make decisions resolve those issues quickly, and with a minimal degree of interference with the ongoing development process.

Scrum is, perhaps, one of the better methodologies from an adaptability-to-change perspective. Imagine a situation where a development team has been working on parts of a project for the first week of a two-week (or longer) Sprint. At that point, someone at the stakeholder level suddenly decides that a change needs to be made to one of the stories. There are several possible reasons—good, bad, or indifferent—for that sort of change to be necessary.

Perhaps the functionality that underlies the story is deemed obsolete, and no longer needed at all—if the story hasn't been completed, then it can simply be removed from the Sprint, and another story from the backlog pulled in to be worked on, if one is available that is no larger than the one being removed. If there's already code written against the story, it will probably need to be removed, but that's about it in terms of impact on the code base. If the story is complete, then the related code also gets removed, but no new work (additional stories) gets pulled in.

If the story is changed—the functionality behind it is being altered to better fit user needs or expectations, for example—the story gets withdrawn from the current Sprint in the same fashion as if it were being removed, at the very least. If there is time available to re-scope the story and re-insert it into the Sprint, that can be undertaken, otherwise it will be added to the backlog, probably at or near the top of the list from a priority perspective.

On occasion, it's possible for a Sprint to derail, but the methodology has expectations around how that gets handled as well. If a Sprint cannot complete successfully for any reason, it's supposed to stop, and a new Sprint is planned to pick up from where that one ended.

Some advantageous aspects of Scrum include:

- Scrum is well-suited to work that can be broken down into small, quick efforts. Even in large-scale systems, if additions to or alterations of the large code base can be described in short, low-effort stories, Scrum is a good process to apply.
- Scrum works well for teams that have reasonably consistent skillsets within their domains. That is, if all developers on a team can, for example, write code in the main language of the project without significant assistance, that's a better team dynamic than if only one out of six team members can.

At the same time, because of the structure involved in a Scrum process, there are some caveats:

- Since a Sprint represents a commitment to complete a set of stories and functionality, changing an in-process Sprint, even with a really good reason, is troublesome, time-consuming, and disruptive. That implies, then, that whoever is in the position of making decisions that could require in-process Sprint changes needs to be aware of the potential impacts of those decisions—ideally, perhaps, they would avoid Sprint-disruptive changes without really, really good reasons.
- Scrum may not lend itself well to meeting project- or system-level deadlines until or unless the team has a fair amount of expertise across the entire domain of the system and its code base. Iteration deadlines are at less risk, though they may require altered or reduced scope in order to deliver working software on an iteration-by-iteration basis.

- Development efforts and outputs become less predictable if the team members change—every new team member, especially if they join the team at different times, will have some impact on the team's ability to be predictable until the new team roster has had time to settle in. Scrum can be particularly sensitive to these changes, since new team members may not have all the necessary tribal knowledge to meet an iteration's commitments for a while.

- Scrum may not work well—perhaps not at all—if the members of a team aren't all in the same physical area. With modern teleconferencing, holding the daily stand-up is still possible, as are the other varied meetings, but Scrum is intended to be collaborative, so easier direct access to other team members tends to become important pretty quickly as soon as questions or issues arise.

- Unless it's pretty carefully managed not to, Scrum tends to reinforce skill-set silos in a team—if only one developer knows, for example, how to write code in a secondary language that the system needs, that person will be tapped more frequently or by default for any tasks or stories that need that knowledge in order to meet the iteration's commitments. Making a conscious effort to turn silo-reinforcing stories or tasks into a team or paired development effort can go a long way toward reducing these effects, but if no efforts are made, or if there isn't support for reducing these silos, they will persist.

- Scrum may be challenging if the system has a lot of external dependencies (work from other teams, for example), or a lot of quality control effort that developers have to contend with. This last item can be particularly problematic if those quality control requirements have legal or regulatory requirements associated with them. Assuring that external dependencies are themselves more predictable can go a long way to mitigate these kinds of challenges, but that may be out of the team's control.

Scrum and the phases of the SDLC model

The phases of our SDLC model that are important to the development effort happening during specific parts of a Scrum process are as follows:

- Before development starts:
  - **Requirement** analysis and definition happens during the story creation and grooming portions of the process, often with some follow-up during Sprint planning. The goal is for each story's requirements to be known and available before the story is included in a Sprint.
  - System architecture and design items follow much the same pattern, though it's possible for a story in an iteration to have architecture and/or design tasks too.
- The development process itself:
  - **Development**, obviously, happens during the Sprint.
  - **Quality** assurance activities generally also happen as part of the Sprint, being applied to each story as it's deemed complete by the developers. If testing activities reveal issues, the story would go back to an **In-Development** status, or perhaps an earlier status, on the task board, and would be picked up and corrected as soon as possible.
  - System integration and testing will probably happen during the Sprint as well, assuming that an environment is available to execute these activities with the new code.
  - **Acceptance** can happen on a story-by-story basis as each story makes its way through all the QA and System Integration and Testing activities, or it can happen all at once at an end-of-Sprint demo-and-acceptance meeting.

It's not hard to see why Scrum is popular—from a developer's perspective, with disciplined planning and devoting care and attention to making sure that the developers' time is respected and realistically allocated, their day-to-day concerns reduce down to whatever they're working on at the moment. Given a mature team, who have a reasonably consistent skill set and a good working knowledge of the system and its code base, Scrum will be reasonably predictable from a business perspective. Finally, Scrum, if managed with care and discipline, is self-correcting—as issues or concerns arise, with the process, *or* with the system and code base to some extent, the *process* will provide mechanisms for addressing and correcting those items.

Kanban

Kanban, as a process, has a lot of similarities to Scrum:

- The main unit of effort is a user story.
- Stories have the same sort of story-level process status, to the point where the same sort of task board, real or virtual, is used to track and provide visibility into work in progress.
- Stories should have all of their requirements and other relevant information ready and waiting before work on them commences. That implies that there is some sort of story grooming process, though it may not be as formally structured as the equivalent in Scrum.

Kanban, unlike Scrum:

- Is not time-boxed—there is no Sprint.
- Does not expect or require the daily status/stand-up meeting, though it's a useful enough tool and is thus commonly adopted. Other variants and approaches, perhaps focusing first on blocked items, then concerns on in-progress items, then anything else, are also viable.
- Does not expect or require that stories be sized, though again it's a useful enough tool and is not uncommon, especially if it is a useful criterion for prioritizing stories for development.

Kanban's primary focus might be described as an effort to minimize context changes, which plays out as working on single stories until they are complete before moving on to the next. This frequently results in prioritization of functionality by need, which lends itself well to situations where there are functional dependencies between stories.

That working-until-complete focus is probably going to occur in a Scrum process as well, but it's not actually expected, since the goal in Scrum is to complete all stories in a Sprint, and assistance from others on the team to complete a story may well be necessary at any point to accomplish that goal.

Kanban's entire process is very simple:

- Stories (and their tasks) are made ready, and prioritized for work
- One or more developers selects a story, and works on it until it's complete, then repeats the process with another story, and another, and so on

- While development and work against current stories is underway, new stories are made ready and added to the stack of available work as details become available, and prioritized accordingly

Kanban, with different policies and procedures than Scrum, offers different advantages:

- Kanban is fairly well-suited to efforts where there are significant silos of knowledge or expertise, since it's focused on completion of functionality, no matter how long it might take
- Kanban handles stories and functionality that are both large and not easily divisible into smaller logical or functional chunk, without having to go through the process of subdividing them into Sprint-sized chunks (but see the next section for the drawbacks of this)
- Kanban limits Work In Progress directly, which reduces the likelihood of overworking developers, provided that the flow of the work is planned correctly and well
- Kanban allows the addition of new work by stakeholders at any point in time, and with any priority, though interruption of in-progress work is still best avoided
- Provided that each story is independent and deliverable, each completed story is ready for installation or implementation as soon as it's been accepted

It also has its own set of caveats:

- Kanban can be more prone to bottlenecks in development, particularly if there are large-scale or long-duration dependencies for subsequent stories—an example might be a data storage system that takes three weeks to complete—that is, there is a dependency for a number of small class structures that need it, which could be implemented in a few days if the data storage system were complete.
- Since it doesn't really provide any concrete milestones at a higher level than individual stories, Kanban requires more direct and conscious effort to establish those milestones if they are needed for external business reasons.
- More conscious thought and effort are typically needed for functionality that is being developed in phases in a Kanban process for it to be efficient—any functionality that has **must-have**, **should-have**, and **nice-to-have** capabilities that are all going to be implemented, for example, needs to provide some awareness of, and guidance future phase goals from the beginning to remain efficient.

- Kanban doesn't require that the team as a whole be aware of the design underlying the work, which can lead to misunderstandings, or even development efforts at cross-purposes. Making a conscious effort to **de-silo** design, and raise overall awareness of the larger-scale requirements may be needed, and it may not be apparent that it is needed at first.

Kanban and the phases of the SDLC model

Many Agile processes, especially those that use stories as a basic unit of effort or work, have a lot of similarities. Since most story-related items have been described in some detail in discussing Scrum, any later methodologies that use stories will only note variations on the themes:

- **Before development starts:** Requirement analysis and definition, and system architecture and design, work in much the same way as they do in Scrum, and for many of the same reasons. The primary difference is that there is a less formal structure expected in Kanban to accomplish the attachment of requirements-and-architecture details to stories. It generally happens when there's time and/or a perceived need, such as the development team being close to running out of workable stories.
- **The development process itself:** Development and Quality Assurance processes are part of the flow of a given story as it's being worked to completion. So, too is system integration and testing, and acceptance pretty much has to happen during a story's life cycle, since there isn't an end-of-Sprint meeting to demonstrate development results and acquire acceptance.

With a less formal structure, fewer process rituals, and a readily-understandable just-in-time approach to its process, Kanban is easily understood, and reasonably easily managed. Some additional care at key points, and the ability to identify those key points, helps considerably in keeping things moving smoothly and well, but as long as the ability to recognize and address those key points improves over time, so too will the process.

Other Agile methodologies

Scrum and Kanban aren't the only two Agile methodologies, or even the only two worthy of consideration. Some others that are worth noting include Extreme Programming, as a free-standing methodology, and Feature and Test-Driven Development, either as standalone methodologies or, perhaps as mix-ins to some other methodology.

Extreme programming

The most noticeable aspect of **Extreme Programming** (**XP**) is probably the **paired programming** approach, which can be an integral part of its implementation. The intention/expectation behind it is that two developers, using one computer, work on the code, which, ideally improves their focus, their ability to collaborate, solve any challenges more quickly, and allows for faster, better, and more reliable detection of potential risks that are inherent to the code being produced. In a paired scenario, the two developers alternate with some frequency between being the person writing the code and the person reviewing it as it's being written. Not all XP implementations use the paired approach, but when it's not in play, other processes, such as extensive and frequent code reviews and unit testing, are necessary to maintain at least some of the benefits that are lost by not using that option.

XP as a methodology may not be able to handle highly complex code bases or highly complex changes to code bases without sacrificing some of its development velocity. It also tends to require more intensive planning and requirements than the more just-in-time approaches such as Scrum and Kanban, since the paired developers should, ideally, be able to work on code in as autonomous a fashion as they can manage. The more information the pair team has up-front, the less time they will have to spend trying to track down information they need, and the less disruption will occur to their efforts. XP doesn't really have any method for tracking progress, or keeping efforts and roadblocks visible, but adopting or bolting on something from some other methodology is certainly possible.

Feature-driven development

The primary unit of work in a **Feature-Driven Development** (**FDD**) process is a feature. Those features are the end result of a detailed System Modeling effort, focusing on creating one-to-many domain models in significant detail, mapping out where features live in the system's domain, how (or if) they are expected to interact with each other—the sort of information that should come out of **use cases**, **data structures**, **flow** models, and **Interprocess Communication** models. Once the overall model is established, a feature list is constructed and prioritized, with a specific view to at least trying to keep the implementation time frame of each feature in the list at a reasonable maximum—two weeks seems to be the typical limit. If an individual feature is expected to take more than the longest acceptable time, it is subdivided until it can be accomplished and delivered in that time period.

Once the complete feature list is ready for implementation, iterations around completing those features are planned around a fixed time period. In each iteration, features or sets of features are assigned to developers, singly or in groups. Those developers work out a final implementation design, and review and refine it if needed. Once the design is deemed solid, development and testing of code to implement the design take place, and the resulting new code is promoted to the build- or distribution-ready code base for deployment.

FDD goes hand-in-hand with several development best practices—automated testing, configuration management, and regular builds so that, if they aren't a full, formal **Continuous Integration** process, they are very close to being one. The feature teams are generally small, dynamically formed, and intended to have at least two individuals, at a minimum, on them, with the intention of promoting collaboration and early feedback, especially on a features' designs and implementation quality.

FDD may be a good option for large and complex systems—by breaking work down into small, manageable features, even development in the context of very large, very complex systems is going to be maintainable with a good success rate. The processes around getting any individual feature up and running are simple and easily understood. Barring occasional check-ins to make sure that development isn't stalling for some reason, FDD is very lightweight and non-intrusive. Feature teams will usually have a lead developer associated with them, who has some responsibility for coordinating the development efforts and refining implementation details when and if needed. That does mean, however, that the lead developer is less likely to contribute to the actual code, particularly if they are spending much of their time executing coordination or design-refinement efforts, or mentoring other members of the team.

Test-driven design

Test-Driven Design (TDD), as might be expected from its name, is focused first and foremost on using automated tests of a code base to direct development efforts. The overall process breaks down into the following steps:

- For each functionality goal (new or enhanced feature) being implemented:
    - Write a new test or set of tests that will fail until the code being tested meets whatever contract and expectations are being tested.
    - Assure that the new test(s) fail, as expected, for the reasons expected, and don't raise any other failures.
    - Write code that passes the new test(s). It may be horribly **kludgy** and inelegant initially, but this doesn't matter as long as it meets the requirements embedded in the test(s).
    - Refine and/or re-factor the new code as needed, retesting to assure that the tests still pass, moving it to an appropriate location in the code base if necessary, and generally making sure that it meets whatever other standards and expectations are present for the code base as a whole.
- Run all tests to prove that the new code still passes the new tests, and that no other tests fail as a result of the new code.

TDD offers some obvious benefits as a process:

- All code in a system will be tested, and have a full suite of regression tests, at a minimum
- Since the primary goal of writing the code is just to pass the tests created for it, code will frequently be just enough to achieve that, which usually results in smaller, and easier-to-manage code bases
- Similarly, TDD code tends to be more modular, which is almost always a good thing, and in turn that generally lends itself to better architecture, which also contributes to more manageable code

The main trade-off, also obviously, is that the test suites have to be created and maintained. They will grow as the system grows, and will take longer and longer periods of time to execute, though significant increases will (hopefully) take a while before they manifest. Creation and maintenance of test suites take time, and is a discipline all to itself—some argue that writing good tests is an art form, even, and there's a fair amount of truth to that. On top of that, there's a tendency to look for the wrong sort of metrics to show how well tests perform: metrics such as code coverage, or even just the number of individual test cases, which indicate nothing about the quality of the tests.

Development paradigms

Programming, when it first appeared, was often limited by hardware capabilities and the higher-level languages that were available at the time for simple procedural code. A program, in that paradigm, was a sequence of steps, executed from beginning to end. Some languages supported subroutines and perhaps even simple function-definition capabilities, and there were ways to, for example, loop through sections of the code so that a program could continue execution until some termination condition was reached, but it was, by and large, a collection of very brute-force, start-to-finish processes.

As the capabilities of the underlying hardware improved over time, more sophisticated capabilities started to become more readily available—formal functions as they are generally thought of now, are more powerful , or at least have a flexible loop and other flow control options, and so on. However, outside a few languages that were generally accessible only inside the halls and walls of Academia, there weren't many significant changes to that procedural approach in mainstream efforts until the 1990s, when Object-Oriented Programming first started to emerge as a significant, or even dominant paradigm.

The following is an example of a fairly simple procedural program that asks for a website URL, reads the data from it, and writes that data to a file:

```python
#!/usr/bin/env python
"""
An example of a simple procedural program. Asks the user for a URL,
retrieves the content of that URL (http:// or https:// required),
writes it to a temp-file, and repeats until the user tells it to
stop.
"""

import os
```

```
import urllib.request

if os.name == 'posix':
    tmp_dir = '/tmp/'
else:
    tmp_dir = 'C:\\Temp\\'

print('Simple procedural code example')

the_url = ''
while the_url.lower() != 'x':
    the_url = input(
        'Please enter a URL to read, or "X" to cancel: '
    )
    if the_url and the_url.lower() != 'x':
        page = urllib.request.urlopen(the_url)
        page_data = page.read()
        page.close()
        local_file = ('%s%s.data' % (tmp_dir, ''.join(
            [c for c in the_url if c not in ':/']
            )
        )).replace('https', '').replace('http', '')
        with open(local_file, 'w') as out_file:
            out_file.write(str(page_data))
            print('Page-data written to %s' % (local_file))

print('Exiting. Thanks!')
```

Object-oriented programming

The distinctive feature of Object-Oriented Programming is (no great surprise) that it represents data and provides functionality through instances of objects. Objects are structures of data, or collections of attributes or properties, that have related functionality (methods) attached to them as well. Objects are constructed as needed from a class, through a definition of the properties and methods that, between them, define what an object is, or has, and what an object can do. An OO approach allows programming challenges to be handled in a significantly different, and usually more useful, manner than the equivalents in a procedural approach, because those object instances keep track of their own data.

The following is the same functionality as the simple procedural example shown previously, but written using an Object-Oriented approach:

```python
#!/usr/bin/env python
"""
An example of a simple OOP-based program. Asks the user for a URL,
retrieves the content of that URL, writes it to a temp-file, and
repeats until the user tells it to stop.
"""

# Importing stuff we'll use
import os

import urllib.request

if os.name == 'posix':
    tmp_dir = '/tmp/'
else:
    tmp_dir = 'C:\\Temp\\'
if not os.path.exists(tmp_dir):
    os.mkdirs(tmp_dir)

# Defining the class

class PageReader:
    # Object-initialization method
    def __init__(self, url):
        self.url = url
        self.local_file = ('%s%s.data' % (tmp_dir,
                ''.join(
                [c for c in the_url if c not in ':/']
                )
            )).replace('https', '').replace('http', '')
        self.page_data = self.get_page_data()
    # Method to read the data from the URL
    def get_page_data(self):
        page = urllib.request.urlopen(self.url)
        page_data = page.read()
        page.close()
        return page_data
    # Method to save the page-data
    def save_page_data(self):
        with open(self.local_file, 'w') as out_file:
            out_file.write(str(self.page_data))
            print('Page-data written to %s' % (self.local_file))

if __name__ == '__main__':
    # Almost the same loop...
```

```
    the_url = ''
    while the_url.lower() != 'x':
        the_url = input(
            'Please enter a URL to read, or "X" to cancel: '
        )
        if the_url and the_url.lower() != 'x':
            page_reader = PageReader(the_url)
            page_reader.save_page_data()
print('Exiting. Thanks!')
```

Although this performs the exact same task, and in the exact same fashion as far as the user is concerned, underneath it all is an instance of the `PageReader` class that does all the actual work. In the process, it stores various data, which could be accessed as a member of that instance. That is, the `page_reader.url`, `page_reader.local_file`, and `page_reader.page_data` properties all exist and could be retrieved and used if there were a need to retrieve that data, and the `page_reader.get_page_data` method could be called again to fetch a fresh copy of the data on the page. It's important to note that the properties are attached to the instance, so it'd be possible to have multiple instances of `PageReader`, each with it's own data, that can all do the same things with their own data. That is, if the following code were executed:

```
python_org = PageReader('http://python.org')
print('URL ............... %s' % python_org.url)
print('Page data length ... %d' % len(python_org.page_data))
google_com = PageReader('http://www.google.com')
print('URL ............... %s' % google_com.url)
print('Page data length ... %d' % len(google_com.page_data))
```

It would yield the following output:

```
URL ............... http://python.org
Page data length ... 48892
URL ............... http://www.google.com
Page data length ... 12467
```

Object-Oriented design and implementation make the development of a complex system, with the attendant complex interactions, considerably easier a fair portion of the time, though it may not be a panacea for all development challenges and efforts. If the basic principles of good OO designs are adhered to, however, they will usually make code easier to write, easier to maintain, and less prone to breakage. A full discussion of OO design principles is well beyond the scope of this book, but some of the more fundamental ones that can cause a lot of difficulty if they aren't adhered to are as follows:

- Objects should have a **Single Responsibility**—each should do (or represent) one thing, and do so well
- Objects should be **open** for extension but **closed** for modification—changes to what an instance actually does, unless it's a new functionality that flat-out doesn't exist, should not require modification to the actual code
- Objects should **encapsulate** what varies—it shouldn't require the use of an object to know anything about how it does and what it does, just that it can do it
- Use of objects should be exercises in programming to an interface, not to an implementation—this is a complex topic that's worth some detailed discussion, with some substance and context, so it'll be looked at in some detail in Chapter 9, *Testing the Business-Objects*, while working out the architecture of the hms_sys project

Functional programming

Functional Programming (FP) is a development approach centered around the concept of passing control through a series of pure functions, and avoiding shared state and mutable data structures. That is, the majority of any real functionality in FP is wrapped in functions that will always return the same output for any given input, and don't modify any external variables. Technically, a pure function should not write data to anywhere—neither logging to a console or file, nor writing to a file—and how the need for that sort of output is accommodated is a discussion well outside the scope of this book.

The following is the same functionality that was in the previous two examples, but written using a Functional Programming approach (if only barely, since the task it's performing isn't all that complex):

```python
#!/usr/bin/env python
"""
An example of a simple FP-based program. Asks the user for a URL,
retrieves the content of that URL, writes it to a temp-file, and
repeats until the user tells it to stop.
"""

# Importing stuff we'll use
import os

import urllib.request

if os.name == 'posix':
    tmp_dir = '/tmp/'
else:
    tmp_dir = 'C:\\Temp\\'
if not os.path.exists(tmp_dir):
    os.mkdirs(tmp_dir)

# Defining our functions

def get_page_data(url):
    page = urllib.request.urlopen(url)
    page_data = page.read()
    page.close()
    return page_data

def save_page_data(local_file, page_data):
    with open(local_file, 'w') as out_file:
        out_file.write(str(page_data))
        return('Page-data written to %s' % (local_file))

def get_local_file(url):
  return ('%s%s.data' % (tmp_dir, ''.join(
      [c for c in the_url if c not in ':/']
      )
    )).replace('https', '').replace('http', '')

def process_page(url):
    return save_page_data(
        get_local_file(url), get_page_data(url)
    )

def get_page_to_process():
```

```
        the_url = input(
            'Please enter a URL to read, or "X" to cancel: '
        )
        if the_url:
            return the_url.lower()
        return None

if __name__ == '__main__':
    # Again, almost the same loop...
    the_url = get_page_to_process()
    while the_url not in ('x', None):
        print(process_page(the_url))
        the_url = get_page_to_process()
    print('Exiting. Thanks!')
```

Again, this code performs the exact same function, and it does so with the same discrete steps/processes as the previous two examples. It does so, however, without having to actually store any of the various data it's using—there are no mutable data elements in the process itself, only in the initial input to the process_page function, and even then, it's not usefully mutable for very long. The main function, process_page, also doesn't use any mutable values, just the results of other function calls. All of the component functions return something, even if it's only a None value.

Functional Programming is not a new paradigm, but it hasn't become widely accepted until relatively recently. It has the potential to be as fundamentally disruptive as Object-Oriented Programming was. It's also different, in many respects, so that making a transition to it might well be difficult—it relies, after all, on substantially different approaches, and on a stateless basis that is very atypical in or of other modern development paradigms. That stateless nature, though, and the fact that it enforces a rigid sequence of events during execution, have the potential to make FP-based code and processes much more stable than their OO or procedural counterparts.

Development practices

At least two post-development process automation practices have arisen, either as a result of some incremental development methodologies, or merely at the same time: Continuous Integration and Continuous Delivery (or Deployment).

Continuous integration

Continuous Integration (**CI**), in its simplest description, is a repeatable, automated process for merging new or altered code into a common, shared environment, either on some sort of timed basis, or as a result of some event such as committing changes to a source control system. Its primary goal is to try and detect potential integration problems as early in the code promotion or deployment process as possible, so that any issues that arise can be resolved before they are deployed to a live, production branch. In order to implement a CI process, regardless of any tools that might be used to control or manage it, there are a few prerequisites:

- Code needs to be maintained in a version control system of some sort, and there should be, ideally, one and only one branch that a CI process will execute against.
- The build process should be automated, whether it fires off on a predetermined schedule, or as a result of a commit to the version control system.
- As part of that build process, all automated tests (unit tests in particular, but any integration or system tests that can be usefully executed should at least be considered for inclusion) should execute. When those test fire off may be worth discussing, since there may be two or more windows of opportunity, and they both have their advantages:
    - Tests executed before the commit and build is complete, if the tools and processes can either prevent the commit or build, or roll a commit back to its last good state on a test failure, will prevent code that fails its tests from being committed. The trade-off in this scenario is that it's possible that conflicting changes from two or more code change sources might be significantly tangled and need correspondingly significant attention to remedy. Additionally, if the offending code cannot be committed, that may make it difficult to hand off the offending code to a different developer who might well be able to solve the issue quickly.
    - Tests that execute after a build will allow code that's failed one or more tests to be committed to the collective code base, but with known issues at a minimum. Depending on the shape and scope of those issues, it might well break the build—and that can be disruptive to the whole team's productivity.

- Some sort of notification process needs to be in place to alert developers that there is an issue—particularly if the issue resulted in a broken build.
- The process needs to assure that every commit is tested and successfully buildable.
- The results of a successful build need to be made available in some fashion—whether through some sort of scripted or automated deployment to a specific testing environment, making an installer for the new build available for download, or whatever other mechanism best suits the product's, team's, or stakeholders' needs.

With these in place, the rest of the process is just a case of working out some of the process rules and expectations, and implementing, monitoring, and adjusting them when/if needed:

- When should commits happen? Daily? At the end of development of a story, feature, or whatever unit of work might apply?
- How quickly does the commit-test-build process need to run? What steps can be taken, if any, to keep it quick enough to be useful?

Continuous delivery or deployment

Continuous Delivery or Deployment (CD) is a natural extension or offshoot of the CI process, taking each successful build, collecting all of the components involved, and either deploying it directly (typically for web and cloud-resident applications and systems), or taking whatever steps would be necessary to make the new build available for deployment—creating a final, end user or production-ready installation package, for example—but not actually deploying it.

A complete CD process will allow for the creation, update, or recreation of a production system based solely on information in a source control system. It also likely involves some **Configuration Management** and **Release Management** tools at the system administration side, and those may well impose specific requirements, functionally or architecturally, or both, on a system's design and implementation.

Summary

These last several chapters have hopefully given you at least a glimpse into all of the moving parts (outside the actual writing of code) in development efforts that are useful to be aware of in software engineering. The odds are good that any given team or company will have selected which methodology, and what pre- and post-development processes are going to be in play. Even so, knowing what to expect from them, or what might be causes for concern while working within their various combined contexts, is useful information, and often one of the expectations that divide programmers from software engineers.

With all of that said and out of the way, it's time to start looking in more depth and detail at the meat of any combination of these—the development processes themselves. To do that, we need a system—a project to work on.

The hms_sys System Project

The project that the next several chapters will focus on is being written for an imaginary company, *Hand Made Stuff*, that specializes in connecting consumers with artisans who create and sell a variety of unique handmade items. Those products cover a wide range of materials and purposes, and include furniture, craft, and jewelry items, such as beads and bits and pieces for costuming. Pretty much anything that someone is willing to make and someone else is willing to buy.

Goals for the system

Hand Made Stuff (**HMS**) is now looking for a way to streamline the business process that they use to allow artisans to make their wares available through the main website. At present, when an Artisan has created something that they're willing to sell, they send an email to someone at the *HMS* central office, with one or more attached photos if it's something new, sometimes with new photos if it's a new version or set of a previously-offered products. Someone in the *HMS* central office copies the relevant information into their web system and does a bit of basic setup to make the items available. From there, once a consumer decides that they want to order something an Artisan has made, the order goes through another manual process that involves the *HMS* central office emailing the Artisan with the order information.

All of these manual processes are time-consuming, and sometimes error-prone. On occasion, they have taken so long that more than one customer has tried to purchase the same item because the information was still being processed to get the first order in motion:

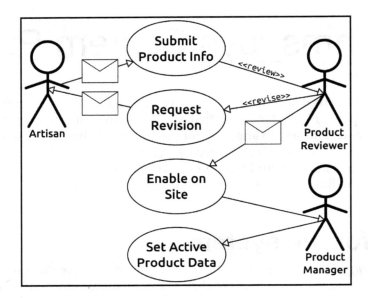

Hand Made Stuff's website runs on an off-the-shelf system that is not easily modifiable. It does have an API, but that API was designed to be used for internal access processes, so there are security concerns about opening access to it up enough to allow artisans to connect to it through new web-application development.

The business that this imaginary company does is, perhaps, not terribly realistic. It certainly doesn't feel like it'd actually be able to compete with existing businesses such as Etsy or (maybe) craigslist or eBay. Even so, the implementation concepts for the system are reasonably realistic, in that they are variations of tasks that need to be implemented across several real-world problem domains. They're just combined in an unusual fashion.

Since the following chapters are intended to represent individual development iterations, in a process that's at least somewhat along the lines of a Kanban methodology, there are some artifacts from the pre-development processes that are worth noting before getting into what those iterations/chapters will look like.

What's known/designed before development starts

The primary goals of the new system center around streamlining and (as much as possible) automating the existing process to get artisans' products into the online catalog. Specifically:

- **artisans** should be able to submit product information without having to go through an email-based process. As part of that change:
  - Some data-entry control will be enforced, to prevent simple mistakes (missing or invalid data).
  - artisans will be able to modify their product data, with some limitations, and with a review still required before those revisions go live. At a minimum, though, they will be able to deactivate live product listings, and activate existing-but-deactivated items as well.
- **Product Reviewers** will be able to make revisions directly (for simple changes, at least), and send items back for major revisions. This part of the process is loosely defined, and may need further detail and definition later in the development cycle.
- **The Product Managers'** data-entry tasks will be reduced significantly, at least as far as the setup of new products is concerned. The new system will take care of most or all of that.

The use-case diagram for the new process, then, looks like the following before any detailed design has taken place:

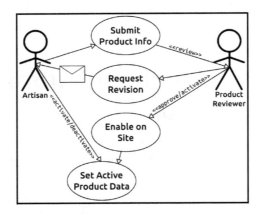

The intention is for each Artisan to be supplied with an installable application that allows them to interact with the *HMS* main office. That local application will connect to an Artisan gateway that will handle the Artisan-to-main-office communications, and store the incoming data from artisans as a sort of staging area for anything that's pending approval. From there, a **Reviewer** (and/or **Product manager**) application will allow **Product reviewers** and managers to move Artisan-supplied products into the main web store, using its native API. The logical architecture, with some rough inter-process communication flows, at this point looks like the following:

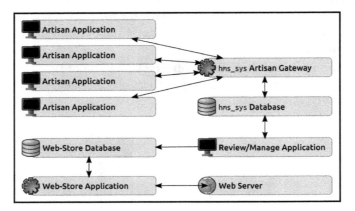

Between these diagrams and the initial concept noted earlier, there are a lot of specific user needs that have already been captured. It's possible that more will arise during development or at least planning for development (as stories for iterations are fleshed out).

The actual data structure behind artisans and their products is not known yet, only that products are distinct elements that can be owned by one and only one Artisan. More detail will be needed to implement these, as well as to determine what data moves where (and when), but the relationship between them is already diagrammable:

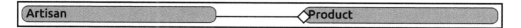

The current lack of information about the inner data structure of these elements also makes any sort of UI design specification difficult, if not impossible. Similarly, it will be difficult to determine any business rules that aren't already implied by the use-case and logical-architecture/data-flow diagrams. Those, too, will require more details before anything more useful can be discerned.

There are a few other varied items that could be inferred from this information and fall into one of the following pre-development steps:

- **Risks**:
    - The fact that the connection between the **Review/Manage Application** and the **Web Store Database** is one-way probably indicates some concern that the data flow needs to be carefully controlled. Realistically, it will probably be necessary for the application to be able to at least read from the database, if only so that existing products can be found and modified, rather than creating new product entries over and over again.
    - The use-case diagram shows that an Artisan can activate or deactivate a product without involving the **Product Reviewer**, but the architecture and flow don't have any obvious way to handle that capability. At a minimum, an examination of a connection from the Artisan gateway to the **Web Store Database** should be undertaken, but that's something that can happen later, during the relevant development iteration. Since the web store system has an API, it may be that the process can be managed by an API call to the **Web Store Application**, from the **Artisan Gateway**, but that hasn't been evaluated yet.

- **Project-management planning data**:
    - If the project has made it to the development shop, the odds are that all of the feasibility, cost-analysis, and other business-level examinations have been made and approved. Though there may not be any specific information needed from these results, knowing that they are probably available if a question arises is a good thing.

What the iteration chapters will look like

In the interest of showing what an Agile process might look like as a system is developed under it, the development of `hms_sys` will be broken down into several iterations. Each iteration, with a single, high-level goal, covers one or more chapters, and is concerned with a common set of Stories. Of the agile methodologies discussed in Chapter 4, *Methodologies, Paradigms, and Practices*, these chapters are closer to being a Kanban approach than anything else, since the number and total sizes of stories being completed in each iteration vary significantly between iterations. In a Scrum setting, these iterations would be time-constrained, broken out into time-limited chunks – that is, each iteration would be planned to last for some specific length of time. The following chapters and their corresponding iterations are goal-oriented instead, with each intended to achieve some milestone of system functionality. In that respect, they are also close to following a **Feature-Driven Development** model.

Each iteration will address the same five items:

- Iteration goals
- Assembly of stories and tasks:
    - Requirement analysis and definition activities from the SDLC model, as/if needed
    - System architecture and design activities, also from the SDLC model, as/if needed
- Writing and testing the code.
- System integration, testing, and acceptance.
- Post-development considerations and impact:
    - Implementation/installation/distribution
    - Operations/use and maintenance
    - Decommissioning

Iteration goals and stories

Each iteration will have a very specific, and reasonably tightly-focused set of goals to be accomplished, building upon the accomplishments of previous iterations until the final system is complete. In order, the goals for each iteration are:

- **Development foundations**: Setting up projects and processes. Each of the functional iterations needs be testable, buildable, and deployable by the time they are finished, so some attention needs to be paid early in the system project to making sure that there is some sort of common foundation to build those on as development progresses.

- **Business object foundations**: Definition and development of business-object data structures and functionality.

- **Business-object data-persistence**: Making sure that the various business objects in use can be stored and retrieved as needed.

- **Service foundations**: Building out the bare-bones functionality for the main office and Artisan services, which will be the backbone of the communication and data-exchange processes for the system as a whole.

- **Service communication**: Defining, detailing, and implementing the actual communication processes between components of the system, particularly the service-layer implementations.

Each of these iterations has a perhaps-surprising amount of design- and implementation-level decision-making that has to happen, and a lot of opportunities to exercise various software-engineering principles across a wide variety of functional, conceptual, and implementation scenarios.

Each iteration's efforts will be captured in a set of user stories, of the type described when examining the Scrum and Kanban methodologies. Each iteration's criteria for being complete will include having all of the stories associated with it complete, or at least resolved. It's possible that some stories will have to be moved to later iterations in order to accommodate functional dependencies, for example, in which case it may not be possible to complete an implementation of those stories until later in the system's development.

Writing and testing the code

Once all of the stories have been defined in sufficient detail to allow development, the code itself will be written, both for the actual functionality associated with each story, and for automated testing of that code – unit-testing with regression-testing capabilities baked in. If possible and practical, integration- and system-testing code will also be written with an eye toward providing the same automated, repeatable testing of new code from those perspectives. The end goal of each iteration will be a deployable and functional code-base that has been tested (and that can be retested on demand). It may not be complete or even usable during the early iterations, but it will be stable and predictable in terms of which capabilities it provides.

This part of the process will form the bulk of the next few chapters. Writing code is, after all, the key aspect of development.

Post-development considerations and impact

The operations/use, maintenance, and decommissioning phases of `hms_sys` will be discussed in some depth after development is complete, but as development unfolds some effort will be made to anticipate specific needs that relate to those parts of the system's life. There may or may not be code written during the core development phases to address concerns in the system's active life, but any expected needs that surface during those efforts could, at a minimum, have some documentation written around them as part of the development effort, targeted for use by system administrators.

Summary

The pre-development and high-level conceptual design items for `hms_sys` are fairly straightforward, at least at the level of detail that's available coming out of the pre-development planning cycle(s). More detail will bubble to the surface once the user stories for the individual iterations' functionalities are fleshed out, along with a host of questions and implementation decisions and details. There's one iteration, though, that will happen first.

That first iteration, as hinted at, is concerned more with the definition of the tools, processes, and practices that will be in play through the real development of the final system. The odds are good that most of the decisions and setup that will be part of that will already have been decided upon by the development team, and by those who manage the team. Even so, it's worth looking at some of the options and decision-making criteria that will hopefully have gone into making those decisions. They can (and often do) have a significant impact on how well things work during development.

Development Tools and Best Practices

5

Before starting on the actual development of `hms_sys`, there are several decisions that need to be made. In a real-world scenario, some (maybe all) of these decisions might be made at a policy level, either by the development team or maybe by management above the team. Some, such as the IDE/code editor program, might be an individual decision by each individual team member; so long as there are no conflicts between different developers' choices, or any issues raised as a result, there's nothing wrong with that. On the other hand, having some consistency isn't a bad thing either; that way, every team member knows what to expect when they're working on code that someone else on the team has touched.

These choices fall into two main categories selection of development tools and what best practices (and standards) will be in play, specifically the following:

- Integrated Development Environment options
- Source Control Management options
- Code and development process standards, including organization of Python code into packages
- Setting up and using of Python virtual environments

Development tools

The two most important tool-oriented decisions that need to be considered are, not surprisingly, centered around creating, editing, and managing the code through the development life cycle.

Integrated Development Environment (IDE) options

It's certainly possible to write and edit code without using a full-blown **Integrated Development Environment** (**IDE**). Ultimately, anything that can read and write text files of arbitrary types or with arbitrary file extensions is technically usable. Many IDEs, though, provide additional, development-centric capabilities that can save time and effort—sometimes a lot of time and effort. The trade-off is, generally, that the more features and functionality that any given IDE provides, the less lightweight it is, and the more complicated it can become. Finding one that every member of a development team can agree on can be difficult, or even painful there are downsides to most of them, and there may not be a single, obvious right choice. It's very subjective.

In looking at code editing and management tools, only real IDEs will be examined. As noted, text editors can be used to write code, and there are a fair few of them out there that recognize various language formats, including Python. However good they are (and there are some that are very good), if they don't provide at least one of the following functional capabilities, they won't be considered. It's just a matter of time until something in this list is needed and not available, and at a minimum, that eventuality will be distracting, and at worst, it could be a critical issue (though that seems unlikely). The feature set criteria are as follows:

- **Large-project support**: A large project, for the purposes of discussion, involves the development of two or more distinct, installable Python packages that have different environmental requirements. An example might include a `business_objects` class library that's used by two separate packages such as an `online_store` and `back_office` that provide different functionality for different users. The best-case scenario for this would include the following :

    - Support for different Python interpreters (possibly as individual virtual environments) in different package projects
    - The ability to have and manage interproject references (in this example, the `online_store` and `back_office` packages would be able to have useful references to the `business_objects` library)

- Less important, but still highly useful, would be the ability to have multiple projects open and editable at the same time, so that as changes in one package project require corresponding changes in another, there's little or no context change needed by the developer making those changes

- **Refactoring support**: Given a long enough period of time, it's inevitable that changes to a system's code without changing how it behaves from an external perspective is going to be necessary. That's a textbook definition of refactoring. Refactoring efforts tend to require, at a minimum, the ability to find and replace entity names in the code across multiple files, possibly across multiple libraries. At the more complex end of the range, refactoring can include the creation of new classes or members of classes to move functionality into a different location in the code, while maintaining the interface of the code.

- **Language exploration**: The ability to examine code that's used by, but not a part of, a project is helpful, at least occasionally. This is more useful than it might sound, unless you are lucky enough to possess an eidetic memory, and thus never have to look up function signatures, module members and so on.

- **Code execution**: The ability to actually run the code being worked on is immensely helpful during development. Having to drop out of an editor into a terminal in order to run code, to test changes to it, is a context change, and those are tedious at the least, and can actually be disruptive to the process under the right circumstances.

These items will be rated on the following scale, from best to worst:

- Superb
- Great
- Good
- Fair
- Mediocre
- Poor
- Terrible

These are the author's opinion, obviously, so take these with an appropriately sized grain of salt. Your personal views on any or all of these, or your needs for any or all of them, may be substantially different.

Many IDEs have various bells and whistles functionality that helps, perhaps substantially, with the processes of writing or managing code, but isn't something that's really critical. Examples of these include the following:

- The ability to navigate to where a code entity is defined from someplace where it's being used
- Code completion and autosuggestion, which allows the developer to quickly and easily select from a list of entities based on the first few characters of an entity name that they've started typing
- Code coloration and presentation, which provides an easy-to-understand visual indication of what a given block of code is – comments, class, function and variable names, that sort of thing

These will also be rated on the same scale, but since they aren't critical functionality, they are presented merely as additional information items.

All of the following IDEs are available across all the major operating systems – Windows, Macintosh, and Linux (and probably most UNIX systems, for that matter) – so that, an important criteria for evaluating the IDE part of a development toolkit is moot across the three discussed.

IDLE

IDLE is a simple IDE, written in Python and using the `Tkinter` GUI, which means that it should run on pretty much anything that Python can run on. It is often, but not always, part of a default Python installation but even when it's not included by default, it's easily installed and doesn't require much of anything in the way of external dependencies or other languages runtime environments.

- **Large-project support**: Poor
- **Refactoring support**: Poor
- **Language exploration**: Good
- **Code execution**: Good
- **Bells and whistles**: Fair

Out of the box, IDLE doesn't provide any project management tools, though there may be plugins that provide some of this capability. Even so, unless there are also plugins available that allow for more than one file to be open at a time without requiring each to be in a separate window, working with code across multiple files will eventually be tedious, at best, and perhaps impractical to the point of being effectively impossible.

Although IDLE's search-and-replace functionality includes one nice feature – regular expression-based searches – that's about it as far as functionality that is meaningful or useful for refactoring purposes. Any significant refactoring effort, or even widespread but smaller scoped changes, will require a relatively high degree of manual effort.

Where IDLE really shines is in its ability to dig into the packages and modules available on the system. It provides both a class browser that allows direct exploration of any importable namespace in the Python path, and a path browser that allows exploration of all available namespaces. The only downsides to these are a lack of search capability and that each class browser has to reside in a separate window. Were these not concerns, a Great rating would not seem out of line.

IDLE allows any open file to be executed with a single keystroke, with the results/output of that run displayed in a single, common Python shell window. There is no facility for passing arguments to those executions, but that's probably only a concern if a project involves some sort of command-line program that accepts arguments. IDLE also provides a syntax check that identifies the first syntax problem detected in the code, which could be of some use.

The only reliably functional bells and whistles item that IDLE offers is coloration of code. There are extensions that are supposed to provide things such as auto-completion and some code authoring assistance (automatic generation of closing parenthesis, for example), but none of them appear to be functional.

The following is a screenshot of IDLE showing the console, a code editing window, class and path browser windows, and a search and replace window:

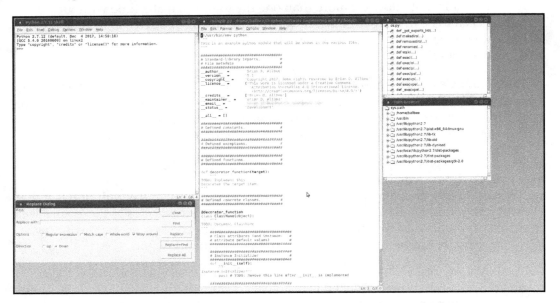

IDLE is probably a reasonable choice for small code efforts – anything that doesn't require having more files open than the user's comfortable with having displayed in their individual windows. It's lightweight, with a reasonably stable (if occasionally quirky) GUI. It's not something that feels like it would work well for projects that involve more than one distributable package, though.

Geany

Geany is a lightweight code editor and IDE with support for a number of languages, including Python. It's available as an installable application across all the major operating systems, though it has some features that aren't available on Windows. Geany is available as a free download from www.geany.org:

- **Large-project support**: Fair
- **Refactoring support**: Mediocre
- **Language exploration**: Mediocre
- **Code execution**: Good
- **Bells and whistles**: Good

This is a screenshot of Geany showing one of several project plugins' sidebars, an open code file, project settings, and search and replace windows:

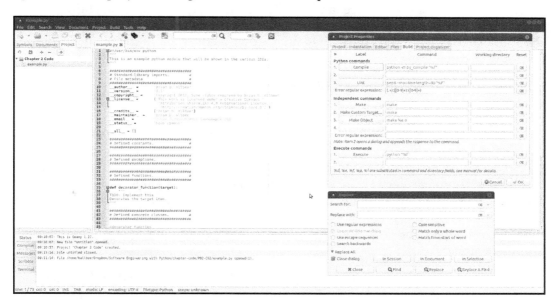

Geany's interface makes working with multiple concurrently open files a great deal easier than the same task would be in IDLE; each open file resides in a single tab in the UI, making multi-file editing quite a bit easier to deal with. It also supports a basic project structure even in its most basic installed configuration, and there are a few different project-oriented plugins that allow for easier/better management and visibility into the files of a project. What it lacks, generally, for large-project support is the ability to actually have multiple projects open at once, though multiple open files across different project source trees is supported. With some careful planning, and judicious configuration of individual projects' settings, it's possible to manage different execution requirements and even specific **Python virtual environments** across a set of related projects, though it requires some discipline to keep those well-isolated and efficient. As can be seen in the screen capture, Geany also provides settings for compilation and build/make commands at a project level, which can be very handy.

Geany's refactoring support is just slightly better than IDLE's, mostly because of its multi-file search and replace capabilities. There is no out-of-the box support for refactoring operations such as renaming a Python module file across an entire project or project set, leaving it as a wholly manual process, but with some care (and, again, discipline) even those aren't difficult to manage correctly, though they may be tedious and/or time consuming.

Geany's language exploration capabilities don't look like they should warrant as high a rating as the *Mediocre* that was given. Short of actually opening every Python namespace that's tied to a given project, which would at least allow exploration of those packages in the **Symbols** panel, there really isn't much obviously available in the way of support for digging into the underlying language. Geany's redemption here is a very robust auto completion capability. Once the first four characters of an identifiable language element are entered – whether that element is part of an open file in the project or part of an imported module – all of the element names that match the currently entered text are shown and selectable, and if the selected item is a function or method, the code hint that comes up for the item includes that item's argument signature.

Geany's code execution capabilities are pretty solid – slightly better than IDLE's in a few respects, if not enough so, or across enough areas, to warrant a higher rating. With some attention to needs and details early on in the project setup, it's possible to configure a given project's **Execute** settings to use a specific Python interpreter, such as one that's part of a specific virtual environment, and allow imports from other projects' virtual environment installations and code bases. The downside is that doing so does require a degree of planning, and it introduces additional complexity in managing the related virtual environments.

Geany's out-of-the box bells and whistles are comparable to those provided by IDLE, with a single significant improvement; a good number of readily-available plugins for a lot of common and useful tasks and needs.

Eclipse variations + PyDev

The Eclipse Platform, managed by the Eclipse Foundation (`www.eclipse.org`), is intended to provide a robust, customizable and fully featured IDE for any number of languages and development focuses. It's an open source project, and has spun off at least two distinct child variants (Aptana Studio, focused on web development), and LiClipse , (focusing on Python development).

The LiClipse installation will be used as the basis of comparison here, since it requires no language-specific setup to begin writing Python code, but it's perhaps worth noting that any Eclipse-derived installation that has access to the same plugins and extensions (PyDev for Python language support, and EGit for Git support) would provide the same functionality. All that said, Eclipse is not, perhaps, for everyone. It can be a very heavy IDE, especially if it's providing support for more than a couple of languages, and can have a significant operational footprint memory and CPU usage – even if its supported languages and functionality set is fairly tightly controlled:

- **Large project support**: Great
- **Refactoring support**: Good
- **Language exploration**: Fair
- **Code execution**: Good
- **Bells and whistles**: Good

Here is a screenshot of LiClipse, showing a code outline view of the open code file, project properties, and a task list automatically generated from TODO comments in the open code files:

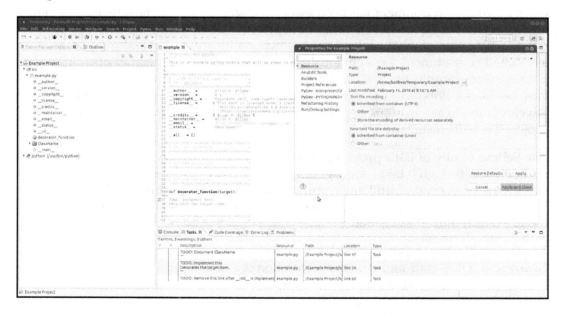

Eclipse's support for large Python projects is very good:

- Multiple projects can be defined and open for modification at the same time
- Each project can have its own distinct Python interpreter, which can be a project-specific virtual environment, allowing distinct package requirements on a per-project basis, while still also allowing execution
- Projects can be set up to use other projects through the Project References settings as dependencies, and code execution will take those dependencies into account; that is, if code is run in a project that has a different project set up as a reference/dependency, the first project will still have access to the second's code and installed packages

Refactoring support across all the Eclipse-derived IDEs is also quite good, providing processes for the renaming of code elements including modules, the extraction of variables and methods, and facilities for the generation of properties and other code constructs. There may be other refactoring capabilities that are context dependent, and thus aren't obviously available at first glance.

Once a Python environment has been associated with a project, the structure of that environment is completely available in the project's UI. By itself, that allows for drill-down exploration of what packages and functionality are available through the associated environment. Less obviously, control-clicking on a member of an installed package (for example, on `urllib.request` in the example code from Chapter 5, *The hms_sys System-Project,* or the `urlopen` function that module provides) will take the developer to the actual member (method or property) of the actual module that the project has in its installation.

The Eclipse family of IDEs provides reasonably good execution capabilities for Python code, though it takes some getting used to. Any module or package file can be executed if or as needed, and any results, be they output or errors, will be displayed. The execution of a specific file also generates an internal run configuration that can be modified or removed as needed.

The Eclipse/PyDev bells and whistles are, for the most part, comparable with those of Geany and IDLE code and structure coloration is available and configurable, autosuggestion and autocompletion is available. The one potentially significant item that LiClipse in particular provides from the get-go is an integrated Git client. LiClipse's Git integration, before any repositories have been cloned, is shown here:

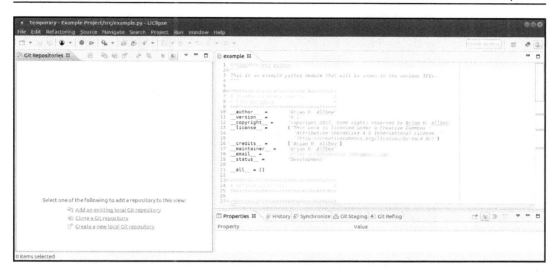

Others

These are not the only IDEs available for Python development, nor are they necessarily the best. Other popular options, based on various professional and semi-professional group polling, include:

- **PyCharm** (Community or Professional version): PyCharm shows up pretty consistently as a popular IDE for Python development. Its feature list includes most of the same bells and whistles that have been noted for Geany and Eclipse/PyDev tools, and it also features out-of-the box integration with Git, Subversion, and Mercurial version control systems, as well as UI and tools for working with various popular RDBMS, such as MySQL and SQL Server in the Professional version. It's probably a good first choice for the development of web applications in Python, provided that its project management functionality isn't going to be overwhelmed by the code base. PyCharm can be downloaded at `www.jetbrains.com/pycharm`.

- **Visual Studio Code**: VS Code is touted as being a lightning fast code editor, and has a lot of functionality available through a large collection of extensions for various languages and purposes. Although it's one of the newer IDEs in the wild with Python support, it's fast becoming a popular choice for scripting tasks, and has a lot of potential for larger, application-centric efforts as well. Visual Studio can be downloaded at `code.visualstudio.com`.

- **Ninja IDE**: Judging by its feature list, Ninja has most of the same base features available through Geany, with the addition of a single, built-in project management subsystem that sounds useful and attractive. Ninja IDE can be downloaded at `ninja-ide.org`

Source Code Management

Whether described as a version or revision control system, **Source Code Management (SCM)**, or some other name, the more common and more popular SCMs provide a host of features and capabilities to make certain aspects of the development process easier, faster, or at a minimum, more stable. These include the following:

- Allowing multiple developers to collaborate on the same parts of the same code base without having to worry (as much) about overwriting each other's work
- Keeping track of all versions of a code base, and who made what changes to it at each point that a new version was committed
- Providing visibility into what changes were made as each new version was committed
- Maintaining different versions of the same code base for specific purposes, probably the most common variation of which is having versions for different environments that code changes are worked on and promoted through, which might include:
  - Local development environments
  - A shared development environment, where all developers' local code changes first mix together
  - A shared test server for QA and broader integration testing

- A **User Acceptance Testing** server, using realistic, production-like data, which can be used to demonstrate functionality to whoever needs to give final approval for changes to be promoted to a live environment or build
- A staging environment that has full access to a complete copy of production data, with an eye towards being able to perform load and other tests that require access to that dataset
- The live environment/build code base

While there are at least a few major variations in how such systems function under the hood, from a developer's perspective, those functional differences may not really matter, so long as they function as expected and function well. Taken together, those basic capabilities, and the permutations of them with various manual efforts, allow the following:

- Developers to roll back to an earlier version of a complete code base, make changes to it, and re-commit those as a new version, which can be useful for:

  - Finding and removing or fixing changes that unexpectedly raised significant issues after being committed or even promoted
  - Creating new branches of the code to experiment with other approaches to committed functionality

- Multiple developers with different areas of expertise to work on parts of the same problem and/or code, allowing them to get that problem solved, or that code written much faster
- Developers with stronger architectural backgrounds or skill sets to define bare-bones code structures (classes and their members, perhaps), then commit them to be fully implemented by someone else
- System domain experts to easily review changes to the code base, identifying risks to functionality or performance before those get promoted to an unforgiving environment
- Configuration managers to access and deploy different versions of the code base to their various target environments

There are probably a lot of other, more specific applications that a good SCM system, especially if it's got good ties to the development and code promotion processes, can help manage.

Typical SCM activities

Probably the most common use pattern for any SCM, no matter which one is in play, and regardless of the specific command variations, is the following sequence of operations:

- Fetching a version of a given code base:
    - Usually, this will be the most recent version, perhaps from a specific branch for development, but any branch or version that needs to be retrieved could be fetched. In any event, the process will make a complete copy of the requested code base in some location on the local file-system, ready to be edited.
- Making changes to the local copy of the code.
- Reconciling any differences prior to committing changes:
    - The goal with this step is to pull down any changes that have been made to the same code base, and find and resolve any conflicts between local changes and any that may have been made by others in the same code. Several current SCMs allow a local commit before committing to a shared repository. In these SCMs, this reconciliation is, perhaps, not as critical until code is being committed to the shared repository, but doing so with every local commit will often break the resolution of conflicts down into smaller, more manageable chunks.
- Committing to the shared repository:
    - Once this has been completed, the changes made are now available for other developers to retrieve (and reconcile conflicts against, if necessary).

This use pattern will probably encompass most development efforts—anything that involves working on an established branch, and that doesn't require a new branch. Creation of new branches is also not unusual, especially if there are major changes expected to substantial portions of an existing code base. It's also not an unusual strategy to have nested branches for different environments, where the deeper branches are still pending some review or acceptance before being promoted up to the more stable branches.

The branch structure is shown here:

The process for promoting code, for example from the `[dev]` branch up to `[test]`, is reduced to an upwards merge, copying code from the lower branch to the higher, followed if necessary by branching from the higher branch back down to the lower again.

It's also not unusual to have separate branches created for specific projects—especially if there are two or more efforts underway that are likely to make widespread and/or significant changes, and most especially if those efforts are expected to conflict with each other. Project-specific branches will usually be taken from a shared development branch, as shown here:

As code is completed for either `[project1]` or `[project2]` branches, it would be committed to its own branch, then merged up into the existing `[dev]` branch, checking for and resolving any conflicts in the process.

There are dozens of SCMs available, about a dozen of which are open source systems and free of cost. The most popular systems are:

- Git (by a wide margin)
- Subversion
- Mercurial

Git

Git is, by a significant margin, the most popular SCM in use at present. It is a distributed SCM system that keeps local branches of code bases and other content very inexpensively, while still providing the ability to push locally committed code into a shared central repository that multiple users can then access and work from. Above all else, it's capable of handling a lot of concurrent commit (or patch) activity—not surprising since it was written to accommodate the Linux kernel development team's efforts, where there might be hundreds of such patches/commits at a time. It's fast and efficient, and the commands for basic functionality that covers most day-to-day needs are fairly easily committed to memory, if using the command line is the preferred approach.

Git has more functionality outside the normal commands and processes than in those processes themselves, that is, there are eight or nine commands that probably encompass the fetch/edit/reconcile/commit steps noted earlier, but Git has 21 commands in total, with the other 12-13 providing functionality that is less commonly needed or used. Anecdotal evidence suggests that most developers, unless they are working on projects over a certain size or complexity, are probably closer to the end of the spectrum that these folks are at:

If that doesn't fix it, git.txt contains the phone number of a friend of mine who understands git. Just wait through a few minutes of 'It's really pretty simple, just think of branches as...' and eventually you'll learn the commands that will fix everything.

https://xkcd.com/1597

There's no shortage of GUI tools for Git either, though many IDEs, whether in an effort to minimize context switches, or for some other reason, provide some sort of interface to Git, even if it's through an optional plugin. The best of those will also detect when problems with some process (a commit or push, for example) crop up, and provide some instruction on how to resolve those problems. There are also free standing Git-GUI applications, and even integrations with built-in system tools such as TortoiseGit (`https://tortoisegit.org/`), which adds Git functionality to the Windows File Explorer.

Subversion

Subversion (or SVN) is an older SCM that's been in play since early in 2004. It's one of the most popular non-distributed SCMs still in use today. Like most SCMs before it, SVN stores a complete local copy of the code and content for each checked-out branch that it's tracking, and uploads those (perhaps in their entirety) during the commit process. It's also a centralized rather than a distributed system, which means that all branching and merging has to happen with respect to the master copy of the code base, wherever it might live.

The various under-the-hood differences and popularity of Git notwithstanding, SVN is a perfectly viable option for managing source code across a team, even if it's less efficient or less popular than Git. It fully supports the typical get-edit-commit work cycle, just not with the same degree of flexibility as Git provides.

Basic workflows for Git and SVN compared

Although the basic checkout, work, merge, and commit workflow is supported by all mainstream SCMs, it's worth looking at some of the additional process steps that Git requires. Each additional step is, obviously, an additional task that a developer will have to perform before code is fully committed, though none of them are necessarily long-running tasks, so the impact is rarely going to be substantial. On the other hand, each additional step involved provides an additional point where additional code modification can be made before it's attached to the master version of the code.

Compare the **Git Workflow** (left) and **SVN Workflow** (right):

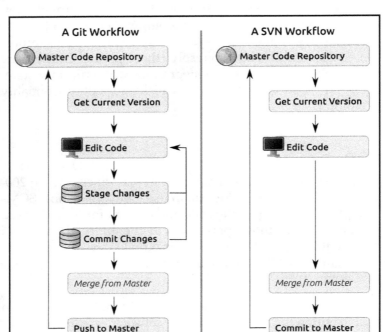

- The processes of getting the current version of the code and editing it are fundamentally the same.

- Git allows the developer to **Stage Changes**. However, perhaps the modifications to the code in three out of five files are complete, and ready to be committed, at least locally, while there are significant efforts still needed on the other two. Since changes must be staged in Git prior to committing, the files that are done can be staged and then committed separately, leaving the others still in progress. Uncommitted staged files can still be edited and re-staged (or not) as needed as well; until a change-set is actually committed, everything is still in an in-progress state.

- Git's **Commit Changes** is to a local repository, which again means that continued editing can happen, as well as manipulation of local commits, until everything is as it needs to be for the final master repository commit.

- Both provide the ability to perform a **Merge from Master** before the final **Push** or **Commit to Master** operations. Realistically, this can happen at any point prior to the final commit, but the granularity of Git's stage-then-commit approach lends itself well to doing so in smaller, more manageable chunks, which will often mean that any merges down from the master source code will also be smaller and easier to manage. There's no reason, on the SVN side, why similar periodic merges down can't be performed, it's just easier to remember to do so during a local commit routine during development.

Other SCM options

Git and SVN are not the only available options, by any means. The next most popular options are the following:

- **Mercurial**: A free, open source SCM, written in Python, that uses a distributed structure like Git, but doesn't require the change staging operation that Git does. Mercurial has been adopted for internal use by Google and Facebook.

- **Perforce Helix Core**: A proprietary, distributed SCM that is at least somewhat compatible with Git commands, targeted for Enterprise clients and use.

Best practices

There are any number of standards and best practices that surround development, at least once the code base(s) involved gets above a certain level of complexity. They are considered as such because they solve (or prevent) various difficulties that will likely arise if they aren't followed. A fair number of them also focus, if indirectly, on some aspect of future-proofing code, at least from the perspective of trying to make it easier for a new developer (or the same developer, maybe years later) to understand what the code does, how to find specific chunks of code, or, perhaps, to extend or refactor it.

Those guidelines fall, roughly, into two categories, no matter the programming language:

- **Standards for code:** Guidelines and concepts that focus on the structure and organization of code, though not necessarily on how that code functions – more on keeping it easily understood and navigable

- **Process standards:** Guidelines and concepts that center around making sure that code is well behaved and that changes to it can be made with the minimum amount of hassle and disruption

Python adds two more items into that mix that don't quite fit into either of those language-agnostic categories; they are the results of capabilities and functional requirements in the context of Python specifically:

- **Package organization:** How best to structure code at a file-system level; where and when to generate new module files and package directories

- **When and how to use Python virtual environments:** What purposes they serve, and how best to leverage them for a given collection of code

Standards for code

Code level standards, at the end of the day, are as much about trying to ensure that the code itself is written and structured in a predictable and easily understood manner as anything else. When those standards are followed, and when they are reasonably well understood by the developers who are working with the code base, it's not unreasonable to expect that any developer, even one who may never have seen a given chunk of code, will nevertheless be able to do the following:

- Read and more easily understand the code and what it's doing
- Find a code element (a class, function, constant, or some other item) that may only be identified by name, or in terms of a namespace, quickly and easily
- Create new code elements in an existing structure that also conform to those standards
- Modify existing code elements and know what standards-related items need to be modified in concert with those changes (if any)

The Python community has one set of guidelines (PEP-8), but there may well be additional internal standards that are in place as well.

PEP-8

At least some of Python's DNA is bound to the observation that code is generally read more often that it is written. That is the basis for significant functional aspects of its syntax, particularly those that relate to the structure of Python code, such as the use of indentation to indicate blocks of functionality. It should, perhaps, then come as no great surprise that one of the earliest **Python Enhancement Proposals** (**PEPs**) is a focused look at how to maintain readability of code where variations in style have no functional significance. PEP-8 is a long specification, some 29 pages if printed directly from the current Python page (www.python.org/dev/peps/pep-0008), but the significant aspects are worth summarizing here.

The first, and perhaps most significant, item therein is the recognition that while it'd be ideal if all Python code followed the same standards, there are a number of defensible reasons not to (see *A Foolish Consistency is the Hobgoblin of Little Minds* in PEP-8). Those include, but are not limited to, the following:

- When applying PEP-8 style guidelines would make the code less readable, even for someone who is used to reading code that follows the standards
- To be consistent with surrounding code that also does not adhere to them (maybe for historic reasons)
- Because there is no reason other than the style guidelines to make changes to the code
- If adherence to the guidelines would break backwards compatibility (let alone functionality, though that seems unlikely)

PEP-8 notes specifically that it is a style guide, and as mentioned in the Style Guide Introduction of Solidity v0.3.0:

"A style guide is about consistency. Consistency with this style guide is important. Consistency within a project is more important. Consistency within one module or function is the most important".

That implies that there may be good (or at least defensible) reasons to not adhere to some or all of the guidelines, even for new code. Examples might include the following:

- Using naming conventions from another language because the functionality is equivalent, such as using JavaScript naming conventions in a Python class library that provides the same **Document Object Model (DOM)** manipulation functionality across a server-side class library for creating and working with DOM objects
- Using very specific documentation string structures or formats to conform to a documentation management system's requirements that applies to all code (Python or otherwise) across the business
- Conforming to other internal standards that contradict the ones advised by PEP-8

Ultimately though, since PEP-8 is a set of style guidelines, not functional ones, the worst that can happen is that someone will complain that the code doesn't stick to the publicly accepted standards. If your code is never going to be shared outside your organization, that may well never be a concern.

There are three loose groupings in PEP-8's guidelines whose members can be summarized briefly:

Code layout:

- Indentation should be four spaces per level:
    - Don't use tabs
    - Hanging indentation should use the same set of rules wherever possible, see the PEP-8 page for specifics and recommendations
- Functional lines should not exceed 79 characters in length and long text strings should be limited to 72 characters per line, including indentation spaces
- If a line has to break around an operator (+, -, *, and, or, and so on), break it before the operator
- Surround top-level functions and class definitions with two blank lines

Comments:

- Comments that contradict the code are worse than no comments—always make a priority of keeping the comments up-to-date when the code changes!
- Comments should be complete sentences. The first word should be capitalized, unless it is an identifier that begins with a lowercase letter (never alter the case of identifiers!).
- Block comments generally consist of one or more paragraphs built out of complete sentences, with each sentence ending in a period.

Naming conventions:

- Packages and modules should have short names, and use the `lowercase` or (if necessary) `lowercase_words` naming convention
- Class names should use the `CapWords` naming convention
- Functions and methods should use the `lowercase_words` naming convention
- Constants should use the `CAP_WORDS` naming convention

Other items that are noted in PEP-8 but are too long to summarize usefully here include the following:

- Source file encoding (which feels like it may soon stop being a concern)
- Imports
- Whitespace in expressions and statements
- Documentation strings (which have their own PEP: `www.python.org/dev/peps/pep-0257`)
- Designing for inheritance

These, along with PEP-8's substantial *Programming Recommendations* section, will be followed in code during the development of the `hms_sys` project where they don't conflict with other standards.

Internal standards

Any given development effort, team, or even company may have specific standards and expectations around how code is written or structured. There may also be functional standards as well, things such as policies that define what types of external systems will be used to provide various functionality that systems consume, which RDBMS engines are supported, what web servers will be used, and so on. For the purposes of this book, the functional standards will be determined during development, but some code structure and format standards will be defined here and now. As a starting point, the PEP-8 code layout, comments, and naming convention standards will apply. Over and above that, there are some code organization and class structure standards that will also be in play.

Code organization in modules

The PEP-8 structure and sequence guidelines will be followed, with a module level doc string, imports from `__future__`, various dunder-names (an `__all__` list to support `from [module] import [member]` use of the module's members, and some standard `__author__`, `__copyright__` and `__status__` metadata about the module), then imports from standard libraries, then third-party libraries, and finally internal libraries.

After that, code will be organized and grouped by member types, in this order, with each element in alphabetical order (unless there are functional reasons why that order isn't viable, such as classes depending on or inheriting from other classes that haven't been defined yet if they are in strict order):

- Module-level constants
- Custom exceptions defined in the module
- Functions
- Abstract base classes that are intended to serve as formal interfaces
- Abstract base classes that are intended to serve as standard abstract classes, or as mixins
- Concrete classes

The goal of all of these structure constraints is to provide some predictability across the entire code base, to make it easy to locate a given module member without having to search for it every single time. Modern IDEs, with the ability to control-click on a member name in code and jump straight to that member's definition, arguably make that unnecessary, but if code is going to be viewed or read by someone without access to such an IDE, organizing it this way still has some value.

Accordingly, module and package header files follow a very specific structure, and that structure is set up in a set of template files, one for general purpose modules, and one for package header (__init__.py) modules. Structurally, they are identical, with only some slight variation between the two in the starting text/content. The module.py template then is the following:

```python
#!/usr/bin/env python
"""
TODO: Document the module.
Provides classes and functionality for SOME_PURPOSE
"""

#######################################
# Any needed from __future__ imports  #
# Create an "__all__" list to support #
#    "from module import member" use  #
#######################################

__all__ = [
    # Constants
    # Exceptions
    # Functions
    # ABC "interface" classes
    # ABC abstract classes
    # Concrete classes
]

#######################################
# Module metadata/dunder-names        #
#######################################

__author__ = 'Brian D. Allbee'
__copyright__ = 'Copyright 2018, all rights reserved'
__status__ = 'Development'

#######################################
# Standard library imports needed     #
#######################################

# Uncomment this if there are abstract classes or "interfaces"
#    defined in the module...
# import abc

#######################################
# Third-party imports needed          #
#######################################
```

```
######################################
# Local imports needed               #
######################################


######################################
# Initialization needed before member #
#   definition can take place        #
######################################


######################################
# Module-level Constants             #
######################################


######################################
# Custom Exceptions                  #
######################################


######################################
# Module functions                   #
######################################


######################################
# ABC "interface" classes            #
######################################


######################################
# Abstract classes                   #
######################################


######################################
# Concrete classes                   #
######################################


######################################
# Initialization needed after member #
#   definition is complete           #
######################################


######################################
# Imports needed after member        #
#   definition (to resolve circular  #
#   dependencies - avoid if at all   #
#   possible                         #
######################################


######################################
# Code to execute if the module is   #
#   called directly                  #
```

```
######################################

if __name__ == '__main__':
    pass
```

The only real differences between a module's template and one for a package header is the initial documentation and that there is a specific callout for including child package and module namespace members in the __all__ list:

```
#!/usr/bin/env python
"""
TODO: Document the package.
Package-header for the PACKAGE_NAMESPACE namespace.
Provides classes and functionality for SOME_PURPOSE
"""

#######################################
# Any needed from __future__ imports  #
# Create an "__all__" list to support #
#    "from module import member" use  #
#######################################

__all__ = [
    # Constants
    # Exceptions
    # Functions
    # ABC "interface" classes
    # ABC abstract classes
    # Concrete classes
    # Child packages and modules
]

#######################################
# Module metadata/dunder-names        #
#######################################

# ...the balance of the template-file is as shown above...
```

Having these available as template files for developer use also makes starting a new module or package a bit quicker and easier. Copying the file, or its contents, to a new file takes a few seconds longer than just creating a new, blank file, but having the structure ready to start coding in makes it a lot easier to maintain the relevant standards.

Structure and standards for classes

Class definitions, whether for concrete/instantiable classes or any of the ABC variants, have a similar structure defined, and will be arranged in sorted groups as follows:

- Class attributes and constants
- Property getter methods
- Property setter methods
- Property deleter methods
- Instance property definitions
- Object initialization (__init__)
- Object deletion (__del__)
- Instance methods (concrete or abstract)
- Overrides of standard built-in methods (__str__)
- Class methods
- Static methods

The property getter, setter, and deleter methods approach was selected, rather than using method decoration, in order to make it easier to keep property documentation in a single location in the class definition. The use of properties (technically, they are managed attributes, but properties is a shorter name, and has the same meaning across several languages) as opposed to general attributes is a concession to unit testing requirements, and to a policy of raising errors as close to their cause as possible. Both will be discussed shortly, in the unit testing part of the *Process standards* section.

The concrete class template then contains the following:

```
# Blank line in the template, helps with PEP-8's space-before-and-
after rule
class ClassName:
    """TODO: Document the class.
Represents a WHATEVER
"""

    ###################################
    # Class attributes/constants      #
    ###################################

    ###################################
    # Property-getter methods         #
    ###################################

#    def _get_property_name(self) -> str:
```

```
#           return self._property_name

    ####################################
    # Property-setter methods          #
    ####################################

#     def _set_property_name(self, value:str) -> None:
#         # TODO: Type- and/or value-check the value argument of the
#         #       setter-method, unless it's deemed unnecessary.
#         self._property_name = value

    ####################################
    # Property-deleter methods         #
    ####################################

#     def _del_property_name(self) -> None:
#         self._property_name = None

    ####################################
    # Instance property definitions    #
    ####################################

#     property_name = property(
#         # TODO: Remove setter and deleter if access is not needed
#         _get_property_name, _set_property_name, _del_property_name,
#         'Gets, sets or deletes the property_name (str) of the
instance'
#     )

    ####################################
    # Object initialization            #
    ####################################

    # TODO: Add and document arguments if/as needed
    def __init__(self):
        """
Object initialization.

self ............. (ClassName instance, required) The instance to
                  execute against
        """
        # - Call parent initializers if needed
        # - Set default instance property-values using _del_...
methods
        # - Set instance property-values from arguments using
        #   _set_... methods
        # - Perform any other initialization needed
        pass # Remove this line
```

```
###################################
# Object deletion                 #
###################################

###################################
# Instance methods                #
###################################

#     def instance_method(self, arg:str, *args, **kwargs):
#         """TODO: Document method
# DOES_WHATEVER
#
# self ............. (ClassName instance, required) The instance to
#                    execute against
# arg .............. (str, required) The string argument
# *args ............ (object*, optional) The arglist
# **kwargs ......... (dict, optional) keyword-args, accepts:
#   - kwd_arg ....... (type, optional, defaults to SOMETHING) The
SOMETHING
#                    to apply
#     """
#         pass

###################################
# Overrides of built-in methods   #
###################################

###################################
# Class methods                   #
###################################

###################################
# Static methods                  #
###################################
# Blank line in the template, helps with PEP-8's space-before-and-
after rule
```

Apart from the __init__ method, which will almost always be implemented, the actual functional elements, the properties and methods, are commented out. This allows the standards expected to be present in the template, and developers can, if they so choose, simply copy and paste whichever code stub(s) they need, uncomment the whole pasted block, rename what needs to be renamed, and start writing code.

The template file for abstract classes is very similar to the concrete class template, with the addition of a few items to accommodate code elements that are not present in a concrete class:

```
# Remember to import abc!
# Blank line in the template, helps with PEP-8's space-before-and-
after rule
class AbstractClassName(metaclass=abc.ABCMeta):
    """TODO: Document the class.
Provides baseline functionality, interface requirements, and
type-identity for objects that can REPRESENT_SOMETHING
"""

    ####################################
    # Class attributes/constants       #
    ####################################

    # ... Identical to above ...

    ####################################
    # Instance property definitions    #
    ####################################

#       abstract_property = abc.abstractproperty()

#       property_name = property(

    # ... Identical to above ...

    ####################################
    # Abstract methods                 #
    ####################################

#       @abc.abstractmethod
#       def instance_method(self, arg:str, *args, **kwargs):
#           """TODO: Document method
# DOES_WHATEVER
#
# self .............. (AbstractClassName instance, required) The
#                     instance to execute against
# arg ............... (str, required) The string argument
# *args ............. (object*, optional) The arglist
# **kwargs .......... (dict, optional) keyword-args, accepts:
#   - kwd_arg ....... (type, optional, defaults to SOMETHING) The
SOMETHING
#                     to apply
#   """
#           pass
```

```
###################################
# Instance methods                #
###################################

# ... Identical to above ...

###################################
# Static methods                  #
###################################
# Blank line in the template, helps with PEP-8's space-before-and-
after rule
```

A similar template is also available for class definitions that are intended to serve as formal interfaces; classes that define functional requirements for an instance of a class, but that don't provide any implementation of those requirements. It looks very much like the abstract class template, barring some name changes and the removal of anything that is or implies a concrete implementation:

```
# Remember to import abc!
# Blank line in the template, helps with PEP-8's space-before-and-
after rule
class InterfaceName(metaclass=abc.ABCMeta):
    """TODO: Document the class.
Provides interface requirements, and type-identity for objects that
can REPRESENT_SOMETHING
"""

    ###################################
    # Class attributes/constants      #
    ###################################

    ###################################
    # Instance property definitions   #
    ###################################

#     abstract_property = abc.abstractproperty()

    ###################################
    # Object initialization           #
    ###################################

    # TODO: Add and document arguments if/as needed
    def __init__(self):
        """
Object initialization.

self .............. (InterfaceName instance, required) The instance to
                   execute against
"""
```

```
        # - Call parent initializers if needed
        # - Perform any other initialization needed
        pass # Remove this line


    ####################################
    # Object deletion                  #
    ####################################


    ####################################
    # Abstract methods                 #
    ####################################

#       @abc.abstractmethod
#       def instance_method(self, arg:str, *args, **kwargs):
#           """TODO: Document method
# DOES_WHATEVER
#
# self .............. (InterfaceName instance, required) The
#                     instance to execute against
# arg .............. (str, required) The string argument
# *args ............ (object*, optional) The arglist
# **kwargs ......... (dict, optional) keyword-args, accepts:
#   - kwd_arg ....... (type, optional, defaults to SOMETHING) The
SOMETHING
#                     to apply
# """
#           pass

    ####################################
    # Class methods                    #
    ####################################


    ####################################
    # Static methods                   #
    ####################################
# Blank line in the template, helps with PEP-8's space-before-and-
after rule
```

Taken together, these five templates should provide solid starting points for writing code for any of the more commonly expected element types expected in most projects.

Function and method annotation (hinting)

If you've worked with Python functions and methods before, you may have noticed and wondered about some unexpected syntax in some of the methods in the template files earlier, specifically the items in bold here:

```
def _get_property_name(self) -> str:

def _set_property_name(self, value:str) -> None:

def _del_property_name(self) -> None:

def instance_method(self, arg:str, *args, **kwargs):
```

These are examples of type hints that are supported in Python 3. One of the standards that `hms_sys` code will also adhere to is that all methods and functions should be type hinted. The resulting annotations may eventually be used to enforce type checking of arguments using a decorator, and even later on may be useful in streamlining unit testing. On a shorter-term basis, there is some expectation that an automatic documentation generation system will pay attention to those, so they're part of the internal standards now.

Type hinting is probably new enough that it's not in common use just yet, so a walk-through of what it does and how it works is probably worth examination. Consider the following unannotated function and its results when executed:

```
def my_function(name, price, description=None):
    """
A fairly standard Python function that accepts name, description and
price values, formats them, and returns that value.
    """
    result = """
name ......... %s
description ... %s
price ........ %0.2f
""" % (name, description, price)
    return result

if __name__ == '__main__':
    print(
        my_function(
            'Product #1', 12.95, 'Description of the product'
        )
    )
    print(
        my_function(
```

```
        'Product #2', 10
    )
)
```

The results from executing that code look good:

```
name ......... Product #1
description ... Description of the product
price ........ 12.95


name ......... Product #2
description ... None
price ........ 10.00
```

This is pretty straightforward, as Python functions go. The `my_function` function expects a `name` and `price`, and also allows for a `description` argument, but that is optional and defaults to `None`. The function itself just collects all those into a formatted string-value and returns it. The `price` argument should be a number value of some sort, and the others should be strings, if they exist. In this case, the expected types of those argument values are probably obvious based on the argument names.

The price argument, though, could be any of several different numerical types, and still function—`int` and `float` values obviously work, since the code runs without error. So too would a `decimal.Decimal` value, or even a `complex` type, as nonsensical as that would be. The type hinting annotation syntax exists, then, to provide a way to indicate without requiring what type or types of values are expected or returned.

Here's the same function, hinted:

```
def my_function(name:str, price:(float,int),
description:(str,None)=None) -> str:
    """
A fairly standard Python function that accepts name, description and
price values, formats them, and returns that value.
    """
    result = """
name .......... %s
description ... %s
price ........ %0.2f
""" % (name, description, price)
    return result
```

```
if __name__ == '__main__':
    print(
        my_function(
            'Product #1', 12.95, 'Description of the product'
        )
    )
    print(
        my_function(
            'Product #2', 10
        )
    )

    # - Print the __annotations__ of my_function
    print(my_function.__annotations__)
```

The only differences here are the type hinting annotations after each argument and the return type hint at the end of the function's first line, which indicate the expected types of each argument, and of the results of calling the function:

```
my_function(name:str, price:(float,int), description:(str,None)=None)
-> str:
```

The output from the function call is identical, but the __annotations__ attribute of the function is shown at the end of the output:

```
name ......... Product #1
description ... Description of the product
price ........ 12.95


name ......... Product #2
description ... None
price ........ 10.00

{
    'return': <class 'str'>, 'description': (<class 'str'>, None),
    'price': (<class 'float'>, <class 'int'>), 'name': <class 'str'>
}
```

All the type-hinting annotations really do is to populate the __annotations__ property of my_function, as shown at the end of the preceding execution. Essentially, they are providing metadata about and attached to the function itself that can be used later.

Taken together then, all of these standards are intended to do the following:

- Help keep code as readable as possible (baseline PEP-8 conventions)

- Keep the structure and organization of code within files predictable (module and class element organization standards)

- Make it easy to create new elements (modules, classes, and so on) that conform to those standards (the various templates)

- Provide some degree of future-proofing against efforts to allow automated documentation generation, type checking of methods and functions, and possibly some unit testing efficiencies to be explored later (type-hinting annotations)

Process standards

Process standards are concerned with what processes are executed against a code base towards any of several purposes. The two that are most common as separate entities are the following:

- **Unit testing:** Ensuring that code is tested and can be re-tested on demand, in an effort to ensure in turn that it works as expected

- **Repeatable build processes:** Designed so that whatever build process you use and probably the installation process as a result, is automated, error free, and repeatable on demand while requiring as little developer time to execute as possible

Taken together, these two also lead to the idea of **integrating unit tests and build processes**, so that, if needful or desired, a build process can ensure that its resulting output has been tested.

Unit testing

It's not unusual for people, even developers, to think of unit testing as a process of making sure that bugs aren't present in a code base. While there is a fair amount of truth to that, at least in smaller code bases, that's actually more a result of the real purpose behind unit testing: unit testing is about ensuring that code behaves in a predictable fashion across all reasonably possible execution cases. The difference can be subtle, but it's still a significant one.

Let's take another look at the preceding `my_function`, this time from a unit testing perspective. It's got three arguments, one that is a required string value, one that is a required number value, and one that is an optional string value. It makes no decisions based on any of those values or their types, it just dumps them into a string and returns that string. Let's assume that the arguments supplied are properties of a product (which is what the output implies, even if that's not really the case). Even without any decision making involved, there are aspects to the functionality that will raise errors, or that probably should in that context:

- Passing a non-numeric `price` value will raise a `TypeError` because the string formatting won't format a non-numeric value with the `%0.2f` format specified
- Passing a negative `price` value probably should raise an error—unless it's actually possible for a product to have a negative price, it just doesn't make sense
- Passing a `price` value that is numeric, but isn't a real number (like a `complex` number) probably should raise an error
- Passing an empty `name` value probably should raise an error—it makes no sense to have what we presume to be a product name accept an empty value
- Passing a multi-line `name` value might be a case that should raise an error
- Passing a non-string `name` value probably ought to raise an error as well, for similar reasons, as would a non-string `description` value

Apart from the first item in the list, these are all potential flaws in the function itself, none of which will raise any errors at present, but all of which could very well lead to undesirable behavior.

Bugs.

 The following basic test code is collected in the `test-my_function.py` module.

Even without bringing a formal unit testing structure into play, it's not difficult to write code that will test a representative set of all good argument values. First, those values have to be defined:

```
# - Generate a list of good values that should all pass for:
#    * name
good_names = [
    'Product',
    'A Very Long Product Name That is Not Realistic, '
        'But Is Still Allowable',
    'None',   # NOT the actual None value, a string that says "None"
]
#    * price
good_prices = [
    0, 0.0, # Free is legal, if unusual.
    1, 1.0,
    12.95, 13,
]
#    * description
good_descriptions = [
    None, # Allowed, since it's the default value
    '', # We'll assume empty is OK, since None is OK.
    'Description',
    'A long description. '*20,
    'A multi-line\n\n description.'
]
```

Then, it's a simple matter of iterating over all the good combinations and keeping track of any errors that surface as a result:

```
# - Test all possible good combinations:
test_count = 0
tests_passed = 0
for name in good_names:
    for price in good_prices:
        for description in good_descriptions:
            test_count += 1
            try:
                ignore_me = my_function(name, price, description)
                tests_passed += 1
```

```
            except Exception as error:
                print(
                    '%s raised calling my_function(%s, %s, %s)' %
                    (error.__class__.__name__, name, price,
description)
                )
    if tests_passed == test_count:
        print('All %d tests passed' % (test_count))
```

The results from executing that code look good:

```
All 90 tests passed
```

Next, a similar approach is taken for defining bad values for each argument, and checking each possible bad value with known good values:

```
# - Generate a list of bad values that should all raise errors for:
#    * name
bad_names = [
    None, -1, -1.0, True, False, object()
]
#    * price
bad_prices = [
    'string value', '',
    None,
    -1, -1.0,
    -12.95, -13,
]
#    * description
bad_description = [
    -1, -1.0, True, False, object()
]

# ...

for name in bad_names:
    try:
        test_count += 1
        ignore_me = my_function(name, good_price, good_description)
        # Since these SHOULD fail, if we get here and it doesn't,
        # we raise an error to be caught later...
        raise RuntimeError()
    except (TypeError, ValueError) as error:
        # If we encounter either of these error-types, that's what
        # we'd expect: The type is wrong, or the value is invalid...
        tests_passed += 1
    except Exception as error:
```

```
        # Any OTHER error-type is a problem, so report it
        print(
            '%s raised calling my_function(%s, %s, %s)' %
            (error.__class__.__name__, name, good_price,
good_description)
        )
```

Even with just the name argument tests in place, we already start seeing issues:

```
RuntimeError raised calling my_function(None, 0, None)
RuntimeError raised calling my_function(-1, 0, None)
RuntimeError raised calling my_function(-1.0, 0, None)
RuntimeError raised calling my_function(True, 0, None)
RuntimeError raised calling my_function(False, 0, None)
RuntimeError raised calling my_function(<object object at 0x7f61840d30a0>, 0, None)
```

And after adding in similar tests for price and description values:

```
for price in bad_prices:
    try:
        test_count += 1
        ignore_me = my_function(good_name, price, good_description)
        # Since these SHOULD fail, if we get here and it doesn't,
        # we raise an error to be caught later...
        raise RuntimeError()
    except (TypeError, ValueError) as error:
        # If we encounter either of these error-types, that's what
        # we'd expect: The type is wrong, or the value is invalid...
        tests_passed += 1
    except Exception as error:
        # Any OTHER error-type is a problem, so report it
        print(
            '%s raised calling my_function(%s, %s, %s)' %
            (error.__class__.__name__, good_name, price,
good_description)
        )

for description in bad_descriptions:
    try:
        test_count += 1
        ignore_me = my_function(good_name, good_price, description)
        # Since these SHOULD fail, if we get here and it doesn't,
        # we raise an error to be caught later...
        raise RuntimeError()
    except (TypeError, ValueError) as error:
        # If we encounter either of these error-types, that's what
        # we'd expect: The type is wrong, or the value is invalid...
```

```
            tests_passed += 1
    except Exception as error:
        # Any OTHER error-type is a problem, so report it
        print(
            '%s raised calling my_function(%s, %s, %s)' %
            (error.__class__.__name__, good_name, good_price,
description)
        )
```

The resulting list of issues is larger still, with a total of 15 items, any of which could lead to a production code bug if they aren't addressed:

```
RuntimeError raised calling my_function(None, 0, None)
RuntimeError raised calling my_function(-1, 0, None)
RuntimeError raised calling my_function(-1.0, 0, None)
RuntimeError raised calling my_function(True, 0, None)
RuntimeError raised calling my_function(False, 0, None)
RuntimeError raised calling my_function(<object object at 0x7f1dd9fe90a0>, 0, None)
RuntimeError raised calling my_function(Product, -1, None)
RuntimeError raised calling my_function(Product, -1.0, None)
RuntimeError raised calling my_function(Product, -12.95, None)
RuntimeError raised calling my_function(Product, -13, None)
RuntimeError raised calling my_function(Product, 0, -1)
RuntimeError raised calling my_function(Product, 0, -1.0)
RuntimeError raised calling my_function(Product, 0, True)
RuntimeError raised calling my_function(Product, 0, False)
RuntimeError raised calling my_function(Product, 0, <object object at 0x7f1dd9fe90b0>)
```

It's not enough, then, just to say that unit testing is a requirement in the development process; some thought has to be given to what those tests actually do, to what the relevant test policies look like, and what they are required to take into account. A good bare-bones starting point test policy would probably include, at a minimum the following:

- What values are used when testing arguments or properties of specific types:
    - Numeric values should probably include even and odd variations, positive and negative values, and zero at a minimum
    - String values should include expected values, an empty string value, and strings that are nothing more than whitespace (" ")
- Some understanding of when each of those values is valid and when they are not, for each element being tested

- Tests must be written for both passing and failing cases
- Tests must be written such that they execute every branch in the element being tested

That last item bears some explanation. Thus far, the code being tested made no decisions—it executes in exactly the same way, no matter what the values of the arguments are. A full unit test executed against code that does make decisions based on the values of arguments must be sure to pass test values for those arguments that invoke all of the decisions that the code can make. It is rare that this need will not be sufficiently accounted for by simply making sure that the good and bad test values are sufficiently varied, but it can become more difficult to ensure when complex class instances enter the picture, and those circumstances warrant closer, deeper attention.

It was noted earlier, in the discussion around class templates, that formal properties (managed attributes) would be used, and that the reason behind that tied in to unit testing policies. We've seen that it's relatively easy to generate tests that can check for specific error types during the execution of a function or method. Since properties are collections of methods, one each for get, set, and delete operation, packaged up by the property keyword, it follows that performing checks against a value passed to a setter method and raising errors if the value or type passed in is invalid (and thus probably going to raise errors elsewhere) is going to make unit testing implementation following the structure/pattern shown earlier at least somewhat faster and easier. A basic structure, using the property_name property from the class-concrete.py template, shows that it's quite straightforward to implement such a property:

```
###################################
# Property-getter methods         #
###################################

def _get_property_name(self) -> str:
    return self._property_name

###################################
# Property-setter methods         #
###################################

def _set_property_name(self, value:(str, None)) -> None:
    if value is not None and type(value) is not str:
        raise TypeError(
            '%s.property_name expects a string or None '
            'value, but was passed "%s" (%s)' % (
                self.__class__.__name__, value,
                type(value).__name__
```

```
        )
     )
   self._property_name = value

####################################
# Property-deleter methods         #
####################################

def _del_property_name(self) -> None:
    self._property_name = None

####################################
# Instance property definitions    #
####################################

property_name = property(
    _get_property_name, _set_property_name, _del_property_name,
    'Gets, sets or deletes the property_name (str|None) of the
instance'
)
```

There are 18 lines of code involved, which is at least 17 lines more than would be required if `property_name` was a simple, unmanaged attribute, and there are probably going to be at least two more lines of code in the __init__ method of the class that uses this property if `property_name` is set during the creation of an instance. The trade-off, though, is that the managed attribute property is going to be self regulating, so there won't have to be much in the way of checking its type or value wherever else it might be used. The fact that it is accessible at all, that the instance it's a member of hasn't thrown an error before the property is being accessed, means that it's in a known (and valid) state.

Repeatable build processes

The idea of having a build process may have originated with languages that require compilation before their code can be executed, but there are advantages to establishing such a process even for languages such as Python that don't. In Python's case, specifically, such a process can collect code from multiple project code bases, define requirements without actually attaching them to the final package, and package code up in a consistent fashion, ready for installation. Since a build process is, itself, another program (or at least a script-like process), it also allows for the possibility of executing other code to whatever end is needed, which means that a build process can also execute automated tests, or even potentially deploy code to a designated destination, locally or remotely.

Python's default installation includes two packaging tools, `distutils`, which is a collection of bare-bones functionality, and `setuptools`, which builds on top of that to provide a more powerful packaging solution. The output of a `setuptools` run, if packaging arguments are supplied, is a ready-to-install package (an egg). The conventional practice for the creation of a package is through a `setup.py` file that makes a call to the setup function that `setuptools` provides, which might look something like this:

```python
#!/usr/bin/env python
"""
example_setup.py

A bare-bones setup.py example, showing all the arguments that are
likely to be needed for most build-/packaging-processes
"""

from setuptools import setup

# The actual setup function call:
setup(
    name='',
    version='',
    author='',
    description='',
    long_description='',
    author_email='',
    url='',
    install_requires=[
        'package~=version',
        # ...
    ],
    package_dir={
        'package_name':'project_root_directory',
        # ...
    },
    # Can also be automatically generated using
    #     setuptools.find_packages...
    packages=[
        'package_name',
        # ...
    ],
    package_data={
        'package_name':[
            'file_name.ext',
            # ...
        ]
    },
```

```
entry_points={
    'console_scripts':[
        'script_name = package.module:function',
        # ...
    ],
},
)
```

The arguments shown all relate to specific aspects of the final package:

- `name`: Defines the base name for the final package file (for example, `MyPackageName`)

- `version`: Defines the version of the package, a string that will also be part of the final package file's name

- `author`: The name of the primary author of the package

- `description`: A short description of the package

- `long_description`: A long description of the package; this is often implemented by opening and reading a file containing the long description data, typically in Markdown format if the package is intended to be uploaded to the Python website's package repository

- `author_email`: The email address of the primary author of the package

- `url`: The home URL for the package

- `install_requires`: A list of package name and version requirements that need to be installed in order to use the code in the package – a collection of dependencies

- `package_dir`: A dictionary that maps package names to source directories; the `'package_name':'project_root_directory'` value shown is typical for projects that have their source code organized under a `src` or `lib` directory, often at the same level in the filesystem as the `setup.py` file itself

- packages: A list of packages that will be added to the final output package; the setuptools module also provides a function, find_packages, that will search out and return that list, with provisions for explicit exclusion of package directories and files using a list of patterns to define what should be left out

- package_data: A collection of non-Python files that need to be included in the package directory that they are mapped to; that is, in the example shown, the setup.py run will look for a package_name package (from the packages list), and include the file_name.ext file in that package because it's been listed for inclusion

- entry_points: Allows the installer to create command-line-executable aliases for specific functions in the code base; what it will actually do is create a small, standard Python script that knows how to find and load the specified function from the package, then execute it

A far more detailed look at the creation, execution, and results from an actual setup.py will be undertaken with the first package created for hms_sys. There are also options for specifying, requiring, and executing automated unit tests that will be explored. If they provide the test execution and stop-on-failure functionality needed, then setuptools.setup will probably suffice for all the needs of hms_sys.

If there are additional needs discovered that a standard Python setup process cannot manage for whatever reason, then a fallback build process will be needed, though it will almost certainly still use the results of a setup.py run as part of its process. In order to keep that fallback as (relatively) simple as possible, and to ensure that the solution is available across as many different platforms as possible, the fallback will use GNU Make.

Make operates by executing command-line scripts for each target that is specified in a Makefile. A simple Makefile, with targets for testing and executing a setup.py file, is very simple:

```
# An example Makefile

main: test setup
        # Doesn't (yet) do anything other than running the test and
        # setup targets

setup:
        # Calls the main setup.py to build a source-distribution
```

```
        # python setup.py sdist

test:

        # Executes the unit-tests for the package, allowing the build-
        # process to die and stop the build if a test fails
```

Running a Make process from the command line is as simple as executing `make`, perhaps with a target specification:

```
$ make
# Executes the unit-tests for the package, allowing the build-
# process to die and stop the build if a test fails
# Calls the main setup.py to build a source-distribution
# python setup.py sdist
# Doesn't (yet) do anything other than running the test and
# setup targets
$
$ make test
# Executes the unit-tests for the package, allowing the build-
# process to die and stop the build if a test fails
$
$ make setup
# Calls the main setup.py to build a source-distribution
# python setup.py sdist
$
```

The first run (`make` without any target specified) executes the first target in the `Makefile`: main. The `main` target, in turn, has the `test` and `setup` targets specified as prerequisite targets to execute before moving ahead with its own processes. The same results would be returned if `make main` were executed. The second and third runs, `make test` and `make setup`, respectively, execute those specific targets.

Make, then, is a very flexible and powerful tool to have available. So long as a given build process step can be executed in the command line, it can be incorporated into a Make-based build. If different processes are needed for different environments (`dev`, `test`, `stage`, and `live`, for example), it's possible to set up Make targets that correspond to those environments, allowing one build process to handle those variations with nothing more complex than executing `make dev, ..., make live`, though some care in target naming will be needed to avoid name collisions between two different but logically sound `test` targets in this case.

Integrating unit tests and build processes

The build process, as hinted earlier, should allow the incorporation and execution of all available automated tests (unit tests at a minimum) that are created for a project. The goal of that integration is to prevent code that's failed its suite of tests from being buildable, and thus deployable, and thus to ensure that only demonstrably good code is available for installation, at least at a live or production code level.

It may be necessary to allow broken code, code that fails its tests, to be buildable at a local or shared development build level, though, if only because developers may well want or need to install a broken build in order to troubleshoot issues. That will be very circumstantial, dependent on whatever policies and procedures are in place to handle circumstances like that. A possible policy set, based on five environments, might boil down to the following:

- **Local development:** No testing required at all

- **Shared development:** Test required, but failed tests do not kill the build process, so broken builds can be promoted to the common dev server(s); broken builds are logged, however, and those logs are easily available in case there's a need to promote code in a hurry

- **QA/test:** As the shared development environment

- **Staging** (and **User Acceptance Testing**) **environments:** Tests must execute and pass for code to be installed or promoted

- **Live/production:** As staging

If the standard `setuptools`-based packaging process will allow tests to run, cause failed tests to abort the packaging effort, and won't require tests to execute during installation, then that provides adequate functional coverage of this sort of policy set, though use of a wrapper (such as Make) to provide environment-specific targets and build processes may be needed to deal with policy conformance/coverage.

If unit testing and build process standards are in place and followed, the end result will tend to be code that is both easily built and deployed, no matter what state it might be in, and that behaves in a known (and provable) fashion under all known circumstances. That doesn't mean that it will be free of bugs, though; it's much less likely to have any significant bugs, so long as the test suite(s) are thorough and complete, but that's not a guarantee.

There is some overhead involved in establishing the associated processes, and, particularly on the unit testing side, still more overhead in maintaining them, but the effects and impact on a system's stability can be amazing.

The author once wrote an asset catalog system for an advertising firm that was in daily use by as many as 300 people every business day following these process guidelines. Over the course of four years, runtime, including an update to a new and significantly changed version of the system, the total number of errors reported that weren't user error, data entry errors, or enterprise-level access permissions was four. These process standards make a difference.

Defining package structures for Python code

The package structure rules in Python are important, since they will determine what code is accessible when an attempt is made to import members from that package. Package structure is also a subset of the overall project structure that can have a significant impact on an automated build process, and it might also have an impact on unit testing setup and execution. Let's start then by examining a possible top-level project structure first, as shown here, and then review what a Python package's requirements are, and see how it fits into the project overall:

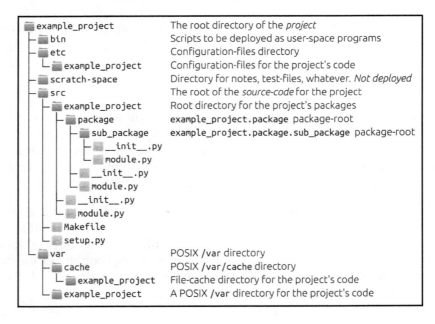

This project structure assumes that the final build will be installed on a POSIX system – most Linux installations, macOS, UNIX, and so on. There may be different needs for, say, a Windows installation, and that will be explored during the `hms_sys` development cycle, when we start working out the remote desktop applications for it. Even so, the structure may still hold up:

- The `bin` directory is intended to collect code and programs that the end user can execute, whether from a command line, or through the GUI of the OS. Those items may or may not use the main package's code, though the odds are good that it will if they are Python executables.

- The `etc` directory is where configuration files are stored, and the `example_project` directory beneath that would then be for a configuration that is very specific to the final installed instance of the project. It may be feasible, or even a better approach, to drop project-specific configurations in the top-level, and so on, directory—that decision will need to be evaluated on a project-by-project basis, and may depend on whether the end user installing the project has permissions to install to global directories.

- The `scratch-space` directory is just a place to collect whatever random files might be useful during development – proof-of-concept code, note files, whatever. It's not intended to be part of a build and won't be deployable.

- The `src` directory is where the project code lives. We'll dig deeper into that shortly.

- The `var` directory is where POSIX systems store program data that needs to be persisted as files. The `cache` directory within it is a standard POSIX location for caching files, and the `example_project` directory within that would therefore be the location specifically for the project's code to cache files. It may be useful to have a dedicated, project-specific directory in `var` that's not in `cache`, and that's also provided.

Packages in a project's context

Within the `src` directory is the package tree for the project. Each directory level at or under the `example_project` directory that has an `__init__.py` file is a formal Python package, and will be accessible through an import statement in Python code. Once this project is built and installed, then, and assuming that the code within it is written to accommodate the relevant import structure, all of the following would be legitimate imports from the project's code:

`import example_project`	Imports the entire `example_project` namespace
`import example_project.package` `from example_project import package`	Imports `example_project.package` and all its members
`from example_project.package import member`	Assuming that `member` exists, imports it from `example_project.package`
`import example_project.package.subpackage` `from example_project.package import subpackage`	Imports `example_project.package.subpackage` and all its members
`from example_project.package.subpackage import member`	Assuming that `member` exists, imports it from `example_project.package.subpackage`

A typical pattern for packages in Python is to group code elements around common realms of functionality. For example, a package that, at a very high level, is focused on DOM manipulation (HTML page structure), and supports XML, XHTML, and HTML5 might group things like so:

- `dom (__init__.py)`
    - `generic (__init__.py)`
        - [General-purpose classes for working with elements]
    - `html (__init__.py)`
        - `generic (generic.py)`
            - [General-purpose classes for working with HTML elements]
        - `forms (forms.py)`

- html5 (__init__.py)
  - [Classes for working with HTML-5-specific elements]
  - forms (forms.py)
- xhtml (__init__.py)
  - [Classes for working with XHTML-specific elements]
  - forms (forms.py)
- xml (__init__.py)

A full implementation, then, of that structure might allow a developer to access an HTML5 Email field object by creating an instance of a class that lived at the dom.html5.forms.EmailField namespace, and whose code lived in .../dom/html5/forms.py as a class named EmailField.

 Deciding where specific classes, functions, constants, and so on should exist in the structure of a code base is a complex topic, and will be explored in greater depth as part of the early architecture and design of hms_sys.

Using Python virtual environments

Python allows a developer to create virtual environments that collect up all the baseline language facilities and functionality into a single location. Once set up, those virtual environments have packages installed in to or removed from them, which allows a project that's executing in the context of the environment to have access to packages and functionality that may not be needed in the base system. A virtual environment also provides a mechanism for keeping track of those installations, which in turn allows a developer to keep track of only those dependencies and requirements that are relevant to the project itself.

Virtual environments can also be used, with some care and thought, to allow a project to be developed against a specific version of the Python language – one that's no longer supported, for example, or that's still too new to be available as a standard installation in the development machine's OS. This last aspect can be very useful in developing Python applications to run in various public clouds such as Amazon's AWS, where the Python version may be newer than what's generally available, and may also have significant syntax differences from earlier versions of the language.

Breaking changes at the language level aren't very common, but they have happened in the past. Virtual environments won't solve those, but they will, at least, allow different versions of code to be maintained with more ease.

Provided that the appropriate Python module (venv in Python 3) is already installed, creating a virtual environment, activating, and deactivating it at a command-line level is pretty straightforward:

```
$ python3 -m venv ~/py_envs/example_ve
$ source ~/py_envs/example_ve/bin/activate
(example_ve) ~$ python
Python 3.5.2 (default, Nov 23 2017, 16:37:01)
[GCC 5.4.0 20160609] on linux
Type "help", "copyright", "credits" or "license" for more information.
>>>
(example_ve) ~$ deactivate
$ python
Python 2.7.12 (default, Dec  4 2017, 14:50:18)
[GCC 5.4.0 20160609] on linux2
Type "help", "copyright", "credits" or "license" for more information.
>>>
```

python3 -m venv ~/py_envs/example_ve

Creates a new, minimal virtual environment at the specified location (in this case, in a directory named example_ve, in a directory named py_envs in the user's home directory):

source ~/py_envs/example_ve/bin/activate

This activates the newly created virtual environment. At this point, launching python shows that it's using version 3.5.2, and the command line interface prefaces each line with (example_ve) to show that the virtual environment is active:

deactivate

This deactivates the active virtual environment. Launching python from the command-line now shows the default Python version, 2.7.12, for the system.

Installing, updating, and removing packages, and showing what packages are installed, are equally straightforward:

```
$ source ~/py_envs/example_ve/bin/activate
(example_ve)~$ pip freeze
pkg-resources==0.0.0
You are using pip version 8.1.1, however version 9.0.1 is available.
You should consider upgrading via the 'pip install --upgrade pip' command.
(example_ve)~$ pip install --upgrade pip
Collecting pip
  Using cached pip-9.0.1-py2.py3-none-any.whl
Installing collected packages: pip
  Found existing installation: pip 8.1.1
    Uninstalling pip-8.1.1:
      Successfully uninstalled pip-8.1.1
Successfully installed pip-9.0.1
(example_ve)~$ pip freeze
pkg-resources==0.0.0
(example_ve)~$ pip install pillow
Collecting pillow
  Downloading Pillow-5.0.0-cp35-cp35m-manylinux1_x86_64.whl (5.9MB)
    100% |████████████████████████████████| 5.9MB 183kB/s
Installing collected packages: pillow
Successfully installed pillow-5.0.0
(example_ve)~$ pip freeze
Pillow==5.0.0
pkg-resources==0.0.0
(example_ve)~$ pip uninstall pillow
Uninstalling Pillow-5.0.0:

# ... Shows a long list of files to be removed if the uninstall is approved

Proceed (y/n)? y
  Successfully uninstalled Pillow-5.0.0
```

This activates the virtual environment again:

```
source ~/py_envs/example_ve/bin/activate
```

This shows the list of currently installed packages. It does not show any of the packages that are part of the core Python distribution, only those that have been added.

```
pip freeze
```

The first run, in this case, also notes that the current version of pip in the environment is old and can be updated, which is done with this command:

```
pip install –upgrade pip
```

The `pip` package itself is part of the base Python installation, and even though it's just been updated, that has no effect on the list of packages returned by calling `pip freeze` again.

To illustrate how `pip` deals with installation of new packages, the `pillow` library, a Python API for working with graphics files, was installed with this:

```
pip install pillow
```

Since `pillow` is not a standard library, it does appear in the results of another `pip freeze` call. The results of `pip freeze` can be dumped to a requirements file (`requirements.txt`, for the purposes of illustration) as part of a project structure, and stored with the project, so that package dependencies don't actually have to live in the source tree of the project, or be stored with it in an SCM. That would allow a new developer on a project to simply create their own virtual environment, then install the dependencies with another `pip` call:

```
pip install -r requirements.txt
```

The `pillow` library was then uninstalled to show what that looks like, with this:

```
pip uninstall pillow
```

 The `pip` program does a good job of keeping track of dependencies, but it may not be foolproof. Even if uninstalling a package removes something that it lists as a dependency, but that's still in use, it's easy enough to re-install it with another `pip` call.

Virtual environments, then, allow for a lot of control over what third-party packages can be associated with a project. They come with a small price, though: they have to be maintained, if rarely, and as changes to those external packages are made by one developer, some discipline needs to be exerted to make sure that those changes are available for other developers working on the same code base.

Summary

There are a fair few factors that can affect how code is written and managed, even before the first line of code is written. Each of them can have some impact on how smoothly a development effort progresses, or on how successful that effort is. Fortunately, there are a lot of options, and a fair amount of flexibility in making the decisions that determine which of them are in play, and how, even assuming that some team or managerial-level policies don't dictate them.

Several of the decisions concerning these items for the `hms_sys` project have been noted, but since the next chapter starts on that development for real, they might be worth calling out once more:

- Code will be written using either Geany or LiClipse as the IDE. They both provide code project management facilities that should handle the multiple-project structure that's expected, and will provide enough of the bells and whistles needed to make navigating across projects relatively painless. Initially, the effort will use Geany, and LiClipse will be held in reserve if Geany becomes too troublesome to work with, or can't handle some aspect of the project after development has progressed.
- Source Code Management will be handled with Git, pointing at an external repository service such as GitHub or Bitbucket.
- Code will follow PEP-8 recommendations until or unless there's a compelling reason not to, or they conflict with any of the internal standards noted.
- Code will be written following the structure laid out in the various template files shown.
- Callables – functions and class methods – will use type-hinting annotations until or unless there is a compelling reason not to.
- All code will be unit tested, though test policy details have yet to be defined other than assuring that all public members are tested.
- Each code project in the system will have its own build process, using standard `setup.py` mechanisms, with `Makefile`-based processes wrapped around them if needed.

- Each build process will integrate unit test results in order to prevent a build from completing if any of the unit tests fail.
- Package structure within the projects has not yet been defined, but will unfold as development gets underway.
- Each project will have and use its own distinct virtual environment, in order to keep the requirements and dependencies associated with each project separate. This may require some build process tweaking, but that remains to be seen.

6
Setting Up Projects and Processes

Our first iteration is all about getting things ready for all of the following iterations, and for any development efforts after the project is initially complete—bug fixes, maintenance, new feature requests, and so on. This sort of preparation will need to be undertaken for any new development effort over a certain expected degree of complexity, but it may not be broken out into its own iteration. Creating many of the foundational structures could be managed as part of other iterations;creating the project's structure when the first development that needs it starts, for example. The trade-off that's tied into taking that approach is that there is a higher probability that early definition work will have to be significantly altered as later development unfolds because that original structure couldn't accommodate multiple Python virtual environments, or the addition of a new project to the system's code base.

 Having some standard structural definitions, like the ones from Chapter 6, *Development Tools and Best Practices*, will minimize a fair number of these concerns going forward, but may not prevent them.

This chapter will cover the setup and preparation items that are common to most projects:

- **Source Code Management (SCM)**
- Project organization
- Unit testing structure
- Build and deploy processes

Iteration goals

The deliverables of this iteration are mostly focused, then, on the following:

- A master repository, stored in a Git server or service (local server, GitHub, or Bitbucket, for example) that contains the complete, empty project structure for the system and its component projects
- A component project for each deployable class library or application in the system
- A unit test suite that can be executed and whose execution passes for each component project in the system
- A build process for each component project – also executable – that results in a deployable package, even if that package starts as something that's essentially useless

Assembly of stories and tasks

The needs of developers can also be expressed as stories, with tasks to execute. These foundational stories may be reused over multiple projects, and if they are, will likely evolve over time to better capture common needs and goals across development efforts—even for radically different systems. These should suffice as a starting point for now:

- As a developer, I need to know how source code for the system is going to be managed and version controlled so that I will be able to appropriately keep/store the code I write:

  1. Create a blank SCM repository for the system—`hms_sys`
  2. Populate the repository with baseline information and documentation needed for ongoing use
  3. Establish and distribute whatever credentials are needed for dev team members to access the repository

- As a developer, I need to know what the full structure of the system looks like, at least at a high level, so that I will be able to write code that fits into that structure. This will involve:

  1. Analyzing the use cases, and the logical and physical architecture, to define the component project's needs and its structure

2. Building out standard project starting points for each component project identified

3. Implementing a minimal `setup.py` for each component project that completes a source package build

4. Determining whether or not to use Python virtual environments for component projects, implement them, and document how they can be reproduced

- As a developer, I need to know how and where to write unit tests for the code base so that I can create unit tests after the code is written. I also need to ensure that the code is thoroughly tested:

    1. Define unit testing standards/requirements (coverage, standard values by type, and so on)

    2. Implement a mechanism for enforcing those standards

    3. Define where unit test code is going to reside in a component project's structure

    4. Implement a basic, top-level test for each component project that executes without any failures

- As a developer, I need to know how to integrate unit tests for a component project into the build process for that component project so that builds can automatically execute unit tests, which involves:

    - Determining how to integrate unit tests into the build process; and

    - Determining how to deal with build/test integration for different environments

Setting Up SCM

Since the balance of the activities that need to happen in this iteration will ultimately need to be stored in SCM, the first story from the list that will be undertaken, with its tasks, is the following one:

- As a developer, I need to know how source code for the system is going to be managed and version controlled, so that I will be able to appropriately keep/store the code I write:

    1. Create a blank SCM repository for the system—`hms_sys`

2. Populate the repository with the baseline information and documentation needed for ongoing use
3. Establish and distribute whatever credentials are needed for dev team members to access the repository

The code for `hms_sys` is going to live in Bitbucket (`https://bitbucket.org`), in a Git repository, so the first step is to set Up a new repository there:

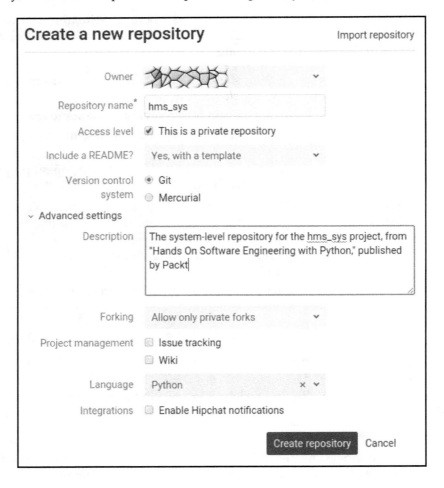

The settings for the new repository are as follows:

- **Owner:** The user who owns the repository. If multiple users have access to the repository through the Bitbucket account, or if there are groups associated with it, those users and groups will be available as options for this setting.

- **Repository name:** The (required) name of the repository. Ideally, a repository name should be easily associated with the system or project that it contains, and since `hms_sys` is both the name of the overall project and it wasn't already taken, that was used.

- **Access level:** Determines whether the repository is public or private. Since `hms_sys` is not intended for public perusal or distribution, the repository has been made private.

- **Include a README?:** Whether the system will create a `README` file as part of the creation process. The options are as follows:

    - **No**: Will require the manual creation of the file later, if one is even needed/desired.
    - **Yes, with a template:** Creates a basic file with minimal information. This option was selected so that a basic `README` file would be created.
    - **Yes, with a tutorial (for beginners).**

- **Version control system:** Allows the repository to use either **Git** or **Mercurial** as its SCM engine. **Git** was selected because that's what we decided to use.

The Advanced settings have to be expanded to be available, and are as follows:

- **Description:** Any description provided here will be added to the `README` file if the **Yes, with a template** option was selected.

- **Forking:** Controls whether/how forking is allowed from the repository. The options are as follows:

    - **Allow forks**: Anyone who has access can fork the repository
    - **Allow only private forks**
    - **No forks**

- **Project management:** Allows the integration of issue tracking and wiki systems with the repository.

- **Language:** Specifies a primary programming language for the code in the repository. This setting doesn't do anything other than categorize the repository by its primary language, at least initially. Some SCM providers will use the language settings to pre-populate Git's `.gitignore` file with commonly ignored file patterns, though, so it's advantageous to specify it if possible.

Once the **Create repository** button is clicked, the repository will be created:

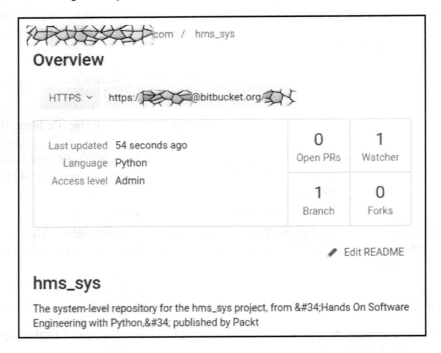

From the overview page for any repository, the HTTPS and SSH options for connecting to and cloning/pulling the repository are available, and anyone who has the requisite permissions can clone it (by whatever means are preferred) to a local copy to work with it:

 There are several ways to initialize a new Git repository. This process, starting at the repository's provider, assures that the repository is well-formed and accessible, as well as allowing for some initial configuration and documentation setup that won't have to be done by hand later.

At this point, two of the tasks from the story are resolved:

1. Create a blank SCM repo for the system—hms_sys.

2. Establish and distribute whatever credentials are needed for dev team members to access the repository. Since the repository was created through the external service provider's interface, the credentials needed for access are managed there, and anyone whose user account is associated with the repository's accounts or groups either has the access they'll need, or can be given it through the user management in the provider's system.

The remaining task, populated with baseline information and the documentation needed for ongoing use, has ties to the project structure that haven't been addressed, but there are still items that can be addressed that are independent of that.

First is the creation and documentation of the base component projects in the top-level repository directory. Initially, it's probably a good idea to create a top-level project, encompassing the entire system code base—this will provide a single project that can be used to organize items that span two or more of the component projects, as well as anything that encompasses the system as a whole.

In Geany, that's accomplished by using **Project → New**, supplying a project name, project file path, and a base path for the project:

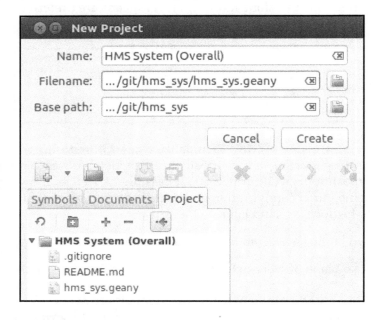

Since Geany project files store filesystem paths that may vary from one machine to another, those need to be added to Git's `.gitignore` file:

```
# .gitignore for hms_sys project
# Geany project-files
*.geany
```

 The `.gitignore` file is, ultimately, a list of files and/or folders that Git will ignore when committing or pushing code to the central repository. Any file or folder that matches one of the paths in `.gitignore` will not be tracked by the SCM.

Additionally, instructions for creating a local `hms_sys.geany` file should probably be documented so that any other developer who needs one can create one as needed. That sort of information can be dropped into the `README.md` file, and similar efforts will be undertaken as the component projects for the system are added:

```
# hms_sys

The system-level repository for the hms_sys project, from "Hands On
Software Engineering with Python," published by Packt.
```

```
## Geany Project Set-up

Geany project-files (`*.geany`) are in the `.gitignore` for the entire
repository, since they have filesystem-specific paths that would break
as they were moved from one developer's local environment to another.
Instructions for (re-)creating those projects are provided for each.

### HMS System (Overall) -- `hms_sys.geany`

This is an over-arching project that encompasses *all* of the
component
projects. It can be re-created by launching Geany, then using
Project → New and providing:

  * *Name:* HMS System (Overall)
  * *Filename:* `[path-to-git-repo]/hms_sys/hms_sys.geany`
  * *Base path:* `[path-to-git-repo]/hms_sys`
```

Once these changes are staged, committed locally, and pushed to the master repository, what should appear there is a revised README.md file and a new .gitignore, but not the hms_sys.geany project file:

As the component projects get added into the code base, the same sort of documentation and setup should be followed, yielding similar results. At this point, the final task of the first story is as complete as it can be, so it would be reviewed and closed if it was judged complete and approved.

Stubbing out component projects

On, then, to the next story:

- As a developer, I need to know what the full structure of the system looks like, at least at a high level, so that I will be able to write code that fits into that structure:

  1. Analyze the use cases, and the logical and physical architecture to define the component project's needs and its structure
  2. Build out standard project starting points for each component project identified
  3. Implement a minimal `setup.py` for each component project that completes a source package build

Component project analysis

The logical architecture, along with the use cases diagram from `Chapter 6`, *Development Tools and Best Practices*, indicates three obvious component projects that will need to be accounted for, one each for the following:

- The **Artisan Application**
- The **Artisan Gateway**
- The **Review/Manage Application**

Each of these component projects, in turn, needs access to some common object types—they all need to be able to handle **Product** instances, and most of them also need to be able to work with **Artisan** and **Order** instances as well:

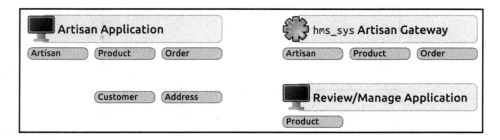

There may well be other business objects that aren't immediately apparent from this breakout, but the fact that there are any is a good sign that there is probably a need for a fourth component project to collect the code that provides those business objects and their functionality. With that in mind, the initial component project structure boils down to this:

- **HMS Core** (`hms-core`): A class library collecting all of the baseline business object definitions to provide representations of objects such as **artisans**, **products**, and **orders**

- **The Central Office Application** (`hms-co-app`): Provides an executable application that allows Central Office staff to perform various tasks that require communication with an **Artisan** about **products**, **orders**, and perhaps other items as well

- **The Artisan Application** (`hms-artisan`): Provides an executable local application that allows an **Artisan** to manage **products** and **orders**, communicating with the Central Office as needed

- **The HMS Artisan Gateway** (`hms-gateway`): Provides an executable service that the **Artisan** Application and Central Office Application use to send information back and forth between the artisans and the Central Office

Component project setup

Some decisions will have to be made later on about how the `hms-core` code will be included in distributions of the other projects that require it, but those don't need to be tackled until they're reached, so they'll be set aside for now. In the meantime, setting Up starting point project structures for each of the component projects is the next step. The basic structure, for now, is identical across all four of the component projects;the only differences will be in the names of the various files and directories.

Using `hms-core` as an example, since that's the first logical code set to start working on, the project structures will look like this:

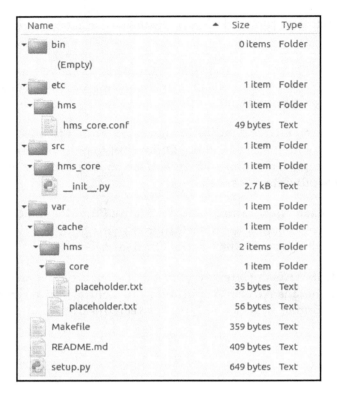

Name		Size	Type
▼ 📁 bin		0 items	Folder
(Empty)			
▼ 📁 etc		1 item	Folder
▼ 📁 hms		1 item	Folder
📄 hms_core.conf		49 bytes	Text
▼ 📁 src		1 item	Folder
▼ 📁 hms_core		1 item	Folder
📄 __init__.py		2.7 kB	Text
▼ 📁 var		1 item	Folder
▼ 📁 cache		1 item	Folder
▼ 📁 hms		2 items	Folder
▼ 📁 core		1 item	Folder
📄 placeholder.txt		35 bytes	Text
📄 placeholder.txt		56 bytes	Text
📄 Makefile		359 bytes	Text
📄 README.md		409 bytes	Text
📄 setup.py		649 bytes	Text

Packaging and build process

Setting up the minimal standard Python packaging for a project and providing the bare-bones build process makes very few changes to the baseline `setup.py` and `Makefile` files that were discussed earlier. There are only a few specifics that are available before code starts being written: the package name and the top-level directory of the main package that `setup.py` will use, and the `setup.py` file itself that can be added to the `Makefile`. The `Makefile` changes are the simplest:

```
# Makefile for the HMS Core (hms-core) project

main: test setup
        # Doesn't (yet) do anything other than running the test and
        # setup targets
```

```
setup:
        # Calls the main setup.py to build a source-distribution
        # python setup.py sdist

test:
        # Executes the unit-tests for the package, allowing the build-
        # process to die and stop the build if a test fails
```

The setup.py file, though it's been populated with some starting data and information, is still pretty much the same bare-bones starting point file that we saw earlier:

```
#!/usr/bin/env python

from setuptools import setup

# The actual setup function call:
setup(
    name='HMS-Core',
    version='0.1.dev0',
    author='Brian D. Allbee',
    description='',
    package_dir={
        '':'src',
        # ...
    },
    # Can also be automatically generated using
    #       setuptools.find_packages...
    packages=[
        'hms_core',
        # ...
    ],
    package_data={
#        'hms_core':[
#            'filename.ext',
#            # ...
#        ]
    },
    entry_points={
#        'console_scripts':[
#            'executable_name = namespace.path:function',
#            # ...
#        ],
    },
)
```

This structure will not acquire any of the various directories and files outside the core package just yet either—at this point, there's no indication that any of them will be needed, so their inclusion will be left until there's an actual need for them. Even without those, though, the setup.py file can successfully build and install the source distribution package, though it throws a few warnings during the build process, and the installed package doesn't provide any functionality yet:

```
~/git/hms_sys/hms-core$ python3 setup.py sdist
running sdist
running egg_info

[Removed for brevity]

creating dist
Creating tar archive
removing 'HMS-Core-0.1.dev0' (and everything under it)

~/git/hms_sys/hms-core$ pip3 install dist/HMS-Core-0.1.dev0.tar.gz
Processing ./dist/HMS-Core-0.1.dev0.tar.gz
Building wheels for collected packages: HMS-Core

[Removed for brevity]

Installing collected packages: HMS-Core
Successfully installed HMS-Core

~/git/hms_sys/hms-core$ python
Python 3.5.2 (default, Nov 23 2017, 16:37:01)
[GCC 5.4.0 20160609] on linux
Type "help", "copyright", "credits" or "license" for more information.
>>> import hms_core
>>> dir()
['__builtins__', '__doc__', ..., 'hms_core']
>>> dir(hms_core)
['__all__', '__author__', '__copyright__', '__doc__', '__status__', ...]
>>> print(hms_core.__doc__)

TODO: Document the package.
Package-header for the hms_core namespace.
Provides classes and functionality for SOME_PURPOSE

>>>
```

In larger (or at least more formally structured) development shops, the build/packaging processes for component projects may well need to accommodate different builds for different environments:

- A local environment, such as the developers' local machines
- A shared development environment, where all developers' local code changes first mix together
- A shared test server for QA and broader integration testing
- A User Acceptance Testing server, using realistic, production-like data that can be used to demonstrate functionality to whoever needs to give final approval for changes to be promoted to a live environment or build
- A staging environment that has full access to a complete copy of production data, with an eye toward being able to perform load and other tests that require access to that dataset
- The live environment/build code base

There is at least *some* potential for needing significant differentiation between these different builds (`local`, `dev`, `test`, `stage`, and `live`, with the user acceptance build assumed to be identical to a stage build for the time being). At this point in the development effort, though, there really isn't anything to differentiate, so the best that can be done is to plan around what will happen if it is needed.

Until there is a need for a completely different package structure for any given environment, the current `setup.py` file will remain untouched. It's highly unlikely that there will be an environment-specific need that isn't common across all environments. If such a need does arise, then the approach will be to create a distinct `setup.py` for each environment that has any distinct needs, and execute that specific `setup.py`, either manually or though the `Makefile`. With some care and thought, this should allow any environment-specific variances to be contained in a single location, and in a reasonably standard fashion.

That, in turn, means that there will have to be changes made to the `Makefile`. Specifically, there will need to be a target for each environment-specific build process (`dev` through `live` again), and some way of managing files that are specific to one of those environments. Since the `make` process can manipulate files, create directories, and so on, the strategy that will be used will be to do the following:

- Identify environment-specific files by prefixing them with the build target/environment name that they relate to. For example, there would be a `dev-setup.py` file in the code base, as well as a `test-setup.py` file, and so on.
- Altering the `Makefile` to make a copy of all relevant files in the project's code tree that can be altered (and destroyed) without impacting the core project files.
- Adding a process that will find and rename all of the environment-specific files in the temporary copy as needed for a specific environment's build, and removing any environment-specific files from the temporary tree that aren't relevant to the build.
- Executing the `setup.py` file as normal.

The changes that would be made to the `Makefile` would look something like this, at least as a starting point.

First, define a common temporary build directory—the local build will be the default, and will simply execute the standard `setup.py` file, just as the original process did:

```
# Makefile for the HMS Core (hms-core) project
TMPDIR=/tmp/build/hms_core_build

local: setup
    # Doesn't (yet) do anything other than running the test and
    # setup targets

setup:
    # Calls the main setup.py to build a source-distribution
    ~/py_envs/hms/core/bin/python setup.py sdist

unit_test:
    # Executes the unit-tests for the package, allowing the build-
    # process to die and stop the build if a test fails
    ~/py_envs/hms/core/bin/python setup.py test
```

A new target, `build_dir`, is created to create the temporary build directory, and to copy all of the project files that can be part of any build into it:

```
build_dir:
    # Creates a temporary build-directory, copies the project-files
    # to it.
    # Creating "$(TMPDIR)"
    mkdir -p $(TMPDIR)
    # Copying project-files to $(TMPDIR)
    cp -R bin $(TMPDIR)
    cp -Ret cetera$(TMPDIR)
    cp -R src $(TMPDIR)
    cp -R var $(TMPDIR)
    cp setup.py $(TMPDIR)
```

A prep target for each environment, as well as the final target for each, will be written to rename and remove files as needed, and to execute the `setup.py` file in the temporary build directory:

```
dev_prep:
    # Renames any dev-specific files so that they will be the "real"
    # files included in the build.
    # At this point, there are none, so we'll just exit

dev: unit_test build_dir dev_prep
    # A make-target that generates a build intended to be deployed
    # to a shared development environment.
    cd $(TMPDIR);~/py_envs/hms/core/bin/python setup.py sdist
```

So, when `make dev` is executed against this `Makefile`, the `dev` target runs the `unit_test` target, and then the `build_dir` target is used to create the temporary copy of the project. Afterwards, `dev_prep` is used to deal with the filename changes and the removal of files from other environments. Then, and only then, will it execute the remaining `setup.py`.

Python virtual environments

The final task to address is determining whether or not to use Python virtual environments for the various component projects, creating them if needed, and documenting how to create them so that other developers will be able to reproduce them if/as needed.

Given the structure across the component projects, what is known about them, and how their installed code is expected to interact with other system members, there isn't an obvious need for different environments, or even an obvious advantage to establishing them. Provided that sufficient care and discipline were exercised during development, making sure that dependencies got added to each component project's `setup.py` or other build process artifacts or configuration, the worst-case scenario that would likely arise is that a missing dependency would be discovered during the process of performing a test installation. In an otherwise bug-free live installation, there might be some trivial inefficiencies that would creep in—the `hms-gateway` project, for example, might install database or GUI libraries that it won't need or doesn't use, or the two component projects might both have message-system libraries that the other users installed, but which aren't needed.

None of these represent any sort of imminent threat to the operation of the individual component project installations, but they do throw unnecessary code into the installations. The potential for significant creep of needless library installations is very real if it isn't carefully watched and managed, and could be a vector for security issues in the future. Worse, any potential security issues might not be visible as a result; if no-one is really aware that something not needed got installed with a given program, then it may not get fixed until it's too late.

 One of the first best steps that can be taken to keep systems secure is to assure that they only have exactly what they need to function installed. That won't cover every possibility, but it will reduce the bandwidth needed to keep current with patches and security issues.

Keeping track of dependencies on a project-by-project basis is something that virtual environments can make a difference in. That's a point in favor of setting them Up for each project individually. Another point in favor of this practice is that some platforms, such as the various public clouds, will require the ability to include dependent packages as part of their deployment process, and a virtual environment will keep those nicely separated from the core system installation package set. In that respect, virtual environments are also, then, a type of future-proofing.

In the context of developing `hms_sys`, then, we'll set up a separate virtual environment for each component project. If they prove unnecessary later on, they can always be deleted. The processes for creating, activating, and deactivating them are pretty straightforward, and can be created wherever is convenient—there isn't really any standard location — the commands vary per Operating System, though, as shown below:

Virtual Environment Activity	Operating system	
	Linux/MacOS/Unix	Windows
Creating	`python3 -m venv ~/path/to-myenv`	`c:\>c:\Python3\python -m venv c:\path\to\myenv`
Activating	`source ~/path/to-myenv/bin/activate`	`C:\> c:\path\to\myenv\Scripts\activate.bat`
Deactivating	`deactivate`	`C:\> c:\path\to\myenv\Scripts\deactivate.bat`

> Once a virtual environment is created and activated, packages can be installed in it with `pip` (or `pip3`), just like outside the virtual environment's context. Installed packages are stored in the virtual environment's libraries, instead of in the global system libraries.

Documenting which virtual environments are associated with which component projects is just a matter of copying the commands needed to create it into project-level documentation somewhere. For `hms_sys`, these will be stored in the `README.md` files for each component project.

Let's review the tasks for this story:

- Analyze the use cases, and the logical and physical architecture to define component-project needs and structure—**Done**
- Build out standard project starting points for each component project identified—**Done**
- Implement a minimal `setup.py` file for each component project that completes a source package build—**Done**
- Determine whether or not to use Python virtual environments for component projects, implement them, and document how they can be reproduced—**Done**
- Providing a unit testing structure

At the end of the previous chapter, it was noted that although an expectation had been set that all code would be unit-tested, with all public members of modules and classes subject to that requirement, it was also noted that no test policy details had been defined yet, which is a good part of what the unit testing story in this iteration is all about:

- As a developer, I need to know how and where to write unit tests for the code base so that I can create unit tests after the code is written. I also need to assure that the code is thoroughly tested:

  1. Define unit testing standards/requirements (coverage, standard values by type, and so on)
  2. Implement a mechanism for enforcing those standards
  3. Define where unit test code is going to reside in a component project's structure
  4. Implement a basic, top-level test for each component project that executes without any failures

 The bulk of this unit testing material was adapted and converted into Python 3 from Python 2.7.x code and a discussion of this is on the author's blog (starting at `bit.ly/HOSEP-IDIC-UT`). Though that code was written for an older version of Python, there may be additional insights to be gained from the unit testing articles there.

It could be argued that all members, not just the public ones, should be tested—after all, if the code in question gets used anywhere, it should also be held to the same standards as far as predictable behavior is concerned, yes? Technically, there's no reason that can't be done, particularly in Python where protected and private class members aren't really protected or private they are merely treated as such by convention—in earlier versions of Python, protected members were accessible, and private members (prefixed with two underscores: `__private_member`) were not directly accessible in derived classes, except by calling them by their mangled name. In Python 3, there is no language-level enforcement of nominally protected or private scope, even though the name mangling is still in play. This is quickly demonstrated. Consider the following class definition:

```
class ExampleParent:

    def __init__(self):
        pass

    def public_method(self, arg, *args, **kwargs):
```

```
        print('%s.public_method called:' % self.__class__.__name__)
        print('+- arg ...... %s' % arg)
        print('+- args ..... %s' % str(args))
        print('+- kwargs ... %s' % kwargs)

    def _protected_method(self, arg, *args, **kwargs):
        print('%s._protected_method called:' %
    self.__class__.__name__)
        print('+- arg ...... %s' % arg)
        print('+- args ..... %s' % str(args))
        print('+- kwargs ... %s' % kwargs)

    def __private_method(self, arg, *args, **kwargs):
        print('%s.__private_method called:' % self.__class__.__name__)
        print('+- arg ...... %s' % arg)
        print('+- args ..... %s' % str(args))
        print('+- kwargs ... %s' % kwargs)

    def show(self):
        self.public_method('example public', 1, 2, 3, key='value')
        self._protected_method('example "protected"', 1, 2, 3,
    key='value')
        self.__private_method('example "private"', 1, 2, 3,
    key='value')
```

If we were to create an instance of `ExampleParent`, and call its `show` method, we'd expect to see all three groups of output and that's exactly what happens:

```
ExampleParent.public_method called:
+- arg ...... example public
+- args ..... (1, 2, 3)
+- kwargs ... {'key': 'value'}
ExampleParent._protected_method called:
+- arg ...... example "protected"
+- args ..... (1, 2, 3)
+- kwargs ... {'key': 'value'}
ExampleParent.__private_method called:
+- arg ...... example "private"
+- args ..... (1, 2, 3)
+- kwargs ... {'key': 'value'}
```

If the `ExampleParent` class structure is examined with `dir(ExampleParent)`, all three of the methods can be seen: `['_ExampleParent__private_method', ...,` `'_protected_method', 'public_method', ...]`. In earlier versions of Python, a class derived from `ExampleParent` would still have access to `public_method` and `_protected_method`, but would raise an error if `__private_method` was called by that name. In Python 3 (and some later versions of Python 2.7.x), that is no longer the case.

```
class ExampleChild(ExampleParent):
    pass
```

Creating an instance of this class, and calling its `show` method yields the same results:

```
ExampleChild.public_method called:
+- arg ...... example public
+- args ..... (1, 2, 3)
+- kwargs ... {'key': 'value'}
ExampleChild._protected_method called:
+- arg ...... example "protected"
+- args ..... (1, 2, 3)
+- kwargs ... {'key': 'value'}
ExampleChild.__private_method called:
+- arg ...... example "private"
+- args ..... (1, 2, 3)
+- kwargs ... {'key': 'value'}
```

Technically then, all members of a Python class are public.

So, what does that mean from the perspective of defining a unit testing policy, if all class members are public? If the public/protected/private convention is adhered to, then the following apply:

- Public members should be tested in the test suite that corresponds to the class they are defined in (their class of origin)
- Most protected members are likely intended to be inherited by derived classes, and should be tested in depth in the test suite that corresponds with the class they are defined in
- Private members should be treated as if they really were private—not accessible at all outside their class of origin—or as if they were implementation details that are subject to breaking changes without warning

- Inherited members shouldn't require any testing again, then, since they will have been tested against their class of origin
- Members that are overridden from their parent classes will be tested in the suite that relates to the class they are overridden in

Setting Up a unit testing process that applies all of these rules is possible, though it's moderately complex and substantial enough that it'd be really advantageous to be able to wrap it Up in some sort of reusable function or class so that it doesn't have to be recreated in every test process, or maintained across dozens or hundreds of copies of it if test policies change. The end goal would be to have a repeatable test structure that's quickly and easily implemented which implies that it could also be templated out in much the same way that modules and package headers were earlier.

First, though, we need something to test. Specifically, we need classes that have methods that fall into the categories that were noted previously:

- Defined locally
- Inherited from a parent class
- Overridden from a parent class

This covers all of the public/protected/private options. Though it wasn't specifically mentioned previously, we should also include a class that has at least one abstract method.Those are still classes, and will also need to be tested; they just haven't been addressed yet. They don't need to be very complex to illustrate the test process, though they should return testable values. With all of that in mind, here is a simple set of classes that we'll use to test against and to generate the core test process:

 These files are in the `hms_sys` code base, in the top-level `scratch-space` directory.

```python
import abc

class Showable(metaclass=abc.ABCMeta):
    @abc.abstractmethod
    def show(self):
        pass

class Parent(Showable):

    _lead_len = 33

    def __init__(self, arg, *args, **kwargs):
```

```
            self.arg = arg
            self.args = args
            self.kwargs = kwargs

        def public(self):
            return (
                ('%s.arg [public] ' % self.__class__.__name__).ljust(
                    self.__class__._lead_len, '.') + ' %s' % self.arg
                )

        def _protected(self):
            return (
                ('%s.arg [protected] ' % self.__class__.__name__).ljust(
                    self.__class__._lead_len, '.') + ' %s' % self.arg
                )

        def __private(self):
            return (
                ('%s.arg [private] ' % self.__class__.__name__).ljust(
                    self.__class__._lead_len, '.') + ' %s' % self.arg
                )

        def show(self):
            print(self.public())
            print(self._protected())
            print(self.__private())

class Child(Parent):
    pass

class ChildOverride(Parent):

    def public(self):
        return (
            ('%s.arg [PUBLIC] ' % self.__class__.__name__).ljust(
                self.__class__._lead_len, '.') + ' %s' % self.arg
            )

    def _protected(self):
        return (
            ('%s.arg [PROTECTED] ' % self.__class__.__name__).ljust(
                self.__class__._lead_len, '.') + ' %s' % self.arg
            )
```

```
def __private(self):
    return (
        ('%s.arg [PRIVATE] ' % self.__class__.__name__).ljust(
            self.__class__._lead_len, '.') + ' %s' % self.arg
    )
```

Creating a quick instance of each concrete class, and calling the `show` method of each instance, shows the anticipated results:

```
Parent.arg [public] ............ parent
Parent.arg [protected] ......... parent
Parent.arg [private] ........... parent
Child.arg [public] ............. child
Child.arg [protected] .......... child
Child.arg [private] ............ child
ChildOverride.arg [PUBLIC] ...... child-override
ChildOverride.arg [PROTECTED] ... child-override
ChildOverride.arg [private] ..... child-override
```

Basic unit testing

Unit testing in Python is supported by the built-in `unittest` module. There may be other modules that also provide unit testing functionality, but `unittest` is readily available, is installed in Python virtual environments by default, and provides all the testing functionality necessary for our purposes, at least as a starting point. The initial test module for the preceding classes is quite simple, even if it doesn't do anything more than define the test case classes that apply to the code being tested:

```
#!/usr/bin/env python

import unittest

class testShowable(unittest.TestCase):
    pass

class testParent(unittest.TestCase):
    pass

class testChild(unittest.TestCase):
    pass

class testChildOverride(unittest.TestCase):
    pass

unittest.main()
```

Each of the classes that begin with `test` (and that are derived from `unittest.TestCase`) will be instantiated by the `unittest.main()` call at the end of the module, and each method within those classes whose name also starts with `test` will be executed. If we add test methods to one of them, `testParent` for example, and run the test module as follows:

```
class testParent(unittest.TestCase):
    def testpublic(self):
        print('### Testing Parent.public')
    def test_protected(self):
        print('### Testing Parent._protected')
    def test__private(self):
        print('### Testing Parent.__private')
```

The execution of the test methods can be seen:

```
### Testing Parent.__private
.### Testing Parent._protected
.### Testing Parent.public
.
----------------------------------------
Ran 3 tests in 0.000s

OK
```

If the `print()` calls are replaced with a pass, as shown in the following code, the output is even simpler, printing a period for each test case's test method that executes without raising an error:

```
class testParent(unittest.TestCase):
    def testpublic(self):
        pass
    def test_protected(self):
        pass
    def test__private(self):
        pass
```

When executed, this yields the following:

```
...
----------------------------------------
Ran 3 tests in 0.001s

OK
```

So far, so good then; we have tests that can be executed, so the next question is how to apply the test policy rules that we want applied. The first policy, having a test module for each source module, is an aspect of project structure rather than one tied to test execution processes. All that we really need to do in order to address that is define where test code will live in any given project. Since we know that we're going to want to address running tests during the build process later on, we need to have a common test directory, a file just inside it (call it `run_tests.py`) that can run all the project's tests on demand, and a test directory and file structure that's accessible to that file should be included, which ends Up looking like this for the `hms_core` component project:

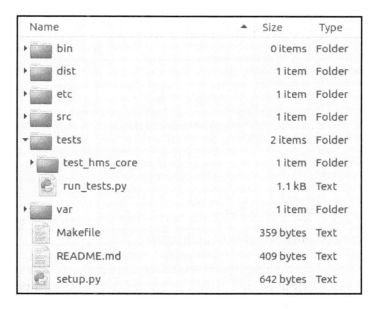

Name		Size	Type
▶ 📁 bin		0 items	Folder
▶ 📁 dist		1 item	Folder
▶ 📁 etc		1 item	Folder
▶ 📁 src		1 item	Folder
▼ 📁 tests		2 items	Folder
	▶ 📁 test_hms_core	1 item	Folder
	🐍 run_tests.py	1.1 kB	Text
▶ 📁 var		1 item	Folder
📄 Makefile		359 bytes	Text
📄 README.md		409 bytes	Text
🐍 setup.py		642 bytes	Text

Identifying missing test case classes

The balance of the testing goals noted earlier all require the ability to examine the code being tested in order to identify module members, and members of those members, that need to be tested. This might sound daunting, but Python provides a module dedicated to that purpose: `inspect`. It provides a very robust collection of functions that can be used to examine Python code at runtime, which can be leveraged to generate collections of member names that can, in turn, be used to determine whether the high-level test coverage meets the standard we're establishing.

For the purposes of illustration, the preceding classes that we need to test will be saved in a module called me.py, which makes them importable, and each step demonstrating the process for finding the needed information about the me module will be collected in inspect_me.py, as this shown here. The corresponding test cases will live in test_me.py, which will start as a near-empty file—no test case classes will be defined there at first.

The first step is identifying the target members of me that we're going to require test case classes for. As things stand right now, all we need is a list of classes in the target module, which can be retrieved as follows:

```python
#!/usr/bin/env python

import inspect

import me as target_module

target_classes = set([
    member[0] for member in
    inspect.getmembers(target_module, inspect.isclass)
])
# target_classes = {
#    'Child', 'ChildOverride', 'Parent', 'Showable'
# } at this point
```

Step by step, what's happening is this:

1. The inspect module is being imported.

2. The me module is being imported, using target_module as an override to its default module-name—we'll want to be able to keep imported module names predictable and relatively constant to make things easier to reuse down the line, and that starts here.

3. The getmembers function of inspect is called against the target_module, using isclass as a filtering predicate. This returns a list of tuples that look like ('ClassName', <class object>). Those results are run through a list comprehension to extract only the class names, and that list is handed off to a Python set to yield a formal set of class names that were discovered.

Python's set type is a very useful basic data type it provides an iterable collection of values that are distinct (never repeated in the set), and that can be merged with other sets (with union), have its members removed from other sets (with difference), and a host of other operations that would be expected from standard set theory.

With those names available, creating a set of expected test case class names is simple:

```
expected_cases = set([
    'test%s' % class_name
    for class_name in target_classes
    ]
)
# expected_cases = {
#     'testChild', 'testShowable', 'testChildOverride',
#     'testParent'
# } at this point
```

This is just another list comprehension that builds a set of class names that start with test from the target class name set. A similar approach to the one that gathered the class names in the target module can be used to find the test case classes that exist in the test_me.py module:

```
import unittest

import test_me as test_module

test_cases = set([
    member[0] for member in
    inspect.getmembers(test_module, inspect.isclass)
    if issubclass(member[1], unittest.TestCase)
])
# test_cases, before any TestCase classes have been defined,
# is an empty set
```

Apart from the `issubclass` check of each member found, which will limit the members of the set to names of classes that are derived from `unittest.TestCase`, this is identical to the process that built the initial `target_classes` set. Now that we have sets that collect what's expected and what's actually defined, determining what test case classes need to be created is a simple matter of removing the defined test case names from the set of expected ones:

```python
missing_tests = expected_cases.difference(test_cases)
# missing_tests = {
#    'testShowable', 'testChild', 'testParent',
#    'testChildOverride'
# }
```

If `missing_tests` is not empty, then its collection of names represents the test case class names that need to be created in order to meet the first part of the "all members will be tested" policy. A simple print of the results at this point will suffice for now:

```python
if missing_tests:
    print(
        'Test-policies require test-case classes to be '
        'created for each class in the code-base. The '
        'following have not been created:\n * %s' %
        '\n * '.join(missing_tests)
    )
```

```
Test-policies require test-case classes to be created for each class in the codebase.
The following have not been created:
 * testShowable
 * testChildOverride
 * testChild
 * testParent
```

Having identified the missing test case class items that need to be created, they can be added to `test_me.py`:

```python
#!/usr/bin/env python

import unittest

class testChild(unittest.TestCase):
    pass

class testChildOverride(unittest.TestCase):
    pass
```

```
class testParent(unittest.TestCase):
    pass

class testShowable(unittest.TestCase):
    pass

if __name__ == '__main__':
    unittest.main()
```

Once they have been added (and once subclasses are derived from
unittest.TestCase, because of the check performed earlier in identifying actual
test case classes), there are no missing test cases that need to be addressed.

A similar approach could be taken for identifying module-level functions that should
arguably also be tested—they are also public members of a module, after all, and
that's what the policy is concerned with, public members of modules. The actual
implementation of tests against functions, or any other callable element, would follow
the structures and processes that will be established later for class methods.

Really, the only public members that may not be easily identified with this sort of
process are unmanaged attributes—module constants or variables that are created at
the module level. While those could still be tested, and arguably should be, the fact
that they are unmanaged, and can be changed at runtime without any checks to
assure that they aren't going to break things somewhere down the line, might well
make any formal testing policy around them little more than a waste of time. That
said, there's no harm in testing them, if only to assure that changes to them,
intentional or accidental, don't pass unnoticed and raise issues and bugs later on.

Identifying missing test methods

The inspect.getmembers function that was used to identify classes in modules
earlier can also be used to identify other member types of other target elements, such
as properties and methods of classes. The process for identifying either is similar to
what's already been shown for identifying classes in modules, and looks like this (for
properties):

```
target_class = target_module.Parent

target_properties = set([
    member[0] for member in
    inspect.getmembers(target_class, inspect.isdatadescriptor)
])
# target_properties = {'__weakref__'}
```

The only significant differences here from the process for finding classes in a module are the target that's being inspected (in this case, the target_class, which we've set to the Parent class) and the predicate (inspect.isdatadescriptor), which filters the results to data descriptors—managed attributes or formal properties.

In Chapter 6, *Development Tools and Best Practices*, when the various internal code standards were being discussed and defined, one aspect of using managed attributes/properties was noted as being significant for unit testing purposes:the ability to know what kinds of values to test with for any given property. This is another advantage of taking that approach: class properties defined using the built-in property() function can be detected as class members that need to be tested. Unmanaged attributes, though they may well be detectable, may not be readily identifiable as members of a class that need to be tested, and that identification is almost certainly not something that can be automated.

A similar inspect.getmembers call can be used to identify class methods:

```
target_functions = set([
    member[0] for member in
    inspect.getmembers(target_class, inspect.isfunction)
])
target_methods = set([
    member[0] for member in
    inspect.getmembers(target_class, inspect.ismethod)
])
target_methods = target_methods.union(target_functions)
# target_methods = {
#    '_Parent__private', 'public', 'show',
#    '_protected', '__init__'
# }
```

Both of these member name collections include items that the test policy doesn't require tests for, though the __weakref__ property is a built-in property of all classes and the _Parent__private method entry ties back to our original __private method, and neither of those need to be included in our lists of required test methods. Some basic filtering can be accomplished by simply adding a check for a leading __ in the property list names (since we'd never be testing a private property according to our test policy). That'd take care of removing __weakref__ from the test list, and allow public and protected properties to appear.

After adding a property declaration (`prop`) to Parent, and adding that filtering criteria, we would get the following:

```
target_properties = set([
    member[0] for member in
    inspect.getmembers(target_class, inspect.isdatadescriptor)
    if not member[0].startswith('__')
])
# target_properties = {'prop'}
```

That same approach would not work well for finding class methods that need to be tested, though;some common methods, such as __init__, have names that would be removed based on name-based filtering, but are members that we'd want to assure have tests required. This simple name-based filtering also doesn't deal with not including member names that exist in a class but aren't defined in that class—like all of the properties and members of the `Child` class. While the name-based filtering is a step in the right direction, it feels like it's time to take a step back and look at a broader solution,one that does account for where a member is defined.

That involves building the list of test names in a more complex fashion, and paying attention to the **Method Resolution Order** (**MRO**) of each class, which can be found in a class built-in __mro__ property. We'll start by defining an empty set and acquiring the MRO of the class, then the same list of property names that were available from the target class:

```
property_tests = set()
sourceMRO = list(target_class.__mro__)
sourceMRO.reverse()
# Get all the item's properties
properties = [
    member for member in inspect.getmembers(
        target_class, inspect.isdatadescriptor)
    if member[0][0:2] != '__'
]
# sourceMRO = [
#    <class 'object'>, <class 'me.Showable'>,
#    <class 'me.Parent'>
# ]
```

We'll also need to keep track of where a property's definition can be found, that is, what class it originates in, as well as the actual implementation of the properties. We'll want to start with a complete data structure for each, which associates the names with the source classes and implementations eventually, but that's initialized with `None` values to start with. That will allow the final structure, once it's populated, to be used to identify members of the class that aren't defined there:

```
propSources = {}
propImplementations = {}
for name, value in properties:
    propSources[name] = None
    propImplementations[name] = None
# Populate the dictionaries based on the names found
for memberName in propSources:
    implementation = target_class.__dict__.get(memberName)
    if implementation and propImplementations[memberName] !=
implementation:
        propImplementations[memberName] = implementation
        propSources[memberName] = target_class
# propImplementations = {
#    "prop": <property object at 0x7fa2f0edeb38>
# }
# propSources = {
#    "prop": <class 'me.Parent'>
# }
# If the target_class is changed to target_module.Child:
# propImplementations = {
#    "prop": None     # Not set because prop originates in Parent
# }
# propSources = {
#    "prop": None     # Also not set for the same reason
# }
```

With that data in hand, the generation of the list of required property test methods is similar to the required test case class list shown earlier:

```
property_tests = set(
    [
        'test%s' % key for key in propSources
        if propSources[key] == target_class
    ]
)
# property_tests = {'testprop'}
# If the target_class is changed to target_module.Child:
# property_tests = set()
```

The process for acquiring and filtering down the method members of a class looks almost the same, though we're going to include all members, even those whose names begin with __, and acquire members that are either functions or methods, just to ensure that we'll include class and static methods of classes:

```
method_tests = set()
sourceMRO = list(target_class.__mro__)
sourceMRO.reverse()
# Get all the item's methods
methods = [
    member for member in inspect.getmembers(
        target_class, inspect.isfunction)
] + [
    member for member in inspect.getmembers(
        target_class, inspect.ismethod)
]
```

The process for constructing the `dict` items used to keep track of method sources and implementations can actively skip local, private members and anything that's been defined as abstract:

```
methSources = {}
methImplementations = {}
for name, value in methods:
    if name.startswith('_%s__' % target_class.__name__):
        # Locally-defined private method - Don't test it
        continue
    if hasattr(value, '__isabstractmethod__') and
value.__isabstractmethod__:
        # Locally-defined abstract method - Don't test it
        continue
    methSources[name] = None
    methImplementations[name] = None
```

The balance of the test name list generation is the same, though:

```
method_tests = set(
    [
        'test%s' % key for key in methSources
        if methSources[key] == target_class
    ]
)
# method_tests = {
#   'testpublic', 'test__init__', 'test_protected',
#   'testshow'
# }
# If the target_class is changed to target_module.Child:
```

```
# method_tests = set()
# If the target_class is changed to target_module.Showable:
# method_tests = set()
```

So, what are the takeaways from all of this exploration? To put it briefly, they are as follows:

- It's possible to automate the process of detecting what members of a module should require test cases to be created
- It's possible to automate the process of verifying that those required test cases exist in the test module that corresponds to a given source module, though it still requires some discipline to assure that the test modules are created
- It's possible to automate the process of detecting what test methods need to be required for any given test case/source class combination, and to do so without requiring the testing of private and abstract members, neither of which make much sense in the context of the test policies we're looking to establish

That's a fair chunk of code, though. 80-odd lines, without some of the actual testing of class members and the announcement of issues, and after stripping out all the comments. That's a lot more code than should ever be copied and pasted around, especially for a process that has the kind of high damage potential or impact that a unit testing process has. It'd be a lot better to be able to keep it all in one place. Fortunately, the `unittest` module's classes provide some options that will make creating module-by-module code coverage tests amazingly easy—though it will require some design and implementation first.

Creating reusable module code coverage tests

A good unit testing framework will allow not just the creation of tests for members of code elements, but will also provide mechanisms for executing code before any of the tests are run, as well as after all tests have executed, successfully or not. Python's `unittest` module handles that in the individual `TestCase` classes, which allow the class to implement the `setUpClass` and `tearDownClass` methods to handle the pre- and post-test setup and teardown, respectively.

That, then, means that it'd be possible to create a test class that could be imported, extended with module-specific properties, and added to a test module that could leverage all of the capabilities just shown to do the following:

- Find all of the classes and functions in the target module
- Determine what test case classes need to exist in the test module, and test them to make sure they exist
- Determine, for each source module member's test case class, what tests need to exist in order to meet our unit testing policies and criteria
- Test for the existence of those test methods

The code coverage test case class will need to know what module to examine in order to find all of that information, but it should be able to manage everything else on its own. Ultimately, it will define just one test of its own that it will execute the one to assure that every class or function in the source module has a corresponding test case class in the test module:

```
def testCodeCoverage(self):
    if not self.__class__._testModule:
        return
    self.assertEqual([], self._missingTestCases,
        'unit testing policies require test-cases for all classes '
        'and functions in the %s module, but the following have not '
        'been defined: (%s)' % (
            self.__class__._testModule.__name__,
            ', '.join(self._missingTestCases)
        )
    )
```

It will also need to be able to provide a mechanism to allow the checks for property and method test methods. Doing so on a fully automated basis is tempting, if it could even be achieved, but there may be cases where that could prove more troublesome bring up than worthwhile. At least for the time being, the addition of those tests will be made available by creating some decorators that will make attaching those tests to any given test case class easy.

 Python's decorators are a fairly detailed topic in their own right. For now, don't worry about how they work just be aware of what using them looks like and trust that they do work.

Our starting point is just a class derived from `unittest.TestCase` that defines the `setUpClass` class method noted earlier, and does some initial checking for a defined class-level `_testModule` attribute—if there is no test module, then all tests should simply skip or pass, since there's nothing being tested:

```
class ModuleCoverageTest(unittest.TestCase):
    """
A reusable unit-test that checks to make sure that all classes in the
module being tested have corresponding test-case classes in the
unit-test module where the derived class is defined.
    """
@classmethod
def setUpClass(cls):
    if not cls._testModule:
        cls._missingTestCases = []
        return
```

 The `@classmethod` line is a built-in class method decorator.

We need to start by finding all the classes and functions available in the target module:

```
cls._moduleClasses = inspect.getmembers(
    cls._testModule, inspect.isclass)
cls._moduleFunctions = inspect.getmembers(
    cls._testModule, inspect.isfunction)
```

We'll keep track of the name of the module being tested as an additional check criteria for class and function members, just in case:

```
cls._testModuleName = cls._testModule.__name__
```

The mechanism for keeping track of the class and function tests is similar to the sources-and-implementations dictionaries in the initial exploration:

```
cls._classTests = dict(
    [
        ('test%s' % m[0], m[1])
        for m in cls._moduleClasses
        if m[1].__module__ == cls._testModuleName
    ]
)
cls._functionTests = dict(
    [
```

```
        ('test%s' % m[0], m[1])
        for m in cls._moduleFunctions
        if m[1].__module__ == cls._testModuleName
    ]
)
```

The list of required test case class names is the aggregated list of all class and function test case class names:

```
cls._requiredTestCases = sorted(
    list(cls._classTests.keys()) + list(cls._functionTests.keys())
)
```

The collection of actual test case classes will be used later to test against:

```
cls._actualTestCases = dict(
    [
        item for item in
        inspect.getmembers(inspect.getmodule(cls),
        inspect.isclass)
        if item[1].__name__[0:4] == 'test'
            and issubclass(item[1], unittest.TestCase)
    ]
)
```

Next, we'll generate the list of missing test case names that the class testCodeCoverage test method uses:

```
cls._missingTestCases = sorted(
    set(cls._requiredTestCases).difference(
        set(cls._actualTestCases.keys())))
```

At this point, that lone test method would be able to execute, and either pass or fail with an output that indicates what test cases are missing. If we write out the test_me.py module as follows:

```
from unit_testing import ModuleCoverageTest

class testmeCodeCoverage(ModuleCoverageTest):
    _testModule = me

if __name__ == '__main__':
    unittest.main()
```

Then after it's been executed, we would get the following:

```
.F
==================================================================
FAIL: testCodeCoverage (__main__.testmeCodeCoverage)
------------------------------------------------------------------

[Removed for brevity]

Unit-testing policies require test-cases for all classes and functions
in the me module, but the following have not been defined:
    (testChild, testChildOverride, testParent, testShowable)

------------------------------------------------------------------
Ran 2 tests in 0.002s
```

All that needs to be done to make that top-level code coverage test pass is to add the missing test case classes:

```python
class testmeCodeCoverage(ModuleCoverageTest):
    _testModule = me

class testChild(unittest.TestCase):
    pass

class testChildOverride(unittest.TestCase):
    pass

class testParent(unittest.TestCase):
    pass

class testShowable(unittest.TestCase):
    pass

if __name__ == '__main__':
    unittest.main()
```

This approach, taking a proactive stance on ensuring code coverage in this fashion, lends itself well to making unit testing a lot less troublesome. If the process for writing tests starts with a common test that will tell the test developer what's missing at every step along the way, then the entire process of writing tests really becomes repeating the following steps until there are no tests failing:

- Execute the test suite
- If there are failing tests, make whatever code changes are needed to make the last one pass:
    - If it's a missing test failure, add the necessary test class or method
    - If it's a failure because of the code in the source, alter that accordingly after verifying that the test values involved in the failure should have passed

Onward!

In order to be able to test for missing property and method tests across all the test case classes in the test module, we'll need to find all of them and keep track of them on a class-by-class basis. This is mostly the same process that we discovered earlier, but the stored values have to be retrievable by class name since we want the single coverage test instance to check all of the source and test case classes, so we'll store them in a couple of dictionaries, propSources for the sources of each, and propImplementations for the actual functionality objects:

```
cls._propertyTestsByClass = {}
for testClass in cls._classTests:
    cls._propertyTestsByClass[testClass] = set()
    sourceClass = cls._classTests[testClass]
    sourceMRO = list(sourceClass.__mro__)
    sourceMRO.reverse()
    # Get all the item's properties
    properties = [
        member for member in inspect.getmembers(
            sourceClass, inspect.isdatadescriptor)
            if member[0][0:2] != '__'
        ]
    # Create and populate data-structures that keep track of where
    # property-members originate from, and what their implementation
    # looks like. Initially populated with None values:
    propSources = {}
    propImplementations = {}
    for name, value in properties:
        propSources[name] = None
```

```
            propImplementations[name] = None
        for memberName in propSources:
            implementation = sourceClass.__dict__.get(memberName)
            if implementation \
                and propImplementations[memberName] != implementation:
                    propImplementations[memberName] = implementation
                    propSources[memberName] = sourceClass
            cls._propertyTestsByClass[testClass] = set(
                [
                    'test%s' % key for key in propSources
                    if propSources[key] == sourceClass
                ]
    )
```

The acquisition of the method tests works in the same way, and uses the same approach from the previous exploration as well:

```
cls._methodTestsByClass = {}
for testClass in cls._classTests:
    cls._methodTestsByClass[testClass] = set()
    sourceClass = cls._classTests[testClass]
    sourceMRO = list(sourceClass.__mro__)
    sourceMRO.reverse()
# Get all the item's methods
methods = [
    member for member in inspect.getmembers(
        sourceClass, inspect.ismethod)
    ] + [
    member for member in inspect.getmembers(
        sourceClass, inspect.isfunction)
    ]
# Create and populate data-structures that keep track of where
# method-members originate from, and what their implementation
# looks like. Initially populated with None values:
methSources = {}
methImplementations = {}
for name, value in methods:
    if name.startswith('_%s__' % sourceClass.__name__):
        # Locally-defined private method - Don't test it
        continue
    if hasattr(value, '__isabstractmethod__') \
        and value.__isabstractmethod__:
        # Locally-defined abstract method - Don't test it
        continue                    methSources[name] = None
        methImplementations[name] = None
    for memberName in methSources:
        implementation = sourceClass.__dict__.get(memberName)
            if implementation \
```

```
                and methImplementations[memberName] != implementation:
                methImplementations[memberName] = implementation
                methSources[memberName] = sourceClass
        cls._methodTestsByClass[testClass] = set(
            [
                'test%s' % key for key in methSources
                if methSources[key] == sourceClass
            ]
        )
    )
```

Once these last two blocks have executed, the code coverage test class will have a complete breakout of all the test methods needed for each test case class in the test module. The property test collection (`cls._propertyTestsByClass`) is sparse, since there's only one property associated with any class, `Parent.prop`:

```
{
    "testChild": set(),
    "testChildOverride": set(),
    "testParent": {"testprop"},
    "testShowable": set()
}
```

The method test structure (`cls._methodTestsByClass`) has a bit more meat to it, though, and is accurately representing that the `public` and `_protected` methods in the `ChildOverride` class need their own test methods, and that the abstract `show` method in `Showable` does not need to be tested:

```
{
    "testChild": set(),
    "testChildOverride": {
        "test_protected", "testpublic"
    },
    "testParent": {
        "test__init__", "test_protected",
        "testpublic", "testshow"
    },
    "testShowable": set()
}
```

That data is all that's needed to handle the tests for the required property and method tests. All that remains is working out a way to attach them to each test case class.

The property and method testing decorators

A decorator can be thought of as a function that takes another function as an argument, and extends or wraps other functionality around the decorated function without actually modifying it. Any callable—a function, an instance method of a class, or (in this case) a class method belonging to a class—can be used as the decorating function. In this case, the code coverage test case class is going to define two class methods (AddPropertyTesting and AddMethodTesting) using a decorator function structure in order to add new methods (testPropertyCoverage and testMethodCoverage) to any classes that are decorated with them. Those two methods, since they are nested members of the main code coverage class, have access to the data in the class—specifically the lists of required property and method test names that were generated. Also, because they are nested members of the decorator functions themselves, they will have access to the variables and data in those methods.

The two decorator methods are almost identical, except for their names, their messaging, and where they look for their data, so only the first, AddMethodTesting, will be detailed. The method starts by checking to make sure that it's a member of a class that extends the ModuleCoverageTest class—this assures that the data it's going to be looking at is limited to only that which is relevant to the combined source and test modules:

```
@classmethod
def AddMethodTesting(cls, target):
    if cls.__name__ == 'ModuleCoverageTest':
        raise RuntimeError('ModuleCoverageTest should be extended '
            'into a local test-case class, not used as one directly.')
    if not cls._testModule:
        raise AttributeError('%s does not have a _testModule defined '
            'as a class attribute. Check that the decorator-method is '
            'being called from the extended local test-case class, not '
            'from ModuleCoverageTest itself.' % (cls.__name__))
```

The target argument that's passed in at the start of the function is a unittest.TestCase class (though it's not explicitly type checked).

It also needs to make sure that the data it's going to use is available. If it's not, for whatever reason, that can be remedied by explicitly calling the class `setUpClass` method ,which was just defined:

```
try:
    if cls._methodTestsByClass:
        populate = False
    else:
        populate = True
except AttributeError:
    populate = True
if populate:
    cls.setUpClass()
```

The next step is defining a function instance to actually execute the test. This function is defined as if it were a member of a class because it will be by the time the decoration process has completed, but because it's nested inside the decorator method, it has access to, and will preserve the values of, all of the variables and arguments defined in the decorator method so far. Of these, the most important is the `target`, since that's the class that's going to be decorated. That `target` value is, essentially, attached to the function that's being defined/created:

```
def testMethodCoverage(self):
    requiredTestMethods = cls._methodTestsByClass[target.__name__]
    activeTestMethods = set(
        [
            m[0] for m in
            inspect.getmembers(target, inspect.isfunction)
            if m[0][0:4] == 'test'
        ]
    )
    missingMethods = sorted(
        requiredTestMethods.difference(activeTestMethods)
    )
    self.assertEquals([], missingMethods,
        'unit testing policy requires test-methods to be created for '
        'all public and protected methods, but %s is missing the '
        'following test-methods: %s' % (
        target.__name__, missingMethods
        )
    )
```

The test method itself is pretty straightforward: it creates a set of active test method names that are defined in the test case class it's attached to, removes those from the required test methods for the test case class that it retrieves from the coverage test class, and if there are any left over, the test will fail and announce what's missing.

All that remains to do is attach the function to the target and return the target so that access to it isn't disrupted:

```
target.testMethodCoverage = testMethodCoverage
return target
```

Once those decorators are defined, they can be applied to the unit testing code like so:

```
class testmeCodeCoverage(ModuleCoverageTest):
    _testModule = me

@testmeCodeCoverage.AddPropertyTesting
@testmeCodeCoverage.AddMethodTesting
class testChild(unittest.TestCase):
    pass

@testmeCodeCoverage.AddPropertyTesting
@testmeCodeCoverage.AddMethodTesting
class testChildOverride(unittest.TestCase):
    pass

@testmeCodeCoverage.AddPropertyTesting
@testmeCodeCoverage.AddMethodTesting
class testParent(unittest.TestCase):
    pass

@testmeCodeCoverage.AddPropertyTesting
@testmeCodeCoverage.AddMethodTesting
class testShowable(unittest.TestCase):
    pass
```

And, with them in place, the test run starts reporting what's missing:

```
...F.FF...
==================================================================
FAIL: testMethodCoverage (__main__.testChildOverride)
------------------------------------------------------------------

Unit-testing policy requires test-methods to be created for all public and protected
methods, but testChildOverride is missing the following test-methods:
    ['test_protected', 'testpublic']

==================================================================
FAIL: testMethodCoverage (__main__.testParent)
------------------------------------------------------------------

Unit-testing policy requires test-methods to be created for all public and protected
methods, but testParent is missing the following test-methods:
    ['test__init__', 'test_protected', 'testpublic', 'testshow']

==================================================================
FAIL: testPropertyCoverage (__main__.testParent)
------------------------------------------------------------------

Unit-testing policy requires test-methods to be created for all public properties,
but testParent is missing the following test-methods:
    ['testprop']

------------------------------------------------------------------
Ran 10 tests in 0.004s

FAILED (failures=3)
```

Creating unit test template files

The bare-bones starting point for the collection of tests just shown would work as a
starting point for any other collection of tests that are concerned with a single
module. The expected code structure for hms_sys, however, includes whole packages
of code, and may include packages inside those packages. We don't know yet,
because we haven't gotten that far. That's going to have an impact on the final unit
testing approach, as well as on the creation of template files to make the creation of
those test modules faster and less error-prone.

The main impact is centered around the idea that we want to be able to execute all of the tests for an entire project with a single call, while at the same time not being required to execute every test in the component project's test suite in cases where the interest is in one or more tests running against something deeper in the package structure. It would make sense, then, to break the tests out in the same sort of organizational structure as the package that they are testing, and allow test modules at any level to import child tests when they are called or imported themselves by a parent higher Up the module tree.

To that end, the template module for unit tests needs to accommodate the same sort of import capabilities that the main code base does, while keeping track of all the tests that result from whatever import process originated with the test run. Fortunately, the `unittest` module also provides classes that can be used to manage that need, such as the `TestSuite` class, which is a collection of tests that can be executed and that can have new tests added to it as needed. The final test module template looks much like the module template we created earlier, though it starts with some search-and-replace boilerplate comments:

```python
#!/usr/bin/env python

# Python unit-test-module template. Copy the template to a new
# unit-test-module location, and start replacing names as needed:
#
# PackagePath  ==> The path/namespace of the parent of the
module/package
#                  being tested in this file.
# ModuleName   ==> The name of the module being tested
#
# Then remove this comment-block

"""
Defines unit-tests for the module at PackagePath.ModuleName.
"""

#######################################
# Any needed from __future__ imports  #
# Create an "__all__" list to support #
#    "from module import member" use  #
#######################################
```

Unlike the packages and modules that provide application functionality, the unit test module template doesn't expect or need to provide much in the way of **all** entries—only the test case classes that reside in the module itself, and any child test modules:

```
__all__ = [
    # Test-case classes
    # Child test-modules
]
```

There are a few standard imports that will occur in all test modules, and there is the potential for third-party imports as well, though that's probably not going to be common:

```
#######################################
# Standard library imports needed     #
#######################################

import os
import sys
import unittest

#######################################
# Third-party imports needed          #
#######################################

#######################################
# Local imports needed                #
#######################################

from unit_testing import *

#######################################
# Initialization needed before member #
#     definition can take place       #
#######################################
```

All the test modules will define a `unittest.TestSuite` instance named `LocalSuite`, which contains all of the local test cases and can be imported by name in parent modules when needed:

```
#######################################
# Module-level Constants              #
#######################################

LocalSuite = unittest.TestSuite()
```

```
########################################
# Import the module being tested       #
########################################

import PackagePath.ModuleName as ModuleName
```

We'll also define boilerplate code that defines the code coverage test case class:

```
########################################
# Code-coverage test-case and          #
# decorator-methods                    #
########################################

class testModuleNameCodeCoverage(ModuleCoverageTest):
    _testModule = ModuleName

LocalSuite.addTests(
    unittest.TestLoader().loadTestsFromTestCase(
        testModuleNameCodeCoverage
    )
)
```

From this point on, everything that isn't part of the __main__ execution of the module should be definitions of the test case classes:

```
########################################
# Test-cases in the module             #
########################################


########################################
# Child-module test-cases to execute   #
########################################
```

If child test modules need to be imported later on, the code structure for doing so is here, commented out and ready to copy, paste, uncomment, and rename as needed:

```
# import child_module
# LocalSuite.addTests(child_module.LocalSuite._tests)
```

There more standard module sections, following the organization structure of the standard module and package templates:

```
########################################
# Imports to resolve circular          #
# dependencies. Avoid if possible.     #
########################################


########################################
```

```
# Initialization that needs to        #
# happen after member definition.     #
######################################

######################################
# Code to execute if file is called   #
# or run directly.                     #
######################################
```

Finally, there's some provision for executing the module directly, running the tests, and displaying and writing out the reports when no failures occur:

```
if __name__ == '__main__':
    import time
    results = unittest.TestResult()
    testStartTime = time.time()
    LocalSuite.run(results)
    results.runTime = time.time() - testStartTime
    PrintTestResults(results)
    if not results.errors and not results.failures:
        SaveTestReport(results, 'PackagePath.ModuleName',
            'PackagePath.ModuleName.test-results')
```

The template provides a handful of items that can be found and replaced when it's first copied to a final test module:

- PackagePath: The full namespace to the module being tested, minus the module itself. For example, if a test module was being created for a module whose full namespace was hms_core.business.processes.artisan, the PackagePath would be hms_core.business.processes

- ModuleName: The name of the module being tested (artisan, using the preceding example)

That search-and-replace operation will also provide a unique name for the ModuleCoverageTest subclass definition that's embedded in the template. As soon as those replacements are completed, the test module can be run, as shown in the preceding example, and will start reporting on missing test cases and methods.

Each test module that follows this structure keeps track of its local tests in a `unittest.TestSuite` object that can be imported by parent test modules, and this can add tests from child `TestSuite` instances as needed a commented-out example of what that would look like is in place of the template file:

```
# import child_module
# LocalSuite.addTests(child_module.LocalSuite._tests)
```

Finally, the template file makes use of some display and reporting functions defined in the custom `unit_testing` module to write summary test result data to the console and (when tests run without failure) to a local file that can be tracked in source control if/as desired.

Integrating tests with the build process

There's only one story/task set remaining how to integrate unit tests with whatever build process will be put into play for the component projects:

- As a developer, I need to know how to integrate unit tests for a component project into the build process for that component project so that builds can automatically execute unit tests:
  - Determine how to integrate unit tests into the build process
  - Determine how to deal with build/test integration for different environments

With the unit testing structures just defined in place in a component project, integrating them into a build process is relatively easily accomplished. In a `setup.py` file-based build, the test modules can be specified in the `test_suite` argument for the `setup` function itself, and tests can be run by executing `python setup.py test`. It will be necessary in the `hms_sys` component projects to add the path for the unit testing standards code to `setup.py` as well:

```
#!/usr/bin/env python

# Adding our unit testing standards
import sys
sys.path.append('../standards')

from setuptools import setup

# The actual setup function call:
setup(
```

```
        name='HMS-Core',
        version='0.1.dev0',
        author='Brian D. Allbee',
        description='',
        package_dir={
            '':'src',
            # ...
        },
        # Can also be automatically generated using
        #       setuptools.find_packages...
        packages=[
            'hms_core',
            # ...
        ],
        package_data={
#           'hms_core':[
#               'filename.ext',
#               # ...
#           ]
        },
        entry_points={
#           'console_scripts':[
#               'executable_name = namespace.path:function',
#               # ...
#           ],
        },
# Adding the test suite for the project
        test_suite='tests.test_hms_core',
)
```

If a Makefile-based build process becomes necessary, the specific call to setup.py test can simply be included in whatever Make targets are relevant:

```
# Makefile for the HMS Core (hms-core) project

main: test setup
        # Doesn't (yet) do anything other than running the test and
        # setup targets

setup:
        # Calls the main setup.py to build a source-distribution
        # python setup.py sdist

test:
        # Executes the unit-tests for the package, allowing the build-
        # process to die and stop the build if a test fails
        python setup.py. test
```

A test suite executed from within `setup.py` will return the appropriate values to stop the Make process if an error is raised or a failure occurs.

Summary

It's probable, barring the setup of a new team or new business, that most of these processes and policies will have been established well before the start of a project—usually before or during the first project that the team undertook. Most development shops and teams will have discovered the needs that underlie the sorts of solutions presented in this chapter, and will have acted upon them.

With all of these items set and committed to the SCM, the foundations are laid for all of the subsequent iterations' development work. The first real iteration will tackle the basic business object's definition and implementation.

Creating Business Objects

7

While examining the logical architecture of hms_sys in Chapter 7, *Setting up Projects and Processes,* a handful of common business object types surfaced across the entire scope of the system:

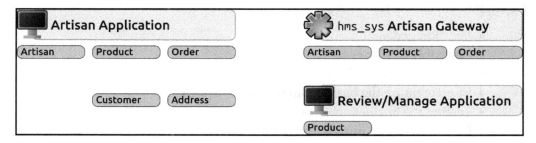

The objects, as displayed in the preceding diagram, are explained as follows:

- An **Artisan** object represents a single **Artisan**—an end user who creates product items to be sold, and who makes those products available to the HMS Central Office through the system. **Artisans** are collected in the Central Office's data structure, and can be managed to a certain extent by Central Office staff, but the majority of their actual data needs to be owned and managed by the individual artisans themselves; that way, they have as much control over their information as possible, and Central Office staff aren't put in the position of managing data changes for artisans if, for example, they change their address, or want to add or change a company name.
- A **Product** is a representation of a physical object, something that an Artisan has created that is for sale.
- An **Order** is the result of a customer placing an order for a Product through the HMS web store.

These three object types also infer two others that were not called out earlier:

- A **Customer**, representing an actual customer that placed an **Order**, and that can be attached to one or more orders
- An **Address**, representing a physical location that something could be shipped to or from, which can also be attached to one or more orders, may be a property of a **Customer**, and almost certainly will be a property of an **Artisan**

This chapter will cover the implementation of those objects as a common class library that can be leveraged by the application and service projects' code, including the design, implementation, automated testing, and build process that turns it into a deployable package.

This chapter covers the following:

- Iteration goals
- Assembly of stories and tasks
- A quick review of classes
- Implementing the basic business objects in `hms_sys`
- Testing the business objects
- Distribution and installation considerations
- Quality assurance and acceptance
- Operation/use, maintenance, and decommissioning considerations

Iteration goals

The deliverable for this iteration, then, is a class library that can be installed alongside or incorporated with the packages and code of the real projects—the user applications and the service—to provide the common representational structure of these business objects:

- The `hms_core` package/library
- Unit tested
- Capable of being built as a free standing package

- Includes base classes that provide baseline representations of the following:

  - Artisans
  - Customers
  - Orders
  - Products

Assembly of stories and tasks

Since the components of the business objects package are intended to be consumed or used by other packages in the system, most of the relevant stories are still focused on providing something that a developer needs:

- As a developer, I need a common definition and functional structure to represent addresses in the system, so that I can incorporate them into the parts of the system that need them:

  - Define a `BaseAddress` **Abstract Base Class (ABC)**
  - Implement the `BaseAddress` ABC
  - Unit test the `BaseAddress` ABC

- As a developer, I need a common definition and functional structure to represent artisans in the system, so that I can incorporate them into the parts of the system that need them:

  - Define a `BaseArtisan` ABC
  - Implement the `BaseArtisan` ABC
  - Unit test the `BaseArtisan` ABC

- As a developer, I need a common definition and functional structure to represent customers in the system, so that I can incorporate them into the parts of the system that need them:

  - Define a `BaseCustomer` ABC
  - Implement the `BaseCustomer` ABC
  - Unit test the `BaseCustomer` ABC

- As a developer, I need a common definition and functional structure to represent orders in the system, so that I can incorporate them into the parts of the system that need them:

  - Define a `BaseOrder` ABC
  - Implement the `BaseOrder` ABC
  - Unit test the `BaseOrder` ABC

- As a developer, I need a common definition and functional structure to represent products in the system, so that I can incorporate them into the parts of the system that need them:

  - Define a `BaseProduct` ABC
  - Implement the `BaseProduct` ABC
  - Unit test the `BaseProduct` ABC

- As an **Artisan**, I need the business objects library to be installed with my application so that the application will work as needed without me having to install dependent components for it:

  - Determine whether `setup.py` based packaging can include packages from outside the local project structure, and implement it if it can
  - Otherwise, implement `Makefile` based processes for including `hms_core` in the other projects' packaging processes

- As a Central Office user, I need the business objects library to be installed with my application so that the application will work as needed without me having to install dependent components of it:

  - Verify that the **Artisan** packaging/installation process will also work for Central Office installations

- As a system administrator, I need the business objects library to be installed with the **Artisan** gateway service so that it will work as needed without me having to install dependent components of it:

  - Verify that the **Artisan** packaging/installation process will also work for **Artisan** gateway installations

It's worth noting that while this design starts by defining a lot of abstract classes, that is not the only way it could have gone. Another viable option would have been to start with simple Concrete Classes in each of the other libraries, then extract the common requirements across those, and create ABCs to enforce those requirements. That approach would yield concrete functionality sooner, while relegating structural and data standards to later, and requiring the movement of a fair chunk of code from the Concrete Classes back down to the ABCs, but it's still a viable option.

A quick review of classes

A class, in any object-oriented language, can be thought of as a blueprint for creating objects—defining what those objects, as instances of the class, are, have, and can do. Classes frequently represent real world objects, be they people, places, or things, but even when they don't, they provide a concise set of data and capabilities/functionality that fits into a logical conceptual unit.

As `hms_sys` development progresses, there will be several classes, both concrete and abstract, that will be designed and implemented. In most cases, the design will start with a class diagram—a drawing of one-to-many classes that shows the structure of each and any relationship between them:

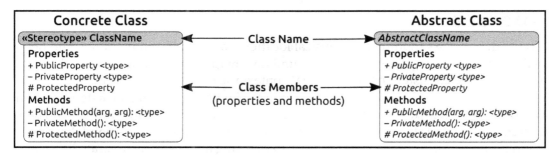

A **Concrete Class** is intended to be instantiated, to have object instances created from the blueprint it provides. An **Abstract Class** provides baseline functionality, interface requirements, and type identity for objects that have specific **Class Members** (concrete or abstract) that will be inherited by, or that require implementation in, classes that derive from them. The scope of those members, both **Properties** and **Methods**, are indicated by + for public members, - for private members, and # for protected members by convention, though as already noted, Python doesn't have truly protected or private members. Still, those at least provide some indication of what the intended scope of a member is.

Implementing the basic business objects in hms_sys

At this point in the development process, we simply don't know whether the exact same functionality for all of the business object classes will be in play in the two applications and the service that are going to be built. The data ownership rules—determination of what users can create, update, or delete what data inside an object—haven't been detailed enough to make those decisions yet. We do, however, have enough information, based solely on the purposes of those objects, to start defining what data they represent, and what constraints should exist around those data points.

We may have enough information here and now to know that certain functionalities need to exist for some of these object types as well—that **Artisan** objects need the ability to add and remove related **Product** objects, for example—even if we don't know yet how that's going to work, or whether there are data ownership rules around those. We can also make some educated guesses around which classes will need to be abstract (because their actual implementations will vary between the applications and the service).

Address

 The `Address` class represents a physical location—a place that something could be mailed or shipped to, or that could be found on a map. The properties of an address are going to be consistent no matter what context the objects are encountered in—that is, an address is an address whether it's associated with an **Artisan**, a **Customer**, or an **Order**—and it feels safe to assume at this point that the whole of any address can be altered by an object that it is a member of, or none of it can be. At this point, barring information to the contrary, it doesn't feel like storing addresses as separate items in the backend data structure will be necessary; although it's possible that they'll have a meaningful independent existence of their own, there's no reason to assume that they will.

With that in mind, making addresses an abstract class doesn't feel like it's necessary, at least not yet:

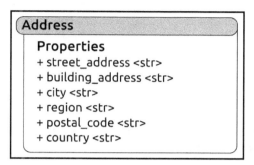

An **Address** is a dumb data object, at least so far; it consists of a data structure, but has no methods or functionality. The properties of the class themselves are fairly simple, and have a few rules around them:

- `street_address` is the street address of the location. It should be a single line string value, is required (cannot be empty), and should probably not allow any whitespace characters other than spaces. An example value of `street_address` would be `1234 Main Street`.

- `building_address` is an optional second line of the address, used to indicate more detail about where at the street address the actual location is. Examples might include an apartment number, a suite or office location or number, and so on. If it's present in any given address, it should be a string value with the same constraints as `street_address`, but, again, it's an optional value.

- `city` is a required string value, also restricted to a single line, and the same whitespace rules as `street_address`.

- `region` is an optional string value, with the same constraints, as are `postal_code` and `country`, at least for the time being.

These last three properties are difficult to generate rules around without some sort of country specific context. It's possible, though it seems unlikely, for addresses in some countries to not have regions or postal codes, while in other countries, they have completely different names and data requirements. By way of example, consider that in the United States, region and `postal_code` represent the **State** and **ZIP Code** (five numbers, with an optional dash and four more numbers), while in Canada they would represent a territory or province and a postal code that is alphanumeric. There may be a solution for some aspects of the requirements on a country by country basis, and that will be examined after the initial property definitions are taken care of.

The initial implementation of `Address` is pretty straightforward; we start by defining a class with the properties that will be available:

```
class Address:
    """
Represents a physical mailing-address/location
    """
    ####################################
    # Class attributes/constants       #
    ####################################

# ... removed for brevity

    ####################################
    # Instance property definitions    #
    ####################################

    building_address = property(
        _get_building_address, _set_building_address,
        _del_building_address,
        'Gets, sets or deletes the building_address (str|None) '
        'of the instance'
    )
    city = property(
        _get_city, _set_city, _del_city,
        'Gets, sets or deletes the city (str) of the instance'
    )
    country = property(
        _get_country, _set_country, _del_country,
        'Gets, sets or deletes the country (str|None) of the '
        'instance'
    )
    region = property(
        _get_region, _set_region, _del_region,
        'Gets, sets or deletes the region (str|None) of the '
        'instance'
```

```
)
postal_code = property(
    _get_postal_code, _set_postal_code, _del_postal_code,
    'Gets, sets or deletes the postal_code (str|None) of '
    'the instance'
)
street_address = property(
    _get_street_address, _set_street_address,
    _del_street_address,
    'Gets, sets or deletes the street_address (str) of the '
    'instance'
)
```

Each of those `property` calls specify a getter, setter, and deleter method that then have to be implemented. The getter methods are all very simple, each returning the associated property value that stores the instance's data for that property:

```
####################################
# Property-getter methods          #
####################################

def _get_building_address(self) -> (str,None):
    return self._building_address

def _get_city(self) -> str:
    return self._city

def _get_country(self) -> (str,None):
    return self._country

def _get_region(self) -> (str,None):
    return self._region

def _get_postal_code(self) -> (str,None):
    return self._postal_code

def _get_street_address(self) -> str:
    return self._street_address
```

The setter methods are also relatively simple, though there's logic that has to be implemented in order to enforce the type and value rules noted earlier. The properties of Address, so far, fall into two categories:

- Required, non-empty, single line strings (such as `street_address`)

- Optional (`None`) or non-empty, single line string values (`building_address`)

The implementation for the required values will all follow the same pattern, using `street_address` as an example:

```python
def _set_street_address(self, value:str) -> None:
    # - Type-check: This is a required str value
    if type(value) != str:
        raise TypeError(
            '%s.street_address expects a single-line, '
            'non-empty str value, with no whitespace '
            'other than spaces, but was passed '
            '"%s" (%s)' %
            (
                self.__class__.__name__, value,
                type(value).__name__
            )
        )
    # - Value-check: no whitespace other than " "
    bad_chars = ('\n', '\r', '\t')
    is_valid = True
    for bad_char in bad_chars:
        if bad_char in value:
            is_valid = False
            break
    # - If it's empty or otherwise not valid, raise error
    if not value.strip() or not is_valid:
        raise ValueError(
            '%s.street_address expects a single-line, '
            'non-empty str value, with no whitespace '
            'other than spaces, but was passed '
            '"%s" (%s)' %
            (
                self.__class__.__name__, value,
                type(value).__name__
            )
        )
    # - Everything checks out, so set the attribute
    self._street_address = value
```

The setter method process, then, from start to finish, is as follows:

1. Make sure that the `value` submitted is a `str` type, and raises a `TypeError` if that's not the case
2. Create a list of forbidden characters—newline, carriage return, and tab, (`'\n'`, `'\r'`, `'\t'`)—that shouldn't be allowed in the value
3. Assume that the value is valid until otherwise determined (`is_valid = True`)

4. Check for the existence of each of those bad characters in the value, and if they are present, flags the value as invalid

5. Check to see if the value is only whitespace (`value.strip()`) or if any invalid characters were found, and if so, raises a `ValueError`

6. If no errors were raised, set the internal storage attribute for the property to the now verified value (`self._street_address = value`)

This same code, with `street_address` changed to `city`, takes care of the city property's setter implementation. This property setter process/flow is going to come up repeatedly, in this iteration and iterations that follow. When it's in use from this point on, it'll be referred to as a standard required text line property setter.

The optional properties use a very similar structure, but check for (and allow) a `None` value first, since setting their values to `None` is technically valid/allowed. The `building_address` property setter serves as an example of this process:

```python
def _set_building_address(self, value:(str,None)) -> None:
    if value != None:
        # - Type-check: If the value isn't None, then it has to
        #   be a non-empty, single-line string without tabs
        if type(value) != str:
            raise TypeError(
                '%s.building_address expects a single-line, '
                'non-empty str value, with no whitespace '
                'other than spaces or None, but was passed '
                '"%s" (%s)' %
                (
                    self.__class__.__name__, value,
                    type(value).__name__
                )
            )
        # - Value-check: no whitespace other than " "
        bad_chars = ('\n', '\r', '\t')
        is_valid = True
        for bad_char in bad_chars:
            if bad_char in value:
                is_valid = False
                break
        # - If it's empty or otherwise not valid, raise error
        if not value.strip() or not is_valid:
            raise ValueError(
                '%s.building_address expects a single-line, '
                'non-empty str value, with no whitespace '
                'other than spaces or None, but was passed '
                '"%s" (%s)' %
```

```
                    (
                        self.__class__.__name__, value,
                        type(value).__name__
                    )
                )
        #  - If this point is reached without error, then the
        #    string-value is valid, so we can just exit the if
        self._building_address = value
```

This setter method process, like the standard required text line property before it, will appear with some frequency, and will be referred to as a standard optional text line property setter.

The deleter methods are also going to be quite simple—all of these properties, if deleted, can be set to a value of None so that they still have a value (thus avoiding instances of AttributeError if they are referenced elsewhere), but one that can be used to indicate that there isn't a value:

```
def _del_building_address(self) -> None:
    self._building_address = None

def _del_city(self) -> None:
    self._city = None

def _del_country(self) -> None:
    self._country = None

def _del_region(self) -> None:
    self._region = None

def _del_postal_code(self) -> None:
    self._postal_code = None

def _del_street_address(self) -> None:
    self._street_address = None
```

With the property definitions and their underlying methods defined, all that remains to make the class usable is the definition of its __init__ method, so that creation of an Address instance can actually accept and store the relevant properties.

It's tempting to just stick to a simple structure, with the various address elements accepted and required in the order that they'd be normally be used in, something like this:

```
def __init__(self,
    street_address,           # 1234 Main Street
    building_address,         # Apartment 3.14
    city, region, postal_code, # Some Town, ST, 00000
    country                   # Country. Maybe.
    ):
```

Another approach, equally valid, would be to allow default values for the arguments that would translate to the optional properties of the instance created:

```
def __init__(self,
    street_address,               # 1234 Main Street
    city,                         # Some Town
    building_address=None,        # Apartment 3.14
    region=None, postal_code=None, # ST, 00000
    country=None                  # Country
    ):
```

Both approaches are perfectly valid from a functional standpoint—it would be possible to create an `Address` instance using either—but the first is probably going to be more easily understood, while the second would allow the creation of a minimal instance without having to worry about specifying every argument value every time. Making a decision about which argument structure to use should probably involve some serious thought about a variety of factors, including these:

- Who will be creating new `Address` instances?
- What do those `Address` creation processes look like?
- When and where will new `Address` instances be needed?
- How will they be created? That is, will there be some sort of UI around the process with any consistency?

The who question has a very simple answer, and one that mostly answers the other questions as well: pretty much any user may need to be able to create a new address. Central Office staff probably will in the process of setting up new **Artisan** accounts. **Artisans** may occasionally need to if they need to change their address. **Customers**, though only indirectly, will need to when they place their first order, and may well need to create addresses for shipping separate from their own default/billing addresses. Even the **Artisan** gateway service will probably need to create `Address` instances as part of the processes for handling movement of data back and forth.

In most of those cases, though, there will be some sort of UI involved: a web store form for the **Customer** and **Order** related items, and whatever GUI is in place in the **Artisan** and Central Office applications. With a UI sitting on top of the address creation process, the onus for passing arguments from that UI to __init__ would only be of importance or concern to the developer. So those questions, though they shed some light on what the functional needs are, really don't help much in making a choice between the two argument form possibilities.

That said, there's no reason that the __init__ can't be defined one way, and another method created for Address to allow the other structure, a standard_address, perhaps:

```
@classmethod
def standard_address(cls,
        street_address:(str,), building_address:(str,None),
        city:(str,), region:(str,None), postal_code:(str,None),
        country:(str,None)
    ):
    return cls(
        street_address, city, building_address,
        region, postal_code, country
    )
```

That then allows __init__ to use the structure that leverages the various default argument values:

```
def __init__(self,
    street_address:(str,), city:(str,),
    building_address:(str,None)=None, region:(str,None)=None,
    postal_code:(str,None)=None, country:(str,None)=None
    ):
    """
Object initialization.

self .............. (Address instance, required) The instance to
                    execute against
street_address .... (str, required) The base street-address of the
                    location the instance represents
city .............. (str, required) The city portion of the street-
                    address that the instance represents
building_address .. (str, optional, defaults to None) The second
                    line of the street address the instance
represents,
                    if applicable
region ............ (str, optional, defaults to None) The region
                    (state, territory, etc.) portion of the street-
```

```
                         address that the instance represents
postal_code .......      (str, optional, defaults to None) The postal-code
                         portion of the street-address that the instance
                         represents
country ..........       (str, optional, defaults to None) The country
                         portion of the street-address that the instance
                         represents
    """
        # - Set default instance property-values using _del_... methods
        self._del_building_address()
        self._del_city()
        self._del_country()
        self._del_postal_code()
        self._del_region()
        self._del_street_address()
        # - Set instance property-values from arguments using
        #   _set_... methods
        self._set_street_address(street_address)
        self._set_city(city)
        if building_address:
            self._set_building_address(building_address)
        if region:
            self._set_region(region)
        if postal_code:
            self._set_postal_code(postal_code)
        if country:
            self._set_country(country)
```

That makes Address functionally complete, at least for the purposes of the story concerning it in this iteration.

As any class is undergoing development, it's quite possible that questions will arise around use cases that the developer envisions, or that simply occur while considering some aspect of how the class works. Some examples that surfaced while Address was being fleshed out are as follows:

- What can/should happen if a non-default property value is deleted in an instance? If a required value is deleted, the instance is no longer well formed and is technically invalid as a result—should it even be possible to perform such a deletion?

- There is a Python module, `pycountry`, that gathers up ISO derived country and region information. Would it be desirable to try to leverage that data in order to ensure that country/region combinations are realistic?

- Will `Address` eventually need any sort of output capabilities? Label text, for example? Or maybe the ability to generate a row in a CSV file?

Such questions are probably worth saving somewhere, even if they never become relevant. If there isn't some sort of project system repository for such things, or some process in place in the development team for preserving them so they don't get lost, they can always be added to the code itself as some kind of comment, perhaps like so:

```
# TODO: Consider whether Address needs some sort of #validation
#       mechanism that can leverage pycountry to assure #that
#       county/region combinations are kosher.
#       pycountry.countries—collection of countries
#       pycountry.subdivisions—collection of regions by #country
# TODO: Maybe we need some sort of export-mechanism? Or a
#       label-ready output?
# TODO: Consider what can/should happen if a non-default #property-
#       value is deleted in an instance. If a required #value is
#       deleted, the instance is no longer well-formed...
class Address:
    """
#Represents a physical mailing-address/location
    """
```

BaseArtisan

The `Artisan` class represents an artisan who participates in the Hand Made Stuff marketplace—a person who creates products that are available to be sold through the Central Office's web store. Knowing that there will almost certainly be different functional rules for each different user's interaction with a final `Artisan` class, it makes sense to make an abstract class in the `hms_core` code base that defines the common functionality and requirements for any concrete `Artisan` in the other packages. We'll name that class `BaseArtisan`.

Like the `Address` class we just completed, the design and implementation of
`BaseArtisan` starts with a class diagram:

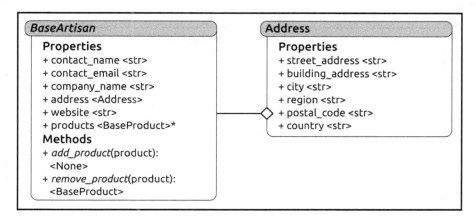

It's not unusual for abstract classes to have a naming convention that
indicates that they are abstract. In this case, the prefix of Base is that
indicator, and will be used for other abstract classes as development
progresses.

`BaseArtisan` is intended to provide a common set of state data rules and
functionality for all of the properties associated with any **Artisan** in any part of the
system. The properties themselves, then, will be concrete implementations.
`BaseArtisan` is also intended to provide some (minimal) functional requirements, in
the form of the `add_product` and `remove_product` methods. It's a given, since
artisans and products relate to each other, that a concrete `Artisan` object will need to
be able to add and remove `Product` objects, but the specifics about how those
processes work may well vary between the two applications and the services that are
making use of that functionality, so they will be abstract—required to be
overridden/implemented in any class that derives from `BaseArtisan`.

This class diagram also includes the `Address` class that was created earlier, with a
diamond ended connector between the two classes. That connection indicates that the
`Address` class is used as an aggregated property of `BaseArtisan`—that is, that the
address property of `BaseArtisan` is an instance of `Address`. That is also indicated in
the address property itself, with an `<Address>` specified as the type of the address
property. In simple terms, a `BaseArtisan` has an `Address`.

It would also be possible to define `BaseArtisan` as inheriting from `Address`. The class diagram for that relationship would be almost identical, except for the connector, as shown here:

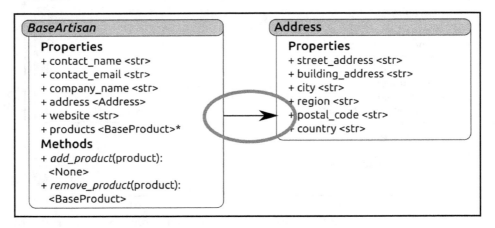

In this relationship, a `BaseArtisan` is an `Address`—it would have all of the properties of an `Address`, as well as any method members that might be added down the line. Both of these relationships are perfectly legal, but there are advantages to using the aggregation (or composition) approach over relying on inheritance that are worth noting before moving on to the implementation of `BaseArtisan`.

OO principles – composition over inheritance

It's probable that the most obvious of those advantages is that the structure is easily understood. An `Artisan` instance will have an address property that is another object, and that object has its own relevant properties. At the `Artisan` level, where there is only one address of any importance, that might not seem significant. Other objects, however, such as `Customer` and `Order`, might have more than one associated address (billing and shipping addresses, for example), or even several: `Customer` might have several shipping addresses that need to be held on to and available.

As a system's object library becomes larger and more complex, using a purely inheritance based design approach will inevitably result in large trees of classes, many of which may do nothing more than provide functionality solely for the purpose of being inherited. A composition based design will reduce that complexity, probably significantly more so in larger and more complex libraries, since the functionality will be encapsulated in single classes, instances of which become properties themselves.

This sort of composition does have some potential drawbacks too, though: deeply nested objects, properties of properties of properties *ad nauseam*, can result in long chains of data structure. For example, if an `order` in the context of `hms_sys` has a `customer` that in turn has a `shipping_address`, finding the `postal_code` of that address from the **Order** would look something like `order.customer.shipping_address.postal_code`. That's not a terribly deep or complex path to get the data involved, and because the property names are easily understood it's not difficult to understand the entire path. At the same time, it's not hard to imagine this sort of nesting getting out of control, or relying on names that aren't as easily understood.

It's also possible (perhaps likely) that a need will arise for a class to provide a local implementation of some composed property class methods, which adds to the complexity of the parent object's class. By way of example, assume that the address class of the `shipping_address` just mentioned has a method that checks various shipping APIs and returns a list of them sorted from lowest to highest cost—call it `find_best_shipping`. If there is a requirement that the `order` objects be able to use that functionality, that will probably end up with a `find_best_shipping` method being defined at the order class level that calls the address-level method and returns the relevant data.

Neither of those are significant drawbacks, however. Provided that there is some discipline exercised in making sure that the design is logical and easily understood, with meaningful member names, they will probably be no worse than tedious.

From a more pure, object oriented standpoint, a more significant concern is the diamond problem. Consider the following code:

```
class Root:
    def method(self, arg, *args, **kwargs):
        print('Root.method(%s, %s, %s)' % (arg, str(args), kwargs))

class Left(Root):
    def method(self, arg, *args, **kwargs):
        print('Left.method(%s, %s, %s)' % (arg, str(args), kwargs))
```

```
class Right(Root):
    def method(self, arg, *args, **kwargs):
        print('Right.method(%s, %s, %s)' % (arg, str(args), kwargs))

class Bottom(Left, Right):
    pass

b = Bottom()
```

Diagrammed, these classes form a diamond shape, hence the diamond problem's name:

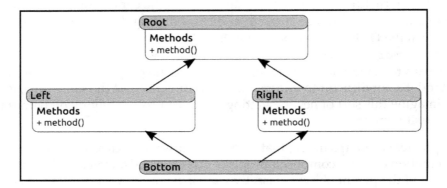

What happens upon the execution of the following:

```
b.method('arg', 'args1', 'args2', keyword='value')
```

Which method will be called? Unless the language itself defines how to resolve the ambiguity, the only thing that is probably safe to assume is that the method of Root will not be called, since both the Left and Right classes override it.

Python resolves ambiguities of this nature by using the order of inheritance specified in the class' definition as a **Method Resolution Order (MRO)**. In this case, because Bottom is defined as inheriting from Left and Right—class Bottom(Left, Right)—that is the order that will be used to determine which method of the several available will actually be executed:

```
# Outputs "Left.method(arg, ('args1', 'args2'), {'keyword': 'value'})"
```

Although it seems unlikely that any of the installable `hms_sys` components will ever reach a level of complexity where inheritance issues would be a significant concern, there is no guarantee that it will never happen. Given that, and that a refactoring effort to move from an inheritance based to a composition based structure would probably be both painful and prone to introducing breaking changes, a composition based approach, even with some of the drawbacks inherent to it, feels like a better design even at this point.

Implementing BaseArtisan's properties

In order to represent an **Artisan** as a person (who may also have a company name), with a location and products, `BaseArtisan` provides six property members:

- `contact_name` is the name of the contact person for an **Artisan**. It should be a standard required text line property, as defined earlier.
- `contact_email` is the email address of the person named in `contact_name`. It should be a well formed email address, and will be required.
- `company_name` is a standard optional text line property (optional because not all **artisans** will have a company name).
- `address` will be required, and will be an instance of `Address`.
- `website` is an optional web site address for the **Artisan**. If it's present, it will need to be a well formed URL.
- `products` will be a collection of `BaseProduct` objects, in much the same way that `address` is a single `Address` instance. Some implementation details around product will be deferred until `BaseProduct` is fully defined.

As before, the process starts with creating the class, and defining the properties whose implementations will be fleshed out next:

```
class BaseArtisan(metaclass=abc.ABCMeta):
    """
Provides baseline functionality, interface requirements, and
type-identity for objects that can represent an Artisan in
the context of the HMS system.
    """
```

The inclusion of `metaclass=abc.ABCMeta` defines `BaseArtisan` as an Abstract Base Class, using the `abc` module's `ABCMeta` functionality:

```
######################################
# Instance property definitions   #
######################################

address = property(
    _get_address, _set_address, _del_address,
    'Gets, sets or deletes the physical address (Address) '
    'associated with the Artisan that the instance represents'
)
company_name = property(
    _get_company_name, _set_company_name, _del_company_name,
    'Gets, sets or deletes the company name (str) associated '
    'with the Artisan that the instance represents'
)
contact_email = property(
    _get_contact_email, _set_contact_email, _del_contact_email,
    'Gets, sets or deletes the email address (str) of the '
    'named contact associated with the Artisan that the '
    'instance represents'
)
contact_name = property(
    _get_contact_name, _set_contact_name, _del_contact_name,
    'Gets, sets or deletes the name of the contact (str) '
    'associated with the Artisan that the instance represents'
)
products = property(
    _get_products, None, None,
    'Gets the collection of products (BaseProduct) associated '
    'with the Artisan that the instance represents'
)
website = property(
    _get_website, _set_website, _del_website,
    'Gets, sets or deletes the URL of the website (str) '
    'associated with the Artisan that the instance represents'
)
```

Since `company_name` and `contact_name` are standard optional and required text line implementations, as were described in creating the `Address` class, their implementations will follow the pattern established there, and will not be examined in any detail. The processes for both are identical to those for `Address.building_address` and `Address.street_address`, respectively—the only things that will change are the names of the getter, setter, and deleter methods and the state data attributes that store the properties' values.

Similarly, the _get_ and _del_ methods that are associated with all of the properties except for products will follow the same basic patterns that've been established already:

- Getter methods will simply return the value stored in the corresponding state storage attribute
- Deleter methods will set the value of the corresponding state storage attribute to None

The getter and deleter method implementations for address, company_name, and contact_email, for example, can be the exact same process as previously shown, even though address is not a simple value property and contact_email hasn't been implemented yet:

```
def _get_address(self) -> (Address,):
    return self._address

def _del_address(self) -> None:
    self._address = None

def _get_company_name(self) -> (str,None):
    return self._company_name

def _del_company_name(self) -> None:
    self._company_name = None

def _get_contact_email(self) -> (str,None):
    return self._contact_email

def _del_contact_email(self) -> None:
    self._contact_email = None
```

This probably feels like a lot of boilerplate, copy and paste code, but that's the cost of being able to perform the type and value checking that's handled by the setter methods. The setter methods themselves are where the magic happens that keeps the high degree of data type and integrity that's desired.

The setter for the `address` property is perhaps surprisingly simple, since all that really needs to be enforced is that any value passed to it must be an instance of the `Address` class. There is no value checking, since any `Address` instance that was successfully created will have performed its own type and value checks as part of the initialization process:

```
def _set_address(self, value:Address) -> None:
    if not isinstance(value, Address):
        raise TypeError(
            '%s.address expects an Address object or an object '
            'derived from Address, but was passed "%s" (%s) '
            'instead, which is not.' %
            (value, type(value).__name__)
        )
    self._address = value
```

The `contact_email` setter could work much like the standard required text line setter process defined in `Address._set_street_address`. It has some of the same data rules associated, after all—it's a required value, cannot be empty, and since it's an email address, it can't be multi-line or have tabs. Since it's an email address, though, it also cannot have spaces in it, and there are other character restrictions that are common to all email addresses that aren't accounted for in that original structure. Since the requirements for the property include it being a well formed email address, there may be other, better ways to validate a value passed to the setter.

 Ideally, an application will want to assure that an email address is both well formed and valid. There's really only one way to do either, though, and it's out of scope for `hms_sys`, even if it makes sense to try and implement it: send a confirmation email, and don't store the value until/unless a confirmation response is received.

There are a number of approaches that will get us most of the way to the validation of a well formed email address. The one that is probably the best place to start is to use a regular expression to match against the value, or to remove everything that is a well formed email address and not allow the value to be set unless there's nothing left after that replacement executes. Using a regular expression probably won't guarantee that the value is well formed, though it will catch a lot of invalid values. Combining that with some standard Python functionality found in the `email.utils` module should at least get the code to a point where testing can be built to look for well formed addresses that fail, and allow modification of the check process.

First, we need to import some items, namely the `parseaddr` function from `email.utils` and the `re` module, in order to create the regular expression object we'll use to test with. Those imports should happen at the top of the module:

```
##########################################
# Standard library imports needed        #
##########################################

import abc # This was already present
import re

from email.utils import parseaddr
```

Next, we'll create a module level constant regular expression object that will be used to check email address values:

```
EMAIL_CHECK = re.compile(
    r'(^[a-zA-Z0-9_.+-]+@[a-zA-Z0-9-]+\.[a-zA-Z0-9-.]+$)'
)
```

This will match whole strings that start with one or more characters *A* through *Z* (upper or lower case), any digit 0-9, or an underscore, period, plus, or dash, followed by @, then most domain names. This structure was found on the internet with a quick search, and may not be complete, but it looks like it should work for most email addresses as it is. All the setter method implementation needs to do now is check that the value is a string, parse a recognizable address out of the string, check the parsed value, and if everything checks out, set the value of the data storage attribute:

```
def _set_contact_email(self, value:str) -> None:
    # - Type-check: This is a required str value
    if type(value) != str:
        raise TypeError(
            '%s.contact_email expects a str value that is a '
            'well-formed email address, but was passed '
            '"%s" (%s)' %
            (
                self.__class__.__name__, value,
                type(value).__name__
            )
        )
    # - Since we know it's a string, we can start by parsing value
    #   with email.utils.parseaddr, and using the second item of
    #   that result to check for well-formed-ness
    check_value = parseaddr(value)[1]
    # - If value is not empty, then there was *something* that was
    #   recognized as being an email address
    valid = (check_value != '')
```

```
        if valid:
            # - Try removing an entire well-formed email address, as
            #   defined by EMAIL_CHECK, from the value. If it works,
            #   there will either be a remnant or not. If there is
            #   a remnant, it's considered badly-formed.
            remnant = EMAIL_CHECK.sub('', check_value)
            if remnant != '' or not value:
                valid = False
    if not check_value or not valid:
        raise TypeError(
            '%s.contact_email expects a str value that is a '
            'well-formed email address, but was passed '
            '"%s" (%s)' %
            (
                self.__class__.__name__, value,
                type(value).__name__
            )
        )
    self._contact_email = value
```

A similar approach should be a good starting point for the website setter method, using the following as the regular expression to test with:

```
URL_CHECK = re.compile(
    r'(^https?://[A-Za-z0-9][-_A-Za-z0-9]*\.[A-Za-z0-9][-_A-Za-
z0-9\.]*$)'
)
```

It starts with the same optional value check that was established in `Address._set_building_address`, but uses the `URL_CHECK` regular expression object to check the value passed in much the same way that `_set_contact_email` does:

```
def _set_website(self, value:(str,None)) -> None:
    # - Type-check: This is an optional required str value
    if value != None:
        if type(value) != str:
            raise TypeError(
                '%s.website expects a str value that is a '
                'well-formed URL, but was passed '
                '"%s" (%s)' %
                (
                    self.__class__.__name__, value,
                    type(value).__name__
                )
            )
        remnant = URL_CHECK.sub('', value)
        if remnant != '' or not value:
```

```
raise TypeError(
    '%s.website expects a str value that is a '
    'well-formed URL, but was passed '
    '"%s" (%s)' %
    (
        self.__class__.__name__, value,
        type(value).__name__
    )
)
self._website = value
```

That leaves just one property to implement: `products`. The products property has aspects to it that may not be apparent at first, but that have potentially significant implications on how it should be implemented. First and foremost, it's a collection of other objects—whether that's a list, a dictionary, or something else hasn't yet been decided—but in any event it's not a single object the way that `address` is. Additionally, it was defined as being a read-only property:

```
products = property(
    _get_products, None, None,
    'Gets the collection of products (BaseProduct) associated '
    'with the Artisan that the instance represents'
)
```

Only the getter method is provided in the `property` definition. This is intentional, but requires some explanation.

Since products is intended to deal with a collection of product objects, it's pretty important that the `products` property itself cannot be changed to something else. For example, if products were settable, it would be possible to execute something like this:

```
# Given artisan = Artisan(...whatever initialization...)
artisan.products = 'Not a product collection anymore!'
```

Now, it's certainly possible to put type and value checking code in place to prevent that sort of assignment—and although there isn't a setter method associated with the property itself, we'll almost certainly want to have one available later on, and it should implement that type and value checking anyway. However, its use will probably be limited to populating an instance's products during the creation of the artisan instance.

The other potential concern is that it would be possible to alter the collection's membership in ways that are both bug prone and difficult to regulate. For example, using the same `artisan` instance, and assuming that the underlying data storage for products is a list, there is nothing to stop code from doing any of the following:

```
artisan.products.append('This is not a product!')
artisan.products[0] = 'This is also not a product!'
```

Similarly, allowing arbitrary deletion of an artisan's products (`del artisan.products`) is probably not a great idea.

At a minimum, then, we want to assure the following:

- Manipulation of the membership of `products` is either not allowed or cannot affect the real, underlying data
- Access to (and perhaps manipulation of) individual `products` members' members is still allowed, that is, given a list of product instances, reading data from and writing data to them is not constrained by the collection they live in

There are a couple of options, even without developing some sort of custom collection type. Since the `products` property uses a getter method to fetch and return the values, it would be possible to alter the data being returned in order to either:

- Return a direct copy of the actual data, in which case altering the membership of the returned collection wouldn't touch the original collection
- Return a copy of the data in a different collection type; if the real data is stored in a list, for example, returning a tuple of that list would provide all of the same iterable sequence capabilities as the original list, but would not allow alteration of the membership of that copy itself

Python keeps track of objects by object reference—that is, it pays attention to where in memory an object actually lives, by association with the name assigned to the object—so when a list or tuple of objects is created from an already existing list of objects, the members of the new collection are the same objects as were present in the original list, for example:

```
# - Create a class to demonstrate with
class Example:
    pass

# -  Create a list of instances of the class
example_list = [
```

```
    Example(), Example(), Example(), Example()
]

print('Items in the original list (at %s):' % hex(id(example_list)))
for item in example_list:
    print(item)

# Items in the original list (at 0x7f9cd9ed6a48):
# <__main__.Example object at 0x7f9cd9eed550>
# <__main__.Example object at 0x7f9cd9eed5c0>
# <__main__.Example object at 0x7f9cd9eed5f8>
# <__main__.Example object at 0x7f9cd9eed630>
```

Creating a copy of the original list will create a new and distinct collection that will still have the same members in it:

```
new_list = list(example_list)
print('Items in the new list (at %s):' % hex(id(new_list)))
for item in new_list:
    print(item)

# Items in the new list (at 0x7f9cd89dca88):
# <__main__.Example object at 0x7f9cd9eed550>
# <__main__.Example object at 0x7f9cd9eed5c0>
# <__main__.Example object at 0x7f9cd9eed5f8>
# <__main__.Example object at 0x7f9cd9eed630>
```

So, too will creating a tuple in a similar fashion:

```
new_tuple = tuple(example_list)
print('Items in the new tuple (at %s):' % hex(id(new_tuple)))
for item in new_tuple:
    print(item)

# Items in the new tuple (at 0x7f9cd9edd4a8):
# <__main__.Example object at 0x7f9cd9eed550>
# <__main__.Example object at 0x7f9cd9eed5c0>
# <__main__.Example object at 0x7f9cd9eed5f8>
# <__main__.Example object at 0x7f9cd9eed630>
```

Returning either a new list or a tuple created from the original state data value would, then, take care of preventing changes made against the property value from affecting the real underlying data. For now the tuple returning option feels like the better choice, since it's more restrictive, in which case _get_products will be implemented as follows:

```
def _get_products(self) -> (tuple,):
    return tuple(self._products)
```

The deleter method _del_products cannot use None as a default with the getter that's now in place. It will have to be changed to something else since trying to return a tuple of a None default value would raise an error. For now, the deleted value will be changed to an empty list:

```
def _del_products(self) -> None:
    self._products = []
```

Finally, here is the setter method, _set_products:

```
def _set_products(self, value:(list, tuple)) -> None:
    # - Check first that the value is an iterable - list or
    #   tuple, it doesn't really matter which, just so long
    #   as it's a sequence-type collection of some kind.
    if type(value) not in (list, tuple):
        raise TypeError(
            '%s.products expects a list or tuple of BaseProduct '
            'objects, but was passed a %s instead' %
            (self.__class__.__name__, type(value).__name__)
        )
    # - Start with a new, empty list
    new_items = []
    # - Iterate over the items in value, check each one, and
    #   append them if they're OK
    bad_items = []
    for item in value:
        # - We're going to assume that all products will derive
        #   from BaseProduct - that's why it's defined, after all
        if isinstance(item, BaseProduct):
            new_items.append(item)
        else:
            bad_items.append(item)
    # - If there are any bad items, then do NOT commit the
    #   changes -- raise an error instead!
    if bad_items:
        raise TypeError(
            '%s.products expects a list or tuple of BaseProduct '
            'objects, but the value passed included %d items '
```

```
                'that are not of the right type: (%s)' %
                (
                    self.__class__.__name__, len(bad_items),
                    ', '.join([str(bi) for bi in bad_items])
                )
            )
        self._products = value
```

Taken together, these variations restrict changes to the products property pretty significantly:

- The property itself is read-only, not allowing the value to be set or deleted
- The value returned from the getter method is identical to, but distinct from, the one that's actually stored in the state data of the object it's being gotten from, and while it still allows access to the members of the original collection, it does not allow the original collection's membership to be altered
- The setter method enforces type checking for the entire collection, assuring that the membership of the collection is composed only of the appropriate object types

What isn't accounted for yet are actual processes for making changes to the collection's members—that capability is in the method members.

Implementing BaseArtisan's methods

BaseArtisan, as it's currently designed, is expected to provide two abstract methods:

- add_product, which requires a mechanism for adding products to the products collection of an instance to be implemented on derived Concrete Classes
- remove_product, which similarly requires a mechanism for removing an item from the products collection of a derived instance

These are specified as abstract methods because, while there will almost certainly be some common functionality involved with each of them across the application and service installables of hms_sys, there will also almost certainly be significant implementation differences across those same components—artisans, for example, may well be the only users who can truly remove items from their products collections.

Typically, in most programming languages that support defining abstract methods, those methods are not expected to provide any actual implementation. It's quite possible, in fact, that the act of defining a method as abstract actually prohibits any implementation. Python does not enforce that restriction on abstract methods, but still doesn't expect any implementation either. As a result, our abstract methods do not need to be any more complicated than this:

```python
@abc.abstractmethod
def add_product(self, product:BaseProduct):
    pass

@abc.abstractmethod
def remove_product(self, product:BaseProduct):
    pass
```

Since we're allowed to put concrete implementation into an abstract method, though, it's possible to leverage that to provide baseline functionality in cases where there is some that's useful to keep in one place. These two methods, add_product and remove_product, fall into that category:

- Adding a product will always need to perform type checking, raise errors when invalid types are presented, and append the new item to the instance's collection
- Removing a product will always involve removing the specified product from the instance's product collection

With those factors in mind, it can actually be beneficial to put those common processes into the abstract method as if they were concrete implementations. Those processes can then be called from derived class instances, with or without additional logic before or after the execution of the baselines themselves. Consider a basic implementation of add_product in BaseArtisan that looks like this:

```python
@abc.abstractmethod
def add_product(self, product:BaseProduct):
    """
Adds a product to the instance's collection of products.

Returns the product added.

self ....... (BaseArtisan instance, required) The instance to
             execute against
product ... (BaseProduct, required) The product to add to the
             instance's collection of products

Raises TypeError if the product specified is not a BaseProduct-
```

```
    derived instance

May be implemented in derived classes by simply calling
    return BaseArtisan.add_product(self, product)
"""
        # - Make sure the product passed in is a BaseProduct
        if not isinstance(product, BaseProduct):
            raise TypeError(
                '%s.add_product expects an instance of '
                'BaseProduct to be passed in its product '
                'argument, but "%s" (%s) was passed instead' %
                (
                    self.__class__.__name__, value,
                    type(value).__name__
                )
            )
        # - Append it to the internal _products list
        self._products.append(product)
        # - Return it
        return product
```

A derived class—an `Artisan` class that lives in the Central Office's application, for example—would be required to implement `add_product`, but could implement it as follows:

```
def add_product(self, product:BaseProduct):
    # - Add any additional checking or processing that might
    #   need to happen BEFORE adding the product here

    # - Call the parent add_product to perform the actual
    #   addition
    result = BaseArtisan.add_product(self, product)

    # - Add any additional checking or processing that might
    #   need to happen AFTER adding the product here

    # - Return the product
    return result
```

There is a trade off to this approach, though: it would be possible for a derived class to implement a completely new `add_product` process, skipping the ready-made validation/business rules. An alternative approach would be to define an abstract validation method (`_check_products`, maybe) that handles the validation process and is called directly by a concrete implementation of `add_product`.

The `remove_product` method can be similarly defined, and could be implemented in a similar fashion in derived class instances:

```
@abc.abstractmethod
def remove_product(self, product:BaseProduct):
    """
Removes a product from the instance's collection of products.

Returns the product removed.

self ....... (BaseArtisan instance, required) The instance to
             execute against
product ... (BaseProduct, required) The product to remove from
             the instance's collection of products

Raises TypeError if the product specified is not a BaseProduct-
  derived instance
Raises ValueError if the product specified is not a member of the
  instance's products collection

May be implemented in derived classes by simply calling
    return BaseArtisan.remove_product(self, product)
    """
        # - Make sure the product passed in is a BaseProduct.
        #   Technically this may not be necessary, since type
        #   is enforced in add_product, but it does no harm to
        #   re-check here...
        if not isinstance(product, BaseProduct):
            raise TypeError(
                '%s.add_product expects an instance of '
                'BaseProduct to be passed in its product '
                'argument, but "%s" (%s) was passed instead' %
                (
                    self.__class__.__name__, value,
                    type(value).__name__
                )
            )
        try:
            self._products.remove(product)
            return product
        except ValueError:
            raise ValueError(
                '%s.remove_product could not remove %s from its '
                'products collection because it was not a member '
                'of that collection' %
                (self.__class__.__name__, product)
            )
```

There may be other methods that would make sense to add to `BaseArtisan`, but if there are, they will probably surface as the implementations of concrete `Artisan` classes are developed. For now, we can call `BaseArtisan` done, after defining its `__init__` method:

```
    def __init__(self,
        contact_name:str, contact_email:str,
        address:Address, company_name:str=None,
        **products
        ):
        """
Object initialization.

self .............. (BaseArtisan instance, required) The instance to
                   execute against
contact_name ...... (str, required) The name of the primary contact
                   for the Artisan that the instance represents
contact_email ..... (str [email address], required) The email address
                   of the primary contact for the Artisan that the
                   instance represents
address ........... (Address, required) The mailing/shipping address
                   for the Artisan that the instance represents
company_name ...... (str, optional, defaults to None) The company-
                   name for the Artisan that the instance represents
products .......... (BaseProduct collection) The products associated
                   with the Artisan that the instance represents
"""
        # - Call parent initializers if needed
        # - Set default instance property-values using _del_...
methods
        self._del_address()
        self._del_company_name()
        self._del_contact_email()
        self._del_contact_name()
        self._del_products()
        # - Set instance property-values from arguments using
        #   _set_... methods
        self._set_contact_name(contact_name)
        self._set_contact_email(contact_email)
        self._set_address(address)
        if company_name:
            self._set_company_name(company_name)
        if products:
            self._set_products(products)
        # - Perform any other initialization needed
```

BaseCustomer

The class that defines what a customer's data structure looks like is very simple, and uses code structures that have already been established in `Address` and `BaseArtisan` for all of its properties. Like the relationship of `BaseArtisan` with concrete `Artisan` instances, `Customer` objects are expected to vary significantly in what they can do, and perhaps what data access is allowed across the different components of the system. Once again, we'll start by defining an ABC—`BaseCustomer`—rather than a concrete `Customer` class:

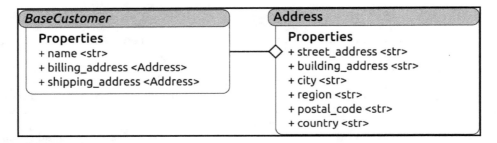

The properties of `BaseCustomer` are:

- `name`, a standard required text line.

- `billing_address` and `shipping_address`, which are, apart from their names, identical to the address property defined in `BaseArtisan`. The `shipping_address` will be made optional, since it's quite possible for a customer to have only one address that's used for both.

The only new aspect of `BaseCustomer` that feels worth mentioning is how the `shipping_address` is annotated during initialization. `BaseCustomer.__init__` is mostly going to follow the same structure/approach that's been shown in previous class definitions:

```
def __init__(self,
    name:str, billing_address:Address,
    shipping_address(Address,None)=None
):
    """
Object initialization.

self ............. (BaseCustomer instance, required) The instance to
                  execute against
```

```
name .............. (str, required) The name of the customer.
billing_address ... (Address, required) The billing address of the
                    customer
shipping_address .. (Address, optional, defaults to None) The shipping
                    address of the customer.
        """
        # - Call parent initializers if needed
        # - Set default instance property-values using _del_...
methods
        self._del_billing_address()
        self._del_name()
        self._del_shipping_address()
        # - Set instance property-values from arguments using
        #   _set_... methods
        self._set_name(name)
        self._set_billing_address(billing_address)
        if shipping_address:
            self._set_shipping_address(shipping_address)
        # - Perform any other initialization needed
```

The shipping_address argument's annotation, (Address, None), is new, after a
fashion. We've used built in types as annotation types before, as well as having a built
in, non-None type and None for optional argument specifications before.
Address.__init__ uses this notation several times. This code, even though it uses a
class that we have defined, works the same way: the Address class is also a type, just
like str is in previous examples. It's just a type that has been defined here in this
project.

BaseOrder

The process of creating pretty much any dumb data object class, or even mostly dumb
ones, is very similar no matter what those classes represent, at least so long as
whatever data structure rules are in play hold true across the entire scope of those
efforts. As more such data oriented classes are created, fewer new approaches to
specific needs will be needed until eventually there will be a concise set of approaches
for implementing various properties of all the various types and value constraints
needed.

The `BaseOrder` class, shown here with `BaseProduct`, is a good example of that effect, at least at first glance:

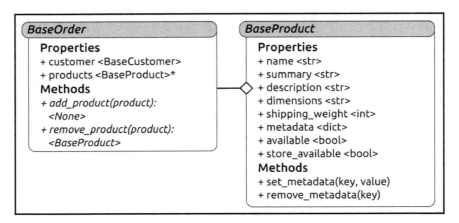

The list of `BaseOrder` properties is very short, since all an order really represents is a customer relationship with a collection of products:

- `customer` is an instance of `BaseCustomer`, which in turn has the `billing_address` and `shipping_address` properties of that **customer**; apart from the fact that the type of the property's value is going to be a `BaseCustomer` instance, it's reasonable to assume that it'll behave in the same way that the `Address` type properties of `BaseCustomer` do

- `products` is a collection of `BaseProduct` instances that can probably behave exactly like the `products` property of `BaseArtisan`—it'll be doing the same sort of thing, after all, storing product instances and preventing mutation of those instances—so the initial implementation of it will be copied directly from `BaseArtisan`

In short, both properties, barring some changing of names in the case of the **customer** property, already have established implementation patterns, so there's nothing substantially new to show in `BaseOrder`.

Copying code directly from one class to another is a contentious topic at times; even if everything works perfectly, it is, by definition, duplicating code, which means that there are now multiple copies of that code to be maintained if something goes awry later on.

BaseProduct

The BaseProduct ABC also has a lot of near boilerplate property code, though only three of its properties fall into implementation patterns that've been established so far:

- name is a standard required text line property.
- summary is a standard required text line property.
- description is an optional string value.
- dimensions is a standard optional text line property.
- shipping_weight is a required number value, which may only be used for determining shipping costs, but could also appear in product displays in the web store.
- metadata is a dictionary of metadata keys (strings) and values (strings also, probably). This is a new data structure, so we'll examine it in detail shortly.
- available is a required Boolean value that allows the artisan to indicate that the product is available to be sold on the HMS web store, though it may be visible to central office staff.
- store_available is also a required Boolean value, indicating that the HMS web store should consider the **product** available. It is intended to be controlled by the Central Office staff, though it may be visible to an artisan.

BaseProduct has only two methods associated so far, both for use in managing the metadata values associated with a product instance:

- set_metadata will set a metadata key/value on the instance
- remove_metadata will remove a metadata key and value from the instance

The name, summary, and dimensions properties, as standard required and optional text lines, will follow those patterns. The description is almost an optional text line implementation; all that needs to be changed there is removing the whitespace character checks, and it's good to go:

```
# These lines aren't needed for description
# - Value-check: no whitespace other than " "
bad_chars = ('\n', '\r', '\t')
for bad_char in bad_chars:
    if bad_char in value:
        is_valid = False
        break
```

The implementation of the `shipping_weight` property varies most significantly in the setter method `_set_shipping_weight`, but is (hopefully) about what would be expected given the normal getter/setter/deleter method structure that is the typical approach for properties in the project:

```python
def _set_shipping_weight(self, value:(int,)):
    if type(value) != int:
        raise TypeError(
            '%s.shipping_weight expects a positive integer '
            'value, but was passed "%s" (%s)' %
            (
                self.__class__.__name__,
                value, type(value).__name__
            )
        )
    if value <= 0:
        raise ValueError(
            '%s.shipping_weight expects a positive integer '
            'value, but was passed "%s" (%s)' %
            (
                self.__class__.__name__,
                value, type(value).__name__
            )
        )
    self._shipping_weight = value
```

The same can be said for the implementation of both of the `available` properties, though it makes sense to allow both formal Boolean (`True` and `False`) values and integer value equivalents (1 and 0) as valid setter value arguments. This gives a bit of wiggle room in cases where the object's state data may not be able to be stored as true Booleans—though that is an unlikely circumstance, it's not out of the realm of possibility, either:

```python
def _set_available(self, value:(bool,int)):
    if value not in (True, False, 1, 0):
        raise ValueError(
            '%s.available expects either a boolean value '
            '(True|False) or a direct int-value equivalent '
            '(1|0), but was passed "%s" (%s)' %
            (self.__class__.__name__, value, type(value).__name__)
            )
    if value:
        self._available = True
        else:
            self._available = False
```

That leaves only the `metadata` property implementation. Metadata is probably best thought of as data about other data—in this case, data about the products that the class is fundamental to representing. In this particular case, the `metadata` property is intended to provide highly flexible data that may vary wildly from one product (or product type) to another, while still being available in a relatively simple manner within a more rigidly defined class/object structure. This will be important in the context of Hand Made Stuff's needs because the products that artisans create and sell through their web store can be virtually anything: beads, wood, or metal furniture, clothing, jewelry, whatever. Though there are a few descriptions that could potentially be applied to any product—what it's made out of, for example, and perhaps some basic items such as color—there are others that make it nearly impossible to categorize products across the entire spectrum available without either requiring a lot more data structures in the current product class structure, or a lot of product types that live in what would almost certainly be a prohibitively complex relationship with each other.

The initial implementation and design will center, then, around maintaining a `dict` based metadata structure with each object. If more stringent requirements arise later (such as requiring that items made of wood must specify the type of wood, for example), a refactoring effort to adjust accordingly may be necessary, but for now a simple `dict` feels reasonable.

Like the products property of `BaseArtisan` and `BaseOrder`, the `metadata` of a `BaseProduct` needs to be difficult to casually or accidentally change—it should require something of a conscious decision to make changes. Given that the `metadata` structure is expected to provide data with which to categorize products, the keys, at the very least, will have some restrictions around what can be used. Metadata names should be meaningful and reasonably short. So, too should `metadata` values, though they will probably be less constrained than their corresponding keys.

Taking all of these items together, the getter and deleter methods are not significantly different from their equivalents for the other properties—the usual name changes and a different deleted default value are about all there is to them:

```
######################################
# Property-getter methods            #
######################################

# ...

def _get_metadata(self) -> (dict,):
    return self._metadata
```

```
# ...

####################################
# Property-deleter methods         #
####################################

# ...

def _del_metadata(self) -> None:
    self._metadata = {}
```

The setter method is, as is most often the case, where the significant differences are; in this case, when it's called, the expectation is that the intention is to clear out any existing metadata and replace it with a new, validated set of keys and values. This changes the entire collection in the property, not just some or all of its members. Since the class will also be providing a dedicated method to allow the addition of new metadata, or changes to existing items in the metadata, and that method will need to perform whatever validation is desired against both keys and values, the _set_metadata property setter method will use the similarly named set_metadata method to assure that all metadata meets the same standards.

The first step is to make sure that the incoming value is a dictionary:

```
####################################
# Property-setter methods          #
####################################
# ...

def _set_metadata(self, value:(dict,)):
  if type(value) != dict:
    raise TypeError(
    '%s.metadata expects a dictionary of metadata keys '
    '(strings) and values (also strings), but was passed '
        '"%s" (%s)' %
    (self.__class__.__name__, value, type(value).__name__)
        )
```

We'll set up a variable to keep track of any invalid values encountered, and clear the current metadata out with the same mechanism that's used to clear it out during initialization, _del_metadata:

```
badvalues = []
self._del_metadata()
```

With those accomplished, we can iterate across the value's keys and values, calling `set_metadata` for each pair until they've all been accounted for, and trapping any errors raised in order to provide more useful error messaging when needed:

```
if value: # Checking because value could be an empty dict: {}
    for name in value:
        try:
            # - Since set_metadata will do all the type- and
            #   value-checking we need, we'll just call that
            #   for each item handed off to us here...
            self.set_metadata(name, value[name])
        except Exception:
            # - If an error was raised,then we want to capture
            #   the key/value pair that caused it...
                badvalues.append((name, value[name]))
```

If any bad values were detected, then we'll want to raise an error and note them. If no errors occur, then the property's been repopulated:

```
if badvalues:
    # - Oops... Something's not right...
    raise ValueError(
        '%s.metadata expects a dictionary of metadata keys '
        '(strings) and values, but was passed a dict with '
        'values that aren\'t allowed: %s' %
            (self.__class__.__name__, str(badvalues))
        )
```

The `set_metadata` method looks a lot like our varied property setter methods—keys and (for now) values in metadata both act like standard required text line properties—so the type and value checking being performed for each will look very familiar:

```
def set_metadata(self, key:(str,), value:(str,)):
    """
Sets the value of a specified metadata-key associated with the product
that the instance represents.

self ............. (BaseProduct instance, required) The instance to
                   execute against
key .............. (str, required) The metadata key to associate a
                   value with
value ............ (str, required) The value to associate with the
                   metadata key
    """
```

Here's the type and value checking for the `key` argument's value:

```python
if type(key) != str:
  raise TypeError(
    '%s.metadata expects a single-line, '
    'non-empty str key, with no whitespace '
    'other than spaces, but was passed "%s" (%s)' %
    (
        self.__class__.__name__, key,
        type(key).__name__
    )
  )
  # - Value-check of key: no whitespace other than " "
      bad_chars = ('\n', '\r', '\t')
      is_valid = True
      for bad_char in bad_chars:
          if bad_char in key:
              is_valid = False
              break
  # - If it's empty or otherwise not valid, raise error
  if not key.strip() or not is_valid:
      raise ValueError(
        '%s.metadata expects a single-line, '
        'non-empty str key, with no whitespace '
        'other than spaces, but was passed "%s" (%s)' %
        (
          self.__class__.__name__, key,
          type(key).__name__
        )
      )
```

And here's the type and value checking for the `value` argument's value:

```python
if type(value) != str:
  raise TypeError(
    '%s.metadata expects a single-line, '
    'non-empty str value, with no whitespace '
    'other than spaces, but was passed "%s" (%s)' %
    (
        self.__class__.__name__, value,
        type(value).__name__
    )
  )
  # - Value-check of value: no whitespace other than " "
    bad_chars = ('\n', '\r', '\t')
    is_valid = True
    for bad_char in bad_chars:
        if bad_char in value:
```

```
            is_valid = False
            break
    # - If it's empty or otherwise not valid, raise error
        if not value.strip() or not is_valid:
            raise ValueError(
                '%s.metadata expects a single-line, '
                'non-empty str value, with no whitespace '
                'other than spaces, but was passed "%s" (%s)' %
                (
                    self.__class__.__name__, value,
                    type(value).__name__
                )
            )
        self._metadata[key] = value
```

The removal of metadata requires considerably shorter and simpler code, though it also assumes that if an attempt is made to remove metadata that doesn't exist, no error need be raised. There might be a need to allow such an error to occur, but for now the assumption is that it won't be needed:

```
def remove_metadata(self, key):
    """
Removes the specified metadata associated with the product that the
instance represents, identified by the key

self ............. (BaseProduct instance, required) The instance to
                    execute against
key .............. (str, required) The key that identifies the
                    metadata value to remove
    """
        try:
            del self._metadata[key]
        except KeyError:
            pass
```

With BaseProduct complete, the required scope of the hms_core class library is fulfilled. Unit testing still needs to be written, and any issues that surface as a result.

Dealing with duplicated code – HasProducts

`BaseArtisan` and `BaseOrder` have `products` properties that behave the same way, to the extent that the original implementation of those properties involved essentially copying and pasting the code from one into the other. While that's probably not such a big deal in this particular case (since the `hms_core` class library is small, with few members, and there are only two places where that duplicate code would have to be maintained), in larger libraries, or if there was a lot of duplication of that code, it could become very problematic very quickly. Since Python allows classes to inherit from multiple parent classes, we can leverage that capability to define a new ABC—`HasProducts`—that will keep all of the product property related code in one place:

```
HasProducts

Properties
+ products <BaseProduct>*
Methods
+ add_product(product):
    <None>
+ remove_product(product):
    <BaseProduct>
```

 This approach is a variation of an object oriented principle that's usually referred to as a mixin—a class that contains concrete implementations of functionality for use in other classes.

The implementation of `HasProducts` is, essentially, just a collection or repackaging of the product properties code of `BaseArtisan` and `BaseOrder`:

```python
class HasProducts(metaclass=abc.ABCMeta):
    """
Provides baseline functionality, interface requirements, and
type-identity for objects that can have a common products
property whose membership is stored and handled in the same
way.
    """
```

The getter, setter, and deleter methods:

```
######################################
# Property-getter methods            #
######################################

def _get_products(self) -> (tuple,):
    return tuple(self._products)

######################################
# Property-setter methods            #
######################################

def _set_products(self, value:(list, tuple)) -> None:
# - Check first that the value is an iterable - list or
#   tuple, it doesn't really matter which, just so long
#   as it's a sequence-type collection of some kind.
 if type(value) not in (list, tuple):
    raise TypeError(
      '%s.products expects a list or tuple of BaseProduct '
      'objects, but was passed a %s instead' %
      (self.__class__.__name__, type(value).__name__)
          )
  # - Start with a new, empty list
  new_items = []
  # - Iterate over the items in value, check each one, and
  #   append them if they're OK
 bad_items = []
for item in value:
  # - We're going to assume that all products will derive
  #   from BaseProduct - That's why it's defined, after all
        if isinstance(item, BaseProduct):
            new_items.append(item)
        else:
            bad_items.append(item)
  # - If there are any bad items, then do NOT commit the
  #   changes -- raise an error instead!
        if bad_items:
            raise TypeError(
            '%s.products expects a list or tuple of BaseProduct'
            'objects, but the value passed included %d items '
            'that are not of the right type: (%s)' %
            (
                self.__class__.__name__, len(bad_items),
                ', '.join([str(bi) for bi in bad_items])
            )
        )
    self._products = value
```

```
####################################
# Property-deleter methods         #
####################################

   def _del_products(self) -> None:
     self._products = []
```

The `products` **property definition:**

```
####################################
# Instance property definitions    #
####################################

products = property(
_get_products, None, None,
'Gets the products (BaseProduct) of the instance'
)
```

Object initialization:

```
####################################
# Object initialization            #
####################################

def __init__(self, *products):
        """
Object initialization.

self ............. (HasProducts instance, required) The instance to
                     execute against
products ......... (list or tuple of BaseProduct instances) The
                     products that were ordered
""" 
        # - Call parent initializers if needed
        # - Set default instance property-values using _del_...
methods
        self._del_products()
        # - Set instance property-values from arguments using
        #   _set_... methods
        if products:
            self._set_products(products)
        # - Perform any other initialization needed

####################################
# Abstract methods                 #
####################################
```

The abstract methods for adding and removing products:

```
    @abc.abstractmethod
    def add_product(self, product:BaseProduct) -> BaseProduct:
        """
Adds a product to the instance's collection of products.

Returns the product added.

self ....... (HasProducts instance, required) The instance to
             execute against
product ... (BaseProduct, required) The product to add to the
             instance's collection of products

Raises TypeError if the product specified is not a BaseProduct-
  derived instance

May be implemented in derived classes by simply calling
    return HasProducts.add_product(self, product)
        """
        # - Make sure the product passed in is a BaseProduct
        if not isinstance(product, BaseProduct):
            raise TypeError(
                '%s.add_product expects an instance of '
                'BaseProduct to be passed in its product '
                'argument, but "%s" (%s) was passed instead' %
                (
                    self.__class__.__name__, value,
                    type(value).__name__
                )
            )
        # - Append it to the internal _products list
        self._products.append(product)
        # - Return it
        return product

    @abc.abstractmethod
    def remove_product(self, product:BaseProduct):
        """
Removes a product from the instance's collection of products.

Returns the product removed.

self ....... (HasProducts instance, required) The instance to
             execute against
product ... (BaseProduct, required) The product to remove from
             the instance's collection of products
```

```
    Raises TypeError if the product specified is not a BaseProduct-
        derived instance
    Raises ValueError if the product specified is not a member of the
        instance's products collection

    May be implemented in derived classes by simply calling
        return HasProducts.remove_product(self, product)
    """
        # - Make sure the product passed in is a BaseProduct.
        #   Technically this may not be necessary, since type
        #   is enforced in add_product, but it does no harm to
        #   re-check here...
        if not isinstance(product, BaseProduct):
            raise TypeError(
                '%s.add_product expects an instance of '
                'BaseProduct to be passed in its product '
                'argument, but "%s" (%s) was passed instead' %
                (
                    self.__class__.__name__, value,
                    type(value).__name__
                )
            )
        try:
            self._products.remove(product)
            return product
        except ValueError:
            raise ValueError(
                '%s.remove_product could not remove %s from its '
                'products collection because it was not a member '
                'of that collection' %
                (self.__class__.__name__, product)
            )
```

Using `HasProducts` in `BaseArtisan` and `BaseOrder` is not difficult, though it involves refactoring them to remove code that is already in place that will override the common code in `HasProducts`. It starts with making sure that the class using `HasProducts` inherits from it:

```
    class BaseArtisan(HasProducts, metaclass=abc.ABCMeta):
        """
    Provides baseline functionality, interface requirements, and
    type-identity for objects that can represent an Artisan in
    the context of the HMS system.
        """
```

The __init__ method of the derived class has to be altered to call the __init__ of
HasProducts as well, in order to assure that it performs all the relevant initialization
tasks:

```
def __init__(self,
    contact_name:str, contact_email:str,
    address:Address, company_name:str=None,
    **products
    ):
        """
Object initialization.
    """
    # - Call parent initializers if needed
# This is all that's needed to perform the initialization defined
# in HasProducts
        HasProducts.__init__(self, *products)
```

The processes of setting default values and instance values for the new class no longer
have to worry about handling the products property setup, since that's handled by
HasProducts.__init__:

```
        # - Set default instance property-values using _del_...
methods
        self._del_address()
        self._del_company_name()
        self._del_contact_email()
        self._del_contact_name()
# This can be deleted, or just commented out.
#        self._del_products()
    # - Set instance property-values from arguments using
        #   _set_... methods
        self._set_contact_name(contact_name)
        self._set_contact_email(contact_email)
        self._set_address(address)
        if company_name:
            self._set_company_name(company_name)
# This also can be deleted, or just commented out.
#        if products:
#            self._set_products(products)
```

Finally, the `products` property in each, along with their associated getter, setter, and deleter methods, can just be removed from the derived classes:

```
# This also can be deleted, or just commented out.
#    products = property(
#          _get_products, None, None,
#          'Gets the products (BaseProduct) of the instance'
#    )
```

With `HasProducts` implemented, the full structure and functionality of the `hms_core` package is tentatively complete—tentatively because it hasn't been unit tested yet. The class diagram for the entire package shows all of the moving parts, and the relationships between them:

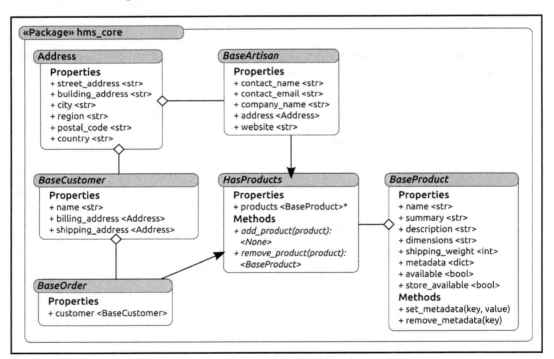

Summary

Overall, these classes provide definitions that could be described as dumb data objects. They provide little or no functionality that isn't directly related in some fashion to the definition and regulation of a specific data structure. Even `HasProducts`, and the classes that derive from it, fall into this category since the functionality provided there is strictly concerned with providing a data structure and controlling how that structure can be manipulated. As other classes are created that derive from these classes, those classes will start to become smarter, starting with persistence of the data for individual objects.

First, though, unit tests for these classes need to be written, to assure that they have been tested, and that they can be retested on demand. Since that represents a significant shift in coding goals, and will involve some in depth examination of testing goals and how to accomplish them, this first unit testing pass warrants its own chapter.

8
Testing Business Objects

Once the core business objects have been defined and tested, they can be used in other packages as foundations for classes to provide concrete class functionality. There are at least two advantages to taking this approach:

- The core classes keep all of the code that deals with data types, data structure, and data validation in a single place, which reduces the complexity of the other code bases that rely upon them
- Once unit tests have been created that pass for the core objects, none of the functionality that they provide will have to be tested elsewhere
- Those tests, written so that they can be executed on demand, can be integrated into a final build process, providing a complete set of regression tests that ensure that changes made in the future don't break existing functionality before executing a build

The process of building out those unit tests, using the test extensions noted earlier, while not difficult, will be time consuming at first. The entire process will be examined in this chapter, establishing some testing patterns that we'll reuse in later chapters, before integrating them into the package build process.

This chapter covers the following:

- Testing business objects
- Distribution and installation considerations
- Quality assurance and acceptance
- Operation/use, maintenance, and decommissioning considerations

Starting the unit testing process

Using the standard unit testing structure/framework that we defined in the chapter before last allows us to start the unit testing of any code base very quickly and easily. It also lends itself well to an iterative test development process. The starting point test module, once the configuration items have been set within it by the couple of search and replace operations, immediately starts reporting on what test cases and methods are reporting. Our initial test module is little more than the following (with some comments removed to keep the listing short):

```python
#!/usr/bin/env python
"""
Defines unit-tests for the module at hms_core.
"""
#######################################
# Standard library imports needed     #
#######################################

import os
import sys
import unittest

#######################################
# Local imports needed                #
#######################################

from idic.unit_testing import *

#######################################
# Module-level Constants              #
#######################################

LocalSuite = unittest.TestSuite()

#######################################
# Import the module being tested      #
#######################################
```

```
import hms_core as hms_core

#######################################
# Code-coverage test-case and         #
# decorator-methods                    #
#######################################

class testhms_coreCodeCoverage(ModuleCoverageTest):
    # - Class constants that point to the namespace and module
    #   being tested
    _testNamespace = 'hms_core'
    _testModule = hms_core

LocalSuite.addTests(
    unittest.TestLoader().loadTestsFromTestCase(
        testhms_coreCodeCoverage
    )
)

#######################################
# Test-cases in the module            #
#######################################

#######################################
# Code to execute if file is called   #
# or run directly.                    #
#######################################

if __name__ == '__main__':
    import time
    results = unittest.TestResult()
    testStartTime = time.time()
    LocalSuite.run(results)
    results.runTime = time.time() - testStartTime
    PrintTestResults(results)
    if not results.errors and not results.failures:
        SaveTestReport(results, 'hms_core',
            'hms_core.test-results')
```

Executing the test module yields the following results:

```
################################################################################
Tests were successful ..... False
Number of tests run ....... 1
  + Tests ran in .......... 0.00 seconds
Number of errors .......... 0
Number of failures ........ 1
Number of tests skipped ... 0
################################################################################
FAILURES
#------------------------------------------------------------------------------#
testCodeCoverage (__main__.testhms_coreCodeCoverage)

[lines removed for brevity]

Unit-testing policies require test-cases for all classes and functions in the
hms_core module, but the following have not been defined:
    (testAddress, testBaseArtisan, testBaseCustomer, testBaseOrder,
    testBaseProduct, testHasProducts)
################################################################################
Unit-test results
################################################################################
Tests were successful ..... False
Number of tests run ....... 1
  + Tests ran in .......... 0.00 seconds
Number of errors .......... 0
Number of failures ........ 1
Number of tests skipped ... 0
################################################################################
```

That test run output informs us, then, that we need to generate test case classes for each of the six classes defined in the module being tested; specifically, we need to create `testAddress`, `testBaseArtisan`, `testBaseCustomer`, `testBaseOrder`, `testBaseProduct`, and `testHasProducts` test case classes. 3

Each of those should, in order to leverage the property and method coverage tests that the standard unit testing structure provides, be decorated with the `AddMethodTesting` and `AddPropertyTesting` decorators that `testhms_coreCodeCoverage` provides:

```
#########################################
# Test-cases in the module              #
#########################################

@testhms_coreCodeCoverage.AddMethodTesting
@testhms_coreCodeCoverage.AddPropertyTesting
class testAddress(unittest.TestCase):
    pass
LocalSuite.addTests(
    unittest.TestLoader().loadTestsFromTestCase(
        testAddress
    )
)

@testhms_coreCodeCoverage.AddMethodTesting
@testhms_coreCodeCoverage.AddPropertyTesting
class testBaseArtisan(unittest.TestCase):
    pass
LocalSuite.addTests(
    unittest.TestLoader().loadTestsFromTestCase(
        testBaseArtisan
    )
)

@testhms_coreCodeCoverage.AddMethodTesting
@testhms_coreCodeCoverage.AddPropertyTesting
class testBaseCustomer(unittest.TestCase):
    pass
LocalSuite.addTests(
    unittest.TestLoader().loadTestsFromTestCase(
        testBaseCustomer
    )
)
```

```
@testhms_coreCodeCoverage.AddMethodTesting
@testhms_coreCodeCoverage.AddPropertyTesting
class testBaseOrder(unittest.TestCase):
    pass
LocalSuite.addTests(
    unittest.TestLoader().loadTestsFromTestCase(
        testBaseOrder
    )
)
@testhms_coreCodeCoverage.AddMethodTesting
@testhms_coreCodeCoverage.AddPropertyTesting
class testBaseProduct(unittest.TestCase):
    pass
LocalSuite.addTests(
    unittest.TestLoader().loadTestsFromTestCase(
        testBaseProduct
    )
)

@testhms_coreCodeCoverage.AddMethodTesting
@testhms_coreCodeCoverage.AddPropertyTesting
class testHasProducts(unittest.TestCase):
    pass
LocalSuite.addTests(
    unittest.TestLoader().loadTestsFromTestCase(
        testHasProducts
    )
)
```

Once those are in place, rerunning the test module will generate a (long!) list of items that need to be addressed before the test policy tests will pass. The full list of requirements was long enough that including it in the book directly would've just ended up with 2-3 pages of a bulleted list. The full results, however, are included in the `hms_core` code base, in `miscellany/initial-test-run.txt`. The entire initial output was far too long to reproduce in its entirety here, but the start and end of the output is reproduced as follows, and specifies a total of 105 test methods that need to be implemented across the six test case classes:

```
############################################################################
FAILURES
testMethodCoverage (__main__.testAddress)
# ...
Unit-testing policy requires test-methods to be created for all public and
protected methods, but testAddress is missing the following test-methods:
    ['test__init__', 'test_del_building_address', 'test_del_city',
    'test_del_country', 'test_del_postal_code', 'test_del_region',
    'test_del_street_address', 'test_get_building_address',
    'test_get_city', 'test_get_country', 'test_get_postal_code',
    'test_get_region', 'test_get_street_address',
    'test_set_building_address', 'test_set_city', 'test_set_country',
    'test_set_postal_code', 'test_set_region', 'test_set_street_address',
    'teststandard_address']
#--------------------------------------------------------------------------#
testPropertyCoverage (__main__.testAddress)
# ...
Unit-testing policy requires test-methods to be created for all public
properties, but testAddress is missing the following test-methods:
    ['testbuilding_address', 'testcity', 'testcountry', 'testpostal_code',
    'testregion', 'teststreet_address']
#--------------------------------------------------------------------------#
testMethodCoverage (__main__.testBaseArtisan)
# ... There are similar results for each test-case class,
#     removed for brevity
#--------------------------------------------------------------------------#
testMethodCoverage (__main__.testHasProducts)
# ...
Unit-testing policy requires test-methods to be created for all public and
protected methods, but testHasProducts is missing the following test-methods:
['test__init__', 'test_del_products', 'test_get_products', 'test_set_products']
#--------------------------------------------------------------------------#
testPropertyCoverage (__main__.testHasProducts)
# ...
Unit-testing policy requires test-methods to be created for all public
properties, but testHasProducts is missing the following test-methods:
    ['testproducts']
############################################################################
Unit-test results
############################################################################
Tests were successful ..... False
Number of tests run ....... 13
Number of failures ........ 12
```

From that point on, the test writing process is just a matter of repeating the following cycle until all tests pass:

- Pick a missing test method or set of test methods that need to be written
- Add the test method(s) to the applicable test case class, set up to fail because they aren't implemented
- Run the test module to verify that the tests fail as expected
- For each test method:
    - Write real test code in the method
    - Execute the test module and ensure that the only failure in that method is the explicit one added, correcting any issues that arise
    - Remove the explicit failures

Even with the guidance that is provided by the standard unit testing process, there is no denying that writing out all of the unit tests for a module, even one as relatively short as `hms_core`, can be incredibly tedious. There are a few things that can be done to make the process go at least somewhat faster, though—especially since we know that there are some common value types and formats that we're expecting. We'll start by writing out tests for the `Address` class, which has one of the largest collections of properties that we're going to be dealing with. As many of those tests get built out, some common (and re usable) test values will start to surface.

 This run through of the unit testing process will also yield a test case class template file (`test-case-class.py`) that will be included in the book's code in the code templates directory.

Unit testing the Address class

The `Address` class tests initially report that the following test methods need to be written:

- **Methods:** test__init__, test_del_building_address, test_del_ci ty, test_del_country, test_del_postal_code, test_del_region, te st_del_street_address, test_get_building_address, test_get_c ity, test_get_country, test_get_postal_code, test_get_region, t est_get_street_address, test_set_building_address, test_set_ city, test_set_country, test_set_postal_code, test_set_region, test_set_street_address, **and** test_standard_address

- **Properties:** `testbuilding_address`, `testcity`, `testcountry`, `testpos` `tal_code`, `testregion`, and `teststreet_address`

The primary concern of the test methods for the properties of the class being tested are, arguably, to make sure that the properties use the appropriate methods for their getter, setter, and deleter functionalities. If that is established as being correct, then the actual processes for handling the properties and their values can be tested solely in the test methods for those methods. With that in mind, the bulk of the property tests for `Address` will look like this:

```
def testproperty_name(self):
    # Tests the property_name property of the Address class
    # - Assert that the getter is correct:
    self.assertEqual(
        Address.property_name.fget,
        Address._get_property_name,
        'Address.property_name is expected to use the '
        '_get_property_name method as its getter-method'
    )
        # - If property_name is not expected to be publicly
# settable,
        #    the second item here
        #    (Address._set_property_name) should
        #    be changed to None, and the failure message        #
adjusted
        #    accordingly:
          self.assertEqual(
            Address.property_name.fset,
            Address._set_property_name,
            'Address.property_name is expected to use the '
            '_set_property_name method as its setter-method'
          )
    #    If property_name is not expected to be publicly    #
deletable,
    #    the second item here (Address._del_property_name)    #
should
    #    be changed to None, and the failure message        #
adjusted
      #    accordingly:
      self.assertEqual(
        Address.property_name.fdel,
        Address._del_property_name,
        'Address.property_name is expected to use the '
        '_del_property_name method as its deleter-method'
      )
```

By switching the templated `property_name` in that code block out for
the actual property name, the individual property tests can be created quite quickly,
for example, implementing `testbuilding_address`:

```
def testbuilding_address(self):
# Tests the building_address property of the Address class
# - Assert that the getter is correct:
    self.assertEqual(
        Address.building_address.fget,
        Address._get_building_address,
        'Address.building_address is expected to use the '
        '_get_building_address method as its getter-method'
    )
# - Assert that the setter is correct:
    self.assertEqual(
        Address.building_address.fset,
        Address._set_building_address,
        'Address.building_address is expected to use the '
        '_set_building_address method as its setter-method'
    )
# - Assert that the deleter is correct:
    self.assertEqual(
        Address.building_address.fdel,
        Address._del_building_address,
        'Address.building_address is expected to use the '
        '_del_building_address method as its deleter-method'
    )
```

The getter and deleter method tests will usually also be quite simple—all they need to
do, ultimately, is ensure that they are retrieving data from the correct internal storage
attribute and setting the value of that attribute to the expected default value,
respectively. The `test_del_building_address` test method serves as an example:

```
def test_del_building_address(self):
# Tests the _del_building_address method of the Address
# class
    test_object = Address('street address', 'city')
    self.assertEqual(
        test_object.building_address, None,
        'An Address object is expected to have None as its default '
        'building_address value if no value was provided'
    )
# - Hard-set the storage-property's value, call the
#   deleter-method, and assert that it's what's expected
#   afterwards:
    test_object._building_address = 'a test value'
    test_object._del_building_address()
```

```
        self.assertEqual(
          test_object.building_address, None,
          'An Address object is expected to have None as its '
          'building_address value after the deleter is called'
        )
```

It's worth noting that in order to test the deleter method (as well as the getter and setter methods later on), we actually have to create an instance of the object being tested—that's what the third line of the test method is doing (test_object = Address...). Once that instance is created, if the property whose deleter method is being tested isn't required or supplied as part of that test object's creation, we can (and should) also test the default/deleted value of the instance. Even if there is a value supplied for the test object, testing the deletion process by setting a value in the underlying storage attribute, calling the deleter method, and verifying the results afterwards will remain constant in almost all cases.

Testing the corresponding getter method is going to be similar; again, all it really has to do is provide that the property is retrieving data from the correct storage attribute:

```
def test_get_building_address(self):
# Tests the _get_building_address method of the Address
# class
  test_object = Address('street address', 'city')
  expected = 'a test-value'
  test_object._building_address = expected
  actual = test_object._get_building_address()
  self.assertEqual(
    actual, expected,
    'Address._get_building_address was expected to return '
    '"%s" (%s), but returned "%s" (%s) instead' %
    (
        expected, type(expected).__name__,
        actual, type(actual).__name__,
    )
  )
```

It's often useful to set expected and actual values that can be passed to the core assertion of the test, particularly if retrieving those values involves using a method or function. It won't make a functional difference, but it can be a lot easier to read later on, and keeping things easily understood and readable is, if anything, more important than keeping the code being tested readable and understandable—test code is a quality assurance effort, after all, and would not be well served by having errors creep in because of a cryptic structure.

It's also worth noting that the test methods for `city` and `street_address` properties vary slightly, because they are both properties that are set during the creation of an instance:

```
def test_del_city(self):
    # Tests the _del_city method of the Address class
    expected = 'city'
    test_object = Address('street address', expected)
    self.assertEqual(
      test_object.city, expected,
      'An Address object is expected to have "%s" (%s) as its '
      'current city value, since that value was provided' %
        (expected, type(expected).__name__)
      )
# - Since we have a value, just call the deleter-method,
#   and
#   assert that it's what's expected afterwards:
      test_object._del_city()
        self.assertEqual(
          test_object.city, None,
          'An Address object is expected to have None as its '
          'city value after the deleter is called'
      )
```

The difference is that since the test object being created is expected to provide a value because it was initialized with one, we're setting up the expected value to test against before the test object is created, creating it using that expected value, then testing to ensure that the deleter doesn't delete that initially set value during object creation. The test that it does getting deleted when explicitly told to is essentially the same, though.

Once all of the getter and deleter method tests have been established using those patterns, the test module run starts to show progress. One of the 29 tests being run (and that is one of the failures) is the code coverage test that is picking up the missing test case classes for `BaseArtisan` and the other `hms_core` classes, which have been commented out to make working with the results output of the `testAddress` test methods easier. Of the remaining eight failures, six are the setter method tests for `testAddress`, which we'll implement next, and the other two are `test__init__` and `teststandard_address`, which we'll look at last:

```
################################################################################
Unit-test results
################################################################################
Tests were successful ..... False
Number of tests run ....... 29
 + Tests ran in .......... 0.00 seconds
Number of errors .......... 0
Number of failures ........ 9
Number of tests skipped ... 0
################################################################################
```

The test methods corresponding to the getter and deleter methods are simple because the methods being tested are, themselves, quite simple. They (thus far) make no decisions, and neither do they do any manipulation of the values themselves; they simply return the current value, or replace it without having to make any decisions about what it's being replaced with. On top of that, they also have no arguments to contend with.

The setter methods are more complicated; they will make decisions, will have arguments (if only one), and might be expected to behave differently depending on the types and values of those arguments. Their corresponding test methods, then, might be expected to be more complex too as a result, and that expectation would be well founded. Test complexity will grow as the complexity of the input grows for well designed tests, because those tests must check all of the logical variants of the input. That will start to become apparent as we test the setter methods of our properties, starting with `Address.building_address` again.

Well designed unit tests need to do several things, not all of which may be obvious at first. The most obvious item is probably testing all of the happy path input possibilities: inputs that are of expected types and with expected and valid values, which should execute without errors and yield the expected results, whatever those results may be. Less obviously perhaps, unit tests should also test with a representative sample set of known bad values—values that are expected to raise errors and prevent the process being tested from completing with erroneous data. Let's take another look at the `_set_building_address` method of `Address` with that in mind:

```python
def _set_building_address(self, value:(str,None)) -> None:
    if value != None:
# - Type-check: If the value isn't None, then it has to
#   be a non-empty, single-line string without tabs
    if type(value) != str:
        raise TypeError(
```

```
                '%s.building_address expects a single-line, '
                'non-empty str value, with no whitespace '
                'other than spaces or None, but was passed '
                '"%s" (%s)' %
                (
                    self.__class__.__name__, value,
                    type(value).__name__
                )
            )
        # - Value-check: no whitespace other than " "
        bad_chars = ('\n', '\r', '\t')
        is_valid = True
        for bad_char in bad_chars:
            if bad_char in value:
                is_valid = False
                break
        # - If it's empty or otherwise not valid, raise error
        if not value.strip() or not is_valid:
            raise ValueError(
                '%s.building_address expects a single-line, '
                'non-empty str value, with no whitespace '
                'other than spaces or None, but was passed '
                '"%s" (%s)' %
                (
                    self.__class__.__name__, value,
                    type(value).__name__
                )
            )
        # - If this point is reached without error, then the
        #   string-value is valid, so we can just exit the if
        self._building_address = value
```

The good values that can be reasonably tested include the following:

- None—If None is passed as the value, then it simply passes through and is set in the inner storage attribute.
- Any single line, non-empty string that doesn't contain tabs or other whitespace characters other than spaces.

Viable bad values would include the following:

- Any value that isn't a string.
- An empty string.
- A string that contains any line breaking characters, or any whitespace that isn't a space.

- A string that is nothing but space characters; this item is less obvious, but the code will raise a `ValueError` because such an input would be caught by the `if not value.strip()` that's part of the value checking code. The results of a `.strip()` called against a string that is nothing but whitespace is an empty string, and that would evaluate as `False` (-ish), thus raising the error.

The `_set_building_address` method doesn't try to do any content validation, so we don't currently have to worry about that; we're implicitly assuming that if someone took the effort to enter a well formed `building_address` value then the value entered is going to be accurate.

Earlier, the `business_address` property was classified as a standard optional text line property. If that classification holds true, then it would be both possible and advantageous to generate a single list of good standard optional text line property values, so that those values can be reused for all of the property tests that they'd logically apply to. That list, set up as a constant in the test module, might look something like this:

```
GoodStandardOptionalTextLines = [
    'word', 'hyphenated-word', 'short phrase',
    'A complete sentence.',
    'A short paragraph. This\'s got some punctuation, '
    'including "quoted text."',
    None # Because optional items are allowed to be None
]
```

Testing the good values in `test_set_business_address` then becomes a simple matter of iterating over that list of values, calling the setter method, and asserting that the results of the getter method after the value's been set match the expected value:

```
# - Create an object to test with:
test_object = Address('street address', 'street_address')
# - Test all permutations of "good" argument-values:
    for expected in GoodStandardOptionalTextLines:
        test_object._set_building_address(expected)
        actual = test_object._get_building_address()
        self.assertEqual(
            expected, actual,
            'Address expects a building_address value set to '
            '"%s" (%s) to be retrieved with a corresponding '
            'getter-method call, but "%s" (%s) was returned '
            'instead' %
        (
```

```
expected, type(expected).__name__,
        actual, type(actual).__name__,
    )
)
```

 It would also be valid to perform the assertion against the property instead of the getter method, since we've tested that the property is associated with the getter method elsewhere.

A corresponding bad values list would have to include all of the bad items listed previously, and would look something like this:

```
BadStandardOptionalTextLines = [
    # Bad string values
    'multiple\nlines', 'also multiple\rlines',
    'text\twith\tabs',
    # Values that aren't strings at all
    1, True, 0, False, object(),
    # empty and whitespace-only strings
    '', '   ',
]
```

The corresponding bad value tests are a similar iteration to the good value iteration shown previously, except that they will specifically look for cases where the execution is expected to fail, and fail if those don't happen or happen in an unexpected fashion:

```
# - Test all permutations of "bad" argument-values:
for value in BadStandardOptionalTextLines:
    try:
        test_object._set_building_address(value)
        # - If this setter-call succeeds, that's a
        #    test-failure!
        self.fail(
            'Address._set_business_address should raise '
            'TypeError or ValueError if passed "%s" (%s), '
            'but it was allowed to be set instead.' %
                (value, type(value).__name__)
        )
    except (TypeError, ValueError):
    # - This is expected, so it passes
        pass
    except Exception as error:
        self.fail(
            'Address._set_business_address should raise '
            'TypeError or ValueError if passed an invalid '
            'value, but %s was raised instead: %s.' %
```

```
                    (error.__class__.__name__, error)
        )
```

This test process, by using the `try ... except` blocks, will do the following:

- Explicitly fail if the setter method allows a bad value to be set without raising an error
- Pass if a bad value raises an expected error (`TypeError` or `ValueError` in most cases) while trying to set a bad value in the test object
- Fail if any error other than the two types expected is raised by the setter method during execution

This same test method structure can be used for all of the `Address` properties that are also standard optional text line values/types with no more effort than changing the setter method names. Basically, all of the property setters of an `Address`, except the ones for `city` and `street_address`, which are standard required text line items, are identical, except for those names.

The only difference between the optional and required text line properties, though, is that optional items can allow `None` as a valid argument, while required ones cannot. If we create separate test value lists that account for those differences, and change which list the test method is using, the same structure, just with different good and bad values, will still work:

```
GoodStandardRequiredTextLines = [
    'word', 'hyphenated-word', 'short phrase',
    'A complete sentence.',
    'A short paragraph. This\'s got some punctuation, '
    'including "quoted text."',
]
BadStandardRequiredTextLines = [
    # Bad string values
    'multiple\nlines', 'also multiple\rlines',
    'text\twith\tabs',
    # Values that aren't strings at all
    1, True, 0, False, object(),
    # empty and whitespace-only strings
    '', '   ',
    None # Because optional items are NOT allowed to be None
]

# ...

def test_set_city(self):
    # Tests the _set_city method of the Address class
```

```
        # - Create an object to test with:
        test_object = Address('street address', 'street_address')
        # - Test all permutations of "good" argument-values:
        for expected in GoodStandardRequiredTextLines:
            test_object._set_city(expected)
            actual = test_object._get_city()
            self.assertEqual(
                expected, actual,
                'Address expects a city value set to '
                '"%s" (%s) to be retrieved with a corresponding '
                'getter-method call, but "%s" (%s) was returned '
                'instead' %
                (
                    expected, type(expected).__name__,
                    actual, type(actual).__name__,
                )
            )
        # - Test all permutations of "bad" argument-values:
        for value in BadStandardRequiredTextLines:
            try:
                test_object._set_city(value)
                # - If this setter-call succeeds, that's a
                #   test-failure!
                self.fail(
                    'Address._set_business_address should raise '
                    'TypeError or ValueError if passed "%s" (%s), '
                    'but it was allowed to be set instead.' %
                    (value, type(value).__name__)
                )
            except (TypeError, ValueError):
                # - This is expected, so it passes
                pass
            except Exception as error:
                self.fail(
                    'Address._set_business_address should raise '
                    'TypeError or ValueError if passed an invalid '
                    'value, but %s was raised instead: %s.' %
                    (error.__class__.__name__, error)
                )
```

With all of the setter method tests in place, rerunning the test module shows that there are only three tests failing:

```
###########################################################################
Unit-test results
###########################################################################
Tests were successful ..... False
Number of tests run ....... 29
  + Tests ran in .......... 0.00 seconds
Number of errors .......... 0
Number of failures ........ 3
Number of tests skipped ... 0
###########################################################################
```

Discounting the coverage test for the other test case classes, that leaves only the __init__ and standard_address methods to test.

Testing the __init__ method is not going to be difficult. All it really needs to establish is that the initialization process that is part of creating a new object instance is calling the various property setters in an appropriate fashion. Other tests have already established that the properties connect to their intended getter/setter/deleter methods, and that those methods are doing what they're supposed to. Since we have predefined lists of good values that we can iterate over, it's a simple matter to set up a (large) set of nested loops to check all the possible combinations of those values as they apply to each property. The nesting level of the loops gets pretty deep (enough so that the following code is indented only two spaces per line in order to fit on the page), but it works:

```python
def test__init__(self):
  # Tests the __init__ method of the Address class
  # - Test all permutations of "good" argument-values:
  for building_address in GoodStandardOptionalTextLines:
    for city in GoodStandardRequiredTextLines:
      for country in GoodStandardOptionalTextLines:
        for postal_code in GoodStandardOptionalTextLines:
          for region in GoodStandardOptionalTextLines:
            for street_address in GoodStandardRequiredTextLines:
              test_object = Address(
                street_address, city, building_address,
                region, postal_code, country
              )
              self.assertEqual(test_object.street_address,
street_address)
              self.assertEqual(test_object.city, city)
              self.assertEqual(test_object.building_address,
building_address)
              self.assertEqual(test_object.region, region)
              self.assertEqual(test_object.postal_code, postal_code)
              self.assertEqual(test_object.country, country)
```

The same approach works just as well in implementing `teststandard_address`:

```
def teststandard_address(self):
    # Tests the standard_address method of the Address class
    # - Test all permutations of "good" argument-values:
    for street_address in GoodStandardRequiredTextLines:
        for building_address in GoodStandardOptionalTextLines:
            for city in GoodStandardRequiredTextLines:
                for region in GoodStandardOptionalTextLines:
                    for postal_code in GoodStandardOptionalTextLines:
                        for country in GoodStandardOptionalTextLines:
                            test_object = Address.standard_address(
                                street_address, building_address,
                                city, region, postal_code,
                                country
                            )
                            self.assertEqual(test_object.street_address,
street_address)
                            self.assertEqual(test_object.building_address,
building_address)
                            self.assertEqual(test_object.city, city)
                            self.assertEqual(test_object.region, region)
                            self.assertEqual(test_object.postal_code, postal_code)
                            self.assertEqual(test_object.country, country)
```

That, then, completes the tests for the `Address` class:

```
##############################################################################
FAILURES
#--------------------------------------------------------------------------#
testCodeCoverage (__main__.testhms_coreCodeCoverage)
Unit-testing policies require test-cases for all classes and functions in the
hms_core module, but the following have not been defined:
    (testBaseArtisan, testBaseCustomer, testBaseOrder, testBaseProduct,
    testHasProducts)
##############################################################################
Unit-test results
##############################################################################
Tests were successful ..... False
Number of tests run ....... 29
 + Tests ran in .......... 0.84 seconds
Number of errors .......... 0
Number of failures ........ 1
Number of tests skipped ... 0
##############################################################################
```

The balance of the unit testing process for the module really consists of reactivating the other test case classes, creating the baseline failing test methods for all of them and then just running the test module and writing and correcting tests, as noted earlier. Because of the way that the test process executes, the output generated will be for each test method of each test case class, in alphabetical order. So, the test case class for `HasProducts` will execute last, and within, that the `testproducts` method, preceded by `test_del_products`, `test_get_products`, and `test_set_products`. It takes less time to simply deal with the last failing test case(s) in the output, rather than scrolling through the entire output looking for a single, specific test method that's being worked on, so the remaining tests will be worked on and discussed in that order.

Unit testing HasProducts

The test method for the `products` property, `testproducts`, has to account for the read only nature of the property—remember that the products property is set up to prevent, or at least minimize, the possibility of casual manipulation of the underlying list value. Apart from the changes to the tests of setter and deleter method assignment, it's pretty much the same as previous property test methods, though:

```
def testproducts(self):
    # Tests the products property of the HasProducts class
    # - Assert that the getter is correct:
    self.assertEqual(
        HasProducts.products.fget,
        HasProducts._get_products,
        'HasProducts.products is expected to use the '
        '_get_products method as its getter-method'
    )
    # - Assert that the setter is correct:
    self.assertEqual(
        HasProducts.products.fset, None,
        'HasProducts.products is expected to be read-only, with '
        'no associated setter-method'
    )
    # - Assert that the deleter is correct:
    self.assertEqual(
        HasProducts.products.fdel, None,
        'HasProducts.products is expected to be read-only, with '
        'no associated deleter-method'
    )
```

Testing the methods of an ABC like `HasProducts` is, at one level, the same sort of process as for a concrete class like `Address`: a test object that is an instance of the ABC has to be created, then relevant test values are passed to the methods and their results asserted. An ABC, if it has abstract members, cannot be instantiated, however, so a throwaway derived class that has minimal implementations of the abstract members has to be defined and used in place of the concrete class to create test objects. For the purposes of testing the member methods of `HasProducts`, that class is `HasProductsDerived`, and it looks like this:

```
class HasProductsDerived(HasProducts):
    def __init__(self, *products):
        HasProducts.__init__(self, *products)
# NOTE: These do NOT have to actually *do* anything, they
# merely have to *exist* in order to allow an instance
    #       to be created:
    def add_product(self, product):
        pass
    def remove_product(self, product):
        pass
```

With that class defined, the tests for `_get_products`, `_set_products`, and `_del_products` can be created as straightforward variations of the test strategies used so far, though they require `GoodProducts` and `BadProducts` definitions that make use of the throwaway class first:

```
#   Since we needed this class in order to generate good #  product-
#   setter test-values, but it wasn't defined until now, #   we'll
#   create the GoodProducts test-values here...
GoodProducts = [
    [
        BaseProductDerived('test1', 'summary1', True, True),
        BaseProductDerived('test2', 'summary2', True, True),
    ],
    (
        BaseProductDerived('test3', 'summary3', True, True),
        BaseProductDerived('test4', 'summary4', True, True),
    ),
]
BadProducts = [
    object(), 'string', 1, 1.0, True, None,
    ['list','with','invalid','values'],
    [
        BaseProductDerived('test4', 'summary4', True, True),
        'list','with','invalid','values'
    ],
```

```
        ('tuple','with','invalid','values'),
        (
            BaseProductDerived('test4', 'summary4', True, True),
            'tuple','with','invalid','values'
        ),
    ]
```

Once those are also in place, the test methods are as follows:

```
def test_del_products(self):
# Tests the _del_products method of the HasProducts class
    test_object = HasProductsDerived()
    self.assertEqual(test_object.products, (),
    'HasProducts-derived instances are expected to return '
    'an empty tuple as a default/deleted value'
    )
# - Test all permutations of "good" argument-values:
        test_object._set_products(GoodProducts[0])
        self.assertNotEqual(test_object.products, ())
        test_object._del_products()
        self.assertEqual(test_object.products, ())

def test_get_products(self):
 # Tests the _get_products method of the HasProducts class
        test_object = HasProductsDerived()
 # - Test all permutations of "good" argument-values:
        expected = GoodProducts[1]
        test_object._products = expected
        self.assertEqual(test_object._get_products(), expected)

    def test_set_products(self):
# Tests the _set_products method of the HasProducts class
        test_object = HasProductsDerived()
# - Test all permutations of "good" argument-values:
        for expected in GoodProducts:
            test_object._set_products(expected)
            if type(expected) != tuple:
                expected = tuple(expected)
            self.assertEqual(expected, test_object._get_products())
# - Test all permutations of each "bad" argument-value
#    set against "good" values for the other arguments:
        for value in BadProducts:
            try:
                test_object._set_products(value)
                self.fail(
                    'HasProducts-derived classes should not allow '
                    '"%s" (%s) as a valid products value, but it '
                    'was allowed to be set.' %
```

```
                    (str(value), type(value).__name__)
                )
            except (TypeError, ValueError):
                pass
```

The test method for `HasProducts.__init__` uses much the same sort of approach as `test_set_products`:

```
    def test__init__(self):
        # Tests the __init__ method of the HasProducts class
        # - Test all permutations of "good" argument-values:
            for expected in GoodProducts:
                test_object = HasProductsDerived(*expected)
                if type(expected) != tuple:
                    expected = tuple(expected)
                self.assertEqual(test_object.products, expected)
```

Since `HasProducts` has concrete functionality hidden behind its `add_product` and `remove_product` methods, it would also be possible to test that functionality in the same fashion, but any derived class methods that call those methods would still have to be individually tested anyway, according to our test policy, so there's not much point in making the additional effort at this time.

Unit testing BaseProduct

The test methods for the properties of `BaseProduct` don't require anything new; they follow the same approaches shown for properties with full get/set/delete capabilities, except for the test of the metadata property, which tests as a read-only property like the test for `HasProducts.products` we have just shown.

Many of the test methods for `BaseProduct` will also follow previously established patterns—testing for good and bad value variants of standard required and optional text lines—but there are a few that require new, or at least variant, approaches as well.

The `set_metadata` and `remove_metadata` method tests are just different enough from previous tests that they are worth a closer examination. In order to test the addition of new metadata key/value items, it's necessary to keep track of an expected value that the same addition of keys and values can be performed against. That is achieved in the test method by creating an empty dictionary (`expected = {}`) that is modified in the iteration that calls the `set_metadata` method on the test object. As each iteration progresses, the expected value is altered accordingly, and is compared to the actual value:

```
def testset_metadata(self):
  # Tests the set_metadata method of the BaseProduct class
  test_object = BaseProductDerived('name', 'summary', True, True)
  expected = {}
  # - Test all permutations of "good" argument-values:
  for key in GoodStandardRequiredTextLines:
      value = '%s value'
      expected[key] = value
      test_object.set_metadata(key, value)
      self.assertEqual(test_object.metadata, expected)
```

Tests for bad key and value sets use a single good value for whichever item is not being tested, and iterate over the bad values, making sure that appropriate errors are raised:

```
      # - Test all permutations of each "bad" argument-value
      #   set against "good" values for the other arguments:
      value = GoodStandardRequiredTextLines[0]
      for key in BadStandardRequiredTextLines:
          try:
              test_object.set_metadata(key, value)
              self.fail(
                'BaseProduct.set_metadata should not allow '
                '"%s" (%s) as a key, but it raised no error'
                  % (key, type(key).__name__)
              )
          except (TypeError,ValueError):
              pass
          except Exception as error:
              self.fail(
                'BaseProduct.set_metadata should raise TypeError '
                'or ValueError if passed  "%s" (%s) as a key, '
                'but %s was raised instead:\n    %s' %
                  (
                      key, type(key).__name__,
                      error.__class__.__name__, error
                  )
              )
      key = GoodStandardRequiredTextLines[0]
      for value in BadStandardRequiredTextLines:
          try:
              test_object.set_metadata(key, value)
              self.fail(
                'BaseProduct.set_metadata should not allow '
                '"%s" (%s) as a value, but it raised no error'
                  % (value, type(value).__name__)
              )
          except (TypeError,ValueError):
```

```
            pass
        except Exception as error:
            self.fail(
                'BaseProduct.set_metadata should raise TypeError '
                'or ValueError if passed  "%s" (%s) as a value, '
                'but %s was raised instead:\n    %s' %
                (
                    value, type(value).__name__,
                    error.__class__.__name__, error
                )
            )
```

The test method for the remove_metadata method of BaseProduct uses a similar strategy for keeping track of an expected value to compare test results against. The only significant difference is that the expected value (and the test object's metadata too) need to be populated before trying to remove any metadata values:

```
def testremove_metadata(self):
    # Tests the remove_metadata method of the BaseProduct class
    # - First we need sopme meadata to remove
    test_object = BaseProductDerived('name', 'summary', True, True)
    expected = {
        'materials':'wood',
        'material-names':'cherry,oak',
        'finish':'gloss'
    }
    for key in expected:
        test_object.set_metadata(key, expected[key])
    self.assertEqual(test_object.metadata, expected)
    # - Test all permutations of "good" argument-values:
    keys = list(expected.keys())
    for key in keys:
        del expected[key]
        test_object.remove_metadata(key)
        self.assertEqual(test_object.metadata, expected)
```

The tests for the setter methods of the Boolean value properties of BaseProduct, available, and store_available still use the same good and bad value iteration approach that's been used elsewhere, they just need a different list of good and bad values to test with:

```
GoodBooleanOrIntEquivalents = [
    True, False, 1, 0
]
```

```
BadBooleanOrIntEquivalents = [
    'true', '', (1,2), tuple()
]
```

Similarly, the test method for _set_shipping_weight needs yet another set of value lists, as does the test method for _set_metadata:

```
GoodWeights = [
    0, 1, 2, 0.0, 1.0, 2.0, 1.5
]
BadWeights = [
    -1, -1.0, object(), 'true', '', (1,2), tuple()
]
GoodMetadataDicts = [
    {},
    {'spam':'eggs'}
]
BadMetadataDicts = [
    -1, -1.0, object(), 'true', '', (1,2), tuple()
]
```

The initial test run against _set_shipping_weight also prompted a review of the assumptions around what constitutes a valid shipping weight. On reflection, and without knowing what the measurement units are at this point, it's quite possible that those values will need to allow floating point values, especially if the units of measure need to eventually allow for pounds, kilograms, or even tons of shipping, as unlikely as that might be.

The system shouldn't place any constraints on what a valid shipping weight is, other than ensuring that it's a number (because it always will be) and isn't negative. Products might, after all, include something like a piece of calligraphy, or an illustration on a single sheet of paper, and that's not going to weigh much at all. On the other end of the spectrum, a marble bust or even a large metal sculpture in the dozens of pounds to one or more tons weight range is just as possible.

With all of these considerations in mind, _set_shipping_weight was altered to allow a broader range of value types, and to allow a zero value as well:

```
def _set_shipping_weight(self, value:(int,float)):
    if type(value) not in (int, float):
        raise TypeError(
            '%s.shipping_weight expects a non-negative numeric '
            'value, but was passed "%s" (%s)' %
            (
                self.__class__.__name__,
                value, type(value).__name__
```

```
            )
        )
    if value < 0:
        raise ValueError(
            '%s.shipping_weight expects a non-negative numeric '
            'value, but was passed "%s" (%s)' %
            (
                self.__class__.__name__,
                value, type(value).__name__
            )
        )
    self._shipping_weight = value
```

Testing `_set_description` also requires one additional new value list to test bad values with; a description can be any string value, as it's currently implemented, and there are no bad value lists that adequately capture bad values for that yet:

```
BadDescriptions = [
    # Values that aren't strings at all
    1, True, 0, False, object(),
    # empty and whitespace-only strings
    '', '   ',
]
```

Unit testing BaseOrder

Unit testing `BaseOrder`, according to the coverage test, is only going to be concerned with testing the `customer` property and whatever methods interact with that property. This is because `BaseOrder` inherits from `HasProducts`. Since none of the members of `HasProducts` have been overridden in `BaseOrder`, they are still owned by `HasProducts`, and have been tested accordingly already:

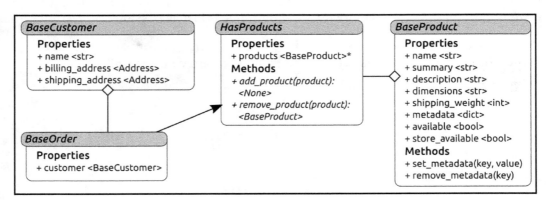

Like the testing processes for `BaseProduct` and `HasProducts`, testing `BaseOrder` requires the creation of a throwaway derived class that can be used to test method members. Since `BaseOrder` also expects a customer instance to be provided during object construction, we'll also need to create a `BaseCustomer` derived class to provide such an object, and good and bad customer values to test with:

```
class BaseCustomerDerived(BaseCustomer):
    pass

GoodCustomers = [
    BaseCustomerDerived('customer name', Address('street-address',
'city'))
]
BadCustomers = [
    '', 'string', 1, 0, True, False, 1.0, 0.0, object(), [],
]
```

The `BaseCustomerDerived` class doesn't have to implement anything, since `BaseCustomer` itself has no abstract members, which raises an interesting thought: if it doesn't have any abstract members, why did we define it as an abstract class to begin with? The original thought behind that decision was that Customer objects are expected to vary significantly in what they can do, and perhaps what data access is allowed across the different components of the system.

That expectation hasn't changed since our initial implementation, so it still feels valid. At the same time, it would be possible to create an actual instance of `BaseCustomer`, simply because it has no abstract members defined, and that has at least some potential to introduce bugs somewhere down the line; if we believe that `BaseCustomer` really is abstract, even though it provides no abstract members, creating a concrete instance of it shouldn't be allowed. That, at least, can be managed, though doing so may feel a bit awkward, by adding a few lines to the `__init__` method of `BaseCustomer`:

```
def __init__(self,
    name:(str,), billing_address:(Address,),
    shipping_address:(Address,None)=None
):

    # ...

    # - Prevent a direct instantiation of this class - it's
    #     intended to be abstract, even though it has no
    #     explicitly-abstract members:
    if self.__class__ == BaseCustomer:
```

```
        raise NotImplementedError(
            'BaseCustomer is intended to be an abstract class, '
            'even though it does not have any explicitly '
            'abstract members, and should not be instantiated.'
        )
```

That, essentially, checks the class type of the object being created, and raises
a NotImplementedError if the object being created is an instance of the abstract
class itself. We'll have to remember to test that when we write
the test__init__ method for that class, so it's worth noting that in the test
method now, so that it doesn't get lost later on:

```
def test__init__(self):
    # Tests the __init__ method of the BaseCustomer class
    # - Test to make sure that BaseCustomer can't be
    #   instantiated on its own!
    # - Test all permutations of "good" argument-values:
    # - Test all permutations of each "bad" argument-value
    #   set against "good" values for the other arguments:
    self.fail('test__init__ is not yet implemented')
```

That aside, the creation of a BaseCustomerDerived class
and GoodCustomers and BadCustomers value lists to test with allows the test-
structures for all of the testBaseOrder test case class to follow the usual patterns
that have been in play so far.

Unit-testing BaseCustomer

All of the property getter, setter, and deleter method tests for BaseCustomer follow
the typical pattern, though the test_object created is usually better handled by
creating individual instances in each test. Doing otherwise leads, pretty quickly, to
one test making changes to a common object that made other tests fail, and creating
individual test objects for each test solves that neatly:

```
test_object = BaseCustomer(
    'customer name', Address('street-address', 'city')
)
```

The test for __init__, which needed to explicitly test whether
a BaseCustomer object could be created, as noted earlier, is still pretty typical of the
test structure established in previous test case classes, even with that addition:

```
def test__init__(self):
# Tests the __init__ method of the BaseCustomer class
# - BaseCustomer is an abstract class, but has no abstract
#   members, so this was set up to keep it from being
#   accidentally used in an inappropriate fashion
    try:
        test_object = BaseCustomer(
        'customer name', Address('street-address', 'city')
        )
        self.fail(
            'BaseCustomer is expected to raise '
            'NotImplementedError if instantiated directly, '
                'but did not do so'
        )
    except NotImplementedError:
            pass
```

The balance of the test method is what would be expected from previous tests, iterating over a relevant set of good values and asserting that they carry through to the properties as expected upon instantiation:

```
# - Test all permutations of "good" argument-values:
    for name in GoodStandardRequiredTextLines:
        for billing_address in GoodAddresses:
            # - Testing without a shipping-address first
            test_object = BaseCustomerDerived(
                name, billing_address
            )
            self.assertEqual(test_object.name, name)
            self.assertEqual(
                test_object.billing_address,
                billing_address
            )
            for shipping_address in GoodAddresses:
                test_object = BaseCustomerDerived(
                    name, billing_address,
                    shipping_address
            )
             self.assertEqual(
                test_object.shipping_address,
                shipping_address
            )
```

Unit testing BaseArtisan

At this point, we've got established patterns that should be used for all of the tests to execute against `BaseArtisan`:

- It's an abstract class, so we need to create a derived class for testing purposes (`BaseArtisanDerived`)
- All of the property getter, setter, and deleter methods follow one of the patterns already established:
  - All of the getter and deleter method tests are standard
  - `address` is almost a direct copy of the tests for billing and shipping address properties in `BaseCustomer`, and uses the same `GoodAddresses`/`BadAddresses` value lists
  - `company_name` is a standard optional text line test, like many of the other properties we've tested already
  - The `contact_email` and `website` setter methods are also follow the standard pattern, though they need new good and bad value lists to test against
  - `contact_name` is a standard required text line property, and is tested like all of the other such properties

The following demonstrates examples of good and bad value lists:

```
GoodEmails = [
    'someone@somewhere.com',
    'brian.allbee+hosewp@gmail.com',
]
BadEmails = [
    '', 'string', -1, -1.0, object(), 'true', '', (1,2), tuple()
]
GoodURLs = [
    'http://www.google.com',
    'https://www.google.com',
]
BadURLs = [
    '', 'string', -1, -1.0, object(), 'true', '', (1,2), tuple()
]
```

The testing of `BaseArtisan`, however, revealed that there was no `website` argument provided in the __init__ method, nor any support for passing a `website` along to an object during construction, so that was altered accordingly:

```python
def __init__(self,
    contact_name:str, contact_email:str,
    address:Address, company_name:str=None,
    website:(str,)=None,
    **products
    ):

    # ...

    # - Call parent initializers if needed
    HasProducts.__init__(self, *products)
    # - Set default instance property-values using _del_... methods
    self._del_address()
    self._del_company_name()
    self._del_contact_email()
    self._del_contact_name()
    self._del_website()
    # - Set instance property-values from arguments using
    #   _set_... methods
    self._set_contact_name(contact_name)
    self._set_contact_email(contact_email)
    self._set_address(address)
    if company_name:
        self._set_company_name(company_name)
    if website:
        self._set_website(website)
```

And that, finally, completes all of the 118 tests for the first module of the system:

```
##############################################################################
Unit-test results
##############################################################################
Tests were successful ..... True
Number of tests run ....... 118
 + Tests ran in .......... 0.85 seconds
Number of errors ......... 0
Number of failures ........ 0
Number of tests skipped ... 0
##############################################################################
```

Unit testing patterns established so far

There's been a lot of exploration of the unit testing of the first module in the system, and that exploration has established some patterns that will appear frequently in unit testing of the other system code as it is written, so they will not be re-examined in any significant detail from this point on unless there's a significant new aspect to them.

Those patterns are as follows:

- Iteration over good and bad value lists that are meaningful as values for the member being tested:
    - Standard optional text line values
    - Standard required text line values
    - Boolean (and numeric equivalent) values
    - Metadata values
    - Non-negative numeric values (for weight values, in this case)
- Verifying property method associations—getter methods in every case so far, and setter and deleter methods where they are expected
- Verifying that getter methods retrieve their underlying storage attribute values
- Verifying that deleter methods reset their underlying storage attribute values as expected
- Verifying that setter methods enforce type and value checks as expected
- Verifying that initialization methods (`__init__`) call all of the deleter and setter methods as expected

Distribution and installation considerations

The default setup.py, with the package name for hms_core added and comments removed, is very basic but still provides all that's needed to build a deployable Python package of the hms_core code base so far. It also provides the ability to execute all of the unit tests that've been created for the package, given the path that they reside in, and the ability to find the unit testing extensions that were put in play:

```python
#!/usr/bin/env python

# - Provide an import-path for the unit-testing standards we're using:
import sys
sys.path.append('../standards')

# - Standard setup.py import and structure
from setuptools import setup

# The actual setup function call:
setup(
    name='HMS-Core',
    version='0.1.dev0',
    author='Brian D. Allbee',
    description='',
    package_dir={
        '':'src',
    },
    packages=[
        'hms_core',
    ],
    test_suite='tests.test_hms_core',
)
```

Execute the following:

```
python setup.py test
```

This will execute the entire test suite living in the `tests/test_hms_core` directory of the project:

```
python setup.py test
running test
running egg_info
writing top-level names to src/HMS_Core.egg-info/top_level.txt
writing src/HMS_Core.egg-info/PKG-INFO
writing dependency_links to src/HMS_Core.egg-info/dependency_links.txt
reading manifest file 'src/HMS_Core.egg-info/SOURCES.txt'
writing manifest file 'src/HMS_Core.egg-info/SOURCES.txt'
running build_ext
testCodeCoverage (idic.unit_testing.ModuleCoverageTest) ... ok
testMethodCoverage (tests.test_hms_core.testAddress) ... ok
testPropertyCoverage (tests.test_hms_core.testAddress) ... ok

# ... There are a LOT of other tests in this output ...
# ... removed for brevity

testproducts (tests.test_hms_core.testHasProducts) ... ok
testCodeCoverage (tests.test_hms_core.testhms_coreCodeCoverage) ... ok


----------------------------------------------------------------------
Ran 119 tests in 0.843s

OK
```

Executing the following:

```
python setup.py sdist
```

This will create a source distribution of the package, which can then be installed with the following:

```
pip install HMS-Core-0.1.dev0.tar.gz
```

This can be done from a Terminal session in the directory that the package file lives in.

The setup.py build process will, at this point, raise a few errors, but none of them will prevent the package from being built, or from being installed:

- warning: sdist: standard file not found: should have one of README, README.rst, README.txt

- warning: check: missing required meta-data: url

- warning: check: missing meta-data: if 'author' supplied, 'author_email' must be supplied too

Once installed, the hms_core package can be used just like any other Python package:

```
$ python
Python 3.5.2 (default, Nov 23 2017, 16:37:01)
[GCC 5.4.0 20160609] on linux
Type "help", "copyright", "credits" or "license" for more information.
>>> import hms_core
>>> dir(hms_core)
[
    'Address', 'BaseArtisan', 'BaseCustomer', 'BaseOrder', 'BaseProduct',
    'EMAIL_CHECK', 'HasProducts', 'URL_CHECK', '__all__', '__author__',
    '__builtins__', '__cached__', '__copyright__', '__doc__', '__file__',
    '__loader__', '__name__', '__package__', '__path__', '__spec__', '__status__',
    'abc', 'parseaddr', 're'
]
>>>
```

Three of the original stories in this iteration, focused on how the build and deploy processes would interact between hms_core and the other component project libraries, have not yet been addressed:

- As an Artisan, I need the business objects library to be installed with my application so that the application will work as needed without me having to install dependent components of it
- As a Central Office user, I need the business objects library to be installed with my application so that the application will work as needed without me having to install dependent components of it

- As a System Administrator I need the business objects library to be installed with the Artisan gateway service so that it will work as needed without me having to install dependent components of it

At this point, because we don't have any other libraries to test with, they realistically cannot be executed against—we'll have to wait for the actual implementation of at least one of the installables' packages before these can be addressed, so they'll go back into the backlog and be picked up when they can actually be worked on.

Quality assurance and acceptance

Since the functionality this library provides is foundational—intended to be consumed by other libraries—there isn't really much in the way of public facing capabilities that could be usefully tested in a formal **Quality Assurance (QA)** process. If such a formal QA process were involved in this iteration, about the most that could be done would be to execute the unit test suite and verify that those tests execute without failures or errors.

Similarly, since the bulk of the stories involved in the iteration were for the benefit of developers, there would be little external acceptance needed; the fact that the various classes in the library exist and function as expected should be sufficient for acceptance of those stories:

- As a developer, I need a common definition and functional structure to represent addresses in the system, so that I can incorporate them into the parts of the system that need them
- As a developer, I need a common definition and functional structure to represent artisans in the system, so that I can incorporate them into the parts of the system that need them
- As a developer, I need a common definition and functional structure to represent customers in the system, so that I can incorporate them into the parts of the system that need them
- As a developer, I need a common definition and functional structure to represent orders in the system, so that I can incorporate them into the parts of the system that need them
- As a developer, I need a common definition and functional structure to represent products in the system, so that I can incorporate them into the parts of the system that need them

The stories focused on installation are in something of an odd state at this point—they were specifically concerned with a single installable package for all the various end users, which is currently the case, but there will be more functionality in other libraries as development progresses. As things stand right now, an argument could be made that these stories meet all the stated requirements, if only because there is only one component installation:

- As an Artisan, I need the business objects library to be installed with my application so that the application will work as needed without me having to install dependent components of it
- As a Central Office user, I need the business objects library to be installed with my application so that the application will work as needed without me having to install dependent components of it
- As a System Administrator, I need the business objects library to be installed with the Artisan Gateway service so that it will work as needed without me having to install the dependent components of it

It could also be argued that these stories, though they are complete here and now, will have to be repeated in the development cycles for the various application and service components that are still to be built. Until those components have their own code, builds, and packages, there are no dependencies that need to be dealt with.

Operation/use, maintenance, and decommissioning considerations

Given how simple this package is, and that it has no external dependencies, there are no obvious considerations or items of even potential concern with regards to the operation and use of the package, or of decommissioning it. In the latter case, decommissioning would be nothing more than uninstalling the package (`pip uninstall HMS-Core`). Maintenance considerations would be similarly limited to updates of the package itself, which would be managed by simply rerunning the original installation process with a new package file.

Summary

This iteration has defined basic business objects representing significant functional aspects of the system, which represent the data elements of the final system. None of them do any more than provide the basic structure and some business rules around what constitutes a valid structure of those elements, though—There is, as yet, no mechanism for storing those elements, retrieving them or interacting with them, except through their properties, directly in code.

The next iteration chapter will start looking in depth at what is required to provide the storage and state data persistence that the system's applications and service layer will require.

Thinking About Business Object Data Persistence

9

It's a given that most programs and systems have a need to store and retrieve data to operate with. The alternative, embedding data into the code itself, is simply not practical, after all. The specific shape of the data storage involved can vary wildly, based on the underlying storage mechanism, the specific needs of an application or service, and even on nominally non-technical constraints such as the need to not require end users to install other software, but the fundamental need remains the same, no matter what those factors add up to.

The various component projects/sub-systems of hms_sys are no exception to this:

- The **Artisan Application** will need to allow **Artisan** users to manage the **products** that the **Artisan** is creating and selling, and to manage at least some of their own business entity data
- The **Artisan Gateway** service will probably need to at least stage data for **artisans**, **products**, and **orders**, with associated **Customer** and **Address** objects, as the data those objects contain moves through various processes
- The **Central Office Application** will need to be able to manage parts of **Artisan** and **Product** data, and may need to read order data, if only for troubleshooting purposes

So far, no specific requirements exist for how this data is going to be persisted, or even where, though it's probable that the **Artisan Application** will need to keep data locally and propagate it up to or through the **Artisan Gateway**, where the **Central Office Application** will access it, as shown in the following diagram:

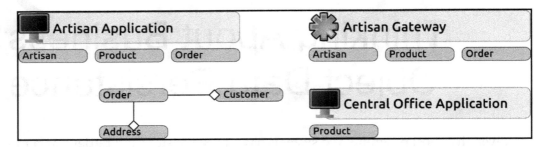

This iteration will work through the requirements, implementation, and testing of the data persistence mechanisms involved for each of the component projects in hms_sys, starting with some basic analysis of the needs and scope that is specific to each component project. However, at this point, we don't have any clear direction as to what the backend data storage even looks like, so we can't really write any stories that provide useful guidance for how to implement data persistence. Clearly, then, more investigation will be needed before planning and executing this iteration.

This chapter will examine the following topics:

- How an iterative (Agile) process usually handles stories that don't have sufficient information to execute against
- What data storage and persistence options are available, in general
- What data access strategies should be examined, before making a decision about how the various hms_sys component projects will deal with data access

Iterations are (somewhat) flexible

In many Agile methodologies, there are specific artefacts and/or processes intended to handle the kinds of scenario that this iteration is starting in—there is a need, even if it's only implied, for some functionality, but not enough information is available to actually make any development progress against that need. There might even be stories already in place that appear to be complete, but that are lacking some nuts-and-bolts details that are needed for development to progress. In this case, those stories might resemble the following:

- As an **Artisan**, I need my **Product** data to be stored locally, so that I can work with it without having to worry about connecting to an external system that I may not have ready access to at the moment
- As a **Product Manager/Approver**, I need to be able to access **Product** information across any/all **artisans** so that I can manage the availability of those products in the web store
- As a **System Administrator**, I need the **Artisan Gateway** to store **Product** and related data separate from the main **Web Store** application so that it can be safely staged before being released to the public site

All of these stories might look complete in that they are defining what needs to happen from each user's perspective, but they lack any information about how those should function.

Enter the Spike.

Spikes, which originated with the XP methodology and have been adopted (officially or otherwise) across several other Agile methodologies, are essentially stories whose purpose is to research and return usable planning details for other stories. Ideally, stories that need Spikes generated around them will be identified before they enter an iteration—if that doesn't occur, stories whose information is lacking will be unworkable, and some sort of shuffle will inevitably take place to either defer the incomplete stories until their spikes have been completed, or incorporate the spikes and their results into a revised iteration plan. The former will frequently be the more likely of the two, though, since without the information from the Spike estimating the target stories will be difficult at best, and perhaps impossible. The spike stories that relate to the original stories that we mentioned previously might be written like so:

- As a developer, I need to know how **Artisan Application** data is to be stored and retrieved so that I can write code for those processes accordingly
- As a developer, I need to know how **Central Office Application** data is to be stored and retrieved so that I can write code for those processes accordingly
- As a developer, I need to know how **Artisan Gateway** data is to be stored and retrieved so that I can write code for those processes accordingly

In order to work through and resolve these spikes, and to finalize the stories for this iteration, it'll be helpful to know what options are available. Once those have been explored, they can be weighed in the context of the applications and the service layer of the system, and some final decisions about implementation approaches can be made, along with some final stories being written to work against.

Data storage options

All of the options that will be given serious consideration have a few common properties:

- They will allow data to be stored offline, so that the application or service program doesn't need to be running constantly in order to ensure that the relevant data isn't lost
- They have to allow the applications and service to perform at least three of the four standard **CRUD** operations:
    - **Create**: Allowing data for new objects to be stored.
    - **Read**: Allowing access to data for existing objects, one at a time, all at once, and possibly with some filtering/searching capabilities.
    - **Update**: Allowing existing data to be altered when/if needed.
    - **Delete**: Allowing (perhaps) the ability to remove data for objects that are no longer relevant. At a minimum, flagging such data so that it's not generally available will work as well.

They should also be examined and evaluated in terms of **ACID** characteristics, though not all of these properties may be essential in the context of the data needs of hms_sys. None should be unachievable, however:

- **Atomicity**: Data transactions should be all or nothing, so that if part of a data-write fails, the entire dataset being written should also fail, leaving data in a stable state
- **Consistency**: Data transactions should always result in a valid data state across the entire dataset, observing and obeying any storage system rules (application-level rules are the responsibility of the applications, though)
- **Isolation**: Data transactions should always result in the same end state that would occur if their component changes were executed one at a time in the same order
- **Durability**: Data transactions should, once committed, be stored in a fashion that prevents loss due to system crashes, power-down, and so on

Relational databases

Relational Database Management Systems (**RDBMSes**) are one of the more mature data storage approaches available for applications, with options that have been in common use for decades. They typically store data as individual records (sometimes called **rows**) in tables (or relations*)* that define field names (**columns**) and types for all member records. Tables often define a primary key field that provides a unique identifier for each record in the table. A simple example of a table that defines user records might resemble the following:

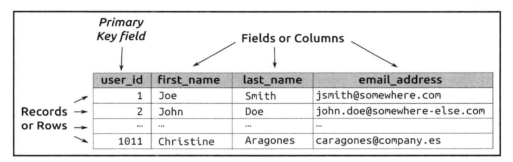

Each record in a table is, then, a consistent structure of data—all users in the preceding example would have `user_id`, `first_name`, `last_name`, and `email_address` values, though the values for the fields other than `user_id` might be empty, or `NULL`. The data from any table can be accessed or assembled through a query without having to change the tables themselves, and it's possible to join tables in a query so that, say, users in one table can be associated with records that they own in another—orders, perhaps.

 This structure is often referred to as a schema, and it both defines structure and enforces data constraints such as value type and size.

The most common query language for relational databases is the **Structured Query Language** (**SQL**)—or at least some variant of it. SQL is an ANSI standard, but there are a number of variants available. There may be others, but SQL is almost certainly the most popular option, and is very mature and stable.

 SQL is a complex enough topic in its own right, even setting aside its variations across database engines, to warrant a book of its own. We'll explore a little bit of SQL as `hms_sys` iterations progress, though, with some explanation of what is happening.

Advantages and drawbacks

One of the more significant advantages of a relational database data store is its ability to retrieve related records in a single query request—the user/orders structure mentioned earlier, for example. Most relational databases systems will also allow multiple queries to be made in a single request, and will return a collection of records for each of those queries as a single result set. The same user- and orders-table structure could, for example, be queried to return a single user and all of that user's orders, which has some advantages in application object structures where one object type has one or more collections of objects associated with them.

Another potentially significant advantage to most relational database engines is their support for transactions—allowing a potentially complex set of changes to, or insertions of data, to roll back as a whole if any single data manipulation fails for any reason. This is virtually guaranteed to be available in any SQL RDBMS, and is a very significant advantage when dealing with financial systems. Support for transactions may be a functional requirement for systems that deal with moving money around—if it isn't, it's probably worth asking why it isn't. Support for transactions that encompass multiple operations is a key aspect of full ACID compliance—without it, the atomicity, consistency, and (to some extent) isolation criteria will be suspect. Fortunately, almost any relational database system that's worthy of being called one at all will provide transaction support sufficient enough for any need likely to arise.

Many relational database systems also support the creation of views and stored procedures/functions that can make data access faster and more stable as well. Views are, for all practical purposes, predefined queries, often across multiple tables, and are often built to retrieve specific data subsets across the tables they are tied to. Stored procedures and functions can be thought of as approximate equivalents to application functions, accepting certain input, performing some set of tasks, and perhaps returning data that was generated by the execution of those tasks. At a minimum, stored procedures can be used in place of writing queries, which has some performance and security benefits.

The schema inherent to tables in most relational databases is both an advantage and a drawback, potentially. Since that schema enforces data constraints, there is less likelihood of having bad data living in a table. Fields that are expected to be string values, or integer values, will always be string or integer values, because it's simply not possible to set a string field to a non-string value. Those constraints ensure data type integrity. The trade-off for that, though, is that value types (and sometimes the values themselves) may have to be checked and/or converted when going into or coming out of the data store.

If relational databases have a downside, it's probably that the structures of the tables containing data are fixed, so making changes to those requires more time and effort, and those changes can have effects on the code that accesses them. Changing a field name in a database, for example, may well break application functionality that references that field name. Most relational database systems also require separate software installations, and server hardware that is operational at all times, like associated applications are. This may or may not be a concern for any given project, but can be a cost consideration, particularly if that server lives in someone else's infrastructure.

Scaling an RDBMS may be limited to adding more horsepower to the server itself—improving the hardware specifications, adding RAM, or moving databases to new, more powerful servers. Some of the aforementioned database engines have additional packages that can provide multi-server scale, though, such as scaling horizontally into multiple servers that still act like a single database server.

MySQL/MariaDB

MySQL is a popular RDBMS that started as an open source project in the mid 1990s. MariaDB is a community-maintained fork of MySQL, intended to serve as a drop-in replacement for MySQL, and to remain available as an open source option in case MySQL (now owned by Oracle) every ceases to be released under an open source license. MySQL and MariaDB are, at the time of writing this book, interchangeable.

Both use the same variant of SQL, with mostly trivial syntax differences from standard SQL that are typically very straightforward. MySQL is—and MariaDB is presumed to be—more optimized for reading/retrieving data than for writing it, but for many applications, those optimizations will likely not be noticeable.

MySQL and MariaDB can be horizontally scaled through the use of clustering and/or replication software additions to a base installation to meet high availability or load needs, though for this to really be effective additional servers (real or virtual) are necessary.

There are several Python libraries for connecting to and interacting with MySQL, and since MariaDB is intended to be able to directly replace MySQL, those same libraries are expected to work without modification for MariaDB access.

MS-SQL

Microsoft's SQL Server is a proprietary SQL-based DBMS, using its own variant of standard SQL (T-SQL—like MySQL's variants, the differences are generally trivial, at least for simple to somewhat complex needs).

MS-SQL also has clustering and replication options for high availability and load scenarios, with the same need for discrete servers to maximize the effectiveness of horizontal scaling.

There are at least two Python options for connecting to and working with MS-SQL databases:

- `pymssql`: This specifically leverages the **Tabular Data Stream** (**TDS**) protocol used by MS-SQL, and allows more direct connection to a backend engine
- `pyodbc`: This provides database connectivity through the **Open Database Connectivity** (**ODBC**) protocol, which Microsoft has placed its confidence in as of mid-2018

PostgresQL

PostgreSQL is another open source database option—an object-relational database system that is designed with an emphasis on standards compliance. As an ORDBMS, it allows data structures to be defined in a more object-oriented fashion, with tables that act like classes with the ability to inherit from other tables/classes. It still uses SQL—its own variant, but again, with mostly trivial differences for most development purposes—and has several Python options for connecting to and working with a database. It also has replication and clustering support, with the same sort of caveats noted for previous options.

NoSQL databases

At the time of writing, there were dozens of NoSQL database options available, both as standalone/local service installations and as cloud database options. The driving factors behind the designs of most of them include an emphasis on the following:

- **Support for massive numbers of users:** Tens of thousands of concurrent users, maybe millions—and supporting them should have as small a performance impact as possible

- **High availability and reliability:** Being able to interact with the data even if one or more database nodes were to go completely offline
- **Supporting highly fluid data structures:** Allowing structured data that isn't bound to a rigid data schema, perhaps even across records in the same data store collection

From a development perspective, the last point in this list is perhaps the most significant, allowing almost arbitrary data structures to be defined as needed.

If the concept of a table in a RDBMS is a storage model, there are a number of alternative storage models across the NoSQL database continuum:

- **Document stores:** Each record equivalent is a document containing whatever data structure it was created with. Documents are often JSON data structures, and as such allow for some differentiation between different data types—strings, numbers, and booleans as simple values, nested lists/arrays and objects for more complex data structures—and also allow for the use of a formal `null` value.

- **Key/Value stores:** Each record equivalent is simply a value, of whatever type, and is identified by a single unique key. This approach could be thought of as a database that is equivalent to a single Python `dict` structure.

- **Wide column stores:** Each record could be thought of as belonging to a RDBMS table with a very large (infinite?) number of columns available, perhaps with a primary key, or perhaps not.

There are also some variants that feel like they combine aspects of these basic models. Creating a data store in Amazon's DynamoDB, for example, starts by defining a table, which requires a key field to be defined, and allows a secondary key field to be defined as well. Once those have been created, though, the contents of those tables acts like a document store. The net result, then, act like a key/document store (a key/value store where each key points to a document).

NoSQL databases are typically non-relational, though there are exceptions to this. From a development perspective, this implies that one of at least three approaches needs to be taken into consideration when dealing with application data that is stored and retrieved from a NoSQL data store:

- Never use data that relates to other data—assure that every record contains everything it needs as a single entity. The trade-off here is that it will be difficult, if not impossible, to account for situations where a record (or the object that the record is associated with) is shared by two or more other records/objects. An example of that might be a user group that multiple users are a member of.
- Deal with the relationships between records in the code that works with those records. Using the same users/groups concept just mentioned, that might involve a `Group` object, reading all the relevant `User` records and populating a `users` property with `User` objects from that data during instantiation. There might be some risk of concurrent changes interfering with each other, but not significantly more than the same sort of process would risk in a RDBMS-backed system. This approach also implies that data will be organized by object type—a distinct collection of `User` object data and a distinct collection of `Group` object data, perhaps—but any mechanism that allows the different object types to be differentiated will work.
- Pick a backend data store engine that provides some sort of relational support.

NoSQL databases are also less likely to support transactions, though again there are options that do provide full ACID-compliant transaction capabilities, and the criteria/options for dealing with transactional requirements at the data store level are very similar to those mentioned previously, that is, dealing with relational capabilities. Even those without any transaction support are still going to be ACID-compliant for single records—at that level of complexity, all that is required to be compliant is that the record is successfully stored.

Advantages and drawbacks

Given the high availability and concurrent user focus behind most NoSQL options, it should come as no great surprise that they are better suited than their RDBMS counterparts for applications where availability and the ability to scale is important. Those properties are even more important in big data applications, and applications that live in the cloud—as evidenced by the fact that the major cloud providers all have their own offerings in that space, as well as providing starting-points for some well-known NoSQL options:

- Amazon (AWS):
    - DynamoDB
- Google:
    - Bigtable (for big data needs)
    - Datastore
- Microsoft (Azure):
    - Cosmos DB (formerly DocumentDB)
    - Azure Table Storage

The ability to more or less arbitrarily define data structures can also be a significant advantage during development, since it eliminates the need for defining database schemas and tables. The trade-off for that, potentially, at least, is that since data structures can change just as arbitrarily, code that uses them has to be written to be tolerant of those structure changes, or some sort of conscious effort may have to be planned to apply the changes to existing data items without disrupting systems and their usage.

Consider, as an example, the `User` class mentioned earlier—if a `password_hash` property needs to be added to the class, in order to provide authentication/authorization support, the instantiation code will likely have to account for it, and any existing user-object records won't have the field already. On the code side, that may not be that big a deal—making `password_hash` an optional argument during initialization would take care of allowing the objects to be created, and storing it as a null value in the data if it hasn't been set would take care of the data storage side, but some sort of mechanism would need to be planned, designed, and implemented to prompt users to supply a password in order to store the real value. The same sort of process would have to occur if a similar change were made in an RDBMS-backed system, but the odds are good enough that there would be established processes for making changes to database schemas, and those would probably include both altering the schema and assuring that all records have a known starting value.

Given the number of options available, it should also not be surprising that there are differences (sometimes significant ones) between them with respect to performing similar tasks. That is, retrieving a record from the data, given nothing more than a unique identifier for the item to be retrieved (`id_value`), uses different libraries and syntax/structure based on the engine behind the data store:

- In MongoDB (using a `connection` object):
  - `connection.find_one({'unique_id':'id_value'})`
- In Redis (using a `redis connection`):
  - `connection.get('id_value')`
- In Cassandra (using a `query` value and a `criteria` list, executing against a Cassandra `session` object):
  - `session.execute(query, criteria)`

It's quite possible that each different engine will have its own distinct methods for performing the same tasks, though there may be some common names that emerge—there are only so many alternatives for function or method names, like get or find, that make sense, after all. If a system needs to be able to work with multiple different data store backend engines, those are good candidates for designing and implementing a common (probably abstract) data store adapter.

Since relational and transactional support varies from one engine to another, this inconsistency can be a drawback to a NoSQL-based data store as well, though there are at least some options that can be pursued if they are lacking.

MongoDB

MongoDB is a free, open source, NoSQL document store engine—that is, it stores whole data structures as individual documents that are, if not JSON, very JSON-like. Data sent to and retrieved from a `MongoDB` database in Python uses Python-native data types (`dict` and `list` collections, any simple types such as `str` and `int`, and probably other standard types like `datetime` objects).

MongoDB was designed to be usable as a distributed database, supporting high availability, horizontal scaling, and geographic distribution out of the box.

Like most NoSQL data storage solutions, MongoDB is schema-less, allowing documents within a MongoDB collection (roughly equivalent to a table in an RDBMS) to have totally different structures.

Other NoSQL options

There are, as noted, dozens of NoSQL database options to pick and choose from. Three of the more popular options for locally installed NoSQL databases with Python drivers/support are as follows:

- **Redis**: A key/value store engine
- **Cassandra**: A wide-column store engine
- **Neo4j**: A graph database

Other data storage options

Another option—one that is probably not going to work well for large quantities of data, or under significant concurrent user-load—is simply to store application data locally as one to many files on the local machine. With the advent of simple structured data representation formats such as JSON, this can be a better option than it might seem at first glance, at least for certain needs: JSON, in particular, with its basic value-type support and the ability to represent arbitrarily complex or large data structures, is a reasonable storage format.

The most significant impediment is making sure that data access has at least some degree of ACID compliance, though, as with NoSQL databases, if all transactions are single records, ACID compliance can still be counted on, for the same reason—the sheer simplicity of the transaction.

The other significant concern that would have to be addressed in using files to store application data is how the language or the underlying OS handles file locking. If either allows a file that's open for writing to be read while the write is in process or incomplete, it's just a matter of time until a read of an incomplete data file misreads the data available, then commits the bad data to the file, probably resulting in loss of data at a minimum, and perhaps breaking the entire data store in the process.

That would be bad, obviously.

Speed of access could be a concern as well, since file access is slower than access to and from data stored in memory.

That said, there are strategies that can be applied to make a local file-based data store immune to that sort of failure, provided that the data is only accessed from a single source in the code. Addressing the potential access-speed concern can also be accomplished in the same process, which would resemble the following:

- The program that uses data starts:
    - Data is read into memory from a persistent file system data store
- The program is used, and a data-access occurs:
    - Data is read from the copy in memory, and passed off to the user
- Data is altered in some fashion:
    - The alteration is noted, and the change(s) is/are committed to the file system data store before returning control to the user
- The program is shut down:
    - Before terminating, all data is checked to assure that no changes are still pending
    - If there are changes, wait for them to complete
    - If necessary, re-write all data to the file system data store

Selecting a data storage option

Looking at the logical architecture for `hms_sys`, and allowing for a local data store for the **Artisan Application** that wasn't in the original diagram, there are three databases that development needs to be concerned with:

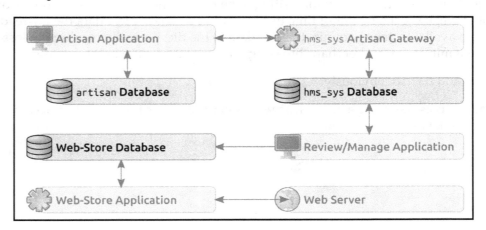

The **Web-Store Database** is attached to the **Web-Store Application**, and cannot be modified as a result. The current expectation is that modifications to data in that database will be handled by a call to the API that the **Web-Store Application** makes available. At this point, then, data access to and from this database can be set aside.

The artisan **Database**, on the other hand, doesn't exist yet at all, and will have to be created as part of the development of hms_sys. It feels safe to assume, given the artisan-level, installation-related stories from the first iteration, that keeping the number of software installations they need to perform to the minimum possible is preferable. That, in turn, suggests that a local file system data store is probably going to be the preferred option at the **Artisan Application** level. That allows for the following:

- The data store is generated locally during the installation or initial setup of the application
- The **Artisan**'s can manage their data locally, even if they are offline
- Data storage to be managed without any additional software installation on the part of the **Artisan**

Since the **Artisan Application** is expected to be a local desktop application, this fits neatly into the set of processes noted previously for making a file-based data store safe and stable. There is some risk of data conflicts if the **Artisan** has more than one **Artisan Application** installed (one each on multiple machines, for example), but that risk would exist for any local data store option, realistically—short of moving the data store to a common online database, there really isn't a way to mitigate that particular concern, and that's outside the development scope for hms_sys at present.

 The idea of centralizing data and applications alike will be examined in more detail later. For now, everything at the Artisan level will reside locally with the Artisan Application.

The hms_sys **Database** also doesn't exist at all yet. Unlike the artisan **Database**, though, it is intended to allow multiple concurrent users—any number of central office users might be reviewing or managing products at any given time as artisans are submitting product information to be reviewed, and orders relayed or pulled from the web store could be set in motion to the relevant artisans while those activities are going on, too. Taken together, these are sufficient to rule out the local file store approach—it might well still be doable, and might even be viable at current levels of usage, but could quickly run into scaling concerns if the usage/load grew too much.

Given that, even if we don't really know what backend engine will be in use, knowing that it won't be the same storage mechanism that the **Artisan Application** uses confirms the idea noted earlier that we'd be well-served to define a common data access method set, generate some sort of abstraction around that structure, and define concrete implementations at each application- or service-object level. The advantages of taking that approach really boil down to variations of the same **Object-Oriented Design Principle (OODP)**: polymorphism.

Polymorphism (and programming to an interface)

Polymorphism, in its simplest terms, is the ability for objects to be interchangeable in the code without breaking anything. In order to accomplish that, those objects must present common public interface members—the same accessible properties and methods—across the board. Ideally, those common interface members should be the only interface members as well, otherwise there is a risk of breaking the interchangeability of those objects. In a class-based structure, it's usually a good idea to have that interface defined as an individual abstraction—an ABC in Python, with or without concrete members. Consider the following collection of classes for making connections to and querying against various relational database backends:

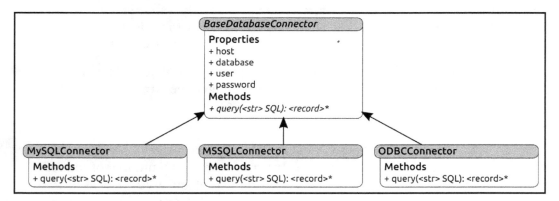

Where:

- BaseDatabaseConnector is an abstract class that requires a query method to be implemented by all derived classes, and provides host, database, user, and password properties that will be used to actually connect to a given database

- The concrete classes, `MySQLConnector`, `MSSQLConnector`, and `ODBCConnector`, each implement the required `query` method, allowing instances to actually execute queries against the database that the instance is connected to

Provided that the connection properties (`host`, ..., `password`) were stored in a configuration file (or anywhere outside the actual code itself, really), along with some way to specify which connector type to use, it wouldn't be difficult to allow those different connection types to be defined at runtime, or maybe even switched out during execution.

This interchangeability, in turn, allows code to be written that doesn't need to know anything about how a process works, just how it should be called, and what it's expected to return as a result. This is a practical illustration of the idea of programming to an interface, not to an implementation, which was mentioned in `Chapter 5`, *The hms_sys System Project,* as well as the concept of encapsulating what varies. The two often go hand-in-hand, as they do in this case.

There is another benefit to the ability to replace objects in this fashion, which might be called future-proofing a code base. If, at some time in the future, the code that uses the data connectors shown previously were suddenly in need of being able to connect to and use a database engine that wasn't available already, the level of effort to make it available would be relatively small, provided that it used the same connection arguments and a similar connection process as the ones that were already in place. All that would need to be done, for example, to create a `PostgreSQLConnector` (used to connect to a `PostgreSQL` database), would be to create the class, derive it from `BaseDatabaseConnector`, and implement the required `query` method. It would still require some development effort, but not as much as would probably be needed if each database connection process had its own distinct classes to contend with.

Data access design strategies

The last bit of analysis that we need to undertake before we can start writing out the stories for this iteration involves determining where the responsibility for object data access is going to live. In a script or another purely procedural context, it would probably suffice to simply connect to a data source, read the data from it as needed, modify it as needed, and write any changes back out again, but that would only be viable because the entire procedure would be relatively static.

In an application or service such as `hms_sys`, data use is very much a random-access scenario—there may be common procedures that might even look a lot like a simple script's step-by-step implementations, but those processes could (and will) be initiated in a fashion that may be totally unpredictable.

That, then, means that we need to have data access processes that are easily called and repeatable with minimal effort. Given that we already know that at least two different data storage mechanisms will be in play, it would also make future support and development a lot easier if we could design these processes so that the exact same method calls could be used, no matter what the underlying data store looks like—again, abstracting the processes, and allowing code to use interfaces, not implementations.

One option that would accomplish this sort of abstraction starts at the data source, making each data source aware of the object-types that are in play, and storing the information that it needs to be able to perform CRUD operations for each object-type somewhere. That's technically a workable implementation, but it will get very complicated very quickly, because each combination of data store and business object type needs to be accounted for and maintained. Even if the initial class set is limited to three data store variants (the file system data store of the **Artisan Application**, a generic RDBMS data store, and a generic NoSQL data store), that's four operations (CRUD) across three data store types for four business objects, for a total of 48 permutations ($4 \times 3 \times 4$) that have to be built, tested, and maintained. Each new operation added into the mix, such as, say, the ability to search a business object data store, as well as each new business object type to be persisted and each new data store type, increases that permutation count multiplicatively—adding one of each increases the count to 75 items ($5 \times 3 \times 5$) that have to be dealt with—which could easily get out of control.

If we take a step back and think about what we actually need for all of those combinations, a different and more manageable solution is possible. For each and every business object that needs to be persisted, we need to be able to do the following:

1. Create a record for a new object.
2. Read a record for a single object, identified somehow, and return an instance for that item.
3. Update the record for a single object after changes have been made to it.
4. Delete the record for a single object.
5. Find and return zero-to-many objects based on matches to some criteria.

It might also be useful to be able to flag objects as being in specific states—active versus inactive, and deleted (without actually deleting the underlying record), perhaps. Tracking created and/or updated dates/times is also a common practice—it's sometimes useful for sorting purposes, if nothing else.

All of the CRUD operations relate directly to the object type itself—that is, we need to be able to create, read, update, delete, and find `Artisan` objects in order to work with them. The various object properties of those instances can be retrieved and populated as needed in the context of the instance's creation, created as part of the instance's creation process, or updated with the owning instance or individually as needed. With those subordinate actions in mind, keeping track of whether an object's record needs to be created or updated will probably be useful as well. Finally, we'll need to keep track of some unique identifier for each object's state data record in the data store. Putting all of those together, the following is what a `BaseDataObject` ABC might look like:

```
┌─────────────────────────────────────────────┐
│ ╭─────────────────╮                          │
│ │ BaseDataObject   │                         │
│ ├─────────────────┴──────────────────────────┤
│ │ Properties                                  │
│ │ + oid <UUID>                                │
│ │ + created <datetime>                        │
│ │ + is_active <bool>                          │
│ │ + is_deleted <bool>                         │
│ │ + is_dirty <bool>                           │
│ │ + is_new <bool>                             │
│ │ + modified <datetime>                       │
│ │ Methods                                     │
│ │ # create()                                  │
│ │ + matches(criteria) <bool>                  │
│ │ + save()                                    │
│ │ + to_data_dict() <dict>                     │
│ │ # update()                                  │
│ │ + delete(*oids)                             │
│ │ + from_data_dict(data_dict) <object>        │
│ │ + get(*oids, **criteria) <object>*          │
│ │ + sort(objects, sort_by) <object>*          │
│ └─────────────────────────────────────────────┘
```

The properties are all concrete, with implementations baked in at the `BaseDataObject` level:

- `oid` is the unique identifier of the object, and is a `UUID` value that will be stored as, and converted from, a string during data access.

- `created` and `modified` are Python `datetime` objects, and may also need to be converted to and from string-value representations during data access.
- `is_active` is a flag that indicates whether or not a given record should be considered active, which allows for some management of active/inactive state for records and thus for objects that those records represent.
- `is_deleted` is a similar flag, indicating whether the record/object should be considered as deleted, even if it really still exists in the database.
- `is_dirty` and `is_new` are flags that keep track of whether an object's corresponding record needs to be updated (because it's been changed) or created (because it's new), respectively. They are local properties, and will not be stored in a database.

Using a `UUID` instead of a numeric sequence requires a bit more work, but has some security advantages, especially in web application and service implementations—`UUID` values are not easily predictable, and have 16^{32} possible values, making automated exploits against them much more time-consuming.

There may be requirements (or at least a desire) to not really delete records, ever. It's not unusual in certain industries, or for publicly traded companies who are required to meet certain data-audit criteria, to want to keep all data, at least for some period of time.

`BaseDataObject` defines two concrete and three abstract instance methods:

- `create` (abstract and protected) will require derived classes to implement a process for creating and writing a state data record to the relevant database.
- `matches` (concrete) will return a Boolean value if the property values of the instance that it's called from match the corresponding values of the criteria passed to it. This will be instrumental in implementing criteria-based filtering in the get method, which will be discussed shortly.
- `save` (concrete) will check the instance's `is_dirty` flag, calling the instance's `update` method and exiting if it's `True`, then check the `is_new` flag, calling the instance's `create` method if it is `True`. The net result of this is that any object deriving from `BaseDataObject` can simply be told to `save` itself, and the appropriate action will be taken, even if it's no action.

- `to_data_dict` (abstract) will return a `dict` representation of the object's state data, with values in formats and of types that can be written to the database that state data records live in.
- `update` (abstract and protected) is the update implementation counterpart to the `create` method, and is used to update an existing state data record for an object.

`BaseDataObject` also defines four class methods, all of which are abstract—each of these methods, then, is bound to the *class* itself, not to instances of the class, and must be implemented by other classes that derive from `BaseDataObject`:

- `delete` performs a physical record deletion for each record identified by the provided `*oids`.
    - `from_data_dict` returns an instance of the class, populated with the state data in the `data_dict` provided, which will usually result from a query against the database that those records live in. It's the counterpart of the `to_data_dict` method, which we already described.

- `get` is the primary mechanism for returning objects with state data retrieved from the database. It's been defined to allow both specific records (the `*oids` argument list) and filtering criteria (in the `**criteria` keyword arguments, which is expected to be the criteria argument passed to matches for each object), and will return an unsorted list of object instances according to those values.
- `sort` accepts a list of objects and sorts them using a callback function or method passed in `sort_by`.

`BaseDataObject` captures all of the functional requirements and common properties that would need to be present in order to let the business object classes and instances take responsibility for their data storage interactions. Setting aside any database engine concerns for the moment, defining a data persistence-capable business object class such as an `Artisan` in the **Artisan Application** becomes very simple—the final, concrete `Artisan` class just needs to inherit from `BaseArtisan` and `BaseDataObject`, as follows, and then implement the nine required abstract methods that are required by those parent classes:

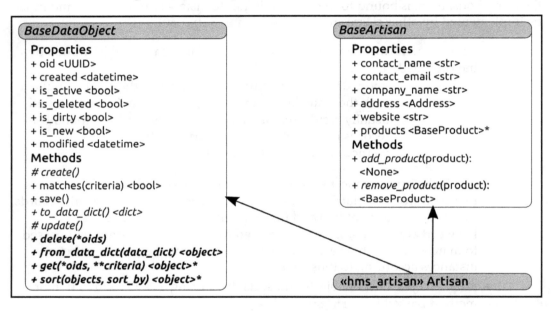

This approach would suffice if it could be safely assumed that any given application or service instance will always use the same data store backend for each business object type. Any engine-specific needs or capabilities could simply be added to each final concrete class. It would also be possible, though, to collect any properties needed by specific data store engines (MongoDB and MySQL, for example) into an additional layer of abstraction, then have the final concrete objects derive from one of those instead:

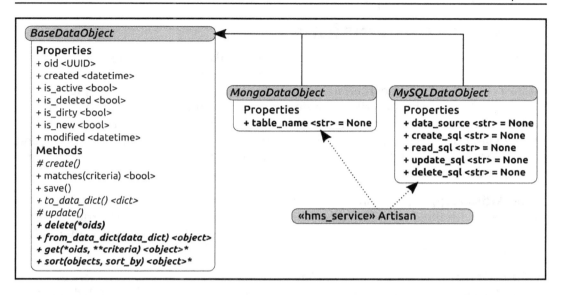

In this scenario, the final `Artisan` class could derive from either `MongoDataObject` or `MySQLDataObject`, and those could enforce the provision of any data required to execute the data access methods against those specific backend engines. Those middle-layer ABCs might also provide some helper methods for tasks that are relevant for each engine type—taking the template SQL in the `create_sql` class attribute, for example, and populating it with instance data values from `to_data_dict()` results in being able to create the final SQL for a MySQL call to create an instance. This approach would keep most of the data access information needed by any given business object class in that class, and associated with the business object itself, which doesn't feel like a bad idea, though it has the potential to get complex if a lot of combinations need to be supported. It would also keep the level of effort involved in adding adding new functionality to all data objects (at the `BaseDataObject` level of the class tree) more manageable—the addition of new abstract functionality would still require implementation in all derived concrete classes, but any concrete changes would simply be inherited and immediately available.

Data access decisions

With all of these factors in mind, then, it's time to make some decisions about how the various component projects' objects will deal with keeping track of their data. In the interests of having a single interface around all object data access, we'll implement the `BaseDataObject` ABC described previously, or something very similar to it, and derive our final data-persisting concrete classes from a combination of that ABC and the relevant business object class built in the previous iteration. Finally what we'll end up with are classes for what we'll call data objects, which are capable of reading and writing their own data.

In the **Artisan Application**, since we don't need to worry about concurrent users interacting with the data at the same time, and since we don't want to burden an **Artisan** user with additional software installations unless there's no better alternative, we'll construct a data persistence mechanism by using local files to store object data.

In the code that will be running in a Central Office context, we will have concurrent users, at least potentially, so data storage will need to be centralized in a dedicated database system. There's no discernible need for a formal, database resident schema (though having one wouldn't be a bad thing), so using a NoSQL option should allow shorter development time, and allow some flexibility in case data structures need to change unexpectedly. We'll reexamine those options in more detail when we get to that portion of the development effort.

Why start from scratch?

This functional structure is going to be built from the ground up, but there are other options that might work as well, or even better in other contexts. There are, for example, several **Object Relational Mapper** (**ORM**) packages/libraries available that would allow the definition of databases and structure to be defined in code and propagated out to a data store, some of which are integrated into full application frameworks. These include Django's `models` module, which is part of the overall Django web application framework, a common and popular option for developing web applications. Other variants include SQLAlchemy, providing an abstraction layer over SQL operations and an ORM to work with an object's data.

There are also specific driver libraries for several database options (SQL and NoSQL both), some of which may provide ORM functionality, but all of which provide at least the basic capability to connect to a data source and execute queries or perform operations against those data sources. It's quite possible to write code that simply executes SQL against an RDBMS such as MySQL or MariaDB, or executes functions that correspond to that SQL against a NoSQL engine like MongoDB or even cloud-resident data stores such as Amazon's DynamoDB. For simple applications, that may actually be a better approach, at least initially. It would keep the development time down, since the various abstraction layers that we've explored so far simply wouldn't be in the picture at all, and the code itself would have a certain type of simplicity, since all it would need to do is execute basic CRUD operations, and maybe not even all of those.

The data objects structure that is being developed for `hms_sys` will expose a lot of the underlying principles that go into the design of a data access framework, and that's part of the reason that the from-the-ground-up approach it entails was selected. Another reason is that, because it will live somewhere between a full-on ORM approach and the a low-level "execute a query against a connection" implementation strategy, it will show a lot of the relevant aspects of both of those approaches.

Summary

There are a lot of options available for data access mechanisms and processes, and while there will occasionally be requirements in play that more or less mandate one of them over the others, there may not be a single right approach across all development efforts. In particular, if time is of the essence, looking for an off-the-shelf solution is probably a good place to start, but if requirements or other constraints don't allow for one of those to be easily applied, creating a custom solution is not out of the question either.

The logical starting point, before getting into the weeds with specific data storage mechanisms, is probably to define the abstraction layer over the collective data access needs— that is, defining the `BaseDataObject` ABC—so that's what we'll tackle next.

10
Data Persistence and BaseDataObject

This chapter will focus exclusively on the development and testing of the `BaseDataObject` ABC (Abstract Base Class), which we'll need in both the `hms_artisan` (**Artisan Application**) and `hms_gateway` (**Artisan Gateway** service) component projects. It is possible that the `hms_co` (**Central Office Application**) code base will also need to utilize the same functionality. We'll look at that in some depth later, while working through the `hms_co` code.

At present, we're expecting `BaseDataObject` to look something like this:

```
┌─────────────────────────────────────────────┐
│ BaseDataObject                               │
├─────────────────────────────────────────────┤
│ Properties                                   │
│ + oid <UUID>                                 │
│ + created <datetime>                         │
│ + is_active <bool>                           │
│ + is_deleted <bool>                          │
│ + is_dirty <bool>                            │
│ + is_new <bool>                              │
│ + modified <datetime>                        │
│ Methods                                      │
│ # create()                                   │
│ + matches(criteria) <bool>                   │
│ + save()                                     │
│ + to_data_dict() <dict>                      │
│ # update()                                   │
│ + delete(*oids)                              │
│ + from_data_dict(data_dict) <object>         │
│ + get(*oids, **criteria) <object>*           │
│ + sort(objects, sort_by) <object>*           │
└─────────────────────────────────────────────┘
```

The story that drives the design and implementation of the `BaseDataObject` that was described earlier is as follows:

- As a developer, I need a common structure for providing persistence of state data for business objects that are available across the entire system so that I can build the relevant final classes

`BaseDataObject` is not functionally related to the business object definitions in `hms_core`, but the functionality it provides still needs to be available to all of the real code bases – the ones for the applications and the **Artisan Gateway** service – it makes sense that it should live in the `hms_core` package, but perhaps not with the business object definitions from the previous iteration. In the long run, it will be easier to understand and maintain the `hms_core` package if its various members are organized into modules that group elements into common purposes or themes. Before the end of this iteration, the current `hms_core.__init__.py` module will be renamed to something more indicative of the purposes it serves, and it will live next to a new module that will contain all of the data objects' classes and functionality: `data_object.py`.

There are two additional stories that relate to the structure of `BaseDataObject` and capabilities, whose needs will be noted as they are met during the development of the class:

- As any data consumer, I need to be able to create, read, update and delete individual data objects, so that I can perform basic data management tasks against those objects.
- As any data consumer, I need to be able to search for specific data objects so that I can then work with the resulting items found.

The BaseDataObject ABC

The bulk of the properties of `BaseDataObject` are Boolean values, flags that indicate whether an instance of the class is in a specific state. The implementations of those properties all follow a simple pattern that's already been shown in the definition of the `available` property of `BaseProduct` in the previous iteration. That structure looks like this:

```
#####################################
# Property-getter methods           #
#####################################
```

```
def _get_bool_prop(self) -> (bool,):
    return self._bool_prop

####################################
# Property-setter methods          #
####################################

def _set_bool_prop(self, value:(bool,int)):
    if value not in (True, False, 1, 0):
        raise ValueError(
            '%s.bool_prop expects either a boolean value '
            '(True|False) or a direct int-value equivalent '
            '(1|0), but was passed "%s" (%s)' %
            (self.__class__.__name__, value, type(value).__name__)
        )
    if value:
        self._bool_prop = True
    else:
        self._bool_prop = False

####################################
# Property-deleter methods         #
####################################

def _del_bool_prop(self) -> None:
    self._bool_prop = False

####################################
# Instance property definitions    #
####################################

bool_prop = property(
    _get_bool_prop, _set_bool_prop, _del_bool_prop,
    'Gets sets or deletes the flag that indicates whether '
    'the instance is in a particular state'
)
```

The deleter methods behind those properties, since they are also used to set the default values for an instance during initialization, should yield specific values when the properties are deleted (calling those methods):

```
####################################
# Property-deleter methods         #
####################################

def _del_is_active(self) -> None:
    self._is_active = True
```

```
    def _del_is_deleted(self) -> None:
        self._is_deleted = False

    def _del_is_dirty(self) -> None:
        self._is_dirty = False

    def _del_is_new(self) -> None:
        self._is_new = True
```

Unless overridden by a derived class, or by a specific object creation process, any instance derived from `BaseDataObject` will start with these:

- `is_active == True`
- `is_deleted == False`
- `is_dirty == False`
- `is_new == True`

So a newly created instance will be active, not deleted, not dirty, and new , the assumption being that the process of creating a new object will usually be with the intention of saving a new, active object. If any state changes are made between the creation of the instance, those may set the `is_dirty` flag to `True` in the process, but the fact that `is_new` is `True` means that the object's record needs to be created rather than updated in the backend datastore.

The only significant deviation from that standard Boolean property structure is in the documentation of the properties themselves during their definition:

```
####################################
# Instance property definitions    #
####################################

is_active = property(
    _get_is_active, _set_is_active, _del_is_active,
    'Gets sets or deletes the flag that indicates whether '
    'the instance is considered active/available'
)
is_deleted = property(
    _get_is_deleted, _set_is_deleted, _del_is_deleted,
    'Gets sets or deletes the flag that indicates whether '
    'the instance is considered to be "deleted," and thus '
    'not generally available'
)
is_dirty = property(
    _get_is_dirty, _set_is_dirty, _del_is_dirty,
    'Gets sets or deletes the flag that indicates whether '
```

```
        'the instance\'s state-data has been changed such that '
        'its record needs to be updated'
    )
    is_new = property(
        _get_is_new, _set_is_new, _del_is_new,
        'Gets sets or deletes the flag that indicates whether '
        'the instance needs to have a state-data record created'
    )
```

Two of the properties of `BaseDataObject`, `created` and `modified`, are shown in the class diagram as `datetime` values – objects that represent a specific time of day on a specific date. A `datetime` object stores the year, month, day, hour, minute, second, and microsecond of a date/time, and provides several conveniences over, say, working with an equivalent value that is managed strictly as a timestamp number value, or a string representation of a date/time. One of those conveniences is the ability to parse a value from a string, allowing the `_set_created` and `_set_modified` setter methods behind the property to accept a string value instead of requiring an actual `datetime`.

Similarly, `datetime` provides the ability to create a `datetime` instance from a timestamp – the number of seconds elapsed from a common starting date/time. In order to fully support all those argument types, it's necessary to define a common format string that will be used to parse the `datetime` values from strings and to format them into strings. That value, at least for now, feels like it's probably best stored as a class attribute on `BaseDataObject` itself. That way, all classes that derive from it will have the same value available by default:

```
class BaseDataObject(metaclass=abc.ABCMeta):
    """
Provides baseline functionality, interface requirements, and
type-identity for objects that can persist their state-data in
any of several back-end data-stores.
    """

    ####################################
    # Class attributes/constants       #
    ####################################

    _data_time_string = '%Y-%m-%d %H:%M:%S'
```

The setter methods are somewhat longer than most, since they are dealing with four different viable value types, though there are only two subprocesses required to cover all of those variations. The setter process starts by type checking the supplied value and confirming that it's one of the accepted types first:

```
def _set_created(self, value:(datetime,str,float,int)):
    if type(value) not in (datetime,str,float,int):
```

```
        raise TypeError(
            '%s.created expects a datetime value, a numeric '
            'value (float or int) that can be converted to '
            'one, or a string value of the format "%s" that '
            'can be parsed into one, but was passed '
            '"%s" (%s)' %
            (
                self.__class__.__name__,
                self.__class__._data_time_string, value,
                type(value).__name__,
            )
        )
```

Handling either of the numeric types that are legitimate is fairly straightforward. If an error is detected, we should provide more specific messaging around the nature of the encountered problem:

```
if type(value) in (int, float):
    # - A numeric value was passed, so create a new
    #   value from it
    try:
        value = datetime.fromtimestamp(value)
    except Exception as error:
        raise ValueError(
            '%s.created could not create a valid datetime '
            'object from the value provided, "%s" (%s) due '
            'to an error - %s: %s' %
            (
                self.__class__.__name__, value,
                type(value).__name__,
                error.__class__.__name__, error
            )
        )
```

The subprocess for handling string values is similar, apart from its call to datetime.strptime instead of datetime.fromtimestamp, and its use of the _data_time_string class attribute to define what a valid date/time string looks like:

```
elif type(value) == str:
    # - A string value was passed, so create a new value
    #   by parsing it with the standard format
    try:
        value = datetime.strptime(
        value, self.__class__._data_time_string
        )
    except Exception as error:
```

```
raise ValueError(
    '%s.created could not parse a valid datetime '
    'object using "%s" from the value provided, '
    '"%s" (%s) due to an error - %s: %s' %
    (
        self.__class__.__name__,
        self.__class__._data_time_string,
        value, type(value).__name__,
        error.__class__.__name__, error
    )
)
```

If the original value was an instance of datetime, then neither of the previous subprocesses would have executed. If either of them executed, then the original value argument will have been replaced with a datetime instance. In either case, that value can be stored in the underlying property attribute:

```
# - If this point is reached without error,then we have a
#   well-formed datetime object, so store it
self._created = value
```

For the purposes of BaseDataObject,
both created and modified should always have a value, and if one isn't available when it's needed – generally only when a data object's state data record is being saved – one should be created then and there for the current value, which can be accomplished in the getter method with datetime.now():

```
def _get_created(self) -> datetime:
    if self._created == None:
        self.created = datetime.now()
    return self._created
```

That, in turn, implies that the deleter method should set the property storage attribute's value to None:

```
def _del_created(self) -> None:
    self._created = None
```

The corresponding property definitions are standard, except that
the created property doesn't allow deletion directly; it makes no sense to allow an object to delete its own created date/time:

```
###################################
# Instance property definitions   #
###################################
```

```
created = property(
    _get_created, _set_created, None,
    'Gets, sets or deletes the date-time that the state-data '
    'record of the instance was created'
)

# ...

modified = property(
    _get_modified, _set_modified, _del_modified,
    'Gets, sets or deletes the date-time that the state-data '
    'record of the instance was last modified'
)
```

The last property of `BaseDataObject` is, perhaps, the most critical `oid`, which is intended to uniquely identify the state data record for a given data object. That property is defined as a **Universally Unique Identifier (UUID)** value, which Python provides in its `uuid` library. There are at least two advantages to using a UUID as a unique identifier instead of some of the more traditional approaches, such as a serial record number:

- **UUIDs are not dependent on a database operation's success to be available:** They can be generated in code, without having to worry about waiting for a SQL INSERT to complete, for example, or whatever corresponding mechanism might be available in a NoSQL data store. That means fewer database operations, and probably simpler ones as well, which makes things easier.

- **UUIDs are not easily predictable:** A UUID is a series of 32 hexadecimal digits (with some dashes separating them into sections that are not relevant for this discussion), such as `ad6e3d5c-46cb-4547-9971-5627e6b3039a`. If they are generated with any of several standard functions provided by the `uuid` library, their sequence, if not truly random, is at least random enough to make finding a given value very difficult for a malicious user, with 3.4×10^{34} possible values to look for (16 values per hex digit, 31 digits because one is reserved).

The unpredictability of UUIDs is especially useful in applications that have data accessible over the internet. Identification of records by sequential numbering makes it *much* easier for malicious processes to hit an API of some sort and just retrieve each record in sequence, all else being equal.

There are some caveats, though:

- Not all database engines will recognize UUID objects as viable field types. That can be managed by storing actual UUID values in the data objects, but writing and reading string representations of those values to and from the database.
- There may be very slight performance impacts on database operations that use UUIDs as unique identifiers as well, especially if a string representation is used instead of the actual value.
- Their inherent unpredictability can make legitimate examination of data difficult if there aren't other identifying criteria that can be used – human-meaningful data values that can be queried against (against other identifying criteria).

Even setting the advantages aside, `BaseDataObject` will use UUIDs for object identity (the `oid` property) because of a combination of requirements and expected implementations:

- The **Artisan Application** won't have a real database behind it. It'll probably end up being a simple, local document store so the generation of a unique identifier for any given data object must be something that's self-contained and not reliant on anything other than the application's code base.

- The same `oid` values need to propagate to and from the **Artisan Application** and the **Artisan Gateway** service. Trying to coordinate identities across any number of artisans could lead, very quickly, to identity collisions, and mitigating that would probably require more work (maybe a lot more) without making significant changes to the requirements of the system, or at least how the various installables in the system interact. The likelihood of collisions between any two randomly-generated UUIDs is extremely low (if not impossible for all practical purposes), simply because of the number of possible values involved.

Implementation of the `oid` property will follow a pattern similar to the one established for the ones based on `datetime`. The getter method will create one on demand, the setter method will accept `UUID` objects or string representations of it and create actual `UUID` objects internally, and the deleter method will set the current storage value to `None`:

```python
def _get_oid(self) -> UUID:
    if self._oid == None:
        self._oid = uuid4()
    return self._oid

# ...

def _set_oid(self, value:(UUID,str)):
    if type(value) not in (UUID,str):
        raise TypeError(
            '%s.oid expects a UUID value, or string '
            'representation of one, but was passed "%s" (%s)' %
            (self.__class__.__name__, value, type(value).__name__)
        )
    if type(value) == str:
        try:
            value = UUID(value)
        except Exception as error:
            raise ValueError(
                '%s.oid could not create a valid UUID from '
                'the provided string "%s" because of an error '
                '%s: %s' %
                (
                    self.__class__.__name__, value,
                    error.__class__.__name__, error
                )
            )
    self._oid = value

# ...

def _del_oid(self) -> None:
    self._oid = None
```

Most of the methods of `BaseDataObject` are abstract, including all of the class methods. None of them has any concrete implementations that might be reused in derived classes, so they are all very basic definitions:

```python
###################################
# Abstract methods                #
###################################
```

```python
    @abc.abstractmethod
    def _create(self) -> None:
        """
Creates a new state-data record for the instance in the back-end
data-store
        """
        raise NotImplementedError(
            '%s has not implemented _create, as required by '
            'BaseDataObject' % (self.__class__.__name__)
        )

    @abc.abstractmethod
    def to_data_dict(self) -> (dict,):
        """
Returns a dictionary representation of the instance which can
be used to generate data-store records, or for criteria-matching
with the matches method.
        """
        raise NotImplementedError(
            '%s has not implemented _create, as required by '
            'BaseDataObject' % (self.__class__.__name__)
        )

    @abc.abstractmethod
    def _update(self) -> None:
        """
Updates an existing state-data record for the instance in the
back-end data-store
        """
        raise NotImplementedError(
            '%s has not implemented _update, as required by '
            'BaseDataObject' % (self.__class__.__name__)
        )

    ###################################
    # Class methods                   #
    ###################################

    @abc.abstractclassmethod
    def delete(cls, *oids):
        """
Performs an ACTUAL record deletion from the back-end data-store
of all records whose unique identifiers have been provided
        """
        raise NotImplementedError(
            '%s.delete (a class method) has not been implemented, '
            'as required by BaseDataObject' % (cls.__name__)
        )
```

```
        @abc.abstractclassmethod
        def from_data_dict(cls, data_dict:(dict,)):
            """
Creates and returns an instance of the class whose state-data has
been populate with values from the provided data_dict
    """
            raise NotImplementedError(
                '%s.from_data_dict (a class method) has not been '
                'implemented, as required by BaseDataObject' %
                (cls.__name__)
            )


        @abc.abstractclassmethod
        def get(cls, *oids, **criteria):
            """
Finds and returns all instances of the class from the back-end
data-store whose oids are provided and/or that match the supplied
criteria
    """
            raise NotImplementedError(
                '%s.get (a class method) has not been implemented, '
                'as required by BaseDataObject' % (cls.__name__)
            )
```

The to_data_dict instance method and the from_data_dict class method are
intended to provide mechanisms to represent an instance's complete state data as
a dict, and create an instance from such a dict representation, respectively.
The from_data_dict method should facilitate record retrieval and conversion into
actual programmatic objects across most standard RDBMS-connection libraries in
Python, especially if the field names in the database are identical to the property
names of the class. Similar usage should be viable in NoSQL data stores as well.
Though the to_data_dict method may or may not be as useful in writing records to
a data store, it will be needed to match objects based on criteria (the matches method,
which we'll get to shortly).

PEP-249, the current **Python Database API Specification,** defines an
expectation that database queries in libraries that conform to the
standards of the PEP will, at a minimum, return lists of tuples as
result sets. Most mature database connector libraries also provide a
convenience mechanism to return a list of dict record values,
where each dict maps field names as keys to the values of the source
records.

The _create and _update methods are simply requirements for the record creation and record update processes, and will eventually be called by the save method. The need for separate record creation and record update processes may not be applicable to all data store engines, though; some, especially in the NoSQL realm, already provide a single mechanism for writing a record, and simply don't care whether it already exists. Others may provide some sort of mechanism that will allow an attempt to create a new record to be made first, and if that fails (because a duplicate key is found, indicating that the record already exists), then update the existing record instead. This option is available in MySQL and MariaDB databases, but may exist elsewhere. In any of those cases, overriding the save method to use those single-point-of-contact processes may be a better option.

The delete class method is self-explanatory, and sort probably is as well.

The get method requires some examination, even without any concrete implementation. As noted earlier, it is intended to be the primary mechanism for returning objects with state data retrieved from the database, and to accept both zero-to-many object IDs (the *oids argument list) and filtering criteria (in the **criteria keyword arguments). The expectation for how the whole get process will actually work is as follows:

- If oids is not empty:

    1. Perform whatever low-level query or lookup is needed to find objects that match one of the provided oids, processing each record with from_data_dict and yielding a list of objects
    2. If criteria is not empty, filter the current list down to those objects whose matches results against the criteria are True
    3. Return the resulting list

- Otherwise, if criteria is not empty:

    - Perform whatever low-level query or lookup is needed to find objects that match one of the provided criteria values, processing each record with from_data_dict and yielding a list of objects
    - Filter the current list down to those objects whose matches results against the criteria are True
    - Return the resulting list

- Otherwise, perform whatever low-level query or lookup is needed to retrieve all available objects, again processing each record with `from_data_dict`, yielding a list of objects and simply returning them all

Taken together, the combination of the `oids` and `criteria` values will allow the `get` class method to find and return objects that do the following:

- Match one or more `oids`: `get(oid[, oid, ..., oid])`
- Match one or more `oids` and some set of `criteria`: `get(oid[, oid, ..., oid], key=value[, key=value, ..., key=value])`
- Match one or more `criteria` key/value pairs, regardless of the `oids` of the found items: `get(key=value[, key=value, ..., key=value])`
- That simply exist in the backend data store: `get()`

That leaves the `matches` and `save` methods, the only two concrete implementations in the class. The goal behind `matches` is to provide an instance-level mechanism for comparing the instance with criteria names/values, which is the process that the `criteria` in the `get` method uses and relies upon to actually find matching items. Its implementation is simpler than it might appear at first, but relies on operations against `set` objects, and on a Python built-in function that is often overlooked (`all`), so the process itself is heavily commented in the code:

```
######################################
# Instance methods                   #
######################################

def matches(self, **criteria) -> (bool,):
    """
Compares the supplied criteria with the state-data values of
the instance, and returns True if all instance properties
specified in the criteria exist and equal the values supplied.
    """
    # - First, if criteria is empty, we can save some time
    #   and simply return True - If no criteria are specified,
    #   then the object is considered to match the criteria.
    if not criteria:
        return True
    # - Next, we need to check to see if all the criteria
    #   specified even exist in the instance:
    data_dict = self.to_data_dict()
    data_keys = set(check_dict.keys())
    criteria_keys = set(criteria.keys())
```

```
# - If all criteria_keys exist in data_keys, then the
#   intersection of the two will equal criteria_keys.
#   If that's not the case, at least one key-value won't
#   match (because it doesn't exist), so return False
if criteria_keys.intersection(data_keys) != criteria_keys:
    return False
# - Next, we need to verify that values match for all
#   specified criteria
return all(
    [
        (data_dict[key] == criteria[key])
        for key in criteria_keys
    ]
)
```

The `all` function is a nice convenience it returns `True` if all of the items in the iterable it's passed evaluate to `True` (or at least true-ish, so non-empty strings, lists, tuples, and dictionaries, and non-zero numbers, would all be considered `True`). It returns `False` if any members of the iterable aren't `True`, and returns `True` if the iterable is empty. The results of `matches` will be `False` if these conditions occur:

- Any key in the `criteria` doesn't exist in the instance's `data_dict` – a criteria key that cannot be matched, essentially
- Any value specified in `criteria` doesn't exactly match its corresponding value in the instance's `data_dict`

The `save` method is very simple. It just calls the instance's `_create` or `_update` methods based on the current state of the instance's `is_new` or `is_dirty` flag properties, respectively, and resets those flags after either executes, leaving the object clean and ready for whatever might come next:

```
def save(self):
    """
Saves the instance's state-data to the back-end data-store by
creating it if the instance is new, or updating it if the
instance is dirty
    """
    if self.is_new:
        self._create()
        self._set_is_new = False
        self._set_is_dirty = False
```

```
        elif self.is_dirty:
            self._update()
            self._set_is_dirty = False
            self._set_is_new = False
```

The initialization of a `BaseDataObject` should allow values for all of its properties, but not require any of those values:

```
def __init__(self,
    oid:(UUID,str,None)=None,
    created:(datetime,str,float,int,None)=None,
    modified:(datetime,str,float,int,None)=None,
    is_active:(bool,int,None)=None,
    is_deleted:(bool,int,None)=None,
    is_dirty:(bool,int,None)=None,
    is_new:(bool,int,None)=None,
):
```

The actual initialization process follows the previously established pattern for optional arguments for all arguments in that case: calling the corresponding _del_ method for each, then calling the corresponding _set_ method for each if the argument isn't `None`. Let's use the `oid` argument as an example:

```
        # - Call parent initializers if needed
        # - Set default instance property-values using _del_...
methods

        # ...

        self._del_oid()
        # - Set instance property-values from arguments using
        #   _set_... methods
        if oid != None:
            self._set_oid(oid)

        # ...

        # - Perform any other initialization needed
```

This initializer method's signature is getting pretty long, with seven arguments (ignoring `self`, since that will always be present, and will always be the first argument). Knowing that we'll eventually define concrete classes as combinations of `BaseDataObject` and one of the business object classes defined, the signature for `__init__` on those concrete classes could get much longer, too. That, though, is part of the reason why the initialization signature of `BaseDataObject` makes all of the arguments optional. Taken in combination with one of those business object classes, `BaseArtisan`, for example, with an `__init__` signature of:

```
def __init__(self,
    contact_name:str, contact_email:str,
    address:Address, company_name:str=None,
    website:(str,)=None,
    *products
    ):
```

The combined `__init__` signature for an `Artisan` that's derived from both, while long...

```
        def __init__(self,
            contact_name:str, contact_email:str,
            address:Address, company_name:str=None,
            website:(str,)=None,
            oid:(UUID,str,None)=None,
            created:(datetime,str,float,int,None)=None,
            modified:(datetime,str,float,int,None)=None,
            is_active:(bool,int,None)=None,
            is_deleted:(bool,int,None)=None,
            is_dirty:(bool,int,None)=None,
            is_new:(bool,int,None)=None,
            *products
            ):
```

... only requires the `contact_name`, `contact_email`, and `address` arguments that `BaseArtisan` requires, and allows all of the arguments to be passed as if they were keyword arguments, like this:

```
        artisan = Artisan(
            contact_name='John Doe', contact_email='john@doe.com',
            address=my_address,
        oid='00000000-0000-0000-0000-000000000000',
            created='2001-01-01 12:34:56', modified='2001-01-01
        12:34:56'
        )
```

Allows the entire parameter set to be defined as a single dictionary and passed whole-cloth to the initializer using the same syntax that passing a keyword argument set would use:

```
artisan_parameters = {
    'contact_name':'John Doe',
    'contact_email':'john@doe.com',
    'address':my_address,
    'oid':'00000000-0000-0000-0000-000000000000',
    'created':'2001-01-01 12:34:56',
    'modified':'2001-01-01 12:34:56'
}
artisan = Artisan(**artisan_parameters)
```

That syntax for passing arguments in a dictionary using `**dictionary_name` is a common form of argument parameterization in Python, especially in functions and methods where the full collection of arguments is unreasonably long. It requires some thought and discipline on the design side of the development process, and an eye toward being very restrictive with respect to required arguments, but in the long run, it's more helpful and easier to use than might appear at first glance.

This last structure will be critical in the implementation of the `from_data_dict` methods of the various classes derived from `BaseDataObject` – in most cases, it should allow the implementation of those methods to be little more than this:

```
@classmethod
def from_data_dict(cls, data_dict):
    return cls(**data_dict)
```

Unit testing BaseDataObject

Unit testing of `BaseDataObject` is going to be... interesting, as it stands right now. Testing the `matches` method, a concrete method that depends on an abstract method (`to_data_dict`), which, in turn depends on the actual data structure (`properties`) of a derived class, is either not possible or meaningless in the context of the test case class for `BaseDataObject` itself:

- In order to test `matches`, we have to define a non-abstract class with a concrete implementation of `to_data_dict`, and some actual properties to generate that resulting `dict` from/with
- That derived class, unless it also happens to be an actual class needed in the system, has no relevance in the final system's code, so tests there do not assure us that other derived classes won't have issues in `matches`
- Even setting the testing of the `matches` method completely aside, testing `save` is similarly pointless, for much the same reason it's a concrete method that depends on methods that are, at the `BaseDataObject` level, abstract and undefined

Back when `BaseArtisan` was being implemented, we defined its `add_product` and `remove_product` methods as abstract, but still wrote usable concrete implementation code in both, in order to allow derived classes to simply call the parent's implementation. In effect, we required an implementation of both in all derived classes, but provided an implementation that could be called from within the derived class methods. The same sort of approach, applied to the `matches` and `save` methods in `BaseDataObject`, would essentially enforce testing requirements on each derived concrete class, while still permitting the use of a single implementation until or unless a need arose to override that implementation. It might feel a bit hacky, but there don't appear to be any downsides to that approach:

- The methods processed in this fashion still have to be implemented in the derived classes.
- If they need to be overridden for whatever reason, testing policies will still require them to be tested.
- If they are implemented as nothing more than a call to the parent class method, they will function and testing policy code will still recognize them as local to the derived class. Our testing policy says those are in need of a test method, and that allows test methods to execute against the specific needs and functionality of the derived class.

Testing `save` doesn't have to take that approach, however. Ultimately, all we're really concerned with as far as that method is concerned is that we can prove that it calls the `_create` and `_update` abstract methods and resets the flags. If that proof can be tested and established in the process of testing `BaseDataObject`, we won't have to test it elsewhere unless the test policy code detects an override of the method. That would, in turn, allow us to avoid having the same test code scattered across all the test cases for all of the final, concrete classes later on, which is a good thing.

Starting the unit tests for the `data_objects` module is simple enough:

1. Create a `test_data_object.py` file in the project's `test_hms_core` directory
2. Perform the two name replacements noted in the header comments
3. Add a reference to it in `__init__.py` in that same directory
4. Run the test code and go through the normal iterative test writing process

The reference to the new test module in `__init__.py` follows the structure that already exists in our unit test module template making a copy of the two lines starting with `# import child_module` in the existing code, then uncommenting them and changing `child_module` to the new test module:

```
#######################################
# Child-module test-cases to execute  #
#######################################

import test_data_objects
LocalSuite.addTests(test_data_objects.LocalSuite._tests)

# import child_module
# LocalSuite.addTests(child_module.LocalSuite._tests)
```

That addition adds all of the tests in the new `test_data_objects` module to the tests already present in the top-level `__init__.py` test module, allowing that top-level test suite to execute the child module tests:

```
###############################################################################
FAILURES
#----------------------------------------------------------------------------#
testCodeCoverage (test_data_objects.testdata_objectsCodeCoverage)
Unit-testing policies require test-cases for all classes and functions in the
hms_core.data_objects module, but the following have not been defined:
    (testBaseDataObject)
###############################################################################
Unit-test results
###############################################################################
Tests were successful ..... False
Number of tests run ....... 119
  + Tests ran in .......... 0.87 seconds
Number of errors .......... 0
Number of failures ........ 1
Number of tests skipped ... 0
###############################################################################
```

The tests in `test_data_objects.py` can also be executed independently, yielding the same failure, but without executing all of the other existing tests:

```
###############################################################################
FAILURES
#----------------------------------------------------------------------------#
Unit-testing policies require test-cases for all classes and functions in the
hms_core.data_objects module, but the following have not been defined:
    (testBaseDataObject)
###############################################################################
Unit-test results
###############################################################################
Tests were successful ..... False
Number of tests run ....... 1
  + Tests ran in .......... 0.00 seconds
Number of errors .......... 0
Number of failures ........ 1
Number of tests skipped ... 0
###############################################################################
```

The iterative process for writing unit tests for `data_objects.py` is no different than the process that was used for writing tests for the base business objects in the previous iteration: run the test module, find a test that's failing, write or modify that test, and re-run until all tests pass. Since `BaseDataObject` is an abstract class, a throwaway, derived concrete class will be needed to perform some tests against it. With the exception of the value-oriented testing of the `oid`, `created`, and `modified` properties of `BaseDataObject`, we have established patterns that cover everything else:

- Iteration over good and bad value lists that are meaningful as values for the member being tested:

    - (Not applicable yet) standard optional text-line values
    - (Not applicable yet) standard required text-line values
    - Boolean (and numeric-equivalent) values
    - (Not applicable yet) non-negative numeric values

- Verifying property method associations – getter methods in every case so far, and setter and deleter methods where they are expected
- Verifying getter methods retrieve their underlying storage attribute values
- Verifying deleter methods reset their underlying storage attribute values as expected
- Verifying that setter methods enforce type checks and value checks as expected
- Verifying that initialization methods (__init__) call all of the deleter and setter methods as expected

Those same three properties (`oid`, `created`, and `modified`), apart from not having an established test pattern already defined, share another common characteristic: all three of them will create a value if the property is requested and doesn't already have one (that is, the underlying storage attribute's value is `None`). That behavior requires some additional testing beyond the normal confirmation that the getter reads the storage attribute that the test methods start with (using `test_get_created` to illustrate):

```
def test_get_created(self):
    # Tests the _get_created method of the BaseDataObject class
    test_object = BaseDataObjectDerived()
    expected = 'expected value'
    test_object._created = expected
    actual = test_object.created
    self.assertEquals(actual, expected,
```

```
        '_get_created was expected to return "%s" (%s), but '
        'returned "%s" (%s) instead' %
        (
            expected, type(expected).__name__,
            actual, type(actual).__name__
        )
    )
```

Up to this point, the test method is pretty typical of a getter method test it sets an arbitrary value (because what's being tested is whether the getter retrieves the value, nothing more), and verifies that the result is what was set. Next, though, we force the storage attribute's value to None, and verify that the result of the getter method is an object of the appropriate type a datetime in this case:

```
    test_object._created = None
    self.assertEqual(type(test_object._get_created()), datetime,
        'BaseDataObject._get_created should return a '
        'datetime value if it\'s retrieved from an instance '
        'with an underlying None value'
    )
```

The test method for the property setter method (_set_created in this case) has to account for all of the different type variations that are legitimate for the property – datetime, int, float, and str values alike for _set_created – and set the expected value accordingly based on the input type before calling the method being tested and checking the results:

```
def test_set_created(self):
    # Tests the _set_created method of the BaseDataObject class
    test_object = BaseDataObjectDerived()
    # - Test all "good" values
    for created in GoodDateTimes:
        if type(created) == datetime:
            expected = created
        elif type(created) in (int, float):
            expected = datetime.fromtimestamp(created)
        elif type(created) == str:
            expected = datetime.strptime(
                created, BaseDataObject._data_time_string
            )
        test_object._set_created(created)
        actual = test_object.created
        self.assertEqual(
            actual, expected,
            'Setting created to "%s" (%s) should return '
            '"%s" (%s) through the property, but "%s" (%s) '
            'was returned instead' %
```

```
                    (
                        created, type(created).__name__,
                        expected, type(expected).__name__,
                        actual, type(actual).__name__,
                    )
                )
        # - Test all "bad" values
        for created in BadDateTimes:
            try:
                test_object._set_created(created)
                self.fail(
                    'BaseDataObject objects should not accept "%s" '
                    '(%s) as created values, but it was allowed to '
                    'be set' %
                    (created, type(created).__name__)
                )
            except (TypeError, ValueError):
                pass
            except Exception as error:
                self.fail(
                    'BaseDataObject objects should raise TypeError '
                    'or ValueError if passed a created value of '
                    '"%s" (%s), but %s was raised instead:\n'
                    '    %s' %
                    (
                        created, type(created).__name__,
                        error.__class__.__name__, error
                    )
                )
```

The deleter method test is structurally the same test process that we've implemented before, though:

```
def test_del_created(self):
    # Tests the _del_created method of the BaseDataObject class
    test_object = BaseDataObjectDerived()
    test_object._created = 'unexpected value'
    test_object._del_created()
    self.assertEquals(
        test_object._created, None,
        'BaseDataObject._del_created should leave None in the '
        'underlying storage attribute, but "%s" (%s) was '
        'found instead' %
        (
            test_object._created,
            type(test_object._created).__name__
        )
    )
```

The exact same structure, with `created` changed to `modified`, tests the underlying methods of the `modified` property. A very similar structure, changing names (`created` to `oid`) and expected types (`datetime` to `UUID`), serves as a starting point for the tests of the property methods for the `oid` property.

Testing `_get_oid`, then looks like this:

```
def test_get_oid(self):
    # Tests the _get_oid method of the BaseDataObject class
    test_object = BaseDataObjectDerived()
    expected = 'expected value'
    test_object._oid = expected
    actual = test_object.oid
    self.assertEquals(actual, expected,
        '_get_oid was expected to return "%s" (%s), but '
        'returned "%s" (%s) instead' %
        (
            expected, type(expected).__name__,
            actual, type(actual).__name__
        )
    )
    test_object._oid = None
    self.assertEqual(type(test_object.oid), UUID,
        'BaseDataObject._get_oid should return a UUID value '
        'if it\'s retrieved from an instance with an '
        'underlying None value'
    )
```

And testing `_set_oid` looks like this (note that the type change also has to account for a different expected type and value):

```
def test_set_oid(self):
    # Tests the _set_oid method of the BaseDataObject class
    test_object = BaseDataObjectDerived()
    # - Test all "good" values
    for oid in GoodOIDs:
        if type(oid) == UUID:
            expected = oid
        elif type(oid) == str:
            expected = UUID(oid)
        test_object._set_oid(oid)
        actual = test_object.oid
        self.assertEqual(
            actual, expected,
            'Setting oid to "%s" (%s) should return '
            '"%s" (%s) through the property, but "%s" '
            '(%s) was returned instead.' %
```

```
                    (
                        oid, type(oid).__name__,
                        expected, type(expected).__name__,
                        actual, type(actual).__name__,
                    )
                )
        # - Test all "bad" values
        for oid in BadOIDs:
            try:
                test_object._set_oid(oid)
                self.fail(
                    'BaseDatObject objects should not accept '
                    '"%s" (%s) as a valid oid, but it was '
                    'allowed to be set' %
                    (oid, type(oid).__name__)
                )
            except (TypeError, ValueError):
                pass
            except Exception as error:
                self.fail(
                    'BaseDataObject objects should raise TypeError '
                    'or ValueError if passed a value of "%s" (%s) '
                    'as an oid, but %s was raised instead:\n'
                    '    %s' %
                    (
                        oid, type(oid).__name__,
                        error.__class__.__name__, error
                    )
                )
```

With all of the data object tests complete (for now), it's a good time to move the class definitions that were living in the package header file (hms_core/__init__.py) into a module file just for them: business_objects.py. While it's purely a namespace organizational concern (since none of the classes themselves are being changed, just where they live in the package), it's one that makes a lot of sense, in the long run. With the move completed, there is a logical grouping to the classes that reside in the package:

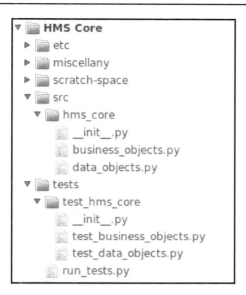

Business object definitions, and items that tie directly to those types, will all live in the `hms_core.business_objects` namespace, and can be imported from there, for example:

```
from hms_core.business_objects import BaseArtisan
```

All members of `hms_core.business_objects` could be imported, if needed, with:

```
import hms_core.business_objects
```

Similarly, functionality that relates to the data object structure that's still in development will all live in the `hms_core.data_objects` namespace:

```
from hms_core.data_objects import BaseDataObject
```

Or, again, all members of the module could be imported with:

```
import hms_core.data_objects
```

With the basic data object structure ready and tested, it's time to start implementing some concrete, data persisting business objects, starting with the ones living in the Artisan Application.

Summary

The implementation of `BaseDataObject` provides mechanisms for all of the common data access needs we identified earlier (all the CRUD operations):

- It allows derived data objects, once they've been instantiated, to create and update their state data
- It provides a single mechanism that allows one or more data objects to be read from the data store, and as a bonus allows for some degree of object retrieval based on criteria other than just the `oid` of the data objects in question
- It provides a single mechanism for the deletion of object data

The actual implementation of those methods is the responsibility of the data objects themselves, which will relate directly to the storage mechanism that each object type uses.

The data storage for the Artisan Application, reading and writing data to local files on the user's machine, is, in many respects, the simpler of the two data storage options to implement, so we'll start with that.

11
Persisting Object Data to Files

At first glance, the process of reading and writing data to and from a file system-resident data store probably looks much simpler than the equivalent processes for many database-backed storage mechanisms. Reading and writing files, after all, is a very basic process. In reality, it's a slightly more complex process, though. There are precautions that need to be taken to deal with things such as file system permissions, hard shutdowns of the application using data access, and even system crashes, to some degree. While these complicate development somewhat, they are perhaps more challenging to identify as possibilities than they are to implement safeguards around.

This chapter will cover the following:

- The basic component project setup for `hms_artisan`
- A further abstraction layer to encapsulate the file system-based data storage needs involved
- The development of data objects in the `hms_artisan` component project for the following:
  - Artisans
  - Products
  - Orders

Setting up the hms_artisan project

With all of the foundation classes we need (so far) defined in `hms_core`, we can start building out the concrete classes that correspond to them in other projects. Since the plan is for the **Artisan Application** to have a custom, local data storage mechanism, and that's likely going to be more complicated than the equivalents in the Central Office application and the Artisan Gateway service, it arguably makes the most sense to start with that project, and by creating a project structure to meet the needs of this story:

- As a developer, I need a project for the Artisan Application so that I have a place to put the relevant code and build the application.

Initially, the code for the `hms_artisan` classes could start in the `hms_artisan/__init__.py` file, just as the business object ABCs in `hms_core` started in its root `__init__.py` file, but it seems reasonable to assume that some variant of the reason why those were just moved to their own `business_objects.py` module would be likely in the Artisan Application codebase. With that in mind, we'll create an `artisan_objects.py` module to keep them grouped and organized. That will also make it easier to keep any data storage classes that we might need that aren't themselves data objects in a separate module in the same package. We could just as easily put all of the Artisan Application code into a single module (`hms_artisan.py`) instead of having a package directory and the attendant files therein. There's no functional reason for not doing so, but unless there's some certainty that there would never be a need to change from that single module file implementation to a package structure, it raises the longer-term risk of having to reorganize the entire namespace file structure. The starting project structure looks very much like the default defined in `Chapter 7`, *Setting Up Projects and Processes:*

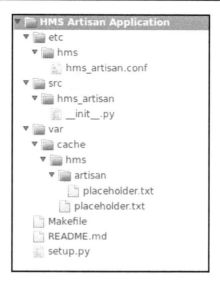

That sort of reorganization is not difficult, but it is time consuming, all the more so if unit test modules also have to be reorganized. When such a reorganization is under way, it has the potential to limit other work against a codebase by anyone who isn't part of the reorganization effort. It also has a lot of potential to make source control management very messy until it's complete, which isn't a great situation for a member of a dev team with other tasks to execute against that codebase to be in.

The odds are good that we'll want or need a separate module for the actual application anyway, though, so it just makes sense to start subdividing code into logical groupings at the outset.

Creating a local file system data store

Artisans' needs for storing data are captured in two stories:

- As an Artisan, I need a local data store for all of my system data, so that I don't have to be connected to the internet to make changes
- As an Artisan, I need my local data store to be as simple as possible, requiring no additional software installations, so that I don't have to worry about installing and maintaining a database system as well as the Artisan Application

The final relationships between the various Artisan Application data objects and `BaseDataObject` could be as simple as having each Artisan-level class derive directly from `BaseDataObject`. Indeed, if there were only one such class at the Artisan level, and no expectation of that changing in the foreseeable future, it would make a lot of sense to take that approach. The code that would handle the creation of record files, updating the data therein, reading it, or deleting it could live in a lone class. Since there are three object types that we need to be concerned with, though, there is at least some potential benefit to collecting a common functionality for file-based data stores into another abstract class that lives between `BaseDataObject` and the concrete `hms_artisan` classes, such as `hms_artisan..Artisan`:

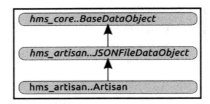

That intermediary class, `JSONFileDataObject`, would extend `BaseDataObject`, adding functionality and data that is specific to the task of managing object state data that lives in a collection of JSON-formatted files. At the same time, it would preserve the abstraction requirements from `BaseDataObject`, or provide a concrete implementation of them and make them available to classes such as `hms_artisan..Artisan`. The net benefit of this inheritance structure is that, ideally, all of the functionality necessary to perform CRUD operations against a JSON-backed data store of objects would be able to reside in one place. Realistically, some of the specifics may have to live in the concrete class implementations – otherwise, they could all be wrapped into a single class, after all – but there will almost certainly be substantial commonalities that can be implemented in that middle inheritance level.

A more complete collection of goals for any class derived from `JSONFileDataObject` would include the following, at a minimum:

- All of the stored data for any derived class should probably live in one location
- Instance data for each object type (class) should probably live in a common location within the top-level location
- Data for any given instance should probably reside in a single, distinct file, whose name can be uniquely related to the instance whose data it stores

Additionally, there are some should-have or nice-to-have functionalities that are worth considering:

- Data reading operations would be faster if the process didn't involve finding, opening, reading, and creating objects for every file every time a data read was executed. A trade-off for this is that any time data-altering operations are executed, they have to be responsible for making the appropriate alterations to whatever data is involved, in all the places it lives. If there is an in-memory collection of objects that were read from the persistent files, for example:
  - Create operations would have to add new objects to the in-memory store
  - Updates would have to write to the data-store file and update the in-memory object

  - Deletions would have to remove the relevant file and remove the appropriate object from the in-memory store

None of these are particularly difficult to implement, though.

Implementing JSONFileDataObject

Defining the JSONFileDataObject abstract class starts with a standard ABCMeta metaclass specification, and some class-level attributes for various purposes:

```
class JSONFileDataObject(BaseDataObject, metaclass=abc.ABCMeta):
    """
Provides baseline functionality, interface requirements, and
type-identity for objects that can persist their state-data as
JSON files in a local file-system file-cache
    """

    ####################################
    # Class attributes/constants       #
    ####################################

    _file_store_dir = None
    _file_store_ready = False
    _loaded_objects = None
```

Where:

- `_file_store_dir` is a default file system directory specification that will eventually need to be read from a configuration file in the final installable application. For the time being, and for unit testing purposes, it will have a hardcoded value set that can be used during development and testing, and we'll look at the configuration setup when we get to the Artisan Application's implementation.

- `_file_store_ready` is a flag value that will be used to indicate to the class whether it's loaded all of the available objects from the data files, and thus whether it needs to load them before performing any CRUD operations.

- `_loaded_objects` is where the collection of objects loaded by the class will be stored. The actual object stores will be a `dict` of object instances, but until the loading operation has completed, it's defaulted to `None` in order to make the determination between unloaded (`None`) and loaded-with-no-objects (an empty `dict`) states later on.

Since it inherits from `BaseDataObject`, the class will start with the abstraction requirements defined there, and could not be instantiated without fulfilling those requirements. However, since we want `JSONFileDataObject` to also be abstract, it also has the standard ABC metaclass specification, and is itself abstract.

The signature of the initialization method of `JSONFileDataObject` is identical to that of the `BaseDataObject` it derives from, but it performs a few additional tasks during that process:

```
#######################################
# Object initialization               #
#######################################

def __init__(self,
    oid:(UUID,str,None)=None,
    created:(datetime,str,float,int,None)=None,
    modified:(datetime,str,float,int,None)=None,
    is_active:(bool,int,None)=None,
    is_deleted:(bool,int,None)=None,
    is_dirty:(bool,int,None)=None,
    is_new:(bool,int,None)=None,
):
    """
```

```
Object initialization.

self ............. (JSONFileDataObject instance, required) The
                   instance to execute against
oid .............. (UUID|str, optional, defaults to None)
created .......... (datetime|str|float|int, optional, defaults to
None)
modified ......... (datetime|str|float|int, optional, defaults to
None)
is_active ........ (bool|int, optional, defaults to None)
is_deleted ....... (bool|int, optional, defaults to None)
is_dirty ......... (bool|int, optional, defaults to None)
is_new ........... (bool|int, optional, defaults to None)
"""
```

The first new functionality involved is checking for a non-None value for
the _file_store_dir class attribute. Since the whole point of these classes is to be
able to save object data to JSON files, and that requires a place for those files to
actually reside, not having one specified is a critical issue that would prevent any
useful execution of CRUD operations, so an error is raised if a problem is detected:

```
# - When used by a subclass, require that subclass to
#   define a valid file-system path in its _file_store_dir
#   class-attribute - that's where the JSON files will live
   if self.__class__._file_store_dir == None:
       raise AttributeError(
           '%s has not defined a file-system location to '
           'store JSON data of its instances\' data. Please '
           'set %s._file_store_dir to a valid file-system '
           'path' %
           (self.__class__.__name__, self.__class__.__name__)
       )
```

Similarly, even if the file storage location is specified, that location has to exist, and be
accessible to the code as it runs under the user's account with the attendant
permissions. Each class, then, needs to check for the location's existence (and create it
if it doesn't exist), and make sure that files can be written, read, and deleted. This
checking process could fire off every time an instance of the class is created, but if the
process has completed once already, it should be satisfactory to skip it from that point
on:

```
if not self.__class__._file_store_ready:
   # - The first time the class is used, check the file-
   #   storage directory, and if everything checks out,
   #   then re-set the flag that controls the checks.
if not os.path.exists(self.__class__._file_store_dir):
   # - If the path-specification exists, try to
```

```
#   assure that the *path* exists, and create it
#   if it doesn't. If the path can't be created,
#   then that'll be an issue later too, so it'll
#   need to be dealt with.
 try:
     os.makedirs(self.__class__._file_store_dir)
   except PermissionError:
       raise PermissionError(
           '%s cannot create the JSON data-store '
           'directory (%s) because permission was '
           'denied. Please check permissions on '
           'that directory (or its parents, if it '
           'hasn\'t been created yet) and try '
           'again.' %
            (
               self.__class__.__name__,
               self.__class__._file_store_dir
            )
       )
```

It's worth noting that since the _file_store_ready value is a class attribute, that value will persist for an entire Python run. That is, using the Artisan Application as an example, the following will happen:

1. The application is started
2. At some point, a data object class instance is initialized (say, a Product), and the checking process runs, successfully verifying all the data storage needs for product objects and setting the _file_store_ready to True accordingly
3. The user does things with the application that don't interact with any product objects
4. Another product object is initialized, but because the _file_store_ready flag has been set to True, the check process is skipped

As soon as the application is shut down, though, that flag value goes away, so the next time the application is started up, the check process is repeated the first time a product object is initialized.

File access permissions are, as noted already, also checked by first writing a file:

```
#  - Check to make sure that files can be
#    created there...
    try:
        test_file = open(
        '%s%stest-file.txt' %
        (self.__class__._file_store_dir, os.sep),
            'w'
        )
        test_file.write('test-file.txt')
        test_file.close()
    except PermissionError:
        raise PermissionError(
            '%s cannot write files to the JSON data-'
            'store directory (%s) because permission was '
            'denied. Please check permissions on that '
            'directory and try again.' %
            (
                self.__class__.__name__,
                self.__class__._file_store_dir
            )
        )
```

Then, by reading the file that was just written:

```
#  - ... that files can be read from there...
    try:
        test_file = open(
        '%s%stest-file.txt' %
        (self.__class__._file_store_dir, os.sep),
            'r'
        )
        test_file.read()
        test_file.close()
        except PermissionError:
            raise PermissionError(
                '%s cannot read files in the JSON data-'
                'store directory (%s) because permission was '
                'denied. Please check permissions on that '
                'directory and try again.' %
                (
                    self.__class__.__name__,
                    self.__class__._file_store_dir
                )
            )
```

And finally, by deleting that file:

```
# - ... and deleted from there...
try:
    os.unlink(
        '%s%stest-file.txt' %
        (self.__class__._file_store_dir, os.sep)
    )
except PermissionError:
    raise PermissionError(
        '%s cannot delete files in the JSON data-'
        'store directory (%s) because permission was '
        'denied. Please check permissions on that '
        'directory and try again.' %
        (
            self.__class__.__name__,
            self.__class__._file_store_dir
        )
    )
# - If no errors were raised, then re-set the flag:
self._file_store_ready = True
```

The balance of __init__() follows the same structure established earlier. Since the class has a parent class – BaseDataObject – it calls that initializer, but since there are no local properties to initialize or set values for, there aren't any of those calls. All of the other properties' initializations are handled by the call to BaseDataObject.__init__:

```
# - Call parent initializers if needed
BaseDataObject.__init__(
    self, oid, created, modified, is_active, is_deleted,
    is_dirty, is_new
)
# - Set default instance property-values using _del_... methods
# - Set instance property-values from arguments using
#   _set_... methods
# - Perform any other initialization needed
```

Three of the methods, either required by the abstraction in BaseDataObject or with concrete implementations, need to be addressed in JSONFileDataObject. The _create and _update methods are required by BaseDataObject, but don't make a lot of sense in the context of this class because the same basic operation would take place whether the operation involved was a creation or update effort. Both of those, while implemented, do nothing more than raise an error with some information that would be useful for developers who encounter it:

```
def _create(self) -> None:
    """
Creates a new state-data record for the instance in the back-end
data-store
    """
        # - Since all data-transactions for these objects involve
        #   a file-write, we're just going to define this method
        #   in order to meet the requirements of BaseDataObject,
        #   make it raise an error, and override the save method
        #   to perform the actual file-write.
        raise NotImplementedError(
            '%s._create is not implemented, because the save '
            'method handles all the data-writing needed for '
            'the class. Use save() instead.' %
            self.__class__.__name__
        )

def _update(self) -> None:
    """
Updates an existing state-data record for the instance in the
back-end data-store
    """
        # - Since all data-transactions for these objects involve
        #   a file-write, we're just going to define this method
        #   in order to meet the requirements of BaseDataObject,
        #   make it raise an error, and override the save method
        #   to perform the actual file-write.
        raise NotImplementedError(
            '%s._update is not implemented, because the save '
            'method handles all the data-writing needed for '
            'the class. Use save() instead.' %
            self.__class__.__name__
        )
```

Those changes, then, put all the responsibility for writing data to files on the `save` method, no matter whether the data being saved represents a new/create action or an edit/update one. Although it's not likely, it's not impossible for the permissions of the directory where data files are stored to change while the program is running. They were checked initially, but that only means that they were valid at the time they were checked, so the process of writing data to files should check them as well, independently:

```
def save(self):
    """
Saves the instance's state-data to the back-end data-store by
creating it if the instance is new, or updating it if the
instance is dirty
```

```
"""
        if self.is_new or self.is_dirty:
```

It does need to confirm that objects have been loaded into memory
first with `_load_objects`; at execution time, this will always be an instance of the
class calling a class method that's inherited, so the class has to be explicitly passed as
an argument:

```
# - Make sure objects are loaded:
self.__class__._load_objects(self.__class__)
```

Then, it saves the data and confirms that the object itself is stored in memory:

```
# - Try to save the data:
 try:
  # - Open the file
  fp = open(
    '%s%s-data%s%s.json' %
        (
            self.__class__._file_store_dir, os.sep,
            self.__class__.__name__, os.sep,
            self.oid
        ), 'w'
    )
        # - Write the instance's data-dict to the file as JSON
        json.dump(fp, self.to_data_dict(), indent=4)
        # - re-set the new and dirty state-flags
        self._set_is_dirty(False)
        self._set_is_new(False)
        # - Update it in the loaded objects
        self.__class__._loaded_objects[self.oid] = self
```

If the file write fails (the `json.dump` call) with a permissions-related error, none of the
in-memory updates will be committed, and a more end user-friendly error message
should be raised, in case it needs to be displayed to that end user:

```
except PermissionError:
    # - Raise a more informative error
        raise PermissionError(
            '%s could not save an object to the JSON data-'
            'store directory (%s) because permission was '
            'denied. Please check permissions on that '
            'directory and try again.' %
        (
            self.__class__.__name__,
            self.__class__._file_store_dir
```

```
    )
      )
# - Any other errors will just surface for the time being
```

The same common storage location file system path values that allow
the save method to be made concrete also allow the `delete` and `get` class methods to
be made concrete class methods of `JSONFileDataObject`. Because the class
properties define what's needed to find the data files relevant to any/all object
instances, delete code can directly make the needed file-deletion efforts, with the
appropriate error handling:

```
@classmethod
def delete(cls, *oids):
    """
Performs an ACTUAL record deletion from the back-end data-store
of all records whose unique identifiers have been provided
    """
    # - First, ensure that objects are loaded
    cls._load_objects(cls)
    # - For each oid specified, try to remove the file, handling
    #   any errors raised in the process.
    failed_deletions = []
    for oid in oids:
        try:
            # - Try to delete the file first, so that deletion
            #   failures won't leave the files but remove the
            #   in-memory copies
            file_path = '%s%s%s-data%s%s.json' %(
                cls._file_store_dir, os.sep,
                cls.__name__, os.sep, oid
            )
            # - Delete the file at file_path
            os.unlink(file_path)
            # - Remove the in-memory object-instance:
            del cls._loaded_objects[str(oid)]
        except PermissionError:
            failed_deletions.append(file_path)
    if failed_deletions:
        # - Though we *are* raising an error here, *some* deletions
        #   may have succeeded. If this error-message is displayed,
        #   the user seeing it need only be concerned with the
        #   items that failed, though...
        raise PermissionError(
            '%s.delete could not delete %d object-data %s '
            'because permission was denied. Please check the '
            'permissions on %s and try again' %
            (
```

```
                cls.__name__, len(failed_deletions),
                ('files' if len(failed_deletions) > 1 else 'file'),
                ', '.join(failed_deletions)
            )
        )
```

The `get` method doesn't need read access to the files directly – the `_load_objects` class method handles that, loading all the data that `get` relies upon – and once the relevant objects exist in memory, finding them, even with criteria or a combination of object IDs and criteria, is quite simple and fast:

```python
@classmethod
def get(cls, *oids, **criteria):
    """
Finds and returns all instances of the class from the back-end
data-store whose oids are provided and/or that match the supplied
criteria
    """
    # - First, ensure that objects are loaded
    cls._load_objects(cls)
```

If `oids` have been supplied, the process has to account for those, and for `criteria` if it was supplied:

```python
    # - If oids have been specified, then the initial results are all
    #   items in the in-memory store whose oids are in the supplied
    #   oids-list
    if oids:
        oids = tuple(
            [str(o) for o in oids]
        )
        # - If no criteria were supplied, then oids are all we need
        #   to match against:
        if not criteria:
            results = [
                o for o in cls._loaded_objects.values()
                if str(o.oid) in oids
            ]
        # - Otherwise, we *also* need to use matches to find items
        #   that match the criteria
        else:
            results = [
                o for o in cls._loaded_objects.values()
                if str(o.oid) in oids
                and o.matches(**criteria)
            ]
        # - In either case, we have a list of matching items, which
```

```
#    may be empty, so return it:
return results
```

If no `oids` were supplied, but `criteria` was, the process is similar:

```
#  - If oids were NOT specified, then the results are all objects
#    in memory that match the criteria
elif criteria:
    results = [
        o for o in cls._loaded_objects
        if o.matches(**criteria)
    ]
    return results
#  - If neither were specified, return all items available:
else:
    return list(cls._loaded_objects.values())
```

In both branches, any filtering based on `criteria` is handled by the individual object's `matches` method, making the process of searching for objects by specific property values very easy.

All of these rely, then, on the `_load_objects` class method to retrieve and populate the in-memory copies of all objects whose data has been persisted as JSON files, and attaching them to the relevant class, in the `_loaded_objects` dictionary that was defined as a common class attribute:

```
def _load_objects(cls, force_load=False):
    """
Class-level helper-method that loads all of the objects in the
local file-system data-store into memory so that they can be
used more quickly afterwards.

Expected to be called by the get class-method to load objects
for local retrieval, and other places as needed.

cls .......... (class, required) The class that the method is
               bound to
force_load ... (bool, optional, defaults to False) If True,
               forces the process to re-load data from scratch,
               otherwise skips the load process if data already
               exists.
    """
```

If the data has not been loaded (indicated by the _loaded_objects attribute containing a None value), or if an explicit reload of data was called for (a True value received in the force_load argument), the method retrieves a list of all files in the class data directory, after verifying that the relevant directories exist, trying to create them if they don't, and raising errors if they need to be created but cannot be:

```
if cls._loaded_objects == None or force_load:
    if not os.path.exists(cls._file_store_dir):
        # - If the path-specification exists, try to
        #   assure that the *path* exists, and create it
        #   if it doesn't. If the path can't be created,
        #   then that'll be an issue later too, so it'll
        #   need to be dealt with.
        try:
            os.makedirs(cls._file_store_dir)
        except PermissionError:
            raise PermissionError(
                '%s cannot create the JSON data-store '
                'directory (%s) because permission was '
                'denied. Please check permissions on '
                'that directory (or its parents, if it '
                'hasn\'t been created yet) and try '
                'again.' %
                (cls.__name__, cls._file_store_dir)
            )
    class_files_path = '%s%s%s-data' % (
        cls._file_store_dir, os.sep,
        cls.__name__
    )
    if not os.path.exists(class_files_path):
        try:
            os.makedirs(class_files_path)
        except PermissionError:
            raise PermissionError(
                '%s cannot create the JSON data-store '
                'directory (%s) because permission was '
                'denied. Please check permissions on '
                'that directory (or its parents, if it '
                'hasn\'t been created yet) and try '
                'again.' %
                (cls.__name__, class_files_path)
            )
    # - Get a list of all the JSON files in the data-store
    #   path
    files = [
        fname for fname in os.listdir(
            '%s%s%s-data' % (
```

```
                cls._file_store_dir, os.sep,
                cls.__name__
            )
        ) if fname.endswith('.json')
    ]
```

If there are any files found, then an attempt is made to read each one, convert it from the JSON-encoded `data_dict` expected into an actual instance of the class, and add the instance to the `_loaded_objects` attribute. Since `_loaded_objects` is a class attribute, loaded values will persist for as long as that class definition is active. Barring an explicit purge or redefinition of the class itself, this will persist for the duration of the Python interpreter that's running the code, allowing the data read in by the process to persist for as long as the code that's using it is running:

```
    cls._loaded_objects = {}
    if files:
        for fname in files:
            item_file = '%s%s-data%s%s' % (
            self.__class__._file_store_dir, os.sep,
            self.__class__.__name__, os.sep, fname
            )
        try:
          # - Read the JSON data
          fp = open(item_file, 'r')
          data_dict = json.load(fp)
          fp.close()
          # - Create an instance from that data
          instance = cls.from_data_dict(data_dict)
          # - Keep track of it by oid in the class
          cls._loaded_objects[instance.oid] = instance
```

Since it's possible, even if it's unlikely, for the file system permissions of the data files themselves or of the parent directories of the file to change while the Artisan Application is running, file reads could throw `PermissionError` exceptions, so those are caught and tracked until the process is complete:

```
      # - If permissions are a problem, raise an
      #   error with helpful information
        except PermissionError as error:
            raise PermissionError(
                '%s could not load object-data from '
                'the data-store file at %s because '
                'permission was denied. Please check '
                '(and, if needed, correct) the file- '
                'and directory-permissions and try '
```

```
                    'again' %
                    (cls.__name__, item_file)
                )
```

Similarly, if the content of a data file is invalid, an error is raised, though in this case it's immediate. The rationale for the immediacy is that data has been corrupted, and that needs to be resolved before allowing any changes to occur:

```
#  -  If data-structure or -content is a problem,
#     raise an error with helpful information
        except (TypeError, ValueError) as error:
            raise error.__class__(
                '%s could not load object-data from '
                'the data-store file at %s because '
                'the data was corrupt or not what '
                'was expected (%s: %s)' %
                (
                    cls.__name__, item_file,
                    error.__class__.__name__, error
                )
            )
#  -  Other errors will simply surface, at
#     least for now
```

Any other errors will cascade out to the calling code, to be handled there or allowed to abort the application's execution.

The original goals, including the should-have or nice-to-have functionalities, have all been accounted for at this point, in a complete set of CRUD operation mechanisms:

- All of the stored data for any derived class should probably live in one location. This is enforced by the `_file_store_dir` class attribute.
- Instance data for each object type (class) should probably live in a common location within the top-level location and data for any given instance should probably reside in a single, distinct file, whose name can be uniquely related to the instance whose data it stores. These are managed by ensuring that all the file paths used contain the class name, so that, for example, all product instance data will be stored in `_file_store_dir/Product-data/*.json` files.

- Data reading operations would be faster if the process didn't involve finding, opening, reading, and creating objects for every file every time that a data read was executed. The _load_objects class method performs the load, and making sure that it gets called before any CRUD operations are executed takes care of making them available. The create, update, and delete processes all take into account both the persistent data files and the in-memory instances that relate to those instances.

The concrete business objects of hms_artisan

The final definition of the concrete classes in the Artisan Application really just boils down to the following:

- Defining each concrete class:
    - Deriving from the corresponding base class in hms_core
    - Deriving from JSONFileDataObject that was just defined
- Collecting the arguments for the new class __init__ method, which needs to account for all of the arguments of the parent classes.
- Implementing any of the abstract instance and class methods required by the parent classes, many of which have already been set up to allow the derived class to call the parent's abstract method.
- Setting up a _file_store_dir class attribute value that can be used by instances of the classes until the final application configuration is worked out.

These relationships may make more sense if they are diagrammed:

hms_artisan..Artisan

hms_core..BaseArtisan
Properties
+ contact_name <str>
+ contact_email <str>
+ company_name <str>
+ address <Address>
+ website <str>

JSONFileDataObject
Methods
create()
+ save()
# update()
+ delete(*oids)
+ get(*oids, **criteria) <object>*

hms_artisan..Customer

hms_core..BaseCustomer
Properties
+ name <str>
+ billing_address <Address>
+ shipping_address <Address>

BaseDataObject
Properties
+ oid <UUID>
+ created <datetime>
+ is_active <bool>
+ is_deleted <bool>
+ is_dirty <bool>
+ is_new <bool>
+ modified <datetime>
Methods
 # create()
+ matches(criteria) <bool>
+ save()
+ to_data_dict() <dict>
 # update()
+ delete(*oids)
+ from_data_dict(data_dict) <object>
+ get(*oids, **criteria) <object>*
+ sort(objects, sort_by) <object>*

hms_artisan..Order

hms_core..BaseOrder
Properties
+ customer <BaseCustomer>

hms_artisan..Product

hms_core..BaseProduct
Properties
+ name <str>
+ summary <str>
+ description <str>
+ dimensions <str>
+ mass <str>
+ metadata <dict>
+ available <bool>
+ store_available <bool>
Methods
+ set_metadata(key, value)
+ remove_metadata(key)

Dealing with is_dirty and properties

BaseDataObject provides is_dirty, a property that's intended to indicate when the state data of an object has been changed (for example, it should be set to True when any of the various _set_ or _del_ methods have been called). Since the concrete objects' property setter and deleter methods, as defined in their corresponding base classes, aren't aware of that capability at all, it's up to the concrete objects to implement that functionality.

However, since those setter and deleter methods can be called in the derived concrete class definitions, the implementation is very straightforward. Using the `address` property of `Artisan` as an example, we essentially define local setter and deleter methods that call their counterparts in `BaseArtisan`:

```
###################################
# Property-setter methods         #
###################################

def _set_address(self, value:Address) -> None:
    # - Call the parent method
    result = BaseArtisan._set_address(self, value)
    self._set_is_dirty(True)
    return result

# ...

###################################
# Property-deleter methods        #
###################################

def _del_address(self) -> None:
    # - Call the parent method
    result = BaseArtisan._del_address(self)
    self._set_is_dirty(True)
    return result
```

Once those are defined, the property itself has to be redefined in order to point to the appropriate methods. Without this step, the `Artisan` objects' properties would still point to the `BaseArtisan` setter and deleter methods, so the `is_dirty` flag would never get set, and data changes would never be saved:

```
###################################
# Instance property definitions   #
###################################

address = property(
    BaseArtisan._get_address, _set_address, _del_address,
    'Gets, sets or deletes the physical address (Address) '
    'associated with the Artisan that the instance represents'
)
```

This same pattern will play out for all of the properties of the `hms_artisan` classes.

That also means, however, that all of those classes, since they all use their various _del_ methods to initialize instance values during the execution of their __init__ methods, may also need to explicitly reset is_dirty to False when an object is created.

This is a very simplistic approach to handling the dirty state of object instances. The fundamental assumption behind this implementation is that any property setting or deletion that occurs will make a change to the applicable state value, so the instance is dirty as a result. Even if the new value was the same as the old value of a property, this would be the case. In systems where there is an actual monetary cost for each database transaction (some cloud-based data stores), it might be worth the additional effort of checking the property value before executing the set code or delete code, and not even making the change, let alone setting the is_dirty flag, if the incoming new value isn't different from the existing one.

hms_artisan.Artisan

Artisans need to be able to manipulate their own data in the Artisan Application:

- As an Artisan, I need to be able to create, manage, and store my own system data so that I can keep it up to date

The initial code for the Artisan class that provides the data structure and persistence that fulfills this story's needs is very lightweight, since most of the functionality is inherited from hms_core, BaseArtisan (for properties and data-structure), and JSONFileDataObject (for methods and persistence functionality). Not counting comments and documentation, it's just under 60 lines of real code:

```
class Artisan(BaseArtisan, JSONFileDataObject, object):
    """
Represents an Artisan in the context of the Artisan Application
    """

    #####################################
    # Class attributes/constants        #
    #####################################

    # TODO: Work out the configuration-based file-system path
    #       for this attribute
    _file_store_dir = '/tmp/hms_data'
```

The __init__ method has a long and detailed argument signature, with 12 arguments (three of which are required), and the products arglist. It may seem daunting, but is not expected to be needed for most use cases (more on that shortly). All it really needs to do is call the parent initializers to set the applicable property values:

```
#####################################
# Object initialization             #
#####################################

# TODO: Add and document arguments if/as needed
def __init__(self,
    # - Required arguments from BaseArtisan
    contact_name:str, contact_email:str, address:Address,
    # - Optional arguments from BaseArtisan
    company_name:str=None, website:(str,)=None,
    # - Optional arguments from BaseDataObject/JSONFileDataObject
    oid:(UUID,str,None)=None,
    created:(datetime,str,float,int,None)=None,
    modified:(datetime,str,float,int,None)=None,
    is_active:(bool,int,None)=None,
    is_deleted:(bool,int,None)=None,
    is_dirty:(bool,int,None)=None,
    is_new:(bool,int,None)=None,
    # - the products arglist from BaseArtisan
    *products
):
    """
Object initialization.

self ............. (Artisan instance, required) The instance to
                   execute against
contact_name ...... (str, required) The name of the primary contact
                   for the Artisan that the instance represents
contact_email ..... (str [email address], required) The email address
                   of the primary contact for the Artisan that the
                   instance represents
address ........... (Address, required) The mailing/shipping address
                   for the Artisan that the instance represents
company_name ...... (str, optional, defaults to None) The company-
                   name for the Artisan that the instance represents
website ........... (str, optional, defaults to None) The the URL of
                   the website associated with the Artisan that the
                   instance represents
oid ............... (UUID|str, optional, defaults to None)
created ........... (datetime|str|float|int, optional, defaults to
None)
```

```
    modified ......... (datetime|str|float|int, optional, defaults to
    None)
    is_active ........ (bool|int, optional, defaults to None)
    is_deleted ....... (bool|int, optional, defaults to None)
    is_dirty ......... (bool|int, optional, defaults to None)
    is_new ........... (bool|int, optional, defaults to None)
    products ......... (BaseProduct collection) The products associated
                       with the Artisan that the instance represents
    """
        # - Call parent initializers if needed
        BaseArtisan.__init__(
            self, contact_name, contact_email, address,
            company_name, website, *products
        )
        JSONFileDataObject.__init__(
            self, oid, created, modified, is_active,
            is_deleted, is_dirty, is_new
        )
        # - Set default instance property-values using _del_...
methods
        # - Set instance property-values from arguments using
        #   _set_... methods
        # - Perform any other initialization needed
```

The bulk of the instance methods can call the original abstract methods (with their existing implementations) in the classes that they originate from:

```
####################################
# Instance methods                 #
####################################

def add_product(self, product:BaseProduct) -> BaseProduct:
    return HasProducts.add_product(self, product)

def matches(self, **criteria) -> (bool,):
    return BaseDataObject.matches(self, **criteria)

def remove_product(self, product:BaseProduct) -> BaseProduct:
    return HasProducts.remove_product(self, product)
```

The exception to that is the `to_data_dict` method, which must be customized for each concrete class. All that it needs to do, though, is return a `dict` of all the properties and values that should be persisted, and that can be used in the initialization of an object. The `address` property has an issue with it, from the perspective of being able to store it in a JSON file, and that will be examined shortly.

The datetime and UUID properties are converted to string values for the outgoing data dictionary, and they are already situated during the initialization of an Artisan object to be converted back to their native data types:

```
def to_data_dict(self) -> (dict,):
    return {
        # Properties from BaseArtisan:
        'address':self.address,
        'company_name':self.company_name,
        'contact_email':self.contact_email,
        'contact_name':self.contact_name,
        'website':self.website,
        # - Properties from BaseDataObject (through
        #   JSONFileDataObject)
        'created':datetime.strftime(
            self.created, self.__class__._data_time_string
        ),
        'is_active':self.is_active,
        'is_deleted':self.is_deleted,
        'modified':datetime.strftime(
            self.modified, self.__class__._data_time_string
        ),
        'oid':str(self.oid),
    }
```

The single class method, like the bulk of the preceding instance methods, also uses the original abstract class methods that have implementations within them:

```
####################################
# Class methods                    #
####################################

@classmethod
def from_data_dict(cls, data_dict:(dict,)):
    return cls(**data_dict)
```

The long argument signature of Artisan.__init__ may feel a bit daunting at first glance. There are a lot of arguments, after all, and Python's language stipulation that requires that arguments have to go before optional ones in method and function argument definitions means that three of those arguments have to come first (though their sequence with respect to each other is up to the developer).

Most of the time, however, that __init__ method will probably not be called directly. The creation of an instance from data retrieved from the data store is expected to be handled with the `from_data_dict` method of the class, probably looking something like this:

```
# - open the data-file, read it in, and convert it to a dict:
with open('data-file.json', 'r') as artisan_file:
    artisan = Artisan.from_data_dict(json.load(artisan_file))
```

An `Artisan` instance could also be created directly by passing a dictionary of values:

```
artisan = Artisan(**data_dict)
```

The only considerations for that approach are that the required arguments must have valid entries in the `data_dict` being passed, and that `data_dict` cannot contain keys that don't exist as argument names in the __init__ method – essentially, that object creation is equivalent to the following:

```
artisan = Artisan(
    contact_name='value', contact_email='value', address=<Address
Object>
    # ... and so on for any relevant optional arguments
)
```

It was noted that there were issues with the `address` property when it came to creating JSON output for an `Artisan` instance. The core issue is that the `Address` class is not directly serializable into JSON:

```
import json
address = Address('12345 Main Street', 'City Name')
a = Artisan('John Smith', 'j@smith.com', address)
print(json.dumps(a.to_data_dict(), indent=4))
```

If the preceding code is executed, `TypeError: <hms_core.business_objects.Address object> is not JSON serializable` is raised.

Although there are several possible solutions for this issue, since we've already established a pattern of converting objects to and reading/creating them from dictionary values, the one that is most like that pattern is to implement the `to_dict` and `from_dict` methods on the original `Address` class in `hms_core`, and change the `to_data_dict` result to use the `to_dict` of the instance's `address`. The new `Address` methods are simple:

```
####################################
# Instance methods                 #
####################################

    def to_dict(self) -> (dict,):
        return {
            'street_address':self.street_address,
            'building_address':self.building_address,
            'city':self.city,
            'region':self.region,
            'postal_code':self.postal_code,
            'country':self.country
        }

####################################
# Class methods                    #
####################################

    @classmethod
    def from_dict(cls, data_dict):
        return cls(**data_dict)
```

As is the change to `Artisan.to_data_dict`:

```
    def to_data_dict(self) -> (dict,):
        return {
            # Properties from BaseArtisan:
            'address':self.address.to_dict() if self.address else
None,
            'company_name':self.company_name,
            'contact_email':self.contact_email,
            'contact_name':self.contact_name,
            'website':self.website,
            # - Properties from BaseDataObject (through
            #   JSONFileDataObject)
            'created':datetime.strftime(
                self.created, self.__class__._data_time_string
            ),
            'is_active':self.is_active,
            'is_deleted':self.is_deleted,
            'modified':datetime.strftime(
                self.modified, self.__class__._data_time_string
            ),
            'oid':str(self.oid),
        }
```

With those changes in place, rerunning the code that raised the `TypeError` before now yields usable JSON, meaning that the results of a `to_data_dict` call can be used to directly write the JSON files needed to persist `Artisan` data to the file system data store:

```
{
    "website": null,
    "is_active": true,
    "contact_email": "j@smith.com",
    "address": {
        "region": null,
        "postal_code": null,
        "building_address": null,
        "street_address": "12345 Main Street",
        "country": null,
        "city": "City Name"
    },
    "modified": "2018-05-20 09:21:48",
    "contact_name": "John Smith",
    "created": "2018-05-20 09:21:48",
    "oid": "52267e19-8668-4f9e-b8b7-53d650682a46",
    "company_name": null,
    "is_deleted": false
}
```

hms_artisan.Product

Artisans have a similar data persistence need for `Product` object data:

- As an Artisan, I need to be able to create, manage, and store `Product` data, so that I can keep `product` information current in the central office system

The `hms_artisan..Product` class, like the `Artisan` class of the package, leverages its corresponding `hms_core` base class (`BaseProduct`) and the `JSONFileDataObject` ABC to minimize the amount of actual code needed in the concrete implementation.

In fact, the only real differences are in the __init__ method (with different arguments, and calling a different parent initialization method set):

```
def __init__(self,
    # - Required arguments from BaseProduct
    name:(str,), summary:(str,), available:(bool,),
    store_available:(bool,),
    # - Optional arguments from BaseProduct
    description:(str,None)=None, dimensions:(str,None)=None,
    metadata:(dict,)={}, shipping_weight:(int,)=0,
    # - Optional arguments from BaseDataObject/JSONFileDataObject
    oid:(UUID,str,None)=None,
    created:(datetime,str,float,int,None)=None,
    modified:(datetime,str,float,int,None)=None,
    is_active:(bool,int,None)=None,
    is_deleted:(bool,int,None)=None,
    is_dirty:(bool,int,None)=None,
    is_new:(bool,int,None)=None,
    ):
    """
Object initialization.

self ............. (Product instance, required) The instance to
                   execute against
name ............. (str, required) The name of the product
summary .......... (str, required) A one-line summary of the
                   product
available ........ (bool, required) Flag indicating whether the
                   product is considered available by the artisan
                   who makes it
store_available ... (bool, required) Flag indicating whether the
                   product is considered available on the web-
                   store by the Central Office
description ....... (str, optional, defaults to None) A detailed
                   description of the product
dimensions ........ (str, optional, defaults to None) A measurement-
                   description of the product
metadata .......... (dict, optional, defaults to {}) A collection
                   of metadata keys and values describing the
                   product
shipping_weight ... (int, optional, defaults to 0) The shipping-
                   weight of the product
    """
        # - Call parent initializers if needed
        BaseProduct.__init__(
            self, name, summary, available, store_available,
            description, dimensions, metadata, shipping_weight
        )
```

```
JSONFileDataObject.__init__(
    self, oid, created, modified, is_active,
    is_deleted, is_dirty, is_new
)
# - Set default instance property-values using _del_...
    methods
# - Set instance property-values from arguments using
#   _set_... methods
# - Perform any other initialization needed
```

The `to_data_dict` method (which has to account for the different properties of the class):

```python
def to_data_dict(self) -> (dict,):
    return {
        # Properties from BaseProduct:
        'available':self.available,
        'description':self.description,
        'dimensions':self.dimensions,
        'metadata':self.metadata,
        'name':self.name,
        'shipping_weight':self.shipping_weight,
        'store_available':self.store_available,
        'summary':self.summary,
        # - Properties from BaseDataObject (through
        #   JSONFileDataObject)
        'created':datetime.strftime(
            self.created, self.__class__._data_time_string
        ),
        'is_active':self.is_active,
        'is_deleted':self.is_deleted,
        'modified':datetime.strftime(
            self.modified, self.__class__._data_time_string
        ),
        'oid':str(self.oid),
    }
```

A similar simple creation of a `Product` object, and a dump of its `to_data_dict` results, yield viable JSON output:

```python
p = Product('name', 'summary', True, True)
print(json.dumps(p.to_data_dict(), indent=4))
```

This yields the following:

```
{
    "available": true,
    "created": "2018-05-20 09:40:10",
    "description": null,
    "dimensions": null,
    "is_active": true,
    "is_deleted": false,
    "metadata": {},
    "modified": "2018-05-20 09:40:10",
    "name": "name",
    "oid": "1b4f226a-8616-4141-be6f-a69cdccf6572",
    "shipping_weight": 0,
    "store_available": true,
    "summary": "summary"
}
```

hms_artisan.Order

The ability for Artisans to have locally saved order data is also needed:

- As an Artisan, I need to be able to create, manage, and store `Order` data so that I can fulfill orders when they are relayed to me, and flag them as fulfilled for the Central Office

Order data, though, is a bit different from the `Artisan` and `Product` data that we have explored so far at a structural level:

- An `Order`, when it comes right down to it, is an association of one customer with one-to-many products.
- There's no expected need for Artisans to keep track of individual customers, except as they relate to orders, so Artisans need `Customer` objects that aren't also data objects, in much the same way that `Artisan` objects have an `Address` associated with them that aren't themselves data objects.
- The `Customer` object that is part of an `Order` also has an `Address` that has to be accounted for.

- The products associated with an order imply at least the possibility of a quantity associated with them – a customer may want to order two of one product, five of another, and one of a third, for example – and don't really need to have all of the `Product` data transmitted, so long as the `oid` for each `Product` in the order is supplied. That would be sufficient information for the Artisan Application to look up products from its local `Product` data store.

That last item, in retrospect, calls into question some of the structure of `BaseOrder` in `hms_core`, or at least whether it's relevant in the scope of the Artisan Application. As it's currently defined, it derives from `hms_core` ... `HasProducts`, with the original intention that actual `Product` objects would be associated with an `Order`. That might make sense in a Central Office or gateway service context, but it's not going to be terribly useful in the context of the Artisan Application. A better order-to-product relationship is probably to store the `oids` and quantities of each `Product` in an `Order`, and let the applications and service look them up when necessary:

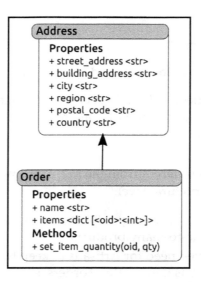

Taking a step back and looking at what an Artisan Application's `Order` really is, it would seem to be an `Address`, with the addition of a `name` property (who the order is for), and some `Product` quantity data. The association between `oid` product specifications and quantity values is easily managed in a `dict` property, and the processes for adding and removing order items can be wrapped in a single method that accepts the `oid` and a quantity value.

That feels like a much better solution for Artisans' order data. They don't really need to know anything more than the data this structure covers:

- Who the order is for (name)
- Where it gets sent to (the properties derived from Address)
- What products are part of the order, and in what quantities (items)

The Order class, then, starts by deriving from Address and JSONFileDataObject, with the usual class attributes:

```
class Order(Address, JSONFileDataObject, object):
    """
Represents an Order in the context of the Artisan Application
    """
    ####################################
    # Class attributes/constants       #
    ####################################

    # TODO: Work out the configuration-based file-system path
    #       for this attribute
    _file_store_dir = '/tmp/hms_data'
```

The property definitions, getter, setter, and deleter methods, and the property declarations follow the pattern we've used everywhere else so far, with _get_items returning a copy of the current property in order to prevent unwanted manipulation of the actual data. The setter and deleter methods also have to explicitly call _set_is_dirty(True) to ensure that the is_dirty flag of the instance gets changed appropriately when a local property is deleted or set, and the properties themselves, with their setter and deleter methods that are inherited from Address, have to be overridden. There are two local getter methods:

```
    ####################################
    # Property-getter methods          #
    ####################################

    def _get_items(self) -> dict:
        return dict(self._items)

    def _get_name(self) -> (str,None):
        return self._name
```

Most of the setter methods call their ancestor methods, set `is_dirty`, and `exit`, but the two that correspond to the local getters are full implementations:

```python
#####################################
# Property-setter methods          #
#####################################

def _set_building_address(self, value:(str,None)) -> None:
    result = Address._set_building_address(self, value)
    self._set_is_dirty(True)
    return result

def _set_city(self, value:str) -> None:
    result = Address._set_city(self, value)
    self._set_is_dirty(True)
    return result

def _set_country(self, value:(str,None)) -> None:
    result = Address._set_country(self, value)
    self._set_is_dirty(True)
    return result

def _set_items(self, value:(dict,)) -> None:
    if type(value) != dict:
        raise TypeError(
            '%s.items expects a dict of UUID keys and int-'
            'values, but was passed "%s" (%s)' %
            (self.__class__.__name__, value,type(value).__name__)
        )
    self._del_items()
    for key in value:
        self.set_item_quantity(key, value[key])
    self._set_is_dirty(True)

def _set_name(self, value:(str,)) -> None:
    self._name = value
    self._set_is_dirty(True)

def _set_region(self, value:(str,None)) -> None:
    result = Address._set_region(self, value)
    self._set_is_dirty(True)
    return result

def _set_postal_code(self, value:(str,None)) -> None:
    result = Address._set_postal_code(self, value)
    self._set_is_dirty(True)
    return result
```

```
def _set_street_address(self, value:str) -> None:
    result = Address._set_street_address(self, value)
    self._set_is_dirty(True)
    return result
```

The deleter methods follow the same pattern:

```
#####################################
# Property-deleter methods          #
#####################################

def _del_building_address(self) -> None:
    result = Address._del_building_address(self)
    self._set_is_dirty(True)
    return result

def _del_city(self) -> None:
    result = Address._del_city(self)
    self._set_is_dirty(True)
    return result

def _del_country(self) -> None:
    result = Address._del_country(self)
    self._set_is_dirty(True)
    return result

def _del_items(self) -> None:
    self._items = {}
    self._set_is_dirty(True)

def _del_name(self) -> None:
    self._name = None
    self._set_is_dirty(True)

def _del_region(self) -> None:
    result = Address._del_region(self)
    self._set_is_dirty(True)
    return result

def _del_postal_code(self) -> None:
    result = Address._del_postal_code(self)
    self._set_is_dirty(True)
    return result
```

```
def _del_street_address(self) -> None:
    result = Address._del_street_address(self)
    self._set_is_dirty(True)
    return result
    self._set_is_dirty(True)
```

And the properties follow suit:

```
####################################
# Instance property definitions    #
####################################

building_address = property(
    Address._get_building_address, _set_building_address,
    _del_building_address,
    'Gets, sets or deletes the building_address (str|None) '
    'of the instance'
)
city = property(
    Address._get_city, _set_city, _del_city,
    'Gets, sets or deletes the city (str) of the instance'
)
country = property(
    Address._get_country, _set_country, _del_country,
    'Gets, sets or deletes the country (str|None) of the '
    'instance'
)
items = property(
    _get_items, None, None,
    'Gets the items associated with the order, a dict of OID '
    'keys with quantity values'
)
name = property(
    _get_name, _set_name, _del_name,
    'Gets, sets or deletes the name associated with the order'
)
region = property(
    Address._get_region, _set_region, _del_region,
    'Gets, sets or deletes the region (str|None) of the '
    'instance'
)
postal_code = property(
    Address._get_postal_code, _set_postal_code, _del_postal_code,
    'Gets, sets or deletes the postal_code (str|None) of '
    'the instance'
)
street_address = property(
    Address._get_street_address, _set_street_address,
```

```
        _del_street_address,
        'Gets, sets or deletes the street_address (str) of the '
        'instance'
    )
```

The initialization process (`__init__`) has a long signature again, since it has to accommodate all of the arguments from its parent classes, plus arguments for the local properties:

```
######################################
# Object initialization              #
######################################

def __init__(self,
    name:(str,),
    # - Required arguments from Address
    street_address:(str,), city:(str,),
    # - Local optional arguments
    items:(dict,)={},
    # - Optional arguments from Address
    building_address:(str,None)=None, region:(str,None)=None,
    postal_code:(str,None)=None, country:(str,None)=None,
    # - Optional arguments from BaseDataObject/JSONFileDataObject
    oid:(UUID,str,None)=None,
    created:(datetime,str,float,int,None)=None,
    modified:(datetime,str,float,int,None)=None,
    is_active:(bool,int,None)=None,
    is_deleted:(bool,int,None)=None,
    is_dirty:(bool,int,None)=None,
    is_new:(bool,int,None)=None,
    ):
        """
Object initialization.

self ............. (Order instance, required) The instance to
                   execute against
name ............. (str, required) The name of the addressee
street_address .... (str, required) The base street-address of the
                    location the instance represents
city ............. (str, required) The city portion of the street-
                    address that the instance represents
items ............ (dict, optional, defaults to {}) The dict of
                   oids-to-quantities of products in the order
building_address .. (str, optional, defaults to None) The second
                    line of the street address the instance
represents,
                    if applicable
region ........... (str, optional, defaults to None) The region
```

```
                         (state, territory, etc.) portion of the street-
                         address that the instance represents
        postal_code ....... (str, optional, defaults to None) The postal-code
                         portion of the street-address that the instance
                         represents
        country .......... (str, optional, defaults to None) The country
                         portion of the street-address that the instance
                         represents
        oid .............. (UUID|str, optional, defaults to None)
        created .......... (datetime|str|float|int, optional, defaults to
        None)
        modified ......... (datetime|str|float|int, optional, defaults to
        None)
        is_active ........ (bool|int, optional, defaults to None)
        is_deleted ....... (bool|int, optional, defaults to None)
        is_dirty ......... (bool|int, optional, defaults to None)
        is_new ........... (bool|int, optional, defaults to None)
        """
        # - Call parent initializers if needed
        Address.__init__(
            self, street_address, city, building_address, region,
            postal_code, country
        )
        JSONFileDataObject.__init__(
            self, oid, created, modified, is_active,
            is_deleted, is_dirty, is_new
        )
        # - Set default instance property-values using _del_...
methods
        self._del_items()
        self._del_name()
        # - Set instance property-values from arguments using
        #   _set_... methods
        self._set_name(name)
        if items:
            self._set_items(items)
        # - Perform any other initialization needed
        self._set_is_dirty(False)
```

The matches method can still just call the matches method
of BaseDataObject; there's no expectation that any matching will need to happen
that would require anything more or different:

```
def matches(self, **criteria) -> (bool,):
    return BaseDataObject.matches(self, **criteria)
```

The process for setting item quantities in an order has a fair amount of type and value checking to do, but those all follow patterns that have been used in earlier code, including checking for types, conversion of `oid` string values to `UUID` objects, and checking for valid values:

```python
    def set_item_quantity(self, oid:(UUID,str), quantity:(int,)) ->
None:
        if type(oid) not in (UUID, str):
            raise TypeError(
                '%s.set_item_quantity expects a UUID or string '
                'representation of one for its oid argument, but '
                'was passed "%s" (%s)' %
                (self.__class__.__name__, oid, type(oid).__name__)
            )
        if type(oid) == str:
            try:
                oid = UUID(oid)
            except Exception as error:
                raise ValueError(
                    '%s.set_item_quantity expects a UUID or string '
                    'representation of one for its oid argument, but '
                    'was passed "%s" (%s) which could not be '
                    'converted into a UUID (%s: %s)' %
                    (
                        self.__class__.__name__, oid,
                        type(oid).__name__, error.__class__.__name__,
                        error
                    )
                )
        if type(quantity) != int:
            raise TypeError(
                '%s.set_item_quantity expects non-negative int-value '
                'for its quantity argument, but was passed "%s" (%s)'
                % (
                    self.__class__.__name__, quantity,
                    type(quantity).__name__
                )
            )
        if quantity < 0:
            raise ValueError(
                '%s.set_item_quantity expects non-negative int-value '
                'for its quantity argument, but was passed "%s" (%s)'
                % (
                    self.__class__.__name__, quantity,
                    type(quantity).__name__
                )
            )
```

If the `quantity` specified for a given item is zero, the item in question is removed entirely rather than leaving what is essentially a line item in the order for zero items of a given product:

```
if quantity != 0:
    self._items[oid] = quantity
else:
    try:
        del self._items[oid]
    except KeyError:
        pass
```

The data dictionary generation actively converts the instance's items into a dictionary with string value keys instead of `UUID` objects, but is otherwise pretty typical of the implementations written so far:

```
def to_data_dict(self) -> (dict,):
    return {
        # - Local properties
        'name':self.name,
        'street_address':self.street_address,
        'building_address':self.building_address,
        'city':self.city,
        'region':self.region,
        'postal_code':self.postal_code,
        'country':self.country,
        # - Generate a string:int dict from the UUID:int dict
        'items':dict(
            [
                (str(key), int(self.items[key]))
                for key in self.items.keys()
            ]
        ),
        # - Properties from BaseDataObject (through
        #   JSONFileDataObject)
        'created':datetime.strftime(
            self.created, self.__class__._data_time_string
        ),
        'is_active':self.is_active,
        'is_deleted':self.is_deleted,
        'modified':datetime.strftime(
            self.modified, self.__class__._data_time_string
        ),
        'oid':str(self.oid),            }
```

The _load_objects and from_data_dict class methods are identical to those put in play in earlier code. The Address class standard_address method cannot be left as it is inherited by Order, since any attempt to call it would result in an error – it would not have the new, required name argument – so it is overridden with a new class method with a nearly identical argument set (adding the name), that can be used to generate a new Order instance with no items added, but all of the other relevant information:

```python
####################################
# Class methods                    #
####################################

@classmethod
def standard_address(cls,
        name:(str,), street_address:(str,),
        building_address:(str,None), city:(str,),
        region:(str,None), postal_code:(str,None),
        country:(str,None)
    ):
    return cls(
        name=name, street_address=street_address, city=city,
        building_address=building_address, region=region,
        postal_code=postal_code, country=country
    )
```

The results of these data storage operations can be seen in the file system:

Barring any corrections or changes prompted by unit testing later in the iteration, that accounts for all of the classes in the Artisan Application that have any anticipated need to persist data. Basic testing of the data persistence functionality by creating a minimal data instance of each shows that they do, indeed, write JSON data to the expected location, and that the data written is at least superficially correct. Detailed unit testing will still have to be undertaken to ensure that the data really is accurately written and retrievable without loss or corruption, but the bulk of the main development for these objects is complete.

The relationships between these concrete classes and the hms_core equivalents has changed somewhat, with the creation of Order as a class no longer attached to hms_core..BaseOrder, and the removal of the Customer class at the Artisan Application level:

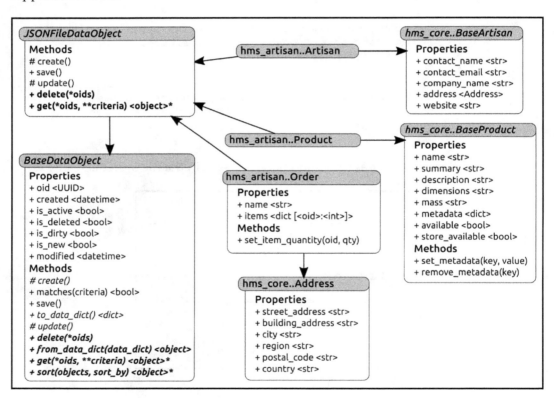

The underlying data storage residing in structured JSON data could also be repurposed to providing data access and CRUD operations against a remote API of some sort. A RESTful/JSON web service, for example, that returned the same JSON structures or accepted them as payloads for creation and update requests, could almost certainly use these objects with only a little bit of modification, in most cases. That sort of approach might be worth looking at in this system, were it ever to go further than it will in this book.

Summary

Though it still needs to be thoroughly tested, which will be addressed in `Chapter 14`, *Testing Data Persistence*, preliminary testing of the JSON-based data file persistence feels pretty solid at this point. The CRUD operations that are required by `BaseDataObject`, passing through `JSONFileDataObject` to all of the concrete data objects, are all present and accounted for, and they appear to be fully functional. The change to the structure of the `Order` class might be cause for some concern with respect to the original design, but was not difficult to deal with. That change should be specifically called out during the approval process for the iteration, since it represents a change to the original design, but it doesn't feel like it will be a cause for any major concerns at this time.

With one data persistence mechanism done, and while the concepts are still fresh, it's time to look at the equivalent processes, backed by a real database engine, for the Central Office applications and service.

12
Persisting Data to a Database

With the file system-backed data persistence of the Artisan Application under our belt, it's time to turn our attention to their equivalents on the Central Office side of the system. We'll be reusing the `BaseDataObject` ABC that was defined previously to ensure that all data object functionality can be called in the same way (for example, using the `get` method to read the data and `save` to write it, for example), but because the underlying data storage process is significantly different in its implementation, that is where most of the similarities will end. We'll still have to decide which of the database options we're going to use, as well.

This chapter will cover the following topics:

- Analyzing database options in depth and selecting a database engine for data object persistence
- Defining a data access strategy for the code that's expected to run at the Central Office
- Designing and implementing some supporting classes for the data access and persistence that are required
- Implementing the concrete data objects required at the Central Office:
  - Artisan
  - Product

There are also some data access considerations that will postpone at least some of the concrete implementations, and those will be discussed in detail.

The Artisan Gateway and Central Office application objects

The **Artisan Gateway** and **Central Office application** both need project structures, so that we will have a place to put the code that's specific to each of them. This need is captured in two stories:

- As a developer, I need a project for the Central Office application, so that I have a place to put the relevant code and build the application
- As a developer, I need a project for the Artisan Gateway, so that I have a place to put the relevant code and build the service

The aforementioned structures can start with nothing more than the basic project template, as follows:

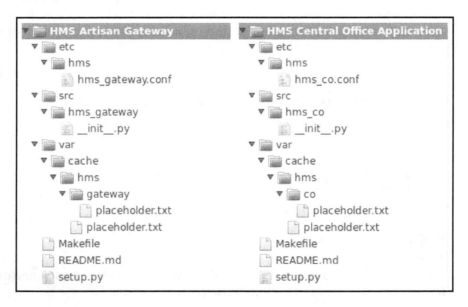

As functionality is built out for the data persistence of business objects in the Artisan Gateway and Central Office application, more modules can be added, as they were in the Artisan Application's project structure. Whether that will be required can be impacted substantially by the selection of the data store engine, but for the time being, this should suffice.

Picking out a backend datastore engine

The story that drives the selection of the backend data store engine for the Artisan Gateway and Central Office application doesn't really mandate any particular engine, just what that engine needs to provide:

- As a consumer of business object data at the HMS Central Office, I need business object data to be stored in a shared data store, so that data will be accessible by multiple consumers simultaneously, with transactional support/protection, and to the ends that they need access to it for.

In a real-world scenario, there might well be specific database engines that are allowed, are encouraged, or are not allowed, based on any number of factors—what system administrators are willing to install and support; what options are available, based on the operating systems in use in the business; and possibly other external factors. There can also be developmental constraints; perhaps the preferred database doesn't have a reliable driver/library in the language being used, or data structure requirements are having a direct impact on the viable options.

Another consideration, and one that does have some representation in the preceding scenario, is how data is accessed (locally versus over a network). In this case, since multiple users can access the system's data at the same time, having a central database (of whatever flavor) that is accessible over the internal network is the easiest solution, in a number of respects:

- It would rely on database engines that are independently installable.
- Those engines, as prepackaged installations, do not require developer effort to create or maintain.
- Their functionality can be tested externally, and thus, it can be trusted to behave as expected; therefore, development doesn't have to test the engine, but only interact with it.

Taken together, these factors would allow for one of several options; a standard, SQL-based RDBMS would work, as would many of the available NoSQL database engines.

Another factor to consider is how the object data structure would be represented in the various database options. Simple objects, such as the `Address` in `hms_core`, can be represented quite easily in any RDBMS with a single table. More complicated objects, such as an `Artisan` with its embedded `Address`, or a `Product` with variably sized and variable content property data (`metadata`), require either discrete tables for related properties (with relationships defined so that the objects' related properties can be retrieved) or support for dynamic, structured data.

As they'd be built in a typical RDBMS implementation, the relationships are very simple; each `Artisan` has one address, and each `Product` has zero-to-many `metadata` items, which would look something like the following:

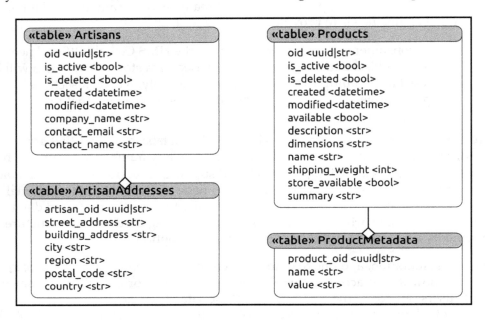

Complications start to arise when we consider how to implement different data retrieval processes, using the possible permutations from the `BaseDataObject.get` class method and assuming that the real work happens at the database engine side of things:

- Getting one `Artisan` and its `address`, or one `Product` and its `metadata`, isn't too complicated; assuming an `oid` value, it boils down to variations of the following:
    - Getting the artisan or product record that matches the `oid`, then converting it to a `dict` so that we can use the `from_data_dict` class method to create an instance
    - For an `Artisan`: Getting the related `address` record, converting it to a `dict`, and inserting it into the first `dict`, created as `address`
    - For a `Product`: Getting the related `metadata` records, converting the records returned to a key/value `dict`, and inserting it into the first `dict`, created as `metadata`

- Creating the instance by calling the appropriate `from_data_dict` class method.
- Getting multiple instances based on only a list of `oid` values isn't much different; it simply starts with retrieving all of the records with matching `oid` values, then sorting out the data and creating and returning a list of instances. Realistically, if this process and the single-`oid` process used the same code, returning one (or zero) objects for a single `oid` (and no results if there was no matching `oid`), it wouldn't be horrible to work with.

- Getting zero-to-many instances based on one local `criteria` value alone—finding an `Artisan` or `Product` by `company_name` or `name`, respectively, is also not difficult by itself. The actual process at the database side of the operation is significantly different from the pure `oid`-based retrievals, as follows:

    - You find all of the matches based on the `criteria` passed, and keep track of the `oid` values for each match

    - Then, you return the items identified by those `oid` values

- Finding items by `address` or `metadata` values is similar, but it gets the initial list of `oid` values identifying results from the child table.

- Getting multiple `criteria` values from a single table, parent, or child is yet another permutation that has to be handled.

- Another permutation is getting `criteria` values from parent and child tables in the same criteria set.

The preceding list shows six different variations that have to be accounted for, assuming that the intentions of `BaseDataObject.get` are honored. These don't address how updates to (or deletions of) data are handled across related tables, either, which adds more complexity.

While it may be possible to implement all of them in SQL on the database side, such an implementation is going to be complicated. If the developers aren't pretty experienced database administrators, it may not be feasible at all; and, even if it is, it will still be a complex solution, with all of the potential risks that follow.

A trade-off approach that could be easily implemented, but would incur more processing time and/or memory usage, would be similar to the approach taken in the Artisan Application: loading all of the objects for any call made to `BaseDataObject.get`, then sorting out the results in the code. As the dataset involved grows, the data being retrieved and sent back will grow, and the time required to usefully retrieve the data that isn't just a simple "get me objects with any of these `oid` values" request will take longer to find in the database and transmit to the application. Given enough time, or enough data, it will start to suffer from scalability issues. This approach is probably feasible, and it will probably work (if for a limited time), provided that multi-table updates and the deletion of child records can be managed in some fashion. The updating side of things would probably be managed purely in the application code, and related record deletion could be managed on the database side or in the application code.

Another option that's still in the realm of an RDBMS-based solution is to use an engine that has support for structured but schema-less data; MySQL and MariaDB, for example, have JSON field types that would allow entire Artisan and Product records to be represented with a very simple table structure, as follows:

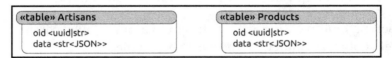

Provided that those JSON fields allow for queries to execute against the data structure within them, all of the options that `BaseDataObject.get` needs to provide are supported, and without the concern of having to manage child tables. For all practical purposes, this specific approach would pretty much involve using MySQL as a replacement for a document store NoSQL database such as MongoDB, but without some of the functionality that a document store database likely already has.

All things considered, that's a lot of complexity that could be considered disadvantageous for an RDBMS-based data store. However, there are some advantages, too, even if they may not seem like significant ones at first glance. An RDBMS data store will generally allow for multiple queries to be executed in one pass. So, the multiple queries that are involved with the retrieval of data from multiple tables can be written as multiple query statements that are executed as a single call to the engine.

Most SQL-based databases also allow for some sort of precompiled/prepared functionality to be written: stored procedures or user functions; views; and, perhaps, other constructs that can move substantial chunks of functionality out of the application code and into the database. Those are usually quicker to execute, and, although SQL may not support extensive functionality (even in procedures and functions), there might be enough available to make their use worthwhile. Finally, and perhaps most significantly, the enforced data structure of tables, combined with the relational capabilities of pretty much any RDBMS worthy of the name, allows for pretty much any data in the system to be queried as needed, while enforcing solid data integrity across all system data if the databases are reasonably well designed.

If an SQL-based RDBMS were to be selected as the engine for object state data persistence, the classes that used that engine to persist their state data would need some (or all) of the following properties to be specified:

- A `host` specification: The hostname (FQDN, machine network name, or IP address) where the database resides
- A `database` name: The name of the database on the specified host that state data will be read from and written to
- A `user`: This will be used to connect to the database on the host
- A `password`: This will be used to connect to the database on the host

Instances would also need to be able to make connections to the database, which could be implemented with a method (`get_connection`, perhaps) or a property (`connection`, which could be lazily instantiated, and written so that an active `connection` could be deleted and recreated, when needed). It would also need a method to execute queries against the database once the connection had been established (`query`, perhaps). If this seems familiar, it's because this is the exact structure that was mentioned earlier, when discussing the idea of a `BaseDatabaseConnector` class.

On the NoSQL side, all of the standard NoSQL advantages apply, as follows:

- Since there aren't any hard and fast table structures involved in the database, there's no significant development time required to make changes to the data structure being stored. Once the data structure at the application side has been changed, any new or updated records will be adjusted when they are saved.

- Most of the NoSQL options already have the functionality to deal with the sort of data retrieval that `BaseDataObject.get` is promising to provide, and that has so much potential complexity in a more traditional RDBMS solution. That will probably translate to less development time and simpler code to maintain, both of which are good things.

- The data writing (creation and update) processes will be simpler to implement, as well, since the relationships that require separate tables or unusual data structures in an RDBMS-based approach just go away, really—data-writes can store an entire data structure all at once, and don't have to worry about making sure that failures in a child table prevent the parent table from being written to.

Of the two options, the NoSQL option feels like it will be easier to manage, while still fulfilling all of the requirements of the data persistence stories. Of the various NoSQL options, MongoDB feels like it will require the fewest changes to data structures, as object data is read from and written to the database; so, MongoDB will be the backend data store engine that we'll use.

The data access strategy for the Central Office projects

Having selected the database engine, another decision that needs to be made is where that engine will ultimately live, in relation to the Artisan Gateway and Central Office application. Both of those will need to be able to read and write the same data from the same location. Since MongoDB can be used across a network, the data store could live pretty much anywhere that's accessible over that network (even on the same machine as one of the two components).

The logical architecture perspective of the relationships between the Artisan Gateway, several instances of the Central Office application, and the `hms_sys` database, then, would look something like the following diagram (allowing for any number of application instances, but showing only three):

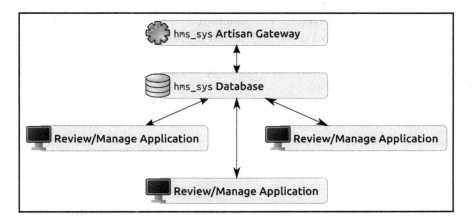

The physical architecture is less significant from a development perspective, provided that each logical component has a readily identifiable physical location. During development, all of those physical locations can be on a developer's local computer. Once deployed, the Artisan Gateway service and the hms_sys database might be installed to different machines, or they might reside on the same machine. This arrangement would allow all of the application instances and the service to share common data, reading from and writing to the hms_sys database from wherever they might live.

Supporting objects for data persistence

It's almost unheard of for a database installation to not require some credentials for access in a production system, and there are other parameters that need to be kept track of across the various object types whose data will be saved in the data store. Since those parameters will be common for all of the different object types in use (for the most part), creating a mechanism that can be used to gather them all up seems like a logical first step. The common parameters that will most likely be needed were noted in the RDBMS exploration earlier, and are as follows:

- host
- port
- database
- user
- password

By the time `hms_sys` is deployed to a production environment, these will almost certainly be saved in some sort of configuration file, and it doesn't hurt to get that logic in place now, rather than waiting to do so later. All of the data store configuration and connection parameters can be captured in a single object instance—a `DatastoreConfig`:

```
class DatastoreConfig:
    """
Represents a set of credentials for connecting to a back-end
database engine that requires host, port, database, user, and
password values.
    """
```

With the exception of the `port` property, which only allows `int` values from `0` through `65535` (the normal range of valid ports in a TCP/IP connection), there's nothing substantially new in the property getter-, setter-, and deleter-methods. The `_set_port` method's value checking is very straightforward, as follows:

```
def _set_port(self, value:int) -> None:
    if type(value) != int:
        raise TypeError(
            '%s.port expects an int value from 0 through 65535, '
            'inclusive, but was passed "%s" (%s)' %
            (self.__class__.__name__, value, type(value).__name__)
        )
    if value < 0 or value > 65535:
        raise ValueError(
            '%s.port expects an int value from 0 through 65535, '
            'inclusive, but was passed "%s" (%s)' %
            (self.__class__.__name__, value, type(value).__name__)
        )
    self._port = value
```

The `__init__` method is also very straightforward, though it has no required arguments, because not all database engines will need all of the parameters, and the class is intended to be very generic. Connection issues that occur as a result of incomplete or invalid configuration will have to be handled at the relevant object level:

```
#####################################
# Object initialization             #
#####################################

def __init__(self,
    host=None, port=None, database=None, user=None, password=None
):
```

```
        """
Object initialization.

self .............. (DatastoreConfig instance, required) The instance
                    to execute against
host .............. (str, optional, defaults to None) the host-name
                    (FQDN, machine network-name or IP address) where
                    the database that the instance will use to persist
                    state-data resides
port .............. (int [0..65535], optional, defaults to None) the
                    TCP/IP port on the host that the database
                    connection will use
database .......... (str, optional, defaults to None) the name of
                    the database that the instance will use to persist
                    state-data
user .............. (str, optional, defaults to None) the user-name
                    used to connect to the database that the instance
                    will use to persist state-data
password .......... (str, optional, defaults to None) the password
                    used to connect to the database that the instance
                    will use to persist state-data
        """
```

Since there will eventually be a need to read configuration data from a file, a class method (from_config) is defined to facilitate that, as follows:

```
####################################
# Class methods                    #
####################################

@classmethod
def from_config(cls, config_file:(str,)):
    # - Use an explicit try/except instead of with ... as ...
    try:
        fp = open(config_file, 'r')
        config_data = fp.read()
        fp.close()
    except (IOError, PermissionError) as error:
        raise error.__class__(
            '%s could not read the config-file at %s due to '
            'an error (%s): %s' %
            (
                self.__class__.__name__, config_file,
                error.__class__.__name__, error
            )
        )
    # - For now, we'll assume that config-data is in JSON, though
    #   other formats might be better later on (YAML, for
```

```
instance)
        load_successful = False
        try:
            parameters = json.loads(config_data)
            load_successful = True
        except Exception as error:
            pass
        # - YAML can go here
        # - .ini-file format here, maybe?
        if load_successful:
            try:
                return cls(**parameters)
            except Exception as error:
                raise RuntimeError(
                    '%s could not load configuration-data from %s '
                    'due to an %s: %s' %
                    (
                        cls.__name__, config_file,
                        error.__class__.__name__, error
                    )
                )
        else:
            raise RuntimeError(
                '%s did not recognize the format of the config-file '
                'at %s' % (cls.__name__, config_file)
            )
```

The local MongoDB connections for development can then be created as instances of `DatastoreConfig`, with the minimum parameters needed to connect to a local database, as follows:

```
# - The local mongod service may not require user-name and password
local_mongo = DatastoreConfig(
    host='localhost', port=27017, database='hms_local'
)
```

Reading and writing data against a Mongo database, using the `pymongo` library, requires a few steps, as follows:

1. A connection to the Mongo engine has to be established (using a `pymongo.MongoClient` object). This is where the actual credentials (the username and password) will apply, if the Mongo engine requires them. The connection (or client) allows the specification of...

2. The database where the data is being stored has to be specified. The `database` value in the configuration takes care of specifying the name of the database, and the database itself, a `pymongo.database.Database` object, once returned by the client/connection allows the creation of…

3. The collection where the actual documents (records) reside (a `pymongo.collection.Collection` object), and where all of the data access processes actually occur.

A very simple, functional example of the connection/database/collection setup for `hms_sys` development might include the following:

```
client = pymongo.MongoClient()      # Using default host and port
database = client['hms_sys']        # Databases can be requested by name
objects = database['Objects']       # The collection of Object
# documents/records
```

At this point, the `objects` object, as a Mongo `Collection`, provides methods for reading, writing, and deleting documents/records in the `Objects` collection/table.

The organization of documents in a collection can be very arbitrary. That `objects` collection could be used to store `Artisan`, `Product`, and `Order` state data documents all in the same collection. There's no functional reason that prevents it. Over a long enough period of time, though, reading data from that collection would slow down more than reads from collections that, for example, grouped those same `Artisan`, `Product`, and `Order` state data documents into separate collections—one collection for each object type. There might be other considerations that will make such a grouping beneficial, as well. Keeping objects of the same type would probably make managing them through a GUI tool easier, and might be similarly beneficial for command-line management tools.

Taking all of the preceding factors together, a fairly optimal integration of data storage and parameters across the objects in the `hms_sys` data store would include the following:

- One or more client connections to a common MongoDB instance, whose credentials and parameters are all configurable and are eventually controlled by a configuration file
- One database specification that is common to all of the objects in the Central Office code bases, from the same configuration that the client setup uses

- One collection specification per object type, which could be as simple as using the name of the class

Having made all of these decisions, we can create an ABC that central-office application and service objects can derive from in much the same way that Artisan Application data objects derived from `JSONFileDataObject`, as we saw in `Chapter 12`, *Persisting Object Data to Files,*—call it `HMSMongoDataObject`. Since it will need to be available to both the Artisan Gateway service and the Central Office application, it needs to live in a package that is available to both. Without creating another package project solely for this purpose, the logical place for it to live would be in a new module in `hms_core`; and, if the naming convention established in the Artisan code base is followed, that module would be named `data_storage.py`.

Diagrammed, the relationship between `HMSMongoDataObject` and the final central-office data objects looks much like the Artisan Application's counterparts, although `hms_co .. Order` is not included, because it may need some special consideration that we haven't explored:

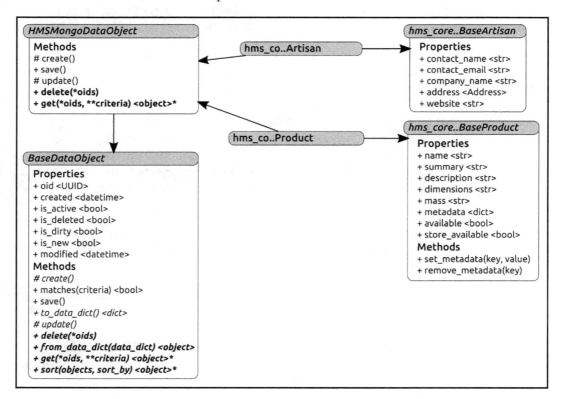

The implementation of HMSMongoDataObject starts by inheriting
from BaseDataObject, and then it includes the following:

```
class HMSMongoDataObject(BaseDataObject, metaclass=abc.ABCMeta):
    """
    Provides baseline functionality, interface requirements, and
    type-identity for objects that can persist their state-data to
    a MongoDB-based back-end data-store.
    """
```

Since we'll be using a DatastoreConfig object to keep track of a common
configuration for all derived classes, that becomes a class attribute
(_configuration), as follows:

```
####################################
# Class attributes/constants       #
####################################

# - Keeps track of the global configuration for data-access
_configuration = None
```

MongoDB documents, when they are created, have an _id value that, if passed to a
normal from_data_dict to create an instance of the class, will throw an error.
There hasn't been an _id argument in any of our implementations so far, and there's
no reason to expect one to surface anywhere down the line, because we're using our
own oid property as the unique identifier for object records. In order to prevent that
from happening, from_data_dict will need to either explicitly remove
that _id value from its object creation process, or keep track of all of
the valid arguments that can exist, and filter things accordingly. Of those two options,
the latter, while slightly more complicated, also feels more stable. In the (unlikely)
event that more fine-grained filtering of data is needed during object creation
in from_data_dict, tracking the valid arguments will be easier to maintain than
having to modify a long list of key removals:

```
# - Keeps track of the keys allowed for object-creation from
#   retrieved data
_data_dict_keys = None
```

Since we have decided that all objects of any given type should live in a collection with a meaningful and related name, the approach that needs the least effort is simply using the class name as the name of the MongoDB collection that state data for instances of the class live in. We can't rule out a potential need to change that, though, so another class attribute that allows that default behavior to be overridden feels like a sensible precaution:

```
# - Allows the default mongo-collection name (the __name__
#   of the class) to be overridden. This should not be changed
#   lightly, since data saved to the old collection-name will
#   no longer be available!
_mongo_collection = None
```

The properties of `HMSMongoDataObject` look relatively normal at first glance, but there is a significant difference that may not be obvious at first. Since data access for any given class is focused on instances of that class, and creation of database connections and collections could be computationally expensive, having a single connection for all data object classes is a tempting idea—that implementation would have the instance-level connection and database properties' underlying storage attributes be members of `HMSMongoDataObject`, not of the derived classes themselves, or instances of those classes.

That would, in effect, require that all data objects for `hms_sys` live in the same database and be accessed through the same MongoDB instance at all times. While that's not an unreasonable requirement, it could make moving live system data problematic. The entire system might need to be shut down for such a data move. As a compromise, the `connection` and `database` properties of each class will be members of that class, instead – which would, for example, allow `Artisan` object data to be moved independently of `Product` data. This may not be a likely consideration in the near future of the system, but it doesn't feel like a bad compromise to make if it has the potential of reducing effort somewhere down the line:

```
######################################
# Property-getter methods            #
######################################

def _get_collection(self) -> pymongo.collection.Collection:
    try:
        return self.__class__._collection
    except AttributeError:
        # - If the class specifies a collection-name, then use that
        #   as the collection...
```

```
            if self.__class__._mongo_collection:
                self.__class__._collection = self.database[
                    self.__class__._mongo_collection
                ]
            # - Otherwise, use the class-name
            else:
                self.__class__._collection = self.database[
                    self.__class__.__name__
                ]
            return self.__class__._collection

    def _get_configuration(self) -> DatastoreConfig:
        return HMSMongoDataObject._configuration

    def _get_connection(self) -> pymongo.MongoClient:
        try:
            return self.__class__._connection
        except AttributeError:
            # - Build the connection-parameters we need:
            conn_config = []
            # - host
            if self.configuration.host:
                conn_config.append(self.configuration.host)
                # - port. Ports don't make any sense without a
                #   host, though, so host has to be defined first...
                if self.configuration.port:
                    conn_config.append(self.configuration.port)
            # - Create the connection
            self.__class__._connection =
pymongo.MongoClient(*conn_config)
            return self.__class__._connection

    def _get_database(self) -> pymongo.database.Database:
        try:
            return self.__class__._database
        except AttributeError:
            self.__class__._database = self.connection[
                self.configuration.database
            ]
            return self.__class__._database
```

The collection, connection, and database properties are also handled differently, for the purposes of deletion. The actual objects that are retrieved by the getter methods are lazily instantiated (created when they are needed, in order to reduce system load when they aren't going to be used), and, because they don't exist until they are first created (by a reference to them), it's just easier to truly delete them, rather than set them to some default value, such as None:

```python
####################################
# Property-deleter methods         #
####################################

def _del_collection(self) -> None:
    # - If the collection is deleted, then the database needs
    #   to be as well:
    self._del_database()
    try:
        del self.__class__._collection
    except AttributeError:
        # - It may already not exist
        pass

def _del_connection(self) -> None:
    # - If the connection is deleted, then the collection and
    #   database need to be as well:
    self._del_collection()
    self._del_database()
    try:
        del self.__class__._connection
    except AttributeError:
        # - It may already not exist
        pass

def _del_database(self) -> None:
    try:
        del self.__class__._database
    except AttributeError:
        # - It may already not exist
        pass
```

The property definitions are slightly different than what we've used in the past, because those properties can be retrieved or deleted, but not set. This corresponds to the idea that the database and collection can only be retrieved (opened) or closed (deleted). Accordingly, they have no setter methods defined or attached to the properties themselves, and the configuration property takes that a step further – it is read-only:

```
#####################################
# Instance property definitions     #
#####################################

collection = property(
    _get_collection, None, _del_collection,
    'Gets or deletes the MongoDB collection that instance '
    'state-data is stored in'
)
connection = property(
    _get_connection, None, _del_connection,
    'Gets or deletes the database-connection that the instance '
    'will use to manage its persistent state-data'
)
database = property(
    _get_database, None, _del_database,
    'Gets or deletes the MongoDB database that instance '
    'state-data is stored in'
)
configuration = property(
    _get_configuration, None, None,
    'Gets, sets or deletes the configuration-data '
    '(DatastoreConfig) of the instance, from HMSMongoDataObject'
)
```

The __init__ method looks very much like
the __init__ method of JSONFileDataObject, with the same arguments (and for the same reasons). Since we have no properties that require default values to be set, however, the only thing that it needs to do is call its own parent constructor, as follows:

```
#####################################
# Object initialization             #
#####################################

def __init__(self,
    oid:(UUID,str,None)=None,
    created:(datetime,str,float,int,None)=None,
    modified:(datetime,str,float,int,None)=None,
    is_active:(bool,int,None)=None,
```

```
            is_deleted:(bool,int,None)=None,
            is_dirty:(bool,int,None)=None,
            is_new:(bool,int,None)=None,
        ):
            """
Object initialization.

self ............. (HMSMongoDataObject instance, required) The
                   instance to execute against
    """
            # - Call parent initializers if needed
            BaseDataObject.__init__(self,
                oid, created, modified, is_active, is_deleted,
                is_dirty, is_new
            )
            # - Perform any other initialization needed
```

Like `JSONFileDataObject`, the `_create` and `_update` methods
for `HMSMongoDataObject` aren't necessary. MongoDB, like the JSON file approach
that was used earlier, doesn't distinguish between creating and updating a document.
Both processes will simply write all of the object data to the document, creating it if
necessary. Since they are required by `BaseDataObject` but aren't of use in this
context, the same implementation, simply raising an error with developer-useful
information, will suffice:

```
        ####################################
        # Instance methods                 #
        ####################################

        def _create(self) -> None:
            """
Creates a new state-data record for the instance in the back-end
data-store
    """
            raise NotImplementedError(
                '%s._create is not implemented, because the save '
                'method handles all the data-writing needed for '
                'the class. Use save() instead.' %
                self.__class__.__name__
            )

        def _update(self) -> None:
            """
Updates an existing state-data record for the instance in the
back-end data-store
    """
            raise NotImplementedError(
```

```
        '%s._update is not implemented, because the save '
        'method handles all the data-writing needed for '
        'the class. Use save() instead.' %
        self.__class__.__name__
    )
```

The implementation of `save`, supported by the class-level `collection` and its `database` and `connection` ancestors, is very simple. We need to acquire the `data_dict` for the instance and tell the MongoDB connection to `insert` that data. The one complicating factor in this process is the standard MongoDB `_id` value that was mentioned earlier. If we did nothing more than calling `insert`, there would be no `_id` value for the MongoDB engine to use to identify that a document that already exists does, in fact, exist. The inevitable result of that would be the creation of new document records for existing items on every update (instead of replacing existing documents), polluting the data with out-of-date instances on every update.

Under normal circumstances, the easiest solution for this would be to either change the `oid` property to `_id` during data writing processes and from `_id` back to `oid` during data reads, or to simply change the `oid` properties that have been established thus far to `_id` in the classes defined thus far. The first option would require only a bit of effort in each `to_data_dict` and `from_data_dict` method, including the ones already defined in the `Artisan` data objects, but it would tend to be more error-prone, as well, and it would require additional testing. It's a viable option, but it may not be the best one. Changing the names of the `oid` properties to `_id` across the board would be simpler (little more than a wide-scale search-and-replace operation, really), but it would leave the classes with what would look like a protected property name that would actually be a public property. Functionally, that's not such a big deal, but it flies in the face of Python code standards, and it is not a preferred option.

Another option is to simply assure that the `hms_sys` `oid` properties and the `_id` values that MongoDB generates are identical. While that does mean that individual document record sizes will increase, that change is trivial – on the order of 12 bytes per document record. Since that could be handled by the `save` method's process, as a simple addition to the `data_dict` value being saved (and would need to be ignored, or otherwise dealt with, during `from_data_dict` retrievals, as a part of that process), there would only be two places where it would have to be written or maintained.

That feels like a much cleaner option, even with the additional data being stored. The final implementation of save, then, would be as follows:

```
def save(self):
    if self._is_new or self._is_dirty:
        # - Make sure to update the modified time-stamp!
        self.modified = datetime.now()
        data_dict = self.to_data_dict()
        data_dict['_id'] = self.oid
        self.collection.insert_one(data_dict)
        self._set_is_dirty(False)
        self._set_is_new(False)
```

The corresponding change in from_data_dict uses the _data_dict_keys class attribute that was defined earlier. Since _data_dict_keys may not have been defined, but needs to be, checking that it's been defined and raising a more detailed error message will make debugging those (hopefully rare) occasions easier. Once that's been verified, the incoming data_dict will simply be filtered down to only those keys that match an argument in the __init__ method of the class, and will be passed to __init__ to create the relevant instance:

```
@classmethod
def from_data_dict(cls, data_dict):
    # - Assure that we have the collection of keys that are
    #   allowed for the class!
    if cls._data_dict_keys == None:
        raise AttributeError(
            '%s.from_data_dict cannot be used because the %s '
            'class has not specified what data-store keys are '
            'allowed to be used to create new instances from '
            'retrieved data. Set %s._data_dict_keys to a list '
            'or tuple of argument-names present in %s.__init__' %
            (cls.__name__, cls.__name__, cls.__name__,
cls.__name__)
        )
    # - Remove any keys that aren't listed in the class'
    #   initialization arguments:
    data_dict = dict(
        [
            (key, data_dict[key]) for key in data_dict.keys()
            if key in cls._data_dict_keys
        ]
    )
    # - Then create and return an instance of the class
    return cls(**data_dict)
```

In order to allow all `HMSMongoDataObject`-derived classes to be configured at once, we need to provide a class method to that end. The one caveat to the implementation of this method is that all of the derived classes will also have the method available, but the method changes the `_configuration` attribute of the `HMSMongoDataObject` class, even if it's called from a derived class. It can be reasonably expected that calling, say, `Artisan.configure`, would configure data access for only `Artisan` objects – but that is not what should happen, so we'll raise an error to make sure that it doesn't go unnoticed if it's attempted:

```
###################################
# Class methods                   #
###################################

@classmethod
def configure(cls, configuration:(DatastoreConfig)):
    """
Sets configuration values across all classes derived from
HMSMongoDataObject.
    """
    if cls != HMSMongoDataObject:
        raise RuntimeError(
            '%s.configure will alter *all* MongoDB configuration,
            'not just the configuration for %s. Please use '
            'HMSMongoDataObject.configure instead.' %
            (cls.__name__, cls.__name__)
        )
    if not isinstance(configuration, DatastoreConfig):
        raise TypeError(
            '%s.configure expects an instance of '
            'DatastoreConfig, but was passed "%s" (%s)' %
            (
                cls.__name__, configuration,
                type(configuration).__name__
            )
        )
    HMSMongoDataObject._configuration = configuration
```

Since all of the class methods that interact with the data store will need the relevant connection, and it may not have been created by an instance before the call was made, having a helper class method to acquire the connection will be useful. It is also possible to force the acquisition of all of the relevant data store objects by creating an instance, but that feels cumbersome and counter-intuitive:

```
@classmethod
def get_mongo_collection(cls) -> pymongo.collection.Collection:
```

```
        """
Helper class-method that retrieves the relevant MongoDB collection for
data-access to state-data records for the class.
        """
        # - If the collection has already been created, then
        #   return it, otherwise create it then return it
        try:
            return cls._collection
        except AttributeError:
            pass
        if not cls._configuration:
            raise RuntimeError(
                '%s must be configured before the '
                'use of %s.get will work. Call HMSMongoDataObject.'
                'configure with a DatastoreConfig object to resolve '
                'this issue' % (cls.__name__, cls.__name__)
            )
        # - With configuration established, we can create the
        #   connection, database and collection objects we need
        #   in order to execute the request:
        # - Build the connection-parameters we need:
        conn_config = []
        # - host
        if cls._configuration.host:
            conn_config.append(cls.configuration.host)
            # - port. Ports don't make any sense without a
            #   host, though, so host has to be defined first...
            if cls._configuration.port:
                conn_config.append(cls.configuration.port)
        # - Create the connection
        cls._connection = pymongo.MongoClient(*conn_config)
        # - Create the database
        cls._database = cls._connection[cls._configuration.database]
        # - and the collection
        if cls._mongo_collection:
            cls._collection = cls._database[cls._mongo_collection]
        # - Otherwise, use the class-name
        else:
            cls._collection = cls._database[cls.__name__]
        return cls._collection
```

The implementation of the `delete` class method is very simple; it boils down to iterating over the provided `oids`, and deleting each one in the iteration. Since `delete` is interacting with the data store, and it's a class method, it calls the `get_mongo_collection` class method that we defined first:

```python
@classmethod
def delete(cls, *oids):
    """
Performs an ACTUAL record deletion from the back-end data-store
of all records whose unique identifiers have been provided
    """
    # - First, we need the collection that we're working with:
    collection = cls.get_mongo_collection()
    if oids:
        for oid in oids:
            collection.remove({'oid':str(oid)})


@classmethod
def from_data_dict(cls, data_dict):
    # - Assure that we have the collection of keys that are
    #   allowed for the class!
    if cls._data_dict_keys == None:
        from inspect import getfullargspec
        argspec = getfullargspec(cls.__init__)
        init_args = argspec.args
        try:
            init_args.remove('self')
        except:
            pass
        try:
            init_args.remove('cls')
        except:
            pass
        print(argspec)
        if argspec.varargs:
            init_args.append(argspec.varargs)
        if argspec.varkw:
            init_args.append(argspec.varkw)
        raise AttributeError(
            '%s.from_data_dict cannot be used because the %s '
            'class has not specified what data-store keys are '
            'allowed to be used to create new instances from '
            'retrieved data. Set %s._data_dict_keys to a list '
            'or tuple of argument-names present in %s.__init__ '
            '(%s)' %
            (
                cls.__name__, cls.__name__, cls.__name__,
```

```
                        cls.__name__, "'" + "', '".join(init_args) + "'"
                )
        )
        # - Remove any keys that aren't listed in the class'
        #   initialization arguments:
        data_dict = dict(
            [
                (key, data_dict[key]) for key in data_dict.keys()
                if key in cls._data_dict_keys
            ]
        )
        # - Then create and return an instance of the class
        return cls(**data_dict)
```

The result of a failed check of _data_dict_keys is
an AttributeError that includes a list of the arguments of
the __init__ method of the class, using
the getfullargspec function of the inspect module.
Python's inspect module provides a very thorough set of functions
for examining code within the code that's running. We'll take a more
in-depth look at the module when we start to look at
metaprogramming concepts.

The get method of HMSMongoDataObject also starts by assuring that the
relevant collection is available. Structurally, it looks a lot like its counterpart
in JSONFileDataObject, which should come as no great surprise, since it's
performing the same sort of actions, and uses the same method signature that was
defined in BaseDataObject. Because MongoDB has more capabilities available than
the file system, there are some noteworthy differences:

```
@classmethod
def get(cls, *oids, **criteria) -> list:
    # - First, we need the collection that we're working with:
    collection = cls.get_mongo_collection()
    # - The first pass of the process retrieves documents based
    #   on oids or criteria.
```

Rather than try to work out a (probably complex) mechanism for dynamically
generating arguments for the find functionality of pymongo that include
both oids and criteria, we'll handle requests based on the combination
of oids and criteria that are present. Each branch in the code will result in a list
of data_dict items that can be converted to a list of object instances later on.

If `oids` are provided, then the initial request will only concern itself with those. At present, the expectation is that `get` calls with `oids` will usually have only a few `oids` involved (usually just one, in fact), so using very basic functionality to get each document that corresponds to a single `oid` in the list should suffice, at least for now:

```
#  - We also need to keep track of whether or not to do a
#    matches call on the results after the initial data-
#    retrieval:
post_filter = False
if oids:
    #  - oid-based requests should usually be a fairly short
    #    list, so finding individual items and appending them
    #    should be OK, performance-wise.
    data_dicts = [
        collection.find_one({'oid':oid})
        for oid in oids
    ]
```

If, somewhere down the line, there is a need to handle longer collections of `oids`, `pymongo` supports that, as well; so, we'll leave a comment about that in place, just in case we need it later:

```
#  - If this becomes an issue later, consider changing
#    it to a variant of
#    collection.find({'oid':{'$in':oids}})
#    (the oids argument-list may need pre-processing first)
```

If `oids` and `criteria` are both provided, the eventual list of objects will need to be filtered with the `matches` method, so the presence of `criteria` will have to be monitored and tracked. If `oids` and `criteria` are both supplied, then we'll need to know that later, in order to filter the initial results:

```
if criteria:
    post_filter = True
```

If only `criteria` is passed, then the entire set of `data_dicts` can be retrieved with a single call, using a list comprehension to gather the found items from the cursor that `find` returns:

```
        elif criteria:
            # - criteria-based items can do a find based on all
criteria
            #   straight away
            data_dicts = [
                item for item in collection.find(criteria)
            ]
```

If neither `oids` nor `criteria` is passed, then we will want to return everything available, as follows:

```
        else:
            # - If there are no oids specified, and no criteria,
            #   the implication is that we want *all* object-records
            #   to be returned...
            data_dicts = [
                item for item in collection.find()
            ]
```

Once the initial `data_dict` has been generated, it will be used to create the initial list of object instances, as follows:

```
    # - At this point, we have data_dict values that should be
    #   able to create instances, so create them.
    results = [
        cls.from_data_dict(data_dict)
        for data_dict in data_dicts
        if data_dict # <-- This could be None: check it!
    ]
```

And, if we still need to filter those results down even more (if we set `post_filter` to `True` earlier), then the same filter process that was used in `JSONFileDataObject` can be used now, calling the `matches` method of each object in the initial results and only adding it to the final results list if it returns `True`, as follows:

```
        # - If post_filter has been set to True, then the request
        #   was for items by oid *and* that have certain criteria
        if post_filter:
            results = [
                obj for obj in results if obj.matches(**criteria)
            ]
        return results
```

All of the basic CRUD operations that are needed for Artisan Gateway and Central Office data objects should be easy to implement at this point, by simply deriving them from the corresponding `Base` class in `hms_core` and `HMSMongoDataObject`:

1. Create and update operations still happen simply by calling the `save` method of any instance.

2. Read operations are handled by the `get` class method, which also allows for a fair bit of functionality for finding objects, though there might be the need for additional functionality that supports more complex capabilities later on.

3. Delete operations are handled by the `delete` class method; again, there may be the need for deletion capabilities that aren't based on the `oid`, but for now, this will suffice.

RDBMS implementations

So far, both of the data object implementations that we've created have overridden the `_create` and `_update` methods that were required in `BaseDataObject`. It would be fair, under the circumstances, to question why those were put in place at all. The short answer to that question is that both of the implementations that have come together so far use the same process at the data store level for creating and updating records and documents. As a result, they simply haven't been needed. If it was expected that `hms_sys` would never need any other database backend, we'd be justified in removing them from the entire code base.

However, what would've happened if the decision to use MongoDB had gone a different way, and the preferred (or mandated) backend data store engine was an RDBMS such as Microsoft SQL Server? Or, worse, what if that sort of change was mandated after the system was operational?

Setting aside the data migration planning that would have to happen and focusing on only the application and service code, what would that kind of change require? Not much, when it comes right down to it. A generic SQL/RDBMS engine ABC (`HMSSQLDataObject`) might look something like the following, for a given RDBMS API/library:

```
class HMSSQLDataObject(BaseDataObject, metaclass=abc.ABCMeta):
    """
Provides baseline functionality, interface requirements, and
type-identity for objects that can persist their state-data to
a (GENERIC) SQL-based RDBMS back-end data-store.
    """
```

The `HMSSQLDataObject` class that is shown here is by no means complete, but should serve as a reasonable starting point for building a full implementation of such a class, which connects to and uses data from any of several RDBM systems. The complete code, such as it is, can be found in the `hms_core/ch-10-snippets` directory of the project code.

The same `_configuration` class property would probably be in use, serving the same purpose. It's possible that the `_data_dict_keys` class attribute would also be of use in reducing record fields to a valid argument dictionary in `from_data_dict`. Since SQL, for the various CRUD operations, or at least for specific starting points for those CRUD operations, would need to be stored and accessible to the classes, a viable option for doing so would be to attach them as class-attributes, as well:

```
####################################
# Class attributes/constants       #
####################################

# - Keeps track of the global configuration for data-access
_configuration = None
# - Keeps track of the keys allowed for object-creation from
#   retrieved data
_data_dict_keys = None
# - SQL for various expected CRUD actions:
_sql_create = """Some SQL string goes here"""
_sql_read_oids = """Some SQL string goes here"""
_sql_read_all = """Some SQL string goes here"""
_sql_read_criteria = """Some SQL string goes here"""
_sql_update = """Some SQL string goes here"""
_sql_delete = """Some SQL string goes here"""
```

Since the SQL for the various CRUD operations would include the tables that the data is stored in, and the process of connecting to the database in most RDBMS' handles the equivalents to the `connection` and `database` in our MongoDB approach, only the `connection` itself needs to be tracked and available as a property:

```
####################################
# Property-getter methods          #
####################################

def _get_connection(self):
    try:
        return self.__class__._connection
    except AttributeError:
        # - Most RDBMS libraries provide a "connect" function, or
        #   allow the creation of a "connection" object, using the
        #   parameters we've named in DatastoreConfig, or simple
        #   variations of them, so all we need to do is connect:
        self.__class__._connection = RDBMS.connect(
            **self.configuration
        )
        return self.__class__._connection
```

Like its equivalent in the Mongo-based implementation, a `connection` is lazily instantiated and performs an actual deletion, rather than resetting to default values, as follows:

```
####################################
# Property-deleter methods         #
####################################

def _del_connection(self) -> None:
    try:
        del self.__class__._connection
    except AttributeError:
        # - It may already not exist
        pass
```

The related property declaration is identical, and is shown as follows:

```
###################################
# Instance property definitions   #
###################################

connection = property(
    _get_connection, None, _del_connection,
    'Gets or deletes the database-connection that the instance '
    'will use to manage its persistent state-data'
)
```

Object initialization is also identical, as follows:

```
###################################
# Object initialization           #
###################################

def __init__(self,
    oid:(UUID,str,None)=None,
    created:(datetime,str,float,int,None)=None,
    modified:(datetime,str,float,int,None)=None,
    is_active:(bool,int,None)=None,
    is_deleted:(bool,int,None)=None,
    is_dirty:(bool,int,None)=None,
    is_new:(bool,int,None)=None,
):
    """
Object initialization.

self .............. (HMSMongoDataObject instance, required) The
                    instance to execute against
oid ............... (UUID|str, optional, defaults to None) The unique
                    identifier of the object's state-data record in
the
                    back-end data-store
created ........... (datetime|str|float|int, optional, defaults to
None)
                    The date/time that the object was created
modified .......... (datetime|str|float|int, optional, defaults to
None)
                    The date/time that the object was last modified
is_active ......... (bool|int, optional, defaults to None) A flag
                    indicating that the object is active
is_deleted ........ (bool|int, optional, defaults to None) A flag
                    indicating that the object should be considered
                    deleted (and may be in the near future)
is_dirty .......... (bool|int, optional, defaults to None) A flag
```

```
                            indicating that the object's data needs to be
                            updated in the back-end data-store
        is_new .......... (bool|int, optional, defaults to None) A flag
                            indicating that the object's data needs to be
                            created in the back-end data-store
        """
            # - Call parent initializers if needed
            BaseDataObject.__init__(self,
                oid, created, modified, is_active, is_deleted,
                is_dirty, is_new
            )
            # - Perform any other initialization needed
```

The significant, substantial differences are mostly in the methods that handle the
CRUD operations. The original `save` method, as implemented in `BaseDataObject`,
is left in place, and will call the `_create` or `_update` methods, as determined
by the `is_dirty` or `is_new` property values for the instance. Each of these methods
is responsible for acquiring the SQL template from the appropriate class attribute,
populating it, as needed, with current state data values, sanitizing the resultant SQL,
and executing it against the connection:

```
        ###################################
        # Instance methods                #
        ###################################

        def _create(self):
            # - The base SQL is in self.__class__._sql_create, and the
            #   field-values would be retrieved from self.to_data_dict():
            data_dict = self.to_data_dict()
            SQL = self.__class__._sql_create
            # - Some process would have to add the values, if not the
    keys,
            #   into the SQL, and the result sanitized, but once that was
            #   done, it'd become a simple query-execution:
            self.connection.execute(SQL)

        def _update(self):
            # - The base SQL is in self.__class__._sql_update, and the
            #   field-values would be retrieved from self.to_data_dict():
            data_dict = self.to_data_dict()
            SQL = self.__class__._sql_update
            # - Some process would have to add the values, if not the
    keys,
            #   into the SQL, and the result sanitized, but once that was
            #   done, it'd become a simple query-execution:
            self.connection.execute(SQL)
```

Sanitizing SQL is a very important security precaution, reducing the risk of a system being vulnerable to an SQL injection attack. These attacks can compromise data confidentiality and integrity, at a minimum, and can also raise the risk of authentication and authorization compromises, perhaps even across multiple systems, depending on password policies and the enforcement of them. Most RDBMS APIs will have some mechanism for sanitizing SQL before executing it, and some will also support query parameterization that can also reduce the risk of vulnerabilities. As a basic rule of thumb, if data supplied by a user is being passed into a query, or even into a stored procedure, it should be sanitized wherever/whenever possible.

The `delete` class method is simple:

```
####################################
# Class methods                    #
####################################

@classmethod
def delete(cls, *oids):
    # - First, we need the database-connection that we're
    #   working with:
    connection = cls.get_connection()
    SQL = cls._sql_delete % oids
    # - Don't forget to sanitize it before executing it!
    result_set = connection.execute(SQL)
```

Most of the pattern and approach behind the `get` method should look familiar; again, it's got the same signature (and is intended to perform the same activities) as the methods that have been created so far, which implement the required functionality of the `BaseDataObject`:

```
@classmethod
def get(cls, *oids, **criteria) -> list:
    # - First, we need the database-connection that we're
    #   working with:
    connection = cls.get_connection()
    # - The first pass of the process retrieves documents based
    #   on oids or criteria.
    # - We also need to keep track of whether or not to do a
    #   matches call on the results after the initial data-
    #   retrieval:
    post_filter = False
```

```
#  - Records are often returned as a tuple (result_set)
#    of tuples (rows) of tuples (field-name, field-value):
#    ( ..., ( ('field-name', 'value' ), (...), ... ), ...)
```

The branch that handles oid requests is as follows:

```
if oids:
    # - Need to replace any placeholder values in the raw SQL
    #   with actual values, AND sanitize the SQL string, but
    #   it starts with the SQL in cls._sql_read_oids
    SQL = cls._sql_read_oids
    result_set = connection.execute(SQL)
    if criteria:
        post_filter = True
```

The criteria branch is as follows:

```
elif criteria:
    # - The same sort of replacement would need to happen here
    #   as happens for oids, above. If the query uses just
    #   one criteria key/value pair initially, we can use the
    #   match-based filtering later to filter further as
    needed
    key = criteria.keys()[0]
    value = criteria[key]
    SQL = cls._sql_read_criteria % (key, value)
    result_set = connection.execute(SQL)
    if len(criteria) > 1:
        post_filter = True
```

The default branch that simply gets everything else is as follows:

```
else:
    SQL = cls._sql_read_all
    result_set = connection.execute(SQL)
```

All of the branches generate a list of data_dict values that can be used to create object instances, though they may not be returned from the backend data store as dictionary values.

The lowest common denominator results of a query are, as noted in the preceding code comments, a tuple of tuples of tuples, which might look something like the following:

```
# This is the outermost tuple, collecting all of the
# rows returned into a result_set:
(
    # Each tuple at this level is a single row:
```

```
    (
        # Each tuple at this level is a key/value pair:
        ('oid', '43d240cd-4c9f-44c2-a196-1c7c56068cef'),
        ('first_name', 'John'),
        ('last_name', 'Smith'),
        ('email', 'john@smith.com'),
        # ...
    ),
    # more rows could happen here, or not...
)
```

If the engine, or the Python API to the engine, provides a built-in mechanism for converting rows returned into dictionary instances, that's probably the preferred approach to use to make the conversion. If there isn't anything built in to handle that, converting the nested tuples to a series of dictionaries isn't difficult to do:

```
# - We should have a result_set value here, so we can convert
#   it from the tuple of tuples of tuples (or whatever) into
#   data_dict-compatible dictionaries:
data_dicts = [
    dict(
        [field_tuple for field_tuple in row]
    )
    for row in result_set
]
```

From this point on, the process is pretty much the same as in the previous implementations, in `JSONFileDataObject` and `HMSMongoDataObject`:

```
# - With those, we can create the initial list of instances:
results = [
    cls.from_data_dict(data_dict)
    for data_dict in data_dicts
]
# - If post_filter has been set to True, then the request
#   was for items by oid *and* that have certain criteria
if post_filter:
    results = [
        obj for obj in results if obj.matches(**criteria)
    ]
```

Another (potentially major) difference concerns how child objects, such as the `products` in an `Artisan` object, will have to be handled. If there is a need to fetch those child objects as objects and populate the parent object with them, assuming that they use the same `BaseDataObject`-derived interface, each child type will have a class associated with it, each of those classes will have a `get` method, and that `get` method will allow the `oid` of the parent object to be specified as criteria. That will allow for a process that looks like the following, used to retrieve and attach any child objects, as needed (using `Artisan` and `Product` classes as an example):

```
# - Data-objects that have related child items, like the
#   Artisan to Product relationship, may need to acquire
#   those children here before returning the results. If
#   they do, then a structure like this should work most
#   of the time:
for artisan in results:
    artisan._set_products(
        Product.get(artisan_oid=artisan.oid)
    )
return results
```

The other members of a final business/data object class that derives from `HMSSQLDataObject` should, for the most part, be expected by now, since they are also required for the implementation of final data objects derived from the other two `DataObject` ABCs. They would include the concrete implementations of `to_data_dict` and `matches` instance methods and the `from_data_dict` class method, and the various class-specific variables (mostly the `_sql` class attributes).

The concrete business objects of the Central Office projects

Up to this point, there's been a lot of effort concerning the foundations, but it's about to pay off, as the creation of the initial Central Office classes gets under way. At present, since the assumption is that the Central Office application and the Artisan Gateway service will be using the same business object classes, and that they need to reside in a common package that's not a part of the package set for either of those code bases, the best option for where they should live appears to be in the `hms_core` component project:

- It was already in the design plan for `hms_core` to be included as a part of the build or deployment of all the other packages, anyway

- Although it would certainly be possible to create yet another component project/package specifically for the data access that these concrete classes will provide, that's a fair amount of overhead for what will probably be a single module, with only three classes (so far)

If, at some point in the future, there is a need or desire to move them to a different package/project—say, if it's decided to change the Central Office application's data access to a web service call to the Artisan Gateway—it won't be difficult to move the code accordingly, although it will be somewhat tedious.

It will probably be easier to understand how the work regarding the foundations is going to pay off by diving right in to one of the concrete classes, so we'll do that now, starting with `hms_core.co_objects.Artisan`.

hms_core.co_objects.Artisan

The Story that's driving the concrete, state data persisting `Artisan` class is as follows:

- As an Artisan manager, I need to be able to manage (create, modify, and delete) artisans in the system, so that their statuses and information can be kept current.

As with the `hms_artisan` equivalent, this is about being able to manage the data, not the UI around that data management process. The various moving parts of any of the data objects in `co_objects` will involve the following:

- The properties of the object type, which will originate with the corresponding `Base` class in `hms_core.business_objects`

- The data persistence-related properties of all data objects in the system, provided or required by `HMSMongoDataObject` or its parent `BaseDataObject`

- Concrete implementations of any abstract members inherited by the concrete class, from any of the classes it derives from

Using the concrete `Artisan` class as an example, the relationships involved are shown in the following diagram:

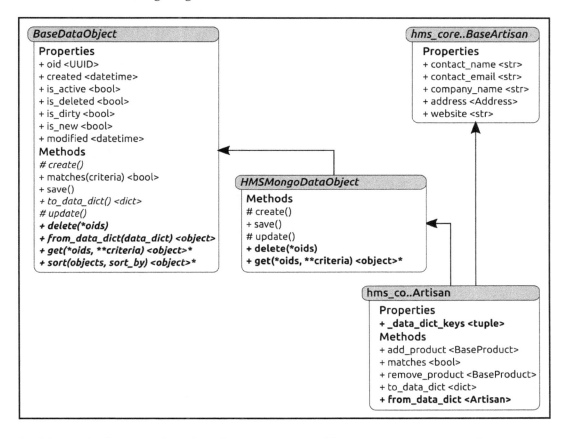

In this particular case, there is only one property (the `_data_dict_keys` class attribute that needs to be overridden from `HMSMongoDataObject`) that needs to be created. Three of the four instance methods (`add_product` and `remove_product`, and `matches`) have concrete implementations in the abstract methods that require their implementation, and can be implemented as nothing more than a call to the original methods in the classes that they originate in.

The `to_data_dict` method for any class deriving from `BaseDataObject` will have to be implemented locally (that's just the nature of the structure that's been developed), but that implementation is not going to be much more than creating and returning a `dict` value.

That leaves `from_data_dict`, the class method that data objects use to create instances from dictionaries; those dictionaries are, in turn, being supplied by data retrievals from the backend data store. In cases where the data object doesn't have any child objects, the baseline method that `BaseDataObject` provides and requires should simply work as an inherited class method. Object types (such as `Artisan`) that do have child object properties will have to accommodate those, and that will happen as a local override of the original class method from `BaseDataObject`.

So, all told, implementing most of these data objects will only involve the following:

- Creating the `_data_dict_keys` class attribute, which can (more or less) be copied and pasted from the argument list of the class' `__init__` method

- Implementing the `matches` method with a call to the method defined in `BaseDataObject` that carries through to `HMSMongoDataObject`

- Implementing `to_data_dict` from scratch

- Implementing a `from_data_dict` class method from scratch, if a customized method is needed

- Creating an `__init__` method that shouldn't need to do anything more than call the relevant parent class `__init__` methods

For most classes, then, the worst-case scenario, to get from nothing to a full, concrete implementation, is two detailed methods to develop, and a few copy-and-paste operations.

Those two methods play out in `hms_core.co_objects.Artisan`, as follows:

```
class Artisan(BaseArtisan, HMSMongoDataObject):
    """
Represents an Artisan in the context of the Central Office
applications and services
    """
```

The `_data_dict_keys` object is a fairly trivial effort, as follows:

```
######################################
# Class attributes/constants         #
######################################

_data_dict_keys = (
    'contact_name', 'contact_email', 'address', 'company_name',
```

```
            'website', 'oid', 'created', 'modified', 'is_active',
            'is_deleted', 'products'
    )
```

The __init__ method still has a fairly complicated argument list, but they can be
copied from their source classes whole-cloth, unless those source
classes' __init__ methods have an argument list (*products, in this case) or a
keyword argument list (which has been avoided, in order to
keep __init__ signatures as simple as possible):

```
#####################################
# Object initialization             #
#####################################

    # TODO: Add and document arguments if/as needed
    def __init__(self,
        contact_name:str, contact_email:str,
        address:Address, company_name:str=None,
        website:(str,)=None,
        # - Arguments from HMSMongoDataObject
        oid:(UUID,str,None)=None,
        created:(datetime,str,float,int,None)=None,
        modified:(datetime,str,float,int,None)=None,
        is_active:(bool,int,None)=None,
        is_deleted:(bool,int,None)=None,
        is_dirty:(bool,int,None)=None,
        is_new:(bool,int,None)=None,
        *products
    ):
        """
Object initialization.

self ............. (Artisan instance, required) The instance to
                   execute against
contact_name ...... (str, required) The name of the primary contact
                    for the Artisan that the instance represents
contact_email ..... (str [email address], required) The email address
                    of the primary contact for the Artisan that the
                    instance represents
address ........... (Address, required) The mailing/shipping address
                    for the Artisan that the instance represents
company_name ...... (str, optional, defaults to None) The company-
                    name for the Artisan that the instance represents
oid ............... (UUID|str, optional, defaults to None) The unique
                    identifier of the object's state-data record in
the
                    back-end data-store
```

```
created .......... (datetime|str|float|int, optional, defaults to
None)
                  The date/time that the object was created
modified ......... (datetime|str|float|int, optional, defaults to
None)
                  The date/time that the object was last modified
is_active ........ (bool|int, optional, defaults to None) A flag
                  indicating that the object is active
is_deleted ....... (bool|int, optional, defaults to None) A flag
                  indicating that the object should be considered
                  deleted (and may be in the near future)
is_dirty ......... (bool|int, optional, defaults to None) A flag
                  indicating that the object's data needs to be
                  updated in the back-end data-store
is_new ........... (bool|int, optional, defaults to None) A flag
                  indicating that the object's data needs to be
                  created in the back-end data-store
products ......... (BaseProduct collection) The products associated
                  with the Artisan that the instance represents
"""
        # - Call parent initializers if needed
        BaseArtisan.__init__(self,
            contact_name, contact_email, address, company_name
        )
        HMSMongoDataObject.__init__(self,
            oid, created, modified, is_active, is_deleted,
            is_dirty, is_new
        )
        if products:
            BaseArtisan._set_products(*products)
        # - Perform any other initialization needed
```

The instance methods that can call the parent classes' methods are all one-liners, returning the results of calling the parent class' method with the appropriate arguments:

```
####################################
# Instance methods                 #
####################################

def add_product(self, product:BaseProduct) -> BaseProduct:
    return Hasproducts.add_product(self, product)

def matches(self, **criteria) -> (bool,):
    return HMSMongoDataObject.matches(self, **criteria)

def remove_product(self, product:BaseProduct) -> None:
    return Hasproducts.remove_product(self, product)
```

The `to_data_dict` method could be daunting, but, since the sequence of the keys in the resultant dictionary is irrelevant, grouping them by the classes they originate from allows several of them (the data store-related ones) to be copied around as needed:

```
def to_data_dict(self):
    return {
        # - BaseArtisan-derived items
        'address':self.address.to_dict() if self.address else
None,
        'company_name':self.company_name,
        'contact_email':self.contact_email,
        'contact_name':self.contact_name,
        'website':self.website,
        # - BaseDataObject-derived items
        'created':datetime.strftime(
            self.created, self.__class__._data_time_string
        ),
        'is_active':self.is_active,
        'is_deleted':self.is_deleted,
        'modified':datetime.strftime(
            self.modified, self.__class__._data_time_string
        ),
        'oid':str(self.oid),
    }
```

 In retrospect, it might have been a better design to provide a method or property of each of the classes that would be responsible for generating their part of a final `data_dict`. That would've kept the code for generating those dictionary items in a single place, at a minimum, and would've allowed the final `data_dict` values to be assembled from all of the parent class values for each instance.

The `from_data_dict` for the Artisan class uses the same logic and process as the original class method in `HMSMongoDataObject`, but has to account for the `address` property, which is either `None` or contains an `Address` instance:

```
###################################
# Class methods                   #
###################################

@classmethod
def from_data_dict(cls, data_dict):
    # - This has to be overridden because we have to pre-process
    #   incoming address and (maybe, eventually?) product-list
    #   values...
```

```
        if data_dict.get('address'):
            data_dict['address'] =
Address.from_dict(data_dict['address'])
        ####### NOTE: Changes made here, for whatever reason might
        #       arise, may also need to be made in
        #       HMSMongoDataObject.from_data_dict - it's the same
        ####### process!
        # - Assure that we have the collection of keys that are
        #   allowed for the class!
        if cls._data_dict_keys == None:
            from inspect import getfullargspec
            argspec = getfullargspec(cls.__init__)
            init_args = argspec.args
            try:
                init_args.remove('self')
            except:
                pass
            try:
                init_args.remove('cls')
            except:
                pass
            print(argspec)
            if argspec.varargs:
                init_args.append(argspec.varargs)
            if argspec.varkw:
                init_args.append(argspec.varkw)
            # FullArgSpec(varargs='products', varkw=None
            raise AttributeError(
                '%s.from_data_dict cannot be used because the %s '
                'class has not specified what data-store keys are '
                'allowed to be used to create new instances from '
                'retrieved data. Set %s._data_dict_keys to a list '
                'or tuple of argument-names present in %s.__init__ '
                '(%s)' %
                (
                    cls.__name__, cls.__name__, cls.__name__,
                    cls.__name__, "'" + "'", "'".join(init_args) + "'"
                )
            )
        # - Remove any keys that aren't listed in the class'
        #   initialization arguments:
        data_dict = dict(
            [
                (key, data_dict[key]) for key in data_dict.keys()
                if key in cls._data_dict_keys
            ]
        )
```

```
# - Then create and return an instance of the class
return cls(**data_dict)
```

With a total of seven items to implement concretely, and only two of them that aren't manageable by calling a parent class' equivalent or writing very simple code, the implementation is pretty painless.

hms_core.co_objects.Product

The corresponding Story for concrete `Product` object data persistence is as follows:

- As a product manager, I need to be able to manage products in the system, so that their statuses and information can be kept current.

The code that fulfills this scenario is even simpler than the code for `Artisan` objects; it doesn't need any special handling of object properties, so `from_data_dict` can simply fall back to the default, defined in `HMSMongoDataObject`. It doesn't have any extraneous methods that are required, either, so a full, functional implementation really just boils down to the `_data_dict_keys` class attribute and the `__init__`, `matches`, and `to_data_dict` methods, with `matches` being implemented as a call to `HMSMongoDataObject.matches`:

```
class Product(BaseProduct, HMSMongoDataObject):
    """
Represents a Product in the context of the Central Office
applications and services
    """
    ###################################
    # Class attributes/constants      #
    ###################################

    _data_dict_keys = [
        'name', 'summary', 'available', 'store_available',
        'description', 'dimensions', 'metadata', 'shipping_weight',
        'oid', 'created', 'modified', 'is_active', 'is_deleted'
    ]
```

The `__init__` method has a long argument set, which should come as no surprise:

```
    ###################################
    # Object initialization           #
    ###################################

    def __init__(self,
```

```
            # - Arguments from HMSMongoDataObject
            name:(str,), summary:(str,), available:(bool,),
            store_available:(bool,),
            # - Optional arguments:
            description:(str,None)=None, dimensions:(str,None)=None,
            metadata:(dict,)={}, shipping_weight:(int,)=0,
            # - Arguments from HMSMongoDataObject
            oid:(UUID,str,None)=None,
            created:(datetime,str,float,int,None)=None,
            modified:(datetime,str,float,int,None)=None,
            is_active:(bool,int,None)=None,
            is_deleted:(bool,int,None)=None,
            is_dirty:(bool,int,None)=None,
            is_new:(bool,int,None)=None,
    ):
        """
Object initialization.

self ............. (Product instance, required) The instance to
                  execute against
name ............. (str, required) The name of the product
summary .......... (str, required) A one-line summary of the
                  product
available ........ (bool, required) Flag indicating whether the
                  product is considered available by the artisan
                  who makes it
store_available ... (bool, required) Flag indicating whether the
                  product is considered available on the web-
                  store by the Central Office
description ....... (str, optional, defaults to None) A detailed
                  description of the product
dimensions ....... (str, optional, defaults to None) A measurement-
                  description of the product
metadata ......... (dict, optional, defaults to {}) A collection
                  of metadata keys and values describing the
                  product
shipping_weight ... (int, optional, defaults to 0) The shipping-
                  weight of the product
oid .............. (UUID|str, optional, defaults to None) The unique
                  identifier of the object's state-data record in
the
                  back-end data-store
created .......... (datetime|str|float|int, optional, defaults to
None)
                  The date/time that the object was created
modified ......... (datetime|str|float|int, optional, defaults to
None)
                  The date/time that the object was last modified
```

```
is_active ......... (bool|int, optional, defaults to None) A flag
                    indicating that the object is active
is_deleted ........ (bool|int, optional, defaults to None) A flag
                    indicating that the object should be considered
                    deleted (and may be in the near future)
is_dirty .......... (bool|int, optional, defaults to None) A flag
                    indicating that the object's data needs to be
                    updated in the back-end data-store
is_new ............ (bool|int, optional, defaults to None) A flag
                    indicating that the object's data needs to be
                    created in the back-end data-store
"""
        # - Call parent initializers if needed
        BaseProduct.__init__(
            self, name, summary, available, store_available,
            description, dimensions, metadata, shipping_weight
        )
        HMSMongoDataObject.__init__(self,
            oid, created, modified, is_active, is_deleted,
            is_dirty, is_new
        )
        # - Perform any other initialization needed
```

The implementations of `matches` and `to_data_dict` are very straightforward, as follows:

```
####################################
# Instance methods                 #
####################################

def matches(self, **criteria) -> (bool,):
    return HMSMongoDataObject.matches(self, **criteria)

def to_data_dict(self):
    return {
        # - BaseProduct-derived items
        'available':self.available,
        'description':self.description,
        'dimensions':self.dimensions,
        'metadata':self.metadata,
        'name':self.name,
        'shipping_weight':self.shipping_weight,
        'store_available':self.store_available,
        'summary':self.summary,
        # - BaseDataObject-derived items
        'created':datetime.strftime(
            self.created, self.__class__._data_time_string
        ),
```

```
                    'is_active':self.is_active,
                    'is_deleted':self.is_deleted,
                    'modified':datetime.strftime(
                        self.modified, self.__class__._data_time_string
                    ),
                    'oid':str(self.oid),
                }
```

The `matches` method may need to be reexamined later on, either during the creation of the Artisan Gateway service or when the various application UIs are being built, because while it works for most cases, it will not currently allow a `get` with any metadata criteria to return results unless `criteria` is the only value being searched for (no `oids` are passed). It's worth a more detailed look here and now, though, because it shows some aspects of how the data object code interacts with MongoDB.

First, let's create some example `Product` objects and save them, as follows:

```
# - An example product - A copper-and-emerald necklace:
product = Product(
    'Necklace #1',
    'Showing some Product.get aspects', True, True,
    metadata={
        'metal':'Copper',
        'gemstone':'Emerald',
    }
)
product.save()
# - Silver-and-emerald necklace:
product = Product(
    'Necklace #2',
    'Showing some Product.get aspects', True, True,
    metadata={
        'metal':'Silver',
        'gemstone':'Emerald',
    }
)
product.save()
# - Copper-and-sapphire necklace:
product = Product(
    'Necklace #3',
    'Showing some Product.get aspects', True, True,
    metadata={
        'metal':'Copper',
        'gemstone':'Sapphire',
    }
)
product.save()
```

```
# - Silver-and-sapphire necklace:
product = Product(
    'Necklace #4',
    'Showing some Product.get aspects', True, True,
    metadata={
        'metal':'Silver',
        'gemstone':'Sapphire',
    }
)
product.save()
```

Finding products that have metadata indicating that they are made of silver and have sapphire gemstones is fairly straightforward, although it requires criteria specifications that look a little odd:

```
# - importing json so we can usefully print the results:
import json
criteria = {
    'metadata':{
        'metal':'Silver',
        'gemstone':'Sapphire',
    }
}
```

Creating the criteria as a dict allows them to be passed to Product.get as a single keyword argument set, and allows the criteria specification to be as detailed as we need. We could, for example, add other metadata, specify a product name, or add any other object properties that appear in the data-dict representation of a Product (as returned by to_data_dict). The results will come back as a list of objects, and, by printing the data-dict representations of them, we can see the results:

```
products = Product.get(**criteria)
print(json.dumps(
    [product.to_data_dict() for product in products],
    indent=4, sort_keys=True)
)
```

Executing the preceding code yields the dataset for the one matching the `Product`, our silver and sapphire necklace, as follows:

```
[
    {
        "available": true,
        "created": "2018-06-02 06:23:38",
        "description": null,
        "dimensions": null,
        "is_active": true,
        "is_deleted": false,
        "metadata": {
            "gemstone": "Sapphire",
            "metal": "Silver"
        },
        "modified": "2018-06-02 06:23:38",
        "name": "Necklace #4",
        "oid": "c886c6d9-98f3-4f03-b326-0c9bad613f89",
        "shipping_weight": 0,
        "store_available": true,
        "summary": "Showing some Product.get aspects"
    }
]
```

It's worth mentioning that passing `criteria` doesn't have to be a multi-level `dict`, even for `metadata` values. Using `criteria` in this format is as follows:

```
criteria = {
    'metadata.metal':'Silver',
    'metadata.gemstone':'Sapphire',
}
```

This criteria structure works just as well. The underlying `find()` method provided by a `pymongo connection` object treats **dot-notation** specifications of this sort as references to a nested object structure that looks much like the `dict` value shown previously, and will process the request accordingly.

Other hms_core.co_objects classes

There could have been Stories and tasks in this iteration to deal with the data persistence of `Customer` and `Order` objects, as well. Those would have probably taken the same basic shape as the stories for the `Artisan` and `Product` objects, looking something like the following `Order` example:

- As an order manager, I need to be able to manage orders in the system, so that their statuses and information can be kept current.

To do so, I would do the following:

- Design and implement an `Order` class for the Central Office data store that allows object data to be persisted.

- Unit test the `Order` class.

Normally, in an Agile, iterative process, a story would have to be accepted before being included in an iteration, and the process of it being accepted would involved enough review and analysis that a full understanding of the tasks involved would be reached, and the stories and tasks written and planned accordingly. In this case, though, since there is a significant dependency on an external system (the Web Store Application) and on an order acceptance and processing workflow that hasn't been detailed yet, there's not a lot that can be done, beyond a bare-bones implementation of the `Customer` and `Order` classes. The workflow, in particular, was going to be somewhat dependent on the data structure that artisans need, which wasn't defined until this iteration.

For all of the preceding reasons, there are no stories to deal with these objects and their data persistence in this iteration. The data persistence aspects of the final classes created for the Artisan Gateway and/or Central Office application will be handled as parts of stories to implement the order processing workflow. In the meantime, though, we can at least stub out the bare minimum structure for those classes in a separate file (in `future/co_objects.py`, in the code for this chapter) while the data object definition process is fresh in our minds, to save some effort later.

Accounting for the other CRUD operations

Up to this point, we've only accounted for two of the CRUD operations that all of our data objects need: `create` and `read`. The `delete` operations, across the board, are accounted for, but not yet proven; however, since that process is very simple, it can wait until we unit test everything, to prove that everything works. The missing item, then, is the `update` operation, at least in part. The various object documents that have been written to the database with every `save()` call have shown that the process of writing object data is working, but we haven't actually tried to update anything yet; and, if we were to try now, it would fail (and fail silently). The reason behind that failure is very simple, and can be seen in the code from `HMSMongoDataObject.save`:

```python
def save(self):
    if self._is_new or self._is_dirty:
        # - Make sure to update the modified time-stamp!
        self.modified = datetime.now()
        data_dict = self.to_data_dict()
        data_dict['_id'] = self.oid
        self.collection.insert_one(data_dict)
        self._set_is_dirty(False)
        self._set_is_new(False)
```

In a nutshell, it's because we're checking for the status of `_is_new` and `_is_dirty`, and only calling the database write if one of them is `True`. By default, when a data object is created, its `_is_dirty` flag value is set to `False`. If that value doesn't get changed somewhere along the line, when an object's property values are altered, the `save` method will never actually write the changed dataset to the database.

There are at least two different ways to resolve this. The more complex solution would be to redefine each of the setter and deleter methods for each property of each concrete data object class, and the property declarations for each of them, so that the methods call their parent methods and the instance's `_set_is_dirty` methods in the process. This is the approach that was taken for the corresponding objects in the Artisan project. See the following code snippet, which uses the `Product.name` property as an example:

```python
def _set_name(self, value):
    BaseProduct._set_name(self, value)
    self._set_is_dirty(True)

# ...

def _del_name(self):
    BaseProduct._del_name(self)
```

```
        self._set_is_dirty(True)

#  ...

name = property(
        # - Using the "original" getter-method and the "local" setter-
        #   and deleter methods
        BaseProduct._get_name, _set_name, _del_name,
        'Gets, sets or deletes the name of the Product'
)
```

Taking this approach would not be difficult (or even terribly time-consuming), but it would add some additional unit testing requirements, since each of those method and property overrides would register as new, local class members that need to be tested. That's not a bad thing, though, since those tests would ultimately only be concerned with verifying that the is_dirty state change happened when it was supposed to.

The other approach would be to simply remove the is_new and is_dirty check condition from HMSMongoDataObject.save. That is a much simpler solution, in many respects, but it comes with at least one caveat: it puts the responsibility of making sure that the save of any changed object is called in the code that's making those changes. Without some careful monitoring of how and when the code is making and saving changes, there is a good possibility that many save calls will be made, incrementally updating the data document for any given object. That may or may not be a significant concern (it's unlikely to have a significant impact on performance for small sets of data changes, for example), but it could get out of control quickly, if not closely monitored. If the data store had a cost per query associated with it, as unlikely as that might seem, that inefficiency would also cost more money on a long-term basis.

Since the actual use cases involving updating the data haven't yet been developed (or even had stories presented that could guide the decision), for now, in order to close these stories, the latter solution will be taken. This keeps things simple for the time being, and we know what will be involved for a more complex solution, should the need for it arise. That, then, revises HMSMongoDataObject.save as follows:

```
def save(self):
        # TODO: For the time being, we're going to assume that save
        #        operations don't need to care about whether the
        #        object's data is new or dirty, that we wouldn't be
        #        calling save unless we already knew that to be the
        #        case. If that changes, we'll want to check is_dirty
        #        and is_new, as shown below, *and* make sure that
        #        they get modified accordingly.
#     if self._is_new or self._is_dirty:
```

```
# - Make sure to update the modified time-stamp!
self.modified = datetime.now()
data_dict = self.to_data_dict()
data_dict['_id'] = self.oid
self.collection.insert_one(data_dict)
self._set_is_dirty(False)
self._set_is_new(False)
```

Summary

As with the Artisan Application's data persistence, we've accounted for (if not proven) all of the CRUD operation requirements for data objects living in the Central Office code bases. Because the interface requirements are also defined by the same `BaseDataObject` inheritance, even though there is additional functionality provided between that ABC and the concrete data objects, the processes for reading and writing data across all of the data objects look the same across the entire system – at least so far.

None of the data access has been unit tested yet, however, and that's a critical item for the system; at the end of the day, the data is, if not the most important part of the system, certainly one of the most import aspects of it. It's time, then, to change the context and write those unit tests, which we'll do in the next chapter.

13
Testing Data Persistence

Repeatable unit testing of code is rarely more critical than in the case of data persistence. Code can change or be replaced over time, perhaps even to the point of changing to a completely different system, written in a completely different language, but once data exists, it can potentially outlive any number of code bases that make use of it. The data in a system, it could be argued, is where the real business value usually exists, so testing of the processes that interact with it, and have the potential to destroy that value, is extremely important.

With that in mind, the bulk of this chapter will be focused on the following:

- Writing the unit tests for the data object and related classes created in this iteration:
  - The new `hms_artisan` classes
  - The new `hms_core` classes
- Integration of those tests with the build process

There's also been enough new functionality added that some attention will have to be paid to the following:

- Other effects of the new code on the build process
- Demonstration of the new code, and how acceptance of the related stories might be facilitated
- How the new code affects operations, use, maintenance, and decommissioning concerns

Writing the unit tests

Most of the process of writing the unit tests for the new data object classes can simply follow the process established in previous iterations:

1. Create the top-level test module for the package being tested.
2. Identify the child modules of the package being tested, and create a corresponding test module for each.
3. Add references to the child test modules to the package test module and import their tests.
4. For each child test module:
   - Execute the module and create test case classes for each item reported as missing
   - Execute the module and create tests methods for each member (property or method) reported as missing

There are several test modules that need to be created, one for each module that was created in the `src` directories across the projects this iteration touched, yielding the following:

- `hms_core/../data_objects.py` → `test_hms_core/test_data_objects.py` (already tested, but listed here for the sake of having a complete list)
- `hms_artisan/../data_storage.py` → `test_hms_artisan/test_data_storage.py`
- `hms_artisan/../artisan_objects.py` → `test_hms_artisan/test_artisan_objects.py`
- `hms_core/../co_objects.py` → `test_hms_core/test_co_objects.py`

Testing hms_artisan.data_storage

The unit tests for `hms_artisan.data_storage` are, at this point, all concerned with testing the `JSONFileDataStore` class. Because of what that class actually does, the typical patterns for unit testing apply poorly, if at all. It has no properties to test, and the one class attribute that can be tested (`_file_store_dir`) is overridden by derived classes.

It's probably worth asserting that the default attribute is what's expected, though, since if it doesn't default to None, that could cause failures in derived classes and instances of those classes:

```
def test_file_store_dir(self):
    self.assertEqual(
        JSONFileDataObject._file_store_dir, None,
        'JSONFileDataObject._file_store_dir is expected to provide '
        'a None default value that must be overridden by derived '
        'classes, but it is set to "%s" (%s)' %
        (
            JSONFileDataObject._file_store_dir,
            type(JSONFileDataObject._file_store_dir).__name__
        )
    )
```

As far as the testing of methods is concerned, while there are several, they are somewhat intertwined, and they also frequently rely upon implementations of methods that are abstract themselves and thus not available in the ABC itself:

- get, delete, and save all call the _load_objects helper class method
- That _load_objects method relies on a concrete implementation of from_data_dict in order to generate the collection of objects that the other methods refer to
- The save method also requires a concrete implementation of the to_data_dict method

Since unit testing is about proving predictable functionality, the question then becomes: what can we prove?

The first, and probably most obvious, item is that object initialization works in pretty much the same fashion that it does in BaseDataObject:

```
class testJSONFileDataObject(unittest.TestCase):

    ##################################
    # Tests of class methods         #
    ##################################

    def test__init__(self):
        # Tests the __init__ method of the JSONFileDataObject class
        # - All we need to do here is prove that the various
        #   setter- and deleter-method calls are operating as
        #   expected -- same as BaseDataObject
        # - deleters first
```

```
test_object = JSONFileDataObjectDerived()
self.assertEquals(test_object._created, None)
self.assertEquals(test_object._is_active, True)
self.assertEquals(test_object._is_deleted, False)
self.assertEquals(test_object._is_dirty, False)
self.assertEquals(test_object._is_new, True)
self.assertEquals(test_object._modified, None)
self.assertEquals(test_object._oid, None)
# - setters
oid = uuid4()
created = GoodDateTimes[0]
modified = GoodDateTimes[1]
is_active = False
is_deleted = True
is_dirty = True
is_new = False
test_object = JSONFileDataObjectDerived(
    oid, created, modified, is_active, is_deleted,
    is_dirty, is_new
)
self.assertEquals(test_object.oid, oid)
self.assertEquals(test_object.created, created)
self.assertEquals(test_object.is_active, is_active)
self.assertEquals(test_object.is_deleted, is_deleted)
self.assertEquals(test_object.is_dirty, is_dirty)
self.assertEquals(test_object.is_new, is_new)
self.assertEquals(test_object.modified, modified)
```

The `GoodDateTimes` test values are the same values we used to test `BaseDataObject`.

Since the `_create` and `_update` methods aren't going to be used, we can prove that they raise the expected errors when called:

```
def test_create(self):
    # Tests the _create method of the JSONFileDataObject class
    test_object = JSONFileDataObjectDerived()
    try:
        test_object._create()
        self.fail(
          'JSONFileDataObject is not expected to raise '
          'NotImplementedError on a call to _create'
        )
    except NotImplementedError:
        pass
```

```
        except Exception as error:
            self.fail(
                'JSONFileDataObject is not expected to raise '
                'NotImplementedError on a call to _create, but %s '
                'was raised instead:\n - %s' %
                (error.__class__.__name__, error)
            )

    def test_update(self):
        # Tests the _update method of the JSONFileDataObject class
        test_object = JSONFileDataObjectDerived()
        try:
            test_object._update()
            self.fail(
                'JSONFileDataObject is not expected to raise '
                'NotImplementedError on a call to _update'
            )
        except NotImplementedError:
            pass
        except Exception as error:
            self.fail(
                'JSONFileDataObject is not expected to raise '
                'NotImplementedError on a call to _update, but %s '
                'was raised instead:\n - %s' %
                (error.__class__.__name__, error)
            )
```

The individual CRUD operations, plus the `_load_objects` method, since they are
joined at the hip, would end up with a lot of overlap – tests for one method would
have to execute tests for other methods as part of their own testing process in order to
really prove that everything was working as expected. Tests of that complexity are
tedious to write, but more importantly, require more effort and discipline to maintain,
and are thus more prone to getting out of touch with the code they are testing. A
better option, in this case, might be to skip those tests, and create one larger, unified
test of all the related functionality. Python's stock `unittest` module provides a `skip`
decorator function that provides the ability to tag tests to be skipped by standard unit
testing runs, and calling that requires that we log a reason for the test being skipped.
In this case, the reason is that all of the methods in question will be tested in one large
pass in a different test method:

```
    @unittest.skip(
        'Since the file-load process provided by _load_objects is '
        'used by many of the CRUD operations, it is tested  as part of '
        'testCRUDOperations'
    )
    def test_load_objects(self):
```

```
        # Tests the _load_objects method of the JSONFileDataObject class
            self.fail('test_load_objects is not yet implemented')

    @unittest.skip(
        'Since deleting a data-file is part of the CRUD operations, '
        'it is tested as part of testCRUDOperations'
    )
    def testdelete(self):
        # Tests the delete method of the JSONFileDataObject class
            self.fail('testdelete is not yet implemented')

    @unittest.skip(
        'Since reading data-files is part of the CRUD operations, '
        'it is tested as part of testCRUDOperations'
    )
    def testget(self):
        # Tests the get method of the JSONFileDataObject class
        self.fail('testget is not yet implemented')

    @unittest.skip(
        'Since creating a data-file is part of the CRUD operations, '
        'it is tested as part of testCRUDOperations'
    )
    def testsave(self):
        # Tests the save method of the JSONFileDataObject class
            self.fail('testsave is not yet implemented')
```

That leaves the responsibility for testing most of `JSONFileDataObject` in the hands of a single test-method – one that's not required by the code that enforces the standard test policy, but that represents the best compromise between individual class-member test coverage and maintainability: `testCRUDOperations`. There's not a lot of opportunity for elegance in it; it has to brute-force its way through a lot of conditions and object states simply because of the nature of the methods being tested. If it's well thought out, though, it leaves the tests for the classes derived from it free to not have to test the common functionality.

The first thing that it has to do is ensure that there's a clean object repository, both in memory and on the filesystem. In order to do that, a throwaway class has to be defined, with the bare minimum of the required functionality needed to assure that all the necessary method classes are being made. That class, `JSONFileDataObjectDerived`, looks like this:

```
class JSONFileDataObjectDerived(JSONFileDataObject):
```

We're providing a file storage location that is not in use by any real objects, which can be deleted and recreated with object data however and whenever we need to:

```
_file_store_dir = '/tmp/hms_artisan_test'
```

Because these tests are concerned with file system data-persistence, they were written for the OS that system development was undertaken on—a Linux installation—though they would execute without modification on any Unix-like OS. Converting them to run under Windows isn't difficult:
Create a test-data directory (C:\TestData, for example), and change all filesystem references that start with /tmp/ to C:\\TestData\\ (note the double-backslashes), and alter the remaining filesystem paths to use Windows' filesystem notation (C:\\TestData\\path\\to\\some\\file.ext, note the double-backslashes again).

We supply the bare minimum required functionality, using defaults or proven/provable functionality from parent classes wherever possible, or the simplest possible implementations:

```
def matches(self, **criteria) -> (bool,):
    return BaseDataObject.matches(self, **criteria)

@classmethod
def from_data_dict(cls, data_dict:(dict,)):
    return cls(**data_dict)
```

Where no default or inheritable functionality is available, we keep to the bare minimum necessary for the tests to be meaningful – in the case of the to_data_dict method, that means sticking to the properties and data structure required by all classes derived from BaseDataObject, including JSONFileDataObject:

```
def to_data_dict(self):
    return {
        'created':datetime.strftime(
        self.created, self.__class__._data_time_string
        ),
        'is_active':self.is_active,
        'is_deleted':self.is_deleted,
        'modified':datetime.strftime(
            self.modified, self.__class__._data_time_string
        ),
        'oid':str(self.oid),
    }
```

That, then, lets us start the `testCRUDOperations` test method by directly clearing the in-memory object cache, and removing any files in the storage location:

```
def testCRUDOperations(self):
    # - First, assure that the class-level data-object collection
    #   (in JSONFileDataObjectDerived._loaded_objects) is None,
    #   and that the file-repository does not exist.
    JSONFileDataObjectDerived._loaded_objects = None
    if os.path.exists(JSONFileDataObjectDerived._file_store_dir):
        rmtree(JSONFileDataObjectDerived._file_store_dir)
```

The `rmtree` function is from a Python package called `shutils`, and recursively deletes files and sub directories from a specified location, raising an error if the target location doesn't exist. The `os.path.exists` call, from the built-in `os` module, checks for the existence of a file or directory at the specified path, returning `True` if something exists there, and `False` otherwise.

We'll need at least one object stored in the newly cleared caches to start our testing process, so the creation of a data object, and saving its state data, comes next:

```
# - Next, create an item and save it
first_object = JSONFileDataObjectDerived()
first_object.save()
# - Verify that the file exists where we're expecting it
self.assertTrue(
    os.path.exists(
        '/tmp/hms_artisan_test/JSONFileDataObjectDerived-'
        'data/%s.json' % first_object.oid
    )
)
# - and that it exists in the in-memory cache
    self.assertNotEqual(
        JSONFileDataObjectDerived._loaded_objects.get(
          str(first_object.oid)
        ), None
    )
```

With one object created and saved, we can verify that the data-write and -read processes allow us to read the same data that we were expecting to be written. We can leverage the `matches` method of the class, since it's inherited from `BaseDataObject`, ultimately, and has been tested earlier.

Since `matches` uses the `data dict` generated by `to_data_dict`, and that doesn't include properties that don't persist, such as `is_dirty` and `is_new`, those need to be checked separately:

```
# - Verify that the item can be retrieved, and has the same
#   data
first_object_get = JSONFileDataObjectDerived.get()[0]
self.assertTrue(
        first_object.matches(**first_object_get.to_data_dict())
)
self.assertEqual(
        first_object.is_dirty, first_object_get.is_dirty
)
self.assertEqual(
        first_object.is_new, first_object_get.is_new
)
```

 A viable alternative, if any concerns arise about using `matches` as a data-structure-verification process, would be to explicitly check each property of the retrieved object against the corresponding property of the original. Using `matches` is a convenience, not a requirement.

Next, we will check to make sure that multiple objects are saved and read as expected. Since the files and the keys for the objects are both functions of the `oid` of the objects, and we now know that the files and in-memory copies of data objects work with the creation of one object, we just need to ensure that multiples don't break anything. Creating two more objects also allows us to re-verify the entire collection later on:

```
# - Create and save two more items
second_object = JSONFileDataObjectDerived()
second_object.save()
third_object = JSONFileDataObjectDerived()
third_object.save()
# - Verify that all three items can be retrieved, and that
#   they are the expected objects, at least by their oids:
#   Those, as part of the file-names, *will* be unique and
#   distinct...
all_objects = JSONFileDataObjectDerived.get()
expected = set(
        [o.oid for o in [first_object, second_object, third_object]]
)
actual = set([o.oid for o in all_objects])
self.assertEqual(expected, actual)
```

We also need to test that deletions behave as expected, removing the deleted object from the in-memory cache and deleting the applicable file. Before performing the deletion, we need to confirm that the file that's going to be deleted exists, in order to avoid a false positive test result once the deletion executes:

```
# - Verify that the file for the second item exists, so the
#   verification later of its deletion is a valid test
self.assertTrue(
    os.path.exists(
        '/tmp/hms_artisan_test/JSONFileDataObjectDerived-'
        'data/%s.json' % second_object.oid
    )
)
```

Then we can delete the item and verify the deletion from both the memory and filesystem:

```
# - Delete the second item
JSONFileDataObjectDerived.delete(second_object.oid)
# - Verify that the item has been removed from the loaded-
#   object store and from the filesystem
self.assertEqual(
JSONFileDataObjectDerived._loaded_objects.get(second_object.oid),
        None
)
self.assertFalse(
os.path.exists(
        '/tmp/hms_artisan_test/JSONFileDataObjectDerived-'
        'data/%s.json' % second_object.oid
    )
)
```

We also need to verify that data writes of updated state data work. We can check that by changing the is_active and is_deleted flags of an existing object, then saving it, and retrieving a copy of it for comparison, and checking with matches:

```
# - Update the last object created, and save it
third_object._set_is_active(False)
third_object._set_is_deleted(True)
third_object.save()
# - Read the updated object and verify that the changes made
#   were saved to the file.
third_object_get = JSONFileDataObjectDerived.get(third_object.oid)[0]
self.assertEqual(
        third_object.to_data_dict(),
        third_object_get.to_data_dict()
    )
```

```
self.assertTrue(
    third_object.matches(**third_object_get.to_data_dict())
)
self.assertEqual(
    third_object.is_dirty, third_object_get.is_dirty
)
self.assertEqual(
    third_object.is_new, third_object_get.is_new
)
```

In the event that other tests might be added to this test case class later, and in the interests of cleaning up files once they are no longer needed, we'll repeat the process of clearing out the in-memory and on-disk object stores. If other tests, created later for whatever ends, need to start with the in-memory and on-disk stores in any particular state, they'll have to make arrangements to get that state set up, but they won't have to worry about clearing it first:

```
# - Since other test-methods down the line might need to start
#   with empty object- and file-sets, re-clear them both
JSONFileDataObjectDerived._loaded_objects = None
if os.path.exists(JSONFileDataObjectDerived._file_store_dir):
    rmtree(JSONFileDataObjectDerived._file_store_dir)
self.fail('testCRUDOperations is not complete')
```

The original `test_file_store_dir` test method did not account for proving that derived classes will not allow themselves to be instantiated without a `_file_store_dir` class attribute that is set to something other than `None`. Revising that, and using another class derived from `JSONFileDataObject`, which is essentially a copy of the `JSONFileDataObjectDerived` class used for CRUD operations testing but without the attribute specification, allows that to be tested as part of the original test method like so:

```
####################################
# Tests of class properties        #
####################################

def test_file_store_dir(self):
    self.assertEqual(
        JSONFileDataObject._file_store_dir, None,
        'JSONFileDataObject._file_store_dir is expected to provide '
        'a None default value that must be overridden by derived '
        'classes, but it is set to "%s" (%s)' %
        (
            JSONFileDataObject._file_store_dir,
            type(JSONFileDataObject._file_store_dir).__name__
        )
    )
```

```
    )
    try:
        test_object = NoFileStoreDir()
        self.fail(
            'Classes derived from JSONFileDataObject are expected '
            'to define a _file_store_dir class-attribute, or cause '
            'instantiation of objects from classes that don\'t '
            'have one defined to fail with an AttributeError'
        )
    except AttributeError:
        pass
```

Testing hms_artisan.artisan_objects

After the initial unit test setup, there are 74 tests that need to be implemented, largely due to the overrides of properties and their setter and deleter methods from their Base counterpart classes in hms_core. Since the main difference between the properties and their overridden methods is the inclusion of an automatic change in the instance's is_dirty property during a set or delete call, that might appear to be the only thing that the property-related tests at this level need to be concerned with:

```
################################################################################
Unit-test results
################################################################################
Tests were successful ..... False
Number of tests run ....... 92
 + Tests ran in .......... 0.01 seconds
Number of errors .......... 0
Number of failures ........ 74
Number of tests skipped ... 0
################################################################################
```

The tests for the properties are all close to the standard structure that has been used so far, essentially verifying that each property has the appropriate getter, setter, and deleter method associations. The only real difference is in which of those methods are being specified. Looking at the testArtisan.testcontact_name, which tests Artisan.contact_name as an example, the test assertions for the setter and deleter methods are structurally identical to their counterparts from the tests for BaseArtisan – they assert that the Artisan setter and deleter methods are associated with the property's set and delete actions.

The getter method assertion is where things get different:

```python
def testcontact_name(self):
    # Tests the contact_name property of the Artisan class
    # - Assert that the getter is correct:
    self.assertEqual(
        BaseArtisan.contact_name.fget,
        Artisan._get_contact_name,
        'Artisan.contact_name is expected to use the '
        'BaseArtisan._get_contact_name method as its getter-method'
    )
    # - Assert that the setter is correct:
    self.assertEqual(
        Artisan.contact_name.fset,
        Artisan._set_contact_name,
        'Artisan.contact_name is expected to use the '
        '_set_contact_name method as its setter-method'
    )
    # - Assert that the deleter is correct:
    self.assertEqual(
        Artisan.contact_name.fdel,
        Artisan._del_contact_name,
        'Artisan.contact_name is expected to use the '
        '_del_contact_name method as its deleter-method'
    )
```

Since the `Artisan` class provided overridden methods for each setter and deleter method, but not for the getter method, the assertion for that aspect of the property is pointing instead to the original getter method, in this case, the one defined in and inherited from `BaseArtisan`. The same basic pattern holds true even for properties without a local setter or deleter method, such as `Product.metadata`, tested by `testProduct.testmetadata`:

```python
def testmetadata(self):
    # Tests the metadata property of the Product class
    # - Assert that the getter is correct:
    self.assertEqual(
        Product.metadata.fget,
        BaseProduct._get_metadata,
        'Product.metadata is expected to use the '
        'BaseProduct._get_metadata method as its getter-method'
    )
    # - Assert that the setter is correct:
    self.assertEqual(
        Product.metadata.fset,
        None,
        'Product.metadata is expected to be read-only, with no setter'
```

```
    )
    # - Assert that the deleter is correct:
    self.assertEqual(
        Product.metadata.fdel,
        None,
        'Product.metadata is expected to be read-only, with no
deleter'
    )
```

The tests for the setter and deleter methods themselves can also be very simple, with a caveat. If the fundamental assumptions are that:

- All the properties inherited from a `Base` class in `hms_core.business_objects` will be tested (which is true as things stand right now)
- Those tests can be trusted to prove the predictable behavior of those properties when they are set or deleted
- The local setter and deleter methods will always call back to their tested counterparts

Then all that needs to be done in testing the local methods is checking that they set `is_dirty` accordingly. There may not be any way, realistically, to verify that those assumptions are in play as part of a unit-test set, though. It becomes a matter of knowing that these items are expected, standard procedure, and maintaining those procedures as new code is developed. If those principles and procedures can be counted upon, the tests for the derived class property-method overrides don't need to go through the same level of effort/detail that their ancestors do, and can be as simple as these:

```
def test_del_address(self):
    # Tests the _del_address method of the Artisan class
    test_object = Artisan('name', 'me@email.com', GoodAddress)
    self.assertEqual(test_object.is_dirty, False,
        'A newly-created instance of an Artisan should '
        'have is_dirty of False'
    )
    test_object._del_address()
    self.assertEqual(test_object.is_dirty, True,
        'The deletion of an Artisan address should set '
        'is_dirty to True'
    )

# ...

def test_set_address(self):
```

```
# Tests the _set_address method of the Artisan class
test_object = Artisan('name', 'me@email.com', GoodAddress)
self.assertEqual(test_object.is_dirty, False,
    'A newly-created instance of an Artisan should '
    'have is_dirty of False'
)
test_object._set_address(GoodAddresses[0])
self.assertEqual(test_object.is_dirty, True,
    'Setting an Artisan address should set '
    'is_dirty to True'
)
```

The data-dict methods (`to_data_dict` and `from_data_dict`) are common across all of the data objects, and show up in the list of tests to be implemented across all of the test case classes as a result. All of them have their own particular challenges to writing good, thorough unit tests. The variations of `to_data_dict` all follow a pretty consistent pattern:

1. Iterate over a (hopefully short) list of representative values for each property that should appear in the output
2. Create an expected dictionary value that can be used to compare the output against
3. Assert that the expected dictionary and the results of `to_data_dict` are the same

In theory, the best way to ensure that all possible good and bad value combinations get tested is to iterate over all those possible combinations, nesting loops within other loops so that, for example, all possible combinations of `name`, `street_address`, `city` values are tested. In practice, tests built using that strategy will take a long time to execute, with a large number of combinations to test (the number of `name` values × the number of `street_address` values × the number of `city` values, and so on). The class with the fewest properties that needs to appear in a data-dict representation is the `Order` class, with five local properties in addition to the ones that are inherited from other classes that are already tested. An incomplete start of the relevant `testto_data_dict` method, with only one of those properties included in the mix, comes to 72 lines:

```
def testto_data_dict(self):
    # Tests the to_data_dict method of the Order class
    for name in GoodStandardRequiredTextLines[0:2]:
        for street_address in GoodStandardRequiredTextLines[0:2]:
            for city in GoodStandardRequiredTextLines[0:2]:
                # - At this point, we have all the required
                #   arguments, so we can start testing with
```

```
    #   partial expected dict-values
    test_object = Order(
        name, street_address, city,
    )
    expected = {
        'name':name,
        'street_address':street_address,
        'city':city,
        # - The balance are default values...
        'building_address':None,
        'region':None,
        'postal_code':None,
        'country':None,
        'items':{},
        # - We also need to include the data-object
        #   items that should appear!
        'created':datetime.strftime(
                test_object.created,
                test_object._data_time_string
            ),
        'modified':datetime.strftime(
                test_object.modified,
                test_object._data_time_string
            ),
        'oid':str(test_object.oid),
        'is_active':test_object.is_active,
        'is_deleted':test_object.is_deleted,
    }
    self.assertEqual(
        test_object.to_data_dict(), expected
    )
```

Each additional property that needs to be tested results in another loop inside the current loop, and the creation of a new test object, making sure to include the new property item/argument being tested:

```
for items in GoodOrderItems:
  test_object = Order(
        name, street_address, city,
        items=items,
    )
```

Each sub-loop has to create its own `expected` value:

```
expected = {
    'name':name,
    'street_address':street_address,
    'city':city,
```

```
        'building_address':None,
        'region':None,
        'postal_code':None,
        'country':None,
        'items':items,
        'created':datetime.strftime(
            test_object.created,
            test_object._data_time_string
        ),
        'modified':datetime.strftime(
            test_object.modified,
            test_object._data_time_string
        ),
        'oid':str(test_object.oid),
        'is_active':test_object.is_active,
        'is_deleted':test_object.is_deleted,
    }
```

Each sub-loop also has to perform its own assertion to test `expected` against the actual value returned by the `test_object.to_data_dict` call:

```
self.assertEqual(
    test_object.to_data_dict(), expected
)
```

There are, at this point, four more properties that have to be tested, each of which will start with its own nested loop:

```
for building_address in GoodStandardOptionalTextLines[0:2]:
    for region in GoodStandardOptionalTextLines[0:2]:
        for postal_code in GoodStandardOptionalTextLines[0:2]:
            for country in GoodStandardOptionalTextLines[0:2]:
                pass
```

Forcing a failure, with a notation that the test-method is not complete, helps prevent false positives from sneaking in, and can also help to track down which test is being worked on in a large list of results:

```
self.fail('testto_data_dict is not complete')
```

The tests for the various `from_data_dict` methods are similarly complex and deeply nested, for a variation of the same reason – they have to account for reasonable possibilities for all of the values that could be supplied. An incomplete start to testing that method in the `Order` class shows the pattern that's started to take shape in 72 lines:

```
def testfrom_data_dict(self):
    # Tests the from_data_dict method of the Order class
```

Since there should always be default `None` values for certain results in the expected values of each iteration segment, we can define them once, then add them to the expected at each point needed:

```
defaults = {
    'building_address':None,
    'region':None,
    'postal_code':None,
    'country':None,
    'items':{},
}
```

The collection of nested loops themselves is identical to the ones for testing `to_data_dict`, starting with variants of all of the required properties/arguments:

```
for name in GoodStandardRequiredTextLines[0:2]:
    for street_address in GoodStandardRequiredTextLines[0:2]:
        for city in GoodStandardRequiredTextLines[0:2]:
```

Each loop segment needs to create a `data_dict` with the current values in it, and create a test object:

```
# - At this point, we have all the required
#   arguments, so we can start testing with
#   partial expected dict-values
data_dict = {
    'name':name,
    'street_address':street_address,
    'city':city,
}
test_object = Order.from_data_dict(data_dict)
```

Since we'll also be testing `to_data_dict`, we can assume that it's trustworthy for the purposes of comparison to the test object's `data-dict`. If the `to_data_dict` tests fail, they will raise those failures on their own, and not allow the test run to pass until those failures are resolved, with the same net result tests failing:

```
actual = test_object.to_data_dict()
```

Creation of the expected value is a bit more complicated. It starts with a copy of the preceding `defaults` values (since we don't want test iterations to pollute the master defaults values). We also need to capture the expected values from the instance, as we'd expect them to appear in the final data dict:

```
# - Create a copy of the defaults as a starting-point
expected = dict(defaults)
instance_values = {
    'created':datetime.strftime(
        test_object.created,
        test_object._data_time_string
    ),
    'modified':datetime.strftime(
        test_object.modified,
        test_object._data_time_string
    ),
    'oid':str(test_object.oid),
    'is_active':test_object.is_active,
    'is_deleted':test_object.is_deleted,
}
```

Building the `expected` value at this point, then, is simply a matter of updating it with the data dict and instance values. With that done, we can perform the actual test assertion:

```
expected.update(instance_values)
expected.update(data_dict)
self.assertEqual(expected, actual)
```

As before, each property/argument that needs to be tested requires its own nested loop, and a copy of the same process from the topmost loop. At each successive loop level, the `data_dict` value has to include more and more data to pass to the `from_data_dict` method, but the balance of each sub-loop is otherwise identical:

```
for items in GoodOrderItems:
    # - Same structure as above, but adding items
    data_dict = {
        'name':name,
        'street_address':street_address,
```

```
        'city':city,
        'items':items,
    }
    test_object = Order.from_data_dict(data_dict)
    actual = test_object.to_data_dict()
    expected = dict(defaults)
    instance_values = {
        'created':datetime.strftime(
                test_object.created,
                test_object._data_time_string
            ),
        'modified':datetime.strftime(
                test_object.modified,
                test_object._data_time_string
            ),
        'oid':str(test_object.oid),
        'is_active':test_object.is_active,
        'is_deleted':test_object.is_deleted,
    }
    expected.update(instance_values)
    expected.update(data_dict)
    self.assertEqual(expected, actual)
    for building_address in GoodStandardOptionalTextLines[0:2]:
    for region in GoodStandardOptionalTextLines[0:2]:
    for postal_code in GoodStandardOptionalTextLines[0:2]:
    for country in GoodStandardOptionalTextLines[0:2]:
        pass
self.fail('testfrom_data_dict is not complete')
```

Testing the `matches` method turns out to be less complicated than might be expected at first glance. A complete test, after all, needs to test for both `True` and `False` results, across all the properties of an object instance, with criteria that might be 1 value or 12, or (theoretically) dozens or hundreds. Fortunately, by using the same nested loop structure that's been used for `to_data_dict` and `from_data_dict` tests, but varying it to create the criteria being used for the test and determining what the expected value needs to be at every step along the way, it's actually not that difficult. The test process starts by creating an object with known functional data in every attribute:

```
def testmatches(self):
    # Tests the matches method of the Order class
    # - First, create an object to test against, with as complete
    #   a data-set as we can manage
    test_object = Order(
        name = GoodStandardRequiredTextLines[0],
        street_address = GoodStandardRequiredTextLines[0],
        city = GoodStandardRequiredTextLines[0],
        building_address = GoodStandardOptionalTextLines[0],
```

```
        region = GoodStandardOptionalTextLines[0],
        postal_code = GoodStandardOptionalTextLines[0],
        country = GoodStandardOptionalTextLines[0],
    )
```

The nested loop structure iterates over a range of numbers (0 and 1), and retrieves the test value from the appropriate list based on the type of value that the property in the loop relates to, creates or adds to the criteria, and determines whether the expected result should be `True` or `False` based on any previous expected value and the comparison of the loop's criteria value against the corresponding object property. All that remains after that is the assertion that the expected value equals the actual value from calling the test object's `matches` method:

```
# - Then we'll iterate over some "good" values, create criteria
for name_num in range(0,2):
    name = GoodStandardRequiredTextLines[name_num]
    criteria = {'name':name}
    expected = (name == test_object.name)
    self.assertEqual(expected, test_object.matches(**criteria))
```

The reason that each sub-loop pays attention to the `expected` value set in its parent is to make sure that `False` results at a higher loop level won't get overridden by a potential `True` result at the current loop level. For example, at this point in the test iterations, if `name` results in a `False` result (because it doesn't match `test_object.name`), even if `street_address` does match, it should still return a `False` result:

```
for str_addr_num in range(0,2):
    street_address = GoodStandardRequiredTextLines[str_addr_num]
    criteria['street_address'] = street_address
    expected = (expected and street_address ==
test_object.street_address)
    self.assertEqual(expected, test_object.matches(**criteria))
```

The pattern for each sub-loop is, apart from the name of the property value being added to the criteria, and the redefinition of the `expected` value, identical all the way down the tree of loops:

```
for city_num in range(0,2):
    city = GoodStandardRequiredTextLines[city_num]
    criteria['city'] = city
    expected = (expected and city == test_object.city)
    self.assertEqual(expected, test_object.matches(**criteria))
    for bldg_addr_num in range(0,2):
        building_address = GoodStandardOptionalTextLines[bldg_addr_num]
        criteria['building_address'] = building_address
```

```
            expected = (
                expected and
                building_address == test_object.building_address
            )
            self.assertEqual(expected,
test_object.matches(**criteria))
            for region_num in range(0,2):
                for pc_num in range(0,2):
                    for cntry_num in range(0,2):
country=GoodStandardOptionalTextLines[cntry_num]
self.fail('testmatches is not complete')
```

The last remaining method that's common to all of the new data objects is the _load_objects helper class method. Initial unit testing raised some syntax concerns that made it necessary to remove the abstraction on the method in JSONFileDataObject, and implement an overriding class method in each of the subordinate classes, all of which call the original class method as follows:

```
@classmethod
def _load_objects(cls, force_load=False):
    return JSONFileDataObject._load_objects(cls, force_load)
```

That, in turn, started raising test-method requirements for the methods in the test runs. The implementation of those tests was not difficult, building to some extent on the original test method written for JSONFileDataObject, where it originated. The structure for that test against the Order class is the simplest example, and starts much the same way, but forcing the on-disk and in-memory data stores to clear, but after setting the on-disk location to a disposable directory:

```
def test_load_objects(self):
    # Tests the _load_objects method of the Order class
    # - First, forcibly change Order._file_store_dir to a disposable
    #   temp-directory, and clear the in-memory and on-disk stores
    Order._file_store_dir = '/tmp/test_artisan_objects/'
    Order._loaded_objects = None
    if os.path.exists(Order._file_store_dir):
        rmtree(Order._file_store_dir)
    self.assertEqual(Order._loaded_objects, None)
```

Again, in order to test the loading process, it's necessary to create and save some objects:

```
    # - Iterate through some objects, creating them and saving them.
    for name in GoodStandardRequiredTextLines[0:2]:
        for street_address in GoodStandardRequiredTextLines[0:2]:
            for city in GoodStandardRequiredTextLines[0:2]:
```

```
test_object = Order(name, street_address, city)
test_object.save()
```

As each object is created, its presence in the in-memory and on-disk stores is verified:

```
# - Verify that the object exists
#    - in memory
self.assertNotEqual(
    Order._loaded_objects.get(str(test_object.oid)),
    None
)
#    - on disk
file_path = '%s/Order-data/%s.json' % (
    Order._file_store_dir, test_object.oid
)
self.assertTrue(
    os.path.exists(file_path),
    'The file was not written at %s' % file_path
)
```

It's also necessary to clear the in-memory store, reload it, and verify that the newly created object is still there. This happens in each object-creation iteration:

```
# - Make a copy of the OIDs to check with after clearing
#    the in-memory copy:
oids_before = sorted([str(key) for key in
Order._loaded_objects.keys()])
# - Clear the in-memory copy and verify all the oids
#    exist after a _load_objects is called
Order._loaded_objects = None
Order._load_objects()
oids_after = sorted(
    [str(key) for key in Order._loaded_objects.keys()]
)
self.assertEqual(oids_before, oids_after)
```

Verification that the deletion process removes in-memory and on-disk objects works by iterating over a list of instances, selecting one at random, deleting that instance, and verifying its removal the same way that the initial creation was verified:

```
# - Delete items at random and verify deletion and load after each
instances = list(Order._loaded_objects.values())
while instances:
    target = choice(instances)
    Order.delete(target.oid)
    # - Verify that the object no longer exists
    #    - in memory
    self.assertEqual(
```

```
        Order._loaded_objects.get(str(test_object.oid)),
        None
    )
    #    - on disk
    file_path = '%s/Order-data/%s.json' % (
        Order._file_store_dir, target.oid
    )
    self.assertFalse(
        os.path.exists(file_path),
        'File at %s was not deleted' % file_path
    )
    # - Make a copy of the OIDs to check with after clearing
    #   the in-memory copy:
    oids_before = sorted(
        [str(key) for key in Order._loaded_objects.keys()]
    )
    # - Clear the in-memory copy and verify all the oids
    #   exist after a _load_objects is called
    Order._loaded_objects = None
    Order._load_objects()
    oids_after = sorted([str(key) for key in
Order._loaded_objects.keys()])
    self.assertEqual(oids_before, oids_after)
```

The list of instances is updated at the end of each iteration:

```
instances.remove(target)
```

Finally, any files that might remain are deleted, just to be safe:

```
# - Clean up any remaining in-memory and on-disk store items
Order._loaded_objects = None
if os.path.exists(Order._file_store_dir):
    rmtree(Order._file_store_dir)
```

Most of the balance of the test methods follow patterns established previously:

- The various properties and their getter, setter, and deleter methods use the structure noted at the beginning of this section
- The various __init__ methods still create and assert argument-to-property settings for a reasonable subset of good values for all arguments/properties

There are a few outliers, though. First and foremost, the `sort` class method that was defined without implementation, as an abstract class method in `BaseDataObject`, has surfaced. At this point, we don't even know whether we're going to need it, let alone what shape it will need to take. Under the circumstances, deferring both its implementation and the testing of that implementation feels prudent. In order to allow the required unit test to be ignored, it can be decorated with `unittest.skip`:

```python
@unittest.skip(
    'Sort will be implemented once there\'s a need for it, '
    'and tested as part of that implementation'
)
def testsort(self):
    # Tests the sort method of the Artisan class
    # - Test all permutations of "good" argument-values:
    # - Test all permutations of each "bad" argument-value
    #   set against "good" values for the other arguments:
    self.fail('testsort is not yet implemented')
```

Two more outliers surfaced in the Artisan class: `add_product` and `remove_product`, which had no testable concrete implementation before now. With the addition of the `Goodproducts` and `Badproducts` value lists to test with, `testadd_product` is very similar to previous test methods utilizing value lists to test against:

```python
def testadd_product(self):
    # Tests the add_product method of the Artisan class
    test_object = Artisan('name', 'me@email.com', GoodAddress)
    self.assertEqual(test_object.products, ())
    check_list = []
    for product in Goodproducts[0]:
        test_object.add_product(product)
        check_list.append(product)
        self.assertEqual(test_object.products, tuple(check_list))
    test_object = Artisan('name', 'me@email.com', GoodAddress)
    for product in Badproducts:
        try:
            test_object.add_product(product)
            self.fail(
                'Artisan.add_product should not allow the '
                'addition of "%s" (%s) as a product-item, but '
                'it was allowed' % (product, type(product).__name__)
            )
        except (TypeError, ValueError):
            pass
```

The process for testing `remove_product` starts by using that same process to create a collection of products, then removes them one at a time, verifying the removal at each iteration:

```python
def testremove_product(self):
    # Tests the remove_product method of the Artisan class
    test_object = Artisan('name', 'me@email.com', GoodAddress)
    self.assertEqual(test_object.products, ())
    for product in Goodproducts[0]:
        test_object.add_product(product)
    check_list = list(test_object.products)
    while test_object.products:
        product = test_object.products[0]
        check_list.remove(product)
        test_object.remove_product(product)
        self.assertEqual(test_object.products, tuple(check_list))
```

Because `hms_artisan..Order` was built from the ground up, its property method tests needed to explicitly perform that same sort of `is_dirty` check noted earlier, but also had to implement any of several standard property tests. A typical deleter and setter method test looks like this:

```python
def test_del_building_address(self):
    # Tests the _del_building_address method of the Order class
    test_object = Order('name', 'street_address', 'city')
    self.assertEqual(
        test_object.building_address, None,
        'An Order object is expected to have None as its default '
        'building_address value if no value was provided'
    )
    # - Hard-set the storage-property's value, call the
    #   deleter-method, and assert that it's what's expected
    #   afterwards:
    test_object._set_is_dirty(False)
    test_object._building_address = 'a test value'
    test_object._del_building_address()
    self.assertEqual(
        test_object.building_address, None,
        'An Order object is expected to have None as its '
        'building_address value after the deleter is called'
    )
    self.assertTrue(test_object.is_dirty,
        'Deleting Order.building_address should set is_dirty to True'
    )

    # ...
```

```
def test_set_building_address(self):
    # Tests the _set_building_address method of the Order class
    # - Create an object to test with:
    test_object = Order('name', 'street_address', 'city')
    # - Test all permutations of "good" argument-values:
    for expected in GoodStandardOptionalTextLines:
        test_object._set_building_address(expected)
        actual = test_object._get_building_address()
        self.assertEqual(
            expected, actual,
            'Order expects a building_address value set to '
            '"%s" (%s) to be retrieved with a corresponding '
            'getter-method call, but "%s" (%s) was returned '
            'instead' %
            (
                expected, type(expected).__name__,
                actual, type(actual).__name__,
            )
        )
    # - Test is_dirty after a set
    test_object._set_is_dirty(False)
    test_object._set_building_address(GoodStandardOptionalTextLines[1])
    self.assertTrue(test_object.is_dirty,
        'Setting a new value in Order.business_address should '
        'also set the instance\'s is_dirty to True'
    )
    # - Test all permutations of "bad" argument-values:
    for value in BadStandardOptionalTextLines:
        try:
            test_object._set_building_address(value)
            # - If this setter-call succeeds, that's a
            #    test-failure!
            self.fail(
                'Order._set_business_address should raise '
                'TypeError or ValueError if passed "%s" (%s), '
                'but it was allowed to be set instead.' %
                (value, type(value).__name__)
            )
        except (TypeError, ValueError):
            # - This is expected, so it passes
            pass
        except Exception as error:
            self.fail(
                'Order._set_business_address should raise '
                'TypeError or ValueError if passed an invalid '
                'value, but %s was raised instead: %s.' %
                (error.__class__.__name__, error)
            )
```

The final test-run report for all tests for the `hms_artisan` namespace shows that all the tests were run except the seven that were explicitly skipped, with no test failures:

```
###########################################################################
Unit-test results
###########################################################################
Tests were successful ..... True
Number of tests run ....... 113
 + Tests ran in .......... 0.25 seconds
Number of errors .......... 0
Number of failures ........ 0
Number of tests skipped ... 7
###########################################################################
SKIPPED
#--------------------------------------------------------------------#
testsort (test_artisan_objects.testArtisan)
testsort (test_artisan_objects.testOrder)
testsort (test_artisan_objects.testProduct)
 - Sort will be implemented once there's a need for it, and tested as part of
   that implementation
test_load_objects (test_data_storage.testJSONFileDataObject)
testdelete (test_data_storage.testJSONFileDataObject)
testget (test_data_storage.testJSONFileDataObject)
testsave (test_data_storage.testJSONFileDataObject)
 - Since the file-load process provided by _load_objects is used by many of
   the CRUD operations, it is tested  as part of testCRUDOperations
###########################################################################
```

Testing the new hms_core Classes

After going through the usual setup process for the unit tests of a module (creating the test module, executing the test module, creating test case classes for each item reported as missing, executing the test module, and creating test methods for each item reported as missing), the initial results show far fewer tests in need of implementation than in previous unit test modules, with only 11 tests that need to be populated:

```
###########################################################################
Unit-test results
###########################################################################
Tests were successful ..... False
Number of tests run ....... 16
 + Tests ran in .......... 0.00 seconds
Number of errors .......... 0
Number of failures ........ 11
Number of tests skipped ... 0
###########################################################################
```

There is a caveat to these results, though: they **do not** include tests of the data object methods required by `BaseDataObject` and `HMSMongoDataObject`, just of the properties and methods defined as part of the `Artisan` and `Product` classes that were created. Those, living in their own test module, add another 33 tests that need to be implemented:

```
########################################################################
Unit-test results
########################################################################
Tests were successful ..... False
Number of tests run ....... 47
 + Tests ran in .......... 0.01 seconds
Number of errors ......... 0
Number of failures ........ 33
Number of tests skipped ... 0
########################################################################
```

Unit testing hms_core.data_storage.py

The bulk of the testing for the `DatastoreConfig` class follows testing patterns that've been established earlier. The noteworthy exception is in testing its `from_config` class method, which requires actual config files to be written to test against. Testing all of the good values by creating a config file full of them doesn't look that much different from other test methods that involve creating an object instance from a `dict` value, though – the same sort of iteration over all the good test values starts it off:

```
# - Test all permutations of "good" argument-values:
config_file = '/tmp/datastore-test.json'
for database in good_databases:
    for host in good_hosts:
        for password in good_passwords:
            for port in good_ports:
                for user in good_users:
                    config = {
                        'database':database,
                        'host':host,
                        'password':password,
                        'port':port,
                        'user':user,
                    }
```

This is where the temporary configuration file is created:

```
fp = open('/tmp/datastore-test.json', 'w')
json.dump(config, fp)
fp.close()
```

Then `from_config` is called, and the various assertions are executed:

```
test_object = DatastoreConfig.from_config(config_file)
self.assertEqual(test_object.database, database)
self.assertEqual(test_object.host, host)
self.assertEqual(test_object.password, password)
self.assertEqual(test_object.port, port)
self.assertEqual(test_object.user, user)
os.unlink(config_file)
```

A similar approach/structure is used in testing the various bad values for each argument/property (`database`, `host`, `password`, `port`, and `user`). They all look much like the test of bad database values:

```
# - Test all permutations of each "bad" argument-value
#   set against "good" values for the other arguments:
# - database
host = good_hosts[0]
password = good_passwords[0]
port = good_ports[0]
user = good_users[0]
for database in bad_databases:
    config = {
        'database':database,
        'host':host,
        'password':password,
        'port':port,
        'user':user,
    }
    fp = open('/tmp/datastore-test.json', 'w')
    json.dump(config, fp)
    fp.close()
    try:
        test_object = DatastoreConfig.from_config(config_file)
        self.fail(
            'DatastoreConfig.from_config should not '
            'accept "%s" (%s) as a valid database config-'
            'value, but it was allowed to create an '
            'instance' % (database, type(database).__name__)
        )
    except (RuntimeError, TypeError, ValueError):
        pass
```

Much of the testing processes for HMSMongoDataObject are also in the vein of previously established test-writing patterns:

- Because the class derives from BaseDataObject, there are many of the same required test methods that depend on abstract functionality being implemented, so a derived class is created to test against, if only to ensure that the dependent method calls are successful

- The tests of the _create and _update methods are essentially identical to those created while testing their hms_artisan counterparts, since they too simply raise NotImplementedError

 Testing the functionality of any HMSMongoDataObject-derived class requires an operational MongoDB installation. Without one, the tests may raise errors (which would hopefully at least indicate what the problem is), or may just sit waiting for a connection to a MongoDB to resolve until the connection-effort times out.

The local properties, since they all use actual deletion of their underlying storage attributes, and are lazily instantiated (created when they are needed if they aren't already available), require a different approach than previous property tests. In the interests of keeping all of the related test code in one spot, the test_del_ methods have been skipped, and the testing of the deletion aspects of the properties merged in with the test_get_ methods. Using test_get_connection as an example:

```
def test_get_connection(self):
    # Tests the _get_connection method of the HMSMongoDataObject class
    # - Test that lazy instantiation on a new instance returns the
    #   class-attribute value (_connection)
    test_object = HMSMongoDataObjectDerived()
    self.assertEqual(
        test_object._get_connection(),
        HMSMongoDataObjectDerived._connection
    )
    # - Test that deleting the current connection and re-aquiring it
    #   works as expected
    test_object._del_connection()
    self.assertEqual(
        test_object._get_connection(),
        HMSMongoDataObjectDerived._connection
    )
    # - There may be more to test later, but this suffices for now...
```

The process for each is similar:

1. Create a `test_object` instance
2. Assert that the tested property getter returns the common class attribute value when called (`HMSMongoDataObjectDerived._connection` in this case)
3. Call the deleter method
4. Reassert that the common class attribute value is returned when the getter is called again

It might also be a good idea to assert, between the deleter and getter method calls, that the class attribute value is deleted, but it's not really necessary so long as the final getter call assertion still passes.

There are several items in the test case class for `HMSMongoDataObject` that depend on an actual database connection in order to be even remotely useful. In addition, there are test methods that directly relate to that dependency that can be skipped, or whose implementation is noteworthy. Since we'll need a database connection, that has to be configured every time that the test case class runs. Ideally, it should not run for every test that needs a connection, though – it's not a big deal if it does, at least not at the scale of the system so far, but in larger-scale systems, creating a new database for every test method that needs it could slow things down. Maybe substantially.

Fortunately, the standard Python `unittest` module provides methods that can be used to both initialize the database connection data, and delete the database used for testing after all the tests are complete. Those are, respectively, the `setUp` and `tearDown` methods. `setUp` need do nothing more than configure the data access, since `HMSMongoDataObjects` will take care of creating the `connection`, `database`, and `collection` objects it needs when they are needed:

```
def setUp(self):
    # - Since we need a database to test certain methods,
    #   create one here
    HMSMongoDataObject.configure(self.__class__.config)
```

`tearDown` is responsible for completely deleting the test database that will have been created for the test case class, and simply creates a `MongoClient`, then uses it to drop the database specified in the configuration:

```
def tearDown(self):
    # - delete the database after we're done with it, so that we
    #   don't have data persisting that could bollix up subsequent
    #   test-runs
```

```
from pymongo import MongoClient
client = MongoClient()
client.drop_database(self.__class__.config.database)
```

The setUp and tearDown methods won't behave the same way as a typical test method if we try to assert any expected values or behavior – any assertions made that fail will simply raise errors. That, then, means that while we could assert that configuration has completed accurately, it doesn't really do anything useful from the perspective of reporting. In this case, if the configuration call doesn't raise any errors, and the various test methods that rely on it pass, it can be taken as proof that configuration is doing what it's expected to do. In that case, we can skip the relevant test methods:

```
@unittest.skip(
    'The fact that the configuration works in setUp is sufficient'
)
def test_get_configuration(self):
    # Tests the _get_configuration method of the HMSMongoDataObject
class
    # - Test all permutations of "good" argument-values:
    # - Test all permutations of each "bad" argument-value
    #   set against "good" values for the other arguments:
    self.fail('test_get_configuration is not yet implemented')

@unittest.skip(
    'The fact that the configuration works in setUp is sufficient'
)
def testconfigure(self):
    # Tests the configure method of the HMSMongoDataObject class
    self.fail('testconfigure is not yet implemented')
```

In order to fully test the delete, get, and save methods, we have to implement a throwaway derived class – HMSMongoDataObjectDerived:

```
class HMSMongoDataObjectDerived(HMSMongoDataObject):

    _data_dict_keys = (
        'name', 'description', 'cost', 'oid', 'created', 'modified',
        'is_active', 'is_deleted'
    )
```

We'll want some local properties that can be used to test `get`, in particular, but they don't need to be anything more than simple attributes that are set during initialization and that appear in the results of a `to_data_dict` call:

```
def __init__(self, name=None, description=None, cost=0,
    oid=None, created=None, modified=None, is_active=None,
    is_deleted=None, is_dirty=None, is_new=None
):
    HMSMongoDataObject.__init__(
    self, oid, created, modified, is_active, is_deleted,
    is_dirty, is_new
)
    self.name = name
    self.description = description
    self.cost = cost

def to_data_dict(self):
    return {
        # - "local" properties
        'name':self.name,
        'description':self.description,
        'cost':self.cost,
        # - standard items from HMSMongoDataObject/BaseDataObject
'created':self.created.strftime(self.__class__._data_time_string),
        'is_active':self.is_active,
        'is_deleted':self.is_deleted,
'modified':self.modified.strftime(self.__class__._data_time_string),
        'oid':str(self.oid),
    }

def matches(self, **criteria):
    return HMSMongoDataObject.matches(self, **criteria)
```

In order to test the `delete` method, we need to first create and save some objects:

```
def testdelete(self):
    # Tests the delete method of the HMSMongoDataObject class
    # - In order to really test get, we need some objects to test
    #   against, so create a couple dozen:
    names = ['Alice', 'Bob', 'Carl', 'Doug']
    costs = [1, 2, 3]
    descriptions = [None, 'Description']
    all_oids = []
    for name in names:
        for description in descriptions:
            for cost in costs:
                item = HMSMongoDataObjectDerived(
                    name=name, description=description, cost=cost
```

```
    )
    item.save()
    all_oids.append(item.oid)
```

We'll want to test that we can delete multiple items and single items alike, so we'll take the last half of the collection of objects created, delete those, then take the last half of the remaining items, and so on, until we're down to a single object. In each iteration, we delete the current collection of `oid`, and verify that they don't exist after they've been deleted. Finally, we verify that all of the created objects have been deleted:

```
# - Delete varying-sized sets of items by oid, and verify that
#   the deleted oids are gone afterwards...
while all_oids:
    try:
        oids = all_oids[len(all_oids)/2:]
        all_oids = [o for o in all_oids if o not in oids]
    except:
        oids = all_oids
        all_oids = []
    HMSMongoDataObjectDerived.delete(*oids)
    items = HMSMongoDataObjectDerived.get(*oids)
    self.assertEqual(len(items), 0)
# - Verify that *no* items exist after they've all been deleted
items = HMSMongoDataObjectDerived.get()
self.assertEqual(items, [])
```

A similar approach is taken for testing `get` – creating several items with easily identifiable property values that can be used as `criteria`:

```
def testget(self):
    # Tests the get method of the HMSMongoDataObject class
    # - In order to really test get, we need some objects to test
    #   against, so create a couple dozen:
    names = ['Alice', 'Bob', 'Carl', 'Doug']
    costs = [1, 2, 3]
    descriptions = [None, 'Description']
    for name in names:
        for description in descriptions:
            for cost in costs:
                HMSMongoDataObjectDerived(
                    name=name, description=description, cost=cost
                ).save()
```

Then we can iterate over those same values, creating a `criteria` set to use, and verifying that the returned objects have the `criteria` values that we passed. One `criteria` value first:

```
# - Now we should be able to try various permutations of get
#   and get verifiable results. These tests will fail if the
#   _data_dict_keys class-attribute isn't accurate...
for name in names:
    criteria = {
        'name':name,
    }
    items = HMSMongoDataObjectDerived.get(**criteria)
    actual = len(items)
    expected = len(costs) * len(descriptions)
    self.assertEqual(actual, expected,
        'Expected %d items returned (all matching name="%s"), '
        'but %d were returned' %
        (expected, name, actual)
    )
    for item in items:
        self.assertEqual(item.name, name)
```

Then we test with multiple `criteria`, to assure that more than one `criteria` value behaves as expected:

```
for cost in costs:
    criteria = {
        'name':name,
        'cost':cost,
    }
    items = HMSMongoDataObjectDerived.get(**criteria)
    actual = len(items)
    expected = len(descriptions)
    self.assertEqual(actual, expected,
        'Expected %d items returned (all matching '
        'name="%s" and cost=%d), but %d were returned' %
        (expected, name, cost, actual)
    )
    for item in items:
        self.assertEqual(item.name, name)
        self.assertEqual(item.cost, cost)
```

Between the tests of the `delete` and `get` methods, we've effectively already tested the `save` method as well – we had to save objects to get or delete them, after all – so `testsave` is arguably not really needed. In the interest of having an actual test, rather that an entry for another skipped test, we'll implement it anyway, and use it to test that we can also get an object by its `oid` value:

```
# - Noteworthy because save/get rather than save/pymongo-query.
#   another option would be to do a "real" pymongo query, but that
#   test-code would look like the code in get anyway...?
def testsave(self):
    # Tests the save method of the HMSMongoDataObject class
    # - Testing save without using get is somewhat cumbersome, and
    #   perhaps too simple...?
    test_object = HMSMongoDataObjectDerived()
    test_object.save()
    expected = test_object.to_data_dict()
    results = HMSMongoDataObjectDerived.get(str(test_object.oid))
    actual = results[0].to_data_dict()
    self.assertEqual(actual, expected)
```

The final test output, once everything is implemented and passes, shows 47 tests, with five skipped:

```
################################################################################
Unit-test results
################################################################################
Tests were successful ..... True
Number of tests run ....... 47
 + Tests ran in .......... 0.41 seconds
Number of errors .......... 0
Number of failures ........ 0
Number of tests skipped ... 5
################################################################################
SKIPPED
#-----------------------------------------------------------------------------#
test_del_collection (__main__.testHMSMongoDataObject)
 - Tested in test_get_collection
test_del_connection (__main__.testHMSMongoDataObject)
 - Tested in test_get_connection
test_del_database (__main__.testHMSMongoDataObject)
 - Tested in test_get_database
test_get_configuration (__main__.testHMSMongoDataObject)
 - The fact that the configuration works in setUp is sufficient
testconfigure (__main__.testHMSMongoDataObject)
 - The fact that the configuration works in setUp is sufficient
################################################################################
```

Unit testing hms_core.co_objects.py

The `Artisan` and `Product` classes in `co_objects`, like their counterparts in the `artisan_objects` module of `hms_artisan`, had to be overridden in order to provide the appropriate `is_dirty` behavior when any of those properties that are part of a state data record are altered. As a result, their corresponding test methods had to be created, just as happened when testing their counterparts in the `hms_artisan` package. Effectively, the same changes were made in both modules, and as a result the test classes and the test methods within them for classes that exist in both packages turned out to be identical.

Unit tests and trust

It was noted earlier that the real purpose of unit testing code is about ensuring that code behaves in a predictable fashion across all possible execution cases. In a very real way, it is also about establishing a measure of trust in a code base. In that context, there is a line that has to be drawn with respect to where that trust can simply be taken as a given. For example, the various unit tests in this iteration have focused on ensuring that the code created for data persistence gets everything that is necessary to and from the database engine. It has not been concerned with whether the library to connect to the database engine is trustworthy; for our purposes, we assume that it is, at least until we encounter a test failure that cannot be explained in any other way.

Unit tests provide that trust for others who might consume our code – knowing that everything that needs to be tested has been, and that all the tests have passed.

Building/distribution, demonstration, and acceptance

The build process for the individual modules will not have changed much, though with unit tests now available, those can be added to the `setup.py` files that are used to package the individual Python packages. The `setup` function that's already in place can, with minimal changes, be used to execute the entire test suite simply by providing a `test_suite` argument that points to the root test suite directory.

It may be necessary to ensure that the path to the test suite directory has been added to `sys.path` as well:

```
#!/usr/bin/env python

import sys
sys.path.append('../standards')
sys.path.append('tests/test_hms_core') # <-- This path
```

The current `setup` function call, then, includes `test_suite` like this:

```
setup(
    name='HMS-Core',
    version='0.1.dev0',
    author='Brian D. Allbee',
    description='',
    package_dir={
        '':'src',
    },
    packages=[
        'hms_core',
    ],
    test_suite='tests.test_hms_core',
)
```

The entire test suite can then be executed with `python setup.py test`, which returns a line-by-line summary of the tests executed and their results:

```
python setup.py test
running test
running egg_info
writing dependency_links to src/HMS_Core.egg-info/dependency_links.txt
writing top-level names to src/HMS_Core.egg-info/top_level.txt
writing src/HMS_Core.egg-info/PKG-INFO
reading manifest file 'src/HMS_Core.egg-info/SOURCES.txt'
writing manifest file 'src/HMS_Core.egg-info/SOURCES.txt'
running build_ext
testCodeCoverage (idic.unit_testing.ModuleCoverageTest) ... ok
testCodeCoverage (tests.test_hms_core.testhms_coreCodeCoverage) ... ok
testCodeCoverage (idic.unit_testing.ModuleCoverageTest) ... ok


...


testsort (tests.test_hms_core.test_co_objects.testProduct) ... skipped
    "Sort will be implemented once there's a need for it, and tested
    as part of that implementation"
teststore_available (tests.test_hms_core.test_co_objects.testProduct) ... ok
testsummary (tests.test_hms_core.test_co_objects.testProduct) ... ok
testto_data_dict (tests.test_hms_core.test_co_objects.testProduct) ... ok
testCodeCoverage (tests.test_hms_core.test_co_objects.testco_objectsCodeCoverage) ... ok

-------------------------------------------------------------------
Ran 261 tests in 1.324s

OK (skipped=9)
```

Packaging the code in a component project still uses `python setup.py sdist` from within the individual project directories, and still yields an installable package:

Demonstrating the new data-persistence functionality could be done in several ways, but requires the creation of disposable/temporary demo data objects in a disposable/temporary database. There's code in the `test_co_objects` test module that does just that, so creating a minimal data object class based on that structure (calling it `ExampleObject` for demonstrative purposes), then running:

```
HMSMongoDataObject.configure(
    DatastoreConfig(database='demo_data')
)

print('Creating data-objects to demo with')
names = ['Alice', 'Bob', 'Carl', 'Doug']
```

```
costs = [1, 2, 3]
descriptions = [None, 'Description']
for name in names:
    for description in descriptions:
        for cost in costs:
            item = ExampleObject(
                name=name, description=description, cost=cost
            )
            item.save()
```

It takes care of generating a dataset that can be examined. From that point, any tool – the command-line `mongo` client or a GUI, such as **Robo3T** – can be used to view and verify that data was, in fact, persisted:

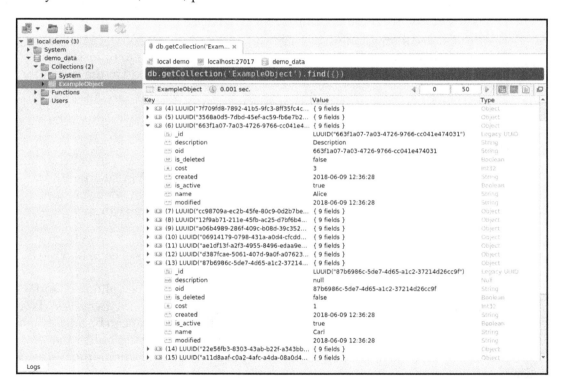

If more detailed acceptance examples are needed – such as examples for each of the business object types – a similar script could be written to create `Artisan` and `Product` instances and save them as well. Similarly, with respect to the `hms_artisan` data object classes, simply showing the files written for objects in an example/demo environment should suffice.

Operations/use, maintenance, and decommissioning considerations

There is no substantial change yet as these items are concerned:

- The packages, though there are now three of them, are still very simple.
- Although we've added an external dependency with the inclusion of the `pymongo` library, we're not yet at a point where we need to worry about how that dependency will be handled.
- There will obviously need to be a MongoDB installation, but until the code is ready to be integrated to some shared environment, even that is a non-issue – local development can use local database engines for now.
- From a decommissioning perspective, uninstalling the software hasn't really changed except that there are now three packages to uninstall – but the process for each is a variation of the process as it stood at the end of the last iteration (`pip uninstall HMS-Core`).

Summary

While there may be other data-access and data-persistence tweaks in later iterations, and there are a few data objects whose specific details aren't known yet because of integration concerns with other systems, the bulk of the data objects work is complete.

Thus far, the development iterations against the `hms_sys` code bases have had most of their attention focused on what might be thought of as system functionality – ensuring that data structures are well formed, can be validated, and will live longer than a single user session or Python run. Interaction with system data from a user perspective hasn't been addressed yet at all. Before that can be addressed, though, there is another layer that needs to be at least analyzed, if not built – the Artisan Gateway service, which acts as a central point where data from remote artisans and Central Office staff comes together.

14
Anatomy of a Service

The next logical chunk of functionality to attack in `hms_sys` is the Artisan Gateway Service. This service waits for input from either Artisan or Central Office end users, creating or updating object data as needed, and perhaps synchronizing that data with the web store system's database. Both of the end user applications are expected to communicate with the Artisan Gateway Service on a completely random basis; whenever someone wants to make a change to the data, it'll be ready and waiting to process that request.

Before we can really implement this service, however, we need to work out how any service can or should work, written in Python. To that end, we will have to examine and understand the following:

- The basic implementation of the structure of a service, including the following:
    - Options for managing the configuration of a service instance
    - How a service can read and respond to requests
- How and when a service is launched in the following environments:
    - A reasonably modern, POSIX-compliant system (Linux, for example)
    - Windows
- Whether there are other, better designs that will work in any OS that Python is available on

In order to better understand these facets of the implementation and execution of a service, we'll build a basic service structure from the ground up, which can then be used as a foundation for the final Artisan Gateway Service.

What is a service?

Services, at their most basic, are simply programs that run in the background on a computer. They typically wait for input from somewhere, perform some actions based on that input, and return data that, at a minimum, indicates that the actions that were undertaken either succeeded or failed. At the most basic level, the input might not even be something that is visible to a user; services that wait for network activities, monitor filesystems, or even just run on some sort of timer-controlled basis, are very common in many operating systems today.

Services should always be available, running continuously, for as long as the host machine is running; this has some implications for how they are written and implemented, as follows:

- They have to be very fault-tolerant: a service that crashes and dies every time something unexpected happens, and has to be restarted as a result, is of little use.
- They should, arguably, be as functionally self-contained as is possible; external dependencies that could fail (and cause a running service to crash as a result) should be examined with a critical eye.
- Because their operations may be completely invisible to the user, there is a lot of potential for a poorly designed or implemented service to overrun system resources, which could eventually take down an entire machine. Even if there is no multi-processing involved, care needs to be taken and discipline exercised, in order to avoid things such as loops that never terminate or functionality that leaves orphan objects, data, or functions in memory. If these occur, it's just a matter of time (or load on the service) until the memory or available CPU dwindles to nothing.

Service structure

All that said, services aren't necessarily all that complex. If there are operating system facilities available to manage the actual code execution (startup and shutdown), they might not be any more complex, structurally, than the following code:

```python
#!/usr/bin/env python
"""
A simple daemon-like function that can be started from the command-
line.
"""
    import syslog
```

```
from time import sleep

def main_program():
    iterations = 0
    syslog.syslog('Starting %s' % __file__)
    while True:
        # TODO: Perform whatever request-acquisition and response-
        #       generation is needed here...
        syslog.syslog('Event Loop (%d)' % iterations)
        sleep(10)
        iterations += 1
    syslog.syslog('Exiting %s' % __file__)

if __name__ == '__main__':
    main_program()
```

When the preceding code is run, it generates no user-visible output, but watching the system logs (using `tail -f /var/log/syslog`, on a Linux machine) shows that it is doing what it's supposed to, as follows:

- It writes the starting message to the log file before entering the main loop.
- In each pass through the loop, it does the following:
  - Writes a message to the log, with the iteration number
  - Sleeps for 10 seconds
  - Increments the iteration counter

The exiting message is not being written to the log file, but that's expected at this point, since the only way to stop the main loop is to kill the program itself, and that terminates the program without exiting the loop. A typical log output, from startup through a few iterations, looks as follows:

```
$ tail -f /var/log/syslog | grep ".*py_daemon_func\.py"
py_daemon_func.py: Starting py_daemon_func.py
py_daemon_func.py: Event Loop (0)
py_daemon_func.py: Event Loop (1)
py_daemon_func.py: Event Loop (2)
py_daemon_func.py: Event Loop (3)
py_daemon_func.py: Event Loop (4)
py_daemon_func.py: Event Loop (5)
```

This isn't much of a service, to be sure, but it illustrates what might be considered the bare minimum of the functionality that would be common to any service.

At the heart of most services is a loop that runs until the service is shut down or killed. Within that loop is where the service will actually check for input, in one of several ways. Some of the more common variants include the following:

- It could be waiting on a request coming in over a network socket (a web service would use this approach).
- It could be waiting on incoming data from standard input (`stdin`).
- It could actively poll for incoming messages from an external queue system, such as RabbitMQ, or cloud-based equivalents, such as AWS's SQS or Google Cloud Platform's Cloud Pub/Sub.

 These are only a few of the possibilities for service input. Other mechanisms that don't lend themselves to a direct waiting-for-something model could always push events into a local queue, and have the service watching or polling from that queue mechanism.

In all but the most basic of services, incoming requests will have to be evaluated, to determine what functionality has to be called in order to handle the request. The most common mechanism for associating incoming request data to a specific functionality is probably a large `if...elif...else` structure that passes the responsibility for handling a request to specific and dedicated functions, looking something like the following:

```
# - Evaluate the incoming request:
    if request['path'].startswith('/product'):
        return handle_product_request(request)
    elif request['path'].startswith('/artisan'):
        return handle_artisan_request(request)
    elif request['path'].startswith('/customer'):
        return handle_customer_request(request)
    else:
# - Invalid request, so return an error
        return handle_invalid_request(request)
```

Each of the `handle_{something}_request` functions, then, would be responsible for taking the incoming request, determining what to do with it, and returning the resultant data.

There is a standard Python library, `python-daemon`, that takes this basic approach a step further, allowing a function to be wrapped in a basic daemon context. The same basic function, with a `python-daemon DaemonContext` wrapped around it, is very similar, and is shown in the following snippet:

```python
#!/usr/bin/env python
"""

A bare-bones daemon implementation.
"""
    import syslog
    from daemon import DaemonContext
    from time import sleep

    def main_program():
        iterations = 0
        syslog.syslog('Starting %s' % __file__)
        while True:
        # TODO: Perform whatever request-acquisition and response-
        #       generation is needed here...
            syslog.syslog('Event Loop (%d)' % iterations)
            sleep(10)
            iterations += 1
        syslog.syslog('Exiting %s' % __file__)

    if __name__ == '__main__':
        with DaemonContext():
            main_program()
```

 The terms **service** and **daemon** are, for the purposes of this book, interchangeable; they both refer to the same sort of background process program.

The execution of this code yields almost identical results (barring the filename that appears in the log messages, it is identical, in fact). The actual differences are effectively invisible, once the daemon code is running. Using `DaemonContext` provides some operational aspects that the bare-bones, function-only code does not deal with, which are considered to be best practices for daemon processes:

- Assuring that any open files associated with the command during startup get closed
- Changing the working directory for the process to a known and/or secure directory
- Setting the file-creation permissions mask, so that the files created by the processes will have a known (and securable) permissions set
- Performing system-level process setup, to allow the process itself to run in the background
- Dissociating the process from any Terminal activity, so that it won't respond to Terminal input once the daemon process is launched

Although `python-daemon` is a standard library, it may not be part of a standard Python installation. If not, it can be installed with `pip install python-daemon`.

The `python-daemon` module, then, provides a very easy way to manage a lot of the best-practice operations for writing daemons and services. There is, however, a potential problem with using it. It won't work on systems that don't have a Unix-like password database (it depends on the `pwd` module, which is Unix-only). That rules it out for services that need to run on Windows systems, at the very least.

Ultimately, though, knowing that a service implementation doesn't have to be much more than a single function call with a perpetual loop, the main concern (outside of the implementation of the service's logic) is probably how to get the host operating system to start, stop, and manage the service instance. We'll examine that in considerably more detail at the end of the chapter, but there are a few other common service implementation patterns and concerns that bear some examination, first.

Configuration

Services frequently have to be configurable without making changes to the actual service code, so that the end users or managers of active services don't have to be developers themselves, in order to be able to effectively manage running service instances. There are several options that can be used to read configuration and setting values from files, each with its own strengths and weaknesses. In order to better compare and contrast them, let's examine the variations that provide the configuration for a service that does the following:

- Logs information, warning, error, and critical level messages:
  - Information and warning level messages to a console
  - Everything, including information and warning level messages, to a single, common log file, whose location is configurable
- Listens for input messages from a queue service, such as RabbitMQ, or a cloud-based queue service, such as AWS's SQS or Google Cloud Platform's Pub/Sub, and needs to know the following:
  - A queue name or URL to listen to
  - How often to check for incoming messages
  - The credentials for access to the queue in question

Windows-style .ini files

Python has a standard package for working with INI files (or, at least, files that are similar to basic Windows INI files): `configparser`. A compatible INI-like file that provides the configuration for previously listed items might look something such as the following:

```
[DEFAULT]
# This section handles settings-values that are available in other
# sections.
# - The minimum log-level that's in play
log_level:      INFO
queue_type:     rabbit
queue_check:    5

[console_log]
# Settings for logging of messages to the console
# - Message-types to log to a console
capture:        INFO, WARNING

[file_log]
# Settings for file-logging
log_file:       /var/log/myservice/activity.log

[rabbit_config]
# Configuration for the RabbitMQ server, if queue_type is "rabbit"
server:         10.1.10.1
port:           5672
queue_name:     my-queue
user:           username
password:       password
```

Some of the advantages of an INI-style configuration file include the following:

- The file structure allows for comments to be used. Any line starting with a # or ; is a comment, and is not parsed, which allows for configuration files to be documented inline.
- Values specified in the [DEFAULT] section are inherited by all of the other sections, and are available as specified originally, or to be overridden in later sections.
- The format itself has been around for a long time, so it's very mature and stable.

This configuration file's values can be examined with a simple script, listing the available values in each configuration section and showing some of the potential disadvantages of the format, as parsed with `configparser` tools:

```
-- DEFAULT ----------------------------------------------------------------
 + log_level ........... (str) INFO
 + queue_type .......... (str) rabbit
 + queue_check ......... (str) 5
-- console_log ------------------------------------------------------------
 + capture ............ (str) INFO, WARNING
 + log_level .......... (str) INFO
 + queue_type ......... (str) rabbit
 + queue_check ........ (str) 5
-- file_log ----------------------------------------------------------------
 + log_file ........... (str) /var/log/myservice/activity.log
 + log_level .......... (str) INFO
 + queue_type ......... (str) rabbit
 + queue_check ........ (str) 5
-- rabbit_config ----------------------------------------------------------
 + server ............. (str) 10.1.10.1
 + port ............... (str) 5672
 + queue_name ......... (str) my-queue
 + user ............... (str) username
 + password ........... (str) password
 + log_level .......... (str) INFO
 + queue_type ......... (str) rabbit
 + queue_check ........ (str) 5
```

The script that generated this output is in the code for *Iteration 3*, at `hms-gateway/scratch-space/configuration-examples/ini_config.py`.

Some of the potential disadvantages of the format include the following:

- The values in the [DEFAULT] configuration section are inherited by all other sections, even if they are not relevant. The `queue_type` and `queue_check` values are available in the `console_log` and `file_log` sections, for example, where they aren't really relevant.

- All configuration values are strings, and would probably have to be converted to their real value types: an `int` for `queue_check` and `rabbit_config:port`, probably a `list` of `str` values for `console_log:capture`, a conversion to `bool` values for any that might appear, and so on.
- The format only really supports two levels of configuration data (sections and their members).

None of these constraints are likely to be too problematic, though. Knowing that they exist is generally going to be enough to plan for how they will be accommodated, and the shape of that accommodation might be nothing more complicated than having no `[DEFAULT]` section, and grouping configuration values into more coherent sections, such as `logging` and `queue`.

JSON files

JSON data structures are also a viable candidate for storing configuration file data. JSON supports data of different types, and complex data structures. Both are advantages, however trivial they might be, over the basic INI-file structure. There is no predefined organizational structure, though, so figuring out how configuration values should be grouped or organized is something that developers will have to give some thought to. There is also no inheritance of configuration data across sections, because there are no sections to inherit from. Still, it's a simple, robust, and reasonably easy-to-understand option. An approximate JSON equivalent of the preceding INI-flavored configuration file might look something such as the following:

```json
{
    "logging": {
        "log_level": "INFO",
        "console_capture": ["INFO","WARNING"],
        "log_file": "/var/log/myservice/activity.log"
    },
    "queue": {
        "queue_type": "rabbit",
        "queue_check": 5,
        "server": "10.1.10.1",
        "port": 5672,
        "queue_name": "my-queue",
        "user": "username",
        "password": "password"
    }
}
```

If JSON has any disadvantages (with respect to its use as a configuration-file format), they'd include the fact that there isn't a good way to allow in-file comments. The `load` and `loads` functions provided by Python's `json` module (for converting a JSON string and a JSON file, respectively) raise an error, `JSONDecodeError`, if there is anything other than data structure in the JSON data being parsed. That's not a deal-breaker, but there are definitely advantages to having the ability to add comments (and thus, documentation) to a configuration file, especially if that configuration is going to be managed by someone that isn't a developer, or isn't willing (or able) to dig into the code itself, in order to work out how to configure some aspect of a system.

YAML files

Another good contender for configuration files is YAML. YAML acts like JSON in many respects, in that it provides structured and typed data representations, and can support complex, nested data structures. In addition, it allows for inline comments, and the `pyyaml` module supports hinting for data structures that would not be usable at all in a JSON-based approach. YAML, like Python, uses indentation as a structural organization mechanism, indicating (in YAML's case) the key/value relationship between items. An equivalent to the preceding JSON configuration file (with comments, and breaking all elements (objects, list members, and so on) into discrete items in the file), would look like this:

```
# Logging configuration
logging:
    console_capture:
        - INFO
        - WARNING
    log_file: /var/log/myservice/activity.log
    log_level: INFO
# Queue configuration
queue:
    queue_type: rabbit
    # Credentials
    user: username
    password: password
    # Network
    server: 10.1.10.1
    port: 5672
    # Queue settings
    queue_name: my-queue
    queue_check: 5
```

We'll build on the idea of using YAML to configure a service later in this chapter. YAML obviously isn't the only option, but it's one of the better ones, allowing for a good combination of ease of understanding, the ability to comment/document, and the availability of more than one value type.

Logging service activities

Since services often run invisibly, in the background, they usually log their activities in some fashion, if only to provide some visibility into what happened during a service call where something went awry. Python provides a module, logging, that allows for a lot of flexibility for logging events and messages from a running program. The following is a very simple, brute-force example of a reasonably complete logging process:

```python
import logging

# - Define a format for log-output
formatter = logging.Formatter(
    '%(asctime)s - %(name)s - %(levelname)s - %(message)s'
)
# - Get a logger. Once defned anywhere, loggers (with all their
#   settings and attached formats and handlers) can be retrieved
#   elsewhere by getting a logger instance using the same name.
logger = logging.getLogger('logging-example')
logger.setLevel(logging.DEBUG)
# - Create a file-handler to write log-messages to a file
file_handler = logging.FileHandler('example.log')
file_handler.setLevel(logging.DEBUG)
file_handler.setFormatter(formatter)
# - Attach handler to logger
logger.addHandler(file_handler)

# - Log some messages to show that it works:
logger.critical('This is a CRITICAL-level message')
logger.debug('This is a DEBUG-level message')
logger.error('This is an ERROR-level message')
logger.info('This is an INFO-level message')
logger.warn('This is a WARNING-level message')
```

When executed, the preceding script generates the following log output:

```
2018-07-08 10:21:30,215 - logging-example - CRITICAL - This is a CRITICAL-level message
2018-07-08 10:21:30,215 - logging-example - DEBUG - This is a DEBUG-level message
2018-07-08 10:21:30,216 - logging-example - ERROR - This is an ERROR-level message
2018-07-08 10:21:30,216 - logging-example - INFO - This is an INFO-level message
2018-07-08 10:21:30,216 - logging-example - WARNING - This is a WARNING-level message
```

A Python `Logger` object (which is what's returned by the `getLogger` call) can be set up to pay attention to log messages of varying priority levels. In order from the least to the most critical (from a production-system standpoint), the default levels available (and some typical uses for them) are as follows:

- `DEBUG`: Recording information about processes as they run, steps they undertake, and the like, with an eye toward providing some visibility into the details of how the code was executed.
- `INFO`: Informational items, such as the start and end times of request-handling processes; and perhaps details or metrics on the processes themselves, such as what arguments were passed, or if a given execution took longer than expected, but still completed.
- `WARNING`: Conditions that didn't prevent processes or operations from completing, but that were suspect for some reason, such as taking a lot longer than expected to complete.
- `ERROR`: Actual errors that were encountered as the code executed, perhaps including detailed trace-back information that would help a developer figure out what actually caused the error in question.
- `CRITICAL`: Recording information that was intercepted before a critical/fatal failure of the running code – something that actually killed the execution. In well-designed and implemented code, especially for a service that is intended to always be available, this level of message recording should rarely be needed. Errors would be captured and logged as `ERROR`-level items, any cleanup that would be required after the error was encountered would be undertaken, a response indicating that an error occurred would be sent back to the requester, and the service would just keep going, waiting for the next request.

The actual handling and recording of the messages of any given level are controlled by the `Logger` object, and/or by its various handlers. The `Logger` object itself will not accept messages with a priority lower than its set priority.

Having `logger.setLevel(logging.DEBUG)` in the example code would allow any of the standard message priorities, while changing it to `logger.setLevel(logging.ERROR)` would only allow `ERROR` and `CRITICAL` messages to be accepted. Similarly, the handlers will ignore any incoming messages that fall below the priority they've been configured to accept – `file_handler.setLevel(logging.DEBUG)`, in the previous example.

By combining detailed logging in the code itself, including `DEBUG`-level items wherever it is necessary, and some configuration of the allowed message-priorities, the same code can fine-tune its own log output for different environments. For example:

```python
def some_function(*args, **kwargs):
    logger.info('some_function(%s, %s) called' % (str(args),
str(kwargs)))
    if not args and not kwargs:
        logger.warn(
            'some_function was called with no arguments'
        )
    elif args:
        logger.debug('*args exists: %s' % (str(args)))
        try:
            x, y = args[0:2]
            logger.debug('x = %s, y = %s' % (x, y))
            return x / y
        except ValueError as error:
            logger.error(
                '%s: Could not get x and y values from '
                'args %s' %
                (error.__class__.__name__, str(args))
            )
        except Exception as error:
            logger.error(
                '%s in some_function: %s' %
                (error.__class__.__name__, error)
            )
    logger.info('some_function complete')
```

This code set logs the following, depending on the differences in logging priorities set up in the `logger`:

```
# Results with logging set to logging.DEBUG on a local dev-environment:
-----------------------------------
2018-07-08 11:00:49,791 - logging-example - INFO - Calling with no arguments
2018-07-08 11:00:49,791 - logging-example - INFO - some_function((), {}) called
2018-07-08 11:00:49,791 - logging-example - WARNING - some_function was called with
    no arguments
2018-07-08 11:00:49,791 - logging-example - INFO - some_function complete
2018-07-08 11:00:49,791 - logging-example - INFO - Calling with x and y values
2018-07-08 11:00:49,791 - logging-example - INFO - some_function((1, 2), {}) called
2018-07-08 11:00:49,791 - logging-example - DEBUG - *args exists: (1, 2)
2018-07-08 11:00:49,792 - logging-example - DEBUG - x = 1, y = 2
2018-07-08 11:00:49,792 - logging-example - INFO - Calling with a bad y-value
2018-07-08 11:00:49,792 - logging-example - INFO - some_function((1, 0), {}) called
2018-07-08 11:00:49,792 - logging-example - DEBUG - *args exists: (1, 0)
2018-07-08 11:00:49,792 - logging-example - DEBUG - x = 1, y = 0
2018-07-08 11:00:49,792 - logging-example - ERROR - ZeroDivisionError in
    some_function: division by zero
2018-07-08 11:00:49,792 - logging-example - INFO - some_function complete

# Results with logging set to logging.ERROR on a production environment:
-----------------------------------
2018-07-08 11:00:49,792 - logging-example - ERROR - ZeroDivisionError in
    some_function: division by zero
```

The complete script that generates this log information is in the *Iteration 3* code, at `hms-gateway/scratch-space/logging-examples/logging-example.py`.

Like YAML configuration, we'll build on this logging structure later in this chapter, as a part of building a reusable base daemon structure.

Handling requests and generating responses

Most services will follow some sort of a request-response process model. A request is received, whether from a human user interacting with the service or some other process; the service then reads the request, determines what to do with it, performs whatever actions are needed, and generates and returns a response.

There are at least three distinct request types that are common enough to warrant a detailed examination – filesystem, HTTP/web message, and queue-based – each with its own baseline assumptions about how requests will be presented to a service, and each with its own resultant implications for design and execution.

The responses generated for any given request type usually imply a response mechanism of the same basic type. That is, a request that comes in from some filesystem variant will usually generate a response that is also expressed as some sort of filesystem output. That may not always be the case, but the odds are good that it will be in many (perhaps most) cases.

Filesystem – based

Requests and responses from and to the local filesystem are typically (and unsurprisingly) concerned with reading and writing data from and to local files. The simplest request-and-response structure of this type is a service that reads data from one file, processes it, and writes the results out to another file, possibly deleting or flushing out the incoming file on every read, and either replacing the output file on every write, or appending to it as each response is generated and returned. Implementations for single input and output files may leverage the `stdin` and `stdout` functionality of Python's `sys` module, or override either (or both) of them.

Both Windows and POSIX operating systems (Linux, macOS) have special file types, called **named pipes,** that reside on the filesystem and act like files, in that they can be opened, read from, and written to by using standard file-access code. The main difference is that a named pipe file can be opened and written to/read from by multiple different processes at the same time. That, then, allows for any number of processes to add requests to a file, queuing them up for a service to read and handle. Named pipes can also be used for service output.

Another variant is monitoring for changes to files in the local filesystem, including the creation of new files, and changes to (or even the deletion of) existing files in a given location. At its most basic, this would involve generating and maintaining a list of files to keep track of, and periodically checking the actual filesystem structure for those files' existence and modified time. An implementation that follows this pattern might have a common input-file directory, and, as each iteration through the main service loop occurred, it would check for new files, read them, execute, and remove the file once processing was complete (in order to keep the number of files being monitored reasonably small).

For scenarios where the number of files being monitored is large enough that creating and refreshing that list is too computationally expensive to be practical, monitoring filesystem events with functionality from the `pyinotify` library is a viable alternative, though there have been differences in what's available between POSIX/Linux and Windows versions of the library.

HTTP- or web-based

HTTP-based services (web services), as the name implies, use the HTTP protocol to receive requests and transmit responses to those requests. As a subset of network-aware services, web services allow access to the service from machines other than the one that the service is actually running on. Web services don't have to be accessible on the public internet; they can live entirely in a local network, and operate just as well inside of those boundaries. They do, however, have to conform to some basic minimum standards, and could benefit from adhering to others.

It is likely that the most important of those standards is adhering to the request methods of the HTTP protocol. The methods that are most commonly seen in websites, and that are supported by any web browser worthy of the name, are as follows:

- `GET`: Used to retrieve data
- `POST`: Used to create data using an attached payload, even though `POST` is typically used in web applications, for both `create` and `update` operations

There are several other methods available in the protocol, including:

- `PUT` and `PATCH`: Intended to update data using an attached payload, in whole or in part, respectively

- `DELETE`: Intended to delete data

- `OPTIONS`: Intended to provide data that indicates what methods are available, especially methods that can create or alter data on the receiving system, such as `POST`, `PUT`, and `DELETE` requests, and, most especially, if a request is being made to the service from somewhere other than the service's domain itself

Other methods that might come into play include HEAD, CONNECT, and TRACE. Depending on the design and implementation of the service, each HTTP method can be implemented as specific functions or methods of a class, allowing each request type to be able to enforce any requirements specific to it, while still allowing some functionality for common needs, such as the extraction of a payload for POST, PUT, and PATCH requests.

A response from a web-service call, even if it's an empty response, is effectively required; otherwise, the calling client will wait until the request times out. Web service responses are limited to data types that can be transmitted by the HTTP protocol, which isn't very limited, but may require some additional development effort to support binary-resource responses (for example, images). As things stand, at the time of writing this book, most responses that can be represented purely in text seem to be returned as JSON data structures, but XML, HTML, and plain-text responses are also in the realm of possibilities.

Although it's certainly possible to write a full-blown web service purely in Python, there are a fair number of protocol-related items that might be better handled by any of several libraries, packages, or frameworks, if only because doing so would reduce the volume of code to be written, tested, and maintained. Options include, but are not limited to, the following:

- Writing a web service as a **Web Server Gateway Interface** (**WSGI**) application that is accessible through an Apache or NGINX web server
- Using the Django REST framework
- Using the Flask-RESTful extension to the Flask framework

A web- server- and framework-based solution will also benefit from security updates to the underlying web server and framework software, without requiring in-house security audits.

 If a web service is expected to be exposed to the public internet, any of these are much better options than writing a service from the ground up, for that reason alone. It won't eliminate the need to be conscious of potential security concerns, but it will reduce the scope of those concerns to the code for the service's functionality itself.

Message- queue-based

Message queue systems, such as RabbitMQ and the various cloud-based options, have several advantages going for them for certain types of applications. They generally allow pretty much any message format to be used, provided that it can be expressed as text, and they allow messages to remain in a pending state until they are explicitly retrieved and dealt with, keeping messages safe and ready to use until the final consumer of those messages is ready to consume them. By way of example, consider the following scenario:

1. Two users are sending messages to a service through a distributed queue that lives on the **Message-Queue Server**
2. **User #1** sends their first message
3. The service receives and acts on that message, but may not have deleted it in the queue yet
4. The service is restarted for some reason – to update it to a new version, perhaps, or because the server itself is being rebooted
5. In any case, before the service comes back online, **User #2** sends their first message.
6. **User #1** sends another message

Before the target service completes its startup, the scenario looks as follows:

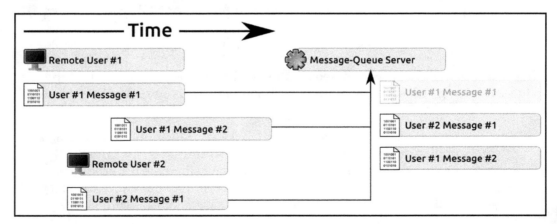

Once the target service has completed its startup, all it has to do to fulfill the pending requests in those messages is poll the **Message-Queue Server** to retrieve any pending messages, and execute against them, just like it was doing before it was restarted.

From the perspective of **User #1** and **User #2**, there has been no interruption in access to the service (though there may have been a noticeable, or even significant, delay in getting their responses back). That would hold true whether the inactive period for the target service was a few seconds, or a few hours. Either way, the messages/commands that the end users sent were saved until they could be acted upon, so no effort was lost.

If the responses to those requests are also transmitted through a queue-based process, the same persistence of messages would hold true. So, as soon as the responses have been generated and sent by the target service, the users are able to receive them, even if they shut down and went home for the day before they were sent. Response messages would wait until the receiving system was active again, at which point they'd be delivered and acted upon.

Queue-based request-and-response cycles are, then, *very* well suited for managing log running and/or asynchronous processes, provided that the code that's acting on the messages takes that possibility into account.

Other request types

Python provides access to enough general-purpose networking functionality that services can be written from scratch to read and respond to pretty much any sort of network traffic desired. The web- and queue-based service types are specific applications of that functionality, under the hood, supported to varying degrees by additional libraries that address some of the needs specific to each, as follows:

- Web services will probably make at least some use of the functionality provided by the `http.server`, or `socket` modules; the `http.server.HTTPServer` or `socketserver.TCPServer` classes are the most likely starting points, but `http.server.ThreadingHTTPServer` is also potentially viable.
- Queue-based services may have libraries available that are specifically built to interact with the underlying queue service they're attached to, including the following:
  - `pika`, for RabbitMQ queue-services
  - `boto3`, for AWS SQS services, starting with creating a `boto3.SQS.Client` object

Socket-based services that don't have some sort of supporting library available will probably start with the `socketserver.TCPServer` class noted in the previous lists, or perhaps with its UDP equivalent, `socketserver.UDPServer`. There are also `Threading` and `Forking` mix-in classes available, which can be used to provide basic server classes that support threading or (on POSIX-compliant systems) forking for servers, in order to handle larger user load levels.

Request and response formats

From a purely technical/functional perspective, service implementations can be data- and format-agnostic. That is, there's no functional reason why a service cannot accept raw binary data input and return raw binary output. Data is data, after all. However, even in cases where a service really is concerned with data that isn't readily readable by human beings, there are advantages to formatting the incoming requests and outgoing responses, to afford some degree of human readability. At a minimum, it makes the debugging of requests and responses easier.

In that respect, request and response data share a lot of the concerns that were noted about the needs of configuration files, as follows:

- Being able to pass structured and typed data around is similarly advantageous
- Allowing that data structure to be at least somewhat comprehensible to a casual reader/observer feels like a good thing, too
- The ability to represent reasonably complex data structures—lists and nested objects—also feels advantageous

Given the same types of concerns, a similar solution to address them makes sense, which means that using a serialization format, such as JSON or YAML, also makes sense. Doing so introduces a bit of additional development effort overhead; for example, converting incoming data from JSON to a native data structure, or an outbound native data structure response to JSON. That effort will generally be pretty trivial, though.

Of those two formats, JSON is arguably a better general-purpose solution. It's well established, and it's directly supported across a wider range of potential service clients, if only because it is, essentially, a native data format for web browsers. YAML is still a viable alternative, though, particularly in cases where there is no web browser client support needed.

A generic service design

Given the configuration and logging possibilities that we've explored so far, the bare-bones service-as-a-function approach feels less and less viable, unless it's reasonable to expect that only one service will ever need to be written. Taking that basic approach is still possible, to be sure, but if there's ever a need to create another service, it'd be more efficient (and, at least, a somewhat more effective use of developer time) if there were a common starting point for creating any service, no matter what it's expected to do. To that end, then, we'll define a set of **abstract base classes** (**ABC**) that define the lowest common denominators of features and functionality that we'll expect from any service or daemon going forward, and we'll use that as our starting point for the Artisan Gateway Service of hms_sys.

The rationale for defining a service as a class, rather than as a function, is centered around the fact that we can reasonably expect at least a handful of properties and methods that would be common to all services/daemons, that would be difficult, tedious, and/or hard to maintain in a simple, function-based design. These include the following:

- A centralized logging facility, built along the lines of the example logging code presented earlier
- A strong possibility that configuration values for the service will need to be accessible across multiple endpoints, which is probably easier to manage with a class-based design
- The ability to use what might be called pluggable request, response, and formatting mechanisms will almost certainly be a lot easier to develop and maintain, since those would be represented by classes that encapsulate all of the necessary functionality

The classes defined here do not leverage any of the available standard library entities that were noted earlier (for example, normal, threaded, or forking variants of socketserver.TCPServer). They are, instead, a baseline starting point for *any* service, at least at one level, and could potentially use any of those server classes as additional mix-ins, if desired. At another level, they could be considered purely illustrative of the kinds of functionality needed in a service class, though they are also viable for use as a service class, for some applications.

These classes are also purely synchronous. They handle one request at a time, processing it to completion and returning a response, before acquiring the next request and handling it. That will probably suffice for low-load scenarios, of the sort expected in the context of the hms_sys system projects, but might not be enough for other use cases, especially if real-time responses and higher computational-cost processes get involved. We'll examine some options for dealing with those kinds of scenarios in chapter 19, *Multiprocessing and HPC in Python*, while discussing local process-scaling options.

The collection of ABCs that we're going to build is as follows:

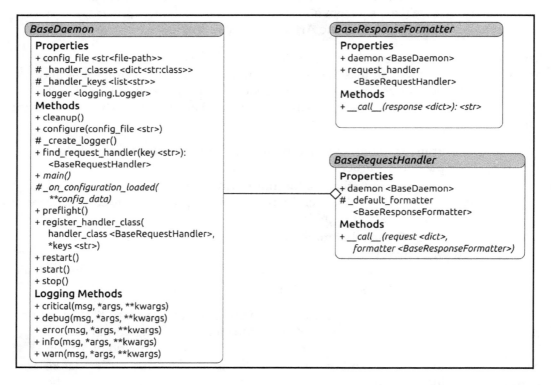

Consider the following:

- BaseDaemon is a starting point for creating classes that actually provide the service itself
- BaseRequestHandler provides a starting point for defining callable objects that will be used to actually handle an incoming request, and that will be responsible for formatting the results using an instance of a class derived from BaseResponseFormatter

- `BaseResponseFormatter` is a similar, callable-object class that will convert a response data structure into a serialized string value, ready to be returned as a message in a queue, an HTTP response, or whatever other format is best suited for the specific response requirement

The BaseDaemon ABC

The implementation of `BaseDaemon` starts, unsurprisingly, with a standard ABC definition, and some class-level attributes/constants, as follows:

```
class BaseDaemon(metaclass=abc.ABCMeta):
    """
    Provides baseline functionality, interface requirements, and type-
    identity for objects that can act as a daemon/service managed by
    facilities in the local OS
    (like systemd) or by third-party service-configurators (like NSSM)
    """

    ####################################
    #   Class attributes/constants     #
    ####################################

    _handler_classes = {}
    _handler_keys = []
```

Since logging is a critical aspect of any service, making sure that some logging parameters are always available is a good idea. That starts with setting up a class-level constant that stores the default logging configuration, as follows:

```
    # - Default logging information
    _logging = {
        'name':None,
        'format':'%(asctime)s - %(name)s - %(levelname)s -
%(message)s',
        'file':{
            'logfile':None,
            'level':logging.INFO,
        },
        'console':{
            'level':logging.ERROR,
        }
    }
```

Those defaults are used by a common `_create_logger` method, provided as a concrete method by the class, to assure that logging will always be available, but that the parameters that control it can be overridden:

```python
def _create_logger(self):
    """
Creates the instance's logger object, sets up formatting for log-
entries, and
handlers for various log-output destinations
    """
    if not self.__class__._logging.get('name'):
        raise AttributeError(
            '%s cannot establish a logging facility because no '
            'logging-name value was set in the class itself, or '
            'through configuration settings (in %s).' %
            (self.__class__.__name__, self.config_file)
        )
```

After checking to see whether a logger name has been specified, the `_logging` class attribute is used to define a common log output format, as follows:

```python
try:
    logging_settings = self.__class__._logging
    # - Global log-format
    formatter = logging.Formatter(logging_settings['format'])
    # - The main logger
    self._logger = logging.getLogger(
        logging_settings['name']
    )
    # - By default, the top-level logger instance will accept
anything.
    #   We'll change that to the appropriate level after checking
the
    #   various log-level settings:
    final_level = logging.DEBUG
```

The same logging settings allow for independent control of the file and console output for logging. The file-based log output needs a `logfile` specification, and allows for an independent `level`, as well:

```python
        if logging_settings.get('file'):
            # - We're logging *something* to a file, so create a
handler
            #    to that purpose:
            if not self.__class__._logging['file'].get('logfile'):
                raise AttributeError(
                    '%s cannot establish a logging facility because no
```

```
                        'log-file value was set in the class itself, or '
                        'through configuration settings (in %s).' %
                        (self.__class__.__name__, self.config_file)
                    )
                    # - The actual file-handler
                    file_handler = logging.FileHandler(
                        logging_settings['file']['logfile']
                    )
                    # - Set the logging-level accordingly, and adjust
final_level
                    file_handler.setLevel(logging_settings['file']['level'])
                    final_level = min(
                        [
                            logging_settings['file']['level'],
                            final_level
                        ]
                    )
                    # - Set formatting and attach it to the main logger:
                    file_handler.setFormatter(formatter)
                    self._logger.addHandler(file_handler)
```

As each logging output is created and attached, the logging level is used to reset the `final_level` value, which will eventually allow the setup process to fine-tune the logging level for the logger object that the output is being attached to. The console logger output setup looks much the same as the file logger output, minus the filename, which it doesn't need:

```
            if logging_settings.get('console'):
                # - We're logging *something* to the console, so create a
                #   handler to that purpose:
                # - The actual console-handler
                console_handler = logging.StreamHandler()
                # - Set the logging-level accordingly, and adjust final_level
                console_handler.setLevel(
                    logging_settings['console']['level']
                )
                final_level = min(
                    [
                        logging_settings['console']['level'],
                        final_level
                    ]
                )
                # - Set formatting and attach it to the main logger:
                console_handler.setFormatter(formatter)
                self._logger.addHandler(console_handler)
                # - For efficiency's sake, use the final_level at the logger
```

```
itself.
        #    That should (hopefully) allow logging to run (trivially)
        #    faster, since it'll know to skip anything that isn't
handled by
        #    at least one handler...
        self._logger.setLevel(final_level)
```

In order to assure that logging will always be available, all of the setup so far executes in a try...except structure. If any errors occur during the process of setting up logging, a final RuntimeError is raised, with the intention of stopping all execution, so that whatever's causing the logging failures must be fixed:

```
except Exception as error:
    raise RuntimeError(
        '%s could not complete the set-up of its logging '
        'facilities because %s was raised: %s' %
        (
                self.__class__.__name__, error.__class__.__name__,
                error
        )
    )
# - Log the fact that we can log stuff now :-)
    self.info(
        'Logging started. Other messages may have been output to '
        'stdout/terminal prior to now'
    )
```

Once the instance's logger object property has been created, logging any message is simply a matter of calling one of the instance's various logging methods. Those methods – critical, debug, error, info, and warn – all look more or less alike, and will write the message supplied to the various pieces of logger output with the appropriate priority, or will fall back to printing the message, if the logger hasn't been created yet:

```
####################################
#        Logging methods           #
####################################

def critical(self, msg, *args, **kwargs):
    if self.logger:
        self.logger.critical(msg, *args, **kwargs)
    else:
        print('CRITICAL - %s' % msg)

def debug(self, msg, *args, **kwargs):
    if self.logger:
        self.logger.debug(msg, *args, **kwargs)
```

```
    else:
        print('DEBUG    - %s' % msg)
```

The properties of the class are, for the most part, typical of the structures and patterns that have been used in earlier code, with typical type and value checking attached to their related setter methods:

```
###################################
#  Instance property definitions  #
###################################

config_file = property(
    _get_config_file, None, None,
    'Gets the configuration-file used to set up the instance'
)
logger = property(
    _get_logger, None, None,
    'Gets the logger for the instance'
)
```

The setter method for the `config_file` property is worth a closer look, perhaps, since it performs some checking, to make sure that the value passed is a readable file:

```
def _set_config_file(self, value:(str,)):
    if type(value) != str:
        raise TypeError(
            '%s.config_file expects a string value that points '
            'to a readable configuration-file on the local file-'
            'system, but was passed "%s" (%s)' %
            (self.__class__.__name__, value, type(value).__name__)
        )
    if not os.path.isfile(value):
        if type(value) != str:
            raise TypeError(
                '%s.config_file expects a string value that '
                'points to a readable configuration-file on the '
                'local file-system, but was passed "%s" (%s), '
                'which is not a file' %
                (
                    self.__class__.__name__, value,
                    type(value).__name__
                )
            )
    if not os.access(value, os.R_OK):
        if type(value) != str:
            raise TypeError(
                '%s.config_file expects a string value that '
                'points to a readable configuration-file on the '
```

```
                        'local file-system, but was passed "%s" (%s), '
                        'which is not a READABLE file' %
                        (
                            self.__class__.__name__, value,
                            type(value).__name__
                        )
                    )
            self.debug(
                '%s.config_file set to %s' % (self.__class__.__name__, value)
            )
            self._config_file = value
```

Once the configuration file has been verified as ready for use, another concrete method provided by the class, `configure`, can be called to read and apply it to an instance of the class. The `configure` method is responsible for reading the file, converting it to a common data structure, and handing it off to a required/abstract method that actually applies the configuration data to the instance: _on_configuration_loaded.

This division of responsibilities allows for a single common method, `configure`, to be consistently available, while allowing for the specific needs of any given class to be abstracted and made the responsibility of the derived class, _on_configuration_loaded:

```
    def configure(self):
        """
Reads the instance's configuration-file, converts it to a dictionary
of values, then hands the responsibility for actually configuring the
instance off to its required _on_configuration_loaded method
        """
        try:
            self.info('Loading configuration for %s' %
self.__class__.__name__)
        except RuntimeError:
            # - This should only happen during start-up...
            print('Loading configuration for %s' %
self.__class__.__name__)
        try:
            fp = open(self.config_file, 'r')
            config_data = yaml.load(fp)
            fp.close()
        except Exception as error:
            raise RuntimeError(
                '%s.config could not read configuration-data from '
                '%s, %s was raised: %s' %
                (
                    self.__class__.__name__, config_file,
```

```
            error.__class__.__name__, error
        )
    )
    # - With the configuration read, it's time to actually
    #   configure the instance
    self._on_configuration_loaded(**config_data)
```

The `_on_configuration_loaded` method can contain some concrete code that other
classes may choose to use, as follows:

```
@abc.abstractmethod
def _on_configuration_loaded(self, **config_data):
    """
Applies the configuration to the instance. Since there are
configuration values that may exist for any instance of the class,
this method should be called by derived classes in addition to any
local configuration.
    """
    if config_data.get('logging'):
        # - Since the class' logging settings are just a dict, we can
        #   just update that dict, at least to start with:
        self.__class__._logging.update(config_data['logging'])
        # - Once the update is complete, we do need to change any
logging-
        #   level items, though. We'll start with the file-logging:
        file_logging = self.__class__._logging.get('file')
        if file_logging:
            file_level = file_logging.get('level')
            if not file_level:
                file_logging['level'] = logging.INFO
            elif type(file_level) == str:
                try:
                    file_logging['level'] = getattr(
                        logging, file_level.upper()
                    )
                except AttributeError:
                    file_logging['level'] = logging.INFO
        # - Similarly, console-logging
        console_logging = self.__class__._logging.get('console')
        if console_logging:
            console_level = console_logging.get('level')
            if not console_level:
                console_logging['level'] = logging.INFO
            elif type(console_level) == str:
                try:
                    console_logging['level'] = getattr(
                        logging, console_level.upper()
                    )
```

```
        except AttributeError:
            console_logging['level'] = logging.INFO
```

If this standard configuration is used, it will be looking for a YAML configuration file that might look something like the following:

```
logging:
    console:
        level: error
    file:
        level: debug
        logfile: /var/log/daemon-name.log
    format: '%(asctime)s - %(name)s - %(levelname)s - %(message)s'
    name: daemon-name
```

It is worth noting that the various configuration methods may well deal with logging settings, and need to log messages before logging is complete. That is why the logging methods shown earlier have the fall-back-to-printing functionality.

The default implementation that was just shown does exactly that. That accounts for all of the code that executes when an instance of `BaseDaemon` is created. The initialization itself is pretty basic, though there are a couple of new and noteworthy items in it, as follows:

```
def __init__(self, config_file:(str,)):
    """
Object initialization.
self .............. (BaseDaemon instance, required) The instance to
                    execute against
config_file ....... (str, file-path, required) The location of the
                    configuration-file to be used to configure the
                    daemon instance
    """
    # - Call parent initializers if needed
    # - Set default instance property-values using _del_... methods
    self._del_config_file()
    self._del_logger()
    # - Set instance property-values from arguments using
    #   _set_... methods
    self._set_config_file(config_file)
    # - Perform any other initialization needed
    # - Read configuration and override items as needed
    self.configure()
    # - Set up logging
    self._create_logger()
    # - Set up handlers to allow graceful shut-down
    signal.signal(signal.SIGINT, self.stop)
```

```
signal.signal(signal.SIGTERM, self.stop)
self.debug(
    'SIGINT and SIGTERM handlers for %s created' %
    (self.__class__.__name__)
)
# - Set up the local flag that indicates whether we're expected
#   to be running or not:
self._running = False
```

The first items of note are the calls to `signal.signal()`. These use Python's `signal` module to set up signal-event-handling processes, so that a running instance of the class, if it's killed at the OS level or interrupted in a Terminal session, will not just immediately die. Instead, those calls trap the termination (`SIGTERM`) and interruption (`SIGINT`) signals that the OS has issued, and allow the running code to react to them before terminating execution. In this case, they both call the instance's `stop` method, which gives the service instance the opportunity to tell its `main` loop to terminate, and thus allows for a graceful shutdown.

The easiest way for that to be implemented is to have an instance value (`self._running`, in this case) that is used by the main loop of the service to determine whether to continue. That flag value is set at the end of the previous __init__ method.

Although the `main` loop method of a service class is the most important aspect of the class (without one, the service doesn't actually do anything, after all), that `main` loop is something that is going to be specific to the derived class. It's required, but it cannot really be implemented at the ABC's level, so it's made an abstract method, as follows:

```
@abc.abstractmethod
def main(self):
    """
The main event-loop (or whatever is equivalent) for the service
instance.
    """
    raise NotImplementedError(
        '%s.main has not been implemented as required by '
        'BaseDaemon' % (self.__class__.__name__)
    )
```

In order to allow for processes that need to fire off before a service starts and after it terminates, we're providing concrete methods for each `preflight` and `cleanup`. These methods were made concrete, rather than abstract, so that they'd always be available, but could be overridden on an as-needed basis. They do nothing more than log that they have been called in their default implementations:

```python
def cleanup(self):
    """
Performs whatever clean-up actions/activities need to be executed
after the main process-loop terminates. Override this in your daemon-
class if needed, otherwise it can be left alone.
    """
    self.info('%s.cleanup called' % (self.__class__.__name__))

def preflight(self):
    """
Performs whatever pre-flight actions/activities need to be executed
before starting the main process. Override this in your daemon-class
if needed, otherwise it can be left alone.
    """
    self.info('%s.preflight called' % (self.__class__.__name__))
```

The `preflight` method might be useful for implementing a `reload` method (a process that, without stopping the service instance, reacquires any local, potentially altered data, before resuming), for services that could benefit from one.

Finally, service instances need to be able to be started, stopped, and maybe restarted, with single, simple commands. The methods that correspond to those are quite simple, as follows:

```python
def start(self):
    """
Starts the daemon/service that the instance provides.
    """
    if self._running:
        self.info(
            '%s instance is already running' %
(self.__class__.__name__)
        )
        return
    self.preflight()
    self.info('Starting %s.main' % self.__class__.__name__)
    self.main()
    self.cleanup()

def stop(self, signal_num:(int,None)=None,
frame:(FrameType,None)=None):
```

```
        """
Stops the daemon-process. May be called by a signal event-handler, in
which case the signal_num and frame values will be passed. Can also be
called directly without those argument-values.

signal_num ........ (int, optional, defaults to None) The signal-
number, if any, that prompted the shutdown.
frame ............. (Stack-frame, optional, defaults to None) The
associated stack-frame.
        """
        self.info('Stopping %s' % self.__class__.__name__)
        self.debug('+- signal_num ... %s' % (signal_num))
        self.debug('+- frame ........ %s' % (frame))
        self._running = False

def restart(self):
        """
Restarts the daemon-process by calling the instance's stop then start
methods. This may not be directly accessible (at least not in any
useful fashion) outside the running instance, but external
daemon/service managers should be able to simply kill the running
process and start it up again.
        """
        self.info('Restarting %s' % self.__class__.__name__)
        self.stop()
        self.start()
```

This class uses several packages/libraries that need to be included, so we have to make sure to include them in the module that the class lives in, as follows:

```
######################################
#   Standard library imports needed  #
######################################

import atexit
import logging
import os
import signal
import yaml

from types import FrameType    # Used by the signal handlers
```

With this code available, creating a new service class (equivalent to the simple, function-based example at the start of the chapter) is quite simple:

```
class testdaemon(BaseDaemonizable):
    def _on_configuration_loaded(self, **config_data):
        try:
            BaseDaemonizable._on_configuration_loaded(self,
**config_data)
            self.info('%s configuration has been loaded:' %
                (self.__class__.__name__)
            )
        except Exception as error:
            self.error('%s: %s' % (error.__class__.__name__, error))
    def main(self):
        iteration = 0
        self._running = True
        self.info('Starting main daemon event-loop')
        while self._running:
            iteration += 1
            msg = 'Iteration %d' % iteration
            self.info(msg)
            sleep(10)
        self.info('%s main loop terminated' %
(self.__class__.__name__))
```

The following screenshot shows the output and logged messages from starting testdaemon, and from killing it after a few iterations. It shows all of the behavior we'd expect from the code in place:

```
$ python testdaemon.py;tail -f /tmp/daemon-name.log

DEBUG    - testdaemon.config_file set to example-config.yaml
INFO     - Loading configuration for testdaemon
INFO     - testdaemon configuration has been loaded:

{timestamp} - daemon-name -  INFO - Logging started. Other messages may have been \
    output to stdout/terminal prior to now
{timestamp} - daemon-name - DEBUG - SIGINT and SIGTERM hanlders for testdaemon \
    created
{timestamp} - daemon-name -  INFO - testdaemon.daemonize called
{timestamp} - daemon-name - DEBUG - +- Initial fork completed
{timestamp} - daemon-name - DEBUG - +- Decoupling from parent environment complete
{timestamp} - daemon-name - DEBUG - +- Second fork completed
{timestamp} - daemon-name - DEBUG - +- PID (18194) written to /tmp/testdaemon.pid
{timestamp} - daemon-name -  INFO - testdaemon.daemonize complete
{timestamp} - daemon-name -  INFO - testdaemon.preflight called
{timestamp} - daemon-name -  INFO - testdaemon.preflight complete
{timestamp} - daemon-name -  INFO - Starting testdaemon.main
{timestamp} - daemon-name -  INFO - Starting main daemon event-loop
{timestamp} - daemon-name -  INFO - Iteration 1
{timestamp} - daemon-name -  INFO - Iteration 2

pkill -f testdaemon.py;tail -f /tmp/daemon-name.log

{timestamp} - daemon-name -  INFO - Iteration 5
{timestamp} - daemon-name -  INFO - Stopping testdaemon
{timestamp} - daemon-name - DEBUG - +- signal_num ... 15
{timestamp} - daemon-name - DEBUG - +- frame ........ <frame object at 0x7fab9a44f210>
{timestamp} - daemon-name -  INFO - testdaemon main loop terminated
{timestamp} - daemon-name -  INFO - testdaemon.cleanup called
```

This basic service doesn't use any request handler classes—it's just too simple to need them—but a more realistic service implementation will almost certainly need that ability. Each handler class will need to be registered before the service instance is started, and will need a way to associate some property or value from an incoming request, to identify a handler class to create, in order to generate a response to the request.

During execution, as requests come in, those requests will have to be examined in order to identify the key that determines what handler class will be used to create an instance. Execution can then be handed off to that instance to create the response.

The handler class registration process is not difficult, but has a fair amount of type and value checking within it, to avoid bad, ambiguous, or conflicting results later on. It's implemented as a class method, so that the association between the keys (endpoints, commands, message types, or whatever applies to an incoming request), and the handler classes behind those keys, can be established before the service is even instantiated:

```python
@classmethod
def register_handler(cls, handler_class:(type,), *keys):
    """
Registers a BaseRequestHandler *class* as a candidate for handling
requests for the specified keys
    """
    if type(handler_class) != type \
            or not issubclass(handler_class, BaseRequestHandler):
        raise TypeError(
            '%s.register_handler expects a *class* derived from '
            'BaseRequestHandler as its handler_class argument, but '

            'was passed "%s" (%s), which is not such a class' %
            (cls.__name__, value, type(value).__name__)
        )
    if not keys:
        raise ValueError(
            '%s.register_handler expects one or more keys, each '
            'a string-value, to register the handler-class with, '
            'but none were provided' % (cls.__name__)
        )
    # - Check for malformed keys
    bad_keys = [
        key for key in keys
        if type(key) != str or '\n' in key or '\r' in key
        or '\t' in key or key.strip() != key or not key.strip()
    ]
    if bad_keys:
        raise ValueError(
            '%s.register_handler expects one or more keys, each a

            'single-line, non-empty string-value with no leading '
            'or trailing white-space, and no white-space other '
            'than spaces, but was passed a list including %s, '
            'which do not meet these criteria' %
            (cls.__name__, '"' + '", "'.join(bad_keys) + '"')
        )
    # - Check for keys already registered
    existing_keys = [
        key for key in keys if key in cls._handler_classes.keys()
```

```
        ]
        if existing_keys:
            raise KeyError(
                '%s.register_handler is not allowed to replace
handler-'
                'classes already registered, but is being asked to do
'
                'so for %s keys' %
                (cls.__name__, '"' + '", "'.join(existing_keys) + '"')
            )
        # - If this point is reached, everything is hunky-dory, so add
        #   the handler_class for each key:
        for key in keys:
            cls._handler_classes[key] = handler_class
```

The process for finding a class to instantiate to handle a given request, given a key, is also not difficult; see the following code:

```
def find_request_handler(self, key:(str,)):
    """
Finds a registered BaseRequestHandler class that is expected to be
able
to handle the request signified by the key value, creates an instance
of the class, and returns it.
    """
    # - Set up the _handler_keys if it hasn't been defined yet.
    #   The goal here is to have a list of registered keys, sorted
from
    #   longest to shortest so that we can match based on the
    #   longest registered key/path/command-name/whatever that
    #   matches the incoming value:
    if not self.__class__._handler_keys:
        self.__class__._handler_keys = sorted(
            self.__class__._handler_classes.keys(),
            key=lambda k: len(k),
            reverse=True
        )
    # - Find the first (longest) key that matches the incoming key:
    for candidate_key in self.__class__._handler_keys:
        if candidate_key.startswith(key):
            # - If we find a match, then create an instance of
            #   the class and return it
            result = self.__class__._handler_classes[candidate_key]
            return result(self)
    return None
```

This method will return an instance of the first class that it can find that matches an incoming request key, and it will return for the longest key-match it can find, in order to both allow the same class to handle multiple keys, and to (hopefully) eliminate the possibility of a bad key-match. Consider a web service that interacts with `client` objects that can have subordinate `client` objects, allowing access to those clients by using paths that include the following:

- `/client/{client_id}`: Uses a `client_handler` object to handle requests
- `/client/{client_id}/client/{subordinate_id}`: Uses a `subordinate_handler` object to handle requests

In order to make sure that a request that should be handled by a `subordinate_handler` doesn't accidentally acquire and use a `client_handler`, the matching process iterates over the list of endpoint keys, from longest to shortest, matches the longer one first, and returns the appropriate class.

The BaseRequestHandler and BaseResponseFormatter ABCs

Without a concrete implementation derived from these classes, there's really not much to them. They use the same standard property structure that has been in play throughout this book for their properties, with typical type checking. The only new concept that they present is a combination of abstraction (which is nothing new) and the utilization of Python's `__call__` magic method.

 We'll look at these classes (indirectly, at least) when the concrete implementations derived from them are created for the `hms_sys` Artisan Gateway Service, in the next chapter.

When a class has a `__call__` method, instances of that class can be called as if they were functions, with the required arguments defined in the signature of the `__call__` method itself. In effect, callable class-instances can be thought of as **configurable functions**. Each instance of a callable class can have completely different state data that remains consistent within its own scope. As a simple example, consider the following code:

```
class callable_class:
    def __init__(self, some_arg, some_other_arg):
        self._some_arg = some_arg
```

```
            self._some_other_arg = some_other_arg

        def __call__(self, arg):
            print('%s(%s) called:' % (self.__class__.__name__, arg))
            print('+- self._some_arg ........ %s' % (self._some_arg))
            print('+- self._some_other_arg ... %s' %
    (self._some_other_arg))
```

Suppose that we create an instance and call it the following:

```
    instance1 = callable_class('instance 1', 'other arg')
    instance1('calling instance 1')
```

We will then get the following output:

```
callable_class("calling instance 1") called:
+- self._some_arg ........ instance 1
+- self._some_other_arg ... other arg
```

We can create additional instances, and call them, too, without affecting the results of the first instance:

```
    instance2 = callable_class('instance 2', 'yet other arg')
    instance2('calling instance 2')
```

The preceding code yields the following:

```
callable_class("calling instance 2") called:
+- self._some_arg ........ <__main__.callable_class object at 0x7f5d9d375550>
+- self._some_other_arg ... True
```

By making the __call__ method of these two classes abstract, we are effectively requiring them to implement a __call__ method that allows each instance to be called as if it were a function, while simultaneously allowing each instance to access the properties and methods available to any instances of the class.

Applying that to BaseRequestHandler, it means that each instance would have a direct reference to the daemon instance, with all of its logging facilities, its start, stop, and restart methods, and the original configuration file; therefore, the following would apply:

- A request handler instance wouldn't have to do anything terribly complicated to log process details as a request was being handled

- Configuration of individual request handlers would be feasible, and could even live in the same configuration file that the daemon itself used, although at present, the configuration would still have to be read and acted upon

- It'd be possible to write one or more handlers (with appropriate caution, including authentication and authorization) that would allow a service request to restart the service

Other service daemons, with more/other functionality at the level of the service instance itself, could also provide a common functionality that would be accessible to each endpoint. Structurally, then, a service that uses a full set of these request handler and response formatter objects would entail the following:

- A single service instance, derived from `BaseDaemon`, that has the following:
    - One to many `BaseRequestHandler`-derived classes registered and available to be instantiated and called in response to incoming requests, each of which can, in turn, create and call instances of any of several `BaseResponseFormatter`-derived classes, to generate the final output data
- With an implementation of `main` that determines which class to create and call for each request, based on the registration of those classes.

The flow of a request-response cycle for the Artisan Gateway Service, implemented with request handlers for Artisan and product interactions and response formatters, might look something like the following:

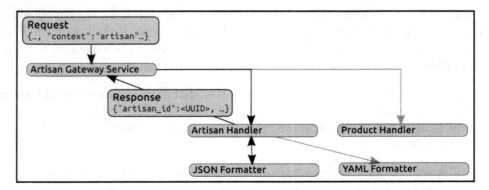

Step by step:

1. A **Request** is sent to the **Artisan Gateway Service**
2. The service determines, from some predefined `context` in the **Request**, that the **Artisan Handler** class should be instantiated and called
3. That handler knows that it needs to generate JSON output, so, after performing whatever processing is needed to generate a response that can be formatted, it acquires a **JSON Formatter** instance and calls the instance to generate the final **Response**
4. The Response is returned to the **Artisan Handler**
5. The **Artisan Handler** returns the **Response** to the **Artisan Gateway Service**
6. The **Artisan Gateway Service** returns the **Response** to the originator of the **Request**

Most of that process hinges on concrete implementation that is not provided by the `BaseRequestHandler` and `BaseResponseFormatter` classes. They are, as shown in the preceding diagram, very simple. `BaseRequestHandler` starts with a standard abstract class structure, as follows:

```
class BaseRequestHandler(metaclass=abc.ABCMeta):
    """
Provides baseline functionality, interface requirements, and
type-identity for objects that can process daemon/service requests,
generating and returning a response, serialized to some string-based
format.
    """
```

Each derived class can have a default formatter class associated with it, so that the eventual call of the instances of the class doesn't require a formatter to be specified, as follows:

```
###################################
#    Class attributes/constants   #
###################################

_default_formatter = None
```

Request handlers could benefit from having access to the service/daemon instance that they were created by. If nothing else, that allows the handler classes to use the daemon's logging facilities. Accordingly, then, we'll keep track of that daemon as a property of the instance, as follows:

```python
####################################
#     Property-getter methods      #
####################################

def _get_daemon(self) -> (BaseDaemon,):
    return self._daemon
####################################
#     Property-setter methods      #
####################################

def _set_daemon(self, value:(BaseDaemon,)) -> None:
    if not isinstance(value, BaseDaemon):
        raise TypeError(
            '%s.daemon expects an instance of a class derived '
            'from BaseDaemon, but was passed "%s" (%s)' %
            (self.__class__.__name__, value, type(value).__name__)
        )
    self._daemon = value

####################################
#     Property-deleter methods     #
####################################

def _del_daemon(self) -> None:
    self._daemon = None

####################################
#  Instance property definitions   #
####################################

daemon = property(
    _get_daemon, None, None,
    'Gets, sets or deletes the daemon associated with the
instance'
    )
```

The initialization of an instance has to provide an argument to set the instance's `daemon` property, but there's not much else to it:

```
###################################
#      Object initialization      #
###################################

def __init__(self, daemon:(BaseDaemon,)):
    """
Object initialization.
self .............. (BaseRequestHandler instance, required) The
                    instance to execute against
daemon ........... (BaseDaemon instance, required) The daemon that
the
                    request to be handled originated with.
    """
# - Set default instance property-values using _del_... methods
    self._del_daemon()
# - Set instance property-values from arguments using
#   _set_... methods
    self._set_daemon(daemon)
```

Since the whole point of the ABC is to require instances to be callable by the service that created them, we'll require a `__call__` method. Any time an instance is called, it will have an incoming request that needs to be processed and responded to. It also feels like a good idea to allow a `formatter` to be passed that could override the default `formatter` type, specified as a class attribute. As concrete implementations of handler classes are written, some thought will need to be given to how to handle cases where the class doesn't specify a `formatter` type, and no `formatter` type is provided in the call itself. That may well vary considerably across request types, though, so there's little point in going into any depth on that concern just yet:

```
###################################
#         Abstract methods        #
###################################

@abc.abstractmethod
def __call__(self, request:(dict,), formatter=None) -> (str,):
    """
Makes the instance callable, providing a mechanism for processing the
supplied request, generating a data-structure containing the response
for the request, formatting that response, and returning it.
self .............. (BaseRequestHandler instance, required) The
instance to execute against
```

```
request .......... (dict, required) The request to be handled
formatter ........ (BaseResponseFormatter instance, optional, if not
"""
        pass
```

The `BaseResponseFormatter` ABC also starts as a standard abstract class. It also
uses the same `daemon` property, and adds a `request_handler` property that uses a
similar setter method, allowing a formatter instance to access the request instance that
created it, as well as the daemon instance that the request was received by:

```
    def _set_request_handler(self, value:(BaseRequestHandler,)) ->
None:
        if not isinstance(value, BaseRequestHandler):
            raise TypeError(
                '%s.request_handler expects an instance of a class '
                'derived from BaseRequestHandler, but was passed '
                '"%s" (%s)' %
                (self.__class__.__name__, value, type(value).__name__)
            )
        self._request_handler = value
```

The `request_handler`, then, needs to be required when creating an instance, for
much the same reason that `daemon` is required:

```
    def __init__(self,
        daemon:(BaseDaemon,),
        request_handler:(BaseRequestHandler,),
    ):
"""
Object initialization.

self .............. (BaseResponseFormatter instance, required) The
                    instance to execute against
daemon ........... (BaseDaemon instance, required) The daemon that
the
                    request to be handled originated with.
request_handler ... (BaseRequesthandler instance, required) The
request-handler object associated with the instance.
"""
        # - Set default instance property-values using _del_...
methods
        self._del_daemon()
        self._del_request_handler()
        # - Set instance property-values from arguments using
        #   _set_... methods
        self._set_daemon(daemon)
        self._set_request_handler(request_handler)
```

Finally, as with `BaseRequestHandler`, we'll require a `__call__` method to be implemented by any derived classes:

```
@abc.abstractmethod
def __call__(self, response:(dict,)) -> (str,):
    """
Makes the instance callable, providing a mechanism for formatting a
standard response-dictionary data-structure.

self .............. (BaseRequestHandler instance, required) The
                    instance to execute against
response .......... (dict, required) The response to be formatted
    """
        pass
```

In general, classes (especially if they are concrete classes) that are this simple (having only one method, plus their initializer, `__init__`) are not the best implementation approach. A class with a single method can usually be handled as a single function instead, even if the function has a more complex set of arguments. The formatter classes may well end up falling into this category as concrete implementation progresses. If they do, refactoring them into (hopefully simple) functions will be undertaken, but for now, `BaseResponseFormatter` will be left standing, as it has been written.

The `BaseRequestHandler` ABC is less of a concern on that count. Requests that interact with different backend data objects can be grouped into handlers for those object types; for example, an `ArtisanHandler` for artisans and a `ProductHandler` for products. It's not a great stretch to anticipate that each of those handlers will have, at a minimum, methods for various CRUD operations that will be called, as requests are handled by the `__call__` method, but other needs arise in specific use cases and service contexts, as follows:

- In a web service context, there could be as many as five additional methods to be implemented – one each for HEAD, CONNECT, OPTIONS, TRACE, and PATCH HTTP methods
- In service contexts that don't have such a rigidly defined set of operations as the HTTP methods of a web service, there is even more potential for additional methods – even as many as one per business process that requests need to be supported for

Even with these levels of complexity, implementing functions to handle the request/response cycles would be feasible. They'd just be larger, more complex functions, with a strong potential for being more difficult to change or maintain on a long-term basis.

Integrating a service with the OS

The last substantial piece of the service implementation puzzle, before getting into the concrete functionality, is getting a service program written in Python, to actually execute as a service at the OS level. The specifics of that process vary, unsurprisingly, across different operating systems (and even vary, to some extent, across different versions of some operating systems – Linux, in particular), but there are common operations that must be addressed across the board, as follows:

- Services need to be started when the machine they run on boots up
- Services need to stop gracefully, when the machine they run on is powered down or rebooted
- Services need to be able to be restarted (which is generally little more than a stop-then-start process)

Some service models might also benefit from being able to reload their data and/or configurations without interrupting service access in the process, particularly if the equivalent reload process that would occur from a restart is time-consuming. There may be other useful operations for specific scenarios.

An exploration of these mechanisms will use the `testdaemon` class that was shown earlier.

Running a service using systemctl (Linux)

Linux distributions are moving away from their old System V-style startup processes to a newer mechanism, the `systemd` daemon, and its associated `systemctl` command-line tool. Services managed by `systemd`/`systemctl` require, at a minimum, a configuration file that defines startup and shutdown processes, a type definition that controls how those processes will be handled by the OS, and whatever executables are needed to start or stop the service processes. A bare-bones `testdaemon.service` configuration file could be as simple as the following:

```
[Unit]
Description=testdaemon: a simple service example written in Python
```

```
[Service]
Type=forking
ExecStart=/usr/bin/python /usr/local/bin/testdaemon.py
ExecStop=/usr/bin/pkill -f testdaemon.py
```

In the preceding code, the following apply:

- The Unit/Description entry is simply a short description of the service, often nothing more than a name.

- Service/Type defines how the startup process will be handled by the systemd daemon. In this case, the execution will be forked, so that whatever process called it is no longer associated with it, and can terminate without stopping the service itself.

- Service/ExecStart defines a process for starting the service, in this case, by executing the testdaemon.py file as a Python script.

- Service/ExecStop defines a process for stopping the service, in this case, by killing all of the processes with testdaemon.py in their name.

Assuming that the actual testdaemon class can be imported from some installed package, the testdaemon.py script that starts the service can be as simple as the following:

```python
#!/usr/bin/env python

# - Import the service-class
from some_package import testdaemon
# - The location of the config-file
config_file = '/path/to/config.yaml'
# - Create an instance of the service class
d = testdaemon(config_file)
# - Start it.
d.start()
```

With both of those files in place, the commands for starting, restarting, and stopping the service from the command line are, respectively, as follows:

```
systemctl start testdaemon.service

systemctl restart testdaemon.service

systemctl stop testdaemon.service
```

The services managed by `systemd` must be enabled in order to start at boot, as follows:

```
systemctl enable testdaemon.service
```

The preceding command requires that an install specification be added to the corresponding `systemd` `.service` file, as follows:

```
...
ExecStop=/usr/bin/pkill -f testdaemon.py

[Install]
WantedBy=multi-user.target
```

There are a lot of other options available to `systemd` service configurations, but these bare-bones settings will allow a service to be auto-started and managed with standard command-line tools.

Running a service using NSSM (Windows)

The easiest way to install services written in Python on a Windows machine is to use **Non-Sucking Service Manager** (**NSSM**). NSSM provides a simple way to wrap a specific executable (the main `python.exe` file, in this case), along with arguments (the `testdaemon.py` script), and make them available as a Windows service. Starting NSSM with `nssm install` provides a window with all of the fields needed for basic service setup, as follows:

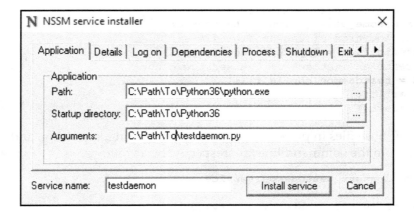

Once the **Install service** button is clicked, the service is available in the Windows Services manager, where its **Startup Type** can be altered, if needed, along with all of the other standard Windows service settings and properties:

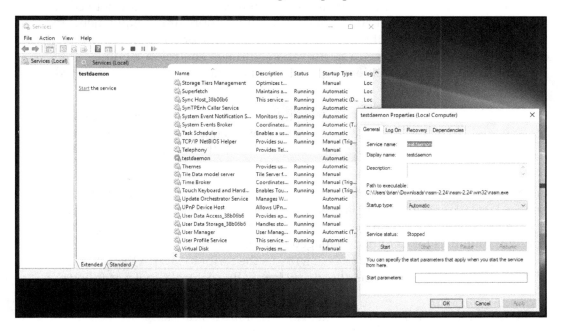

Changes can also be made to the NSSM-created properties of the service, by running `nssm install <service-name>`, which presents the same UI that was used to create the service entry.

If an NSSM-packaged service fails to start, it will log useful information to the standard Windows Event Log; debugging startup problems should start there. Odds are good that if there are any issues, they will be permissions-related, such as the service's account not having access to the script file, a configuration file, and so on.

macOS, launchd, and launchctl

The **Macintosh operating system** (**macOS**) is, under the hood, a Unix variant, so in many respects, there will be fewer issues or differences than there are between Linux and Windows service installations. macOS provides approximate equivalents to `systemd` and `systemctl`: the `launchd` and `launchctl` programs, respectively. They provide the same sort of service startup and shutdown control capabilities, at a minimum, with a lot of additional options for handling service processes, based on all kinds of system events.

 Disclaimer: While writing this book, no macOS machine was available to test with, so, while this section should be complete and usable as it stands, there may be issues that weren't identified before publication

A bare-bones `launchd`-compatible service configuration file needs to contain a service label, the program that is executed when the service starts up, and any arguments that the program needs: exactly what `systemd` needs, although the configuration files for `launchd`-managed services are XML files. A basic starting point configuration, using `testdaemon.py` as the script to launch the actual service object and providing both run-at-load and keep-alive controls, looks as follows:

```xml
<?xml version="1.0" encoding="UTF-8"?>
<!DOCTYPE plist PUBLIC "-//Apple//DTD PLIST 1.0//EN"
"http://www.apple.com/DTDs/PropertyList-1.0.dtd">
<plist version="1.0">
    <dict>
        <key>Label</key>
        <string>testdaemon</string>
        <key>Program</key>
        <string>/path/to/python</string>
        <key>ProgramArguments</key>
        <string>/path/to/testdaemon.py</string>
        <key>RunAtLoad</key>
        <true/>
        <!--
            A very basic keep-alive directive. There may be better
options:
            See "SuccessfulExit" and "Crashed" subkeys
        -->
        <key>KeepAlive</key>
        <true/>
    </dict>
</plist>
```

That configuration, once in one of the standard locations for `launchd` files, allows the service to be started, restarted, and stopped, respectively, as follows:

```
launchctl start testdaemon.service

launchctl restart testdaemon.service

launchctl stop testdaemon.service
```

Managing services on other systems

Although the current trend for managing service processes in Linux systems is, as noted, moving toward `systemd`/`systemctl`, there may be operational systems that still use System V-style initialization scripts. A bare-bones starting point for such a script would look something like the following:

```
#!/bin/sh

# - The action we're concerned with appears as $1 in a standard
#   bash-script
    case $1 in
        start)
            echo "Starting $0"
            /usr/bin/python /usr/local/bin/testdaemon.py
            ;;
        stop)
            echo "Stopping $0"
            /usr/bin/pkill -f testdaemon.py
            ;;
        restart)
            echo "Restarting $0"
            /usr/bin/pkill -f testdaemon.py
            /usr/bin/python /usr/local/bin/testdaemon.py
            ;;
    esac
```

In a System V-managed context, the service itself has to take responsibility for making sure that it detaches from whatever process called it – a Terminal session, or the startup processes of the OS itself. Otherwise, the service process may simply start, then terminate before it actually does anything.

 Since this scenario should be less and less common as time goes on, but is still possible, there is a class in the `daemons` module, `BaseDaemonizable`, that handles daemonizing a service class instance, including writing the **process ID (PID)** to a file in a known location, in case that's needed for some part of a service process. Deriving a service class from that, instead of `BaseDaemon`, should take care of the majority of the different needs, while still preserving the `BaseDaemon` structure.

Summary

The service foundations that were created in this chapter should provide a solid, common starting point for nearly any service, although tweaks to the structure or overrides of existing functionality may be required for specific use cases. With the foundations in place, the path is clear to actually creating the Artisan Gateway Service in `hms_sys`, which will connect the Artisan and Central Office data flows in the next chapter.

15
The Artisan Gateway Service

In order to implement the end user and Gateway-daemon communications, we need to examine and make some decisions on several operational aspects of the daemon – how it's going to work, how data gets sent and received, and how that data is acted upon. In this chapter, we'll examine that in detail, and write code to implement processes based on those decisions.

The chapter covers the following topics:

- Defining what the data structure (messages) being sent back and forth looks like, and what it needs to provide, including a signed-message implementation that should work no matter what mechanism is used to send the data
- Examining two fundamental options for sending and receiving data: message queues and web services
- How messages will be handled, independently of the transmission mechanism
- The basic structures needed to implement a message-queue-based transmission mechanism
- What variations would be encountered (and how to deal with them) in a web-service-based approach
- What the traffic to and from the Artisan Gateway will look like
- A minimal integration of those traffic patterns into existing data objects' current processes

Overview and goal

In the context of the `hms_sys` system, the Artisan Gateway has been only loosely defined thus far – it's been described as acting as a central contact point for communication between Artisans and the Central Office, especially with respect to the `Product` and `Order` objects – what its role is, in effect. The specifics of how it works, and when, haven't really been touched upon, though at least some of the latter are probably very obvious, following a simple rule that might be stated as changes made (by whomever) need to propagate to all relevant parties as soon as is feasible. Those changes are largely dependent on who is making them. At a minimum, the following processes feel likely:

- Artisans can create new `Product` data
- Artisans can update current `Product` data
- Artisans can delete a `Product` outright
- Central Office staff can mark a `Product` as available – which is just a specialized variant of a `Product` update process
- Central Office staff can also make content changes to Products – also an update variant – with some constraints on what can be altered
- Customer end users can indirectly create `Order` objects, which need to propagate out to Artisans in some fashion
- Artisans can update Orders as part of the process of fulfilling them

All of these processes are variants of CRUD operations on the `Product` and/or `Order` objects, and will probably not need much more functionality than is already provided by the `_create` or `_update` methods of the related classes within each subsystem. They should cover most, perhaps all, of how the data changes are actually stored.

The transmission of those data changes, no matter what the timing or protocol ends up looking like, has some common factors as well, with a process that will need to handle the role-specific variations of the following steps:

- A data change (create, update, or delete) is made locally, in one of the user-level applications
- The data change is validated, to assure that the data is well formed and conforms to data-structure requirements

- The data change is stored locally (if applicable)
- The data change is serialized and transmitted to the Artisan Gateway service, where whatever actions need to be undertaken are executed

These steps do not address the possibility of conflicting changes, such as an Artisan and someone in the Central Office making different changes to the same data in the same data-change timeframe. A strategy for dealing with that possibility may not even be necessary, depending on the specific data-change business rules in play, but will have to be examined as well.

That leaves only the decision about the transmission method itself to be made. Since the individual users that will be making changes to data are not expected to be in the same physical location, we need a network-transmission protocol of some sort – a web service or message-queue-based process, as discussed in Chapter 15, *Anatomy of a Service*. A web service, if it were written from scratch, would probably be a significantly larger undertaking, potentially requiring code to handle authentication, authorization, and processes for handling specific HTTP methods and tying them to specific CRUD operations against individual data object types. There's enough complexity between those alone to warrant looking at an existing service-capable framework, such as Flask or Django, rather than writing (and having to test) all of the relevant code.

Given that the system only needs to be concerned with the seven actions identified earlier (Artisan: create, update, or delete Products, and so on), it feels simpler to write those seven functions, and allow messages in a queue-based protocol to simply call them when necessary. The potential concerns around authentication and authorization can be mitigated significantly by assigning each Artisan its own distinct queue, and perhaps signing each message originating with an Artisan. Between those two approaches, an Artisan's identity can be determined simply by the fact that a message is coming in from a given queue that's associated with them. Coupling that with a signature on each message, as long as it can be generated by the Artisan's application and verified by the Artisan Gateway service without transmitting any secret data with the message, provides a reasonably robust authentication mechanism. Authorization concerns in this context are nearly trivial – any given channel, given that it can be associated with a user type, or even a specific user, can simply be allowed access to (and thus execution of) the operations that are relevant to that user or type only.

At a high level, the data flows for Artisan/Product operations, no matter which transmission mechanism is selected, would look like this:

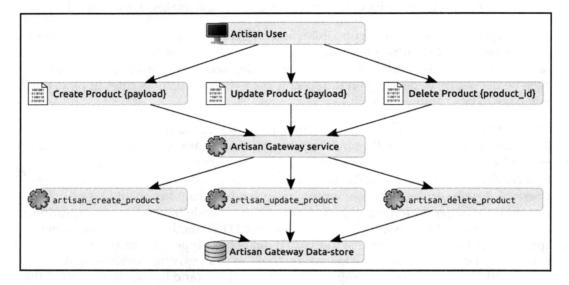

Where:

- The various messages (**Create Product**, **Update Product**, and **Delete Product**) with their respective {**payload**} data (or a {**product_id**} for deletion operations) are created by the local **Artisan Application**, transmitted to the **Artisan Gateway** service
- Those messages are read, validated, and used to determine which service method (`artisan_create_product`, and so on) should be called
- The relevant method deals with whatever data storage is needed in the **Artisan Gateway Datastore** during execution

Similar data flows would exist for all of the operations that Central Office users could execute against `Product` objects, and for `Artisan` and `Order` object interactions, at a minimum. In addition, there may well be related operations that need to be made available for more specific data-object operations in more specific Central Office roles. The Central Office staff will need to be able to manage `Artisan` objects, at a minimum, and maybe `Order` objects as well.

Iteration stories

Although there are at least *some* aspects of many of these stories that rely on some UI implementation that hasn't been examined yet, there are non-UI functional aspects to each of them that can be usefully examined and worked. With that in mind, the stories relevant for this iteration, at least initially, are as follows:

- As an Artisan, I need to be able to send data changes to the Artisan Gateway so that those changes can be propagated and acted upon as needed
- As a Central Office user, I need to be able to send data changes to the Artisan Gateway so that those changes can be propagated and acted upon as needed
- As an Artisan Manager, I need to be able to create `Artisan` objects so that I can manage Artisans
- As an Artisan Manager, I need to be able to delete `Artisan` objects so that I can manage Artisans
- As an Artisan Manager, I need to be able to update `Artisan` objects so that I can manage Artisans
- As an Artisan, I need to be able to create `Product` objects so that I can manage my Product offerings
- As an Artisan, I need to be able to delete `Product` objects so that I can manage my Product offerings
- As an Artisan, I need to be able to update `Order` objects so that I can indicate to the Central Office when my part of an Order is fulfilled
- As an Artisan, I need to be able to update `Product` objects so that I can manage my Product offerings
- As an Artisan, I need to be able to update my own `Artisan` object so that I can manage my information at HMS Central Office
- As a Product Manager, I need to be able to activate `Product` objects so that I can manage Product availability
- As a Product Manager, I need to be able to deactivate `Product` objects so that I can manage Product availability
- As a Product Manager, I need to be able to update `Product` objects so that I can manage Product information that an Artisan can't
- As any user sending messages across, to, or from the Artisan Gateway service, I need those messages to be signed so that they can be validated before being acted upon

With the exception of the last item, these have been grouped more or less in the order that they would need to be executed in a real use case: Central Office users (acting as Artisan Managers) would need to create objects representing Artisans before those Artisans could be expected to do anything, and Artisans have to be able to create `Product` objects before Central Office users (acting as Product Managers) could be expected to do anything with those objects.

Messages

Before taking a serious look at the transmission-mechanism options, it would be beneficial to have a solid definition of what, exactly, constitutes a message being transmitted. At a minimum, given what the data flows coming into the Artisan Gateway service look like, and with some idea of what the actual data for a typical data object being transmitted entails, it's apparent that a message needs to be able to handle structured data. Internally, that's probably best represented by a `dict`, if only because they are easy to serialize and un-serialize into at least two different formats that are easily transmissible: JSON and YAML. We've already established data dictionary structures for the objects whose state data can be stored. A `Product`, for example, from an Artisan's perspective, whose data dictionary has been rendered into JSON looks like this:

```
{
    "oid": "a7393e5c-c30c-4ea4-8469-e9cd4287714f",
    "modified": "2018-08-19 07:13:43",
    "name": "Example Product",
    "created": "2018-08-19 07:13:43",
    "description": "Description  TBD",
    "metadata":{
        "wood": "Cherry, Oak"
    },
    "available": false,
    "dimensions": "2½\" x 4\" x ¾\"",
    "shipping_weight": 0.5,
    "summary": "Summary TBD",
}
```

This provides all of the data needed for any create or update operation of a `Product` initiated by an Artisan, but doesn't specify what operation needs to be performed with the data. It also doesn't have any signature data associated with it, which we'll want to provide to complete the last of the iteration stories noted earlier. Both of those items, operation and signature, need to be added to the message, but not to the message data, so that creating an instance of the `Product` object on the receiving end doesn't have to deal with removing non-product data from the incoming data structure.

In the context of a message, they are both metadata: data about the data, in this case describing what is to be done with the real data, and what signature should be used to verify the integrity of the message. A more complete message, intended to update an existing product (providing a description and summary, and making the item available) would look something like this (assuming that all product-data is transmitted during an update operation):

```
{
    "data":{
        "oid": "a7393e5c-c30c-4ea4-8469-e9cd4287714f",
        "modified": "2018-08-19 07:41:56",
        "name": "Example Product",
        "created": "2018-08-19 07:13:43",
        "description": "Cherry and oak business-card holder",
        "metadata": {
            "wood": "Cherry, Oak"
        },
        "available": true,
        "dimensions": "2½\" x 4\" x ¾\"",
        "shipping_weight": 0.5,
        "summary": "Cherry and oak business-card holder",
    },
    "operation":"update",
    "signature":"{Hash hexdigest}"
}
```

That data structure as an output goal gives us enough information to implement a `DaemonMessage` class to represent any message going to or coming from the Artisan Gateway service. `DaemonMessage` is a concrete class, and lives in the `hms_core.daemons` module. It starts with a typical class declaration, and has a class constant defined that will be used later for encoding string values into byte values, in both instance and class methods:

```
class DaemonMessage(object):
    """
    Represents a *signed* message being sent to or received from a
```

```
BaseDaemon instance.
"""
    ###################################
    # Class attributes/constants      #
    ###################################

    # - class-constant encoding-type for signature processes
    __encoding = 'utf-8'
```

Most of the properties of `DaemonMessage` follow the standard getter, setter, and deleter method/property-declaration pattern we've been using so far. One of them, the `signature` property, needs to return a calculated value every time it's called, and simply has a getter method definition – `_get_signature`:

```
    ###################################
    # Property-getter methods         #
    ###################################

# ...

    def _get_signature(self) -> str:
        if not self.data:
            raise RuntimeError(
                '%s.signature cannot be calculated because there is '
                'no data to sign' % (self.__class__.__name__)
            )
        if not self.signing_key:
            raise RuntimeError(
                '%s.signature cannot be calculated because there is '
                'no key to sign data with' % (self.__class__.__name__)
            )
        return sha512(
            bytes(
                # - We're using json.dumps to assure a consistent
                #   key-order here...
                json.dumps(self.data, sort_keys=True), self.__encoding
            ) + self.signing_key
        ).hexdigest()
```

The `_get_signature` method has several noteworthy aspects in its implementation. First, since a signature should only be available if there is data to sign, and a signing key value to sign the data with, it actively checks for those values, raising `RuntimeError` if either is not set. Secondly, its return value has to ensure that hashes of the data structure will always be the same for the same data structure. Python's `dict` data structures do not guarantee the same sequence of keys across multiple `dict` values, even if the same keys exist across them.

Since the hashing mechanism requires a `bytes` value, and rendering a `dict` into `bytes` (using a `str()` conversion as an intermediate translation mechanism) will not always return the same `bytes` sequence to be hashed, some mechanism for ensuring the instance's `data` dict is always rendered into a consistent `str`/`bytes` sequence is needed. Since the value going into the hashing process for generating the signature could start as a string, and since `json.dumps` provides a mechanism for recursively sorting the output's keys, that was a quick and simple solution.

The selection of `json.dumps` was made based on simplicity and convenience. It might be better in the long run to create an `OrderedDict` instance (from the `collections` module), add each element, in order, to the new instance, then hash the string value of that instead. If nothing else, that would alleviate any potential concerns with data structures to be hashed containing values that cannot be serialized into JSON. Another option would be to hash a YAML value instead, since it deals with data types that aren't directly serialize-able in a cleaner fashion.

The property setter and deleter methods are typical-enough implementations that they don't warrant much in the way of explanation, though the setter method corresponding to the operation property (`_set_operation`) checks the incoming value against a limited set of options.

One significant deviation from the typical properties pattern we've used so far is that `DaemonMessage` exposes most of its properties as settable and deletable. The rationale behind that decision is that it seems likely that the `data`, `operation`, and `signing_key` values of a message may not all be known when the message first needs to be created, or they may even need to be altered before the message is being sent by some other process. Allowing them to be set or deleted on the fly alleviates any such concerns in later implementations that use instances of `DaemonMessage`. In combination with the on-the-fly, calculated-value implementation of signature (and its checking for required property-values before returning), this allows as much flexibility as we should need later, while still preserving the type- and value-checking of those properties:

```
###################################
# Instance property definitions   #
###################################

data = property(
    _get_data, _set_data, _del_data,
    'Gets, sets, or deletes the data/content of the message'
)
```

```
        operation = property(
            _get_operation, _set_operation, _del_operation,
            'Gets, sets, or deletes the operation of the message'
        )
        signature = property(
            _get_signature, None, None,
            'Gets the signature of the message'
        )
    signing_key = property(
            _get_signing_key, _set_signing_key, _del_signing_key,
            'Gets, sets, or deletes the signing_key of the message'
        )
```

Accordingly, the initialization of a `DaemonMessage` doesn't require any of those properties to be supplied to construct an instance, but it allows all of them:

```
        ####################################
        # Object initialization            #
        ####################################

        def __init__(self,
            operation:(str,None)=None, data:(dict,None)=None,
            signing_key:(bytes,str,None)=None
        ):
            """
Object initialization.

self .............. (DaemonMessage instance, required) The instance to
                    execute against
operation ......... (str, optional, defaults to None) The operation
                    ('create', 'update', 'delete' or 'response') that
                    the message is requesting
data .............. (dict, optional, defaults to None) The data of the
                    message
signing_key ....... (bytes|str, optional, defaults to None) The raw
                    data of the signing-key to be used to generate the
                    message-signature.
            """
            # - Call parent initializers if needed
            # - Set default instance property-values using _del_...
methods
            self._del_data()
            self._del_operation()
            self._del_signing_key()
            # - Set instance property-values from arguments using
            #   _set_... methods
            if operation:
                self.operation = operation
```

```
        if data:
            self.data = data
        if signing_key:
            self.signing_key = signing_key
```

Since the purpose of the `DaemonMessage` class is to provide a simple, consistent way
to generate messages serialized into JSON, and that requires a `dict` value to serialize
from, we provide methods to do both:

```
    def to_message_dict(self):
        return {
            'data':self.data,
            'operation':self.operation,
            'signature':self.signature,
        }

    def to_message_json(self):
        return json.dumps(self.to_message_dict())
```

Similarly, we'll need a way to unserialize messages from JSON, with an intermediate
from dictionary method. These are implemented as class methods, allowing
a message instance to be created and validated with a signing key. The critical aspects
of that functionality all reside in the `from_message_dict` class method:

```
    @classmethod
    def from_message_dict(cls,
        message_dict:(dict,), signing_key:(bytes,str)
    ):
        """
message_dict ...... (dict, required) The incoming message as a dict,
                    that is expected to have the following structure:
                    {
                        'data':dict,
                        'operation':str, #
(create|update|delete|response)
                        'signature':str # (hash hex-digest)
                    }
signing_key ....... (bytes|str, optional, defaults to None) The raw
                    data of the signing-key to be used to generate the
                    message-signature.
        """
```

Typical type- and value-checking is performed against the incoming arguments first:

```
        if type(message_dict) != dict:
            raise TypeError(
                '%s.from_message_dict expects a three-element '
                'message_dict value ({"data":dict, "signature":str, '
```

```
                      '"operation":str}), but was passed "%s" (%s)' %
                      (cls.__name__, data, type(data).__name__)
                )
            if type(signing_key) not in (bytes,str):
                raise TypeError(
                      '%s.from_message_dict expects a bytes or str
signing_key '
                      'value, but was passed "%s" (%s)' %
                      (cls.__name__, signing_key,
type(signing_key).__name__)
                )
            if type(signing_key) == str:
                      signing_key = bytes(signing_key, cls.__encoding)
```

A new `DaemonMessage` instance is created from the data and operation values of the incoming `message_dict`, and from the `signing_key` argument after ensuring that all data is present and well formed:

```
            _data = message_dict.get('data')
            if not _data:
                raise ValueError(
                      '%s.from_message_dict expects a three-element dict '
                      '({"data":dict, "signature":str, "operation":str}), '
                      'but was passed "%s" (%s) which did not include a '
                      '"data" key' %
                      (cls.__name__, data, type(data).__name__)
                )
            _signature = message_dict.get('signature')
            if not _signature:
                raise ValueError(
                      '%s.from_message_dict expects a three-element dict '
                      '({"data":dict, "signature":str, "operation":str}), '
                      'but was passed "%s" (%s) which did not include a '
                      '"signature" key' %
                      (cls.__name__, data, type(data).__name__)
                )
            _operation = message_dict.get('operation')
            if not _operation:
                raise ValueError(
                      '%s.from_message_dict expects a three-element dict '
                      '({"data":dict, "operation":str, "operation":str}), '
                      'but was passed "%s" (%s) which did not include a '
                      '"operation" key' %
                      (cls.__name__, data, type(data).__name__)
                )
            result = cls(_operation, _data, signing_key)
```

Once the new `DaemonMessage` instance exists, provided that its data has the same keys and values, and that the local `signing_key` used to generate the signature is the same as the `signing_key` that was used to create the original message before it was transmitted, the signature values of both messages should be identical. If they aren't, then there is something suspect with the message. There are not many possible causes for a signature failure:

- The `data` in the message has gotten corrupted/altered in some fashion

- The local and remote `signing_key` values are different

In either case, no action should be taken – either the data itself is suspect, or the authenticity of the message cannot be verified. In any signature-failure condition, we raise a custom error, `InvalidMessageError`:

```
if result.signature == _signature:
    return result
raise InvalidMessageError(
    'The message %s, with a signature of "%s" did not match '
    'the expected signature. Message DENIED' %
    (_data, result.signature)
)
```

The conversion from a JSON-serialized message to a `DaemonMessage` instance simply decodes the incoming JSON, then feeds the resultant `dict` data structure into `from_message_dict`, returning the resultant object:

```
@classmethod
def from_message_json(cls, json_in:(str,),
signing_key:(bytes,str)):
    return cls.from_message_dict(json.loads(json_in), signing_key)
```

Serializing messages to and from JSON doesn't impact our options for how the Artisan Gateway service actually transmits those messages. Both of the options mentioned, web service and message queue approaches, can handle JSON message formats – so this message strategy is *very* portable in that respect.

The signing process of `DaemonMessage` relies heavily on the idea of creating and managing signing keys for messages – messages cannot be sent or read without them – and there are some significant considerations that should be discussed before moving on.

Like any cryptographic process, hash-based signatures rely on a secret value (`signing_key`, in this case) that has to be created and secured. With respect to creating a `signing_key`, there are several factors to bear in mind, but the two most significant areas follows:

- The longer the value is, the harder it will be to crack
- The more varied the characters in it are, the harder it will be to crack

The math underlying these is fairly straightforward: it takes less time to iterate over 10 values than it does over 100, so the more variations that are possible in a secret value of any kind, the longer it will take to iterate over them all. The number of possible values can be expressed mathematically as (the number of values per character)$^{\text{(the number of characters in the string)}}$, so a 128-character `signature_key`, with 255 possible characters would entail 255^{128} possible values, or about 1.09×10^{308} combinations that would have to be checked to guarantee the calculation of a `signature_key` of that size and scope. At one billion such calculations per second, or about 3.15×10^{16} calculations per year, it's still technically/mathematically possible to crack such a `signing_key`, but assuming that the hashing algorithm doesn't have any significant flaws that can be exploited, it's impractical, at best.

The creation of a `signature_key` of whatever length is desired is fairly straightforward. Python's `os` module provides a function, `urandom`, that returns a character sequence (as a `bytes` object) suitable for cryptographic use, and of whatever length is desired, so generation of even a very long key is as simple as calling the following:

```
os.urandom(1024)
```

The results can be converted to a hexadecimal string value for storage, if needed, and converted back from that hexadecimal string with `bytes.fromhex()`:

```
import os

example_key = os.urandom(1024)
print(example_key)

example_key_hex = example_key.hex()
print(example_key_hex)

example_from_hex = bytes.fromhex(example_key_hex)
print(example_from_hex == example_key)

# Yields:
# b'!\x0cW\xe5\x89\x7fan ... a LOT more gibberish-looking
```

```
characters...'
# 210c57e5897f616ec9157f759617e7b4f ... a LOT more hexadecimal
digits...
# True
```

Securing secret values is usually concerned with some combination of the following:

- Assuring that they are encrypted at rest, so that even if the data store that secrets reside in is compromised, the secrets themselves cannot be easily used
- Assuring that they are encrypted in motion, to prevent man-in-the-middle exploits from being able to access easily usable keys
- Changing (rotating) them on a reasonably frequent basis, to reduce the likelihood that a captured secret can be compromised before it's no longer useful

The creation and management of `signing_key` values for Artisans (and perhaps for Central Office-to-Artisan communications as well), and the possibility of implementing some sort of key-rotation process will be examined in more detail in `Chapter 17`, *Handling Service Transactions*.

Ensuring that they are encrypted in motion could be a significant factor in deciding how messages will be transmitted, though. In-flight encryption will require the creation of an encryption certificate for either a web-service or locally hosted message-queue implementation. A message-queue approach may allow a private certificate to be used, while a web service might require a certificate from a public Certificate Authority.

 Encryption in motion should always be implemented when transmitting any secret information, and a `signing_key` definitely falls into that category!

Encryption at rest feels like it might be overkill for a system of this scope, though it could be implemented in code with libraries such as PyCrypto, and/or by configuring the MongoDB engine to use its Encrypted Storage Engine (available in MongoDB Enterprise). It would also add more complexity to the system than seems warranted at this point, including (again) key-creation and management.

Deciding on a message-transmission mechanism

With the structure of the messages being passed now resolved, it's a good time to take a deeper look at the options for how those messages could be transmitted. Ultimately, a decision needs to be made regarding how to implement a process to deal with the stories:

- As an Artisan, I need to be able to send Product and Order data changes to the Artisan Gateway so that those changes can be propagated and acted upon as needed
- As a Central Office user, I need to be able to send Artisan and Product data changes to the Artisan Gateway so that those changes can be propagated and acted upon as needed

Of the two options discussed earlier (web service or message-queue-based implementations), using message queues feels like a better fit:

- Given the limited number of operations expected, a queue-based approach would involve less development effort, and probably less complexity than a web-service implementation:

  - There's no need to handle any of the protocol-level details (HTTP methods, variations of data-payload structures, and so on) that would have to be dealt with in implementing a web service
  - There's no need to write a full-blown HTTP server (either from the ground up, or using one of the server classes provided by the `http.server` package), or to integrate functionality/code with any of several web-framework options (Flask, or the Django REST Framework, for example)

- Messages can be sent and will simply wait in their queues until they are retrieved and acted upon, so:

  - All end users can continue to use their applications without interruption so long as the queue server is accessible
  - The Artisan Gateway itself could be taken down (for maintenance, updating, or even to be moved to a different server) at any point

There are some caveats/trade-offs to this approach, though:

- Messages that contain conflicting data changes, though they will still be retrieved and processed, could require additional manual attention to reconcile those changes. The same thing could happen in a web-service context, but it's at least somewhat more likely with message queues.
- Message-retrieval, as an active process over a network, could take somewhat longer than simply reading an incoming request made directly to the Artisan Gateway. As a result, service throughput may be impacted, but even if a complete message-operation cycle took 10 seconds, that would allow for 360 operations per hour (over 8,600 operations per day, or 3,1000,000 over the course of a year), assuming they were not performed in parallel.
- If the message-queue provider goes down, preventing messages from being delivered in the first place, that could interrupt end user application usage.

- Allocation of message queues will have to be given some consideration:

    - If each Artisan has their own queues, into and out of the Artisan Gateway, at least some data about those queues has to be stored and managed, and each Artisan-to-Gateway queue will have to be checked individually
    - If all Artisans share one inbound queue to the Artisan Gateway, identification of which Artisan a given message originated with will have to be implemented for each operation

- Since there is no implicit response requirement in the message protocol to indicate that it has been acted upon (or couldn't be because of an error), any response to a message that needs to be sent to a user will have to be actively/independently sent.

- As an Artisan, I need a message queue created for and assigned to me so that I can send my data changes to the Artisan Gateway.

Message-queue implementation with RabbitMQ

The `hms_sys` projects will use RabbitMQ as its message-queue provider. RabbitMQ is actively maintained, and is a zero-cost solution, with paid support and consultation options, making it a good low-budget choice. Additionally, there is a ready-to-roll Python library, `pika` (installed with `pip install pika`) that provides all the critical functionality needed to send and receive messages from a RabbitMQ server, without having to get too far into the weeds implementing a solution from scratch. The makers of RabbitMQ, Pivotal Software, also offer a commercial version that includes additional management features along with support agreements.

There are other options available for message-queue implementations, including cloud-based solutions from Amazon (SQS), Microsoft (Azure Service Bus), and Google (Cloud Pub/Sub), all of which have corresponding Python libraries available for use. Locally installable options include Apache Kafka and ActiveMQ, and Kestrel. There is also a general-purpose AMQP library available (`amqp`) that should allow connection to and interaction with any message queue service that uses at least a basic AMQP protocol.

Sending a message to a RabbitMQ instance with `pika` is fairly straightforward. Here's a simple example, using the `DaemonMessage` class to generate and sign messages:

```python
#!/usr/bin/env python
# - scratch-space/rabbitmq-sender.py
# - Derived from RabbitMQ - RabbitMQ tutorial - "Hello world!"
#   https://www.rabbitmq.com/tutorials/tutorial-one-python.html

# The pika library is for communicating with RabbitMQ
import pika

# Use DaemonMessage to format our messages
from hms_core.daemons import DaemonMessage
```

Since we're transmitting a `DaemonMessage`, we need to generate a signing key and message data:

```python
# Message-items
# - Signing-key
signing_key = '!:iLL>S@]BN;h%"h\'<2cPGsaKA 3vbGJ'
# - Message data (a dict)
```

```
message_data = {
    'hello':'Hello from %s' % __file__,
    'random_number':3, # not a random number yet
}
```

Then we create the message:

```
# - The actual message to be sent
message = DaemonMessage(
    'response', message_data, signing_key
)
```

Next, we establish a connection to the RabbitMQ server:

```
# RabbitMQ connection and related items
# - Create a connection
connection = pika.BlockingConnection(
    pika.ConnectionParameters('localhost')
)
# - Create (or at least specify) a channel
channel = connection.channel()
# - Create or specify a queue
channel.queue_declare(queue='hello')
```

Then the message is sent, and the connection is closed:

```
# Send the message
channel.basic_publish(
    exchange='', routing_key='hello',
    body=message.to_message_json()
)

# Close the connection
connection.close()
```

Executing this script doesn't generate any output, but verification that the message has been sent can be performed with the rabbitmqctl command-line tool:

```
root# rabbitmqctl list_queues
Listing queues ...
hello 1
```

Running the script a second time, and then the `rabbitmqctl list_queues` tool, shows another message ready and waiting in the queue:

```
root# rabbitmqctl list_queues
Listing queues ...
hello 2
```

RabbitMQ requires the provision of a channel (or perhaps queue name is as good a description) that provides organizational grouping for messages on the server, and that we'll consider using to segregate messages by specific Artisans later on. Consider the following queue-name declarations:

```
# - Create or specify a queue
channel.queue_declare(queue='hello')

# Send the message
channel.basic_publish(
    exchange='', routing_key='hello',
    body=message.to_message_json()
)
```

Here, the preceding queue-name declarations are changed to the following:

```
# - Create or specify a queue
channel.queue_declare(queue='queue_name') # Changed here

# Send the message
channel.basic_publish(
    exchange='', routing_key='queue_name',  # Changed here also
    body=message.to_message_json()
)
```

When we review the queues and message counts with `rabbitmqctl list_queues`, we see that a new queue (`queue_name`) has appeared, with one message in it:

```
root# rabbitmqctl list_queues
Listing queues ...
hello 2
queue_name 1
```

Reading messages from a queue is a bit more complex, but not significantly so. An example script to read the messages sent to our queue by the previous runs of the `rabbitmq-sender.py` script starts much the same way:

```
#!/usr/bin/env python
# - scratch-space/rabbitmq-receiver.py
# - Derived from RabbitMQ - RabbitMQ tutorial - "Hello world!"
#   https://www.rabbitmq.com/tutorials/tutorial-one-python.html

import pika

from pprint import pprint
from hms_core.daemons import DaemonMessage
```

We need to use the same signing-key value, otherwise the messages being retrieved won't be allowed to be read:

```
signing_key = '!:iLL>S@]BN;h%"h\'<2cPGsaKA 3vbGJ'
```

Message-handling is dealt with by providing a callback function that accepts all of the message properties that are returned by the process of fetching a message from the queue:

```
# - Define a message-handler function
def message_handler(ch, method, properties, body):
    print('Handling a message:')
    # - Some print-output removed to keep the listing here shorter
```

It's important that we wrap functionality for message-handling in a `try … except` block, so that if something does go awry during the message-handling process, it doesn't kill the main message-polling loop that we'll set up later. In this case, at least one error could be raised: the `InvalidMessageError` error we defined earlier—it gets thrown if a `DaemonMessage` cannot be created because of an invalid signature:

```
    try:
        message = DaemonMessage.from_message_json(
            body.decode(), signing_key
        )
        print(
            '+- message ........ (%s) %r' %
            (type(message).__name__, message)
        )
        print(
            '    +- operation ... (%s) %r' %
            (type(message.operation).__name__, message.operation)
        )
        print(
```

```
                '    +- signature ... (%s) %r' %
                (type(message.signature).__name__, message.signature)
            )
            print(
                '    +- data ........ (%s)' %
                (type(message.data).__name__)
            )
            print('-- Message-data '.ljust(80,'-'))
            pprint(message.data)
            print('='*80)
        except Exception as error:
            print('%s: %s' % (error.__class__.__name__, error))
```

The processes for creating a connection, and associating a channel or queue name to it, are the same:

```
# Create a connection
connection = pika.BlockingConnection(
    pika.ConnectionParameters('localhost')
)
# - Create (or at least specify) a channel
channel = connection.channel()
# - Create or specify a queue
channel.queue_declare(queue='hello')
```

In this case, though, we're consuming messages, rather than sending them, so we need to set that up:

```
# - Set up a consumer
channel.basic_consume(
    message_handler, queue='hello', no_ack=True
)
```

Finally, we can start listening for messages:

```
# - Listen for messages
print('Listening for messages:')
print('='*80)
channel.start_consuming()
```

On execution, this script sets up its own event loop, listening for messages on the queue/channel specified. This is approximately equivalent to the event loop that `BaseDaemon.main` requires of derived daemon classes, though an actual daemon implementation might not use it. As soon as this script is run, it reads and outputs the content of the two messages sent earlier by the first script:

```
Listening for messages:
==============================================================
Handling a message:
+- ch (channel) ... (BlockingChannel) <BlockingChannel>
+- method ......... (Deliver) <Basic.Deliver>
+- properties ..... (BasicProperties) <BasicProperties>
+- message ........ (DaemonMessage) <hms_core.daemons.DaemonMessage object>
    +- operation ... (str) 'response'
    +- signature ... (str) '59237... (a lot more hex-digits) ... 904'
    +- data ........ (dict)
-- Message-data ----------------------------------------------
{'hello': 'Hello from rabbitmq-sender.py', 'random_number': 3}
==============================================================
Handling a message:
+- ch (channel) ... (BlockingChannel) <BlockingChannel>
+- method ......... (Deliver) <Basic.Deliver>
+- properties ..... (BasicProperties) <BasicProperties>
+- message ........ (DaemonMessage) <hms_core.daemons.DaemonMessage object>
    +- operation ... (str) 'response'
    +- signature ... (str) '59237... (a lot more hex-digits) ... 904'
    +- data ........ (dict)
-- Message-data ----------------------------------------------
{'hello': 'Hello from rabbitmq-sender.py', 'random_number': 3}
==============================================================
```

This also allows us to verify that the signatures of the two messages, with identical content and using the same signing key, are identical. This is expected behavior, given that message data and the signing key input did not change between sending the two messages.

Imagine we change the signing key:

```
#!/usr/bin/env python
# - scratch-space/rabbitmq-bad-sender.py
# - Derived from RabbitMQ - RabbitMQ tutorial - "Hello world!"
#   https://www.rabbitmq.com/tutorials/tutorial-one-python.html

# ... Interim script-code removed for brevity

# Message-items
# - Signing-key
signing_key = 'Invalid signing key'

# ...
```

Then rerun the same script; we get different results from our message listener:

```
================================================================================
Handling a message:
+- ch (channel) ... (BlockingChannel) <BlockingChannel>
+- method ........ (Deliver) <Basic.Deliver>
+- properties ..... (BasicProperties) <BasicProperties>
InvalidMessageError: The message
    {'hello': 'Hello from rabbitmq-bad-sender.py'},
    with a signature of "036e8… (a lot more hex-digits) … 4cc" did not match
    the expected signature. Message DENIED
```

This serves as additional verification that the message-signing process will work as expected: Not allowing messages with invalid signatures to be created, and thus not being acted upon.

That message-handling functionality, with one minor change, can serve as the basis for the `main` loop of the main class for the Artisan Gateway:

```
class ArtisanGatewayDaemon(BaseDaemon):
    """
Provides the main ArtisanGateway daemon/service.
    """
```

We still need a message-handling function, but now it's defined as a method of the service class:

```
    def _handle_message(self, message:(dict,)) -> None:
        self.info(
            '%s._handle_message called:' % self.__class__.__name__
        )
        self.info(str(message))
```

The `main` loop of the `ArtisanGatewayDaemon` class can start as a simple re-casting of the original functionality from the receiver script:

```
def main(self):
    """
The main event-loop (or whatever is equivalent) for the service
instance.
    """
```

Initially, just to establish that the functionality needed is viable, we'll use the same `signing_key`, `connection`, and `channel` values established earlier. Eventually, these will depend on configuration values – specifying the signing key, or at least where or how to get it – and depending on whether the final implementation goes down the path of having individual Artisan queues, there might be several queue-names/channels, or just the one. For now, having just the one that was used in the earlier script allows us to establish basic queue-reading functionality:

```
signing_key = '!:iLL>S@]BN;h%"h\'<2cPGsaKA 3vbGJ'
connection = pika.BlockingConnection(
    pika.ConnectionParameters('localhost')
)
channel = connection.channel()
channel.queue_declare(queue='hello')
```

The base structure of the loop that `main` executes is similar to the structure of the main loop from the `testdaemon` of Chapter 15, *Anatomy of a Service* – so long as the class' internal _running flag is `True`, the loop continues, performing the queue check and processing incoming messages. Once the loop is terminated, whether by the `stop` method of the class or by one of the signals that was registered during the execution of `BaseDaemon.__init__` by `ArtisanGatewayDaemon.__init__`, control exits and the `cleanup` method of the class is called before it terminates completely.

The primary difference, as should be expected, is what actually happens during each iteration through the loop. In this case, the `channel` is polled for the next available message, and if one is detected, it's read, converted to a `DaemonMessage`, acknowledged, and handed off to the message-handler method defined earlier. It requires the same sort of `connection` and `channel`:

```
# - To start with, we're just going to use the same
#   parameters for our pika connection and channel as
#   were used in the rabbitmq-sender.py script.
connection = pika.BlockingConnection(
    pika.ConnectionParameters(
        self.connection_params['host'],
        self.connection_params.get('port'),
```

```
                  self.connection_params.get('path'),
        )
    )
    # - Create (or at least specify) a channel
    channel = connection.channel()
    # - Create or specify a queue
    channel.queue_declare(queue=self.queue_name)
```

Once those are established, the `main` loop is very straightforward:

```
    # - Normal BaseDaemon main-loop start-up:
    self._running = True
    self.info('Starting main daemon event-loop')
    # - Rather than use a channel-consumer (see the example in
    #   rabbitmq-reciever.py), we're going to actively poll for
    #   messages *ourselves*, in order to capture just the
    #   message-body - that's what we really care about in
    #   this case...
    while self._running:
        try:
            # - Retrieve the next message from the queue, if
            #   there is one, and handle it...
            method_frame, header, body = \
    channel.basic_get(self.queue_name)
            if method_frame:
                # - Any actual message, valid or not, will
                #   generate a method_frame
                self.debug('received message:')
                message = DaemonMessage.from_message_json(
                    body.decode(), self.signing_key
                )
                self.debug('+- %s' % message.data)
                # - If we've received the message and processed
                #   it, acknowledge it on basic principle
                channel.basic_ack(method_frame.delivery_tag)
                self._handle_message(message)
        except InvalidMessageError as error:
            # - If message-generation fails (bad signature),
            #   we still need to send an acknowledgement in order
            #   to clear the message from the queue
            err = '%s: %s' % (error.__class__.__name__, error)
            self.error(err)
            channel.basic_ack(method_frame.delivery_tag)
        except Exception as error:
            # Otherwise, we just log the error and move on
            err = '%s: %s' % (error.__class__.__name__, error)
            self.error(err)
            for line in traceback.format_exc().split('\n'):
```

```
                 self.error(line)
        self.info('%s main loop terminated' % (self.__class__.__name__))
```

In order to test this, a quick, basic configuration file was assembled, mostly for logging information, and an instance of the new class was created with that configuration and started. The log output from startup to shutdown, including sending a good message, a bad message, then another good message, shows that everything operates as expected:

```
# Start-up of daemon

{date/time} - hms_ag - INFO - Logging started. Other … (truncated) … prior to now
{date/time} - hms_ag - INFO - ArtisanGatewayDaemon.preflight called
{date/time} - hms_ag - INFO - Starting ArtisanGatewayDaemon.main
{date/time} - hms_ag - INFO - Starting main daemon event-loop

# Sending the first valid message

{date/time} - hms_ag - INFO - ArtisanGatewayDaemon._handle_message called:
{date/time} - hms_ag - INFO - <hms_core.daemons.DaemonMessage object at 0x7fb4b11371d0>

# Sending an invalid message (signature failure)

{date/time} - hms_ag - ERROR - InvalidMessageError:
                            The message {'hello': 'Hello from rabbitmq-bad-sender.py'},
                            with a signature of "036e8… (a lot more hex-digits) … 4cc"
                            did not match the expected signature.
                            Message DENIED

# Sending a second copy of the good message

{date/time} - hms_ag - INFO - ArtisanGatewayDaemon._handle_message called:
{date/time} - hms_ag - INFO - <hms_core.daemons.DaemonMessage object at 0x7fb4b11372b0>

# Shutting the daemon down

{date/time} - hms_ag - INFO - Stopping ArtisanGatewayDaemon
{date/time} - hms_ag - INFO - ArtisanGatewayDaemon main loop terminated
{date/time} - hms_ag - INFO - ArtisanGatewayDaemon.cleanup called
```

The quick, basic configuration for this daemon instance is very simple:

```
# Logging configuration
# scratch-space/hms_ag_conf.yaml
logging:
  format: "%(asctime)s - %(name)s - %(levelname)s - %(message)s"
  name: hms_ag
  console:
    level: info
  file:
```

```
level: info
logfile: "/tmp/hms_ag.log"
```

The queue parameters should reside in the configuration file as well, and be acquired by the daemon instance. The additional configuration values end up looking like this:

```
queue:
  type: rabbit
  connection:
    host: localhost
    port: 5672
    path: /
  queue_name: "central-office"
signing_key: "0T*)B{Y#.C3yY8J>;1#<b\\q^:.@ZQjg2 tG~3(MJ&b_"
```

The process for loading those values involves the addition of some instance properties that mostly follow the normal pattern in use thus far:

- `connection_params`: A dict value whose values are retrieved from the connection section of the config file that is used to create the RabbitMQ connection
- `queue_name`: A string, it is the queue-name/channel that the instance will listen to
- `signing_key`: A `bytes` or `str` value, it is the signing key that the instance will use to create `DaemonMessage` instances sent on or received from its queue

Actually getting and storing those values involves nothing more than adding to the `_on_configuration_loaded` method of the class. Originally, all it did was call the same method of the `BaseDaemon` parent class in order to set up logging capabilities, and that remains the same:

```
def _on_configuration_loaded(self, **config_data):
    # - Call the BaseDaemon function directly to set up logging,
    #   since that's provided entirely there...
    BaseDaemon._on_configuration_loaded(self, **config_data)
```

Queue-specific items are retrieved next. Although there's no expectation at this point that other queue systems will be needed, we can't rule out that possibility in the future, so the code starts with the assumption that we'll want to allow for that in the future:

```
queue_config = config_data.get('queue')
if queue_config:
    try:
```

```
            if queue_config['type'] == 'rabbit':
                self._connection_params =
queue_config['connection']
                self.info(
                    'Connection-parameters: %s' %
                    self.connection_params
                    )
                self._queue_name = queue_config['queue_name']
                self.info(
                    'Main queue-name: %s' % self.queue_name
                    )
            # If other queue-types are eventually to be supported,
            # their configuration-load processes can happen here,
            # following this pattern:
            # elif queue_config['type'] == 'name':
            #     # Configuration set-up for this queue-type...
            else:
                raise RuntimeError(
                    '%s could not be configured because the '
                    'configuration supplied did not specify a '
                    'valid queue-type (%s)' %
                    (self.__class__.__name__,
queue_config['type'])
                    )
        except Exception as error:
            raise RuntimeError(
                '%s could not be configured because of an '
                'error -- %s: %s' %
                (
                    self.__class__.__name__,
                    error.__class__.__name__, error
                )
            )
    else:
        raise RuntimeError(
            '%s could not be configured because the configuration

'
            'supplied did not supply message-queue configuration'
%
            (self.__class__.__name__)
            )
```

The signing key is also in the configuration file, so acquiring and storing it comes next:

```
        # - The signing-key is also in configuration, so get it too
        try:
            self._signing_key = config_data['signing_key']
```

```
except Exception as error:
    raise RuntimeError(
        '%s could not be configured because of an error '
        'retrieving the required signing_key value -- %s: %s'
    %
    (
        self.__class__.__name__,
        error.__class__.__name__, error
    )
    )
```

At least for the time being, that takes care of all of the configuration needed to remove the hardcoded values that were in use in main, while keeping the class functional. Execution of a variant of the original message-sending script (in `scratch-space/rabbitmq-sender-daemon-queue.py` of the chapter code) showed that the daemon still functioned as expected with these changes – listening for and acting upon valid messages.

Handling messages

In order to actually do something with the data of a message, we'll need to define what a well-formed command message actually looks like, implement methods to execute the commands that are allowed, and implement functionality that knows how to call those methods, given a well-formed and verified message to do so. The first item from that list is quite simple, but could have a lot of different valid implementation patterns. Consider that, at this point, we're allowed to transmit four different operation actions by `DaemonMessage`: `'create'`, `'update'`, `'delete'`, and `'response'`. These operation actions correspond directly to standard CRUD operations, except for the `'response'` value, though even that is, perhaps, roughly equivalent to a `read` operation. For any given data object type, those operations would, respectively, need to execute the same processes:

1. Create a new instance of the relevant class, populated with state data from the message, using the `from_data_dict` class method (or a new equivalent class method, perhaps), and `save` the new instance

2. Retrieve an existing instance of the relevant class, using the `get` class method, update any of that instance's state data with new values from the message (which would probably benefit from having a new method created, perhaps `update_from_message`), and `save` the instance

3. Find and delete the instance specified by the message data with the `delete` class method

4. Retrieve and return the data dict representation of the instance specified by the message data, using the `get` class method to perform the retrieval, and the `to_data_dict` method of the found instance to generate the data structure of the message

The daemon, then, needs to have as many as 16 `{action}_{object}` methods, one for each action/object combination, just to ensure that all of the combinations are accounted for. For each object type (Artisans, Customers, Orders, and Products), the set of methods would look something like this (the method names are self-explanatory):

- `create_artisan`

- `update_artisan`

- `delete_artisan`

- `response_artisan`

The one critical piece of data that isn't yet accounted for, and is needed to determine which of those methods to execute on receipt of a command message, is the object type. The `DaemonMessage` class doesn't have a specific property for object types, because the initial thought was that doing so could needlessly limit future uses of it to messages that have both an `operation` and an object type. Revising `DaemonMessage` to allow an object-type specification wouldn't be difficult. It would involve little more than adding an optional property, allowing another optional argument in the `__init__` method, and any other methods that call it, and accounting for it in the dictionary output methods. Going to those lengths, though, seems unnecessary: the messages themselves, as structured data, can just as easily contain the necessary data. As an example, consider a "create Artisan" message that looks like this:

```
{
    "data":{
        "target":"artisan",
        "properties":{
            "address":"1234 Main Street, etc.",
            "company_name":"Wirewerks",
            "contact_email":"jsmith@wirewerks.com",
            "contact_name":"John Smith",
            "website":"http://wirewerks.com",
        }
    },
    "operation":"create",
```

```
        "signature":"A long hex-string"
    }
```

If any command message has an operation and indicates in its data an object type (the `target` value) with the properties to be used in the operation as a standard structure, that would work just as well. Similar data structures will also work for update operations:

```
{
    "data":{
        "target":"artisan",
        "properties":{
            "address":"5432 West North Dr, etc.",
            "modified":"2019-06-27 16:42:13",
            "oid":"287db9e0-2fcc-4ff1-bd59-ff97a07f7989",
        }
    },
    "operation":"update",
    "signature":"A long hex-string"
}
```

For delete operations:

```
{
    "data":{
        "target":"artisan",
        "properties":{
            "oid":"287db9e0-2fcc-4ff1-bd59-ff97a07f7989",
        }
    },
    "operation":"delete",
    "signature":"A long hex-string"
}
```

As well as for response operations:

```
{
    "data":{
        "target":"artisan",
        "properties":{
            "oid":"287db9e0-2fcc-4ff1-bd59-ff97a07f7989",
        }
    },
    "operation":"response",
    "signature":"A long hex-string"
}
```

Determining which method to call based on the message's operation and
`data.target` values is simply a long chain of `if...elif...else` decisions:

```
def _handle_message(self, message:(dict,)) -> None:
    self.info(
        '%s._handle_message called:' % self.__class__.__name__
    )
```

Since we'll need the target (for decision-making later) and the properties (to pass as
arguments to the method), get those first:

```
target = message.data.get('target')
properties = message.data.get('properties')
```

Each combination of `operation` and `target` looks very much like the others.
Starting with `create` operations:

```
if message.operation == 'create':
```

If the target is one of the known, allowed types, then we can just call the appropriate
method:

```
if target == 'artisan':
    self.create_artisan(properties)
elif target == 'customer':
    self.create_customer(properties)
elif target == 'order':
    self.create_order(properties)
elif target == 'product':
    self.create_product(properties)
```

If the `target` is not known, we want to throw an error:

```
else:
    raise RuntimeError(
        '%s error: "%s" (%s) is not a recognized '
        'object-type/target' %
        (
            self.__class__.__name__, target,
            type(target).__name__
        )
    )
```

The other operations work much the same way – `update` operations, for example:

```
elif message.operation == 'update':
    if target == 'artisan':
        self.update_artisan(properties)
```

```
        elif target == 'customer':
            self.update_customer(properties)
        elif target == 'order':
            self.update_order(properties)
        elif target == 'product':
            self.update_product(properties)
        else:
            raise RuntimeError(
                '%s error: "%s" (%s) is not a recognized '
                'object-type/target' %
                (
                    self.__class__.__name__, target,
                    type(target).__name__
                )
            )
```

The `delete` and `response` operations are similar enough that there's little point in reproducing them here, but they are present in the code. Finally, we also capture cases where the operation isn't recognized, and raise an error in those cases as well:

```
        else:
            raise RuntimeError(
                '%s error: "%s" (%s) is not a recognized '
                'operation' %
                (
                    self.__class__.__name__, operation,
                    type(operation).__name__
                )
            )
```

The actual operation methods are, as a result of the data object design/structure and the structure of the incoming messages, relatively simple. Creation of an `Artisan`, for example:

```
def create_artisan(self, properties:(dict,)) -> None:
    self.info('%s.create_artisan called' % self.__class__.__name__)
    self.debug(str(properties))
    # - Create the new object...
    new_object = Artisan.from_data_dict(properties)
    #    ...and save it.
    new_object.save()
```

Update of an `Artisan`:

```
def update_artisan(self, properties:(dict,)) -> None:
    self.info('%s.update_artisan called' % self.__class__.__name__)
    self.debug(str(properties))
    # - Retrieve the existing object, and get its data-dict
```

```
#   representation
existing_object = Artisan.get(properties['oid'])
data_dict = existing_object.to_data_dict()
# - Update the data-dict with the values from properties
data_dict.update(properties)
# - Make sure it's flagged as dirty, so that save will
#   *update* instead of *create* the instance-record,
#   for data-stores where that applies
data_dict['is_dirty'] = True
# - Create a new instance of the class with the revised
#   data-dict...
new_object = Artisan.from_data_dict(data_dict)
#   ...and save it.
new_object.save()
```

Deletion of an `Artisan`:

```
def delete_artisan(self, properties:(dict,)) -> None:
    self.info('%s.delete_artisan called' % self.__class__.__name__)
    self.debug(str(properties))
    # - Delete the instance-record for the specified object
    Artisan.delete(properties['oid'])
```

`Artisan` **response:**

```
def response_artisan(self, properties:(dict,)) -> dict:
    self.info('%s.response_artisan called' % self.__class__.__name__)
    self.debug(str(properties))
    # - Since get allows both oids and criteria, separate those
    #   out first:
    oid = properties.get('oid')
    criteria = {
        item[0]:item[1] for item in properties.items()
        if item[0] != 'oid'
    }
    return Artisan.get(oid, **criteria)
```

Queues and related Artisan properties

Since Artisans will communicate with the Gateway over specific queues, and those queues have to be identified and consistently associated with their respective Artisans, we'll need to have mechanisms in the various code bases to store queue identifiers, and to associate them with their Artisan owners.

The queue specifications themselves can be implemented simply by adding a property (`queue_id`) to the `Artisan` objects' classes. Since the Artisan objects at both the Gateway service and Artisan application will make use of `queue_id`, it makes sense to implement that in the `hms_core.business_objects.BaseArtisan` class, where it will be inherited everywhere it's needed. The property getter and deleter methods are typical implementations, as is the `property` declaration, though it follows a read-only property pattern. The setter method is pretty typical also:

```python
def _set_queue_id(self, value:(str)) -> None:
    if type(value) != str:
        raise TypeError(
            '%s.queue expects a single-line printable ASCII '
            'string-value, but was passed "%s" (%s)' %
            (
                self.__class__.__name__, value,
                type(value).__name__
            )
        )
    badchars = [
        c for c in value
        if ord(c)<32 or ord(c) > 127
        or c in '\n\t\r'
    ]
    if len(badchars) != 0:
        raise ValueError(
            '%s.queue expects a single-line printable ASCII '
            'string-value, but was passed "%s" that contained '
            'invalid characters: %s' %
            (
                self.__class__.__name__, value,
                str(tuple(badchars))
            )
        )
    self._queue_id = value
```

Artisans will also need to keep track of a signing key property that is unique to each Artisan, but exists in both the local `Artisan` objects at the Artisan Application side of the message-transmission process and at the Artisan Gateway side. Signing keys, as `bytes` values, may not be easily stored in their native value types, though: `bytes` values are not natively JSON-serializable, which is problematic for the local Artisan data storage already implemented, and could be problematic for the MongoDB storage in use elsewhere.

Fortunately, the `bytes` type provides instance and class methods to serialize and unserialize values to and from hexadecimal string values. Serializing a byte's value is as simple as calling the `hex()` method of the value, and creating a bytes value from a hex string is accomplished by calling `bytes.fromhex(hex_string)`. A simple example of a complete serialization/unserialization of a bytes value using `hex()/fromhex()` shows that the value is preserved as needed:

```
import os

raw_key=os.urandom(24)
print('raw_key (%s)' % type(raw_key).__name__)
print(raw_key)
print()

serialized = raw_key.hex()
print('serialized (%s)' % type(serialized).__name__)
print(serialized)
print()

unserialized = bytes.fromhex(serialized)
print('unserialized (%s)' % type(unserialized).__name__)
print(unserialized)
print()

print('unserialized == raw_key: %s' % (unserialized == raw_key))
```

The output of this code will look like the following:

```
raw_key (bytes)
b'\x95|\xcea\xdd\r\xa1\xd6^U\xa9)\xe5\xbc\xbc\x9c<S\x13\xc6\xe2\xf7\x12W'

serialized (str)
957cce61dd0da1d65e55a929e5bcbc9c3c5313c6e2f71257

unserialized (bytes)
b'\x95|\xcea\xdd\r\xa1\xd6^U\xa9)\xe5\xbc\xbc\x9c<S\x13\xc6\xe2\xf7\x12W'

unserialized == raw_key: True
```

The corresponding property of the Artisan classes (`signing_key`) follows the typical read-only property structure too, and apart from its setter method, is nothing unusual. The setter method has to allow both raw `bytes` values and hex string representations of `bytes` values, and *stores* a `bytes` value:

```
def _set_signing_key(self, value:(bytes,str)):
    if type(value) not in (bytes,str):
        raise TypeError(
            '%s.signing_key expects a bytes-value of no less '
            'than 64 bytes in length, or a hexadecimal string-'
            'representation of one, but wa passed "%s" (%s)' %
            (self.__class__.__name__, value, type(value).__name__)
        )
```

If it's passed a string, it tries to convert that using `bytes.fromhex()`:

```
    if type(value) == str:
        try:
            value = bytes.fromhex(value)
        except:
            raise ValueError(
                '%s.signing_key expects a bytes-value of no '
                'less than 64 bytes in length, or a hexadecimal '
                'string-representation of one, but wa passed '
                '"%s" (%s), which could not be converted from '
                'hexadecimal into bytes' %
                (
                    self.__class__.__name__, value,
                    type(value).__name__)
                )
            )
```

It also enforces a minimum length of the signing key, arbitrarily set to 64 bytes (512 bits):

```
    if len(value) < 64:
        raise ValueError(
            '%s.signing_key expects a bytes-value of no less '
            'than 64 bytes in length, or a hexadecimal string-'
            'representation of one, but wa passed "%s" (%s), '
            'which was only %d bytes in length after conversion' %
            (
                self.__class__.__name__, value,
                type(value).__name__, len(value)
            )
        )
    self._signing_key = value
```

The corresponding final `Artisan` objects have to account for these new properties in their `to_data_dict` methods and `__init__` methods. The `to_data_dict` changes look the same – using `hms_core.co_objects.Artisan` as an example, and showing the new properties added to the end of the dict result returned, they end up looking like this:

```python
def to_data_dict(self) -> (dict,):
    return {
        # - BaseArtisan-derived items
        'address':self.address.to_dict() if self.address else None,
        'company_name':self.company_name,
        'contact_email':self.contact_email,
        'contact_name':self.contact_name,
        'website':self.website,
        # - BaseDataObject-derived items
        'created':datetime.strftime(
            self.created, self.__class__._data_time_string
        ),
        'is_active':self.is_active,
        'is_deleted':self.is_deleted,
        'modified':datetime.strftime(
            self.modified, self.__class__._data_time_string
        ),
        'oid':str(self.oid),
        # Queue- and signing-key values
        'queue_id':self.queue_id,
        'signing_key':self.signing_key.hex(),
    }
```

The changes to the `__init__` methods vary somewhat: since the new `queue_id` and `signing_key` properties are assigned as `BaseArtisan.__init__` executes, that method has to actually call the deleter and setter methods:

```python
def __init__(self,
    contact_name:str, contact_email:str,
    address:Address, company_name:str=None,
    queue_id:(str,None)=None, signing_key:(bytes,str,None)=None,
    website:(str,None)=None
    *products
    ):
    """Doc-string omitted for brevity"""
    # - Call parent initializers if needed
    # ... omitted for brevity
    # - Set instance property-values from arguments using
    #    _set_... methods
    self._set_contact_name(contact_name)
    self._set_contact_email(contact_email)
```

```
        self._set_address(address)
        # New queue_id and signing_key properties
        self._set_queue_id(queue_id)
        self._set_signing_key(signing_key)
        if company_name:
            self._set_company_name(company_name)
        if website:
            self._set_website(website)
```

Since `queue_id` and `signing_key` are technically required properties, if time allowed, moving them into the required-arguments portion of the `__init__` signature, between `address` and `company_name`, would be the right thing to do. In this case, it's more a matter of space constraints than time, so they're being added into the signature at an easy location to deal with instead, rather than having to review, modify, and reshow all of the various `BaseArtisan.__init__` calls that already exist in the code. They'll still work as required properties, though, since the setter methods won't accept the default `None` values, and they're being called without the sort of checking that `company_name` and `website` use.

The `__init__` methods of `co_objects.Artisan` and `artisan_objects.Artisan` only have to be updated to include the new arguments in their signatures and pass those along to their `BaseArtisan.__init__` calls. The revisions to `co_objects.Artisan.__init__` look like this:

```
    def __init__(self,
        contact_name:str, contact_email:str,
        address:Address, company_name:str=None,
# New queue_id and signing_key arguments
        queue_id:(str,None)=None,
        signing_key:(bytes,str,None)=None,
        website:(str,None)=None
        # - Arguments from HMSMongoDataObject
        oid:(UUID,str,None)=None,
        created:(datetime,str,float,int,None)=None,
        modified:(datetime,str,float,int,None)=None,
        is_active:(bool,int,None)=None,
        is_deleted:(bool,int,None)=None,
        is_dirty:(bool,int,None)=None,
        is_new:(bool,int,None)=None,
        *products
    ):
        """Doc-string omitted for brevity"""
        # - Call parent initializers if needed
```

```
BaseArtisan.__init__(self,
    contact_name, contact_email, address, company_name,
# New queue_id and signing_key arguments
    queue_id, signing_key,
    website
)
# ... other initialization omitted for brevity
# - Perform any other initialization needed
```

Requirements for a web-service-based daemon

If we were to pursue a web-service-based implementation for the Artisan Gateway instead, there are several common factors, and a few hurdles that would have to be overcome. Arguably the most significant hurdle would be in implementing the full set of HTTP methods – POST, GET, PUT, and DELETE – the official and standards-compliant methods that correspond to the Create, Read, Update, and Delete CRUD operations we're expecting to use.

If the medium that commands are transmitted in is to remain the serialized and signature-bearing message output of the DaemonMessage class, we'd need to be able to pass a complete, signed message in at least two different ways:

- In a query string format for the GET and DELETE operations: GET isn't intended to support the same sort of payload capabilities that POST and PUT methods allow, and though there doesn't seem to be any official stance as to whether DELETE should or should not support it, it's probably safest to assume that it won't, and write code accordingly.

- In as many as two different payload formats for POST and PUT operations. Thus far, we haven't addressed any of the Product data in any detail; even if there is no requirement to support the transmission of product images, it's just a matter of time until one would surface. The HTTP POST and PUT operations allow a payload to be sent in the request body, and allow that payload to be sent in two different formats (encodings) in a standard web form request context:

  - As a key-value string list that looks very much like the equivalent in a GET request

- As a more detailed encoding, where each field in the request has the same name and data as the key-value list, but also allows fields to specify that they contain specific data types – Files, for example, with other data, such as the filename

The latter encoding is seen in web pages that allow file uploads as an `enctype="multipart/form-data"` attribute in the relevant `<form>` tag. Submitting such a form, with two files included in the payload, will generate an `HTTP` request that might look something like this:

```
Content-Type: multipart/form-data; boundary=---------------------------{field-separator}
Content-Length: {content-length}

---------------------------{field-separator}
Content-Disposition: form-data; name="{field-name}"

{field-value}
---------------------------{field-separator}
Content-Disposition: form-data; name="{field-name}"; filename="{file-name}"
Content-Type: {MIME-type}

{file-data}

---------------------------{field-separator}
Content-Disposition: form-data; name="{field-name}"; filename="{file-name}"
Content-Type: {MIME-type}

{file-data}

---------------------------{field-separator}--
```

In this example:

- `{field-separator}` is a random string that uniquely identifies the beginning of each field's dataset
- `{content-length}` is the total size of the payload
- `{field-name}` is the name of the field whose data is wrapped in the section
- `{field-value}` is text data from a field that is not a file-upload field
- `{file-name}` is the name of the file being uploaded, as it existed on the client machine

- {MIME-type} is an indicator of the type of file being transmitted, for example image/png
- {file-data} is the data of the file corresponding to the field

In order to support a payload with just these three chunks of data, we'd have to find or create code that can reliably parse out each data section and handle each data chunk that gets spat back out. While there is at least one such library, requests-toolbelt, there are known issues with it in certain core Python versions (3.3.0 and 3.3.1), so it may or may not be a viable option depending on what Python version is in play. Writing (and testing) code from scratch to deal with multipart/form-data payloads would be a time-consuming process at best.

Assuming that all of that is dealt with, although it's not difficult to write network listeners that would be able to capture and handle an incoming request, that too could involve a fair chunk of time, particularly on the testing side of things, just to be able to reliably (and provably) handle incoming requests. In a web service scenario, it would almost certainly be a better option to start with one of the well-established web application packages that already deals with all of those needs and requirements, and write code that simply maps incoming requests to the handler methods, in much the same way that the message-queue implementation does. On the plus side, the signed messages should be usable in that context, and the underlying operation methods would likely not have to be modified to any significant degree.

Traffic to and from the service

The message-receiving aspect of the communication chain by the service is already in place, in the main method of ArtisanGateway, but no message-sending functionality has been implemented yet, apart from the bits and pieces focused around message generation. Each data object type, when modified, created, or deleted, is going to need to send a relevant command message to its counterpart subsystem. For example, if an Artisan creates a new Product, the act of creating that Product object needs to send a "create product" message to the Gateway service. Likewise, if a change is made to a Product by Central Office staff, the Gateway service needs to send an "update product" message to the appropriate Artisan Application instance.

On the Artisan Application side of those scenarios, all of the queue parameters needed to send any message are going to be constant. They will always send messages to the same queue server, on the same port, using the same connection and channel. Rather than requiring all of the message-queue settings to be passed to all of the various data objects during initialization, which could complicate them significantly, and make the code difficult to deal with if a different message-transport mechanism were needed later on, we can create another class that contains all of those and provides a method for sending arbitrary messages to the queue server: RabbitMQSender. In the process of defining that class, we can also leverage certain aspects of Python class/instance relationships to make the creation of sender instances considerably easier:

- An instance of a Python class that has defined class attributes also has instance attributes with the same name and value. That is, if RabbitMQSender has a class attribute named _host, with a value of localhost, all instances of RabbitMQSender will, when created, have a _host attribute with the same localhost value.

- Changing an instance attribute's value will have no effect on the class attribute's value.
- Changing a class attribute's value will also change the corresponding instance values, provided that they haven't been explicitly set in those instances. So, if an instance of RabbitMQSender is created, then RabbitMQSender._host is changed, and the _host value of the instance will be updated accordingly.

Taken together, and with some caution in design when applied, these allow RabbitMQSender to be defined so that the *class* can be configured, allowing a usable instance of the class to be created with nothing more than the most basic of calls, along the lines of my_sender = RabbitMQSender().

If a different message-transport mechanism were to be needed later, it would probably be a good idea to introduce a layer of abstraction that RabbitMQSender would derive from – BaseMessageSender, perhaps – that would require the message-sending method and all of the relevant transport-mechanism properties. That would provide a common interface for all transport mechanisms, and make it a lot easier to switch between them if/as needed.

`RabbitMQSender`, then, starts as a typical class-definition, with the various connection properties and any other message-transmission constants defined as protected class attributes:

```
class RabbitMQSender(object):
    """
Provides baseline functionality, interface requirements, and
type-identity for objects that can send messages to a RabbitMQ
message-queue that shares configuration across all derived
classes
    """
    #####################################
    # Class attributes/constants        #
    #####################################

    # - Common RabbitMQ parameters
    _host = None
    _port = None
    _queue_name = None
    _virtual_host = None
```

The properties that correspond to those have only getter methods, so that they cannot be easily/accidentally altered:

```
    def _get_host(self):
        return self._host

    def _get_port(self):
        return self._port

    def _get_queue_name(self):
        return self._queue_name

    def _get_virtual_host(self):
        return self._virtual_host
```

They are associated with property names in a typical read-only property structure:

```
    host = property(
        _get_host, None, None,
        'Gets the host (FQDN or IP-address) of the RabbitMQ '
        'server that derived objects will send messages to'
    )
    port = property(
        _get_port, None, None,
        'Gets the TCP/IP port on the RabbitMQ server that '
        'derived objects will send messages to'
    )
```

```
queue_name = property(
    _get_queue_name, None, None,
    'Gets the name of the queue on the RabbitMQ server that '
    'derived objects will send messages to'
)
virtual_host = property(
    _get_virtual_host, None, None,
    'Gets the "virtual_host" on the RabbitMQ server that '
    'derived objects will send messages to'
)
```

The `connection` and `channel` properties follow a typical lazy-instantiation pattern, being created on the first request for either of them, and are also exposed as read-only properties:

```
def _get_channel(self):
    try:
        return self._channel
    except AttributeError:
        # - Create (or at least specify) a channel
        self._channel = self.connection.channel()
        # - Create or specify a queue
        self._channel.queue_declare(queue=self._queue_name)
        return self._channel

def _get_connection(self):
    try:
        return self._connection
    except AttributeError:
        self._connection = pika.BlockingConnection(
            # Parameters
            pika.ConnectionParameters(
                host=self._host,
                port=self.port,
                virtual_host=self.virtual_host
            )
        )
        return self._connection
# ...

channel = property(
    _get_channel, None, None,
    'Gets the channel that the instance will send messages to'
)
```

```
connection = property(
    _get_connection, None, None,
    'Gets the connection that the instance will send messages '
    'with/through'
)
```

There are no property-setter or -deleter methods needed, nor is there any functionality needed in __init__ for the class. All of an instance's properties will effectively refer back to the class attribute values, which can be set with a single class method call:

```
@classmethod
def configure(cls,
    queue_name:(str), host:(str,), port:(int,None)=None,
    virtual_host:(str,None)=None
):
    cls._queue_name = queue_name
    cls._host = host
    if port:
        cls._port = port
    if virtual_host:
        cls._virtual_host = virtual_host
```

In the context of an Artisan Application, all that needs to be done to preconfigure all instances of RabbitMQSender is to call RabbitMQSender.configure with the appropriate settings, probably taken from the configuration file of the Artisan Application instance:

```
RabbitMQSender.configure(
    queue_name = configuration['queue_name'],
    host = configuration['host'],
    port = configuration.get('port'),
    virtual_host = configuration.get('virtual_host'),
)
```

Finally, the process of sending messages is provided by a single method:

```
def send_message(self, message:(DaemonMessage)):
    """
Sends the supplied message to the RabbitMG server common to
all RabbitMQSender objects

self ............ (RabbitMQSender instance, required) The
                    instance to execute against
message .......... (DaemonMessage, required) The message to send.
    """
        # - Note that exchange is blank -- we're just using the
```

```
#    default exchange at this point...
self.channel.basic_publish(
    exchange='', routing_key=self.queue_name,
    body=message.to_message_json()
)
```

On the Artisan Application side of the message-transfer processes, the creation of a `RabbitMQSender` instance and calling its `send_message` method should take care of the actual message transmission we'll need. On the Artisan Gateway side, when sending messages to Artisan Application instances, the process will be similar – simplified in some ways, possibly not needing the `RabbitMQSender` (or an equivalent) class, or perhaps needing a similar variant in order to better handle multiple outgoing queues. We'll integrate the Artisan-side processes and examine the Gateway needs in more detail in `Chapter 17`, *Handling Service Transactions*.

Impacts on testing and deployment

At this point in the iteration, apart from standard unit-testing for various properties and methods that aren't involved in any message transmission, there's not much that can be done from a testing standpoint. We have yet to integrate messaging with data changes, which we'll examine in `Chapter 17`, *Handling Service Transactions*, and without a complete send-and-receive process available, in either direction, there's not much that can be done, even from a manual-testing perspective, that hasn't already been explored.

It also feels premature to work out any deployment details for the Artisan Gateway daemon just yet, for similar reasons, though at this point, it feels like a very basic `setup.py/Makefile` arrangement will probably handle everything we'll need.

Summary

Although we now have all the foundations needed to work through and close the 14 stories that the iteration stated with, only three are even potentially closed:

- As an Artisan, I need to be able to send data changes to the Artisan Gateway so that those changes can be propagated and acted upon as needed
- As a Central Office user, I need to be able to send data changes to the Artisan Gateway so that those changes can be propagated and acted upon as needed
- As any user sending messages across to or from the Artisan Gateway service, I need those messages to be signed so that they can be validated before being acted upon

Those foundations include, however, a functional (if untested) Artisan Gateway daemon/service, a mechanism for generating command messages that can be acted upon by that service and the remote applications, and the basic processes for actually transmitting those command messages. Between those accomplishments, the odds are good that we've actually closed these three stories, but until they are tested, we cannot prove that they can be.

The requisite testing to prove closure, and the balance of the stories still to be implemented, all rely on integrating the various CRUD operations at the data-object level in the Artisan and Central Office applications with the requisite messaging to propagate those data changes to the Artisan Gateway, and (where needed) from the Gateway to the remote Artisan and Central Office applications, which we'll address in the next chapter.

16
Handling Service Transactions

There is a substantial amount of interaction potential between system components and the data objects that they individually manage. While we've worked out some of the mechanisms that determine what transmitting a data change or command message looks like, we've not yet started to explore the specifics of those interactions. In a nutshell, we still need to address what the data flows (and, thus, message transmissions) look like for all of the local CRUD operations.

In this chapter, we will cover the following topics:

- Creation of products by artisans
- Activation and deactivation of products by artisans and Central Office staff
- Making changes to Product data by artisans and Central Office staff
- Deletion of products by artisans
- Creation of artisans by Central Office staff
- Making changes to Artisan data by artisans and Central Office staff
- Deletion of artisans by Central Office staff
- Creation of orders by the Web Storefront, and relaying that information to artisans for fulfillment
- Cancellation of orders from the Web Storefront, and relaying that information to artisans
- Order-item fulfillment by artisans

Remaining stories

Since our work in `Chapter 16`, *The Artisan Gateway Service,* only (tentatively) closed three stories, there are still several (eleven) that need to be addressed. The implementation of `RabbitMQSender` and the RabbitMQ message transmission strategy that was adopted also raised questions about how to propagate some of the artifacts needed for those processes—the signing key in particular—and there's also a decision pending about whether the Artisan Gateway will use one message queue for inbound traffic from artisans, or one per Artisan, and that may add another story:

> • As an Artisan, I need a message queue created and assigned to me so that I can send my data changes to the Artisan Gateway

The bulk of the stories still pending each represent a data flow process, a data transaction tied to a specific action that's undertaken by a specific user in the context of the system. Each process, in turn, is some variation of a CRUD operation—generally creating, updating, or deleting one or more data objects, as instructed by the relevant message. In reviewing the possibilities of all of the various CRUD operations against all of the business objects available to each user role in the system, five new stories surfaced:

> • As an Artisan, I need to be able to deactivate `Product` objects so that I can manage `Product` availability (which may be handled by a general Update operation)
> • As an Artisan, I need to be informed when an Order has been placed that includes one of my Product offerings so that I can fulfil my part of that Order (ultimately, the creation of an Artisan-resident `Order` object, triggered by some activity on the Central Office side)
> • As a Customer, I need the relevant parts of my Order to be relayed to the appropriate artisans so that they can fulfill their part of my Order (the other half of the previous story, but it might add some functional needs to that)

- As a Customer who's canceled an Order, I need the relevant parts of that cancellation to be relayed to the appropriate artisans so that they won't fulfill their part of the Order (essentially a deletion of an Artisan-resident `Order`-object, but with notification on the Artisan Application side)
- As an Artisan, I need to be informed when an Order has been canceled that includes one of my Product offerings so that I can stop any in-process fulfillment activities related to it and update my `Product` status as needed (again, the other half of the previous story)

All of these transactions follow a similar pattern:

- The relevant **message data** of the **Object** whose data needs to be sent along is used to create a **message** (with `DaemonMessage`).
- That **message** is sent by a sender (an instance of `RabbitMQSender`) to the **Artisan Gateway service**.
- The service reads the **message**, and calls the appropriate `[process-method]`, which will probably interact with the **Artisan Gateway data store**.
- The `[process-method]` itself may need to send other messages, either back to the **Artisan Gateway service** itself for further local processing, or through the service back to an Artisan. The processes for sending subsequent messages will be very similar, with the potential for an additional variation—the destination of the new message:

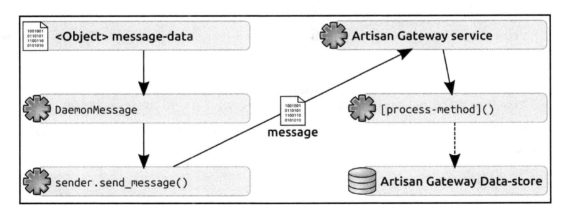

The primary points of variation are, then, in the **message data** itself, and those variations should be shaped, in turn, by business rules around what the user role is allowed to do to those objects.

A bit of reorganization

Before digging into the details of the individual transactions, some minor reorganization of recent code seems in order. The `RabbitMQSender` and `DaemonMessage` classes were originally written in the `hms_core.daemons` module, because that seemed a logical place to keep them—they are still relevant to the daemon, but also have relevance to parts of the Artisan Application (and perhaps the Central Office application) that don't have any ties to the various daemon classes themselves. Since we've also uncovered a need for various objects to be able to generate message data structures, and that feels like it should be handled by a different abstraction, it feels logical to move those two classes into a new `hms_core` module (`hms_core.messaging`), and add the new abstraction there instead—that way, all of the messaging-related classes are in one place. Moving the custom exception, `InvalidMessageError`, to the new module also feels like a sensible step, since it is also strictly message-related.

Those code moves require some trivial changes to the Artisan Gateway service's main module, such as changing the original imports from this:

```
from hms_core.daemons import BaseDaemon, DaemonMessage, \
    InvalidMessageError
from hms_core.daemons import BaseDaemon
```

To the following:

```
from hms_core.daemons import BaseDaemon
from hms_core.messaging import DaemonMessage, InvalidMessageError
```

Similar changes are also necessary in any of the test scripts that have been generated in order for them to still be useful.

This sort of code reorganization is probably inevitable, at least on a long-term basis: it's just a matter of time before something just doesn't feel right where it lives, and needs to be moved to a better location. In general, the earlier the need for a reorganization like this is caught, the better, as it will tend to be less troublesome or disruptive because there's less chance of broken interactions with code if there's less code to interact with. It also probably goes without saying, but it's always a good idea to rerun any test code that might have been created to assure that nothing is egregiously broken before moving on. In this case, the final test script for the daemon (`scratch-space/daemon-artisan-tests.py`) revealed some minor issues that had to be resolved—not because of the code-move, but because it wasn't rerun before closing out the code in `Chapter 16`, *The Artisan Gateway Service*. Still, the issue was caught before it became a real bug.

Preparation for object transactions

The preceding code reorganization gives us a solid, logical place to create the new **Abstract Base Class** (**ABC**) that we mentioned earlier. The goal of this new ABC is to require derived classes to be able to provide a message-data-ready data structure that can be passed to `DaemonMessage` as the data argument in its `__init__` method, both streamlining the process of creating a message for any given object that needs one, and allowing the code for that process to exist as part of the individual data object classes themselves. In keeping with the naming convention that's evolved in the code so far, this would probably be best written as an instance method named `to_message_data`. Another option considered was `to_message_dict`, but that method name already exists elsewhere, and it doesn't relate to the `DaemonMessage` argument quite as well.

The `to_message_data` method can be completely abstract, with no concrete implementation provided in the abstract method itself—unlike many of the abstract methods defined thus far in the `hms_sys` code-base, there really isn't any common functionality to fall back on.

And that's it, really. The new ABC doesn't need anything else that comes to mind. It just defines a requirement for the new method. It doesn't even need an __init__ method, since there's nothing that would need to be passed as an instance property value (though it will still inherit the __init__ method from the object class that all classes ultimately derive from). Its entire definition, then, is as follows:

```
class HasMessageData(metaclass=abc.ABCMeta):
    """
Provides interface requirements, and type-identity for objects that
are expected to provide a to_message_data method.
    """

    ####################################
    # Abstract methods                 #
    ####################################

    @abc.abstractmethod
    def to_message_data(self) -> (dict,):
        """
Creates and returns a dictionary representation of the instance
that is safe to be passed to a DaemonMessage instance during or
after creation as the data of that message.

self ............. (HasMessageData instance, required) The
                   instance to execute against
    """
        raise NotImplementedError(
            '%s.to_message_data has not been implemented as '
            'required by HasMessageData' %
            (self.__class__.__name__)
        )
```

An ABC defined with no concrete functionality is about as close as Python code can get to the sort of formal interface declaration that other object-oriented languages provide. It's still just an Abstract Base Class, just like the other ABCs that have been built for the project so far, but all it does is generate a set of functional requirements that derived classes have to implement before they can be instantiated. In this case, when we apply HasMessageData to the various data object classes that have already been defined in the hms_core.co_objects and hms_artisan.artisan_objects namespaces (Artisan and Product classes in both, and Order in the hms_artisan namespace), this immediately establishes a requirement that those classes implement to_message_data, without caring how they get implemented.

In `hms_sys`, since the concrete `Artisan`, `Order`, and `Product` classes all derive from ABCs defined in `hms_core`, we could actually attach `HasMessageData` to those ABCs, rather than to the concrete classes. The end result would be the same—the concrete classes would be required to implement `to_message_data`—and there would be (very slightly) less work. The trade-off would be that any future classes that derived from `BaseArtisan`, `BaseOrder`, or `BaseProduct` would also be required to implement `to_message_data`, even if there was no need for that functionality. While that doesn't feel horrible, it does impose some functional requirements on future development that may not be warranted. For the time being, since we know that the current concrete classes should derive from `HasMessageData`, we'll derive them from it directly—if that needs to be changed in the future, it's a safer effort to move the requirement deeper into the inheritance tree.

The concrete implementations of `to_message_data` provides a logical hook in the code for the implementation of business rule restrictions regarding what each object is allowed to send in a message. That is, neither Artisan nor Central Office users are allowed to alter or set all state data for all objects—they each have specific properties that they control. Even in cases where the user type owns the object type (artisans and products), there are properties that the other user owns (products and `store_available`, for example). Since `to_message_data` will be used to actually generate the message data that will, in turn, be used to make changes on the receiving end of each message transaction, the simple expedient of limiting the data structure generated by it to the values that the user type can create or alter prevents illegal changes to object data by each user. We'll dig into that as we work through the specific transactions for each user/object/action combination.

Product object transactions

Since the set of Product data transactions have the largest number of individual transactions (seven), we'll start with those in the hopes that they will expose any gaps in the design sooner rather than later. Each transaction ties back to one of the original iteration stories, and the specific story that relates to the transaction process will be called out. The specific implementation of `to_message_data` for the user/object combination will be defined in the first transaction for that combination, and refined if/as needed in subsequent transaction details. Any other specific needs for that particular combination will also be addressed.

Since all of the varied operations against any objects require the object to be identified, the one constant in all `to_message_data` outputs is the `oid` property of the object being transmitted. It plays a significant role in each of the operations:

- When creating a new object, the `oid` has to be provided in the message so that we don't end up with different unique identifiers across different application installations or environments. That's already taken care of by the generation of the `oid` value, which is inherited from `BaseDataObject`, where the `oid` is created if it doesn't exist.
- When updating an existing object, the `oid` has to be provided so that the original object can be retrieved and altered.
- When deleting an existing object, the same identification need exists—the `oid` has to be provided in order to identify which object is being deleted.
- Although we don't have a use case yet for a response message (more or less equivalent to a read in the standard CRUD operations structure), it, too would require an `oid` value in order to identify which object should be fetched and returned.

Artisan – creating a product

The relevant story for an Artisan's need to create a Product, from the list earlier, is:

- As an Artisan, I need to be able to create `Product` objects so that I can manage my `Product` offerings

Artisan users own the majority of the data points for a `Product` object. In fact, the only property that they really shouldn't be able to create or alter is the `store_available` flag that controls whether a given Product is available on the Web Storefront that the Central Office runs. As a result, the output of `to_message_data` for `hms_artisan.artisan_objects.Product` looks very much like its `to_data_dict` method:

```
def to_message_data(self) -> (dict,):
    """
Creates and returns a dictionary representation of the instance
that is safe to be passed to a DaemonMessage instance during or
after creation as the data of that message.
    """
    return {
        'oid':str(self.oid),
        # - Properties from BaseProduct:
```

```
        'available':self.available,
        'description':self.description,
        'dimensions':self.dimensions,
        'metadata':self.metadata,
        'name':self.name,
        'shipping_weight':self.shipping_weight,
        'summary':self.summary,
        # - Date/time values, since we may well want/need to
        #   keep those in sync across environments
        'created':datetime.strftime(
            self.created, self.__class__._data_time_string
        ),
        'modified':datetime.strftime(
            self.modified, self.__class__._data_time_string
        ),
    }
```

The `created` and `modified` values are included in this data structure, operating under the assumption that they should also be kept in sync across the Artisan and Central Office data stores—that might, if nothing else, allow the UI logic to more easily detect when something has changed that the UI needs to be aware of before displaying instance data, though it would almost certainly require some standardization of a common time—one across all application and service instances.

Given a new `Product` object (`new_product`) and the signing key for the Artisan (`signing_key`), transmission of the `new_product` to the Artisan Gateway service becomes very simple:

```
new_product_message = DaemonMessage(
    'create', new_product.to_message_data(), signing_key
)
# - Assumes that RabbitMQSender has already been configured...
#   it would be slightly more involved if this were the first time
#   it was used...
sender = RabbitMQSender()
sender.send_message(new_product_message)
```

The Artisan Gateway method that accepts those messages and actually creates the new `Product` is `ArtisanGatewayDaemon.create_product`. Since it's a method in a service, and especially since it makes changes to data (creating new data, in this case), there's nearly as much logging of its processes as there is process itself, though much of it is debugging logging, and will only be logged if the service is configured to log events at that level:

```
def create_product(self, properties:(dict,)) -> None:
    self.info('%s.create_product called' % self.__class__.__name__)
```

```
if type(properties) != dict:
    raise TypeError(
        '%s.create_product expects a dict of Product '
        'properties, but was passed "%s" (%s)' %
        (
            self.__class__.__name__, properties,
            type(properties).__name__
        )
    )
self.debug('properties ... %s:' % (type(properties)))
self.debug(str(properties))
# - Create the new object...
new_object = Product.from_data_dict(properties)
self.debug('New object created successfully')
#    ...and save it.
new_object.save()
self.info(
    'New Product %s created successfully' % new_object.oid
)
```

At this point, the various Gateway methods aren't making any determination about whether the incoming message is authorized to make the changes that the method is making. We'll examine this later on.

Central Office – approving/listing a product

The relevant Story for Central Office staff being able to activate products, from the earlier collection of stories is:

- As a Product Manager, I need to be able to activate Product objects so that I can manage Product availability

The Central Office owns the store_available flag of products, so their version of to_message_dict, living in hms_code.co_objects.Product, is, at least initially, much simpler:

```
def to_message_data(self) -> (dict,):
    """
Creates and returns a dictionary representation of the instance
that is safe to be passed to a DaemonMessage instance during or
after creation as the data of that message.
    """
    return {
        'oid':str(self.oid),
```

```
        # - Properties from BaseProduct:
        'store_available':self.store_available,
        # - Date/time values, since we may well want/need to
        #   keep those in sync across environments
        'modified':datetime.strftime(
            self.modified, self.__class__._data_time_string
        ),
    }
```

The related message transmission, with a `product_to_activate` Product object and the Central Office `signing_key` is just as easy as the new-Product transmission that we looked at prior:

```
product_message = DaemonMessage(
    'update', product_to_activate.to_message_data(), signing_key
)
sender = RabbitMQSender()
sender.send_message(product_message)
```

The same message structure and transmission process will also address the Central Office's need to be able to deactivate products, another of the original iteration stories:

- As a Product Manager, I need to be able to deactivate `Product` objects so that I can manage `Product` availability

The Artisan Gateway method that accepts those messages and updates the relevant `Product` is `ArtisanGatewayDaemon.update_product`. Like `create_product`, it logs fairly extensively through its execution:

```
def update_product(self, properties:(dict,)) -> None:
    self.info('%s.update_product called' % self.__class__.__name__)
    if type(properties) != dict:
        raise TypeError(
            '%s.update_product expects a dict of Product '
            'properties, but was passed "%s" (%s)' %
            (
                self.__class__.__name__, properties,
                type(properties).__name__
            )
        )
    self.debug('properties ... %s:' % (type(properties)))
    self.debug(str(properties))
    # - Retrieve the existing object, and get its data-dict
    #   representation
    existing_object = Product.get(properties['oid'])
    self.debug(
```

```
                'Product %s retrieved successfully' % existing_object.oid
        )
        data_dict = existing_object.to_data_dict()
        # - Update the data-dict with the values from properties
        data_dict.update(properties)
        # - Make sure it's flagged as dirty, so that save will
        #    *update* instead of *create* the instance-record,
        #    for data-stores where that applies
        data_dict['is_dirty'] = True
        # - Create a new instance of the class with the revised
        #    data-dict...
        new_object = Product.from_data_dict(data_dict)
        #    ...and save it.
        new_object.save()
        self.info('Product %s updated successfully' % new_object.oid)
```

Central Office – altering product data

The relevant story for a Central Office need to alter Product data, from the list earlier, is:

- As a Product Manager, I need to be able to update Product objects so that I can manage Product information that an Artisan can't

It's not unreasonable to assume that the Central Office will want to be able to make changes to specific Product properties without having to send them through an Artisan—making minor spelling corrections, or similar, simple changes to Product content that's carried over to their Web Storefront. Since there isn't any solid definition of what properties would be involved, let's assume that those properties include the name, description, and summary of a Product. In that case, the to_message_data that was created for hms_code.co_objects.Product needs to be altered to include those values:

```
def to_message_data(self) -> (dict,):
    """
Creates and returns a dictionary representation of the instance
that is safe to be passed to a DaemonMessage instance during or
after creation as the data of that message.
    """
    return {
        'oid':str(self.oid),
        # - Properties from BaseProduct:
        'description':self.description,
        'name':self.name,
        'store_available':self.store_available,
```

```
'summary':self.summary,
# - Date/time values, since we may well want/need to
#   keep those in sync across environments
'modified':datetime.strftime(
    self.modified, self.__class__._data_time_string
),
}
```

This implementation introduces a potentially unwanted side effect: any update operation executed by a Central Office user can update all of these properties at once. If that behavior is not desired, then there are options that could be pursued:

- Additional methods could be added to `ArtisanGatewayDaemon` to handle more specific actions, such as `set_product_availability`, which would only change the `store_available` flag value. That would likely require the following:

  - The addition of a corresponding allowed `operation` to `DaemonMessage`
  - To check messages that originate with an Artisan so that they can't accidentally or intentionally perform a store availability change that they shouldn't be allowed to

- Filtering of the outbound message data, to remove any elements from it that don't apply to a specific operation, could be implemented as part of the message generation:

  - Helper methods could be added to the concrete `Product` classes to perform that filtering
  - The UI could be made responsible for determining what kind of message should be sent, and it could perform that filtering

At present, there doesn't appear to be any real harm in allowing any update action to update across multiple logical operations, though, so it can be left alone for now.

Alterations by this Central Office role, for now, can be handled by the same message construction, transmission and, handling processes in use by the approval/listing action—it's just another variant of a data update.

Artisan – updating product data

The relevant story for an Artisan's need to update Product data, from the list earlier, is:

- As an Artisan, I need to be able to update `Product` objects so that I can manage my `Product` offerings

The only real difference between Artisan update and create transactions is the `operation` associated with the outgoing message—we've already included the `modified` property in the results of `to_message_data` in Artisan `Product` objects:

```
product_message = DaemonMessage(
    'update', product_to_update.to_message_data(), signing_key
)
sender = RabbitMQSender()
sender.send_message(product_message)
```

Data alterations originating from an Artisan are, from a process standpoint, identical to data changes that originate from a Central Office user—they can use the same `ArtisanGatewayDaemon.update_product` method to actually execute those changes—so there's no new code needed for them.

Since artisans also control a Product availability flag (available), the same considerations noted for the Central Office Product approval listing would apply at the Artisan level. Those encompass two stories that weren't part of the original iteration story set, but should be included for the sake of completeness:

- As an Artisan, I need to be able to activate `Product` objects so that I can manage `Product` availability
- As an Artisan, I need to be able to deactivate `Product` objects so that I can manage `Product` availability

These, too, can be handled by the same, existing data update process already defined, so long as there's no requirement to isolate activation/deactivation changes from other changes to the data structure. Even if such a requirement were to surface, it would be feasible to handle them at the message origination side of the transaction, limiting the content of the message to only the `active` flag and the `oid` that identifies the product to be activated or deactivated.

Artisan – deleting a product

The relevant story for an Artisan's need to delete a Product, from the list earlier, is:

- As an Artisan, I need to be able to delete `Product` objects so that I can manage my `Product` offerings

As noted earlier, deletion actions really only require the `oid` of the item being deleted in order to successfully execute. Any other information would be wasted bandwidth, though if that's not a concern, the code for a deletion really only differs in the `operation` sent in the message again:

```
product_message = DaemonMessage(
    'delete', product_to_delete.to_message_data(), signing_key
)
sender = RabbitMQSender()
sender.send_message(product_message)
```

Executing a more tightly focused message is not difficult—it doesn't require anything more, ultimately, than taking more direct control of the message data, limiting it to just the relevant object ID. One approach would be to create the message data directly, like this:

```
message_data = {
    'oid':str(product_to_delete.oid)
}
product_message = DaemonMessage('delete',message_data, signing_key)
sender = RabbitMQSender()
sender.send_message(product_message)
```

The corresponding deletion method in the Artisan Gateway (`delete_product`) is a lot simpler than those corresponding to the create or update processes for the same reason: all that's really needed is the `oid` of the object whose data is to be deleted:

```
def delete_product(self, properties:(dict,)) -> None:
    self.info('%s.delete_product called' % self.__class__.__name__)
    self.debug(str(properties))
    # - Delete the instance-record for the specified object
    Product.delete(properties['oid'])
    self.debug(
        'Product %s deleted successfully' % properties['oid']
    )
```

Artisan object transactions

The processes for sending `Artisan` object messages will not deviate significantly from the examples shown previously for `Product` objects. The creation and transmission of `create` and `update` messages will typically follow a structure that looks something like this:

```
# - Typical create-object message-creation and -transmission
create_message = DaemonMessage(
    'create', object_to_create.to_message_data(), signing_key
)
sender = RabbitMQSender()
sender.send_message(create_message)

# - Typical update-object message-creation and -transmission
update_message = DaemonMessage(
    'update', object_to_update.to_message_data(), signing_key
)
sender = RabbitMQSender()
sender.send_message(update_message)
```

Deletion messages, depending on what decision is made regarding sending the full object dataset, or just the required `oid` value, will typically follow one of these two structures:

```
# - Transmit the full object-data-set as the delete-message
delete_message = DaemonMessage(
    'delete', object_to_delete.to_message_data(), signing_key
)
sender = RabbitMQSender()
sender.send_message(delete_message)

# - Transmit *only* the required oid as the delete-message:
message_data = {
    'oid':str(product_to_delete.oid)
}
delete_message = DaemonMessage('delete', message_data, signing_key)
sender = RabbitMQSender()
sender.send_message(delete_message)
```

Artisan objects, like Product objects, are not complicated from the standpoint of their CRUD operations methods in the Artisan Gateway service. Indeed, apart from the specifics of which objects are being worked on, and the specific expected structure of the command messages associated with the various methods involved in executing those operations, they are identical to their Product object counterparts. For example, the update_artisan method of the Artisan Gateway service looks like this:

```
def update_artisan(self, properties:(dict,)) -> None:
    self.info('%s.update_artisan called' % self.__class__.__name__)
    if type(properties) != dict:
        raise TypeError(
            '%s.update_artisan expects a dict of Artisan '
            'properties, but was passed "%s" (%s)' %
            (
                self.__class__.__name__, properties,
                type(properties).__name__
            )
        )
    self.debug('properties ... %s:' % (type(properties)))
    self.debug(str(properties))
    # - Retrieve the existing object, and get its data-dict
    #   representation
    existing_object = Artisan.get(properties['oid'])
    self.debug(
        'Artisan %s retrieved successfully' % existing_object.oid
    )
    data_dict = existing_object.to_data_dict()
    # - Update the data-dict with the values from properties
    data_dict.update(properties)
    # - Make sure it's flagged as dirty, so that save will
    #   *update* instead of *create* the instance-record,
    #   for data-stores where that applies
    data_dict['is_dirty'] = True
    # - Create a new instance of the class with the revised
    #   data-dict...
    new_object = Artisan.from_data_dict(data_dict)
    #   ...and save it.
    new_object.save()
    self.info('Artisan %s updated successfully' % new_object.oid)
```

Across the board, then, the various Artisan operations follow the same patterns as those established by/for the Product operations.

Central Office – creating an artisan

The relevant Story for Central Office staff being able to create an Artisan, from the earlier collection of stories is:

- As an Artisan Manager, I need to be able to create `Artisan` objects so that I can manage artisans

`Artisan` objects are unusual, in that while they are logically owned by the Artisan that they represent, they are created by the Central Office. This implies that two radically different message formats will be needed by the Central Office code-base: one to create an `Artisan` and one to update it. If we start with a complete message structure for creation purposes, we can better evaluate whether it presents any risks or complications in the update process later:

```python
def to_message_data(self) -> (dict,):
    """
Creates and returns a dictionary representation of the instance
that is safe to be passed to a DaemonMessage instance during or
after creation as the data of that message.
    """
    return {
        'oid':str(self.oid),
        # - BaseArtisan-derived items
        'address':self.address.to_dict() if self.address else None,
        'company_name':self.company_name,
        'contact_email':self.contact_email,
        'contact_name':self.contact_name,
        'website':self.website,
        # - BaseDataObject-derived items
        'created':datetime.strftime(
            self.created, self.__class__._data_time_string
        ),
        'modified':datetime.strftime(
            self.modified, self.__class__._data_time_string
        ),
        # Queue- and signing-key values
        'queue_id':self.queue_id,
        'signing_key':self.signing_key.hex(),
    }
```

Since the process for creating an `Artisan` should almost certainly involve the creation and storage of the identifier of the message queue that's associated with Artisan (`queue_id`) and an initial `signing_key`, those values are included in the Central Office's `Artisan.to_message_data` method. We still have to define how signing keys and queue identifiers are actually created within the `Artisan` objects, but they will have to be sent along to the Artisan Gateway in some fashion so that they'll be available for use in sending, receiving, and validating messages to and from an Artisan Application instance.

These processes are significant from a security perspective: remember that the signing key is considered a **secret** data value, one that should be treated with caution, and not transmitted needlessly or without some attention to safeguarding the data. In many respects, it's equivalent to a user password—a secret value that is associated with one and only one user. If the signing key is a password, then the queue identifier could be considered roughly equivalent to a username—data that is, perhaps, not quite as secret, but that should still be treated with caution because it potentially uniquely identifies a user, and is associated with a true secret, together forming a set of user credentials. As the implementation- details around `queue_id` and `signing_key` creation and management unfold, it's quite probable that we'll have to revisit this message structure, so for now, we'll leave it in its current state.

Central Office – updating artisan data

The relevant Story for Central Office staff being able to update an Artisan's data, from the earlier collection of stories is:

- As an Artisan Manager, I need to be able to update `Artisan` objects so that I can manage artisans

Once an `Artisan` object has been created, most of its properties are arguably owned by the Artisan that the object represents. Certainly, from a common sense standpoint, the Artisan user is in the best position to know whether their data is current, and it's in their best interests to keep that data current. That said, and setting aside the `queue_id` and `signing_key` properties until their processes have been fleshed out in more detail, the risks of allowing Central Office users to modify Artisan data don't feel significant, provided that changes made are propagated to, and can also be changed by the Artisan users themselves. The caveat to this scenario is that the `oid` property shouldn't be changeable by anyone—Central Office or Artisan users—but that almost goes without saying. It is, after all, the unique identifier for the `Artisan` object, and unique identifiers should never be changed lightly.

With all of that in mind, no modifications to the Central Office's `Artisan.to_message_data` method are needed to fulfil this story yet, though alterations may well surface, as with the creation process, as the `queue_id` and `signing_key` management processes are defined and implemented.

Central Office – deleting an artisan

The relevant Story for Central Office staff being able to delete an Artisan's data, from the earlier collection of stories is:

- As an Artisan Manager, I need to be able to delete `Artisan` objects so that I can manage artisans

Although the process of deleting an Artisan may have other implications—removal, or at least deactivation of all their products, for example—there aren't any that come to mind from the perspective of generating deletion command messages. Like the deletion process for `Product` objects, the only property value that's really needed is the `oid` of the Artisan to be deleted, and whatever decision is made about using the full message body or creating a specific one for deletion process purposes in that context will probably apply to this context as well.

Artisan – updating Artisan data

The relevant Story for Artisan being able to update an Artisan's data, from the earlier collection of stories is:

- As an Artisan, I need to be able to update my own `Artisan` object so that I can manage my information at the HMS Central Office.

No matter what the eventual shape of the processes surrounding the `queue_id` and `signing_key` properties of an `Artisan` turns out to be, those values, as secrets, should never be sent across the open internet without some protection—encrypting them while in motion, at a minimum. Without those values, changes to Artisan data by Artisan users can travel unencrypted, so the base message structure for Artisan updates is nearly a duplicate of the equivalent in the Central Office's namespace:

```
def to_message_data(self) -> (dict,):
    """
Creates and returns a dictionary representation of the instance
that is safe to be passed to a DaemonMessage instance during or
after creation as the data of that message.
```

```
        """
                return {
                    'oid':str(self.oid),
                    # - BaseArtisan-derived items
                    'address':self.address.to_dict() if self.address else
None,
                    'company_name':self.company_name,
                    'contact_email':self.contact_email,
                    'contact_name':self.contact_name,
                    'website':self.website,
                    # - BaseDataObject-derived items
                    'created':datetime.strftime(
                        self.created, self.__class__._data_time_string
                    ),
                    'modified':datetime.strftime(
                        self.modified, self.__class__._data_time_string
                    )
                }
```

Between the Central Office and Artisan code-bases, we're allowing either user type to alter most of an Artisan's data. The majority of it is some variation of contact information, none of which has any functional implications, and the balance has policies that have already been set down, if not implemented yet (oid), or is still pending further definition (queue_id and signing_key). The worst risk that seems even remotely likely with both user types having full control over these properties is either simultaneous conflicting changes (probably best handled at the UI level), or ongoing conflicting changes (one user changing a value, the other changing it back, the first changing it again, and so on).

Order object transactions

orders, and their corresponding objects in the system, haven't been discussed much since the definition of the concrete Order class in the artisan_objects module. In part, this is because the other classes (particularly Artisan and Product) are representations of data that originate in the hms_sys code-bases. Still, the artisan_objects.Order class was left in about as complete a state as could be expected, with full data persistence and a concrete implementation that was expected to deal with all the requirements against it up to that point.

As a result, though, several aspects of orders fell off the radar. The original set of stories for this iteration only included one Order-related story—an Artisan's need to be able to update an Order as part of a fulfillment process—with nothing that provided any path for that Order to get to an Artisan to begin with, let alone anything prior to that. There also wasn't any accommodation for the potential of an order being canceled before its fulfillment was complete. Accounting for the customer-to-gateway and gateway-to-Artisan paths of those items, they adds four new stories that will be addressed first.

Dealing with orders is also complicated somewhat by the fact that the specifics of the Web Storefront system have been left intentionally vague. There are dozens of options available, if not hundreds, written in most of the popular/mainstream languages, and with varying degrees of extensibility. Rather than picking any one, a fundamental assumption was made that `hms_sys` integration could be accomplished in some fashion, which could include at least the following possibilities:

- A brute-force process, executing on a schedule, could acquire new, raw Order information from the store's data, and fire off the Artisan Gateway's Order creation process
- The store system, through some sort of small, custom extension, could fire off a create Order message to the Artisan Gateway, either directly or through the message queue, executing its Order creation process
- If the store system were written in Python (there are at least eleven options in this field), it might actually be able to import whatever `hms_sys` code is needed, perhaps add some configuration, and directly execute the relevant `hms_sys` code

In a real-world scenario, the cross-system integration would probably have been a significant set of very specific requirements—but for the purposes of illustration, and to keep focused on the project, those were intentionally left aside.

Customer – relaying order items to artisans

The relevant Story for Customer being able to relay Order items to artisans, from the earlier collection of stories is:

- As a Customer, I need the relevant parts of my Order to be relayed to the appropriate artisans so that they can fulfill their part of my Order.

orders have a significantly more complex life cycle than any of the other objects in
hms_sys. Unlike Artisan objects, or perhaps Product objects, they are expected to
have a short active lifespan; being created, processed once, then archived or perhaps
even deleted. Artisan objects, in contrast, once created, are expected to persist for as
long as the Central Office/Artisan relationship lasts. Product objects may or may not
persist in an active state for long periods of time, but can also last as long as the
Central Office/Artisan relationship of their owning artisans continues. In both of these
cases, though the length of their life cycles may vary substantially, they are basically
created and persisted (with or without modification) indefinitely.

By contrast, a relatively simple Order, moving through a simple subset of what
hms_sys could support, might look like this:

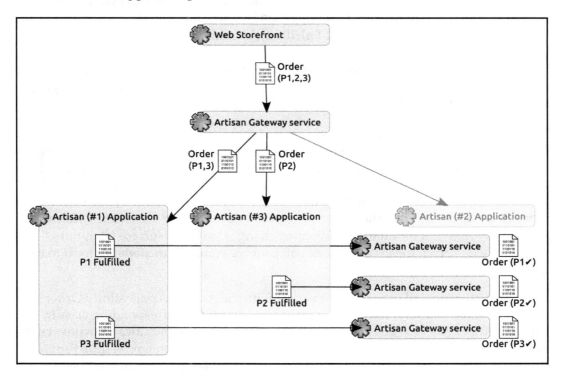

Where:

- The initial **Order** (for `Product` objects **P1, P2,** and **P3**) is created by the **Web Storefront** and is handed off to the **Artisan Gateway** for distribution to and handling by the relevant Artisan users
- The **Artisan Gateway** sends **Order** messages to the **Artisan Applications** associated with the artisans whose products are in the **Order** (**Artisan #2,** in this example, exists, but the Order doesn't contain any of their products):
    - One **Order**, for products **P1** and **P3**, is sent to **Artisan #1**
    - One **Order** for Product **P2** is sent to **Artisan #3**
- **Artisan #1** fulfils the part of the order for Product **P1** (**P1 Fulfilled**), which sends an update message for the **Order** back to the **Artisan Gateway**, where the fulfillment of that portion is noted and stored
- A similar cycle occurs (**P2 Fulfilled**) for **Artisan #3**, with respect to Product **P2** from the original Order
- The final fulfillment cycle (**P3 Fulfilled**) is executed by **Artisan #1**
- The Order, with all of its fulfillment complete, can be archived, deleted, or handled in whatever other way is needed

Since no concrete `Order` class was ever created that the Artisan Gateway service would be able to access, that's the first thing that needs to be done. Without knowing precisely how Order data is going to be relayed to the service, but still needing to be able to perform round trip testing of the process later, there's little more that can be done than to define it as a basic class derived from `HMSMongoDataObject` (like the other data object classes in the `co_objects` module) and from `BaseOrder` (from the `business_objects` module). Additions or changes to it may surface later, but deriving `Order` from those two classes will provide enough functionality for it to be testable.

After going through all of the analysis effort with the Artisan Application's Order class definition, that feels like a better starting point for the corresponding class in the Central Office code (`co_objects`), though it will need some modification/conversion in the process. First and foremost, it needs to derive from `HMSMongoDataObject` instead of `JSONFileDataObject`—but since both of those, in turn, are derived from `BaseDataObject`, a fair portion of the new `Order` class is already implemented with that inheritance change.

TIP

There's enough common code between the two `Order` classes that it would almost certainly be worth spending time moving those common items back down into `BaseOrder`. Designing, or even implementing concrete classes, then gathering their common functionality into common parent classes is just as valid a design or implementation approach as starting from the foundations and building out, though it happened accidentally in this case.

Beyond that, we'll need a mechanism that will allow the Web Storefront system to create an `Order`. So far, we don't have any specifications around that process, but that doesn't stop us from creating a class method that will (hopefully) eventually be used in that capacity. For near future testing purposes, it will be set up to accept a `BaseCustomer` object that's derived as a `customer`, and a list of Product identifiers, with an eye toward the `customer` being revised at some point in the future. To start with, all we're concerned with is a method that can be called to create a complete `Order` with the relevant `Product` objects attached to it:

```
def create_order_from_store(
    cls, customer:(BaseCustomer,str,dict), **order_items
):
    """
Creates and returns a new order-instance, whose state is populated
with data from the

customer .......... (Type TBD, required) The customer that placed
                   the order
order_items ....... (dict [oid:quantity], required) The items and
                   their quantities in the order
    """
```

It feels reasonably safe to assume that the storefront will be able to pass Product identifiers and their quantities in the Order along as some sort of `dict` value, and that it won't be keeping track of entire `Product` objects, at least not in the same structure that `hms_sys` code uses. Given the list of Product `oid` values available in the `keys()` of the `order_items`, retrieving products to be added to the `order` instance on creation is simply a matter of filtering all available products down into a collection of the specific items in the Order, while preserving their associated quantities:

```
# - Get all the products and quantities identified by the
#   incoming oid-values in order_items
products = {
    product:order_items[str(product.oid)]
    for product in Product.get()
```

```
            if str(product.oid) in order_items.keys()
    ]
```

The products generated here are dicts, generated by a dictionary comprehension, whose keys are `Product` objects, and values are the quantities of those products in the Order. Then, we need to acquire the `customer`:

```
# TODO: Determine how customer-data is going to be #provided
# (probably a key/value string, could be a JSON packet
# that could be converted to a dict), and find or create
# a customer object if/as needed. In the interim, for
# testing purposes, accept a BaseCustomer-derived object.
    if not isinstance(customer, BaseCustomer):
        raise NotImplementedError(
            "%s.create_order_from_store doesn't yet accept "
            "customer arguments that aren't BaseCustomer-"
            "derived objects, sorry" % (cls.__name__)
        )
```

Finally, the new `Order` instance is created, saved (assuring that its data is persisted), and returned (in case the calling code needs to reference it immediately after it's been created):

```
# - Create the order-instance, making sure it's tagged
#   as new and not dirty so that the save process will
#   call _create
new_order = cls(
    customer, is_dirty=False, is_new=True, *products
)
# - Save it and return it
new_order.save()
return new_order
```

The `Order` class will also need a `to_message_data` method, just like their Product and Artisan counterparts, and with one defined, can use a message transmission process that is basically identical to what was established earlier:

```
def to_message_data(self) -> (dict,):
    """
Creates and returns a dictionary representation of the instance
that is safe to be passed to a DaemonMessage instance during or
after creation as the data of that message.
    """
    return {
        # - Local properties
        'name':self.name,
        'street_address':self.street_address,
```

```
'building_address':self.building_address,
'city':self.city,
'region':self.region,
'postal_code':self.postal_code,
'country':self.country,
# - Generate a string:int dict from the UUID:int dict
'items':{
    str(key):int(self.items[key])
    for key in self.items.keys()
},
# - Properties from BaseDataObject (through
#   HMSMongoDataObject)
'modified':datetime.strftime(
    self.modified, self.__class__._data_time_string
),
'oid':str(self.oid),
}
```

This process implies a new story that will probably be needed mostly for UI development, but that might have some implications in additional design and implementation of the Artisan Applications:

- As an Artisan, I need to be informed when an Order has been placed that includes one of my Product offerings so that I can fulfill my part of that Order

Since the creation of a new `Order` by the Web Storefront also needs to relay new `Order` objects to each Artisan (looking back at the Order flow diagram), and since it seems reasonable to expect that only the store-to-Gateway-service portion of that flow would be calling `create_order_from_store`, that seems like a reasonable place to implement that messaging at first glance, but in doing so, there would be no access to the service's logging facilities, so any failures in communication between the two systems would potentially be lost. If, instead, the Web Storefront were to issue a create Order message to the Artisan Gateway, the Gateway service could in turn call `create_order_from_store` with the applicable data, and log events as needed/desired while it executes. For the purposes of illustration, this is the approach that is going to be assumed. In this case, `create_order_from_store` is complete as it stands, and the Artisan/Order messaging happens as part of the Gateway service's `create_order` method. The first major chunk of its code looks very much like the other create processes:

```
def create_order(self, properties:(dict,)) -> None:
    self.info('%s.create_order called' % self.__class__.__name__)
    if type(properties) != dict:
```

```
        raise TypeError(
            '%s.create_order expects a dict of Order '
            'properties, but was passed "%s" (%s)' %
            (
                self.__class__.__name__, properties,
                type(properties).__name__
            )
        )
    self.debug('properties ... %s:' % (type(properties)))
    self.debug(str(properties))
# - Create the new object...
    new_order = Order.create_order_from_store(properties)
    self.info(
        'New Order %s created successfully' % new_order.oid
    )
```

Since the `create_order_from_store` method already saves the new Order, we don't need to save it here—it will already exist in the data store, and can be retrieved by other processes as soon as this point in the code has been reached. In order to proceed, and send the necessary `Order` messages to the individual artisans who need to be aware of them, we need to sort out which products (and in what quantities) are associated with each Artisan in the system.

Since the `Artisan` can have a `Product`, but a `Product` doesn't keep track of which `Artisan` they belong to (which might be a good thing to add, in retrospect), the best option we have right now is to load up the `Artisan`, and search for it for each product. This is not optimal, and definitely worth looking at changing, but it will work for now.

The `new_order` variable is holding on to an `Order` object that, if expressed as a dict, would look like this:

```
{
    'oid':<UUID>,
    'name':<str>,
    # - Shipping-address properties
    'street_address':<str>,
    'building_address':<str> or None,
    'city':<str>,
    'region':<str>,
    'postal_code':<str>,
    'country':<str> or None,
    # - order-items
    'items':{
        <Product object #1>:<int>,
```

```
    <Product object #2>:<int>,
    <Product object #3>:<int>,
},
}
```

Rendering that down into a dict of Artisan/item:quantity values is simple, if done in a brute-force manner:

```
artisan_orders = {}
# - Get all the artisans
all_artisans = Artisan.get()
# - Sort out which artisan is associated with each item
#   in the order, and create or add to a list of
#   products:quantities for each
for product in new_order.products:
    try:
        artisan = [
            candidate for candidate in all_artisans
            if product.oid in [
                p.oid for p in candidate.products
            ]
        ][0]
```

If an Artisan is found that's associated with the Product, then one of two cases needs to execute: either the `artisan` already exists as a key in the `artisan_orders` dict, in which case we just append the item data to the current list of items associated with the `artisan`, or they haven't had a Product match yet, in which case we create an entry for the `artisan`, whose value is a list containing the item data in question:

```
item_data = {
  str(oid):new_order.products[product]
}
if artisan_orders.get(artisan):
    artisan_orders[artisan].append(item_data)
else:
    artisan_orders[artisan] = [item_data]
if artisan_orders.get(artisan):
    artisan_orders[artisan].append(product)
else:
    artisan_orders[artisan] = [product]
```

Although it shouldn't happen, it's possible that an Order could come in with a Product that has no identifiable `artisan` to associate with it. The specifics of how that error case should be handled may be dependent on the web store system. Even setting that consideration aside, it should be handled in some fashion that hasn't been defined yet. At a minimum, however, the failure should be logged:

```
except IndexError:
    self.error(
        '%s.create_order could not find an '
        'artisan-match for the product %s' %
        (product.oid)
    )
self.debug('All artisan/product associations handled')
```

Once this sorting has completed, the `artisan_orders` dict will look something like this, with each key in `artisan_orders` being an actual `Artisan` object, with all of the properties and methods of any such instance, with the Product `oid` and quantities associated:

```
{
    <Artisan #1>:{
        <str<UUID>>:<int>,
        <str<UUID>>:<int>,
    },
    <Artisan ...>:{
        <str<UUID>>:<int>,
    },
    <Artisan #{whatever}>:{
        <str<UUID>>:<int>,
        <str<UUID>>:<int>,
    },
}
```

Python dict instances can use *almost* anything as a key: any immutable built-in type (like `str` and `int` values, and even `tuple` values, but not `list` or other `dict` values) can be used as a key in a `dict`. In addition, instances of user-defined classes, or even those classes themselves, are viable. Instances of built-in classes, or the built-in classes themselves, may not be valid `dict` keys, though.

With a complete and well-formed `artisan_orders`, the process of sending Order messages to each Artisan is relatively simple—iterating over each Artisan key, building the message data in the structure that the Artisan Application's `Order` class expects, creating a `DaemonMessage` to sign the message, and sending it:

```
sender = RabbitMQSender()
self.info('Sending order-messages to artisans:')
for artisan in artisan_orders:
# Get the products that this artisan needs to be concerned #with
items = artisan_orders[artisan]
# - Create a message-structure that
#     artisan_objects.Order.from_message_dict can handle
new_order_data = {
    'target':'order',
    'properties':{
        'name':new_order.name,
        'street_address':new_order.street_address,
            'building_address':new_order.building_address,
            'city':new_order.city,
            'region':new_order.region,
            'postal_code':new_order.postal_code,
            'country':new_order.country,
            'items':items,
            'oid':str(new_order.oid),
        },
    }
    # - Create the signed message
    order_message = DaemonMessage(
        'create', new_order_data, artisan.signing_key
    )
```

Sending a message to a specific Artisan requires another change: the `send_message` method of `RabbitMQSender` was not originally built to send messages to a queue other than the default it was configured with. It makes sense for each Artisan to have their own message queue for several reasons, and in order to use that specific queue, it has to be accepted as a `send_message` argument. The Gateway side call to send the message reflects that (passing `artisan.queue_id` as an argument):

```
# - Send the message to the artisan
sender.send_message(order_message, artisan.queue_id)
self.info(
    '+- Sent order-message with %d products to '
    'Artisan %s' % (len(items), artisan.oid)
)
```

The related changes in `RabbitMQSender.send_message` are not complicated: the addition of an optional `queue_name` argument, and a check to see if it has been provided, falling back to the configured default queue name is all that was needed:

```
def send_message(self, message:(DaemonMessage),
        # Added queue_name
        queue_name:(str,None)=None
    ):
    if type(message) != DaemonMessage:
        raise TypeError(
            '%s.send_message expects a DaemonMessage instance '
            'as its message argument, but was passed "%s" (%s)' %
            (
                self.__class__.__name__, message,
                type(message).__name__
            )
        )
    # Using the optional queue_name to override the default
    if not queue_name:
        queue_name = self.queue_name
    # - Note that exchange is blank -- we're just using the
    #   default exchange at this point...
    # - Also note that we're using queue_name instead of the
    #   original self.queue_name default...
    self.channel.basic_publish(
        exchange='', routing_key=queue_name,
        body=message.to_message_json()
    )
```

Customer – canceling an order

The relevant Story for Customer being able to cancel an Order, from the earlier collection of stories is:

- As a Customer who has canceled an Order, I need the relevant parts of that cancellation to be relayed to the appropriate artisans so that they won't fulfill their part of the Order.

Order cancellation has one aspect in common with Order creation: the origin point of a cancellation should be with a customer, almost certainly as some functionality available through the Web Storefront. Operating under the same assumptions that shaped the creation of an Order, so that the Web Storefront will be able to send a message to the Artisan Gateway service to indicate that a cancellation has been initiated, similarly allows the Gateway to handle it in a single message handler method: `delete_order`, in this case.

The `delete_order` message handler method is, ultimately, two tasks that it must perform:

- Given an Order, identified by an `oid`, it has to track down which artisans were involved with the initial Order. That part of the process can be identical to the identification of artisans and products in `create_order`. The Product identification aspect of that code may not be needed, but it doesn't do any harm to include it, and it might even be leveraged later on to prevent the cancellation of orders that have been partially fulfilled.

- It has to generate and send a message to each Artisan Application associated with an Artisan who's associated with the Order: a delete message with the Order's `oid` as the data payload.

 The Artisan/Product association, yielding `artisan_orders` in the `create_order` and `delete_order` code, would probably be worth moving into a common helper method in the `ArtisanGatewayDaemon` class: it's identical to being written in those methods as things stand right now. With only two instances of that code present right now, and those being close together in the code, it's not an imperative, perhaps, but as long as there are two instances of the same code, any changes to one have to be made to the other as well.

Like the Order creation process, Order cancellation implies a new story, again probably needed mostly for UI development, but that might have some additional design and implementation implications for the Artisan Applications:

- As an Artisan, I need to be informed when an Order has been canceled that includes one of my Product offerings so that I can stop any in-process fulfillment activities related to it and update my Product status as needed

The foundation for resolving this story, when it does become active, should be mostly–if not entirely–in place as a result of the Order deletion messaging.

Artisan – fulfilling an item in an order

The relevant Story for Artisan being able to fulfil an item in an Order, from the earlier collection of stories is:

- As an Artisan, I need to be able to update Order objects so that I can indicate to the Central Office when my part of an Order is fulfilled.

Ultimately, the act of fulfilling all or part of an Order by an Artisan is just another update process, at least from a messaging standpoint. So far, though, there isn't a mechanism for keeping track of fulfilled items in any of the `Order` classes, and that's going to be problematic until it's addressed. Fortunately, the model for fulfilled items can be essentially identical to the model for the original Order items—a collection (a `dict`, specifically) of Product `oid` keys and `int` quantities. Adding that property to `artisan_objects.Order`, using the `items` property as a model or guideline, requires the following:

- Including `fulfilled_items`, a `dict`, as an argument in `__init__`, and integrating it the same way that the `items` argument/property is integrated
- Creating the `getter`, `setter`, and `deleter` methods for it
- Creating the `fulfilled_items` property, associated with `_get_fulfilled_items`
- Making sure that the `to_data_dict` method includes a representation of `fulfilled_items` in its output results
- Making sure that the `from_data_dict` class method doesn't need any special handling of an incoming `fulfilled_items` value

Since `fulfilled_items` will follow the same constraints as the `items` property of an `Order`, direct modification of the members of `fulfilled_items` is prohibited. The underlying rationale for that prohibition is similar: we want modifications of those members to be tightly controlled in order to prevent bad data changes as much as possible. At the same time, we need to allow artisans to fulfill Order items (while performing all the relevant checks to make certain that the data changes are valid).

To facilitate that, the `artisan_objects.Order` class needs a method that will be called to allow an Artisan user to mark items as fulfilled:

```
def fulfill_items(self, oid:(UUID,str), quantity:(int,)):
    """
Assigns a number of items fulfilled to a given item-oid, and sets the
is_dirty state of the instance to True
    """
```

Order fulfillment data is, for an Artisan, one of the more important datasets, so we're going to check every argument in several different ways before allowing the change to be saved. The check processes starts with standard type and value checking (stripping the error messaging out to keep the listing short):

```
if type(oid) not in (UUID,str):
    raise TypeError() # Expecting a UUID or str-UUID value
if type(oid) != UUID:
    try:
        oid = UUID(oid)
    except:
        raise ValueError() # Could not convert a str value to a UUID
if type(quantity) != int:
    raise TypeError()
if quantity < 0:
    raise ValueError() # Should not fulfill a negative quantity
```

We're also going to check to make sure that the item being fulfilled is actually part of the Order:

```
if oid not in self._items:
    raise RuntimeError(
        '%s.fulfill_item was asked to fulfill an item '
        '(%s) that doesn\'t exist in the order-items' %
        (self.__class__.__name__, oid)
    )
```

And we'll check to make sure that the fulfillment quantity isn't greater than the quantity in the Order:

```
if quantity > self._items[oid]:
    raise RuntimeError(
        '%s.fulfill_item was asked to fulfill an item '
        '(%s) in a higher quantity (%d) than was '
        'ordered (%d)' %
        (
            self.__class__.__name__, oid, quantity,
            self._items[oid]
```

```
        )
    )
# If everything checks out, then update the quantity, etc.
self._fulfilled_items[oid] = quantity
self._set_is_dirty(True)
```

Similar changes, minus the `fulfill_items` method, will also need to be made to the Central Office `Order` class (`co_objects.Order`) to handle fulfillment messages. For the time being, until we can focus on the round trip message testing in the next chapter, these can be accommodated by simply copying the code from `artisan_objects.Order`.

 Copying that much code around is another argument for refactoring the `Order` classes, re-defining `BaseOrder`, and deriving the concrete classes from it instead. Time and space constraints in this book may not allow for much discussion of this process, but we'll take at least a brief look at it, either during or after testing.

When do messages get sent?

Up until this point, we've spent a fair length of time digging in to how the relevant messaging will be generated and sent, but very little about when it happens, apart from the examination of Order creation and cancellation. Since messages correspond directly to various local CRUD operations, it's tempting to simply add the messaging calls into the `_create` and `_update` methods that they already have, making sure to account for the `is_dirty` and `is_new` flags that we defined in `BaseDataObject`. Before going down that path, though, it would be a good idea to take a look at all of the messaging processes, from origination to completion, to make sure that they have a clear process termination. The scenario that we need to make sure to avoid, using a `Product` update process as an example, looks like this:

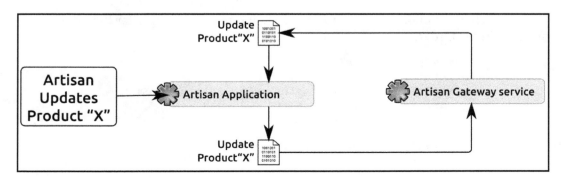

Where:

1. An **Artisan** makes a change to one of their products:
   - The local data change is executed
   - Their **Artisan Application** sends a message to the **Artisan Gateway: Update Product "X"**

2. The **Artisan Gateway** receives the message:
   - The local data change is executed
   - A message is sent to the corresponding **Artisan Application: Update Product "X"**

3. The **Artisan Application** receives the message:
   - The local data change, which likely doesn't have any updated data, is executed
   - A message is sent to the **Artisan Gateway: Update Product "X"**

At the end of the last step, the process would, without some check process or exit condition, jump back to the second step, and into an infinite loop of update messages that don't actually do anything. The same scenario could occur with any of the update processes where more than one origin point for data changes could be in play: the `Artisan` objects can be updated by the artisans they represent and by Central Office staff. `Order` objects are currently exempt, but it's not difficult to imagine a future need for a customer to alter an Order after it's been transmitted to the artisans who'd be fulfilling items in it.

Ultimately, because the `save` methods of the various data object classes have no awareness of where the data change they're executing came from, they cannot make any decisions about whether or not it's appropriate to send a message out after the data change has been executed. A possible solution, then, would be to allow (or even require) an additional argument in each `save` that provides that information, and that could be used to determine whether a message needs to be sent or not. The structure of this modification might look something like this (for a data object living in the Artisan Application's code-base):

```
def save(self, origin:(str,)):
    """
Saves the instance's state-data to the back-end data-store by
creating it if the instance is new, or updating it if the
instance is dirty
    """
    # - Perform the data-save process as it currently exists
    if self.is_new and origin != 'artisan':
        # - Send "create" message
```

```
elif self.is_dirty and origin != 'artisan':
    # - Send "update" message
self._set_is_new(False)
self._set_is_dirty(False)
```

It would be feasible to add an additional abstraction layer between `BaseDataObject` (where `save` is defined currently) and each of the concrete data objects that would override the `BaseDataObject.save` method. This abstraction–an additional ABC–would need to be created in the Artisan Application and Artisan Gateway code-bases, at a minimum, and another variant might be needed in the Central Office application as well, depending on implementation details that haven't been fully explored yet.

The trade-off is that all data objects would have to pay attention to where their data changes originated from. This feels… messy, complicated, and potentially difficult to maintain, at least at first blush.

Another possibility would be to alter `DaemonMessage`: if the messages themselves contain something, such as data that indicates where they originated from, then the handlers for those messages would be able to tell whether or not a message needs to be sent after the data change had been dealt with. In that design scenario, a `Product` update message that originated with an Artisan, including an `origin` specification, might look like this (before being converted to JSON):

```
{
    'operation':'update',
    'origin':'artisan',
    'data': {
        'target':'product',
        'properties':{
            'oid':str(new_order.oid),
            'name':'Revised Product Name',
            # - Other product-data skipped for brevity
        },
    },
    'signature':'signature hex-string'
}
```

The corresponding `update_product` handler method in the `ArtisanGatewayDaemon` service class, along with other handler methods, currently expects a `dict` (`properties`) to act upon, and is called by `ArtisanGatewayDaemon._handle_message` as the `main` loop of the service reads messages to be acted upon. We could change what the individual handler methods expect, passing the original `message` (a `DaemonMessage` instance) instead, making the handler methods responsible for breaking down the incoming `message` into the `properties` and acting upon them as they already do, and giving them the responsibility for determining whether a message needs to be sent and sending it.

Given a `DaemonMessage` with an `origin`, and a globally accessible value to compare that origin with, the decision to send a message or not, and sending it if needed, isn't complex. If it were anywhere in the Gateway service (that is, `self` is the service instance), it would look more or less like this:

```
# self.message_origin is an attribute containing 'gateway'
# - message is the incoming DaemonMessage instance
# - message.origin is 'artisan'
# - artisan is the relevant Artisan object
if message.origin == self.message_origin:
    sender = RabbitMQSender()
    outbound_message = DaemonMessage(
        operation=message.operation,
        origin=self.message_origin,
        data=message.data,
        signing_key=self.signing_key
    )
    sender.send_message(order_message, artisan.queue_id)
```

The data used to create the `outbound_message` might differ, depending on whether the data dictionary or message dictionary of the newly created or recently updated object was used instead.

So, when an incoming `message` is acted upon:

- Its `origin` is checked
- If that `origin` is local, then a corresponding `outbound_message` is created and sent, using the original `operation` of the incoming `message`, the local `origin` and `signing_key`, and whatever `data` is appropriate
- Otherwise, that entire branch is skipped

That's not a lot of code to add—a mere nine lines, assuming that the sender isn't created elsewhere. The changes to DaemonMessage are pretty trivial: adding the origin property and making sure it's accounted for everywhere (basically, anywhere that the operation property is already in use). At this point, this doesn't represent a major change to existing code either—we've only created outbound messages for Order creation and updates so far.

If there is a sticking point, it's in the need to acquire the Artisan instance that relates to the operation so that the outbound message can use the appropriate message queue (artisan.queue_id). This would be necessary no matter what approach we decide to pursue, though, so it's probably a wash in this case (and it would complicate the idea of modifying save, which we saw previously, even more).

Even with that, this feels like a solid approach. The changes to _handle_message are mostly argument and variable name changes at this point:

```python
def _handle_message(self, message:(DaemonMessage,)) -> None:
    self.info(
        '%s._handle_message called:' % self.__class__.__name__
    )
    target = message.data.get('target')
    self.debug('+- target ....... (%s) %s' % (
        type(target).__name__, target)
    )
    self.debug('+- operation .... (%s) %s' % (
        type(message.operation).__name__, message.operation)
    )
    if message.operation == 'create':
        if target == 'artisan':
            self.create_artisan(message)

# ... removed for brevity

    elif message.operation == 'update':
        if target == 'artisan':
            self.update_artisan(message)
        elif target == 'customer':
            self.update_customer(message)
        elif target == 'order':
            self.update_order(message)
        elif target == 'product':
            self.update_product(message)
        else:
            raise RuntimeError(
                '%s error: "%s" (%s) is not a recognized '
                'object-type/target' %
```

```
            (
                self.__class__.__name__, target,
                type(target).__name__
            )
        )

    # ... removed for brevity

    else:
        raise RuntimeError(
            '%s error: "%s" (%s) is not a recognized '
            'operation' %
            (
                self.__class__.__name__, message.operation,
                type(message.operation).__name__
            )
        )
```

The handler methods (using update_product, as an example) remain largely unchanged:

```
def update_product(self, message:(DaemonMessage,)) -> None:
    self.info('%s.update_product called' % self.__class__.__name__)
    if type(message) != DaemonMessage:
        raise TypeError(
            '%s.update_product expects a DaemonMessage '
            'instance, but was passed "%s" (%s)' %
            (
                self.__class__.__name__, message,
                type(message).__name__
            )
        )
```

We still need the properties; we're just acquiring them in the individual handler methods instead of in _handle_message:

```
properties = message.data.get('properties')
self.debug('properties ... %s:' % (type(properties)))
self.debug(str(properties))
```

The code, from that point until the modified object is saved, remains unchanged:

```
#   ... and save it.
new_object.save()
self.info('Product %s updated successfully' % new_object.oid)
```

And then we can check to see if an outbound message needs to be sent, acquire the relevant Artisan, create the message, and send it:

```
if message.origin == self.message_origin:
    # - Acquire the Artisan whose Product this is
    artisan = self.get_artisan_from_product(new_object)
    sender = RabbitMQSender()
    outbound_message = DaemonMessage(
        operation=message.operation,
        origin=message.origin,
        data=message.data,
        signing_key=self.signing_key
    )
    sender.send_message(order_message, artisan.queue_id)
```

Since acquiring an Artisan from a Product is going to be a recurring theme, a helper method (get_artisan_from_product) was created to streamline that process. It also highlights the eventual need for a more direct association between products and artisans, but a data object query-based process will suffice for now:

```
def get_artisan_from_product(
        self, product:(UUID,str,BaseProduct)
    ) -> (Artisan):
    # TODO: Add artisan (owner) to Product classes, and use
    #       that instead. For now, use this approach
    all_artisans = Artisan.get()
    if isinstance(product, BaseProduct):
        product = product.oid
    elif type(product) == str:
        product = UUID(product)
    for artisan in all_artisans:
        if product in [p.oid for p in artisan.products]:
            return artisan
```

A final consideration before ending this chapter: when we started this chunk of development, there was still a decision pending with respect to whether message queues were going to be implemented as a "one for all artisans" or "one for each Artisan." No formal decision was made, but there are other considerations that may have arisen as the messaging processes were being thought out:

- Each Artisan needs at least two separate message queues: one for traffic to the Artisan, and one for traffic from them. If a single queue for all traffic is implemented, then:
    - The code would have to be altered to include both an `origin` (already done) and a `destination` in order to assure that, for example, messages dropped in a queue by the Gateway weren't also read by the Gateway
    - Even with that in place, a message that hasn't been read and acted upon by the appropriate destination would almost certainly block other messages in the queue from being read and acted upon, without still more code changes and the attendant complexity
- If each Artisan has a distinct message queue for inbound and outbound messages, that entire set of complications will simply go away. There is some additional work that will be necessary—providing some means of identifying individual inbound and outbound queues—but if each queue handles only traffic in one direction, to or from one Artisan Application and the Gateway service, this simplifies things considerably, and the development cost should be pretty minimal.
- As a side benefit, since each message in a queue would, simply because it came from that queue, be immediately associable with the Artisan that the queue belongs to.

The only remaining cost in having multiple message queues is that multiple queues would exist—and that, in the main, is a cost that will be borne by the message queue server.

Summary

The development efforts in this chapter have been scattered all over the system's code-base, largely because of some requirement gaps or implementation needs and details that surfaced as specific functionality unfolded. Ideally, in a real-world effort, much of that would have surfaced considerably earlier, and been expressed as specific tasks that were attached to the stories in the iteration, though some might still have occurred—we've made some decisions, both in this chapter and the one before, that shaped how things needed to work, that might not have been captured in an initial story analysis exercise.

As a result, the code at this point is quite probably broken. Perhaps drastically broken. Still, there's been a lot of progress against the iteration's stories, even if none of them can be formally closed yet:

- Fundamental functionality for dealing with all the data flow between system components has been defined, with a few concrete implementations that will serve as starting points for other concrete implementations
- Changes needed to accomplish the transmission and receipt of messages have been scoped, if not implemented
- A solid (if basic) understanding of how and when those messages need to be sent has been established

There's still work to be done on most of the iteration stories before they can be considered complete—even setting aside the UI considerations, we still don't have demonstrable, provable message flows in place. Getting those finalized will be the focus of the next chapter, and it will take a decidedly test-driven approach, even if it's not a formal TDD process.

Testing and Deploying Services 17

Chapter 17, *Handling Service Transactions*, ended with an untested receipt of over-the-wire CRUD operations being implemented for the data objects, originating with the Artisan and Central Office applications. Since proving (and demonstrating) these capabilities is going to be needed for both quality assurance and story approval purposes, and since there was no structured or useful repeatable testing of that code, in this chapter, we will take a detailed look at the following topics:

- Identifying and dealing with the challenges of testing service applications
- What is involved in packaging and deploying the service
- An approach for demonstrating the service's functionality

Additionally, since the functional development of `hms_sys` is very nearly complete, some thoughts and examinations of what's still remaining to be done in `hms_sys` for it to be useful to end users, and some possible future enhancements to it, will be undertaken.

The challenges of testing services

Testing services, while not difficult, can be substantially more elaborate than the relatively basic unit testing that's been shown up to this point. Each point in the general `hms_sys` data flow from an Artisan to the Gateway, for example, has specific and individual testing concerns, but the flow as a whole should, ideally, be as well, so that an end-to-end process verification can be performed on demand.

The end-to-end flow could be pictured like this:

From start to finish, a test plan for this data flow would need to address, at a minimum, the following:

- Creating the `message-data` in a fashion that it could be used to verify the process at its end
- Creating the `DaemonMessage` (though probably not testing that it was created accurately—there should already be unit tests that take care of testing that)
- Sending the resulting **message**
- Verifying that the results of the **Artisan Gateway service** receiving the message are as expected, by comparison with the original `message-data`

Depending on specifics of how the service operates, there are steps that happen between the transmission and receipt of the **message** that may not be practical (or may not be possible) to test:

- Testing the `send_message()` part of the overall process has to take steps to assure that the transmission of the **message** can be verified without some other process (the Gateway service, in this case) consuming the **message** before it can be verified. If the unit testing of `send_message` accounts for that, to the extent that the `send_message` method itself can be considered trustworthy, then the larger scope process test can safely skip testing that part of the whole.

- Similarly, testing of the various [process-method] items should provide adequate trustworthiness with respect to their parts of the whole flow process. The alternative is altering those methods so that their operation can be observed during the process, in which case they really aren't the same methods, and any tests that are applied are potentially meaningless.

Given that each part of the overall process should have their own unit tests, it would be fair to ask these questions: *"What are we actually gaining by testing the whole process, then? Isn't the collection of individual unit tests enough by itself?"* The short answer (though it may be taken as the author's opinion) is **no**—from one vantage point, all of the process tests are, in a very real way, unit tests of the Artisan Gateway's main method—the event loop that makes the decisions about which method to call based on the content of an incoming message. From that perspective alone, and given that ArtisanGatewayDaemon.main is the critical chunk of functionality in the class, it must be thoroughly tested. Also consider that the unit tests required by our testing policy essentially cover all of the boxes in the flow diagram: message-data, DaemonMessage, send_message, and so on. They do not provide any coverage of the arrows in the flow diagram. Though it may be unlikely that the code misses one of the steps that the arrows represent, it's not impossible, so a higher-level, end-to-end process test that would reveal any of those gaps would, in turn, provide proof of the trustworthiness of the processes as a whole. Similarly, the end results of those processes each need to be verifiable—if, for example, an Artisan-Creating-Product process is fired off, some assurance needs to be made that once the process is complete, that new Product object can be retrieved from the data store, with the correct data.

Finally, since the various processes all happen behind the scenes, they will likely be very hard to debug if a bug slips through into production installation:

- There will be little or no visibility into the individual Artisan application installations that are starting the execution of the processes
- The messages that are being sent back and forth, barring extremely detailed logging of their content/data, won't persist long enough to be readable and usable for debugging in a production setting
- Without more detailed logging, the specific daemon process calls are happening invisibly, and their results, if there are any, cannot be checked against the original data that they originated from

The overall testing strategy

Before writing the code that implements the full process testing, an effort needs to be made to complete and successfully execute all of the outstanding unit tests. Once this is complete, we can logically take it as a given that any failures that arise in the *process* tests are because of something in that process, though we may want to take steps to verify sub-process steps, and raise failures for certain conditions. This may well evolve as the process tests are written.

Each business object that has a set of corresponding processes needs to check for any/all of the following processes that apply:

- Creation of the object, and both local and remote persistence of its data:
  - By each role that is allowed to perform an update
  - Making sure to test both valid and invalid update attempts
- Updating the object's data:
  - By each role that is allowed to perform an update
  - Making sure to test both valid and invalid update attempts
- Deletion of the object:
  - By each role that is allowed perform a deletion
  - Making sure to test both valid and invalid deletion attempts
  - Verifying applicable local and remote data changes after the attempt is made

Determining what would constitute an invalid attempt requires consideration of the following questions, at a minimum:

- At any step in the process being tested, what could be corrupted that should prevent the process from completing successfully?
- At any step in the process being tested, what could be altered with malicious intent that should prevent the process from completing successfully?
- What tests are already in place that account for these scenarios?
- What tests need to be created for any scenarios that aren't accounted for?

In the case of the Gateway service, the points with potential for bad data variations are:

- **An invalid attempt is made to create or alter a business object instance:** These should be mostly covered by unit tests on the creation and update processes of the business objects themselves—these tests should assure that, for example, only well-formed data creation and updates are allowed, and having raised an exception there, the message transmission process shouldn't even fire. These cases really can't be tested in the context of the Gateway daemon, but must be tested in the applications that talk to it.

- **An unauthorized data event message is received:** The testing of message signatures in `DaemonMessage` should assure that messages with invalid signatures raise an error. As an extension of that, tests of the data event processes should assure that if an unauthorized message error is raised, it is handled cleanly, and does not execute any data changes.

- **An authorized data event message is received with invalid data:** Provided that the unit tests that are relevant for the data event on the origination side of the message are complete, this may be an indicator of malicious activity. Testing considerations aside for the moment, some review of the logging around this event should probably be undertaken to assure that events in this category are logged. Whether malicious or not, the corresponding unit tests on the receiving end of the message should assure that some kind of exception is raised, and the data event process tests should assure that any exceptions raised are handled cleanly and do not execute any data changes.

Though these tests will not, strictly speaking, be unit tests (they would be formally classified as some mixture of system or integration tests), we can still leverage the functionality of the `unittest` module that has driven all of the automated testing for the system up until this point. This will allow the process tests to be integrated into, and thus run as part of a complete test suite, if there was a desire to do so, or to be run independently, or even individually if needed/desired.

Unit testing variations of note

The bulk of the unit tests that need to be implemented fall fairly neatly into the standard processes that have been in play since the beginning of the `hms_sys` development effort, and there's nothing new to say about those. A relatively small number of others, however, have some noteworthy variations.

With the advent of a substantial amount of new code that relies heavily on either standard Python modules (`atexit`, `logging`, and `signal`, for example, in the `daemons` codebases), or various third-party modules that were installed to meet specific needs (`pika`, for RabbitMQ support), another aspect of testing policy bubbles up: the question of how deeply (or even whether) to test functionality that are little more than wrappers around functionality from other sources. It's not an unreasonable assumption that any packages that are part of the Python distribution itself are thoroughly tested before they're included in the distribution. It's probably not unreasonable to assume that any packages that are available to be installed through the `pip` utility are also thoroughly tested, though that may well vary significantly from package to package.

These are variations on a theme that might be expressed as **trusting the framework**. Essentially, this boils down to operating under the assumption that packages installed through `pip` (or whatever facilities are provided by the OS) are sufficiently tested (for whatever the value of sufficient might be). If these are considered sufficiently tested, they do not need to be categorically tested themselves. Whether the functionality that was developed that uses trusted framework functionality needs to be tested becomes something of a judgment call, perhaps depending on the specifics of how the external functionality is used.

This consideration should be borne in mind as the noteworthy variations of unit tests are listed.

In the `hms_core` package, tests for the `BaseDaemon` and `BaseDaemonizable` ABCs have corresponding concrete classes defined (`BaseDaemonDerived` and `BaseDaemonizableDerived`, respectively), which are used to create test instances as needed. That's not new in and of itself—we've used concrete derived classes to simplify testing of ABCs before. Creating testable instances of either, though, requires a configuration file to be passed during instance construction. The creation and clean up of that file is handled by the `setUpClass` and `tearDownClass` methods, which are defined on the `TestCase` class:

```
class testBaseDaemon(unittest.TestCase):

# ...

    @classmethod
    def setUpClass(cls):
        # - Create a basic config-file that can be used to create
        #   instances of BaseDaemonDerived.
        config_data = """logging:
    format: "%(asctime)s - %(name)s - %(levelname)s - %(message)s"
```

```
    name: example
    console:
      level: info
    file:
      level: debug
      logfile: "/tmp/example.log"
"""
        cls._config_file = 'example.config'
        with open(cls._config_file, 'w') as fp:
            fp.write(config_data)

    @classmethod
    def tearDownClass(cls):
        try:
            os.unlink(cls._config_file)
        except:
            pass
```

When `setUpClass` executes, before any of the test methods fire, it creates a usable config file (`example.config`) in the current working directory, populates it with bare-bones configuration data, and keeps track of the filename in a class attribute (`cls._config_file`) that the test methods can access. The typical pattern for creating a test object within a test method ends up looking like this:

```
    def testmethod(self):
        # Tests the method method of the BaseDaemon class
        test_object = BaseDaemonDerived(self._config_file)
        # - Whatever assertions and other test-processes are needed...
```

A number of tests against members of `hms_core.daemons` were actively skipped. The various control methods (`start`, `stop`, and `restart`) of `BaseDaemon` were skipped grudgingly. The fundamental issue with trying to test those is that, as they stand right now, they are little more than a collection of calls to other methods, many of which will, themselves, be tested. The balance falls into the trust of the framework category. At most, there is one decision point (in start, where a check of the instance's `_running` flag is made) that could, perhaps, be usefully tested, but it would have to happen really quickly before a change to that flag value would terminate the instance's processes. Ultimately, as long as an instance of the daemon starts, stops, and restarts without error, these methods are performing as expected, and there is little to gain by explicitly testing the corresponding methods.

A similar decision was made for the `daemonize`, `preflight`, and `start` methods in `BaseDaemonizable`, for similar reasons, with the added wrinkle that many of the methods being called are provided by standard modules, and themselves would fall into the category of trusting the framework.

All of the logging wrapper methods of `BaseDaemon` (`critical`, `debug`, `error`, `info`, and `warn`) were actively skipped. The rationale behind that decision was that as long as the `Logger` instance that they call is created correctly, those instances fall into the "trust the framework" category.

The properties of `BaseDaemonizable` whose values are filesystem paths (`stdin`, `stdout`, `stderr`, and `pidfile`) almost follow the standard testing structures that we established earlier. The primary difference is that they are filesystem path values, and so the test methods for those properties need to include both valid and invalid paths and paths that were well-formed, but that couldn't be written to or read from because of filesystem permissions. These tests are also tightly bound to the operating system, in a sense: a perfectly valid file path in Windows, for example, is not going to be valid in a POSIX-style filesystem, such as those used by Linux or macOS.

A similar strategy was required for `BaseDaemon.config_file`, and the `configure` method.

The `cleanup` and `preflight` methods of `BaseDaemon` fell into a unique category: by default, all they do is log (at an `info` logging level) that they have been called, so that startup and shutdown activity logging can announce that they were executed. If a derived class doesn't actually override these methods, the baseline functionality provided by `BaseDaemon` will be called, and perform the same logging. If the same standards are applied that were applied to the logging wrapper methods noted earlier, the implication is that `cleanup` and `preflight` both fall into the "trust the framework" classification. But what happens if a future need changes one of those methods, adding something that goes beyond the simple call to log that the method has executed? In that case, if the tests are skipped, there won't be any testing being performed, even if there should be. The simple truth of the matter is that changes made that would impact the associated tests cannot be anticipated, and as a result, a certain amount of expected discipline has to be assumed—that anyone making a substantive change to those base methods will also have to update the corresponding tests accordingly.

In the process of building and executing these unit tests, a handful of classes that were stubbed out earlier in the development cycle, but that were never actually used, surfaced as requiring tests. Since those were never needed (or even implemented, in many cases), the classes themselves have been removed, and the corresponding test requirements went away as a result.

The `RabbitMQSender` class, in `hms_core.messaging`, had one method—`send_message`—that partly fell into the "trust the framework" category. It also needed testing to assure that the type checking for a `DaemonMessage` instance was accounted for, though. Taken together, the complete testing for the method amounted to little more than the type checking test, and assured that the method executed without error. After some consideration, retrieving the sent message, or at least performing the acknowledgement of it so that it won't sit in some test queue forever, was implemented in `send_message` as well.

The remaining outstanding tests needed, all of which followed reasonably simple variations of the standard unit testing processes, were as follows:

- In `hms_core.business_objects` and `hms_artisan.artisan_objects`:
    - Testing the `Artisan.queue_id` and `Artisan.signing_key` properties
- In `hms_core.co_objects`:
    - Testing the `Artisan.to_message_data` method
    - Testing the new `Order` class
- In `hms_core.daemons`:
    - Testing `BaseDaemon._create_logger`
- In `hms_core.messaging`:
    - Testing `DaemonMessage`
    - Testing `HasMessageData`
    - Testing `InvalidMessageError`
    - Testing the standard items of `RabbitMQSender`
- In `hms_artisan.artisan_objects`:
    - Testing the `Artisan.to_message_data` method

With all of the tests in classes outside the `hms_Gateway` namespace accounted for, that leaves the properties and methods of the `ArtisanGatewayDaemon` class, which are ready to be tested. The properties and most of the methods therein, once more, can be tested by following the standard testing policy and process that's been in play. The most noteworthy exception is `ArtisanGatewayDaemon.main`, which will be skipped in the test module, and tested with the end-to-end-process tests that we can build now.

Testing Artisan transactions

The end-to-end process test for an Artisan needs to include the following:

- Creating an Artisan as it would happen if originating from a Central Office staff member
- Updating an Artisan as it would happen if originating from a Central Office staff member
- Updating an Artisan as it would happen if originating with the Artisan themselves
- Deleting an Artisan as it would happen if originating from a Central Office staff member

Since we aren't testing classes, which has been the pattern for all of our unit tests so far, we don't need all of the functionality of our standard unit test extensions, but we will want to use enough of the same structure and at least some of the utilities that were created there in order to integrate the process flow tests with the regular unit test runs for the `hms_Gateway` namespace. With that in mind, the starting point code looks very similar to our previous test modules:

```python
#!/usr/bin/env python
"""
Defines end-to-end process-tests for the ArtisanGatewayDaemon
"""

#######################################
# Standard library imports needed     #
#######################################

import os
import sys
import unittest
```

Since all we really need from the unit testing extensions we've been using is the output and report-saving functionality, we will only import those:

```
#####################################
# Local imports needed              #
#####################################

from idic.unit_testing import PrintTestResults, SaveTestReport
```

The module-level constants stay the same, and since we're going to be testing against a running instance of the ArtisanGatewayDaemon class, we already know that we'll need to import that:

```
#####################################
# Module-level Constants            #
#####################################

LocalSuite = unittest.TestSuite()

#####################################
# Imports needed for testing        #
#####################################

from hms_Gateway.daemons import ArtisanGatewayDaemon
```

The four process flows that we're going to test initially can each be represented by a single test method. Each of these methods will have to provide whatever code needs to be executed for each step of the flow test, but they can start with nothing more than an explicit failure:

```
#####################################
# Test-cases in the module          #
#####################################

class testArtisanProcesses(unittest.TestCase):

    def testArtisanCreateFromCO(self):
        self.fail('testArtisanCreateFromCO is not yet implemented')

    def testArtisanUpdateFromCO(self):
        self.fail('testArtisanUpdateFromCO is not yet implemented')

    def testArtisanUpdateFromArtisan(self):
        self.fail('testArtisanUpdateFromArtisan is not yet
implemented')
```

```
        def testArtisanDeleteFromCO(self):
            self.fail('testArtisanDeleteFromCO is not yet implemented')
```

Since we're using our standard unit testing extensions, we still need to actively add each test case class to the local test suite:

```
LocalSuite.addTests(
    unittest.TestLoader().loadTestsFromTestCase(
        testArtisanProcesses
    )
)
```

Finally, since we'll want to be able to run the process tests module independently, we'll include the same if __name__ == '__main__' code block that's been in all the previous modules, which will provide the output of the test results and save the results to a report file if there are no failures:

```
#######################################
# Code to execute if file is called   #
# or run directly.                    #
#######################################

if __name__ == '__main__':
    import time
    results = unittest.TestResult()
    testStartTime = time.time()
    LocalSuite.run(results)
    results.runTime = time.time() - testStartTime
    PrintTestResults(results)
    if not results.errors and not results.failures:
        SaveTestReport(results, 'hms_Gateway.ModuleName',
            'hms_Gateway.EndToEndProcesses.test-results')
```

Since all of these tests will need a running instance of the ArtisanGatewayDaemon class, we also need to make sure that one is available. Because a running instance of the class is a service, running independently of any other processes, starting up a service instance cannot happen as a normal part of any test method—the main loop would start, and nothing else would progress until it terminated, making it impossible to actually test the processes that main controls.

There are a couple of options that could be pursued to alleviate this issue:

- The test process could, in some fashion, use the operating system service control facilities to start a local service instance in much the same way that it would be controlled once it was deployed. On a long-term basis, this might be a better approach, but at this point in the development process, we aren't able to actually deploy the service code, so that would have to wait for future development. There is a trade-off to this approach, though: the service would have to be deployed, or some equivalent mechanism would have to be created to mimic a deployed service, on each execution of the test suite in order for tests to be accurate.

- Since the service is, ultimately, just an instance of a class, the test process could create an instance and start it, let the tests execute, then terminate the service instance that was used for the tests. Although this is a more complex solution, it feels better in at least one respect: each test suite would be able to execute against a service instance that could be customized specifically for those tests, including having distinct message queues that could, if necessary, be examined while working through issues raised by the test methods, without having to sort through a potentially huge set of messages.

Implementing the second option involves using the `setUpClass` and `tearDownClass` methods that were noted earlier to create the service instance and make it run before any tests execute, and shut the instance down after they've all completed. Since it makes sense to have one test case class for each business object process set, setting up `setUpClass` and `tearDownClass` so that they can be reused by the various test case classes also feels like a good plan. We can simplify this by creating a class that contains all the required logic for both methods, then derive the individual test case classes from that new class and the normal `unittest.TestCase` class that's been the backbone of our test case classes so far:

```
class NeedsArtisanGateway:

    @classmethod
    def setUpClass(cls):
        """
Creates and starts an instance of the ArtisanGatewayDaemon that
can be used during execution of the tests.
        """
```

This, incidentally, shows that it's possible to add helper classes to test suites—classes that provide some functionality or capabilities needed during test execution, but that aren't, themselves, test case classes.

We need to create a configuration file that the service instance will use, but before we do that, we'll store some of the values we're likely to need in the test methods as class attributes so that we can access them later when needed:

```
cls.Gateway_signing_key = os.urandom(64).hex()
cls.Gateway_queue_id = 'hms_ag_%s_process_test' %
cls.queue_name
cls.Gateway_config_file = 'process_test.config'
```

The configuration data can be set up as a string that follows the configuration structure that was established earlier. Customization of the service instance, if needed, can be managed by adding variable/attribute values to the class, and making sure that those values get carried into the string, as was done with the `cls.Gateway_queue_id` and `cls.Gateway_signing_key` attributes here:

```
cls.Gateway_config_data="""# Logging configuration
logging:
  format: "%%(asctime)s - %%(name)s - %%(levelname)s - %%(message)s"
  name: hms_ag_process_test
  file:
    level: debug
    logfile: "/tmp/hms_ag_process_test.log"
queue:
  type: rabbit
  connection:
    host: localhost
    port: 5672
    path: /
  queue_name: "%s"
signing_key: "%s"
""" % (cls.Gateway_queue_id, cls.Gateway_signing_key)
```

The configuration data is written to a temporary config file that's used by the test case class, in much the same way that we did before when testing `BaseDaemon`:

```
with open(cls.Gateway_config_file, 'w') as fp:
    fp.write(cls.Gateway_config_data)
```

Since we may need to access the service instance itself, we'll create and store the instance as another class attribute:

```
cls.Gateway = ArtisanGatewayDaemon(cls.Gateway_config_file)
```

Starting the service instance requires executing its start method so that the process is independent of the running test code. To achieve this, we're going to use the `Process` class, from Python's `multiprocessing` module, telling it what method to call when the `Process` is started, and that the process should be treated as a `daemon`, keeping its execution independent from other running code. Once that's been set up, we can start the `Process`, which executes the start method of the service instance stored in `cls.Gateway`:

```
cls.Gateway_process = Process(target=cls.Gateway.start, daemon=True)
cls.Gateway_process.start()
```

 The `multiprocessing` module will be explored in more detail in *Chapter 19, Multi-processing and HPC in Python*, as we explore various strategies and approaches for scaling computational load across multiple processes and machines.

The teardown is much simpler: having stored the process that controls the running service instance (`cls.Gateway_process`), that `Process` simply needs to be terminated (the `terminate` method call), and the temporary config file deleted so that we don't leave it in the test code. Because the termination of the process may not be complete before the teardown execution is complete, a short delay has been added as well:

```
@classmethod
def tearDownClass(cls):
    # - Stop the service-instance
    cls.Gateway_process.terminate()
    # - Clean up (delete) the temp. config-file
    os.unlink(cls.Gateway_config_file)
    # - Add a short delay to allow the process-termination time
    #   to complete before proceeding with the next item...
    time.sleep(1)
```

Using the `NeedsArtisanGateway` class in the test case classes requires some trivial code changes: each test case class needs to derive from `NeedsArtisanGateway` and `unittest.TestCase`, to begin with:

```
class testArtisanProcesses(NeedsArtisanGateway, unittest.TestCase):
```

Also, since `NeedsArtisanGateway` requires a `queue_name` class attribute to create the `Gateway_queue_id` class attribute, that needs to be defined:

```
queue_name = 'artisan'
```

From that point on, however, all that remains is unchanged:

```
def testArtisanCreateFromCO(self):
    self.fail('testArtisanCreateFromCO is not yet implemented')

# ...
```

Before implementing any of the tests, there is some configuration and setup that needs to happen within the test module. All of the process tests are expected to need data access capabilities, so we need to import the main data store class, as well as the data store configuration class, and configure data access to allow those capabilities:

```
from hms_core.data_storage import DatastoreConfig, HMSMongoDataObject

config = DatastoreConfig(
    database='hms_proc_tests',
)
HMSMongoDataObject.configure(config)
```

Similarly, since the process tests are all concerned with message transmission, we'll need to be able to create sender objects—instances of `RabbitMQSender`—as well as `DaemonMessage` objects. Those, too, need to be imported, and a base `RabbitMQSender.configuration` call needs to be made:

```
from hms_core.messaging import DaemonMessage, RabbitMQSender, \
    MESSAGE_ORIGINS
RabbitMQSender.configure(
    'hms_ag_process_test', 'localhost', 5672, '/'
)
```

`MESSAGE_ORIGINS` in the `import` line is a new module constant, a collection of names and values that can be used to control what values are members of the collection, what names are associated with them, and to determine whether a given value is a member of the collection. It is defined as follows:

```
MESSAGE_ORIGINS = namedtuple(
    'MESSAGE_ORIGINS', ['artisan', 'central_office']
)(
    artisan='artisan',
    central_office='central-office',
)
```

Python does have some official enumeration classes, but the one that would otherwise be best suited to meet this need, `enum.Enum`, does not allow an arbitrary value to check for membership in the enumeration. The differences can be seen in the results shown in the `enumeration-example.py` file in this chapter's code (in `hms_Gateway/scratch-space`).

Lastly, since the test processes will be using classes with the same names from different namespaces (for example, `hms_core.co_objects.Artisan` and `hms_artisan.artisan_objects.Artisan`, both named Artisan), we need to import these and rename them in the process, like so:

```
from hms_core.co_objects import Artisan as COArtisan
from hms_artisan.artisan_objects import Artisan as ARArtisan
```

From this point onward, any creation of a `COArtisan` object will be instances of the `hms_core.co_objects.Artisan` class, and `ARArtisan` objects will be `hms_artisan.artisan_objects.Artisan` instances.

With those out of the way, the implementation of the first process test method can (finally) begin. It starts with the creation of the `sender` object, which will be used to send the test messages:

```
def testArtisanCreateFromCO(self):
    sender = RabbitMQSender()
```

In order to test the Artisan creation process, we have to create an Artisan:

```
parameters = {
    'contact_name':'contact-name',
    'contact_email':'no-one@me.co',
    'address':{
        'street_address':'street-address',
        'city':'city',
    },
    'queue_id':self.Gateway_queue_id,
    'signing_key':self.Gateway_signing_key,
}
new_artisan = COArtisan.from_data_dict(parameters)
```

We then create the `message` to be sent, and send it:

```
message = DaemonMessage(
    operation='create',
    origin=MESSAGE_ORIGINS.central_office,
    data={
        'target':'artisan',
        'properties':new_artisan.to_message_data(),
    },
    signing_key=self.Gateway_signing_key
)
sender.send_message(message, self.Gateway_queue_id)
```

At this point in the code, the message has been sent, but there's no easy way to determine whether it's been received yet, let alone processed. Without actually writing code (possibly a lot of code) to keep track of messages and their status, there's not much in the way of options to pause processing until we're reasonably certain that the message has been delivered and acted upon. The next best option, and one that takes a lot less code effort, though it will slow down the test process, is to simply delay the execution for a short time—long enough to allow the message to be delivered and acted upon, but not so long that running the tests becomes problematically long. Using `time.sleep`, we're going to delay processing for 5 seconds, at least for now. It may need to be increased later, or it might be able to be decreased if a better feel for how long the process takes to complete is required:

```
time.sleep(5)
```

Once the message has been received and acted upon, if all went well, then a `new_artisan` object will be created by the Gateway service, and saved to the database that it's using. The next step in testing the process is to assure that a new object was, in fact, created and stored:

```
try:
    verify_artisan = COArtisan.get(str(new_artisan.oid))[0]
except IndexError:
    self.fail(
        'Although the new artisan (oid: %s) was created, '
        'it could not be retrieved' % (new_artisan.oid)
    )
```

Knowing that the new object was created, we can then check to make sure that the new object's data is identical to the data that was originally sent to create it. Since the data dict representation of any data object is going to be the most comprehensive—it should include all data that gets persisted—that is a simple comparison of the original Artisan and the newly created and retrieved Artisan:

```
self.assertEquals(
    verify_artisan.to_data_dict(), new_artisan.to_data_dict()
)
```

If the test process gets past that check, then we're done with the new_artisan object that we created to test, and we can delete it from the database:

```
COArtisan.delete(str(new_artisan.oid))
```

This concludes the "happy path" testing of the process—where everything was created, formatted, and sent exactly as intended. Testing unauthorized and badly formed messages requires a bit more work, since we'll be circumventing the checking that's performed by the Artisan and DaemonMessage classes. Starting, then, with an unauthorized message, where the signature of the message doesn't match the signature calculated on the receiving end, we need to first create an unauthorized message. We can use the existing message, since it still exists, extract the data we'll be sending, and then alter something—either a data value or the signature will do:

```
unauthorized_message_data = message.to_message_dict()
unauthorized_message_data['data']['properties']['website'] = \
    'http://some-bogus-website.com'
```

Since we already have a sender, we can use its channel, along with the Gateway_queue_id of the instance, to circumvent the normal sending process that expects a DaemonMessage instance. Instead, we'll send the JSON dump of the unauthorized message that we just created:

```
sender.channel.basic_publish(
    exchange='', routing_key=self.Gateway_queue_id,
    body=json.dumps(
        unauthorized_message_data, sort_keys=True
    )
)
```

The test portion of this branch is concerned with whether a data change made it through the Gateway service. If one did, it would have generated a new `Artisan` record, and we could retrieve the corresponding object. If it did, and we can, then something went wrong, and we explicitly cause the test to fail. If the retrieval attempt failed (raising an `IndexError` because the result set that comes back is a zero-length list, and has no element at `[0]`), that's the expected/desired behavior, and we can simply ignore the error, passing that portion of the test:

```
try:
    verify_artisan = COArtisan.get(str(new_artisan.oid))[0]
    self.fail(
        'An unauthorized message should not execute a data-'
        'change'
    )
except IndexError:
    pass
```

Testing an invalid but authorized message works much the same way, but we'll alter the message data, and then use a normal `DaemonMessage/sender` process:

```
invalid_message_data = new_artisan.to_message_data()
# - Alter a data-value, like website
invalid_message_data['website'] = 12.345
invalid_message = DaemonMessage(
    operation='create',
    origin=MESSAGE_ORIGINS.central_office,
    data={
        'target':'artisan',
        'properties':invalid_message_data,
    },
    signing_key=self.Gateway_signing_key
)
sender.send_message(invalid_message, self.Gateway_queue_id)
try:
    verify_artisan = COArtisan.get(str(new_artisan.oid))[0]
    self.fail(
        'An unauthorized message should not execute a data-'
        'change'
    )
except IndexError:
    pass
```

Variations on the same theme for the Central-Office-updating-Artisan and Central-Office-deleting-Artisan processes will look very similar, with each doing the following:

- Creating a local Artisan and saving it in order to have a data object that's going to be manipulated
- Optionally verifying that the newly created Artisan exists in the database before proceeding, though if the `Artisan.save` method is considered trustworthy from other tests, this could be skipped
- Creating an appropriate `message` to execute the process being tested, and sending it
- Testing the results against a second instance of the same Artisan:
    - The update process tests have to make a point of changing all fields that can be legitimately changed by the role that the test is acting in—as a Central Office user/Artisan Manager. In that respect, it might look very much like previous unit tests against methods like `Artisan.to_data_dict`, which return dictionary representations of the objects
    - It should also make a point of trying to make changes to the Artisan that shouldn't be allowed, and verifying that those attempts fail
    - The deletion process test will be considerably simpler, since all it will need to do is try and re-acquire the test object (using something similar to `verify_artisan = COArtisan.get(str(new_artisan.oid))[0]`, which we looked at previously) with the test passing if the retrieval effort fails after deletion is executed

Tests against invalid access attempts, such as an Artisan creating an Artisan, should also be implemented, and would have a code structure similar to portions of the test code shown previously. Before those tests could pass, though, mechanisms to actually check the message in the various operation methods would have to be implemented. Using the `origin` of the incoming `DaemonMessage` for any given operation, this might look something like this, showing a general, any-role-is-allowed check and a specific-role-only check, and using the `create_artisan` method of the Gateway service as an example:

```
def create_artisan(self, message:(DaemonMessage,)) -> None:
    self.info('%s.create_artisan called' % self.__class__.__name__)

    # ...
```

```
    # - Assure that only the appropriate roles can execute this
    #   method. First check against *all* valid origins (at a
    #   minimum, this check should occur in *all* methods)
    if message.origin not in MESSAGE_ORIGINS:
        raise RuntimeError(
            'Malformed message: "%s" is not an accepted '
            'message-origin' % message.origin
        )
    # - Alternately, check against specific roles/origins instead,
    #   if they are limited
    if message.origin != MESSAGE_ORIGINS.central_office:
        raise RuntimeError(
            'Unauthorized Action: "%s" is not allowed to '
            'execute this method' % message.origin
        )
```

Tests against invalid role/action execution variants would look very much like the testing of `invalid_message` that we saw previously, verifying that the operation method doesn't execute when presented with a well-formed message that's attempting to execute an operation that's not allowed by any given role/`origin`.

Testing transaction processes that originate from the application side of a relationship is a bit more complicated, if only because there's been no significant development so far on those applications. To test these processes, a bare-bones mock-up of the application processes would have to be created, at least initially—later on down the line, when there are reasonably complete and tested applications, it might be better to actually run a local instance of them. Both Artisan and Central Office applications would need a mock-up, and would need to provide CRUD operations methods in much the same manner that the Gateway service daemon's class does. A mock-up of the Artisan application might start with code such as this:

```
class ArtisanapplicationMock:

    # ... Properties and initialization would need to be fleshed
    #     out, obviously...

    # CRUD-operation methods to implement
    def update_artisan(self, message:(DaemonMessage,)) -> (None,):
        # TODO: Implement this method
        pass

    def create_order(self, message:(DaemonMessage,)) -> (None,):
        # TODO: Implement this method
        pass

    def update_order(self, message:(DaemonMessage,)) -> (None,):
```

```
        # TODO: Implement this method
        pass

    def delete_order(self, message:(DaemonMessage,)) -> (None,):
        # TODO: Implement this method
        pass

    def update_product(self, message:(DaemonMessage,)) -> (None,):
        # TODO: Implement this method
        pass
```

The structure of the Gateway service could be reused, in part, to provide a method that routes messages to their respective operation methods:

```
    def _handle_message(self, message:(DaemonMessage,)) -> (None,):
        # - This method would look very much like its counterpart
        #   in hms_Gateway.daemons.ArtisanGatewayDaemon
        # TODO: Implement this method
        pass
```

Rather than having a `main` loop, though, the mock-up would be better served by having a single method that acts like a single pass through the Gateway service's `main` loop. For testing purposes, this allows the handling of messages to be more tightly controlled so that any number of test messages can be sent as part of a test process. Then, a single call can be made to the `ArtisanapplicationMock` method to read and handle all messages, which results in the fact that those messages can be tested. This method, `handle_pending_messages`, still looks a lot such as `ArtisanGatewayDaemon.main`, though:

```
def handle_pending_messages(self) -> (None,):
    # - Create a connection
    connection = pika.BlockingConnection(
        pika.ConnectionParameters(
            self.connection_params['host'],
            self.connection_params.get('port'),
            self.connection_params.get('path'),
        )
    )
    # - Create (or at least specify) a channel
    channel = connection.channel()
    # - Create or specify a queue
    channel.queue_declare(queue=self.queue_name)
    # - Get *all* pending messages, and execute against them
    polling = True
    while polling:
        try:
            # - Retrieve the next message from the queue, if
```

```
        #    there is one, and handle it...
        method_frame, header, body =
channel.basic_get(self.queue_name)
        if method_frame:
            # - Any actual message, valid or not, will
            #    generate a method_frame
            message = DaemonMessage.from_message_json(
                body.decode(), self.signing_key
            )
            # - We've received the message, and will
            #    process it, so acknowledge it on basic
            #    principle
            channel.basic_ack(method_frame.delivery_tag)
            self._handle_message(message)
        else:
            polling = False
    except InvalidMessageError as error:
        # - If message-generation fails (bad signature),
        #    we still need to send an acknowledgement in order
        #    to clear the message from the queue
        channel.basic_ack(method_frame.delivery_tag)
```

With that available, and a corresponding mock-up for the Central Office application, the processes for testing transactions that originate with an application passing through the Gateway service to the other application and making changes will be similar to the testing process for simpler transactions, such as creating an Artisan:

1. A message is created for the operation, with the appropriate origin and data
2. That message is sent to the Gateway service
3. Verification of any service-level data changes is performed, possibly after a delay to ensure that there's been time for the message to be delivered and acted upon
4. The `handle_pending_messages` method of the appropriate application mock-up class is called to read and process the incoming message
5. Testing of the expected results is performed—new local data created for creation transactions, changes to existing data for update transactions, and the removal of existing data for deletion transactions

TIP
This entire process—the creation of code that simulates a more complex system or object for testing purposes—is called **Mocking**. Mocking allows tests to be written without having to rely on actual (and often far more complex) real code implementations.

Testing for products and orders, for the most part, can follow similar patterns. The primary differences will, of course, be in what object types are being created and manipulated, and in what various roles are allowed to do to those objects, according to the business rules for each role/operation combination. Additional tests may need to be defined to specifically target certain operations—artisans fulfilling part of an order, for example, which is fundamentally just an update operation. However, this should only alter item fulfilment data, and not all of that data at that. Even so, this will almost certainly follow similar test processes and structures to those outlined here.

Demonstrating the service

A mainstay of many iterative development processes is the requirement that the functionality of code can be demonstrated to stakeholders so that they have sufficient information to agree that requirements for a story have been met, or to point out any gaps in those requirements. Demonstration of a service poses some unique challenges to meeting that requirement:

- Everything that's happening is happening "behind the scenes" invisibly
- Much of what is happening happens so quickly that there simply isn't time to see the interim steps that lead to the final results
- The odds are good that there won't be any sort of user interface associated, or that even if there is one, that it will provide enough visibility into the processes to demonstrate them in enough detail

Sometimes, as is the case of the Gateway service, there are also external systems—databases, message queue services, and so on, that need to be available to the code being run for a demonstration process to actually run successfully. Preparation for demonstration needs to take that into account, and have running instances of any needed external services available, obviously. In this case, since development and testing already relies on those same services being available, this is a non-issue, provided that a code demo can be run from a development environment.

The process tests that have been implemented can be executed to demonstrate that the code is behaving in a predictable fashion, and this a good item to be demonstrated, but it does nothing to address our initial concerns. A very basic approach to show the inner workings of the various processes would be to write a demonstration script that performs the same tasks that occur in the final code, in whatever logical or required order is needed, but in user controllable chunks, with displays of relevant data when and as needed. It's a brute-force, bare-bones approach, but makes the steps in the processes visible (addressing the first concern), and executes each step when a user says to (addressing the second concern). In effect, it's solving the first two concerns by creating a user interface to that specific purpose. Though the full demo script is too long to reproduce here, it will largely look like the process tests:

```python
#!/usr/bin/env python
"""
A (partial) script that runs through the various processes we need
to demo for the Artisan Gateway service.
"""

# - Imports needed for the demo-script
import unittest
import os

from hms_core.co_objects import Artisan as COArtisan
from hms_core.messaging import DaemonMessage, RabbitMQSender, \
    MESSAGE_ORIGINS
```

The configuration of various items, like the data store that the demo process will use or the message queue, would need to be provided at about this point in the code.

Because the unit tests for the entire service live in a package structure (that mirrors the structure of the real code), the entire unit test suite can be imported, and a function can be written to execute them on demand:

```python
from test_hms_Gateway import LocalSuite

def demoUnitTests():
    print(
        '+== Showing that unit-tests run without error '.ljust(79,'=')
+ '+'
    )
    results = unittest.TestResult()
    LocalSuite.run(results)
    print('+== Unit-tests run complete '.ljust(79,'=') + '+\n\n')
```

The demonstrations of each data transaction process can also be wrapped in individual functions in the demo module. With the exception of new code to display information as the demo is running, and to prompt whoever is running the demo to allow it to continue, they will look very much like the corresponding process test methods:

```
def demoArtisanCreateFromCO():
    print(
        '+== Central Office Creating Artisan '.ljust(79,'=') + '+'
    )
```

The code for creating an Artisan test object to work with is nearly identical:

```
parameters = {
    'contact_name':'contact-name',
    'contact_email':'no-one@me.co',
    'address':{
        'street_address':'street-address',
        'city':'city',
    },
    'queue_id':'bogus-queue-id',
    'signing_key':os.urandom(64),
}
new_artisan = COArtisan.from_data_dict(parameters)
```

Since the demo will need to show the initial state of the new_artisan object before the transmission of its create message to show that the data persisted as expected, some simple, brute-force output of the object's data-dict is in order:

```
initial_state = new_artisan.to_data_dict()
print('| Initial state:'.ljust(79, ' ') + '|')
for key in sorted(initial_state.keys()):
    print(
        (
            ('| +- %s ' % key).ljust(24, '.') + ' %s' %
initial_state[key]
        )[0:78].ljust(79, ' ') + '|'
    )
print('+' + '-'*78 + '+')
```

Creating the message, and sending it, looks almost identical, apart from the queue_id that's used to identify which queue it gets sent through. It also has the same time.sleep delay as the corresponding process test, for the same reason:

```
sender = RabbitMQSender()
# - Send the new-COArtisan message to the service
message = DaemonMessage(
```

```
            operation='create',
            origin=MESSAGE_ORIGINS.central_office,
            data={
                'target':'artisan',
                'properties':new_artisan.to_message_data(),
            },
            signing_key=parameters['signing_key']
        )
        sender.send_message(message, parameters['queue_id'])
        # - The message has been sent, but we have to wait for
        #   a bit before it is received and acted upon before we
        #   can verify the creation happened
        time.sleep(5)
```

The display of the results is essentially the same code used to display the initial_state that we saw previously; it's just using the data-dict of the retrieved, database-persisted instance instead of the original instance:

```
        verify_artisan = COArtisan.get(str(new_artisan.oid))[0]
        verify_state = new_artisan.to_data_dict()
        print('| Saved state:'.ljust(79, ' ') + '|')
        for key in sorted(verify_state.keys()):
            print(
                (
                    ('| +- %s ' % key).ljust(24, '.') + ' %s' %
        verify_state[key]
                )[0:78].ljust(79, ' ') + '|'
            )
        print('+' + '='*78 + '+')
```

Since showing the original and persisted data is one logical grouping, the script waits for input from the user before continuing with the next step of the demo:

```
        print('\n')
        input('[Enter] to continue the demo')
        print('\n')
```

Setting aside the remaining items in this demo function, and all of the other demo functions that would likely be needed, the entire demo script can be executed by simply calling each demo function if the module is executed directly (if __name__ == '__main__'):

```
if __name__ == '__main__':
    demoArtisanCreateFromCO()
```

The output with just this first segment of the first demo method in place can already be used to show that data persistence is accurate:

```
+== Central Office Creating Artisan =========================================+
| Initial state:                                                             |
| +- address ........... {'country': None, 'building_address': None, 'city': ' |
| +- company_name ...... None                                                |
| +- contact_email ..... no-one@me.co                                        |
| +- contact_name ...... contact-name                                        |
| +- created .......... 2018-09-29 10:13:33                                  |
| +- is_active ........ True                                                 |
| +- is_deleted ....... False                                                |
| +- modified ......... 2018-09-29 10:13:33                                  |
| +- oid .............. b9bd49e0-d11b-4ba6-9cf5-bc019cb64776                  |
| +- queue_id ......... bogus-queue-id                                       |
| +- signing_key ...... 42ac3040780c20df0e96bda01a0a899cbae4a53fc6ca4ae49a1f8 |
| +- website .......... None                                                 |
+----------------------------------------------------------------------------+
| Saved state:                                                               |
| +- address ........... {'country': None, 'building_address': None, 'city': ' |
| +- company_name ...... None                                                |
| +- contact_email ..... no-one@me.co                                        |
| +- contact_name ...... contact-name                                        |
| +- created .......... 2018-09-29 10:13:33                                  |
| +- is_active ........ True                                                 |
| +- is_deleted ....... False                                                |
| +- modified ......... 2018-09-29 10:13:33                                  |
| +- oid .............. b9bd49e0-d11b-4ba6-9cf5-bc019cb64776                  |
| +- queue_id ......... bogus-queue-id                                       |
| +- signing_key ...... 42ac3040780c20df0e96bda01a0a899cbae4a53fc6ca4ae49a1f8 |
| +- website .......... None                                                 |
+============================================================================+

[Enter] to continue
```

The steps that follow for this first demo function will be similar:

- Wrapping the execution with data displays of before and after whatever changes are made
- Displaying what data changes are being made when applicable, so that there is visibility into those changes
- Demonstrating expected failure cases, such as invalid message data or signatures, and any role-based variants

There will almost certainly be enough similarity between what the process test methods are proving (and executing) and the demonstrations of those same processes that the test methods will supply most of the code needed for all of the demo functions.

Packaging and deploying the service

Since the `hms_Gateway` and `hms_core` projects each have their own `setup.py` file, the packaging and deployment process doesn't need to be any more complicated than doing the following:

- Executing each `setup.py` to generate the installable package
- Moving those package files to the server that is going to run the Gateway service
- Installing them with the following code:
  - `pip install HMS-Core-0.1.dev0.tar.gz`
  - `pip install HMS-Gateway-0.1.dev0.tar.gz`
- Creating, for new installations, the configuration file at the necessary location

The configuration needed to allow the Gateway daemon to start up automatically on system boot and shutdown with a system shutdown will vary based on the OS of the target machine (more on that in a bit).

If, on the other hand, there is a need for a single package, consolidating the `src` directories from all of the relevant projects will need to be undertaken as part of the packaging process. That can be accomplished, if it's not available through some combination of the normal `setuptools.setup` function's arguments, with a `Makefile` and a minor change to the `setup.py` that's in place in the project.

Support for the inclusion of source code outside a project's main source directory has, in the author's experience, had sporadic issues with earlier versions of Python and/or the `setuptools` package. If those issues are resolved in the current version, then it may possible to use the `package_dir` argument of `setuptools.setup`, possibly in combination with the `setuptools.find_package` function to instruct the main `setup` function where you can find other package source trees outside the current project. The `Makefile` approach described here is not as elegant, and can have other (generally minor) issues, but works all the time with only basic `setup.py` functionality/requirements.

The relevant change to the setup.py file is simple, requiring only the addition of the hms_core package name to the list of packages to include in the distribution:

```
# The actual setup function call:
setup(
    name='HMS-Artisan-Gateway',
    version='0.1.dev0',

    # ...

    packages=[
        'hms_Gateway',
        'hms_core',
    ],

    # ...

)
```

Since setup.py doesn't care where it's being run from, a simple brute-force solution to gather all of the relevant source code into a single location as a Makefile target might start with this:

```
full_package:
        # Create a temporary packaging directory to copy all the
        # relevant files to
        mkdir -p /tmp/Gateway-packaging
        # Copy those files
        cp -R src/hms_Gateway /tmp/Gateway-packaging
        cp -R ../hms-core/src/hms_core /tmp/Gateway-packaging
        # - Change to the temporary packaging directory, execute
setup.py
        cd /tmp/Gateway-packaging;python setup.py
        # - Move the resulting package to somewhere outside the
        #       temporary packaging directory, after assuring that the
        #       location exists
        mkdir -p ~/Desktop/HMS-Builds
        mv /tmp/Gateway-packaging/dist/* ~/Desktop/HMS-Builds
        # - Clean up the temporary directory
        rm -fR /tmp/Gateway-packaging
```

Step-by-step, all the target is actually doing is the following:

- Creating a temporary build directory
- Copying the entire package directory from each project into that directory
- Jumping into the directory and executing a typical `setup.py` run (with the modified `setup.py` file)
- Making sure that a directory exists on the filesystem that the final package files can be moved to
- Moving the newly created package files to that directory
- Removing the temporary build directory

The final output of the combined `Makefile/setup.py` process would be a single package file, `HMS-Gateway-0.1.dev0.tar.gz`, that includes both the `hms_Gateway` and `hms_core` package directories, ready for installation with `pip install HMS-Gateway-0.1.dev0.tar.gz`.

Common considerations across all operating systems

No matter what operating system the Gateway service daemon is running under, it will require a full configuration file, at a known location, that stores all of the settings that the service will need to know about when it starts up. The basic, Linux-flavored version of this configuration file (living in `/etc/hms/hms_Gateway.conf` on the target machine the service is running on) looks very much like the bare-bones example used in the *Message-Queue implementation with RabbitMQ* section of `Chapter 16`, *The Artisan Gateway Service*:

```
# HMS Artisan Gateway Service Configuration
# - Used by the hms_Gateway.daemons.ArtisanGatewayDaemon class
#   to launch an active instance of the service
logging:
  format: "%(asctime)s - %(name)s - %(levelname)s - %(message)s"
  name: hms_Gateway
# If console-logging is desired, uncomment these lines
#  console:
#    level: info
  file:
    level: error
    logfile: "/var/log/hms/hms_Gateway.log"
queue:
  type: rabbit
```

```
connection:
  host: rabbitmq.hms.com
  port: 5672
  path: /
queue_name: "central-office"
# Signing-key should be generated and added to configuration
# during installation. It should be a 64-character,
# bytes-type-compatible string-value, and will likely need to be
# explicitly quoted
signing_key: ""
```

This config file is intentionally not part of the packaging process—otherwise, every time an update was installed, there would be some risk of overwriting an existing and operational configuration. Once the final configuration is in place, it should not need to be modified under any reasonably normal circumstances. The only difference between the Linux version of the configuration file and one that would be used on a Windows server is the log file path (`logging:file:logfile`), which would need to be pointed at a Windows filesystem path.

The service management options that we'll examine, under both Windows and Linux operating systems, allow a simple command-line execution to start the service daemon. Older Linux service management might require a separate, freestanding script in Bash or Python to bridge between the operating system's core functionality and the user's and system's interaction with it. With the advent of these more modern options, though, we can launch the service daemon on a production system in much the same way it was launched for testing during its development, by adding a few lines of code to the end of `hms_Gateway/daemons.py`:

```
if __name__ == '__main__':
    daemon = ArtisanGatewayDaemon('/etc/hms/hms_Gateway.conf')
    daemon.start()
```

When a Python module is directly executed by the Python interpreter—`python -m hms_Gateway.daemons`, for example, or `python /path/to/hms_Gateway/daemons.py`—the `if __name__ == '__main__'` condition will evaluate to `True`, and the code within that `if` statement will be executed. In this case, it creates an instance of `ArtisanGatewayDaemon`, passing the hard-coded config file path, then calling the `start` method of the `daemon` object, starting the service.

Linux (systemd) execution

On a reasonably recent Linux system, service management is handled by another service: `systemd`. Configuration is needed for `systemd` to know when and how to launch the service daemon, how to shut it down, and how to restart it, along with some additional information that is used to determine when the service starts during the system's boot process. A bare-bones starting point `systemd` configuration file for the Gateway service would look like this:

```
[Unit]
Description = Artisan Gateway Service
After       = network-online.target

[Service]
# - Start-up process
ExecStart    = python -m hms_Gateway.daemons
# - How to shut the service down
ExecStop     = pkill -f hms_Gateway.daemons
ExecRestart = pkill -f hms_Gateway.daemons;python -m
hms_Gateway.daemons

# - If it stops unexpectedly, do we want it to restart?
Restart      = always

[Install]
# - This corresponds, at least roughly, to runlevel 3, after
#   a complete system start
WantedBy     = multi-user.target
```

Where the roles for he mentioned keywords are as follows:

- `Description` is a simple description of the service
- `After` indicates an operational state target that should be completely established before launching the service daemon—in this case, since the Gateway service requires network access, we are indicating that it should start after the network online target is complete, expecting that all network functionality will be available at that point
- `ExecStart` is a command that can be executed by the OS to start the service

- `ExecStop` is a command that will be used to stop the service—in this case, using the `pkill` OS utility to find (`-f`) and kill any processes that match the `hms_Gateway.daemons` string
- `Restart` allows `systemd` to automatically restart the service if it dies unexpectedly
- `WantedBy` is an OS state indicator that, in this case, defines under what circumstances the service daemon should launch—when a (standard) multi-user-capable run-level is reached, typical of a command-line only server system

Once both of these configuration files are in place, the Gateway service should start automatically after the system boots up, shut down cleanly if the system is shut down, and can be manually started, stopped, and restarted with the following standard commands:

- `systemctl start hms_Gateway`
- `systemctl stop hms_Gateway`
- `systemctl restart hms_Gateway`

Windows (NSSM) execution

Running the Gateway service on a Windows machine requires some middleware to create a service-compatible wrapper around the Python code that's going to be executed. One of the more popular and stable middleware options is the **Non-Sucking Service Manager** (**NSSM**). NSSM provides a GUI for creating, installing, and managing services that are written in a variety of languages—in general, if a program can be run from a command line, NSSM can almost certainly get it running as a Windows service.

NSSM may need to be run with administrative privileges, but in any event, is launched from the command line—`C:\path\to\nssm.exe install` launches the GUI, and all of the settings needed are present under one of the tabs. The **application** tab defines the **Path** to the program to be executed (`python.exe`, in our case) with whatever **Arguments** are needed (the Python script to run), as well as a **Service name**, which is used to identify the service:

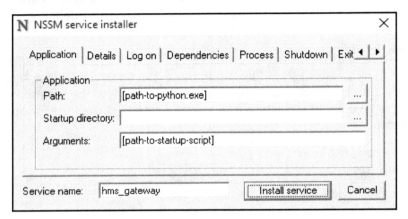

If an existing NSSM-managed service needs to be modified, it can be accessed by executing the NSSM program and specifying the **Service name** in the command: `C:\path\to\nssm.exe install hms_Gateway`, for example.

The **Details** tab allows a **Display name** and **Description** to be provided, which will appear in the Windows Service Administration interface. It also allows for the control of the **Startup type**: whether the service starts automatically, or under other circumstances:

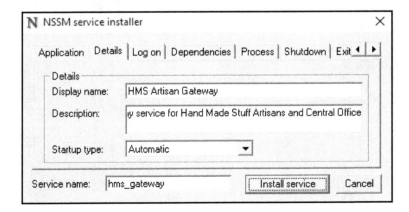

Once the **Install Service** button is clicked, it's done—the new service, wrapped and manageable by NSSM, is available in the Windows Services administrator!

At this point, what might be called the "functional foundations" of hms_sys are pretty complete: all of the data flows that are expected have been accounted for, and if there are restrictions mandated by the business rules that aren't implemented in the business logic, there is at least enough support for making the decisions related to them quick and easy to implement.

We still haven't actually closed most of the stories that the iteration started with, though, in retrospect, those were written with goals that were too broad for them to be closed without UI development. Had they been broken out into two stories (or more) each, one of each set, focusing on the end-user goals and needs would look pretty much the same:

- As an Artisan Manager, I need to be able to create Artisan objects in a GUI so that I can manage artisans quickly and easily
- As an Artisan Manager, I need to be able to delete Artisan objects in a GUI so that I can manage artisans quickly and easily

Each of these would have a corresponding story that focuses more on assuring that there would be some code, some functionality that the GUI-related stories could start with, and build upon. Those would probably have looked something like this:

- As

    - a UI developer, I need a mechanism to send **create Artisan** messages to the Gateway service so that I can create a UI to execute that process
    - As a UI developer, I need a mechanism to send **delete Artisan** messages to the Gateway service so that I can create a UI to execute that process

Alternately, if each of the original stories' development processes had taken the approach of making sure that the entire process for each end user action, from GUI to service to database to (where applicable) amother user application, had tasks associated with it, that would have allowed the stories as they were originally written to be completed in their entirety.

This kind of gap, in a real-world situation, would have been addressed as part of grooming the stories, before they were even put into an active iteration. Story grooming is a development team activity, where incoming stories are examined, fleshed out, and (when necessary) tweaked with the help of any stakeholders to assure that they can be accomplished. Part of this process involves reviewing stories and their attendant tasks to assure that everything needed for the story to be worked to completion is accounted for. A review of that nature would almost certainly have revealed that either the stories, as originally presented here, had tasks that represented everything the story needed, or that splitting the original stories into UI and mechanism stories was necessary.

Still, a few stories from the original set feel like they can be closed, barring tweaks that might surface during the demonstration and review:

- As an Artisan, I need to be able to send data changes to the Artisan Gateway so that those changes can be propagated and acted upon as needed
- As a Central Office user, I need to be able to send data changes to the Artisan Gateway so that those changes can be propagated and acted upon as needed
- As any user sending messages across to or from the Artisan Gateway service, I need those messages to be signed so that they can be validated before being acted upon

Where hms_sys development could go from here

There's still a substantial amount of work needed for hms_sys to be *truly* complete, but all of the design, development, and process principles that needed to be exposed have been at this point, so this feels like a good point to break away from it and move on to other things. Before moving on, though, there are some easily identified items that could be picked up and worked on.

Code review, refactoring, and cleanup

There are at least a couple of items in the code as it stands right now that could be reviewed and remedied.

So far, there's been no call for any request-response process that would need to simply return any of the data objects. There are, however, methods that were stubbed out to address those potential needs (the various `response_{object}` methods in `ArtisanGatewayDaemon`), even though the needs themselves never surfaced. While it doesn't hurt to leave them in place, that would, ultimately, entail having test case classes and/or test methods that are required by the testing policy that don't really serve any purpose. The methods being tested don't do anything, and aren't expected to in the foreseeable future. At a minimum, these methods and any tests associated with them should probably be commented out, but they could even be completely removed, keeping the code cleaner.

Since distinct classes were created for orders in both the Artisan and Central Office contexts, taking some time to winnow out their common functionality and interface, and re-define the `BaseOrder` class in `hms_core` would clean the codebases up a bit too. That would also entail reworking the relevant unit tests, and might (probably trivially) touch other classes that use the current `Order` classes.

The presence of Central Office classes in `hms_core`, while an understandable decision at the time, could present a small data integrity risk on a longer term basis: as members of `hms_core`, they would, at present, be distributed as part of an Artisan application (which depends on `hms_core`), and would be available to a disgruntled Artisan, if that were ever to occur. Though the risk is probably trivial, it's certainly not an impossible scenario, and there's really no reason why an Artisan application should have any code that's intended for use only by Central Office staff. Re-organizing those items into a separate project/module, or altering the build/packaging process to actively remove that module from the Artisan application's codebase, feels like a good idea, eliminating any concerns that might arise about deploying code to users who wouldn't/shouldn't use it.

A similar reorganization effort may be needed later on with respect to where the `daemons.py` module lives, and how it's used. At this point, we don't really have a design for the end user applications–just a collection of functional requirements that have been implemented at a fundamental level, and so there's no real feeling for how the applications themselves will function. It's possible that the design would involve a local service, even if it's only running while the main application is active, in which case keeping `daemons.py` in the `hms_core` namespace makes sense. If, on the other hand, the end-user applications don't use such a service, then there's no reason to deploy the relevant code in either of the end-user applications and moving it into its own deployable package, or into a separate but dependent project would not a bad idea.

There are at least a few unit tests (the ones testing the various `to_data_dict` methods are probably the most obvious ones) that, because of the way the test arguments are used in deeply nested loops, will, over time, take longer and longer to execute. As things stand right now, there are as many as a dozen value variations that are (or could be) tested, and only a few values being used per variation. With three values per variation, and 12 variations to test, each of which lives in its own loop, that's 3^{12}—over half a million—assertions that would be executed on every execution of that test method. This takes time to execute. Reworking the various nested loop test methods so that each value variant is tested individually, un-nesting the loops, would speed up test execution significantly—there would be 36 (3 × 12) assertions instead of the half-million needed now. The trade-off is that the test code will be substantially longer, and potentially (slightly) more difficult to maintain as a result, but the time saved in the long run will be worth the effort.

Developing a UI

There are literally dozens of GUI options available for Python applications, even if the list is limited to those that are usable on more than one OS/platform—a list is maintained on the Python website at `https://wiki.python.org/moin/GuiProgramming`. The more widely used are sufficiently feature-rich, and whole books could be written about each of them. Noteworthy GUI frameworks and toolkits include the following:

- **Tkinter:** Distributed as part of Python installations
- **PyGObject:** A GUI used for many Linux/Gnome applications, related to GnomePython and PyGTK (`https://pygobject.readthedocs.io/en/latest/`)
- **Kivy:** This includes support for Android and iOS (iPhone) applications (`https://kivy.org/`)

Tkinter is the *de facto* standard for Python application GUIs, and has shipped with Python distributions for a long time. While the GUI elements it provides are, in many respects, quite basic, it provides enough of them for a wide range of application needs to be met. As one of the more mature options, there is a lot of documentation available for it (see `https://wiki.python.org/moin/TkInter`), and it is quite stable. There are also a fair number of extension packages available that likely address needs that a baseline Tkinter installation may not fulfil, including **Python Megawidgets** (**PMW**—`http://pmw.sourceforge.net/doc/`). While Tkinter GUIs may not be the most attractive in the world—their appearance is tightly bound to the GUI engine of the underlying OS, with all the variations that entails—they are *eminently* functional.

Tkinter doesn't have complex dependencies, making it extremely portable; a given Tkinter GUI will function without alteration on any OS, and simple tweaks based on the detection of which OS is present are generally not difficult, though they may require significant planning ahead of time.

If you've ever worked on a Linux system that has a Gnome frontend, the odds are good that you've been exposed to a **PyGObject**-based GUI, whether you knew it or not. Although it's part of the open source Gnome Project, and thus perhaps more focused on fulfilling needs for various Linux systems, PyGObject is a viable option on Windows and Macintosh systems as well. Like most of the GUI frameworks available for Python, PyGObject does involve at least some additional software installation, and there may be extensive dependencies involved, even if they aren't directly visible, but those should be managed by the installation process of PyGObject itself. PyGObject assumes at least some control over widget appearance, taking that control away from the underlying GUI engine of the OS in order to provide a more attractive appearance.

Kivy is a popular option, and is often cited as the go-to GUI framework for Python applications needing mobile technology support (Android and iOS applications). Judging by several of the entries in their gallery page (`https://kivy.org/#gallery`), it can provide very clean and attractive GUIs. Kivy uses its own design language to define how a GUI is laid out, and what the elements look like. Mobile application support through Kivy is accomplished by bundling a complete Python installation with each Android `apk` or iOS `app` file.

Another option, though it might sound odd at first, would be to implement the Artisan and Central Office applications as local web servers, and use HTML, CSS, and JavaScript to create the GUI. This isn't as far-fetched as it might sound: Python includes a variety of web server classes in the `http.server` module (`https://docs.python.org/3.6/library/http.server.html`), and even if none of them were ready to use as-is, they could be extended to provide whatever functionality was lacking. Though the servers provided might not be as powerful or feature-rich as a dedicated web server (Apache or IIS), they wouldn't really need to be, since there would be only a handful of users accessing it at any given time.

Order fulfilment and shipping APIs

The basic data changes involved in the order fulfilment process that an Artisan would execute are reasonably detailed and understood, but there is certainly room for improvement. One feature that would be very nice to have would be integration with online APIs for the various shipping companies that would be used to deliver those fulfilled order items. That integration, depending on the shape of all the requirements around it, could be a major development effort all by itself, and could include the following:

- Allowing an Artisan user to provide a package or shipping ID during transactions for both individual and multiple item fulfilment
- Sending a confirmation email (if the APIs don't handle that on their own) to the customer with shipment tracking information
- Sending some sort of notification to the Central Office that order items have been fulfilled, which would be a trigger for whatever manual or automatic process which pays the Artisan for the items shipped

Over and above that, there would be definitions needed for the various shipper APIs (since it's unlikely that any two of them will use the exact same request structure) and testing strategies and implementations for them, quite possibly with extensive mocking, if the APIs themselves don't provide any test harnesses.

Summary

The testing of services, particularly in a repeatable fashion that can be used as ongoing regression testing, has its own particular challenges, but none of them is insurmountable. The methods presented here are a solid starting point, and could be elaborated on in as much detail as required to meet almost any testing requirements. That said, these are reasonably complete, and easily managed/maintained should new testing requirements surface, whether through the discovery and correction of bugs, or the advent of new functional requirements that have to be reflected in tests.

18
Multiprocessing and HPC in Python

High-performance computing (HPC), quite simply, is the use of parallel processing during the execution of an application to spread the computational load across multiple processors, often across multiple machines. There are several MPC strategies to choose from, ranging from custom applications that leverage local multiprocessor computer architecture through to dedicated MPC systems, such as Hadoop or Apache Spark.

In this chapter, we will explore and apply different Python capabilities, building from executing a baseline algorithm against elements in a dataset one element at a time, and look at the following topics:

- Building parallel processing approaches that exploit locally available multiprocessor architectures, and the limitations of those approaches using Python's `multiprocessing` module
- Defining and implementing an approach across multiple machines to parallelize the baseline serial process—essentially creating a basic computational cluster
- Exploring how to use Python code in dedicated, industry-standard HPC clusters

Common factors to consider

Code that executes in a parallel manner has a few additional factors to consider as it's being developed. The first consideration is the input to the program. If the primary operations against any set of data are wrapped in a function or method, then the data is handed off to the function. The function does whatever it needs to do, and control is handed back to the code where the function was called. In a parallel processing scenario, that same function might be called any number of times, with different data, with control passing back to the calling code in a different order than their execution started in. As the datasets get larger, or more processing power is made available to parallelize the function, more control has to be exerted over how that function is called, as well as when (under what circumstances), in order to reduce or eliminate that possibility. There may also be a need to control how much data is being worked on at any given time, if only to avoid overwhelming the machine that the code is running on.

An example of this scenario seems to be in order. Consider three calls to the same function, all within a few milliseconds, where the first and third call complete in one second, but the second call, for whatever reason, takes ten seconds. The order of calls to the function would be as follows:

- Call #1
- Call #2
- Call #3

The order that those return in, though, is as follows:

- Call #1 (in one second)
- Call #3 (also in one second)
- Call #2 (in *ten* seconds)

The potential concern is that if the returns from the function are expected to come back in the same order they were called, even if it's only implicitly, with dependencies on Call #2 needed by Call #3, the expected data won't be present, and Call #3 will fail, probably in a very confusing manner.

This collection of controls over the input data, and as a result over when, how, and how often the parallelized process is executed, has several names, but we'll use the term orchestration here. Orchestration can take many forms, from simple loops over a small dataset, launching parallel processes for each element in the dataset, to large-scale, over-the-wire message-based process request-and-response mechanisms.

The output from a set of parallel processes also has to be considered in some detail. Some of the parallelization methods available in Python simply do not allow the results of a function call to be directly returned to the calling code (at least not yet). Others may allow it, but only when the active process is complete and the code actively attaches to the process, blocking access to any other processes until the targeted one has completed. One of the more common strategies for dealing with output is to create the processes to be parallelized so that they are fire-and-forget calls—calling the function deals with the actual processing of the data and with sending the results to some common destination. Destinations can include multiprocess-aware queues (provided by the multiprocessing module as a `Queue` class), writing data to files, storing the results to a database, or sending some sort of asynchronous message to somewhere that stores the results independent of the orchestration or execution of those processes. There may be several different terms for these processes, but we'll use dispatch in our exploration here. Dispatch may also be controlled to some extent by whatever orchestration processes are in play, or might have their own independent orchestration, depending on the complexity of the processes.

The processes themselves, and any post-dispatch use of their results, also need to be given some additional thought, at least potentially. Since the goal, ultimately, is to have some number of independent processes working on multiple elements of the dataset at the same time, and there is no sure way to anticipate how long any individual process might take to complete, there is a very real possibility that two or more processes will resolve and dispatch their data at different rates. That may be true even if the expected runtime for the relevant data elements is the same. There is no guarantee, then, for any given sequence of elements to be processed, that the results will be dispatched in the same sequence that the processes against those elements were started. This is particularly true in distributed processing architectures, since the individual machines that are actually doing the work may have other programs consuming their available CPU cycles, memory, or other resources that are needed to run the process.

Keeping the processes and the dispatch of their results independent, as much as possible, will go a long way toward mitigating that particular concern. Independent processes won't interact with or depend on any other processes, eliminating any potential for cross-process conflicts, and independent dispatches eliminate the potential for cross-results data contamination. If there is a need for processes that have dependencies, those can still be implemented, but additional effort (most likely in the form of dispatch-focused orchestration) may be needed to prevent conflicts from arising as results from parallel processes become available.

A simple but expensive algorithm

First, we need to solve a problem. In order to keep the focus on the various mechanisms for parallel processing, that domain of that problem needs to be easily understood. At the same time, it needs to allow for processing of arbitrarily large datasets, preferably with unpredictable runtimes per element in the dataset, and with results that are unpredictable. To that end, the problem we're going to solve is determining all of the factors of every number in some range of integer values. That is, for any given positive integer value, x, we want to be able to calculate and return a list of all the integer values that x is evenly divisible by. The function to calculate and return the list of factors for a single number (factors_of) is relatively simple:

```python
def factors_of(number:(int)) -> (list):
    """
Returns a list of factors of the provided number:
All integer-values (x) between 2 and number/2 where number % x == 0
    """
    if type(number) != int:
        raise TypeError(
            'factors_of expects a positive integer value, but was
passed '
            '"%s" (%s)' % (number, type(number).__name__)
        )
    if number < 1:
        raise ValueError(
            'factors_of expects a positive integer value, but was
passed '
            '"%s" (%s)' % (number, type(number).__name__)
        )
    return [
        x for x in range(2, int(number/2) + 1)
        if number % x == 0
    ]
```

Although this function, by itself, only deals with a single number, a process that calls it over and over again for any set of numbers can be scaled out to any number of numbers to process, giving us the arbitrarily large dataset capabilities when needed. The runtimes are somewhat predictable—it should be possible to get a reasonable runtime estimate for numbers across various ranges, though they will vary based on how large the number is. If a truly unpredictable runtime simulation is needed, we'd be able to pre-generate the list of numbers to be processed, then randomly select them, one at a time. Finally, the results on a number-by-number basis aren't predictable.

Some testing setup

It may be useful to capture some runtime information for a sample set of numbers, say from 10,000,000 to 10,001,000, capturing both the total runtime and the average time per number. A simple script (serial_baseline.py), executing the factors_of function against each of those numbers one at a time (serially), is easily assembled:

```python
#!/usr/bin/env python
"""serial_baseline.py

Getting data that we can use to estimate how long a factor_of call
will
take for some sample "large" numbers.
"""

print(
    '# Execution of %s, using all of one CPU\'s capacity' % __file__
)
print('='*80)
print()

import time
from factors import factors_of

# - The number we'll start with
range_start = 10000000
# - The number of calls we'll make to the function
range_length = 1000
# - The number that we'll end with - range *stops* at the number
#   specified without including it in the value-set
range_end = range_start + range_length + 1
# - Keep track of the time that the process starts
start_time = time.time()
# - Execute the function-call the requisite number of times
for number in range(range_start, range_end):
    factors_of(number)
# - Determine the total length of time the process took to execute
run_time = time.time() - start_time
# - Show the relevant data
print(
    '%d iterations executed in %0.6f seconds' %
    (range_length, run_time)
)
print(
    'Average time per iteration was %0.6f seconds' %
```

```
            (run_time/range_length)
    )
```

Assuming that any/all machines involved in the calculation processes are essentially identical in terms of processing power, the output from this script gives a reasonable estimate for how long it takes to perform the `factors_of` calculation against a number near a value of `10,000,000`. The output from a fairly new powerful laptop, where this code was initially tested, looked like this:

```
# Execution of serial_baseline.py, using all of 1 CPU's capacity
===============================================================================

1000 iterations executed in 422.351294 seconds
Average time per iteration was 0.422351 seconds
```

For testing purposes further down the line, we'll also create a constant list of test numbers (`TEST_NUMBERS`), chosen to provide a fairly wide range of processing times:

```
TEST_NUMBERS = [
    11,           # Should process very quickly
    16,           # Also quick, and has factors
    101,          # Slower, but still quick
    102,          # Slower, but still quick
    1001,         # Slower still, but still fairly quick
    1000001,      # Visibly longer processing time
    1000000001,   # Quite a while
]
```

These seven numbers were chosen to provide a good range of larger and smaller numbers, varying the individual runtimes for calls of the `factors_of` function. Since there are only seven numbers, any test runs that make use of them (instead of the 1,000 numbers used in the preceding code) will take substantially less time to execute, while still providing some insight into the individual runtimes if needed.

Local parallel processing

The primary focus for the local parallelization of processing will be on the `multiprocessing` module. There are a couple of other modules that might be usable for some parallelization efforts (and those will be discussed later), but `multiprocessing` provides the best combination of flexibility and power with the least potential for restrictions from the Python interpreter or other OS-level interference.

As might be expected from the module's name, `multiprocessing` provides a class (`Process`) that facilitates the creation of child processes. It also provides a number of other classes that can be used to make working with child processes easier, including `Queue` (a multiprocess-aware queue implementation that can be used as a data destination), and `Value` and `Array`, which allow single and multiple values (of a single type) to be stored in a memory space that is shared across multiple processes, respectively.

The full life cycle of a `Process` object involves the following steps:

1. Creating the `Process` object, defining what function or method will be executed when it is started, and any arguments that should be passed to it
2. Starting the `Process`, which begins its execution
3. Joining the `Process`, which waits for the process to complete, blocking further execution from the calling process until it is complete

For comparison purposes, a multiprocessing-based baseline timing test script, equivalent to the `serial_baseline.py` script, was created. The significant differences between the two scripts start with the import of the multiprocessing module:

```python
#!/usr/bin/env python
"""multiprocessing_baseline.py

Getting data that we can use to estimate how long a factor_of call
will
take for some sample "large" numbers.
"""

print(
    '# Execution of %s, using all available CPU capacity (%d)' %
    (__file__, multiprocessing.cpu_count())
)
print('='*80)

import multiprocessing
import time
```

Because there are multiple processes being created, and because they will need to be polled after all of them have been created, we create a list of processes, and append each new process as it's created. As the process objects are being created, we're specifying a name as well—that has no bearing or impact on the functionality, but does make things a bit more convenient for display purposes, should it be needed in testing:

```
# - Keep track of the processes
processes = []
# - Create and start all the processes needed
for number in range(range_start, range_end):
    process = multiprocessing.Process(
        name='factors_of-%d' % number,
        target=factors_of,
        args=(number,),
    )
    processes.append(process)
    process.start()
```

As soon as process.start() is called for each process, it launches and runs in the background until it's complete. The individual processes don't terminate once they're complete, though: that happens when process.join() is called and the process that has been joined has completed. Since we want all of the processes to start executing before joining to any of them (which blocks the continuation of the loop), we handle all of the joins separately—which also gives every process that has started some time to run until they're complete:

```
# - Iterate over the entire process-set, and use join() to connect
#   and wait for them
for process in processes:
    process.join()
```

The output from this test script on the same machine that the previous script was run on, and with the same programs running in the background, shows some significant improvement in the raw runtime:

```
# Execution of multiprocessing_baseline.py, using all available CPU capacity (4)
================================================================================

1000 iterations executed in 236.325325 seconds
Average time per iteration was 0.236325 seconds
```

This is an improvement, even without any sort of orchestration driving it other than whatever is managed by the underlying OS (it just throws the same 1,000 numbers at `Process` instances that call the `factors_of` function): the total runtime is about 55% of the time that the serial processing took.

 Why only 55%? Why not 25%, or at least close to that? Without some sort of orchestration to control how many processes were being run, this created a 1,000 processes, with all the attendant overhead at the operating system level, and had to give time to each of them in turn, so there was a lot of context shifting going on. A more carefully tuned orchestration process should be able to reduce that runtime more, but might not reduce it by much.

The next step toward a useful multiprocessing solution would be to actually be able to retrieve the results of the child process operations. In order to provide some visibility into what's actually happening, we're going to print several items through the process as well. We'll also randomize the sequence of test numbers so that each run will execute them in a different order, which will (often) show how the processes are interwoven:

```python
#!/usr/bin/env python
"""multiprocessing_tests.py
Also prints several bits of information as it runs, but those
can be removed once their purpose has been served
"""

import multiprocessing
import random
# - If we want to simulate longer run-times later for some reason,
#    this will need to be uncommented
# import time

from datetime import datetime
```

We're going to use TEST_NUMBERS we set up earlier, and randomly arrange them into a list:

```python
# - Use the small, fixed set of numbers to test with:
from factors import TEST_NUMBERS
# - Randomize the sequence of numbers
TEST_NUMBERS.sort(key=lambda i:random.randrange(1,1000000))
```

In order to actually capture the results, we'll need somewhere that they can be sent when they are calculated: an instance of multiprocessing.Queue:

```
queue = multiprocessing.Queue()
```

The resultant queue object, as noted earlier, lives in memory that is shared by and accessible to the top-level process (the multiprocessing_tests.py script) and by all of the child Process objects' processes when they execute.

Since we're going to be storing results in the queue object as they are calculated, we need to modify the factors_of function to handle that. We'll also add in some print() calls to display when the function is called, and when it's done with its work:

```
def factors_of(number:(int)) -> (list):
    """
Returns a list of factors of the provided number:
All integer-values (x) between 2 and number/2 where number % x == 0
    """
    print(
        '==> [%s] factors_of(%d) called' %
        (datetime.now().strftime('%H:%M:%S.%f'), number)
    )
```

The type and value checking remains unchanged:

```
    if type(number) != int:
        raise TypeError(
            'factors_of expects a positive integer value, but was
passed '
            '"%s" (%s)' % (number, type(number).__name__)
        )
    if number < 1:
        raise ValueError(
            'factors_of expects a positive integer value, but was
passed '
            '"%s" (%s)' % (number, type(number).__name__)
        )
    # - If we want to simulate longer run-times later for some reason,
    #   this will need to be uncommented
    #   time.sleep(10)
```

The actual calculation of the factors of `number` remains unchanged, though we're assigning the results to a variable instead of returning them so that we can deal with them differently as the function completes:

```
factors = [
        x for x in range(2, int(number/2) + 1)
        if number % x == 0
    ]
print(
    '<== [%s] factors_of(%d) complete' %
    (datetime.now().strftime('%H:%M:%S.%f'), number)
)
```

Instead of returning the calculated values, we're going to use `queue.put()` to add them to the results that `queue` is keeping track of. The `queue` object doesn't particularly care what data gets added to it—any object will be accepted—but for consistency's sake, and to assure that each result that gets sent back has both the number and the factors of that number, we'll `put` a `tuple` with both of those values:

```
queue.put((number, factors))
```

With all of that prepared, we can start the main body of the test script:

```
print(
    '# Execution of %s, using all available CPU capacity (%d)' %
    (__file__, multiprocessing.cpu_count())
)
print('='*80)
print()
```

We need to keep track of the starting time for the calculation of the runtime later:

```
start_time = time.time()
```

Creating and starting the processes that call `factors_of` is the same basic structure that we used earlier:

```
processes = []
for number in TEST_NUMBERS:
    # - Thread has been created, but not started yet
    process = multiprocessing.Process(
        name='factors_of-%d' % number,
        target=factors_of,
        args=(number,),
    )
    # - Keeping track of the individual threads
    processes.append(process)
```

```
        # - Starting the current thread
        process.start()
```

At this point, we have a set of started but possibly incomplete child processes running
in the background. If the first few that were created and started were for the smaller
numbers, they may have already completed, and are just waiting for a `join()` to
finish their execution and terminate. If, on the other hand, one of the *larger* numbers
was the first to be executed against, that first child process may well still be running
for some time, while the others, with shorter individual runtimes, may be idling in
the background, waiting for a `join()`. In any event, we can simply iterate over the
list of process items, and `join()` each one in turn until they're all done:

```
for process in processes:
    print(
        '*** [%s] Joining %s process' %
        (datetime.now().strftime('%H:%M:%S.%f'), process.name)
    )
    process.join()
```

Once all of the `join()` calls have completed, the `queue` will have all of the results for
all of the numbers, in an arbitrary order. The heavy lifting of the child processes is all
complete, so we can calculate the final runtime and show the relevant information:

```
# - Determine the total length of time the process took to execute
run_time = time.time() - start_time
# - Show the relevant data
print('='*80)
print(
    '%d factor_of iterations executed in %0.6f seconds' %
    (len(TEST_NUMBERS), run_time)
)
print(
    'Average time per iteration was %0.6f seconds' %
    (run_time/len(TEST_NUMBERS))
)
```

Actually accessing the results, which in this case is just for display purposes, requires
calling the `get` method of the queue object—each `get` call fetches and removes one
item that was put into the queue earlier, and for now we can simply print
`queue.get()` until the `queue` is empty:

```
print('='*80)
print('results:')
while not queue.empty():
    print(queue.get())
```

There are several noteworthy items that appear in the results of the test run, as shown in the following screenshot:

```
# Execution of multiprocessing_tests.py, using all available CPU capacity (4)
================================================================================

==> [20:47:47.268985] factors_of(11) called
==> [20:47:47.270272] factors_of(101) called
==> [20:47:47.270984] factors_of(102) called

*** [20:47:47.271755] Joining factors_of-11 process

==> [20:47:47.272125] factors_of(1000000001) called
==> [20:47:47.272729] factors_of(16) called
==> [20:47:47.273174] factors_of(1000001) called
==> [20:47:47.274394] factors_of(1001) called

<== [20:47:57.273740] factors_of(11) complete

*** [20:47:57.276896] Joining factors_of-1000001 process

<== [20:47:57.279912] factors_of(101) complete
<== [20:47:57.280497] factors_of(102) complete
<== [20:47:57.281377] factors_of(16) complete
<== [20:47:57.285299] factors_of(1001) complete
<== [20:47:57.356765] factors_of(1000001) complete

*** [20:47:57.357743] Joining factors_of-101 process
*** [20:47:57.357819] Joining factors_of-102 process
*** [20:47:57.357852] Joining factors_of-1000000001 process

<== [20:48:40.374990] factors_of(1000000001) complete

*** [20:48:40.376157] Joining factors_of-16 process
*** [20:48:40.376216] Joining factors_of-1001 process
================================================================================
7 factor_of iterations executed in 53.109640 seconds
Average time per iteration was 7.587091 seconds
================================================================================
results:
(11, [])
(101, [])
(16, [2, 4, 8])
(102, [2, 3, 6, 17, 34, 51])
(1001, [7, 11, 13, 77, 91, 143])
(1000001, [101, 9901])
(1000000001, [7, 11, <truncated for brevity> , 90909091, 142857143])
```

All of the lines that begin with ==> show where the calls to the factors_of function occurred during the run. Unsurprisingly, they are all near the beginning of the process. The lines beginning with *** show where the processes were joined—one of which happened in the middle of a run of Process creation events. Lines beginning with <== show where the factors_of calls were completed, after which they remained idle until the corresponding process.join() was called.

The randomized sequence of test numbers, judging by the calls to factors_of, was 11, 101, 102, 1000000001, 16, 1000001, and 1001. The sequence of calls completed was 11, 101, 102, 16, 1001, 1000001, and 100000000—a slightly different sequence, and the *joins* sequence (and thus the sequence of the final **results**) was slightly different from that as well. All of these confirm that the various processes were starting, executing, and completing independently of the main process (the for number in TEST_NUMBERS loop).

With the Queue instance in place, and a way established for accessing the results of the child processes, that's everything really needed for basic local multiprocess-based parallelization. There are a few things that could be tweaked or enhanced, if there were functional needs for them:

- If throttling of the number of active child processes were needed, or any finer control over how or when they were created, started, and joined, a more structured Orchestrator of some sort could be constructed:

  - The number of processes allowed could be limited based on the number of available CPUs on the machine, which can be retrieved with multiprocessing.cpu_count().

  - Regardless of how the number of processes allowed was determined, limiting the number of active processes could be managed in several ways, including a Queue for pending requests, another for results, and a third for requests that were ready to be joined. Overriding each Queue object's put so that it would check the other queues' status, and trigger whatever actions/code was appropriate in those other queues, could allow a single queue to control the entire process.

- Orchestration functionality could, itself, be wrapped in a `Process`, as could whatever data handling was needed after the dispatch of the child process data.

- The multiprocessing module also provides other object types that might prove useful for certain multiprocessing scenarios, including the following:

  - The `multiprocessing.pool.Pool` class—objects that provide/control a pool of Worker processes to which jobs can be submitted, with support for asynchronous results, timeouts and callbacks, and more

  - A variety of manager-object options that provide ways to create data that can be shared between different processes—including sharing over a network between processes running on different machines

Threads

Python has another local parallelization library—`thread`. The `thread` objects it provides are created and used in much the same way that `multiprocessing.Process` objects are, but thread-based processes run in the same memory space as the parent process, while `Process` objects, when they are started, actually create a new Python interpreter instance (with some connection capabilities to the parent Python interpreter).

Because threads run in the same interpreter and memory space, they are not capable of accessing multiple processors the same way that a `Process` can.

 A thread's access to multiple CPUs on a machine is a function of the Python interpreter that's used to run the code. The standard interpreter that ships with Python (Cpython) and the alternative PyPy interpreter both share this limitation. IronPython, an interpreter that runs under/in the .NET framework, and Jython, which runs in a Java runtime environment, do not have that limitation.

Thread-based parallelization is also far more likely to encounter conflicts with Python's **global interpreter lock (GIL)**. The GIL actively prevents multiple threads from executing or altering the same Python bytecode at the same time. There are some potentially long-running processes that happen outside the GIL's control—I/O, networking, some image processing functionality, and various libraries such as NumPy—but outside those exceptions, any multithreaded Python program that spends a lot of its execution time interpreting or manipulating Python bytecode will eventually hit a GIL bottleneck, losing its parallelization in the process.

 More information about the GIL, why it exists, what it does, and so on, can be found on the Python wiki at `https://wiki.python.org/moin/GlobalInterpreterLock`.

Parallelizing across multiple machines

Another common parallelization strategy is to spread the workload of computational processes across multiple machines (physical or virtual). Where local parallelization is limited, ultimately, by the number of CPUs, or the number of cores, or the combination of both on a single machine, machine-level parallelization is limited by the number of machines that can be thrown at a problem. In this day and age, with immense reservoirs of virtual machines able to be made available in public clouds and private data centers, it's relatively easy to scale the number of available machines to match the computational needs of a problem.

The basic design for this kind of horizontally scalable solution is more complicated than the design for a local solution—it has to accomplish the same tasks, but separate the ability to do those tasks so that they can be made available on any number of machines, and provide mechanisms for executing processes and accepting the results from the remote tasks as they complete. In order to be reasonably fault-tolerant, there also needs to be more visibility into the status of the remote process machines, and those, in turn, have to be proactive about sending notifications to the central controller when something occurs that will disrupt their ability to do their jobs. A typical logical architecture, at a high level, looks like this:

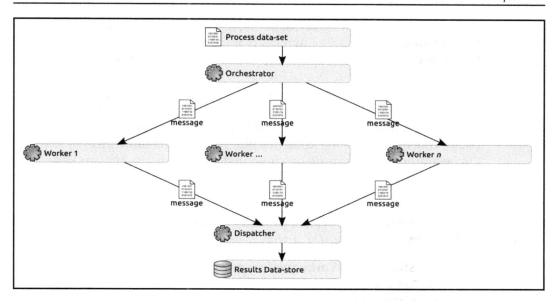

Where:

- The **Orchestrator** is a process running on one machine that is responsible for taking bits of the **Process dataset**, and sending them to the next available **Worker.**
- It also keeps track of what **Worker** nodes are available, and probably what each Worker's capacity is.
- In order to accomplish that, the **Orchestrator** would have to be capable of registering and unregistering **Worker** nodes.
- The **Orchestrator** should probably also keep track of the general health/availability of each of its **Worker** nodes, and be able to associate tasks with those nodes—if one becomes unavailable, and still has pending tasks, it can then reassign those tasks to other, available **Worker** nodes.
- Each **Worker** node is a process running on an individual machine that, while running, accepts process instructions in incoming **message** items, executes the process(es) necessary to generate the results, and sends a results **message** to the **Dispatcher** when complete.
- Each **Worker** node would also have to announce to the **Orchestrator** when it becomes available, in order to be registered, and when it is shutting down normally so that the **Orchestrator** could unregister it accordingly.

- If processing an incoming **message** wasn't possible because of an error, a **Worker** should also be able to relay that information back to the **Orchestrator**, allowing it to reassign the task to another **Worker** when it can.
- The **Dispatcher** is a process running on one machine that is responsible for accepting result message data, and doing whatever needs to be done with it—storing it in a database, writing it to a file, and so on. The **Dispatcher** could, conceivably, be the same machine, or even the same process as the Orchestrator—so long as dispatch-related message items get handled appropriately and without bogging down the orchestration processes, where it lives is a matter of preference.

The basic structure of this kind of system could be implemented with the code that was already shown in Chapter 16, *The Artisan Gateway Service*:

- The **Orchestrator** and **Worker** nodes could be implemented as a daemon, similar to ArtisanGatewayDaemon. If it were determined that the **Dispatcher** needed to be independent, it, too, could be a similar daemon.
- The messaging between them could be handled with a variant of DaemonMessage objects, providing the same signed message security, transmitted over a RabbitMQ message system.
- That message transmission process could leverage the RabbitMQSender class that was already defined (also from Chapter 16, *The Artisan Gateway Service*).

A complete implementation of this approach is outside the scope of this book, but the critical aspects of it can be examined in enough detail to write an implementation if the reader so desires.

Common functionality

The existing DaemonMessage class would need to be altered or overridden to accept different operations at the Orchestrator, Worker, and Dispatcher levels, creating new namedtuple constants that are applicable for each. Initially, the Worker node would only be concerned with accepting calls to its factors_of method, and its allowed operations would reflect this:

```
WORKER_OPERATIONS = namedtuple(
    'WORKER_OPERATIONS', ['factors_of',]
)
(
```

```
        factors_of='factors_of',
    )
```

The corresponding change to the setter method for the operation property could use the appropriate `namedtuple` constant to control accepted values (for example, replacing _OPERATIONS with WORKER_OPERATIONS, in some fashion, for a Worker node's implementation):

```
        def _set_operation(self, value:str) -> None:
    #  - Other operations would need to be added
            if not value in _OPERATIONS:
                raise ValueError(
                    '%s.operation expects a string value (one of '
                    '"%s"), but was passed "%s" (%s)' %
                    (
                        self.__class__.__name__,
                        '", "'.join(_OPERATIONS._fields),
                        value, type(value).__name__
                    )
                )
            self._operation = value
```

Similarly, all three components would potentially need to know about all the possible `origin` values, in order to be able to assign message origins appropriately:

```
MESSAGE_ORIGINS = namedtuple(
    'MESSAGE_ORIGINS', ['orchestrator', 'worker', 'dispatcher']
)
(
    orchestrator='orchestrator',
    worker='worker',
    dispatcher='dispatcher',
)
```

The `main` method of any of the individual daemons would remain essentially unchanged from how `ArtisanGatewayDaemon` implemented it.

In this approach, there are only a few distinct variations of a few class members for each of the daemon classes (Worker Node, Orchestrator, and Dispatcher), but they are worth noting because of their distinct nature. The bulk of the differences is in the `_handle_message` methods of each daemon class, and each would have to implement its own instance methods for the operations they map process requests to as well.

The Worker nodes

All of the operations that were defined in the previous section for a hypothetical Worker daemon would have to be handled in the class' _handle_message method—to start with, that's nothing more than the factors_of method:

```python
def _handle_message(self, message:(DaemonMessage,)) -> None:
    self.info(
        '%s._handle_message called:' % self.__class__.__name__
    )
    target = message.data.get('target')
    self.debug('+- target ....... (%s) %s' % (
        type(target).__name__, target)
    )
    self.debug('+- operation .... (%s) %s' % (
        type(message.operation).__name__, message.operation)
    )
    if message.operation == WORKER_OPERATIONS.factors_of:
        self.factors_of(message)
    else:
        raise RuntimeError(
            '%s error: "%s" (%s) is not a recognized '
            'operation' %
            (
                self.__class__.__name__, message.operation,
                type(message.operation).__name__
            )
        )
```

The implementation of the factors_of method would not be substantially different from the original factors_of function, as defined at the beginning of this chapter, except that it would have to send a results message to the Dispatcher's message queue rather than returning a value:

```python
def factors_of(self, number):

    # ... code that generates the results

    # - Assuming that the configuration for RabbitMQSender
    #   is handled elsewhere, we can just get a new instance
    sender = RabbitMQSender()
    outbound_message = DaemonMessage(
        operation=dispatch_results,
        origin=MESSAGE_ORIGINS.worker,
        data={
            'number':number,
            'factors':factors,
```

```
    },
    signing_key=self.signing_key
)
sender.send_message(outbound_message, self.dispatcher_queue)
```

The Worker node daemons, which need to notify the Orchestrator when they become available and are becoming unavailable, can do so in their `preflight` and `cleanup` methods, respectively:

```
def preflight(self):
    """

Sends a message to the orchestrator to indicate that the instance is
no longer available
    """
    # - Assuming that the configuration for RabbitMQSender
    #   is handled elsewhere, we can just get a new instance
    sender = RabbitMQSender()
    outbound_message = DaemonMessage(
        operation=ORCHESTRATOR_OPERATIONS.register_worker,
        origin=MESSAGE_ORIGINS.worker,
        data={
            'worker_id':self.worker_id,
            'max_capacity':1,
        },
        signing_key=self.signing_key
    )
    sender.send_message(outbound_message, self.orchestrator_queue)

def cleanup(self):
    """

Sends a message to the orchestrator to indicate that the instance is
no longer available
    """
    # - Assuming that the configuration for RabbitMQSender
    #   is handled elsewhere, we can just get a new instance
    sender = RabbitMQSender()
    outbound_message = DaemonMessage(
        operation=DISPATCH_OPERATIONS.unregister_worker,
        origin=MESSAGE_ORIGINS.worker,
        data={
            'worker_id':self.worker_id,
        },
        signing_key=self.signing_key
    )
    sender.send_message(outbound_message, self.orchestrator_queue)
```

They would also have to implement the `dispatcher_queue`, `worker_id`, and `orchestrator_queue` properties that these methods use, providing a unique identifier of the worker node (which could be as simple as a random `UUID`) and the common Orchestrator and Dispatcher queue names (probably from a configuration file that's common to all Worker instances).

The Orchestrator

The Orchestrator would be concerned with registration, unregistration, and pulse operations (allowing the Workers to send messages to the Orchestrator, essentially saying "I'm still alive"):

```
ORCHESTRATOR_OPERATIONS = namedtuple(
    'ORCHESTRATOR_OPERATIONS', [
        'register_worker', 'unregister_worker', 'worker_pulse'
    ]
)
(
    register_worker='register_worker',
    unregister_worker='unregister_worker',
    worker_pulse='worker_pulse',
)
```

The Orchestrator's `_handle_message` would have to map each operation to the appropriate method:

```
def _handle_message(self, message:(DaemonMessage,)) -> None:
    self.info(
        '%s._handle_message called:' % self.__class__.__name__
    )

    # ...

    if message.operation ==
ORCHESTRATOR_OPERATIONS.register_worker:
        self.register_worker(message)
    elif message.operation ==
ORCHESTRATOR_OPERATIONS.unregister_worker:
        self.unregister_worker(message)
    elif message.operation ==
ORCHESTRATOR_OPERATIONS.worker_pulse:
        self.worker_pulse(message)
    else:
        raise RuntimeError(
            '%s error: "%s" (%s) is not a recognized '
```

```
        'operation' %
        (
            self.__class__.__name__, message.operation,
            type(message.operation).__name__
        )
    )
```

The Dispatcher

Initially, the Dispatcher, if it were an independent process and not folded into the Orchestrator, would be concerned with dispatch result operations only:

```
DISPATCH_OPERATIONS = namedtuple(
    'DISPATCH_OPERATIONS', ['dispatch_results',]
)
(
    dispatch_results='dispatch_results',
)
```

Its _handle_message method would be constructed accordingly:

```
    def _handle_message(self, message:(DaemonMessage,)) -> None:
        self.info(
            '%s._handle_message called:' % self.__class__.__name__
        )

        # ...

        if message.operation == DISPATCH_OPERATIONS.dispatch_results:
            self.dispatch_results(message)
        else:
            raise RuntimeError(
                '%s error: "%s" (%s) is not a recognized '
                'operation' %
                (
                    self.__class__.__name__, message.operation,
                    type(message.operation).__name__
                )
            )
```

Integrating Python with large-scale, cluster computing frameworks

Large-scale, cluster computing frameworks, in order to provide as much compatibility with custom written operations as possible, will probably accept input in only two different ways: as command-line arguments, or using standard input, with the latter being more common for systems that are targeted for big data operations. In either case, what's needed to allow a custom process to be executed at and scaled to a clustered environment is a self-contained, command-line executable that usually returns its data to standard output.

A minimal script that accepts standard input—whether by passing data into it with a pipe, or by reading the contents of a file and using that—could be implemented like this:

```
#!/usr/bin/env python
"""factors_stdin.py

A command-line-ready script that allows factors_of to be called with

> {incoming list of numbers} | python factors_stdin.py

which executes factors_of against the provided numbers and prints the
result FOR EACH NUMBER in the format

number:[factors-of-number]
"""
```

Standard input is available through Python's `sys` module as `sys.stdin`. It's a file-like object, and can be both read and iterated over on a line-by-line basis:

```
from sys import stdin
```

The `factors_of` function should probably be included directly in the script code, if only so that the entire script is totally self-contained, and won't require any custom software installation to be usable. For the sake of keeping the code shorter and easier to walk through, though, we'll just import it:

```
from factors import factors_of
```

If the script is executed directly—python factors_stdin.py—then we'll actually execute the process, starting with acquiring all of the numbers from stdin. They may come in as multiple lines, each of which could have multiple numbers, so the first step is to extract all of them so that we end up with one list of numbers to process:

```python
if __name__ == '__main__':
    # - Create a list of stdin lines - multi-line input is
    #   common enough that it needs to be handled
    lines = [line.strip() for line in stdin]
    # - We need the numbers as individual values, though, so
    #   build a list of them that we'll actually execute against
    numbers = []
    for line in lines:
        numbers += [n for n in line.split(' ') if n]
```

With all of the numbers ready, we can iterate over them, convert each value from the string value that was in the input into an actual int, and process them. If a value in the input can't be converted to an int, we'll simply skip it for now, though depending on the calling cluster framework, there may be specific ways to handle—or at least log—any bad values as errors:

```python
for number in numbers:
    try:
        number = int(number)
    except Exception as error:
        pass
    else:
        # - We've got the number, so execute the function and
        #   print the results
        print('%d:%s' % (number, factors_of(number)))
```

The script can be tested by echoing a list of numbers, and piping that into python factors_stdin.py. The results are printed, one result per line, which would be accepted by a calling program as standard output, ready to be passed to some other process that accepted standard input:

```
> echo "4 8 15 16 23 42" | python factors_stdin.py
4:[2]
8:[2, 4]
15:[3, 5]
16:[2, 4, 8]
23:[]
42:[2, 3, 6, 7, 14, 21]
```

If the source numbers are in a file (`hugos_numbers.txt`, in the chapter code), those can be used just as easily, and generate the same results:

```
> cat hugos_numbers.txt | python factors_stdin.py
4:[2]
8:[2, 4]
15:[3, 5]
16:[2, 4, 8]
23:[]
42:[2, 3, 6, 7, 14, 21]
```

If the cluster environment expects command-line arguments to be passed, a script can be written to accommodate that as well. It starts with much the same code:

```python
#!/usr/bin/env python
"""factors_cli.py

A command-line-ready script that allows factors_of to be called with

> python factors_cli.py number [number [number]] ...

which executes factors_of against the provided numbers and
prints the results for each in the format

number:[factors-of-number]
"""

from factors import factors_of
from sys import argv
```

Where it deviates is in acquiring the numbers to be processed. Since they are passed as command-line values, they will be part of the `argv` list (another item provided by Python's `sys` module), after the script name. The balance of this process is identical to the `stdin` based script:

```python
if __name__ == '__main__':
    # - Get the numbers from the arguments
    numbers = argv[1:]
    for number in numbers:
        try:
            number = int(number)
        except Exception as error:
            # - Errors should probably be logged in some fashion,
            #   but the specifics may well vary across different
            #   systems, so for now we'll just pass, skipping anything
            #   that can't be handled.
```

```
        pass
    else:
        # - We've got the number, so execute the function and
        #   print the results
        print('%d:%s' % (number, factors_of(number)))
```

The output, as with the previous script, is simply printed to the console, and would be accepted as standard input by any other processes that it was handed off to:

```
> python factors_cli.py 4 8 15 16 23 42
4:[2]
8:[2, 4]
15:[3, 5]
16:[2, 4, 8]
23:[]
42:[2, 3, 6, 7, 14, 21]
```

Python, Hadoop, and Spark

It's likely that the most common or popular of the large-scale, cluster computing frameworks available is Hadoop. Hadoop is a collection of software that provides cluster computing capabilities across networked computers, as well as a distributed storage mechanism that can be thought of as a network-accessible filesystem.

Among the utilities it provides is Hadoop Streaming (https://hadoop.apache.org/docs/r1.2.1/streaming.html), which allows for the creation and execution of Map/Reduce jobs using any executable or script as a mapper and/or reducer. Hadoop's operational model, at least for processes that can use Streaming, is file-centric, so processes written in Python and executed under Hadoop will tend to fall into the stdin based category that we discussed earlier more often than not.

Apache Spark is another option in the large-scale, cluster computing frameworks arena. Spark is a distributed, general-purpose framework, and has a Python API (pyspark, http://spark.apache.org/docs/2.2.0/api/python/pyspark.html) available for installation with pip, allowing for more direct access to its capabilities.

Summary

In this chapter, we have covered all of the basic permutations (serial and parallel, local and remote/distributed) of multiprocessing in Python, as it would apply to custom HPC operations. The basics needed for integrating a process written in Python to be executed by a large-scale cluster computing system such as Hadoop are quite basic—simple executable scripts—and the integration prospects with those system are as varied as the systems themselves.

19
Programming versus Software Engineering

Development shops often have specific levels, grades, or ranks that their developers fall into, indicating the levels of experience, expertise, and industry wisdom expected of staff at each level. These may vary (perhaps wildly) from location to location, but a typical structure looks something like the following:

- **Junior developers:** A junior developer is typically someone that doesn't have much programming experience. They probably know the basics of writing code, but they are not expected to know much beyond that.

- **Developers:** Mid-level developers (referred to by whatever formal title might apply) usually have enough experience that they can be relied on to write reasonably solid code, with little to no supervision. They probably have enough experience to determine implementation details and strategies, and they will often have some understanding of how different chunks of code can (and do) interact with each other, and what approaches will minimize difficulties in those interactions.

- **Senior developers:** Senior developers have enough experience - even if it's focused on a set of specific products/projects - to firmly grasp all of the technical skills involved in typical development efforts. At this point in their careers, they will almost always have a solid handle on a lot of the non-technical (or semi-technical) skills that are involved, as well—especially policies and procedures, and strategies and tactics that encourage or enforce business values such as stability and the predictability of development efforts. They may not be experts in those areas, but they will know when to call out risks, and they will often have several options to suggest for mitigating those risks.

Above the level of the senior developer, the terminology and definition often varies even more wildly, and the skill set usually starts to focus more on business-related abilities and responsibilities (scope and influence) than on technical capabilities or expertise.

The dividing line between programming and software engineering falls somewhere within the differences between developers and senior developers, as far as technical capabilities and expertise are concerned. At a junior level, and sometimes at a developer level, efforts are often centered around nothing more than writing code to meet whatever requirements apply, and conforming to whatever standards are in play. Software engineering, at a senior developer level, has a big-picture view of the same end results. The bigger picture involves awareness of, and attention paid to, the following things:

- Standards, both technical/developmental and otherwise, including best practices
- The goals that code is written to accomplish, including the business values that are attached to them
- The shape and scope of the entire system that the code is a part of

The bigger picture

So, what does this bigger picture look like? There are three easily-identifiable areas of focus, with a fourth (call it **user interaction**) that either weaves through the other three or is broken down into its own groups.

Software engineering must pay heed to standards, especially non-technical (business) ones, and also best practices. These may or may not be followed but, since they are standards or best practices for a reason, not following them is something that should always be a conscious (and defensible) decision. It's not unusual for business-process standards and practices to span multiple software components, which can make them difficult to track if a certain degree of discipline and planning isn't factored into the development process to make them more visible. On the purely development-related side, standards and best practices can drastically impact the creation and upkeep of code, its ongoing usefulness, and even just the ability to find a given chunk of code, when necessary.

It's rare for code to be written simply for the sake of writing code. There's almost always some other value associated with it, especially if there's business value or actual revenue associated with a product that the code is a part of. In those cases, understandably, the people that are paying for the developmental effort will be very interested in ensuring that everything works as expected (code-quality) and can be deployed when expected (process-predictability).

Code-quality concerns will be addressed during the development of the `hms_sys` project a few chapters from now, and process-predictability is mostly impacted by the developmental methodologies discussed in `Chapter 5`, *The hms_sys System-Project*.

The remaining policy-and-procedure related concerns are generally managed by setting up and following various standards, processes, and best practices during the startup of a project (or perhaps a development team). Those items - things such as setting up source control, having standard coding conventions, and planning for repeatable, automated testing - will be examined in some detail during the set up chapter for the `hms_sys` project. Ideally, once these kinds of developmental process are in place, the ongoing activities that keep them running and reliable will just become habits, a part of the day-to-day process, almost fading into the background.

Finally, with more of a focus on the code side, software engineering must, by necessity, pay heed to entire systems, keeping a universal view of the system in mind. Software is composed of a lot of elements that might be classified as **atomic**; they are indivisible units in and of themselves, under normal circumstances. Just like their real-world counterparts, when they start to interact, things get interesting, and hopefully useful. Unfortunately, that's also when unexpected (or even dangerous) behaviors—bugs—usually start to appear.

This awareness is, perhaps, one of the more difficult items to cultivate. It relies on knowledge that may not be obvious, documented, or readily available. In large or complex systems, it may not even be obvious where to start looking, or what kinds of question to ask to try to find the information needed to acquire that knowledge.

Asking questions

There can be as many distinct questions that can be asked about any given chunk of code as there are chunks of code to ask about—even very simple code, living in a complex system, can raise questions in response to questions, and more questions in response to those questions.

If there isn't an obvious starting point, starting with the following really basic questions is a good first step:

- Who will be using the functionality?
- What will they be doing with it?
- When, and where, will they have access to it?
- What problem is it trying to solve? For example, why do they need it?
- How does it have to work? If detail is lacking, breaking this one down into two separate questions is useful:
    - What should happen if it executes successfully?
    - What should happen if the execution fails?

Teasing out more information about the whole system usually starts with something as basic as the following questions:

- What other parts of the system does this code interact with?
- How does it interact with them?

Having identified all of the moving parts, thinking about "What happens if…" scenarios is a good way to identify potential points where things will break, risks, and dangerous interactions. You can ask questions such as the following:

- What happens if this argument, which expects a number, is handed a string?
- What happens if that property isn't the object that's expected?
- What happens if some other object tries to change this object while it's already being changed?

Whenever one question has been answered, simply ask, What else? This can be useful for verifying whether the current answer is reasonably complete.

Let's see this process in action. To provide some context, a new function is being written for a system that keeps track of mineral resources on a map-grid, for three resources: gold, silver, and copper. Grid locations are measured in meters from a common origin point, and each grid location keeps track of a floating-point number, from 0.0 to 1.0, which indicates how likely it is that resource will be found in the grid square. The developmental dataset already includes four default nodes - at (0,0), (0,1), (1,0), and (1,1) - with no values, as follows:

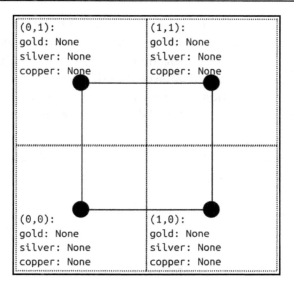

The system already has some classes defined to represent individual map nodes, and functions to provide basic access to those nodes and their properties, from whatever central data store they live in:

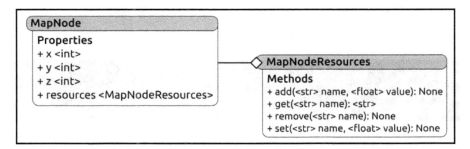

Constants, exceptions, and functions for various purposes already exist, as follows:

- `node_resource_names`: This contains all of the resource names that the system is concerned with, and can be thought of and treated as a list of strings: `['gold', 'silver', 'copper']`
- `NodeAlreadyExistsError`: An exception that will be raised if an attempt is made to create a `MapNode` that already exists
- `NonexistentNodeError`: An exception that will be raised if a request is made for a `MapNode` that doesn't exist

- `OutOfMapBoundsError`: An exception that will be raised if a request is made for a `MapNode` that isn't allowed to exist in the map area
- `create_node(x,y)`: Creates and returns a new, default `MapNode`, registering it in the global dataset of nodes in the process
- `get_node(x,y)`: Finds and returns a `MapNode` at the specified (x, y) coordinate location in the global dataset of available nodes

A developer makes an initial attempt at writing the code to set a value for a single resource at a given node, as a part of a project. The resulting code looks as follows (assume that all necessary imports already exist):

```
def SetNodeResource(x, y, z, r, v):
    n = get_node(x,y)
    n.z = z
    n.resources.add(r, v)
```

This code is functional, from the perspective that it will do what it's supposed to (and what the developer expected) for a set of simple tests; for example, executing, as follows:

```
SetNodeResource(0,0,None,'gold',0.25) print(get_node(0,0))
SetNodeResource(0,0,None,'silver',0.25) print(get_node(0,0))
SetNodeResource(0,0,None,'copper',0.25) print(get_node(0,0))
```

The results are in the following output:

```
<MapNode (0,0) {'silver': None, 'gold': 0.25, 'copper': None}>
<MapNode (0,0) {'silver': 0.25, 'gold': 0.25, 'copper': None}>
<MapNode (0,0) {'silver': 0.25, 'gold': 0.25, 'copper': 0.25}>
```

By that measure, there's nothing wrong with the code and its functions, after all. Now, let's ask some of our questions, as follows:

- **Who will be using this functionality?**: The function may be called, by either of two different application front-ends, by on-site surveyors, or by post-survey assayers. The surveyors probably won't use it often, but if they see obvious signs of a deposit during the survey, they're expected to log it with a 100% certainty of finding the resource(s) at that grid location; otherwise, they'll leave the resource rating completely alone.

- **What will they be doing with it?**: Between the base requirements (to set a value for a single resource at a given node) and the preceding answer, this feels like it's already been answered.

- **When, and where, do they have access to it?**: Through a library that's used by the surveyor and assayer applications. No one will use it directly, but it will be integrated into those applications.

- **How should it work?**: This has already been answered, but raises the question: Will there ever be a need to add more than one resource rating at a time? That's probably worth nothing, if there's a good place to implement it.

- **What other parts of the system does this code interact with?**: There's not much here that isn't obvious from the code; it uses MapNode objects, those objects' resources, and the get_node function.

- **What happens if an attempt is made to alter an existing MapNode?**: With the code as it was originally written, this behaves as expected. This is the happy path that the code was written to handle, and it works.

- **What happens if a node doesn't already exist?**: The fact that there is a NonexistentNodeError defined is a good clue that at least some map operations require a node to exist before they can complete. Execute a quick test against that by calling the existing function, as follows:

```
SetNodeResource(0,6,None,'gold',0.25)
```

The preceding command results in the following:

```
Traceback (most recent call last):
    SetNodeResource(0,6,None,'gold',0.25)

# stripped for brevity ...

map_nodes.NonExistantNodeError
```

This is the result because the development data doesn't have a MapNode at that location yet.

- **What happens if a node can't exist at a given location?**: Similarly, there's an OutOfMapBoundsError defined. Since there are no out-of-bounds nodes in the development data, and the code won't currently get past the fact that an out-of-bounds node doesn't exist, there's no good way to see what happens if this is attempted.

- **What happens if the z-value isn't known at the time?:** Since the `create_node` function doesn't even expect a z-value, but MapNode instances have one, there's a real risk that calling this function on an existing node would overwrite an existing z-altitude value, on an existing node. That, in the long run, could be a critical bug.
- **Does this meet all of the various developmental standards that apply?:** Without any details about standards, it's probably fair to assume that any standards that were defined would probably include, at a minimum, the following:
    - Naming conventions for code elements, such as function names and arguments; an existing function at the same logical level as `get_node`, using `SetNodeResources` as the name of the new function, while perfectly legal syntactically, may be violating a naming convention standard.
    - At least some of the effort towards documentation, of which there's none.
    - Some inline comments (maybe), if there is a need to explain parts of the code to future readers—there are none of these also, although, given the amount of code in this version and the relatively straightforward approach, it's arguable whether there would be any need.
- **What should happen if the execution fails?:** It should probably throw explicit errors, with reasonably detailed error messages, if something fails during execution.
- **What happens if an invalid value is passed for any of the arguments?:** Some of them can be tested by executing the current function (as was done previously), while supplying invalid arguments—an out-of -range number first, then an invalid resource name.

Consider the following code, executed with an invalid number:

```
SetNodeResource(0,0,'gold',2)
```

The preceding code results in the following output:

```
ValueError: set_node_resource expects a float value from
0.0-1.0, or a value that can be converted to one, for
resource_value: 2.0 (float) is not valid
```

Also, consider the following code, with an invalid resource type:

```
SetNodeResource(0,0,'tin',0.25)
```

The preceding code results in the following:

```
ValueError: tin is not a tracked resource
(gold,silver,copper)
```

The function itself can either succeed or raise an error during execution, judging by these examples; so, ultimately, all that really needs to happen is that those potential errors have to be accounted for, in some fashion.

Other questions may come to mind, but the preceding questions are enough to implement some significant changes. The final version of the function, after considering the implications of the preceding answers and working out how to handle the issues that those answers exposed, is as follows:

```
def set_node_resource(x, y, resource_name,
    resource_value, z=None):
    """
Sets the value of a named resource for a specified
node, creating that node in the process if it doesn't
exist.

Returns the MapNode instance.

Arguments:
 - x ............... (int, required, non-negative) The
                     x-coordinate location of the node
                     that the resource type and value is
                     to be associated with.
 - y ............... (int, required, non-negative) The
                     y-coordinate location of the node
                     that the resource type and value is
                     to be associated with.
 - z ............... (int, optional, defaults to None)
                     The z-coordinate (altitude) of the
                     node.
 - resource_name .... (str, required, member of
                      node_resource_names) The name of the
                      resource to associate with the node.
 - resource_value ... (float, required, between 0.0 and 1.0,
                       inclusive) The presence of the
                       resource at the node's location.
```

```
Raises
 - RuntimeError if any errors are detected.
"""
    # Get the node, if it exists
    try:
        node = get_node(x,y)
    except NonexistentNodeError:
        # The node doesn't exist, so create it and
        # populate it as applicable
        node = create_node(x, y)
    # If z is specified, set it
    if z != None:
        node.z = z
# TODO: Determine if there are other exceptions that we can
#       do anything about here, and if so, do something
#       about them. For example:
#    except Exception as error:
#        # Handle this exception
    # FUTURE: If there's ever a need to add more than one
    #    resource-value at a time, we could add **resources
    #    to the signature, and call node.resources.add once
    #    for each resource.
    # All our values are checked and validated by the add
    # method, so set the node's resource-value
    try:
        node.resources.add(resource_name, resource_value)
        # Return the newly-modified/created node in case
        # we need to keep working with it.
        return node
    except Exception as error:
        raise RuntimeError(
            'set_node_resource could not set %s to %0.3f '
            'on the node at (%d,%d).'
            % (resource_name, resource_value, node.x,
            node.y)
        )
```

Stripping out the comments and documentation for the moment, this may not look much different from the original code—only nine lines of code were added—but the differences are significant, as follows:

- It doesn't assume that a node will always be available.
- If the requested node doesn't exist, it creates a new one to operate on, using the existing function defined for that purpose.
- It doesn't assume that every attempt to add a new resource will succeed.
- When such an attempt fails, it raises an error that shows what happened.

All of these additional items are direct results of the questions asked earlier, and of making conscious decisions on how to deal with the answers to those questions. That kind of end result is where the difference between the programming and software engineering mindsets really appears.

Summary

There's more to software engineering than just writing code. Experience; attention to detail; and asking questions about how the code functions, interacts with the rest of a system, and so on; are important aspects of evolving from a programming to a software engineering mindset. The time required to acquire experience can be shortened, perhaps significantly, by simply asking the right questions.

There are also factors completely outside the realm of creating and managing code that require examination and questioning. They mainly focus on what can, or should, be expected from the pre-development planning around a developmental effort, and that starts with understanding a typical software development life cycle.

Other Books You May Enjoy

If you enjoyed this book, you may be interested in these other books by Packt:

Clean Code in Python
Mariano Anaya

ISBN: 978-1-78883-583-1

- Set up tools to effectively work in a development environment
- Explore how the magic methods of Python can help us write better code
- Examine the traits of Python to create advanced object-oriented design
- Understand removal of duplicated code using decorators and descriptors
- Effectively refactor code with the help of unit tests
- Learn to implement the SOLID principles in Python

Mastering Python Design Patterns - Second Edition
Kamon Ayeva

ISBN: 978-1-78883-748-4

- Explore Factory Method and Abstract Factory for object creation
- Clone objects using the Prototype pattern
- Make incompatible interfaces compatible using the Adapter pattern
- Secure an interface using the Proxy pattern
- Choose an algorithm dynamically using the Strategy pattern
- Keep the logic decoupled from the UI using the MVC pattern
- Leverage the Observer pattern to understand reactive programming
- Explore patterns for cloud-native, microservices, and serverless architectures

Leave a review - let other readers know what you think

Please share your thoughts on this book with others by leaving a review on the site that you bought it from. If you purchased the book from Amazon, please leave us an honest review on this book's Amazon page. This is vital so that other potential readers can see and use your unbiased opinion to make purchasing decisions, we can understand what our customers think about our products, and our authors can see your feedback on the title that they have worked with Packt to create. It will only take a few minutes of your time, but is valuable to other potential customers, our authors, and Packt. Thank you!

Index

www.ingramcontent.com/pod-product-compliance
Lightning Source LLC
Chambersburg PA
CBHW060632060326
40690CB00020B/4382